Praise for *To The Sound of the Guns*

Grady Birdsong's book is a combination of well-researched operational history and a moving and deeply personal account of the author's own combat experiences in Vietnam. It is both history and story. The places, the events, and most especially, the Marines and Sailors of whom the author writes, become vividly real, transporting the reader to that distant place and time. A highly-recommended addition to the record of the U.S. Marines in the Vietnam War.

> — **Colonel Len Blasiol, USMC (Ret)**
> Coauthor, *U.S. Marines in Vietnam: The Defining Year 1968*
> Published by the History and Museums Division
> Headquarters, U.S. Marine Corps, Washington, D.C.

~~~

This book is a tribute to the Marines of 1/27 and to all Vietnam War veterans. It is a well-researched and documented history from Fall 1967, all through deployment, until the Fall of 1968. It includes Operation Allen Brook and other events that took place southwest of Da Nang at Liberty Bridge, and Go Noi Island, among others. But beyond good research, this book has the distinctive touch of being written by someone who knew many of the characters, and experienced many of the events. This book will be of special interest to Vietnam veterans, Marines, students of history, alumni and family members of the 27th Regiment.

I met Grady Birdsong in Dec 1966 when we were recruits in boot camp Platoon 2267 at MCRD, San Diego. Grady has always been a straight shooter. In fact, he was our training series high shooter (234) and the platoon honor man at graduation. Serving with 1st ANGLICO from Sept 1967 to Jan 1969, I spent much of 1968 in an adjacent area east of 1/27's area of operations.

> — **Paul D. Carter, Sergeant, 1st ANGLICO**, Vietnam 1967 – 1969
> Professional Engineer, FACI
> Senior Bridge Engineer @ CH2M Hill

~~~

"To the Sounds of Guns" hits a nerve, in the positive sense, for this Hospital Corpsman who served in Echo Company 2nd Battalion 7th Marines in the timeframe this book is written. It pulls one back to that time and experiences, many similar and some different, including the humor and sadness. Historically, it fills in the holes of being young, ignorant and in a world of hurt. In a word, Grady Birdsong's writing is touching!

> — **Dennis E. Sedlack, HM2** Echo 2/7, Vietnam, July 1968 - July 1969

In World War II, the 1st Battalion, 27th Marines created a storied history for itself. A generation later, the unit was ordered to stand up again, this time to fight in the jungles of Vietnam. "To the Sound of the Guns" takes the reader through 1/27's reorganization in Hawaii to deployment on the battlefields of Vietnam—a move expedited by the enemy launching its 1968 Tet Offensive.

The author, Grady Birdsong, chronicles how 1/27's "band of brothers" came together—a battalion of Marines proving every bit as courageous in battles like Hue City as were their World War II counterparts at Iwo Jima. Birdsong's research also delves into the thinking of the political and military leaders who put 1/27 in harm's way, revealing a mindset sometimes lacking cohesiveness—and unwilling to hear about it from others. Detailed, too, is 1/27's impressive operational history and combat record.

Just like the Marines of World War I were "First to Fight," paying a heavy price for doing so, so too did the Marines of 1/27, ultimately losing 112 of their number.

Birdsong's book creates an intriguing account and chronology of men, voluntarily answering their country's call to duty, who transition into warriors. He is able to provide extraordinary insightfulness into 1/27's experiences because he, too, was part of that evolution.

"To The Sound Of The Guns" is a highly recommended read for those who served in 1/27, those interested in Marine Corps history and those just seeking to understand how the mettle of Marines is forged.

— **LtCol James G. Zumwalt USMCR**
Detachment Commander, 4th CAG Vietnam
Author, *Bare Feet, Iron Will—Stories from the Other Side of Vietnam's Battlefields*
Living the Juche Lie—North Korea's Kim Dynasty
Doomsday Iran—the Clock is Ticking
Contributor: *Leadership in Action—Principles Forged in the Crucible of Military Service Can Lead Corporate America Back to the Top; Profiles in Patriotic Leadership*
Writer of hundreds of op-eds on foreign policy and defense-related issues

~~~

"To The Sound Of The Guns" speaks for what it was like to serve in a Marine infantry maneuver battalion in I-Corps during the height of the Vietnam War. I know, I was there in a sister battalion during Operation Allen Brook in the spring-summer of 1968. This history brought back many memories. If a person wants to know what it was like, this is an accurate read. Corporal Grady Birdsong's history of our sister battalion, 1/27, documents not only my story, but the stories of the other Marines I humped with, fought, cried and prayed with in 1968.

— **Wesley S. Love, Sergeant, USMC** Kilo Co, 3/27, Vietnam, 1968

~~~

Grady Birdsong is a trail blazer in the finest traditions of Marine Combat Author's that returned home from their "Trip Down South;" and with impressive success, told their story. Grady fits that template perfectly. His research is scholarly, detailed and focused. The supporting graphs, photos and referenced first-hand battle accounts are well presented and bring the smell of battle and the battle field right into the reading room with you.

Birdsong focuses all his energy and resource's over the past several years documenting the history that clearly highlight his deeply held respect for the Marine Warriors of his beloved 1st Battalion, 27th Marines. On numerous occasions this fighting battalion conducted, literally and figuratively, a passage of lines as they continued the attack into that cordite and gun smoke-shrouded, now hallowed ground known as the Go Noi Island, Liberty Bridge, and other locations in that AO that were then and remain the stuff of legends. His Vietnam battle accounts bring new meaning to the term "Gun Fighters." His riveting book absolutely belongs in the honored and treasured section of the libraries of all those Marines that carried the fight to the VC and NVA while serving in what was always a violent and deadly battle area. "To The Sound Of The Guns" will join Web's, "Fields of Fire" as a classic of that era, time and place.

— **LtCol Ken Pipes USMC (Ret)**
Bravo 6, 1/26. Khe Sanh, TET, 1967/68
Assistant S-3: Hill 55, Liberty Bridge, Go Noi and Dodge City AO's
Reserve Captain, San Diego Sheriff Department 1990--2016

~~~

Grady Birdsong's book is exactly what the American public needs to read! He has done a great service to Marines and the 1st Battalion of the 27th Marine Regiment by digging deep, and sharing his first-hand experience as a rifleman with 27th Marines and other respected units during the peak of the Vietnam War. Through his meticulous and detailed account, we learn in words, pictures, facts, and figures about what this brave battalion endured, and gain a better appreciation for all those who served in Vietnam.

— **Tim Hall, USMC**, Vietnam – 1966-67
Author, *Marines Never Cry: Becoming a Man When It Mattered*

~~~

Grady Birdsong's "To the Sound of the Guns" is a terrific read, but more importantly, it contains stories, information, and photos that will add significant context to the Vietnam War chapter of Marine Corps History.

Shortly after graduating from Boot Camp, PFC Birdsong joined 1st Battalion, 27th Marines, 5th Marine Division. Formed in 1966 at Camp Pendleton, California, the Marines and Sailors of the 2nd and 3rd Battalion trained rigorously for war there, the 1st Battalion at Kaneohe Bay, Hawaii, hoping for the best but preparing for the worst. The explosive actions that took place in late January and early February 1968, known as the Tet Offensive, greatly accelerated their deployment, and they landed in the Republic of Vietnam at the bloody height of the war.

This book contains dozens of personal stories and an exhaustive array of statistics, data, tables of organization, and timelines, as well as hundreds of great photos. Think of this as the largest, most detailed and colorful expeditionary book you've ever read. Semper Fidelis!

— **Nicholas Warr, C Co., 1/5 1967/68**
Author – *Phase Line Green; the Battle for Hue, 1968*
Charlie One Five; One Marine Company's Vietnam War

~~~

This should become one of the definitive narratives of US Marine involvement in Vietnam. Filled with anecdotes that could only come from a first-person participant, catalogs of equipment used, strategic correspondence obtained through meticulous research, this new book by Corporal Grady Birdsong should be sought out and acquired by every serious scholar of the Vietnam War.

— **Mark Hardcastle**, 1982 USAFA graduate,
Persian Gulf War combat pilot, Airline Captain
Author, *The Symphony of Your Life: Restoring Harmony*
When Your World Is Out of Tune, 2014

~~~

Grady Birdsong has written an extremely detailed history of the 1st Battalion, 27th Marines from its reactivation to the unit's deactivation during the Vietnam war.
He has moved past just writing history by filling the pages with multiple stories and pictures of the Marines and Corpsmen, weapons and support equipment, the details of combat and life in an infantry battalion. The book is a great contribution to our Corps' history while honoring those who served in this battalion during 1966-1968.

— **Major General B. Don Lynch, USMC (Ret)**
CO, 8th Communication Battalion, Camp Lejeune, NC (1981-1983)
CG, 1st Force Service Support Group, Camp Pendleton, CA (1992-1993)
Director, Marine Corps Staff, HQ Marine Corps, WDC (1994)
Deputy CG, Marine Corps Combat Development Command, Quantico, VA (1995)

~~~

Grady Birdsong has written far more than the history of the 1st Battalion, 27th Marines from 1966-1968. He has done an excellent job of recording the organization of Marine units and the weapons they carried. The collection of photos from many of the Marines and their families will bring back many memories of the adventures of Marines and Corpsmen in Vietnam during this era.

This book is a great repository of Marine history that should be required reading for Marines. Marines of Battalion 1/27 will see their history but other Marines will receive an understanding of what the peak year of the war in Vietnam was like. The battle of Hue City is one history but there is so very much more.

— **Colonel Frederic L. Tolleson USMC (Ret)**
CO, Echo Co 2/7 Vietnam
CO, 6th Marine Regiment
U. S. Naval Academy, Class of 1955

~~~

For those who were there, Grady Birdsong's *To the Sound Of The Guns* will evoke powerful memories. For those who were not, it will reveal a level of detail found in no other book in my own personal, and extensive, collection of *Vietnamiana*. His scope is mind-boggling, from training in Hawaii through a trans Pac transit by ship and across two tours "in country". There are other books describing in detail, for example, the structure and operation of the ubiquitous UH-1e "Huey" helicopter or the business of using heavy artillery to support troops in contact. But there are no other books drilling down so far as to reveal the second most important item in the infantryman's personal equipment: the tiny and marvellous P-38 can opener we all wore on a chain around our necks with our dog tags, and without which we would have starved. The richness of Birdsong's prose is amplified by copious and informative photographs, map reproductions, and even copies of original orders and unit diary entries. Fittingly, and sobering, he ends with a section on the aftermath of war, stories of how families struggled to cope with the loss of so many fathers, brothers, husbands and sons, a fitting way to end a war story. I did not think a book today could add more to all that has been written about Vietnam, but Grady Birdsong has done just that. If you care about the experience of America and Americans in Vietnam, the country's crux in the last half of the Twentieth Century and crucible in which it was tested, get this book.

Don Moore, Lt - Mike Co, 3/7
Vietnam 1968
Adelaide, South Australia

~~~

"To The Sound Of The Gun" allows the reader to realize the hardships, complete terror and above all else the bond that exists among men that only they and those who have been in combat can understand. Vietnam Veterans have a saying, "Strangers once, Brothers forever!" Grady, well done, Semper Fi!

— *William Purcell, USMC*
Alpha Co., 3rd Platoon
1/1 Hue City-Tet 1968

To The Sound Of The Guns

1st Battalion, 27th Marines from Hawaii to Vietnam 1966-1968

Patch Design by Gary E. Jarvis, Ph.D. ~ 1/27 Delta Company

Grady T. Birdsong

BIRDQUILL LLC

To the Sound of the Guns: 1st Battalion, 27th Marines from Hawaii to Vietnam 1966-1968
by Grady T. Birdsong

Published by

BIRDQUILL LLC

Denver, Colorado

ISBN 978-0-9976068-2-9 (color edition, soft cover)
ISBN 978-0-9976068-3-6 (color edition, hard cover)
ISBN 978-0-9976068-4-3 (black and white edition, soft cover)
Library of Congress Control Number: 2017900692

Book Design and Cover Design by Nick Zelinger, www.nzgraphics.com
Editing by Alexandra O'Connell, www.alexoconnell.com

Genre – BISAC
1. History/Military/Vietnam War HIS027070
2. History/Military/Pictorial HIS027050

Disclaimers

The views expressed in this manuscript are those of the author and his research and do not reflect the official policy or position of the United States Government, Department of Defense, or the United States Marine Corps.

While an effort has been made to ensure the accuracy of the data presented in this manuscript, its total accuracy cannot be guaranteed. Errors were and forever will remain, common among official military reporting and historians. Nonetheless, the greater part of the historical information presented herein is as correct and factual as is humanly possible.

This history is focused on and ultimately dedicated to all who served and sacrificed in the Battalion/ Regiment/Division. Recognizing that not all stories or aspects are covered in this edition, critiques and proposed additions for potential future editions are strongly encouraged. No two people see or remember an event the same way. The intent of this book has been to record the history of the 27th Marines and supporting units in Vietnam as fairly, accurately, and honestly as possible, utilizing as many views of a situation as possible.

Cover Photos:
Front Top: Lance Corporal Geoffrey Thomas Rowson, D Co, 1/27 firing an M60 from a Pagoda rooftop during an operation near Hue City on 14 April 1968. Photographer, Dennis Fisher; DOD photo USMC A371498
Front Lower & Back Cover: Go Noi Island area during Operation Allen Brook, 1968. Photographer, Hal Kennedy, H&S Co, 1/27

This book is dedicated to the Marines and Corpsmen of 1st Battalion, 27th Marine Regiment who were killed in action while serving in Vietnam, and to their families who loved them. It is also intended to be a beacon to the Marines and Corpsmen who lived, endured, and returned to their families. Each of these men willingly and unselfishly volunteered to serve our great nation. We must never forget those who gave all their yesterdays. This History reverently honors all these fine men.

Contents

Note to the reader:

Throughout this book many references are made to Grid Coordinates (e.g., AT995675, the UTM zone and map grid position of 27th Marines HQ Command Post). These two-character zone and six-digit numbers are derived from Defense Mapping Agency L-7014 Series maps (1:50,000 scale). A more detailed explanation of the UTM grid overlay methodology embedded on each L-7014 Series maps for Vietnam can be found in Chapter 4.

CTZ = Corps Tactical Zone. During the Vietnam War, South Vietnam was divided into four Zones for purposes of military operations, based on military regions organized by the French. I Corps was located in the region nearest North Vietnam and adjacent to the DMZ. I CTZ and I Corps are used interchangeably throughout the text to designate the zone where the Marines of 1/27 were deployed.

Foreword

*"Those who expect to reap the blessings of freedom, must, like men,
undergo the fatigues of supporting it."*
~ Thomas Paine, Philadelphia, September 12, 1777

To the Sound of the Guns is a meticulously researched and documented historical account of the First Battalion, 27th Marines' seven-months' service in Vietnam. More than that, it goes beyond most historical accounts in that it includes sections that describe how a Marine infantry battalion is organized and equipped, gripping personal accounts of battles fought by the Marines who fought them, numerous photographs covering the entire time of the deployment and an emotionally moving section that provides input by family and friends concerning some of the members of the battalion killed.

Twenty-three years from the time an earlier generation of the battalion deployed from Hawaii to fight the Iwo Jima battle during World War II, the warriors of 1/27 deployed from Hawaii in February 1968 to fight in another war. They, along with the rest of the 27th Marines, reinforced the First Marine Division following commencement of the Communist Tet Offensive. During the ensuing seven months of heavy combat, the battalion accomplished every assigned mission in the Da Nang, Hue City and Go Noi Island areas, inflicting heavy casualties on enemy forces. This was accomplished at a very high cost, with 112 Marines and Navy Corpsmen killed and 557 wounded, some a second or third time.

Grady Birdsong has done an outstanding job in producing this book and those wanting to learn more about this battalion, specifically, or Marines in war, in general, will enjoy reading, *To the Sound of the Guns.*

Colonel Franklin P. Eller, USMC (Ret)
Executive Officer, 1st Battalion, 27th Marines 1967-68
Annapolis, Class of 1955

The Vietnam War was costly to the U. S. Marine Corps. From 1965 to 1975, nearly 500,000 Marines served in Southeast Asia. Of these, more than 13,000 were killed and 88,000 wounded, nearly a third of American causalities sustained during the war.

United States Marine Corps History Division

Introduction

*"There is a just God who presides over the destinies of nations,
and who will raise up friends to fight our battles for us. The battle, sir,
is not to the strong alone, it is to the vigilant, the active, the brave."*
~ Lt. Gen. Victor H. Krulak, USMC (Ret)

With the passage of time, we Marine and Corpsmen veterans of the Vietnam War have begun to reflect on what transpired during one of the most exhilarating times of our entire lives. This reflection consumed our collective thought processes in the last three-fourths of our existence. Our service influenced how we thought after Vietnam and how we looked upon the society/government which had dispatched us into the breach of the Vietnam War. Vietnam became one of the most consuming, divisive, and inflammatory events of the latter 20th century. For us Marines and Corpsmen it was not only frightening, sometimes boring, at times trying, a lot of the time heartbreaking, but for most of us who came home, one of the most stirring experiences of our lives. Emotions, adrenaline rushes, and raw action were heightened to their peak at the most unsuspecting of times. Some of us made more life-and-death decisions in Vietnam than most people dream of in their entire lives. It was a time in our youth in which we were intensely alive. Truly unforgettable for each of us!

The Marine Corps has for the most part always been a volunteer service. Almost all the military ranks during this time were voluntary. Close to 70 percent of the men and the very few women involved in the total war effort were in Southeast Asia by choice. On the other side of the coin, it was extremely easy not to serve during the war if that was the choice. Most who did not desire to go into the military could stay in college with deferments, and some went to Canada firmly against the war and serving in the military. Those sons of this nation who chose to serve did so with honor, courage, and commitment when their nation called during the 1960s. This is the story of some of those brave men. Men who believed in America and its God-given freedoms.

The actual history and fiber of these Marines and Corpsmen, and their actions within this hallowed unit, cannot be told without telling of how the unit was formed, what it prepared for, what training it went through; and later when deployed, how it was transported, what it encountered, and what it did while in the theater of the northern area, aka "I-Corps" or "Eye Corps," of the Republic of Vietnam.

How did these men find themselves in this war? What circumstances led the United States into this region? Who were the men and families of 1st Battalion, 27th Marines? From where in the heartland did these honorable men originate? How did their families endure while they fought? These are a few of the questions which will be addressed throughout this descriptive and photographic history. It is hoped that the pictures, interpretations, and explanations in this history will impart a significant understanding of the role played by the 1st Battalion, 27th Marines in Vietnam.

The expression "To the Sound of the Guns" became the motto inscribed on the 1st Battalion's patch during World War II. Its appeal: to take aggressive action and go to the heart of the battle. The original expression is believed to have originated during the Battle of Waterloo. The French Cavalry Reserve under the command of Marshall Grouchy heard the noises of Napoleon's "Grand Battery" in the distance. Grouchy's Commanders, especially Etienne-Maurice Gerard, suggested they "march to the sound of the guns." Grouchy decided against that maneuver, pointing out that Napoleon's men already engaged could well deal with Wellington's entrenched Anglo-Allied Army. This delay, and a final blocking action by the Prussian Rearguard on Grouchy's Three Corps in the Hundred Days Campaign, ultimately kept 33,000 French soldiers from reaching the battle of Waterloo, resulting in a French defeat.[1]

During World War II, the Battalion took the latter part of this saying as their adapted motto: "To the sound of the guns!" John Basilone, a prior Medal of Honor recipient and legendary WWII Marine Corps hero, died during the initial assault on Iwo Jima while moving his machine gun and men forward *to the sound of the guns* with Charlie Company, 1/27. Now, here is the continuing history of 1/27.

~ Respectfully, Grady Thane Birdsong, Corporal USMC Vietnam 1968-1969

CHAPTER 1

Training Begins in Hawaii

"These are my recruits. I will train them to the best of my ability. I will develop them into smartly disciplined, physically fit, basically trained Marines, thoroughly indoctrinated in love of Corps and country. I will demand of them, and demonstrate by my own example, the highest of personal conduct, morality, and professional skill."
~ USMC Drill Instructors' Creed

On 26 February 1965, President Lyndon B. Johnson approved sending a contingent of Marines to Da Nang, South Vietnam to provide security for the established U. S. air base from Communist guerillas. Before this, America had sent only advisors and equipment in support of the South Vietnamese. What began as a Marine Expeditionary Brigade (MEB) quickly evolved into a larger Marine Expeditionary Force (MEF), and finally the III Marine Amphibious Force (III MAF) by midsummer of 1965.

The Marines soon began "search-and-destroy" operations outward from the air base. With the consequential buildup of enemy men and material in the northern part of South Vietnam over the next years came a larger requirement for manpower. This forced the Marine Corps to accelerate their manpower and training for combat in South Vietnam. First Battalion, 27th Marine Regiment assumed that assignment beginning in 1967, with the task of enabling a single, integrated unit to organize, deploy, and employ combined arms forces in conjunction with the Navy. In August of 1967, American troop strength was reported to be 478,000 in the Republic of Vietnam (as it was then called) which included approximately 78,000 Marines. It was the beginning of a journey which most did not expect.[1]

Kaneohe Bay Marine Corps Air Station

Prior to World War II, the Army redeveloped the old coastal Army post located on the Mokapu Peninsula on the eastern side of the island of Oahu into an Artillery Defense Command. The Navy eventually took it over, and transitioned the facility into a seaplane base. During the War in the Pacific, this air station became a major training base for aviation headed into the Pacific theater. After the war, it was scaled back again and in 1952 the United States Marine Corps took it over and made it the training ground for all the combined air/ground Fleet Marine Force (FMF) teams operating in the Pacific. This facility would evolve into a training ground for Marines and Corpsmen destined for Vietnam, starting in 1966.

In April of 1946, Kaneohe Naval Air Station evacuated everyone from the area as tsunami waves nearly twenty-five feet in height converged over most of the peninsula, covering most of the land before receding back into the sea. In May of 1949, the K-Bay Naval Air Station was decommissioned and placed in a maintenance status. The Navy put all of the Mokapu Peninsula land up for lease. By 1950, with no development in the future, only a small security detail remained. Then in 1951, the Marine Corps consolidated all of the previous Naval Air Station (NAS) landholdings and in January 1952, commissioned this former NAS as the Marine Corps Air Station Kaneohe Bay. By 1953, the base became the home of the 1st Provisional Marine Air-Ground Task Force. By 1966 and 1967 the area was bustling with Marines training for duty in Vietnam.

The Marines had a long history and a heritage to honor. The 27th Marine Regiment was formed as part of the 5th Marine Division and in January of 1944 saw its first action in combat on Iwo Jima in the Pacific. Lieutenant Keith Wells' men of 3rd Platoon in "Easy" Company of 2nd Battalion, 28th Marine Regiment of the same 5th Division raised the first flag on Iwo Jima's Mount Suribachi in February of 1945 as part of a monumental assault on the island by three Marine Divisions: the 3rd, 4th, and 5th Divisions. The assault by the combined Divisions, called the *V Amphibious Corps*, resulted in more than 23,000 casualties, which sadly included over 5,000 killed in action (KIAs).

The objective in taking Iwo Jima was to capture the airfields on the island and use them for a planned incursion onto the Japanese mainland. First Battalion, 27th Marines was assigned the Motoyama Airfield closest to Suribachi. After the war, the full 5th Marine Division was deactivated in 1946.[2]

The 5th Division, with its 26th, 27th, and 28th Regiments, reactivated again during the Vietnam War (see more information regarding the Divisions in *Exhibit A: An Overview of the USMC Table of Organization*). In June of 1966, 5th Marine Division Headquarters began organizing 2nd and 3rd Battalions of the 27th Marine Regiment at Camp Pendleton, California. The Regiment's 1st Battalion was also reactivated and strategically located at Marine Corps Air Station Kaneohe Bay as part of the 1st Marine Brigade, FMF.

The 26th Regiment, sent to Vietnam in March of 1966, played a dominant role in the northern I CTZ area of South Vietnam.[1] It became attached to both the 1st and 3rd Marine Divisions at various times during its entire deployment. The 27th and 28th Regiments began their role in the training of personnel at Camp Pendleton as replacements for the units already in Vietnam. The 27th Marines were finally ordered to Vietnam in early February of 1968 by President Johnson. The 28th Marine Regiment,

---

[1] CTZ = Corps Tactical Zone. During the Vietnam War, South Vietnam was divided into four Zones for purposes of military operations, based on military regions organized by the French. I Corps was located in the region nearest North Vietnam and adjacent to the DMZ.

activated in Camp Pendleton in January of 1967, served as an on-call Regiment based in California, prepared to ship overseas on a moment's notice.

Battalion Landing Team (BLT) 1/26 (Rein), also part of the 5th Marine Division at Camp Pendleton, was the first of that newly reformed Division's units to embark for Vietnam after conducting *Operation Silver Point I* on the beaches of Del Mar, California in late June 1966. This peacetime operation marked the first amphibious exercise by a 5th Marine Division unit since landing on Iwo Jima in 1945.

MARINES OF 1st Bn., 27 Marines, drop their life jackets as they move across White Beach with the first landing wave.

Operation Alligator Hide in The Pendleton Scout News, May 1967
~ Courtesy of Raul Figueroa, H&S Co, 1/27

On 23 January of 1967, 1/27 left Kaneohe Bay, Hawaii and took part in a full-scale maritime training exercise in the Pacific, the first since its activation. On 14 April 1967, 1/27 left Kaneohe Bay again for Camp Pendleton, California to participate in another amphibious training exercise, Operation *Alligator Hide*, held on the beaches of southern California. The American military was ramping up its training and support for the war in Southeast Asia.

Marine Training Regimen

Before entering actual staging for WestPac (Western Pacific)—the accumulating of men, equipment, and material destined for the Republic of Vietnam—days were spent learning the basics and reminiscing about boot camp days. Without exception, Marines trained each waking day, learning the skills of a rifleman. No one escaped the new grind and everyone remembered their sweat-filled days of boot camp training—physical training, first aid, pugil stick sparring (bayonet training), hand-to-hand combat, hours of close order drill movements on the parade deck, rifle qualification, studying events in Marine Corps history, Universal Code of Military Justice (UCMJ), wearing the uniform, terminology, guard duty, and the General Orders. The training regimen in Hawaii would build on boot camp's core education, adding to its basic cohesion and leadership in fire teams, squads, and platoons, while advancing unit tactics onto what was learned at Infantry Training Regiment (ITR) immediately after boot camp. This unit training in Hawaii was the precursor to entering the "Fleet," or Fleet Marine Force (FMF), as a ready force.

782 Ruck Gear ~ Courtesy of Hugh G. Barton, H&S Co, 1/27

Most of the gear the Marines and Corpsmen possessed was Military issue; however, some items slipped by the scrutiny of superiors or perhaps were overlooked. Skateboarding and surfing had just become popular in the mid-1960s. The Album "Surfin' USA," released March 1963, put the Beach Boys on the charts. Surf rock and the California youth lifestyle became the rage. You couldn't keep Marines from indulging in the culture. Some of these men stubbornly kept mementos of civilian life with them until the last moments before deployment into the combat zone.

Training in the Fleet Marine Force, K-Bay

1st Battalion, 27th Marines spent a large part of 1967 and January of 1968 in rigorous training exercises on the Island of Oahu and Kauai and on the beaches at Camp Pendleton. Daily live fire exercises at Kaneohe Weapons Firing Range began as well as extensive field problems in the jungle, heavy foliage, mountain areas, and sugarcane/pineapple plantations on the Island of Kauai. 1/27 began to transform into a potent fighting unit. The Battalion was a mix of veterans and new "boots" just out of ITR from Camp Pendleton. Not yet a full-strength combat unit, 1/27 struggled daily to fill its ranks with Marines and Corpsmen.

Michael Brown, a Kentucky boy, found himself on an airplane headed west with orders for Fleet Marine Force Pacific (FMFPAC) in 1966. He was one of the first members of the newly formed 1st Battalion, 27th Marines in Hawaii. As he remembered, "1/27 existed mostly on paper." He was one of the first Marines to be assigned to H&S Company in the S-4 section as a supply clerk. As he recalls, "The new 2nd Lieutenant, an excellent Staff Sergeant in the armory, a terrific E-5 Sergeant as warehouse chief, and a fourteen-year professional Corporal in the office all embodied the first remnants of battalion supply. The Gunnery Sergeant of this section was the only Marine that knew how the whole supply system worked and was quite good at it. I really liked this fellow and listened to him and what he told us to do."

Corporal George Schaeffer, Jr. and HM2 Danny Grimshaw rolling up a shelter half in the squad bay during training at Kaneohe Bay, Hawaii 1967

Marines getting ready for liberty in the Squad Bay 1967

~ Courtesy of Linda Lowe, sister of HM3 Robert L. Dodsworth, B Co, 1/27 (KIA 13 April 1968)

Remembering back to the days of residing in the Kaneohe Bay barracks, Corporal George Schaeffer reminisces about living and training amongst other Marines in the squad bays. "The only thing that I remember for sure about the squad bay living was that the poker game, Acey Deucey, were held behind the wall of lockers in the very rear area of the NCO section. I lost my paycheck two paydays in a row before I learned my lesson. And I might add that these losses introduced me to the 10 for 20 per cent principal (loan ten dollars get twenty dollars back) which came in handy sometimes."

William H. "Bill" Drennan, one of the senior NCOs (non-commissioned officers) assigned to Delta Company, recalls his first days in K-Bay and that he only knew one face that he had been with in the past. "Corporal Richard Corson served with an MP unit at Camp Butler, Okinawa with me after a tour in Vietnam. Richard had been wounded two or three times on his first tour with 2nd Battalion, 4th Marines and was a solid Marine. We got to know each other quickly and made steadfast friends. Our new commanding officer was Captain Patrick Kahler, affectionately called 'Captain Skippy' by the troops because he had made rank so quickly."

1st Lieutenant John Bouldin confirmed that his close friend, 1st Lieutenant Patrick Kahler, came by to see him. Kahler commanded the Ontos Platoon at K-Bay before taking over Delta Company when promoted to Captain. Bouldin recalls, "Pat came over to see us and told me, John, I've made Captain so fast that you should not call me

'Skipper' but just call me, 'Skippy.'" Kahler was a deep zone selection, which meant his promotion had been accelerated.

Right away, Delta Company started receiving newly minted Marines just out of boot camp and ITR, ready to begin their tenure with the Fleet Marine Force. As Drennan and other NCOs learned the ins and outs of new Marines, they began the gargantuan task of molding them into capable battlefield warriors ready for the coming challenges.

As Drennan recalls, "Training consisted of dry net training, developing sound squad and fire team maneuvers, interacting with each of them on a personal level by teaching several important drills, i.e., hand grenade throwing, trip wire detection, guerilla tactics, conserving water, first aid basics, etc."

In October of 1967, the entire Battalion was trialed. They loaded onto a troop ship and were transported to another island in the Hawaiian chain, where they disembarked from the ship, hit the beaches in landing craft, engaged an imaginary foe, and were evaluated by the training staff.

William E. "Doc" Carroll recalls arriving in Hawaii and being assigned to Charlie Company. The Doc remembers exactly the one-way conversation he had with his new Company Commander, First Lieutenant Dennis Blankenship. Summoned into his office, Doc received these welcoming words, "Welcome aboard, Doc, you are now a rifleman…You can be a 'Doc,' but first, you're a rifleman with me." Lieutenant Blankenship then went to a storage area and came back with an M14 service rifle, handed it to Carroll and told him that he would learn its use well. Doc Carroll remembers looking at him strangely and thinking, "When I went through Navy basic training the only rifle we got to shoot was a .22 rifle with no recoil at all. I did not know what to think about what he was saying."

Blankenship, a Marine "Mustang" officer was definitely a lead-by-example, Marine. Carroll remembers vividly throughout the training period doing everything he was told. "Everything he did, I did. He was a true leader. He had already done two tours and had become proficient in the Vietnamese language. He had been a recon Marine to boot and

Corporal Robert E. Fuss (KIA 27 April 1968) and Corporal Robert A. Ray (WIA 13 April 1968) prepare for an Alpha Company formation in 1967 while training at K-Bay
~ Courtesy of Howard Matthews, A Co, 1/27

damned if they didn't take him away from us when we landed in Da Nang. He was one of those guys that was short in stature but tall in my eyes…I believe that I am alive today because of him. I will never forget him!"

A Memory of Parris Island Boot Camp 1964

Sergeant Andrew W. Boyko, one of a few Marines who became a member of both the Third and First Battalions of the 27th Regiment, kept a diary of his time at the Marine Corps Recruit Depot at Parris Island, South Carolina. His diary gives the casual reader an idea of what thoughts went through a recruit's mind during the intense recruit training conducted by the United States Marine Corps in the early and mid-1960s. Boyko, a member of Platoon 296, Company K, and 2nd Recruit Training Battalion wrote in his diary almost every day while in training.

2 November – *Today each boot in Platoon 296 got a physical, a series of three shots, and three ounces of blood removed. One private was horsing around and was knocked to the deck by a DI [drill instructor]*

3 November – *We had our bucket issue, and rifle issue. A boot dropped his rifle and had to sleep with it that night. A Marine and his rifle is the deadliest weapon in the world.*

4 November – *Tests all day today. Go to chow and back to being tested. I think I scored well because I was called out to a separate room with another guy to take more tests. I took the Ukrainian language, and a radio test. I am still trying to shake the dots and dashes out of my head.*

5 November – *Today we took a swim test. You had to swim 100 yards to pass. Three recruits almost drowned but were saved by the guards. The rest of the day was spent on the manual of arms. One private called his rifle a gun, and had to reach between his legs with his right hand and grab his "gun" and carry his rifle in his left hand, and walk around the squad bay saying; "This is my rifle, this is my gun, this is for fighting, this is for fun." After that, more drills outside. The sand fleas are terrible. They get at you and almost make you go crazy.*

6 November – *Today was a regular day. Everyone is tired, and I hurt at the shins because I got kicked by the DI for scratching. We also got the "Boot" newspaper here from Parris Island.*

7 November – *Platoon 296 is starting to shape up a little. We can now drill half-assed, and we are getting used to all the hardship. Life is still a reality to me, and I face it the best I can every day. Today we have been at Parris Island one week.*

8 November – *Sunday (Ha Ha) Went to church, drilled, had classes, and in the afternoon, went to a sports meet. Platoons compete against each other for trophies.*

9 November – *Today we were told what war is like. Why we have to know all we are taught. Had more drill, and learned how to take apart the M14 rifle and put it together. I can do it pretty easy.*

10 November – *Marine Corps 189th Birthday. We ran about six times around a field as big as a football field. Saw a football game and had a big meal.*

11 November – *Had a class on the M14 rifle, U.S. Caliber 7.62mm. Stripped it down, and put it back together. Drilled most of the day and cleaned the barracks. The sky outside at night is so beautiful and filled with stars. The night is lovely; I only wish I could enjoy it. Today we also lost a man to motivation platoon.*

12 November – *Things went along pretty fast today. We had a very inspiring talk by a Major on patriotism and the Marine Corps. We also started PT (Physical Torture). Today I referred to the DI as "you" and had to drink a cap full of Whisk soap. We also got three more shots.*

13 November – *It is Friday the 13th. I am not superstitious, but the things that happened today could make anyone superstitious. It seems that all day we ran, and had PT. Guys cursed like you never heard before, yet I in all this hell, while still running after four men dropped out from exhaustion, looked towards the sky, and for the first time in my life, thanked the Lord for letting me take it without too much sweat.*

14 November – *Today we drilled with rifles for the first time, and if I say so myself, we did damn well for the first time. For that, we went to a football game. Cherry Point vs Parris Island. Cherry Point won 33-20. We had drill & PT. When a platoon works together and does things right, you have a sense of pride and things go a lot easier.*

15 November – *Went to church, had a real nice day. Drilled, cleaned my rifle and had a lecture on guard duty. Today I thought of home and how close Christmas was. We also got the "Boot" newspaper.*

16 November – *Had a strength test. I got a perfect score of 250 points. Haircut, PX call [post exchange], and drill. Had a game of "musical bunks" all night.*

17 November – *PT all day, rain, exercise, everything. I have a cramp in my left calf, and it feels as if I'm half dead. I hope the rest of the time won't be this hard.*

18 November – *Swimming rescue drill, and PT. The days are getting harder, but we seem to be taking it. We don't swear so much now. Maybe pretty soon we can take it without a cuss. We also had a class on the "Automatic Pistol, 45 Caliber M1911-A1." I seem to grasp firearms pretty fast. So far, I haven't had any difficulties with any weapon I've handled. We also lost three men. One of them was Jim Murray, a buddy I came here with.*

19 November – *Today ran along pretty smoothly. We were all tired, but not too complaining. The barracks had to be field dayed, rifles cleaned, and manual of arms practiced.*

20 November – *Rifle PT began. It also rained later. Had PT afternoon at 1600. Jim Murray finally returned from ST (Special Training) today. All in all, it was a good day.*

21 November – *It gets cold here very fast. Yesterday it was down to the high 30's. Today it will drop to 29 at night. I have now been here three weeks. One-fourth of my training is over.*

22 November – *Had a field meet and lost. I was on guard duty, and didn't go to church 0600-0800, and will pull another fire watch 2330-0130. Three guys were on UA [unauthorized absence]. Got arrested and will have a Summary Court Martial. The guys are from the topside of my barracks.*

23 November – *Had two fillings put in at dental today. We had bayonet class and ran the obstacle course. We also had to take our rifles apart "blindfolded." A guy from this platoon is getting a medical discharge. He was told to pack tonight. We also did a lot of running, and I saw men drop from exhaustion at the roadside. The DI's just told them to get up and going.*

24 November – *Had to go swimming with utilities, pack, and rifle. Most guys didn't make it, but a lot did. Made a PX call, got paid $7.46 (payday today). It rained all day so we drilled indoors. Another guy is expected to get discharged. This one might be dishonorable. Also, had a lecture on range firing.*

25 November – *Rained in the morning. I had guard duty 0400-0600. Private Shields got a medical discharge today from my platoon. I also saw Private Dempsey. He is also supposed to get a medical discharge. Had classes. Mostly on the 45 (pistol) and PT. Disassembled 45 in squad bay after chow.*

26 November – *Thanksgiving Day. Beautiful chilly morning. I raised the flag on the Iwo Jima Monument. Had PT and drill. A big lunch which got me more filled than any other time here at PI. Field day(ed) the barracks, went to church (morning) and cleaned rifle in the squad bay. I have an infection on my foot and was told to report to sick bay tomorrow. Had guard duty, too.*

27 November – *Went to sick bay. Was there for 4 ½ hours. Got 48-hour light duty. Had marching pack inspection. Today was a pretty day. There is also a lot of talk about the war in Vietnam from the papers. I wonder if I'll be in that war?*

28 November – *Started mess duty. It's not too bad because the time flies. Don't have too much time for anything else.*

29 November – *Was up at 4 AM. Didn't go to church because of mess duty all day. Cleaned rifles on free time. Don't even have enough time to write a letter home.*

30 November – *Mess duty & PT.*

1 December – *It was cold today. Had an inspection at mess duty. Passed with flying colors. PT at 1000. Talked about Christmas.*

2 December – *Private Hennekie is getting a General Discharge we found out today. His nickname is "Private Nervous." Talked about home and people we knew during Mess duty.*

3 December – *Mess duty, PT. Another platoon graduated today. All of them said it was great. Talked about home. Also, got paid $10 (pay day) for Christmas shopping.*

4 December – *Mess duty & PT. Rainstorm all day, everyone was soaked. A Private Polleta went AWOL. Was caught & sent to the Brig. I saw him and he was in sad shape (Poor Bastard).*

5 December – *Mess duty is over. This weekend seemed to have flown by. Made a PX call and thought about White Christmas back home. One we'll never have here.*

6 December – *Went to church, had PT and drill. Washed clothes and had class on UCMJ.*

7 December – *Took first class swim test. Only nine men made it. Had haircut, PT, and bayonet class.*

8 December – *Had PT & bayonet confidence course. Then had pugil stick fights. I whipped the daylights out of my opponent twice. Had a "sex education" class. Guard duty tonight 0200-0400.*

9 December – *Got uniforms, had drill & PT. In the evening, Private York went outside and got his head smashed against the "dipsy dumpster" (accidents do happen).*

10 December – *Had our 21-day test. The lowest score was 90%. I got 100%. Also, had photos taken for ID cards. Had drill, PT, and cleaned rifles.*

11 December – *Had inspection, got shots. Turned in rifles. Got ready to go to rifle range tomorrow. Everyone was pretty busy. Worked all day in preparation to go to the range. Also, had PT and drill.*

12 December – *Field day the barracks, made packs. Went to the rifle range. Got brand new brick barracks, two magazine pouches, three rifle magazines and a shooting jacket.*

16 December – *Was quite busy this week. Monday got rifles, 7 shots, and started snapping in. Tuesday Private Poter passed out on a cleaning detail but was OK. Later more snapping in and PT. Today Private Gerdon went to the hospital because of his foot (won't return). More snapping in and fired in the 900-inch line.*

19 December – *Time. It may mean so little to a civilian, but so much to a Marine. During the weekday, you barely have time to breathe. They don't tell you, you have to do anything, you just do it. You know it is good for you. The platoon pulled butts yesterday and I went to sick bay for stomach cramps. Today we snapped in. It is cold, but we're getting used to it. It seems to be getting easier or else we're getting used to it.*

21 December – *Fired the M14 at the 200-yard line. Slow fire sitting and offhand and rapid fire sitting. Also, fired the 45 Automatic pistol and had PT. Was a fairly good day.*

22 December – *Fired a full course. I got 184, I am not satisfied. Come hell or high water, I am going to qualify. Also, a guy went UA from STB. Had to go looking for him back of the Butts (Target trenches). I don't know what happened to him.*

25 December – *Drilled…snapped in and shined shoes.*

Andrew Boyko quit writing after Christmas of 1964.[3] Like other Marines, Boyko cherished his days in boot camp. He found that he did measure up to the men who went before him. He proudly claimed the title "United States Marine" on graduation day. Boot camp was for him a challenging—both mentally and physically—training program, considered the toughest basic training of the military services.

Barracks Living

What can you say about barracks life during training other than everyone knows just about everything there is to know about you? And you know more about others than you ever wanted to know. It was hard to keep barracks living areas clean and livable, and it wasn't fun when the order came down to "Field Day" the whole squad bay. Some of the men kept an extra set of gear and clothing at the ready, sharp and crisp for that surprise inspection. This was lovingly called a "Junk on the Bunk." The Marine Corps traditionally concentrated on being a highly disciplined, focused, and "squared away" organization, no matter what the circumstance (training, maneuvers, combat). Field Days followed by inspections were part of the Marine Corps everyone knew and loved.

K-Bay HQ and the Enlisted Barracks 1966
~ Photos courtesy of Alioth Glaettli, H&S Co, 1/27

Kaneohe Bay MCAS Campus 1967   Kaneohe Bay MCAS 1966
~ Courtesy of Howard Matthews, A Co, 1/27   ~ Courtesy of William Peck, C Co, 1/27

"Never a dull moment in the Barracks…" as Howie Matthews demonstrates with Alpha Company
Marines in 1967 ~ Courtesy of Howard Matthews, A Co, 1/27

Wolfe, Wochner, Lingo, Hamilton, & Bertelson at K-Bay. They had all earned the
National Defense Ribbon displayed on their left chest ~ Courtesy Charles F. Eckerson, 1/27

National Defense Service Medal/Ribbon

The National Defense Service Medal/Ribbon, commissioned in 1953 by President
Dwight D. Eisenhower, is awarded to members of the U.S. Military who serve
(honorably) during periods of war (also coined "National Emergency"). The timeline authorized for Vietnam was January of 1961 through August of 1974. Anyone
who served during this time was authorized to wear the ribbon.

Marines provide their own security for all situations 24/7, no matter what. This
constant surveillance on any area where Marines serve is known as the "fire watch." A
watch was usually for one or two hours. The National Defense Service Medal/Ribbon
was the first ribbon earned right after recruit training in the mid-1960s. Thus, the term
"fire watch" became associated with the National Defense Service ribbon in most
Marines' minds during this era.

In moments of levity, these ribbons were sometimes referred to by west coast
MCRD-SD (Marine Corps Recruit Depot-San Diego) Marines as the "Battle of Tijuana."
Everyone who served in the southern California area after boot camp took Liberty
and headed south of the border to Tijuana, Mexico for at least one or two of those
Liberty calls. Ah, and the stories that were told…and some that should not be told…

A "quiet and cultural" evening at the Blue Fox in Tijuana 1967
~ Courtesy of Grady Birdsong, H&S Co, 1/27 (seated on left)

The Battalion Training Regimen

Tracy Robeson, Delta Company, remembers the rigorous training regimen the Battalion underwent in 1967. "I remember deploying to an island in Hawaii to participate in jungle warfare training. It was a two-week exercise. We loaded into what we termed 'Cattle Cars' which were trucks. Then we were transported to a Navy embarkation area in Pearl Harbor. The ship we were transported to was the USS Cavalier APA-37. We arrived at the training area on an outlying island on 16 October 1967, late morning. One thing for sure it was a wet landing, and the humidity was stifling and extremely hot. We had executed a typical Marine Corps beachhead landing in a small landing craft with full combat gear and rifles. After a grueling hump into the jungle, we settled in our area and set up our shelter halves. Setting up on a steep slope and blowing up our air mattresses aka 'rubber lady' we soon were in a deep slumber."

Practice for disembarking a Naval vessel
on dry land, Kaneohe Bay 1967
~ Courtesy of Linda Lowe, sister of
HM3 Robert L. Dodsworth, B Co, 1/27
(KIA 13 April 1968)

A torrential rain fell that night and literally washed Marines and air mattresses down the slope, covering them in red, slippery, and slimy mud. Getting soaked and sliding down a mountainside taught a good lesson on where not to set up, Robeson recalls.

Tracy Robeson, Delta Company Kaneohe Bay, Hawaii 1967 ~ Courtesy Tracy Robeson, D Co, 1/27

The next session began an exercise in Escape and Evasion. The Company Commanders took all Marines and Corpsmen to the top of one of the mountains in the training area. Everyone was indoctrinated to the simulated North Vietnamese Prisoner of War camp. The instructors were dressed in black pajamas and the camp replicated the real thing. Robeson remembers, "They instructed us on the exercise and the rules. We were to try and escape and were given 24 hours to reach the designated rally area if we could. It was shown to us on a map. We were to escape and evade or face the consequence of POW interrogations."

Field training in Hawaii ~ Courtesy of Corporal James J. Cox, K Co, 3/5 Vietnam (1/27 Hawaii)

The men were given a compass and map and instructed to form teams of at least four to six men after the escape. Rationed with a canteen of water, and no weapon or food, everyone broke away from the camp in bunches. "It happened that Scott Nesbitt, Billy Frye and I teamed up with one other Marine. I cannot recall the other Marine. We took off through the dense trees, underbrush in that jungle, running like a bunch of squirrels looking for acorns who were going to be shot at. As we made our way down through the heavy jungle we would slide on our asses most of the way down the mountain. It was a very steep drop going down. Finally, we came to the bottom and a clearing. Catching our breath and recovering from an extreme workout coming down we started discussing our next move. Deciding not to cross the open field to our front we decided to skirt its perimeter inside the tree line. Even though it was a longer distance to maneuver around the edge of the huge open field we did make it to our rally point. Along the way, we heard occasional hollering and rounds going off reminding us of the dreaded capture and interrogation. It was an exhausting day and this training I do believe, prepared us in mind and body for the upcoming rigors of Vietnam. The rest of our time on the island was spent patrolling and practicing ambush techniques, testing our ability to adapt."

Escape & Evasion Training Hawaii 1967. L-R: Arthur D. Sinksen (KIA 2 June 1968), UNK, Donald Morehead-Sell, Stephen Austin (KIA 8 June 1968) ~ Courtesy of Donald Morehead-Sell, C Co, 1/27

Liberty Call

Marines have always adapted, improvised, and overcome, no matter where they happen to land. Transportation to go on Liberty in Hawaii was no exception. There were always innovative Marines who acquired a vehicle that would fill the void and provide that necessity. Such was the case with Corporal George Schaeffer while in Hawaii. He happened to purchase the affectionately named "Big Lead Sled" for a bargain price. It provided the means for him and a lot of his buddies to go where they might not have been able to go on such a great Liberty place as Hawaii. As he remembers: "That old '59 Bonneville brought back some great memories. It was the only time in my enlistment that I had my own transportation. It was a common occurrence to have a carload of young Marines heading for Liberty in Waikiki. We would often pull over and enjoy the view from the Pali Mountain Pass.

"In this picture, the waves that day were crashing at an overhead height just five to ten feet off shore. It only took one crushing wave to change my mind about swimming that day. It was because of this car that I visited many of the tourist attractions and could drive around the entire island on day trips.

"As I remember, before our deployment we were told that we would only be gone for a couple of months. The last time that I saw the car was when I put it in a special lot along with others. I was lucky; some of the guys left their families behind. I was to be discharged when our deployment ended so I sold it to a Corpsman who was deploying back to the island. He gave me fifty bucks for it."

"Surfing USA" in Hawaii with Hugh and the boys, 1967 ~ Courtesy Hugh G. Barton, H&S Co, 1/27

"Wait till I tell the folks back home about this…" ~ Courtesy Alioth Glaettli, H&S Co, 1/27

"The Big Lead Sled" used for many a Liberty Call and outings to Kailua Beach (A No Drinking Beach)
~ Courtesy Sergeant George C. Schaeffer Jr., B Co, 1/27

Waikiki Beach

This two-mile stretch of white sand ran from the Hilton Hawaiian Village to Kapiolani Park. In the early morning hours, the beach belonged to walkers and runners and was a quiet place. By midmorning, it had the looks of a resort beach, with rental stands setting up shop. By noon walking down the beach was a challenge.

The Marines of 1/27 often spent leisure time in Waikiki on Kalakaua Avenue, or on the beaches surrounding the base. All sorts of activity abounded during off-base leave. Lovely palm trees and tropical foliage created a perfect setting for this new-found duty station in the Pacific. The fragrance of exotic flowers, the beauty of the dramatic Ko'olau Mountains, and watching surfing or swimming in the shimmering waters of the famous Waikiki Beach made the hours off base go quickly.

Bill Drennan, of Delta Company, recollects that when Liberty call came, "There were times we had an opportunity to blow off steam and go on Liberty. Trips to Honolulu, walking its streets, trying our best to pick up girls...Though Hawaii was beautiful in its own way, the cost

Hal Kennedy on Liberty with absolutely nothing to do ~ Courtesy of Hugh G. Barton, H&S Co, 1/27

was very expensive for most of us. I remember that the only way we were able to afford to get over to the main side was by government busing. We were transported over to Waikiki Beach by United States Marine Corps trucks which we called, 'Cattle Cars' and when we rode in them, we 'mooed' all the way over to Waikiki beach... it was a hoot! I suspect that the locals thought we were truly crazy..."

(Left) Kailua and "K-Bay" Marine Corps Air Station in background
(Right) Marines stroll down Waikiki Beach January 1967
~ Courtesy of Alioth Glaettli, H&S Co, 1/27

Drennan recaptures some of those Liberty Call moments: "Corporal David Harrison and myself spent time at the movies or as he liked to call them, 'Flicks.' *A Fist Full of Dollars*, starring Clint Eastwood, was one that we thought was one of his best... December 1967 rolled around and I took leave and went home to Houston for a family visit and to see my new little brother, David Gregory Drennan, who had been born that October. While home on leave, my parents received a letter from our commanding officer, Lieutenant Colonel Greenwood, detailing that our Battalion would be embarking on a training cruise for six months taking in the Philippines, Okinawa, and Australia and that we would write home once arriving at those destinations." Drennan laughed and thought to himself, "I don't even like writing..."

PFC Michael L. Brown, from Louisville, Kentucky describes what stood out most for him being in Hawaii. "Lots of fun times in Hawaii but it's really kind of weird walking around on Christmas Eve in a short sleeve shirt."

Pat Rider, already a veteran of Vietnam with one tour under his belt, came to Hawaii in 1967. He had been fortunate enough to get an assignment at K-Bay with 1/27. Transferred to Company D, Rider and the most senior Marines separated themselves from the new guys now filling the ranks by hanging a curtain at the far end of the squad bay. He recalls, "Remembering all the company formations, daily drill, 782 gear and rifle inspections, and the field days where we had to scrub and swab the deck [floors] before being allowed liberty chits to go into Honolulu. Most times we rode in 'cattle cars' [military trucks] over the mountain into the downtown area. I can even remember hitchhiking over there one Sunday afternoon. Our Company Commander, Captain Pat Kahler, and his wife stopped and picked us up to give us a ride. We rented rooms at the reef hotels and did a lot of drinking and carrying on and even slept on grass mats right on Waikiki Beach…I think it was safe back then."

Corporal Rider participated in maneuvers on the island of Kauai. He remembers loading "a C-130 aircraft and flying toward the island watching an engine catching fire, mid-air, and landing safely." With more to come on that training exercise, Corporal Rider recalled another of the Delta Company Marines somehow had been bitten by a huge centipede, and his cheek swelled up to the size of a baseball.

"Mustang" Lieutenants Baribeau and Hand attending Mess Night, Kaneohe Bay 1967
~ Courtesy of Jesse Hand, H&S Co, 1/27
("Mustang" infers that an officer was a former enlisted)

Mess Night Camaraderie

Mess Night is a custom which can be traced to victory celebrations by both Viking and Roman legions. The Mess Night is a formal affair steeped in paying respects to Marines who have gone to battle before. It affords a night of well-deserved bonding and socializing in the best dress uniform, with ribbons and medals earned.

The tradition spread throughout the Christian world to monasteries, and to many other military units. The Marine Corps Mess Night customs came from the Royal Marines of England and Regimental Messes within the British Army. Throughout the years, changes in format have been adapted to adhere to the unique character of the Marine Corps.

The atmosphere of dignity maintained during Mess Night contributes to the fraternal bond, unity, and esprit de corps of a combat unit. While dinner is served, the floor is opened for "fines," a Mess custom that allows Marines to accuse members of the Mess of "infractions," ranging from minor uniform discrepancies to the playing of pranks on each other, designed to foster camaraderie and good morale. The designated President of the Mess Night will hear the cases brought up by the members. If the designated President finds guilt in the case, usually he metes out a monetary fine or an order to perform a simple skit or dance. It is also traditional for the President and Vice President to themselves execute an amusing incident or joke to increase the festivity of the night.

All good things must end, and after celebrating established bonds during a well-earned night of revelry, the men of 1st Battalion were up the next day at 0600 for roll call, and continued the serious work of honing the tactical skills of a maneuver Rifle Battalion.

The Buildup

Many of the members of 1/27 found themselves en route to Vietnam without prior notice. William H. Drennan, who already had a tour of Vietnam behind him with 1st Battalion, 3rd Marines, remembers his days as a Military Policeman in the spring-summer of 1967 at Camp Pendleton. "I hated being an MP and was looking forward to leaving it behind…and about late August of 1967 several transfers became available: The Marine Barracks in Fairbanks, Alaska, a tour of duty in the Panama Canal, or Marine Air Security at Kaneohe Bay, 'K-Bay' Hawaii. Having never been there, I chose the Air Security duty, looking forward to going to Hawaii."

Arriving in San Francisco, California to board a flight to Honolulu, he discovered many non-commissioned officers ready to embark on the flight with the same orders for Hawaii as himself. He silently thought, "Even though I had never had a conversation with these Marines and all of them with orders like mine, all going to the same unit, isn't this strange?"

Upon arrival at the Honolulu airport late in the evening, Marine Corps buses loaded the NCOs with their seabags and personal gear and began the long ride to the other side of the island and K-Bay. Drennan recalls, "We arrived late, probably 0900 or 1000 pm, had a formation, in which our new Commanding Officer, Lieutenant Colonel John E. Greenwood, greeted us. He told us that we were a newly formed unit, the 1st Battalion, 27th Marines, part of the 27th Marine Regiment which had been reactivated in June of the previous year, and that we would begin a rigorous training regimen. I for one was just numb to find out I was back in a grunt unit with no Marine Air Security that I had so eagerly anticipated...?"

Gabe Komanec had already served one tour in the Republic of Vietnam with 3/7 and found himself at the Oak Knoll Naval Hospital located in the Oakland, California area in 1967, rehabilitating and then on light duty. As a field radioman (RTO) with 3/7 in 1966, he had caught two bullets in the femur from enemy machine gun fire. After being evacuated from Vietnam, he spent about seven and a half months rehabbing and then serving on light duty as an MP at Naval Station on Treasure Island. After a while, he was transferred to Camp Lejeune, North Carolina and became an MP still on light duty. One day he noticed an application on the company bulletin board for MP duty in Hawaii. He thought to himself, "Boy that is the ticket." To get that duty, a Marine had to be an E-4 and still have two years remaining on their enlistment. He fit the requirements and immediately applied and ended up being sent to Hawaii.

Upon arrival at K-Bay and while beginning to settle in at the MP barracks, a Staff NCO came through their bunk area requesting their paperwork (orders) from each person. Komanec remembers, "He took our orders and came back about an hour later and all the papers had 1st Battalion, 27th Marines, Company C stamped on them. That was 1967."

Komanec became a squad leader due to time-in-grade, a previous tour in Vietnam, and being a senior Corporal. While training, he volunteered for sniper training at the U. S. Army's Schofield Barracks installation, learning the finer points of long-range shooting. After training hard for five months, Komanec and the men he arrived with at K-Bay, along with other line companies, were loaded onto a naval vessel, the USS Vancouver. Komanec distinctly recalls, "We were supposed to float to the Philippine Islands and train with the South Korean Marines. Three days out to sea and they told us we were going to Vietnam... I remember the reporters on the dock asking us, 'How does it feel to go back to Vietnam?' At the time, we didn't believe them..."

Naval Transport of Marines

One thing has remained constant throughout the history of the Marine Corps. Marines depend on ships to arrive on the scene to accomplish the mission. Due to the nature of the war in the Pacific and Europe during World War II, the importance of amphibious forces and their transport was well learned and further developed into the 1960s. Seaborne Marines aboard amphibious assault ships in the Pacific took island after island from the Japanese in some hard-fought battles. Due to these lessons, the means to deploy large numbers of troops logistically on short notice became the essence of the FMF.

Marines had to be able to sail into harm's way and provide quick manpower ashore. Such was the case to transport the Regimental Landing Team (RLT-27) to Vietnam. The battalion in Hawaii had initially planned a training exercise boarding navy vessels at Pearl Harbor and deploying to the Pacific region. The 1/27 Command Chronologies of February 1968 reads, "On 10 February 1968, approximately half of the command, then organized as a Battalion Landing Team, departed Hawaii aboard the USS Vancouver to be followed by the remaining on 12 February 1968 aboard the USS Bexar and the USS Washburn in route (sic) to Okinawa. The battalion was scheduled for a four-month deployment which was to have involved two periods of training on Okinawa and participation in Operation Former Champ in Taiwan and Operation Tamaraw in the Philippines... References (d) and (e) canceled participation in the combined exercises and diverted the BLT to Vietnam for duty."[4]

Designated as a Battalion Landing Team at the time and not yet deployed to Vietnam, the administration and personnel summary in the Command Chronologies reported the following: "BLT 1/27 had not deployed from Hawaii with Vietnam as its destination. Thus, nearly 400 members of the command were non-qualified for duty there once firm deployability criteria were announced. Identifying these non-deployable, processing requests for deferred assignments, obtaining waivers, etc.

were major problems encountered between receipt of reference (d) [orders for Vietnam] and arrival in Vietnam. Their resolution was greatly hampered by the three-way split of the command and separation of many personnel from their records due to the semi-tactical embarkation."[5]

Bravo Company preparing to ship out February 1968
~ Courtesy of Corporal Michael Weymouth, B Co, 1/27

Deployment to the Far East for Further Training

Inspections ensure everyone has all their combat gear before deployment. Each Marine is given a prescribed format in which to properly display gear prior to the event. The essentials to be inspected for each Marine are issued equipment, e.g., rifle, ammo magazines, bayonet, utilities, boots, socks, underwear, helmet, flak jacket, 782 web gear, canteens, shovel, and so on. Support equipment such as field radios, batteries, mortars, support weapons, first aid units, jeeps, generators, rope, and more are also inspected for readiness and use during these appraisals. The health of each Marine and his equipment, ready to deploy on a moment's notice, is essential to the mission's success.

Marine Corps Air Station, Kaneohe Bay, Hawaii's *Windward Marine Newsletter* of 5 January 1968, carried an article titled, "Station, Brigade Troops Prepare for Annual FMFPAC Inspection." It points out that cash sales were doing a booming business; the Main Exchange (PX) was selling brass and shoe polish as if it was going out of style. "This inspection, like all others, demands that personnel have a neat military appearance, that all administrative records are up to date and everyone stationed here be capable of filling his role as a combat-ready Marine…Items to be checked include a troop inspection and drill, staff NCO uniform inspection…Physical Readiness and clothing and equipment."[6]

The rumor mill ran rampant with scenarios that the battalion was indeed slated to deploy to Vietnam. The upper-level brass forged ahead with the intent of training for the distinct possibility of being sent into combat. Everyone knew that a gradual escalation of the war in Southeast Asia was still in process, and that they were in the queue. Marines of 1/27 prepared for the upcoming training exercise in the western Pacific Ocean, while the on-high decision of combat deployment had not yet been made.

Top & Bottom: Battalion Landing Team 1/27 staging departure for exercises in the Pacific, February 1968
~ Courtesy of Linda Lowe, sister of HM3 Robert L. Dodsworth, B Co, 1/27 (KIA 13 April 1968)

1st Lieutenant Jesse Hand, H&S Company Commander, remembered leaving Pearl Harbor and pointed out that, "Most if not all the married officers and senior NCOs of the battalion had their families with them in Hawaii. They had set up personal households, brought along cars, pets, and their children and put them in school, while some wives worked at jobs on and some off the base."

In early February, 1968 battalion personnel said their goodbyes to family and friends and boarded ship to get underway for the planned training operation in the Pacific. Hand recalls, "A few days into the voyage, Colonel Greenwood notified all personnel that he had received orders from higher command to cancel the training operation and proceed to the Republic of Vietnam."

1st Lieutenant Hand, along with others, was a little shocked as a lot of them had already served one tour. More confusion came from a Marine Corps order that mandated there would be a two-year period between assignments in the RVN. Since most of the previous tour veterans had less than two years, the question became, would they be required to serve a second tour so quickly? Jesse recalls, "The question was soon answered while we were steaming west and that order was changed to read one year between tours."

Further turmoil came from a long-standing Marine Corps order, dating back to World War II days, specifically noting that no dependents could remain in government quarters once the unit sponsor was transferred or deployed elsewhere. First Lieutenant Hand pointed out that the married Marines with dependents on the island of Hawaii now on the boat became concerned with the fact that, "Their families will not know the Battalion had been diverted to Vietnam for a few days. The then-Base Commander of MCAS Kaneohe, Hawaii, upon being notified that 1/27 had been deployed to the RVN, went ahead and issued his order, based on the USMC order, for all dependents living in base quarters to immediately evacuate or words to that effect. This caused rumors to run rampant and was at best a serious task to get control of and at worst a chaotic mess."

It turned out that many of the dependent spouses met with the leadership of the Battalion C.O. and X.O.'s wives (Commanding Officer and Executive Officer), and petitioned the Commandant of the Marine Corps to intercede on the behalf of the dependents of 1/27 until it was clear what the commitment of the battalion was going to be in Vietnam. Lieutenant Hand later found that, "Even though this was an unusual happening for dependents to contact the CMC directly, especially for officer wives (bad for a husband's career), the CMC did respond favorably and allowed all dependents to remain put. They also offered government transportation to anyone who desired to leave Hawaii. The order also set up advance pay for any needs of the families and to keep all dependents informed about their Marine's status in the RVN."

During the voyage to Da Nang, 1st Lieutenant Hand was summoned to Colonel Greenwood's quarters. Greenwood informed Hand that he was putting him in charge of H&S Company. Hand's immediate reaction was that he did not want the job! He recalled their conversation: "Colonel Greenwood sharply asked, 'What do you mean, you don't want the job?' I reluctantly replied, 'Well sir, I will take the job if you order me to take it and I will do it to the best of my ability but I will not be happy about it.' The Colonel then shot back at me and asked, what [would] make me take the job and be happy about it? I replied to him, 'Sir, I would request that you personally notify all Battalion Staff that they will support me directly and my orders pertaining to the duties as the commanding officer of H&S Company and the Headquarters Commandant of 1st Battalion, 27th Marines.' He quickly shot back at me, 'Is that all you need, Jesse?' And then said, 'Done, you have my word!'"

Lieutenant Hand understood he was treading dangerous ground. He knew there were potential problems: first and foremost, the battalion staff was mostly Captains and above, and being a junior officer as the Company Commander (Hand was a "Mustang" officer) could pose problems. Hand wanted to know that he had that support.

Another pressing issue when 1/27 landed in Da Nang Harbor would be that not everyone was over eighteen years of age. What to do with the seventeen-year-old Marines they had on board?

A third small group of Marines could not go ashore because of wounds. There were a few who had three Purple Hearts (wounded in action thrice) and a few who were considered sole surviving sons. As Hand remembered, "Administratively and logistically it was a major SNAFU to sort out each of these categories and keep them aboard ship(s) while the rest of the battalion deployed and started staging. It got sorted out and burgeoned into a huge loss of almost 400 personnel. That would deplete the rifle companies of needed manpower at a time when they were being sent into combat."

After arriving in Da Nang Harbor aboard the USS Vancouver, Hand's biggest headache became the "offloading" dilemma. On the way over, due to available space, H&S Company, personnel, and gear were dispersed to three different ships. Once they landed it was Hand's responsibility to get them together, find transportation to RLT-27's base camp south of Da Nang, and set up a working Command Post (CP). Hand described another unforeseen problem. "Most of the Division-level attachments (Engineers, Tanks, Ontos, etc.) were now being detached ('chopped') from us and sent to their parent units already in-country. This created a lot of extra administrative paperwork for my H&S Company personnel."

1/27 Deployment on the USS Bexar 12 February 1968 Pearl Harbor, Hawaii
~ Courtesy of Linda Lowe, sister of HM3 Robert L. Dodsworth, B Co, 1/27

Above: 1/27 Marines and sailors aboard ship watching boxing match
~ courtesy of William Carroll, C Co, 1/27

All Aboard: 1/27 Departs for WestPac Training, Diverts to the Republic of Vietnam

The Navy Ship USS Bexar APA-237

The previous photos taken around and on the USS Bexar APA-237 (pronounced "Bear") by Docs William Carroll and Robert Dodsworth, exemplify life aboard a naval vessel during this time. The Bexar took many trips during its protracted career as an "Auxiliary Personnel, Attack" (APA) naval vessel. It was commonly referred to as an Attack Transport, and was designed to carry up to 1500 Marines and their equipment into a combat area. This ship got its name from Bexar County, Texas, where in the early 1700s the Spanish established an armed garrison near San Antonio. Upon arrival into a debarking area with 1500 Marines and cargo, it could put all its landing craft into the water inside of twenty minutes. Mechanized Landing Craft (LCMs) were capable of hauling light tanks to a beach area. Twenty other LCVPs (Landing Craft, Vehicle and Personnel), were capable of carrying a truck or other cargo each, though most often they moved infantry personnel ashore. Also, the Bexar could employ three LCPs (Landing Craft, Personnel) for command and control purposes when needed.

Ed Singletary of Alpha Company remembers, "We loaded the ship on my birthday. We were supposed to be going first to Okinawa and then to the Philippines and do some amphibious landing training. When we were out to sea and on our way, I remember them announcing that they had a lot of trouble in Vietnam and we were changing course, heading full steam for Da Nang Harbor. Well anyway, most everybody suspected that we were going to Vietnam."

Corporal Pat Rider looks back on this trip with mixed emotion. "I remember the long days and nights on the ship going west into the Pacific Ocean, almost always feeling queasy or nauseous. I did not want to eat much, unusual for me. We gathered each morning for our Company formation to perform Physical Training [PT]. It came to my mind that we had PT every day and the shipboard sailors did not have to partake? Because we engaged in physical exercise, I felt that perhaps maybe us Marines were just a little better. We enjoyed the ongoing boxing matches and of course the PT contests. How could I forget our own Bill Drennan winning the onboard push-up contest? He performed well over a hundred push-ups, pumping them out one after another."

While cruising toward Vietnam, thinking of another combat tour, Rider began feeling uneasy. He had served with Charlie Company, 1/1 in 1966 in the northern I-Corps area, and had come home from his first tour in one piece. He recollected his thoughts back then: "I am going back to Vietnam for the second time, and I was again scared. Raised as a Catholic and attending twelve years of Parochial School, always going to church, Confession, Mass, and Communion, I wanted to 'get it right' with my God before arriving. So, I prayed a lot and wrote my dear Mother telling her that I had done so."

Initially scheduled for a normal training exercise in the Pacific Ocean, in February of 1968 the Bexar changed course, convoying with the USS Washburn (AKA-108) and the USS Vancouver (LPD-2) to Da Nang, Vietnam. These three ships delivered the men of the 1st Battalion, 27th Marines to the I CTZ theater, aka "I-Corps." After "offloading" the Marines and Corpsmen in Da Nang Harbor, the USS Bexar steamed toward Yang Po Rie, Korea to continue joint training exercises with the Korean military.

The Navy Ship USS Washburn AKA-108

The second ship carrying members of 1/27 was the USS Washburn, a Tolland-class attack cargo ship which had been commissioned at Hoboken, New Jersey on 17 May 1945. It was named after Washburn County, Wisconsin. It had participated in the Inchon landing in Korea and supported the Cuban Missile Blockade in the early 1960s. By late February of 1968, the Washburn was in convoy heading to Vietnam, carrying H&S Company of the 1/27 Marines, landing craft, and their supplies to Vietnam. It arrived 28 February 1968 in Da Nang Harbor.

The Navy Ship USS Vancouver LPD-2

The Third ship in convoy with members of 1/27 was a Raleigh class amphibious transport dock, commissioned on 10 May of 1963. The USS Vancouver spent most of the later 1960s in the Western Pacific and near the Vietnam coast carrying Marines. It was designed to carry a portion of a Battalion Landing Team (BLT), a task-organized battalion reinforced with other elements, e.g., artillery, armor like the M50A1 Ontos, and combat engineers. The BLT Marines aboard this type of Navy ship could be landed into any hotspot or developing battle as reserves.

The USS Vancouver was capable of embarking troops via helicopter or landing craft launched from its "well" deck internal to the hull. A Landing Platform Dock (LPD), the Vancouver loaded part of the BLT 1/27 troops at Pearl Harbor on 8 through 10 February, and headed for Okinawa in convoy.

Corporal Raymond Whaley, an Anti-Tank Battalion Marine attached to 1st Battalion in Hawaii, remembers loading his self-propelled tracked vehicle, the M50A1 Ontos Tank Destroyer onto the USS Vancouver in Pearl Harbor that early February. "It was around 0800 in the morning and my driver, Ronnie Williams, a North Carolina boy, and my loader, 'Beany' from Worchester, Massachusetts, were maneuvering our 'beast' onto the Vancouver. Both newly minted Marines had arrived in Hawaii in October of 1967, after finishing Infantry Training Regiment and coming off their first home leave. Neither had any schooling on tracked vehicles and it would be my duty to train these new guys during the upcoming months in the Pacific."

As the Vancouver sailed out of Pearl Harbor that afternoon the sun was still shining in the west, the seas were calm, and the ocean was the most magnificent blue one could imagine. Whaley recollects his thinking at the time. "We were going to have maneuvers with the Philippines Marines and I was anticipating my shore leave in Manila once again. Looking out across the water toward Hawaii, I said my last goodbye to that enchanted Island that I had been on since my last tour of Vietnam

Bunk area below deck ~ Courtesy of Linda Lowe, sister of R. L. Dodsworth, B Co, 1/27

ten months earlier. As we progressed further out to sea, the ship started rolling very slightly, back and forth, left and right, pitching and yawing ever so slightly and wouldn't you know it, I started getting seasick. I just made the toilet bowl in the head [ship's bathroom] and gone were my breakfast and lunch. Needless to say, I was the only one in my group that got seasick that first day."

The next day, the Vancouver was well underway and slicing through the waves like a hot knife through butter. As Corporal Whaley remembers, "The ship was really moving. In a couple of days out to sea, our Battalion Commander came on the horn, to give us some important news. He announced over the loudspeaker that the whole 27th Marine Regiment had been ordered to the Republic of Vietnam immediately, by the President of the United States. We were all down below deck playing cards and my first thought, 'Oh hell, there goes my shore leave in Manila, damn!'"

The seas got progressively worse the further west the Vancouver traveled. Whaley noticed the food on the metal tables in the galley constantly sliding, milk and drinks spilling, milk dispensers rolling, and the Marine and Sailors attending chow did their best to prevent an ongoing disaster. "Now, everyone was sick, except me. There was vomit all over the ladderways, the hand rails, the heads and not much of the living areas were left untouched, including the sleeping areas. I had to go up topside onto the main deck to get away from that putrid and lingering stench."

A few days out to sea the conditions were beyond rough. The Marines and Sailors aboard the Vancouver were restricted to only safe areas topside. Whaley remembers going up to an area close to the bridge and talking with two sailors who were on watch. He recollects, "By now the ship's bow seemed to be diving almost under water as we lunged forward. I asked these two, how tall the waves were and they replied, 'sixty to seventy feet,' with a laugh. They could tell I was uncomfortable. I knew that they were silently laughing at me. Finally, they took pity and calmed me by telling me that there was nothing to worry about. They further assured me that the ship had encountered waves of this magnitude before and would perform well in this typhoon. I then went back to my berthing compartment and tried to sleep. This trip would get better."

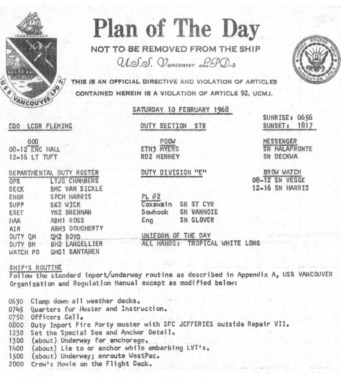

Plan of The Day

NOT TO BE REMOVED FROM THE SHIP

U.S.S. Vancouver LPD-2

THIS IS AN OFFICIAL DIRECTIVE AND VIOLATION OF ARTICLES
CONTAINED HEREIN IS A VIOLATION OF ARTICLE 92, UCMJ.

SATURDAY 10 FEBRUARY 1968

SUNRISE: 0656
SUNSET: 1817

CDO LCDR FLEMING

DUTY SECTION STB

OOD
08-12 ENC HALL
12-16 LT TUFT

POOW
ETN3 MYERS
RD2 HENNEY

MESSENGER
SN MALAFRONTE
SN DECKWA

DEPARTMENTAL DUTY ROSTER
OPS   LTJG CHAMBERS
DECK   BMC VAN SICKLE
ENGR   SPCH HARRIS
SUPP   SK2 WICK
EXEC   YN2 BRENNAN
MAA   ABH1 ROSS
AIR   ABH3 DOUGHERTY
DUTY QM QM2 BOYD
DUTY BM BM2 LANGELLIER
WATCH PO GMG1 SANTANEN

DUTY DIVISION "E"

PL #2
Coxswain SN ST CYR
Bowhook   SN VANNOIE
Eng   SN GLOVER

UNIFORM OF THE DAY
ALL HANDS: TROPICAL WHITE LONG

BROW WATCH
08-12 SN VEGGE
12-16 SN HARRIS

SHIP'S ROUTINE
Follow the standard inport/underway routine as described in Appendix A, USS VANCOUVER
Organization and Regulation Manual except as modified below:

0630 Clamp down all weather decks.
0745 Quarters for Muster and Instruction.
0750 Officers Call.
0800 Duty Inport Fire Party muster with SFC JEFFERIES outside Repair VII.
1230 Set the Special Sea and Anchor Detail.
1300 (about) Underway for anchorage.
1400 (about) Lie to or anchor while embarking LVT's.
1500 (about) Underway; enroute WestPac.
2000 Crew's Movie on the Flight Deck.

USS Vancouver LPD-2 Bulletin, 10 Feb 1968 ~ Courtesy of Raymond Whaley, H&S Co, 1/27, Hawaii

The handout shown above further explained to the Marines of 1/27, "The ship expects to get underway about 1300 today to load LVT's and underway for Okinawa about 1500. Personnel are reminded that the movements of the ship remain classified ... Welcome to the Marines of BLT 1/27. Since you were fortunate enough to make your transit in the USS Vancouver, make the most of it. Enjoy to the maximum your stay on board one of the newest additions to the modern amphibious fleet. There are many facilities on board which are available to all of you and none of which you are excluded. The Vancouver crew is the finest in the Amphibious Forces and will be happy to assist you or answer your questions during the 'settling in' period. There are certain restricted areas on the ship (such as the bridge) which will be made known to you by your respective Company and Platoon Commanders; however, it is certain that you'll find life in the USS Vancouver – with its air conditioning, cleanliness, and good spirit – a far cry from that in other transports you may have been assigned.

"In this same spirit of cooperation, it is asked only that you help us in keeping the ship this way. Our crew will cooperate to the maximum to repair or replace any broken mirrors, bunk lights, rifle straps, etc., but we ask only that you advise someone immediately when such repairs are needed. Finally, the Vancouver is our home and we want it to be yours if you are with us. Accordingly, we naturally expect that you keep this in mind always and treat it as such. This is particularly true about cigarette butts and soft drink paper cups/cans, and we ask that you utilize the receptacles provided for them.

"We realize that we're not the Queen Elizabeth (the ship), but as transports go, you'll go a long way before you can top the USS Vancouver. So, if you must go – better you go first class!"

Signed: E. R. Sands for B. R. Banks

Flight deck of the USS Vancouver LPD-2 ~ Courtesy of "Doc" R. W. McConnell, D Co, 1/27

En Route

Scuttlebutt is a Navy term originating in the days of sailing ships. "Scuttle" means a hole made in the hull which could sink a ship; "butt" was a wooden cask holding fresh water from which a crew could draw their drinking water. The crew gathered around this water source for all the rumors about the voyage, thus gaining all the latest scuttlebutt generated amongst those on board.

Michael L. Brown, H&S Company, remembers some of the boredom of the trip to the RVN. Adding insult to injury, the scuttlebutt on board was that a Russian vessel was following the ship. He remembers, "No excursions above deck allowed in daylight. The Russians already knew we were aboard but we had to stay out of sight anyway due to regulations. Marines condemned to stay below deck for an entire day with no fresh air sucks. That's the Corps for ya!"

Brown also recaptures some of the memorable moments on a boring voyage in the Pacific Ocean. "The trip to Da Nang wasn't without its moments. A few of us learned the hard way about how rogue waves break against the ship's bow in inclement weather. A mountain of salt water drenched us new Marines unexpectedly standing in the chow line, so we decided that this could benefit our future amusement. Keeping our secret about these waves and harsh weather produced a lot of 'gotcha's' in the chow line as we steamed toward Vietnam."

Brown tells that he learned that he could volunteer for other duties to get out of the endless gear inspections. He found out that he could work in the mess hall and ended up as an assistant to the baker. The baker, a Chief in rank, left PFC Brown to himself in the bakery day after day while the ship was steaming toward the Orient. As Brown tells it, "Being trained in supply, naturally I inventoried everything in the bakery just for something to do. One day I came across several cans with no labels and thought what the hell, and opened one of them. It was a full can of blackberries. So, I decided I would make some pies. I did not lack for recipes or required ingredients. I knew what was in the inventory. So, I set about making pies to kill time. When they came out of the oven they smelled heavenly, and I was still all alone...So while they cooled I made my way to my squad bay to inform my buddies about our good fortune...When I returned to the galley the pies were gone. And I was pissed! A note from the officer's mess saying how much they appreciated the fresh blackberry pies didn't make it any better. And later I found out that the Chief took credit for those pies...#%&*%^. So much for volunteering."

Arrival

Pulling into Da Nang Harbor in the early morning hours on 23 February, Corporal Whaley remembers being awakened by strange vibrations. "The ship's slow movement woke me up at 0200 in the morning. I went up on deck to see what was going on. I could see in the distance overhead flares and tracers in the night sky. We could smell the cordite and that familiar smell that was Vietnam. Eventually Ronnie and Beany, my crew, came up on deck to join me. We all watched the night sky and it was quite a sight with the fireworks display. I had come back to Vietnam from being wounded only ten months prior. Later, I would learn from the S-3 NCO that I did not have to stay but could sign a waiver if I wanted to be with my guys...what the hell, I was here.

I signed the waiver. The morning broke through the clouds; it was just another day. We had finally traded the 'Devil and the deep blue sea' for the 1968 Tet Offensive. Good Morning, Vietnam!"

Da Nang Harbor 1968 ~ Courtesy of Ronald G. Oakes, B Co, 1/27

CHAPTER 2

The 1968 Tet Offensive: The Peak Year of Decisions

How had the Vietnam War become so chaotic? On that morning of 12 February 1968, as the sun rose from the ocean's surface, many Marines must have wondered how the war's intensity had increased so quickly.

They had been getting bits and pieces of the latest news. In late January, during the Lunar New Year (or "Tet") holiday, North Vietnamese and Communist forces launched savage attacks throughout South Vietnam. The U.S. and Army of the Republic of Vietnam (ARVN) forces took heavy losses before regrouping and repulsing the North Vietnamese and Viet Cong offensive. Most of the Marines of 1st Battalion, 27th Marines had only half-believed they were heading westward on training exercises in the Western Pacific.

The surprise of the 1968 Tet offensive back in the U. S. hastened underlying political turmoil, student unrest, war protests, and the call by military leaders for more troops. News coverage daily showed film footage of U. S. troops in battle. Several disturbing reports showed troops suffering wounds on-camera. Half-hour newscasts had dramatic effects on television audiences back home. How had the United States become mired in a war that most citizens knew very little about? Where was this country of South Vietnam? What were the realities of this war? How had the nation become bogged down in the rice paddies and jungles of Southeast Asia?

"Hey, Hey, LBJ! How many kids did you kill today?" was a slogan chanted by radical anti-Vietnam War protestors on campuses everywhere in America in 1967-68. The protests were comprised of enormous numbers of college students who were beginning to lose faith in government solving most national problems. By 1968, hippies and radical protestors had alarmed many in Middle America. It was indeed a pivotal year for not only the Marines who signed up to serve their country but for most Americans. Where would it all lead?

The Vietnam War continued raging on despite public opinion. On 13 February 1968, the Department of Defense announced that an Army brigade and a regiment of the 5th Marine Division would be sent to Vietnam. On 17 February, Headquarters Company, two Battalions, the 2nd and 3rd of the 27th Marine Regiment, and the 2nd Battalion, 13th Marines (Artillery), left from El Toro, California for Vietnam via aircraft. The 1st Battalion already aboard troop transport in the Pacific Ocean diverted from a training exercise and began steaming toward Da Nang Harbor. Together, RLT-27 became their alpha-numeric designator. RLT-27 (minus BLT 1/27, stationed in Hawaii) quickly staged for review by the President of the United States before deployment from El Toro on 17 February.

LBJ visits RLT-27 Feb 17, 1968, embarking for Vietnam from El Toro Marine Air Station, California
~ Photo courtesy of USMC base photographer (unknown) given to Andrew Boyko
(second from left, 3/27 and later 1/27)

President Lyndon B. Johnson made the trip to El Toro Marine Corps Air Station in California to see the 2nd and 3rd Battalion Marines embark for Vietnam, and then traveled on to Fort Bragg, North Carolina for the 82nd Airborne's departure the next day. In his brief visit, President Johnson said this to the departing Marines: "Nations—like men—are never privileged to know and never able to choose the precise moment when their destiny is determined. We can only know—and we can only strive to answer—the call of duty when that call comes, and the call has come tonight. The men at Khe Sanh, in I-Corps, need help. They have asked for it. If you were there and they were here, they would come to help you. I have asked you to go and help them. And I know you will do your duty and that you will get the job done. Our hearts and our hopes fly with you as you leave on this weekend. May God bless and keep each of you. We are proud of you. Your Nation is proud of you. And we will be prouder when you come marching home after you have done the job. Thank each of you and good night."[1]

Vietnam War Origins and U. S. Involvement

The Vietnam War expanded like no other America had fought to date. From research, we know the roots of origin for this conflict go back to the days after World War II. It seems that as early as February of 1946, Ho Chi Minh began to lobby the USA, China, Russia, and Britain for support of the Vietnamese people and their independence. His reasoning portrayed the pursuit of world peace and the claim that continued French colonization in Indochina was curtailing that ideal. His proposal to the United Nations was formatted to their ideas for a peaceful existence and begged for intervention and the negotiation of a fair settlement.

There are many theories as to how the United States became involved in Southeast Asia. France colonized the northern regions of Vietnam beginning in the 1880s and held a presence there until the 1950s. The historical facts support that the United States had made a simple financial commitment to its World War II ally, France. This commitment continued to be honored to varying degrees by the Truman, Eisenhower, and Kennedy administrations.

During the Eisenhower presidency and the fall of Dien Bien Phu in 1954, France withdrew militarily from Vietnam, and with the Geneva Accords Agreement signed in 1954, two temporary Vietnams came into existence, one in the north governed by the Viet Minh and the other to the south governed by the State of Vietnam. Elections were scheduled for 1956 and intended to reunite the two Vietnams. The United States did not sign the Geneva Accords, and agreed only to participate as an observer. It was that year in April at a news conference that Eisenhower began emphasizing the Domino Theory in Southeast Asia and Central America. The Domino Theory governed U.S. foreign policy starting in the 1950s, and basically held that a Communist takeover of one nation would lead to a chain reaction in surrounding states, much like falling dominos.

Thus began the shifting of U. S. foreign policy in that region to organize the South-East Asia Treaty Organization (SEATO). SEATO would realign some foreign alliances to protect South Vietnam. The slow trickle of U.S. advisers into South Vietnam began in 1955 to help the "nation building" theme adapted by Eisenhower's administration. In the years following, Eisenhower increased the number of U. S. military advisors in South Vietnam.

When leaving office, Eisenhower cautioned John F. Kennedy of the Communist threat in Southeast Asia. By the early 1960s, America had signed a military and economic aid treaty with South Vietnam. The arrival of U. S. support troops (advisors) and the formation of the United States Military Assistance Command (MACV) had begun in earnest. As the conflict escalated and military aid increased, the U. S. began air raids on North Vietnam and Communist-controlled areas in South Vietnam. By 1966, U. S. troop levels were approaching 200,000 and North Vietnam was starting to receive technical assistance and arms from the Soviet Union and other Communist countries.

The Street Without Joy – A Sign of What Was to Come

An enemy booby trap killed Dr. Bernard B. Fall, one of the foremost authors and authorities on Vietnam, while he tagged along with a Marine patrol during Operation Chinook II in 1967. Ironic that he was a KIA, 21 February, on the "street without joy," the same area he had so prophetically written about and for which his book was named. In looking back, maybe *Street Without Joy: The French Debacle in Indochina* should have been part of all training education for our military. This book warned America of what they would face in Southeast Asia. Some officers and non-coms (senior enlisted) would read his work on their own.

The actual "street without joy" (la Rue Sans Joie) stretched from Hue to Quang Tri in the I-Corps area, and was a segment of the national highway, Route 1. This area had been carefully planned and built by the Viet Minh during the French Colonial period, and was indicative of how the Communists operated against the Americans in Vietnam. An interlocking system of trench lines, tunnels, underground arms caches, ammo, and first-aid supplies were hidden in and around villages along this twenty-mile stretch. Hamlets surrounded by bushes, bamboo trees, and hedgerows made the Communists' pre-planned fields of fire invisible to those ambushed on this stretch of coastal road. During its deployment, 1/27 would come to know Route 1 well.

The Year the War Changed

The Tet Offensive of January 1968 elevated intense-battle campaigns throughout most of South Vietnam. The assaults throughout the northern and central regions of South Vietnam in the early morning hours of January 30th caused plenteous havoc. Before dawn that day, the Saigon and Mekong Delta areas were under heavy attack. The North's leadership fully expected the people of the South to rise in revolt and join them in reuniting as one country.

An estimated 75,000 - 80,000 North Vietnamese Army (NVA) and Viet Cong troops began their somewhat synchronized assaults on the U. S. Embassy, Vietnam's Presidential Palace, the Vietnamese Joint Staff, and the nearby Ton San Nhut Airbase in metropolitan Saigon. Further north, eight enemy battalions under cover of the dark crept into Hue City and the Citadel, a smaller replica of the original Forbidden City in Beijing, China. The ancient city of Hue was to Vietnam what Boston is to America in historical significance.

Three severely understrength Marine Corps battalions, three Army, and eleven South Vietnamese battalions in the Hue area battled almost a month before regaining control. Hundreds of Vietnamese citizens in this area were summarily executed, buried alive, or randomly killed and were not discovered for days.

The entire Viet Cong and NVA throng suffered extensive combat damage, and unbeknownst to the U. S. military, withdrew into their sanctuaries in defeat. However, these wide-scale battles and skirmishes, reported daily in the news media back in the United States, began to seriously erode American public opinion about the Vietnam War.

The United States remained loyal to the South Vietnamese, although domestic opposition to the Vietnam War increased noticeably in 1968, and by 1973 Congressional action forced the cessation of bombing Communist forces in Cambodia (along the Ho Chi Minh Trail). The Case-Church Amendment, signed into law in June of 1973, prohibited U. S. military activity, even though America continued to supply military equipment and economic aid. When the 1st Battalion, 27th Marines stepped onto Vietnamese soil in-country in late February of 1968, a full-scale shooting war had peaked. American sons were committed. There would be no turning back.

News Coverage Back Home

Back in the United States, 1968 began with live-broadcast news events of major North Vietnamese offensives coupled with the intensive antiwar protests being held in the streets of America. The antiwar movement, one of the most divisive undertakings in the twentieth-century alongside the Civil Rights campaigns of the 1960s, captured most Americans' attention. After the Tet Offensive, American public sentiment shifted quite dramatically. American society was clearly in upheaval and citizens began to question escalation and troop levels. The battles appeared in the daily news and nightly TV broadcasts. The Tet Offensive of 1968 undoubtedly contributed to President Johnson's decision to retire and not seek re-election in late March. United States troop strength would top out at almost 550,000 personnel in the Vietnam theater that year.

Most of the Marines and Corpsmen in Vietnam were occupied with a more determined daily existence, that of staying alive and eventually going home whole. The news of the protests trickled slowly to the Marines and Corpsmen engaged in combat. Unbeknownst to them, the beginning of the end began with the Tet Offensive of 1968. The U.S. would be out of Vietnam within five years.

Not portrayed in the media was the fact that the Americans had dealt a heavy blow to the North Vietnamese Army and its Main Force Viet Cong units working in parallel throughout South Vietnam. What also did not get reported were the heavy causalities suffered by the NVA and Viet Cong. Additionally, not being reported in the daily news were the destruction and routing of NVA soldiers who had infiltrated into South Vietnam via the Ho Chi Minh trail, clear-cut American victories, and the Marine Corps Civil Action Programs engaged in "winning hearts and minds" of the local populace.

Walter Cronkite of CBS proclaimed to the world after the battle for the Citadel in Hue City that the U.S. was "mired in a stalemate." It was very likely the North Vietnamese quickly refocused their thinking when they realized that their unsuccessful attacks in the south were being portrayed in the American news media as a stalemate. Senator Eugene McCarthy, running for president against Johnson on the Democratic ticket, ran a campaign against Johnson's war policy calling for halts in the bombing.[2] McCarthy used the success of Communist attacks during the Tet Offensive of 1968 as part of his campaign rhetoric.

The Marines and Corpsmen of 1/27 had yet to know they had other forces (war protesters) at home working against them. As was later learned, those protesters aided and abetted the enemy's morale with their antics. Even though they had suffered a crushing defeat in the Tet of 1968, the North Vietnamese began to realize that they could gradually scale down, continuing smaller operations and continue to rely on the psychological impact of reporting by the American news media and the actions of the American war protesters.

The Pentagon Papers

In 1967, Secretary of Defense Robert McNamara commissioned a study that he hoped would establish a written record of decisions that led to U. S. participation in

Vietnam. He felt the papers would address the key historical points for scholars in the future. This study examined Southeast Asian policy beginning in 1940, through 1968. The papers were "Top Secret" and considered sensitive, especially if they became public. The Administration feared that this study would create turmoil amongst foreign governments and discourage secret assistance to the United States if exposed. Supposedly only fifteen copies existed, which consisted of approximately 7,000 pages (3,000 pages of narrative history and 4,000 pages of supporting documents). The papers were held in the "think tank" of the Rand Corporation in Santa Monica, California.

Based on the investigative reporting of Neil Sheehan, Hedrick Smith, E. W. Kenworthy, and Fox Butterfield, the *NY Times* began publishing a series of articles on these secret papers starting 13 June 1971. An immediate court battle followed. Later that June, the Supreme Court of the United States ruled that the NY Times could continue to publish the articles.[2]

During the Daniel Ellsberg trial for leaking the Pentagon Papers to the *NY Times*, General Victor Krulak was called to be a witness for the federal government. Ellsberg's lawyer, Leonard Weinglass, introduced into the proceedings the idea that U. S. intervention in Vietnam was pre-meditated, and the Gulf of Tonkin incident a concocted event. Krulak later explained those moments in his memoir, *First to Fight*: Weinglass "wanted me to admit that well before we went to Vietnam the Marines were preparing for combat there." General Krulak went on to describe that he surprised Weinglass by admitting that the Marines were indeed preparing for the eventuality of fighting in Vietnam and "even more important, I told him, we were preparing to fight in a lot of other places, too!"[3]

NVA & VC Order of Battle Analysis Prior to 1968

A closer look at the Pentagon Papers study released in the NY Times in 1971 reveals that the Joints Chiefs and General William C. Westmoreland pressured LBJ to nationalize the Vietnam War to secure a quick victory. The ensuing debate and the Tet Offensive brought the opposite of what most of the upper-level brass and Congress sought. The prospect of calling up reserves and putting America economically in a state of full-scale war was not what the President wanted. He was squarely faced with "great domestic dissent, dissatisfaction, and disillusionment about both the purposes and the conduct of the war."[4] On March 31, 1968, two months after the beginning of Tet, President Johnson relieved General Westmoreland, in command MACV, and announced his decision to limit military operations in Vietnam. He shut down the bombing effort in the North and only allowed a small percent of the troop increase asked for by the Generals. Additionally, he told a numbed nation that he would not seek reelection for the presidency.

Research reveals that through much of 1967, the President had not paid full attention to Central Intelligence Agency reports and the Pentagon offices of International Security Affairs. These CIA and Pentagon reports emphasized that the enemy could withstand troop attrition for a long time. LBJ had relied heavily on General

Westmoreland and MACV's analysis of the war effort rather than CIA research. Later findings disclosed that the CIA's analysis was lowered to downplay estimates of Communist force buildup before Tet to more closely comply with MACV estimates.

Samuel Adams, CIA analyst/specialist in NVA/VC troop strengths, produced Telex cables from General Creighton Abrams back to 1967 that substantiated his testimony at General William Westmoreland's libel suit against CBS News in 1982. During the trial, Adams told the court about the political pressure put upon him by the military to depict NVA and VC troop levels as weaker than they were. Westmoreland eventually withdrew his libel suit as these and other discoveries came into focus.

The Tet Offensive had triggered a larger than anticipated political problem for the entire Johnson administration. Westmoreland's staff certainly knew a lot more than they let on, but were surprised by the entirety of the attacks which Hanoi had unleashed. Westmoreland, who had been asking for an additional 200,000 troops to continue prosecuting the war, was finally given a fraction of that manpower by President Johnson in February of 1968. The 27th Marine Regiment (RLT-27) and a Brigade from the 82nd Airborne were ordered to proceed to Da Nang, South Vietnam, in early 1968 as part of that relatively slight increase in manpower.

Major General Donn J. Robertson, the Commanding General of the 1st Marine Division when RLT-27 hastily arrived in Vietnam in February 1968, had ironically been a Battalion Commander in the 27th Marines (3/27) during the battle for Iwo Jima twenty-three years earlier, an engagement for which he received the Navy Cross Medal. He was later the Regimental Executive Officer of 27th Marines during the occupation of Japan. The Division's 24th Frag Order of 1968 (a Frag Order is a change to an existing order; see above) issued on 18 February 1968 by 1st Marine Division, moved Battalions 2/3 and 3/5, deploying them into other Tactical Areas of Operational Responsibility (TAORs). This positioned the 27th Regimental HQ south of Da Nang at the village of Duong Son (2)[1], Quang Nam Province (grid coordinate AT992678).

Command Chronology 1 to 29 February 1968, HQ, 1st Marine Division
(Reinforced), FMF Regimental Landing Team 27's Arrival, in-country

---

[1] Villages were often built together in clusters, with only one name given for a group of villages. The maps used by Marines added numbers to identify a specific village location within the group.

The RLT-27 Battalion's initial responsibility in February of 1968 was to engage in rice denial and airfield security operations. This area would become the TAOR and operating area for most of the RLT-27 for almost seven months. Da Nang airstrip, a short distance to the north, in the late 1960s was considered the busiest airport in the world. The Viet Cong and NVA continued to pour men and materials into the Go Noi staging area, the "Arizona Territory," Hill 55, Que Son Valley, An Hoa basin, and "Dodge City" battlefields southwest and west of the airstrip to destroy the strategic real estate. Unbeknownst to the Marines and Corpsmen of RLT-27, this entire area was one of the most dangerous places in the world in 1968.

Major General Donn J. Robertson, Commanding General, 1st Marine Division receives an award from Lt. General Hoang Xuan Lam, ARVN commander 1968. (DOD Photo USMC 1-171-68-A)

The Politics of Reinforcements

According to the Pentagon Papers, after the start of Tet 1968 there was contention as to whether the President and General Earle G. Wheeler (Chairman of the Joint Chiefs) pressed General Westmoreland to ask for more troops, or if the President asked for Westmoreland's current recommendations. After a few days and no response, General Wheeler reportedly sent a Telex on February 8, in effect asking if Westmoreland "needed reinforcements, we are limited in what we can offer, but we can provide you with the option of an 82nd Airborne Division and a half Marine Corps Division both loaded with Vietnam Veterans." General Wheeler further stressed that the 525,000-troop allotment authorized for 1968 had only reached the 500,000 mark. Wheeler concluded his message: "Query: Do you need reinforcement? Our capabilities are limited."[5]

The same day, Westmoreland responded and requested those additional troops, and additionally asked the President for authorization to launch an amphibious assault with Marines into North Vietnam as a diversionary tactic. General Wheeler replied that he recommended that Westmoreland utilize the 82nd Airborne and the Marines bring them directly to Da Nang, RVN and do so immediately. Nothing was mentioned with respect to the request to launch the amphibious assault north of the DMZ.

The Joint Chiefs of Staff recommended immediate reinforcements be deferred at that time, but that the preparation for possible deployment go forward. The Chiefs focused on and were hoping to get the President to activate the reserves, which at the time they (JCS) thought a more commonsense approach.

On 13 February, LBJ approved the release of 10,500 men through Secretary of Defense, Robert McNamara—a brigade of the 82nd Airborne and a Marine Regimental Landing Team (RLT-27). President Johnson flew both to California and then on to Fort Bragg to personally shake hands with the troops he was deploying. It was reported that the men, many of whom had recently returned from Vietnam, were grim. It has been speculated that this could have had bearing on his decision to not seek reelection a month and a half later.

In 1968, III Marine Amphibious Force in the Republic of Vietnam (III MAF, RVN) had become the equivalent size of a U. S. Corps, consisting of two Army Divisions, two reinforced Marine Divisions, a Marine aircraft wing, and with supporting units in the realm of over 100,000 personnel. Its area of responsibility was the upper one-fourth of the Republic of South Vietnam, the I Corps. At the time, Lieutenant General Robert E. Cushman presided as III MAF's Commanding General. This continued to be one of the more hotly contested areas in the northern part of the RVN due to the Da Nang airfield and seaport.

It is now known that General Westmoreland was not satisfied with the offensive tactics the Marines were employing during that time, and was cautiously concerned with Cushman's strategies. Consequently, Westmoreland rearranged his command structure and had his deputy, Army General Creighton Abrams, take command of the I-Corps Tactical Zone while turning over Marine aviation to an Air Force Commander in April 1968.

Marine leadership vociferously protested, but was rebuked by the Joint Chiefs of Staff. General Westmoreland, steadfast in his views, had no confidence in the Marine Corps upper-echelon leadership. In turn, Lieutenant General Victor H. Krulak, Commanding General FMFPAC, Cushman's boss, had personal misgivings about the direction General Westmoreland was taking.

In a SPECAT EXCLUSIVE Telex for Lieutenant General R. E. Cushman from the Command Chronologies of FMFPAC, General Krulak conveyed his thought process about Westmoreland at that time. The Telex was sent on 21 February 1968, four days after the 82nd Airborne Brigade and RLT-27 had embarked and were en route to Vietnam. Lieutenant General Cushman had Telexed Krulak, asking for guidance in positioning these additional incoming resources. Lieutenant General Krulak emphatically replied as follows:

1. Basically, I see the problem of stating resource requirements to be Westy's [Westmoreland], based on his assessment of the enemy situation and his own strategic analysis of what he will need to do the job. The MACV working paper would suggest that he sees it pretty much that way too, but that he apparently intends to ask for the forces he thinks he needs, without consulting his principal subordinates: your assignment, under the ground rules of the working paper, as I interpret them, is not to tell him what is needed to fight the I CTZ battle, but just to fill the numerical blanks for what you estimate to be necessary USMC program V add-ons, and for a Marine Division (-), plus the proper balance of accompanying Marine aviation and support forces[...]

2. There is no problem in providing the pure arithmetic for you and, time being so short; I am doing so in the message. However, I regard Westy's procedure as a weak way to run the store. It seems to me that you, as Westy's viceroy for I CTZ, should have a chance to tell him what your needs are to fight the battle he wants fought in your region, without regard to whether the forces are Army, Marines, ROK [Republic of Korea], etc. Then he should weigh this with all the corresponding input from other corps areas and come up with his overall conclusion. And finally, I regard it as improper for him to name specific Marine (or Army, for that matter) units as the ones he wants. That is up to his superiors.

Lieutenant General Victor "Brute" Krulak chatting with a convalescent Marine in Hawaii 1968
~ Courtesy of Lieutenant Bill Black, A Co, 1/27

3. Next, as to our own situation. It is simple. There aren't any more forces. We cannot support what we now have deployed for much over four months. If all deployment criteria were reduced to zero, if enlistments were involuntarily extended, 5th Mar Div (-) [meaning RLT-27] and 3d MAW (-) could be put into some sort of shape in a month or so, but only by substantial intra-Marine Corps transfers. If the reserves were called up the Marines could deploy a substantial Air/Ground Force quickly (more than an Air/Ground Brigade, I'd guess). But, as of now, zero.

4. The above should not deter you from advising Westy what is needed to do his bidding in I CTZ; but that advice should be in absolute terms, not in terms of just Marines since, as you know so well, I CTZ is not a pure Marine job, anymore.

5. If you are asked for USMC Program V add-on strengths, here are the figures, as best we can distil them, from phone calls etc., of what you have said that you want. I do not personally subscribe to them all, but a shortage of time precludes detailed analysis now. Will make such an analysis ASAP, and advise you of my specific conclusions. Parenthetically, I point out that the increases need not all be Marines when bumped against I CTZ needs [he pencils in all of the units to make up the USMC Program V resources].[6]

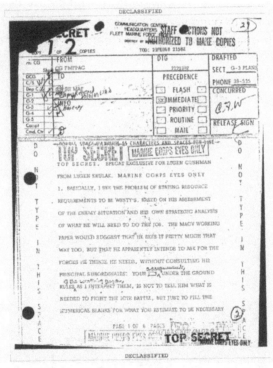

First page of the eight-page Telex sent to Lieutenant General Robert E. Cushman from Lieutenant General Victor Krulak, 21 Feb 1968 at 2158Z time ~ Command Chronologies FMFPAC

In his book, *The Marines In Vietnam 1954-1973: An Anthology and Annotated Bibliography*, Brigadier General Edwin H. Simmons points out that the move by Westmoreland to place his deputy, General Creighton W. Abrams, at MACV Forward (Phu Bai), was interpreted by some in the press corps as Westmoreland's dissatisfaction with the Marine Corps leadership. Simmons goes on to explain that Abrams refrained from giving direct orders to any Army or Marine unit under General Cushman's command. However, scuttlebutt at the higher levels rumored that the rift between Westmoreland and the Marines was still simmering.

General Westmoreland and Lieutenant General R. E. Cushman review the troops in I-Corps
~ Courtesy of Marine Corps History Division (DOD Photo USMC A191509)

Lieutenant General Robert E. Cushman, III MAF CG, with Bob Hope USO show
~ Courtesy of III MAF USMC Photographer (unknown) 1969, copy given to Raul E. Figueroa, III MAF

Per the history, *The Defining Year 1968*, both General Cushman and General Krulak were suspicious about the move of MACV Forward HQ to Phu Bai, and both cautiously transitioned into the new command arrangement, cooperating with General Abrams even though they were not pleased with the new command structure.[7]

Simmons wrote, "Formation of MACV Forward and later of ProvCorps V struck some members of the press as being a manifestation of Army dissatisfaction with Marine Corps Generalship. Old debates, dating back to France in World War I, Saipan and Okinawa in World War II and X Corps in Korea were exhumed. Disclaimers by both Army and Marine Corps spokesmen did not completely still the clamor."[8]

Vietnamese Lt. General Hoang Xuan Lam, Marine Lt. Generals Robert E. Cushman, Jr.,
and Victor H. Krulak, and Army Lt. General William B. Rosson attending dedication
of Camp Bruno A. Hochmuth on 4 April 1968 (DOD Photo USMC A25515)

One of the points made in Robert Coram's book, *Brute: The Life of Victor Krulak, U.S. Marine*, was that Westmoreland often fumed with angst about Krulak, who was delivering speeches to many high-level people in the military, both in Hawaii and back in CONUS (Continental U. S.). Krulak's talks always suggested the Army and its high command was not prosecuting the war to a final win.

General Cushman served as Deputy Commander, III MAF in April of 1967, and in June was promoted to Lieutenant General, thereby assuming full command of III MAF until late February 1968, when General Westmoreland assigned his deputy, Army General Creighton Abrams, to take responsibility of I Corps Tactical Zone at MACV Forward in Phu Bai. Cushman then became a senior advisor and an I Corps Coordinator to Abrams. In 1969, Lieutenant General Cushman became the Deputy Director of the CIA. Following the CIA assignment, he was promoted to General, taking command of the Marine Corps as Commandant in 1972. It was on his watch as Commandant that the last Marine units pulled out of Vietnam.

Strategic Thinking

General Krulak had introduced his controversial Combined Action Program (CAP) strategy in the mid-1960s. As General Krulak explained in his memoir, the basic concept of his strategy was that winning the hearts and minds of the locals would ensure a victory. However, according to Krulak, two drawbacks prevented CAP's success: Westmoreland wouldn't buy into Krulak's "ink blot" Combined Action Program, and, "The enemy enjoyed a privileged sanctuary in the ports of North Vietnam and in Laos, through which a growing cascade of deadly munitions was flowing."

Krulak's CAP began to show signs of progress throughout South Vietnam later in the war. CAP and Counterinsurgency were designed around the idea of protecting the indigenous people, providing security, and helping them promote their economy, a combination Peace Corps/military program. By day, the Marines helped villagers with their civil life, improving water supplies, providing basic health care, and so on, and at night they set up ambushes as well as provided basic security. This made Westmoreland nervous, because he had to answer to a President and Secretary of Defense that liked body-count statistics. And as is pointed out in Coram's, *Brute*, Westmoreland argued that the CAP concept would take too long. At the time, the U.S. military was winning all the regional battles militarily.

In addition to CAP, the Phoenix Program and SOG programs showed success, although they were not instituted quickly enough or in large enough measure. The CIA set up the Phoenix Program to seek and destroy the Viet Cong infrastructure. Military Assistance Command, Vietnam – Studies and Observation Group (MACV-SOG) formed as a highly classified, multi-branch, special operation group, which conducted strategic recon and unconventional warfare. The hierarchy wanted quick results, which ran counter to the methodology of these programs.[9]

Westmoreland began implying the Marines were afraid to take the fight to the enemy. It was commonly known that he was suspicious of the Marines, and especially General Krulak. The rift between Westmoreland and Krulak expanded over time. Westmoreland clashed with General Krulak often and was resolute on keeping an eye on him and his Marines' tactical operations.[10] It was learned that, rather than personally question the authority of Marine Commanders, General Westmoreland preferred to send the Marines orders for specific situations which he felt would get them moving forward.[11]

Lieutenant General Victor H. Krulak (on right), CG FMFPAC inspecting FLC/1st Force Service Regiment, Da Nang on 3 April 1968 (DOD Photo USMC A25618)

In a meeting with General Krulak, Secretary of Defense McNamara told him that CAP was "a good idea," but it was "too slow." Krulak responded in a letter to McNamara dated 11 November 1965, "In the highly populous areas the battleground is in the people's minds. We have to separate the enemy from the people..." Despite these differences, relations between the higher command remained strained but cooperative.[12]

Early on, General Krulak exposed his strategic views to, not only, General Westmoreland but also, by divulging his ideas in writing and circulating them, to people who could act. His appraisal condemned the Westmoreland strategy already in play: "Attrit the enemy to a degree which makes him incapable of prosecuting the war, or unwilling to pay the cost of so doing.... If this is indeed the basis for our strategy, it has to be regarded as inadequate." He further emphasized his ideas in *First To Fight*: "provincial people" were where the battle was, because they were being utilized, terrorized, and exploited by the Viet Cong. Not enough was being done to provide a strong government, and if these "subversion and guerrilla efforts were to disappear" the war would soon end because the enemy would be denied the essentials of "food, sanctuary, and intelligence."[13]

Krulak's appraisals and ideas were never given much consideration until 1970, when the mining of Haiphong Harbor and a renewed bombing campaign were instituted. But as General Krulak points out, it was then too late. By that time, the North had established a gargantuan logistical-supply infrastructure which routed through Laos and Cambodian sanctuaries to the west of Vietnam, rivaling no other present-day army.[14]

It was common knowledge that Krulak was the only high-ranking military officer who confronted LBJ and his war strategy. It has been speculated that LBJ passed Krulak over for the Commandant billet purposefully, and left him in place out of spite. It is documented that Krulak knew he would pay a price for confronting President Johnson, but his conscience would not let him do otherwise. General Krulak was truly one of few in the top rungs of military leadership at the time that put country, Corps, and duty before self.

Early on, even Commandant Wallace M. Greene Jr. aired his differences over Vietnam with Secretary McNamara. It was well known that McNamara looked upon the Joint Chiefs with disdain, unwilling to acknowledge that they were fully trained and most capable of planning military operations in Vietnam. His perceived arrogant attitude irritated the Commandant. In a memorandum found in the Greene Collection of papers, "Escalation of Effort in South Vietnam," 10 July 1965 (Marine Corps History Division), General Greene, a consummate note taker, penciled in a personal note about McNamara: "an arrogant individual who will eventually have his 'comeuppance'!"[15]

North Vietnamese Perspectives

In Bui Tin's book, *From Enemy to Friend*, the Commander of the Ho Chi Minh Trail, General Dong Sy Nguyen, purportedly told Tin that his greatest fear was of American ground forces cutting off the Trail. He told Tin that the U. S. could bomb and it wouldn't matter. American bombers rarely caused major damage, and Nguyen admitted that what worried him was that the Americans would send troops in and disrupt the entire system. Some senior officers of the North Vietnamese Joint Staff confided in Bui Tin that all the Americans had to do was use two to three divisions, both American and Saigon troops, occupy a chunk of the Ho Chi Minh Trail, and the NVA would be in trouble![16]

Colonel Tin went on to tell of a tour on which he accompanied General Giap, Gen. Le Trong Tan (Chief of Joint General Staff), and other senior-level officers to the Soviet Union, Poland, East Germany, Hungary, and China in 1977. During this trip, they discussed the war years. General Giap told the group that he was very worried during 1964-65 that a combined invasion from the sea and air would come to someplace in the northern part of Vietnam. He was not at all confident that the U.S.S.R. would come to North Vietnam's defense. He also mentioned that the Chinese had already told him they would not do any more than they already had been doing.

Giap said that if the Americans attacked the Ho Chi Minh Trail, the destruction of what North Vietnam had put in place for logistics and supply "would totally dislocate" the war effort in the South. He added that the North Vietnamese would have to go on the defense of the homeland, rather than expand their original objectives. Colonel Tin remembered General Giap concluding the discussions with the following: "The war would not have evolved in our favor as it did."[17]

Colonel Robert Fischer, a 1955 Naval Academy graduate who became a "Covan" (advisor) to the Vietnamese Marine Corps in 1966, writes in his memoir, *Guerrilla Grunt*, about General Westmoreland's prosecution of the war: "Like General Paul Harkins before him, he would not hear any criticism and certainly had not read the French Lessons Learned in Southeast Asia. He adamantly refused to admit that his blitzkrieg combat assaults had destroyed too many villages—as well as the potential loyalty of the many villagers he blasted. Those villages and graveyards were ancient and sacred ground. It seems that he truly believed all villagers were 'Viet Cong sympathizers.' During his time, he never merged U.S. and Vietnamese units, preferring separate chains of command that puzzled most Vietnamese officers."[18]

Psychological tactics were part of the North's campaign against the Americans, as can be seen in a propaganda pamphlet from the 1/27 TAOR in 1968 that plays on the emotions of American service members (transcription on the following page).

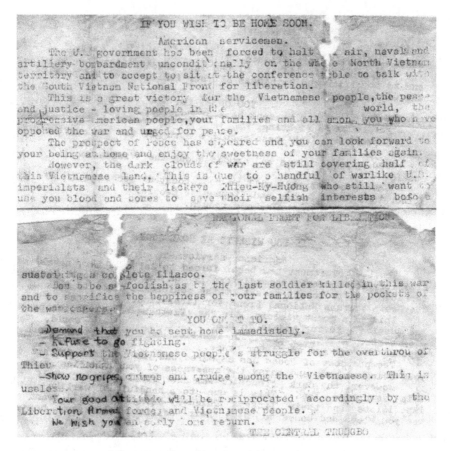

Propaganda pamphlet found in the Go Noi area ~ Courtesy of Sergeant John Decker, Fox Co, 2/7
(Enhanced clarification below)

If You Wish To Be Home Soon.

American servicemen.

The U.S. government has been forced to halt the air, naval and artillery bombardment unconditionally on the whole North Vietnam territory and to accept to sit at the conference table to talk with the South Vietnam National Front for Liberation.

This is a great victory for the Vietnamese poeple, the peace and justice-loving people in the world, the progressive American poeple, your families and all among you who have opposed the war and urged for peace.

The prospect of Peace has appeared and you can look forward to your being at home and enjoy the sweetness of your families again.

However, the dark clouds of war are still covering half of this Vietnamese land. This is due to a handful of warlike U.S. imperialsts and their lackeys Thieu-Ky-Huong who still want to use you blood and bones to save their selfish interests before sustaining a complete fiasco.

Don't be foolish as be the last soldier killed in this war and to sacrifice the happiness of your families for the pockets of the warmongers.

YOU OUGHT TO.
- *Demand that you be sent home immediately.*
- *Refuse to go fighting.*
- *Support the Vietnamese people's struggle for the overthrou of Thieu-Ky-Huong*
- *Show no grips, crimes, and grudge among the Vietnamese. This is useless.*
- *Your good attitude will be reciprocated accordingly by the Liberation Armed forces and Vietnamese people.*

We wish you an early home return.
Signed: **THE CENTRAL TRUNGBO**

Communist forces lost many men during the war; it has been estimated that the number was over one million soldiers. America lost over 58,000, and public opinion played a large part in America's eventual withdrawal from Southeast Asia.

Born of an earlier mindset and schooled for conventional warfare, Westmoreland looked to American firepower and body count for the winning strategy. As was pointed out by Max Boot in *Invisible Armies*, Westmoreland had the power to decide how the war would be prosecuted on the ground. He called the shots for most of the war years.

President Johnson did control the bombing of the North due to his concern over China and the Soviet Union, and feared they would enter with manpower if provoked. But General Westmoreland plodded on with his war of attrition until 1968 when he was relieved and General Creighton Abrams took his place.

A South Vietnamese Perspective

Nguyen Cao Ky, the Prime Minister of the Republic of Vietnam in the 1960s, had an even different view of America's involvement in his country. In his book, *How We Lost the Vietnam War*, he recalls that even though he felt America was heavily involved in the war effort, that his country would have been better suited and equipped had the effort been approached like China and Russia did in their economic and material support to the North Vietnamese. He points out that those powers chose to fight a limited war. The Chinese and Russians supported the North Vietnamese from behind the scenes, never allowing photographs or news articles of their involvement for fear of misinterpretation. Their latest technologies in equipment and supplies were provided to the North Vietnamese in voluminous quantities.

The typical NVA soldier had no idea where his weaponry came from, just that "Uncle Ho" had acquired them. The average NVA soldier did not have the war fought for him by the Chinese or the Russian soldier. For the most part, they received very little advisory support. They were fighting for a charismatic leader, Ho Chi Minh, and for the reunification of Vietnam (nationalism).

On the other side of the coin, Ky felt American over-involvement caused an erosion of morale amongst the South Vietnamese. He points out that his countrymen felt that they participated in a lesser role, and were fighting for the United States in their war. While he believed South Vietnam did need American assistance, he was convinced that the sons and daughters of South Vietnam could have won, had they been provided economic aid and expertise, improving the lot of the average peasant family without the United States being at the forefront. He felt that his armies had been trained for the defensive, and that had there been more emphasis on them taking the offensive, especially during the aftermath of the 1968 Tet, South Vietnam could have perhaps done more damage to the North's war effort.[19]

The Other War

Colonel William R. Corson points out an altogether different opinion in his book *The Betrayal*. He felt that had South Vietnam's leaders and their followers all "bugged out" for the southern parts of France, Vietnam's political system would have been better for it. He felt that once all the corrupt and incompetent elements in Vietnam were gone, the war could have taken a different turn. Corson contends that withdrawing all U. S. advisors and support from the ARVN forces would have made the ARVN feel the need to fight for their own survival. His opinion rested on his experience with the Vietnamese upper echelons, the peasants themselves, and with Marine Corps Combined Action Platoons in South Vietnam.

In the Introduction to *The Betrayal*, William J. Lederer, author of *The Ugly American*, points out that Corson demonstrated rampant corruption within the South Vietnamese government and a hesitation on the part of the U. S. government to recognize that corruption. U.S. high-level officials looked the other way. More importantly, Lederer asserts that Corson, with his 1,200 men spread over seventy-eight hamlets in the northern I CTZ, had for the most part won the "hearts and minds" of the South Vietnamese peasants, who fought beside these Marines in the Tet of 1968. It was later shown that these units more than held their ground in those battles. The people in these areas had a personal stake in winning, regardless of the corruption going on in the higher levels of their government. Lederer made the case for Corson's CAPs, which made conditions better for everyone.

Corson's approach, sometimes called the "Other War" or the "Pacification Program," encompassed the strategic effort of winning the endorsement of the people of I Corps. His program was designed to help them consolidate, stabilize, and give them a hand in their own political system. The Combined Action Platoons that Corson commanded were strategically designed to help put together an economic, political, and social-justice infrastructure for the Vietnamese citizenry.[20]

America Sends Its Best Young Men

America sent its best troops to fight this war. Draftees were not significant in number comparatively. It is now documented that close to 70 percent of the men who served during the Vietnam War were volunteers.[21] Hundreds of thousands of young working-class men volunteered for service during this conflict out of national pride.

An even greater percentage of men in the Marine Corps were volunteers, even though they were taking some draftees to fill the ranks. These volunteers scored stunning victories over the Communists, especially during the peak years of 1968 and 1969. The sacrifices made by these young men and RLT-27 contributed to shattering defeats that almost decimated the NVA and VC during the campaigns of 1968.

It is starting to slowly come to light in the reexamination of the Vietnam War, that America was winning militarily during this timeline despite the media, post-war propaganda, and politics. The Vietnam War was strongly protested at home as immoral and unjust until the draft went away in July of 1973. The issues protested by the draft dodgers and the antiwar activists then dissipated, and the protests mysteriously went away after the draft lottery ended. It now seems that the media strongly influenced societal perception during these times.

Training and Deployment – Orders for Vietnam

The Narrative Summary from 1st Battalion, 27th Marines Command Chronology of February 1968 describes the plan for 1/27 because of President Johnson's decision to send additional troops in 1968 and the events that followed.

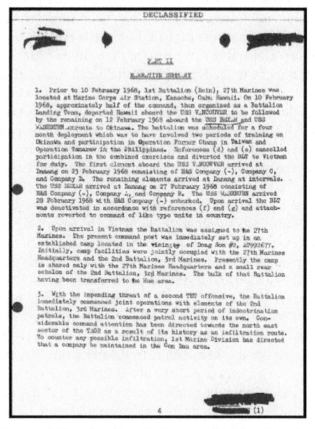

February 1968 Command Chronology Narrative Summary of events. Note: (-) means that a unit is on the light side or not up to full T/O (Table of Organization) strength, or that it is only part of the unit and the other part is elsewhere.

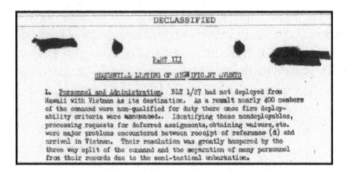

February 1968 Command Chronology Significant Events

There has been much discussion amongst the Marines and Corpsmen of RLT-27 about when the decision was made to place them in harm's way. The above two missives from the February 1968 Command Chronology of 1st Battalion, 27th Marines, along with historical fact and dates from the Pentagon Papers, puts those deployment events in perspective. The upper echelons of Marine Corps leadership did not know RLT-27 was positively headed for Vietnam until 13 February 1968. The additional troop buildup had been an ongoing debate in the upper echelons of the administration and Congress before that, but a firm decision had not been made. RLT-27 leadership dutifully prepared for the inevitable.

Once LBJ decided, General Krulak canceled the training exercise and directed the battalion to steam directly to Da Nang. The Battalion, it was learned, was seriously understrength, with an average of about 120 Marines per Rifle Company instead of 150. Additionally, close to 400 of the Battalion personnel were mixes of seventeen-year-olds, sole surviving sons, Marines returned from RVN under thrice-wounded policy, officers and enlisted with less than four months until discharge, those with less than one year between tour dates, and other criteria that affected deployment back to the RVN.

Krulak rigorously looked throughout the 5th Marine Division and the West Coast for Marines to fill this under-strength Regiment. He reportedly performed some creative paperwork to register RLT-27 generally ready, rather than fully combat ready, as per Marine Corps regulations. To address the frail ranks of 1/27, he culled replacements from staging Battalion and FMFPAC security forces, FMFPAC HQs, and 9th Marine Amphibious Brigade (MAB) to fill its shortfall. It should be noted that three of the 5th Marine Division's regiments served in Vietnam: the 26th, 27th and 13th Marines (Artillery). The 28th Marine Regiment, activated in 1967 along with the others, served on-call but did not deploy. In February of 1968, the 28th Marines transferred twenty-two officers and about 600 enlisted men to the 27th Marines in the shuffle instituted by General Krulak. Especially in 3rd Battalion, 27th Marines, non-infantry MOSs (Military Occupational Specialties) were tapped to fill the line company ranks with infantrymen. The adage, "Every Marine a rifleman, first" once again became the norm.[22]

1/27 Battalion Commander, Lieutenant Colonel John E. Greenwood, wrote to each parent of the Marines in 1/27, explaining this pivotal decision by the Commander-In-Chief and how it affected their son. Below is a copy of that letter.

1st BATTALION (Rein), 27th MARINES
FLEET MARINE FORCE, PACIFIC
FPO SAN FRANCISCO, CALIFORNIA 96602

February 21, 1968

Dear Parents and Friends:

As your son has no doubt informed you his Battalion, the 1st Battalion (Rein), 27th Marines, set out from Hawaii earlier this month for exercises and training in Okinawa, the Philippines, Taiwan, and Japan. We were to be gone for approximately four months and had planned to conduct maneuvers in conjunction with some of our SEATO allies. Now, suddenly and unexpectedly, our plans have been changed. As Battalion Commander I want to take this opportunity to explain our present status and also to make myself available to you in case any questions or problems may arise in which I can be of assistance.

Two days after leaving Hawaii the Battalion was diverted from its original mission and our participation in the exercises cancelled. As a result of recent developments, the President ordered us to go into Vietnam as a part of his prudent build up of forces in that country. The three ships on which the Battalion is embarked, the USS VANCOUVER, the USS BEXAR, and the USS WASHBURN, immediately changed course for our new destination. We left Hawaii in the spirit for which the Marine Corps is famous - fully prepared for any contingency - and when we arrive in Vietnam this Battalion and each man in it should disembark with confidence in our preparedness. As I said in my letter to some of you on December 13, 1967, "Should the time come for us to go, either as a unit or as individuals, we will be ready."

Present policies, however, require that some 300 of our men be reclassified as "nondeployable". These are men who for a variety of reasons cannot go with us. Many of them, your son being one, cannot go because they are only seventeen years old. These men will be sent to Okinawa for further training and will be reassigned to a replacement draft within a few weeks after their eighteenth birthdays.

Our Battalion has been training together as a unit for the past several months and is fortunate to have a large number of Marines in every occupational field and from every rank with past combat experience in South Vietnam. For nearly half of us this will be the second tour. This foundation of experience has been advantageous throughout our training, and it will be equally advantageous in the months ahead. Because of this and because your son has been with the Battalion and is a part of it, I hated to see him pulled out and sent to a strange unit as an individual replacement. I therefore sent a message about the matter to the Commanding General, Fleet Marine Force, Pacific, and have obtained his assurance that your son will rejoin us rather than some other unit after his stay at Okinawa. I am particularly pleased with this, and believe it is the best for him and the whole Battalion.

As you must sense, I am extremely proud of the 1st Battalion (Rein), 27th Marines. I am confident of our ability to meet any eventuality with success in the true tradition of the Marine Corps. In the months ahead if you have problems or questions concerning your son which you want to bring to my attention, I hope you will feel free to do so. My officers and I firmly believe that at no time is anything more important to success in the Marine Corps than the individual Marine.

Sincerely,

J. E. GREENWOOD
Lieutenant Colonel, U.S. Marine Corps
Commanding

Letter courtesy of Colonel Franklin P. Eller, USMC (Ret), XO of 1/27 1967-68

Filling the Ranks of 1/27

Felix Salmeron, a combat-tested veteran of an earlier tour and a Sergeant, found himself assigned to 5th Force Recon, Subunit One (5th Recon was the 5th Marine Division reconnaissance unit) in Camp Pendleton early in 1967. General Krulak had begun beefing up the newly formed 27th Regiment within the 5th Marine Division in anticipation of President Johnson's potential decision to send Westmoreland more troops. In September and October, staff NCOs and officers began to be funneled into the 27th Marines. The 26th Marines were already in Vietnam. The 1st Battalion was forming as a Brigade in Kaneohe Bay, Hawaii. Second and Third Battalions were being formed at Camp Pendleton, California. When Sergeant Salmeron arrived in Hawaii back in the infantry again, the unit had started preparations for a training exercise in the Pacific.

Salmeron remembered, "We really didn't have enough leaders or people to fill the ranks. I remember that troops started coming to us from supporting units. I had a kid that was a mortician, who ended up being one of my Squad Leaders. I had another young Marine that was a cook, who was a Sergeant and he came over and ended up being one of my Squad Leaders. I had another Marine who was a tanker and the whole principle behind this billet filling at the time was for them to get exposure to leadership roles in a combat unit. I don't think there was any initial intent to keep these kids permanently or so we were told. When we returned from the exercise they were to go back to their regular units.

"As you know it turned out we went on to Vietnam. When we arrived in the RVN we had a whole combination of different MOS's in combat roles with no exposure to leadership let alone the infantry. A lot of these kids learned their skills real-time. They did not have the luxury of picking it up in a school. We had them and we had the new kids right out of boot camp and all they knew was that their Squad Leader was a Corporal or a Sergeant and was in charge. So, we had to deal with teaching these Marines infantry tactics in a real combat theater. It was a real challenge. Everyone is a basic infantryman anyway from boot camp. We got through it."

Within Alpha Company, as was the case in other companies, there were some NCOs who had recently served combat tours in the RVN. They were not required to go ashore unless a waiver was signed. A few elected not to return so soon. Sergeant Salmeron and Sergeant Kellams signed waivers to go ashore due to the lack of NCO leadership.

As Salmeron recollected, "We went ashore with a skeleton number of NCOs. I was the senior enlisted Marine [E-5] making the landing with the Company. Captain Jim Panther used to say I was his XO. Both Kellams and I were in line for Staff Sergeant Billets. I remember that Corporal Steven Maher was acting as our First Sergeant. After we arrived and started to stage, the companies got an influx of new officers straight from basic school. The challenge was then to train both the new troops and the new platoon leaders. I had two new Second Lieutenants during the seven months I was there. When you deal with challenges on both sides of the rank ladder you have no one to turn to for advice. You just could not, under any circumstance, show any weakness to anyone. Especially if you lost a Platoon Leader, it is amplified. You feel as if you have failed in some way, but you still have Marines to lead. You had to make hard decisions, suck it up and go forward. It was difficult not to show emotion when you lost a Marine. You still had to be concerned for those who were alive. Most young officers did not understand the dilemma that the experienced NCO leaders were dealing with."

On 10 February 1968, William Drennan, a seasoned Marine Corps NCO with a previous combat tour already under his belt, boarded the USS Vancouver for what he thought would be a fun cruise through the Orient to train with other nationalities practicing war games. The rude awakening came on 13 February when everyone aboard the Vancouver was notified that the Battalion now in the Pacific Ocean and heading for Okinawa had been redirected to Vietnam. Drennan recollects, "Our military records were already being reviewed by upper brass that day. They told me that I did not have to return to Vietnam, but was given time to think it over and could give a yes or no when we arrived at Da Nang harbor. Knowing that I would eventually have to serve another tour, I elected to go ashore with this unit—probably the best thing I possibly could have done."

Maneuver Battalions in Vietnam

Each Marine Corps Rifle Regiment throughout the entire Marine Corps commands three battalions: the First, Second, and Third Battalions. Each rifle battalion within this structure is a tactical unit capable of maneuver, and all movement is entirely on foot, with a minimal number of jeeps, trucks, and Mechanical Mules held back for support roles. All weaponry and ammo is personal and hand-carried.

During this era, a battalion was made up of an H&S Company and four lettered rifle companies. To make it simple, during the Vietnam War the First battalion of any of the Regiments had (using the phonetical alphabet) Alpha, Bravo, Charlie, and Delta companies; the Second Battalion's letter companies were Echo, Foxtrot, Golf, and Hotel; and Third Battalions were India, Kilo, Lima, and Mike. Juliet was not utilized in the Marine's phonetic alphabet.

Each battalion's H&S Companies consisted of a command section, medical support, supply, and administration for the maneuvering rifle companies. Also included in support were a tactical communications network, the 81mm mortar platoons, 106mm recoilless rifles, and the seldom-used flamethrowers.

Within the four lettered companies resided three rifle platoons, a weapons platoon, and a headquarters command section. At full strength, a rifle company would have six officers and 210 enlisted troop billets. This was not always the case in Vietnam due to normal losses caused by heat, wounds, illnesses, R&Rs, transfers, rotations back to the U. S., and KIAs. Later during the tour, platoons within the battalion averaged roughly twenty-five to thirty Marines with a Corpsman, if lucky. These averages fluctuated with circumstances (See Exhibit A in the Appendix, *An Overview of the*

USMC Table of Organization, for a more detailed look at the organization and overview of the entire Marine Corps).

The Decision to Deploy RLT-27

When the decision to send the 82nd Airborne and RLT-27 was finalized, President Johnson reached what would be the peak of American participation in the fighting, with just over a half-million troops deployed in the war effort. He wanted no more escalation of troops, and denied General Westmoreland's request for another 200,000. This request, not known at first, eventually became public and caused widespread consternation for the Administration.

LBJ had sensed that the maximum troop level could not be increased without political resistance and that Americans would not react favorably to sending more of our nation's youth into the killing fields of South Vietnam. Back on 3 August 1967, without much press, the limiting number was officially set at 525,000 by President Johnson. This was less than what Westmoreland had in mind. It has been said that this is the best evidence on record that LBJ was determined to find a way of getting out of the war without sending more troops. It has also been said that Secretary of Defense Clark Clifford, who replaced McNamara, and a few other "wise men" reasoned with LBJ behind the scenes to de-escalate the war and eventually turn it over to the South Vietnamese. This was not widely reported on and certainly was not part of LBJ's public discourse.

We now know 1968 was the beginning of a pivotal and defining year in the Vietnam War. It is recorded that because LBJ had become reluctant to commit further troops to the war effort during 1967-68, Vo Nguyen Giap, Hanoi's top General and strategist, started to believe that his country's strategy of attrition was beginning to pay dividends. Giap expressed to Morley Safer in a 1989 meeting that the most significant thing that came out of the 1968 Tet offensive was that it curtailed the American bombing, and brought both sides into negotiation. Giap felt that this was a victory for the North. Even though the North Vietnamese units were firmly defeated and demoralized in the aftermath of Tet, Americans back home had had enough of the bloodshed. RLT-27 and the 82nd Airborne were the last unit movement of troops in the U.S. buildup of this divisive and unique war.

After taking command from Westmoreland, General Creighton W. Abrams changed strategy and tactics, placing more emphasis on population security and pacification. Pacification meant a reduction in the enemy taxing the civilian population, food supplies taken from villagers, and recruitment by the enemy. With the new direction, a "clear-and-hold strategy" along with the Phoenix and Chieu Hoi programs (to find, capture, interrogate, or encourage Viet Cong and NVA defection), the nature of the war began to change. The Communists' control of the general population and their political organizations began to erode by late 1969. Even though General Abrams did the best he could with what he had inherited, the opposition in Washington was only interested in withdrawing from Vietnam.[23]

Reinforcements Arrive

RLT-27's deployment, originally planned for three to four months, began movement within forty-eight hours of notification. Second Battalion, 27th Marines, commanded by Lieutenant Colonel Louis J. Bacher, arrived in Da Nang by air from Camp Pendleton on 17 February. The next arrival was the 3rd Battalion, commanded by Lieutenant Colonel Tullis J. Woodham, Jr. on 20 February. RLT-27 was commanded by Colonel Adolph G. Schwenk and supported by an Artillery Battalion, the 2nd Battalion, 13th Marines, commanded by Lieutenant Colonel Rhys J. Phillips, Jr.

1st Battalion, 27th Marines, commanded by Lieutenant Colonel John E. Greenwood—whom Colonel Adolph G. Schwenk had not yet met (part of Hawaii-based 1st Marine Brigade)—was in the Pacific Ocean on a planned amphibious exercise. Greenwood's 1/27 arrived between 23 - 28 February 1968.

The Battalions transitioned into the TAOR with elements of the 5th and 3rd Marines for a couple of weeks, before taking over full responsibility for their newly assigned area of operation (AO) on the coastal sector south of Da Nang, which consisted of the Marble Mountains (five of them) and all the way south to just north of Hoi An.[24]

Once RLT-27 settled south of Da Nang, receiving initial indoctrination at their new HQs, the 1st Battalion hastily embarked to the Hue area and began operations under the control of the Commanding General of Task Force X-ray, Brigadier General Foster C. Lahue. 1/27 would run a major clearing operation of all the residual NVA and Viet Cong units left in the Hue City area after the Tet offensive of 1968. These remaining units had engaged in the initial battles which took place in and around

Marines & Sailors "off-loading" into landing craft on cargo nets from an APA (Assault Personnel Attack) to go ashore
~ Courtesy of Charles F. Eckerson, H&S Co, 1/27

the Citadel, and consequently were pushed into the canal areas further to the east. It would be the gargantuan task of 1st Battalion to seek out and destroy those enemy combatants who had established a strong presence in that area.

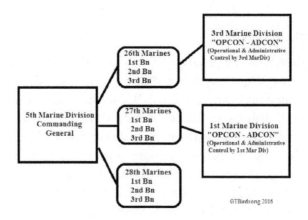

Chart shows 27th Marine Regiment, 5th Marine Division "operationally and administratively controlled" by 1st Marine Division ~ diagram courtesy of Grady Birdsong

Command and Control in the Republic of Vietnam

The acronym OPCON and ADCON came into wide use during this time. Some units were Operationally Controlled—Administratively Controlled, which permitted the interchange of battalions to other regiments, regiments to other divisions.

While 1st Battalion, 27th Marines deployed to the Hue City area during March through May of 1968, 2nd and 3rd Battalions remained in their respective areas under the control of the 1st Marine Division. After accomplishing the mission in the Hue area, 1/27 redeployed back to the south of Da Nang with its sister battalions, and assumed its place in a multi-battalion operation in the Go Noi area during the summer of 1968. The code name for this major operation at the time became widely known as "Allen Brook." Conducted in the area south-southwest of the Da Nang airstrip, Allen Brook became one of the major operations of the year for the Marines in I Corps.

The movement and control of tactical units throughout I CTZ became the norm during the late 1960s, and and provided the Division and Regimental Commanders increased flexibility in Vietnam.

The Marine Commanders during this timeline in history were:

> Commandant of the Marine Corps (CMC) –
> **General Leonard F. Chapman** 1968-71
> Fleet Marine Force Pacific (FMFPAC) CG –
> **Lt. Gen. Victor H. Krulak** 1964-68
> III Marine Amphibious Force (III MAF) CG –
> **Lt. Gen. Robert E. Cushman Jr.** 1967-68
> First Marine Division (1st MarDiv) CG –
> **Major Gen. Donn J. Robertson** 1967-68
> Third Marine Division (3rd MarDiv) CG –
> **Major Gen. Rathvon McC. Tompkins** 1968
> First Marine Aircraft Wing (1st MAW) CG –
> **Major Gen. Norman J. Anderson** 1967-68

"Brute" Krulak, the Commanding General of FMFPAC, became one of the candidates for Commandant of the Marine Corps in the late 1960s. The story goes LBJ sought Krulak's advice on how the war was going in mid-1966. Summoned to the White House, Brute basically told the President that the war tactics were being prosecuted wrongly, and the U. S. military needed to stop the flow of supplies and materials on the Ho Chi Minh Trail from the Communist forces in the North to the South. He then told LBJ, in effect, he should authorize the blockade of all ports and the mining of the Haiphong harbor area. LBJ did not want to hear this advice. After General Krulak told LBJ his views, he was

Lieutenant General Victor H. "Brute" Krulak touring Kaneohe MCAS Rifle Range and 1/27 in Hawaii 1967 ~ Courtesy of Charles F. Eckerson, H&S Co, 1/27

curtly dismissed. It is speculated that Brute never earned that fourth star or became the Marine Corps Commandant because of this meeting.[25]

Action – Losses

In the "Early Bird" section of the Washington Post on 9 March 1968, an article chronicled the troop strength of Marines in Vietnam at 78,000, and the Army about 330,000. February started off with unbelievable Marine KIA and WIA (wounded in action) numbers, compared to the Army. May of 1968 showed distressing KIA numbers for the Marine Corps. Marines historically always engage directly with the enemy; their adopted slogan from World War I was "First to Fight," and many of them paid the ultimate price.

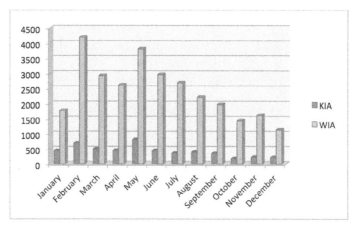

Marine Casualties in Vietnam 1968. February through September were difficult months
~ Chart by the author, Grady Birdsong, compiled from data in The Defining Year 1968, p 576

February shows KIAs of 691 and WIAs at 4,197 in I Corps (includes the small percent of wounds from accidents). The month of May likewise confirms an even tougher month for the Marine Corps with 810 KIAs and 3,812 WIAs. Truly, 1968 became a defining year.[26]

In the meantime, life went on in the field. The life of a Marine rifleman and Corpsman in Vietnam wasn't easy. A full tour lasted thirteen months. Once you had served your time, another "new guy" in the replacement draft would fill your billet.

The typical Marine grunt in Vietnam got much more enemy contact than in World War II or Korea. Completely safe places were non-existent in-country. The rear areas were subject to rocket/mortar attacks at random. Most officers would serve six months in a combat unit and then transfer back to headquarters for a support assignment. The enlisted grunts served with their fire team/squad/platoon the whole tour of duty until wounded, killed, or rotated back to the U.S. The infantry operated in the field constantly, and seldom "stood down" (idle time while realigning).

Think of the hottest day ever with humidity almost matching the temperature. Think of your clothing rotting off your body. Imagine sores, rashes, and insect bites on your arms and legs, and leeches hanging from your lower extremities. To sleep, a Marine would pull what was called a poncho over or under himself. He could sleep in bright sunlight, pouring rain, mud, or wherever. When he had time, the typical grunt would write letters back to loved ones on C-ration boxes torn apart to about the size of a post card. A letter or card home from the combat zone would reach home as free postage. Most patrols ended up being boring and tedious. A firefight might happen suddenly, one never knew. Sometimes a skirmish would seem to last an eternity. Then suddenly everything would go quiet, and a grunt would trudge on to endure another prolonged period of wearisome boredom.

Now, during the "Year of the Monkey" (The Chinese zodiac assigns an animal and its attributes to each year of a recurring 12 year cycle), it was 1st Battalion, 27th Marines; turn: they were the "new guys" coming into the country. It would be up to the Battalion leadership and second-timers to set the stage for learning the ropes and guiding these Marines into the heavy and almost constant combat they would face in the next six months.

CHAPTER 3

Arrival and Staging:
Attached to 1st Marine Division

"Marines die, that's what we're here for. But the Marine Corps lives forever.
And that means you live forever."
~ Gunny Hartman played by Staff Sergeant R. Lee Emery
in the movie, *Full Metal Jacket*, 1987

The area around the village of Duong Son (2), about 10 Kilometers south of Da Nang, was nothing more than an open sandy area along an oiled dirt road heading south called "Liberty Road" when 1st Battalion, 27th Marines arrived in-country to begin familiarization. The area was previously inhabited by another battalion (2/3) and featured existing infrastructure, including administration buildings, a mess hall, a water purification unit, an outdoor movie theater, hooches, tent areas for the grunts, and a Landing Zone (LZ) for choppers. Regiment and its command would stay at Duong Son (2), while 1st Battalion went north assigned (opcon) to Task Force X-Ray and operated in the Hue City TAOR for the months of March, April, and part of May before returning.

A newly-formed combat unit, 1/27 underwent rigorous training even though classified as not a full-strength organization. Hastily molded together in California and Hawaii, the 27th Marines manifested about a 30/70 percent mixture of experience and "newbies" upon arrival. Most of the men, never hearing of this obscure village, had not envisioned they would ever set foot in this part of the world.

Da Nang City during the wet season, 1967 ~ Courtesy of Tony Sarlls, MACG 18, 1st MAW
(submitted by his wife Paula)

L-R: General Westmoreland, General Cushman, Colonel Adolph G. Schwenk, General Donn Robertson
~ Courtesy of Lieutenant Crane Davis, C Co, 1/27

Operational Environment in Da Nang

Named Tourane during earlier French colonial rule, Da Nang flourished as a popular tourist mecca. It was the largest city in central Vietnam, and had one of the most important seaports. To the west was the Annamese Cordillera, which reached elevations of 4,636 feet above sea level. This area fluctuated between two seasons, the wet season from August through December and the dry, from January to July. Due east, the South China Sea revealed white sandy beaches for many miles southward. During the dry season of 1968, the heat was extreme, hot and humid, especially in April, May, and June. Temperatures during this time would sometimes reach upwards of 100 degrees Fahrenheit, with humidity ranges averaging 75-80 percent. Later in the summer of 1968, the battalion would suffer extraordinary manpower losses to not only KIAs and WIAs, but to the maladies of heat stroke and heat exhaustion.

1/27 Battalion Headquarters, Duong Son (2) ~ Courtesy of Ron Oakes, B Co, 1/27

Regimental and Battalion Headquarters

The Duong Son village area (UTM grid coordinates AT992677), in which 1/27 bivouacked beginning in late February of 1968, lies approximately ten kilometers due south of the major seaport area of Da Nang City. Liberty Road became the main thoroughfare for supplies and men going south to all the major areas of operation in the southern areas of Quang Nam Province: Hill 55, Liberty Bridge, An Hoa, "Dodge City Territory," the "Arizona Territory," Charlie Ridge, and Go Noi, to name a few areas in which Marine battalions conducted combat operations. These areas were considered "Indian country" by all Marines. North Vietnamese Army regulars, aka NVA, operated regularly throughout these areas as did the Main Force VC Battalions and the local Viet Cong (VC). Liberty Bridge (AT923532), constructed to enable movement of material and personnel across the ever-changing Thu Bon River to the southern-most tactical area of An Hoa, became a jumping off point for many major operations. The bridge was constantly under attack, and was destroyed multiple times.

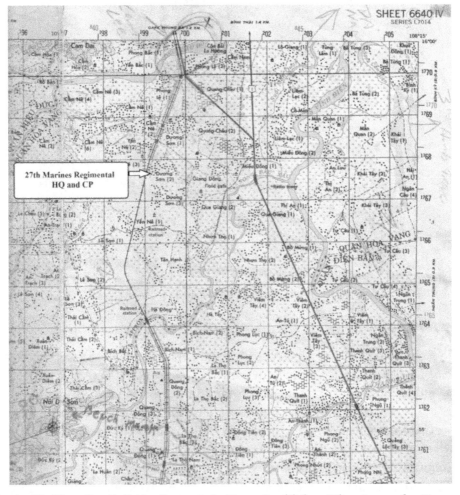

South of Da Nang, Cam Le Bridge (top center) – Duong Son (2) three Kilometers south ~ Map used by Captain Dan Guenther, 3rd Amphibian Tractor Battalion, 1st Marine Division, RVN 1968-69

RLT-27 HQ command and 1st Battalion began staging just below the Cam Le Bridge, about ten Kilometers south of the city of Da Nang. Duong Son (2) was the village located at UTM grid AT992677 on the previous map.

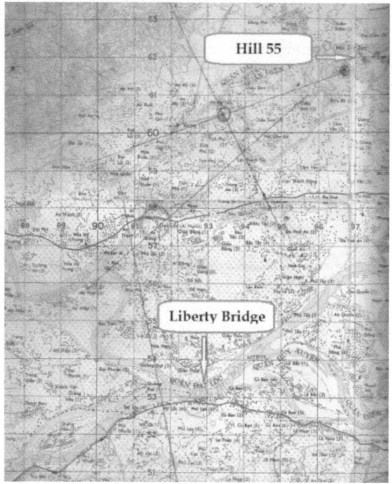

Topo Map, Dai Loc – Sheet 6640 IV, Series L7014 ~ Personal Map used by Captain Dan Guenther, 3rd Amphibian Tractor Battalion, 1st Marine Division, RVN, 1968-69

RLT-27 Tactical Area of Responsibility (TAOR)

Go Noi "Island," east of Liberty Bridge and beginning with the Cu Ban villages, was one of the staging areas more hotly contested by the NVA. Go Noi is not really an island, but surrounded by seasonal rivers out to the coastal area. Further to the east on one of the estuaries of the Thu Bon River was Hoi An, the former harbor town of the original Vietnamese people, the Cham. This harbor had become an extremely important trade center with the Japanese, Chinese, and the Dutch in the 16th and 17th centuries; a truly beautiful small seacoast city.

The Marble Mountain helicopter base, next page, was situated on a peninsula to the southeast of Da Nang, which the Han River separated from the city. There were five marble elevations (top center of photo) jutting out of the landscape to the south of the airstrip, the tallest of which provided what the Marines called the "crow's nest." The crow's nest afforded a 360-degree view of all approaches to both air bases, provided the weather was good. The landmass to the southwest with its many rivers and paddy fields was the second highest rice-producing region in South Vietnam. The Mekong Delta and this area supplied most of the rice for Southeast Asia. Da Nang and the areas south were also some of the most hotly contested areas of ground during the war.

Aerial View of Marble Mountain airstrip looking south and the five Marble Mountains at the top of the photo. RLT-27's TAOR is to the south and west of this photo (DOD photo USMC, A801132)

Liberty Road – Supply Lifeline

Many a jeep, truck, and tank passed through the 1/27 base camp area on Liberty Road. The Battalion closed the road to all traffic through its Command Post (CP) during the night. Every morning a mine sweep by combat engineers, accompanied by flank security grunts, endeavored to open it up so tactical and resupply traffic as well as local commerce could traverse south and north. Logistically, this oiled dirt road was critical to each unit for "beans and bullets," and the units in these areas provided overall security of the airbase. The Da Nang air base was considered the busiest airport in the world from 1968 through 1970.

M48 Patton Tank passing through Duong Son (2) on Liberty Road ~ Courtesy Ron Oakes, B Co, 1/27

The National Railroad tracks ran adjacent to Liberty Road south for a few more "Klicks" (Kilometers) and then veered southeasterly, finally crossing the Song Thu Bon on the eastern side of Go Noi, which became infested with well-constructed and camouflaged enemy fortifications. The underground and hidden NVA staging areas in the Go Noi were constructed from a lot of the reinforcement materials salvaged from the railway by enemy combatants. Every year like clockwork the Marines would have to sweep through the Go Noi Island terrain in force, clearing out NVA combatants and their underground tunnels and bunkers. Their objective was the destruction of the Da Nang airbase.

Liberty Road & North Gate of Duong Son (2) with water purification unit in operation
~ Courtesy of Ron Oakes, B Co, 1/27

Liberty Road ran south out of Da Nang, and went as far as An Hoa combat base, the jumping-off place for a lot of the operations in the southwest sector of the "Rocket Belt" surrounding the Da Nang airstrip. Along the way, it passed Hill 10, Hill 55, Liberty Bridge, and finally the small airfield and base at An Hoa, all of which lay close to the road's periphery. "Dodge City," another heavy-combat area, also bordered on the Song Thu Bon River close to Liberty Bridge. It had affectionately derived its name from the Wild West town in Kansas that was famous for old west gunfights. The "Arizona" territory close by also gained its name from Marines because it looked like the Arizona desert. It was imperative that the 1st Marine Division maintain extensive patrolling throughout all this area.

The area assigned to RLT-27 was immediately south of Da Nang. The 27th Marines established their headquarters in the hamlet of Duong Son (2). The regiment quickly learned from other units' "past lessons" that the most effective and proven tactics were small unit patrols of platoons, squads, or fire teams.

Most of the casualties prior to the regiment's deployment were from enemy mines and booby traps, officially called Surprise Firing Devices (SFD) at the time. Lieutenant Colonel Tullis Woodham, Jr, the 3rd Battalion, 27th Marines Commander, noted that in his area of operations his Marines encountered the highest concentration of mines and booby traps in the history of infantry warfare.[1]

A lot of the enemy in the area were an integral part of the Viet Cong infrastructure; farmers by day and enemy at night. Additionally, the NVA regulars coming down the Ho Chi Minh Trail were staging in the mountainous areas to the west, and in the Go Noi area east of Liberty Bridge. Full-time VC, and the irregulars who belonged to the Communist local "Self-Defense or Secret Self-Defense forces," maintained a healthy presence throughout the area when the 27th Marines came on the scene.[2] Both the NVA and Viet Cong were firmly entrenched in the region and the local populace was sympathetic to them, providing rice, comfort, and intelligence. It would be a long seven months for the Regiment.

Captured VC compliments of Charlie Company
~ Courtesy of William Carroll, C Co, 1/27

Liberty Road & South Gate of Duong Son (2)
~ Courtesy of Hugh G. Barton, H&S Co, 1/27

The obvious buildup of enemy regulars in the southern and western corridors of approach to the Da Nang base, in late 1967 and early 1968, evoked a new focus by the upper command. Operation Ballard kicked off in April in the Charlie Ridge area by a battalion from 7th Marines. Another battalion of the 7th and the 27th Marines prepared for Operation Allen Brook in the Go Noi, followed by 7th Marines launching Operation Mameluke Thrust into the "Arizona" and "Happy Valley" regions to the west and southwest. This signaled a major change from patrolling close to the airbase areas, to going after the enemy in his staging and base camp areas.[3]

Outer perimeter Duong Son (2) base camp
~ Courtesy of R. W. McConnell, D Co, 1/27

Liberty Road: Local Economic Artery

Local Vietnamese bus passengers on Liberty Road ~ Courtesy Hal Kennedy, H&S Co, 1/27

Local bus & military convoy traffic on Liberty Road ~ Courtesy of Ron Oakes, B Co, 1/27

Especially in the mornings just after engineers had cleared it, Liberty Road was bustling with motor scooters, overcrowded buses, and trucks in convoy. These buses, "jalopies" that reminded you somewhat of an old western stagecoach, would weave in and out of the traffic with no concern for their passengers. The road was always well-oiled by the engineers to keep the dust down. Villagers would walk it carrying goods they were taking to market. Some villagers balanced long bamboo poles on their shoulder, rope tied at both ends with hanging baskets of their goods. Roadside stands in the hamlets and villages would open for business as the traffic passed through. Anything from a Coca-Cola, vegetables, and fruit, to fresh French bread loaves and more could be bought. The traffic and commerce continued whether it was raining or the sun was shining.

Public transportation for civilians throughout Vietnam in 1968 was crude at best. Overcrowding of buses such as the one shown above was a common sight. The Vietnamese would endeavor to see how many people, some with chickens, pigs, and other agricultural animals, could be loaded on such a fragile and broken-looking contraption. It was amazing to see one of these vehicles, with three times the load you might think the bus would carry, move forward under its own power. People would be hanging out of the windows, riding on the back bumper, and sometimes on top of these buses.

This ancient land was inhabited for centuries by people using the same methods of farming, doing the same simple tasks which had been passed down from generation to generation. Almost everything was done by hand and was therefore labor-intensive. Technology had not yet blessed this society in 1968.

3rd Battalion Operates Adjacent to 1/27

In the northeastern sector of the Regimental TAOR, 3rd Battalion, 27th Marines began conducting sweeps in the Cau Ha (1) area in March searching for the Viet Cong operating in that area. Lieutenant Gene Schwartzlow, before becoming 1st Battalion's communication officer, began his tour as a Platoon Commander for 1st Platoon, Kilo Company, 3/27. As he recalls his first command assignment in-country, Kilo Company had started to conduct a "sweep operation" to the south and east of the Marble Mountains located close to the helicopter base on the coast. The operational task of positioning his platoon on line with other platoons became the mode for sweeping an area in search of Viet Cong. "As we pushed to the east we crossed vast rice paddies, passing through many villages. When we encountered villagers, our job was to check IDs and determine who were 'friendlies' and who were not. Those that were identified as possible Viet Cong were shuttled off to a team of Vietnamese military interrogators for questioning. The area that my platoon was covering was well known for enemy activity at night."

There was no enemy contact until Schwartzlow's platoon came upon a "spider trap" buried in the sand. A Corporal named Witherspoon discovered the trap, immediately fired his M16 into the hole, and then carefully threw a grenade into the entry orifice. When Lieutenant Schwartzlow arrived to inspect the situation, the Corporal, a two-tour veteran, began discussing alternatives. Another Lance Corporal volunteered to search for booby traps and other hazards in the entrance. Lieutenant Schwartzlow recalls, "No one else would go into the entire tunnel so I went in. I remember well my fears of the undetected explosives that might go off at any time in the small man-made underground bunker...More vivid; however, is my recollection of later feeling the still warm body of our enemy who had lost his battle for survival. Touching and holding the remains of this young man made the outcome of war very clear to me. I felt no ill-will toward him, only sorrow."

Although most villages appeared to be normal during this sweep, Schwartzlow remembers, "One village in my area seemed to be different. As we entered the village, suspicious eyes stared at us from nearly every corner of the village. As we started our interviews it became abundantly clear that it was not a normal village. We were in a leper colony!

"As we brought forth everyone to check their ID, we witnessed a parade of people with missing toes, fingers, ears, and noses. Others were more seriously afflicted. It was a ghastly sight.

Leper Colony during the sweep ~ Courtesy of Colonel Gene Schwartzlow (Ret), H&S Co, 1/27

"We knew that those infected with leprosy could be the Viet Cong we were looking for, but after seeing their plight, we just let them go. They were all dressed in rags and proper hygiene was seriously overlooked which contributed to the spread of the disease. They all appeared to be shunned by the rest of the world.

"I knew nothing of the disease. When I contacted my Company Commander and the Battalion Operations Officer, they had no advice to tell me. The Battalion Surgeon recommended we maintain as little physical contact as possible. It wasn't until years later that I learned that leprosy is most usually transmitted through the mucous membranes of the nose. I also learned that over 90 percent of all humans have a natural immunity to the disease. At the time, we all were very stressed out due to our fear of this unknown malady. Today, leprosy can be cured with the right antibiotics.

"After checking everyone out, everyone in the village was cleared to go about their daily routine. Our platoon Corpsman did what he could to provide medical supplies and help them as best he could.

"As we proceeded further east, we wondered if we would experience any residual effects from our visit. As it turned out, we did not."

"Halt, Who Goes There?"

Ontos (tracked vehicles) Marines Ronnie Williams and Raymond Whaley had been attached to 1/27 in Hawaii at K-Bay. They all had ridden over on the boat with 1/27 and were re-assigned to 1st Tanks in the Da Nang area upon arrival. As noted in the 1st Tank Battalion Command Chronology of February 1968, "The 1st Platoon, Company B, 5th Antitank Battalion, attached to BLT 1/27 was 'chopped' to this battalion (1st Tank Bn) on 23 February. This platoon has four M50A1 Ontos, without the FM series radio. An additional ontos is expected to arrive from Hawaii in the future which will bring the platoon to T/E strength."

Getting settled in their position supporting 2/27, Williams remembers, "We were on watch one night after arriving and had moved one of our tanks closer to a bunker around midnight. We were providing the manpower for standing watch with the tank." As he and another Marine, Robert "Bobby" Walker talked about the day's events on top of the bunker, something moved in the distance inside the wire. Walker had been in-country with Tanks and had experience in this area of operation. The field of vision that night was clear and gave them a frontal view of the area outside the perimeter wire. Walker recalls, "I remember thinking that it was my mind playing tricks on me and that I was imagining movement out there…there was a tree line to the side of the road darkened and with shadows. It was extremely hard to distinguish movement of any kind in that dark area. But I kept seeing something move, and often. Soon I could make out human forms and it was then I notified all the Marines in the wire on guard duty."

Kelly, another Marine on the tank, also confirmed that movement. He woke up the other tank crewman inside the turret and quickly removed a High Explosive (HE) round from the breach and reloaded it with an M377 90 mm anti-personnel flechettes round. These were also known as "Beehive" rounds, because of the array of steel dart-like flechettes which would propel forward from the canister through the tank barrel, much like a shotgun blast.

They all tensely watched as the human forms came slowly toward them. Walker remembered, "Something was strange about them, I could not put my finger on it. It was the way they moved...they were larger than gooks. Kelly brought me back to reality and said he was going to fire a round for everyone to get down. The blasts from these canons were horrific. Before Kelly could fire, I stood up and yelled, 'Halt, who goes there?' as loud as I could...much to my surprise came back a reply, '27th Marines.' I was shocked and couldn't believe it. I yelled out, 'Advance and be recognized,' which they did. Coming close to me, I asked the point man, 'What in the hell are you doing out here?' He told us that they were new in-country and were sent out to patrol the area and had become lost. I told him that we had not been notified of a patrol in the area and had almost fired on them. He was really lost so we showed him where they were on a map and provided directions back to their base area. We were thanking our lucky stars that we did not fire that round at them... I still get the cold chills thinking about it."

1/27 H&S Company – The "Glue" that Held the Battalion Together

1st Lieutenant Jesse Hand, the Commanding Officer of 1st Battalion, Headquarters & Service Company (H&S Co) had been in the area on a prior tour in 1966. He had been in and around Marble Mountain nearby, and relieved his old Unit, 2/3, and moved into the base camp that he helped build on his first tour. Over the next few days and weeks, the rifle companies would work out of the main base camp at Duong Son (2) village (there were three Duong Son villages) doing joint indoctrination patrols with 2/3 personnel. The enemy activity in the area remained mainly small VC units that utilized hit-and-run tactics.

Hand remembered the first Marine killed in action, one of his Marines, Lance Corporal Bobby Lynn Weathers, on 17 March 1968. He recalled, "Weathers was driving a jeep, and when taken under fire by a sniper, sped up and crashed going through a curve, killing him."

The Commanding Officer (CO) of any Marine H&S Company wears several hats; first, he is the company commander, which consists of the mission to assist the Battalion Commander in the command and control of the maneuver battalion. Secondly, he is responsible for managing the physical support of the battalion including the billeting, messing facilities and utilities, and he runs the administrative and training aspects for the Battalion. Additionally, the H&S Company Commander is the only officer on the Headquarters staff other than the Battalion Commander who can dispense punishment under the Uniform Code of Military Justice (UCMJ).

An H&S Company is organized into the following staff sections also called shops:

S-1 ~ Handles all personnel and administrative matters
S-2 ~ Deals with collection of intelligence and security of the battalion
S-3 ~ Provides operations planning and coordination; conducts training
      and combat operations
S-4 ~ Manages supply and logistics; handles equipment distribution
      and replacement

1st Lieutenant Hand reinforced a guiding principle he had learned over the years, "That these officers and enlisted personnel in each shop created the battalion operation order(s) with input from all the Company Commanders which supported and propelled the mission of the Battalion."

The H&S Company Commander of 1st Battalion further functioned as Commandant of the base camp. Since the 27th Marine Regimental Headquarters was also located in this same camp, Regimental Headquarters fell under that command support umbrella as well. First Lieutenant Hand recalls, "I was also responsible for the entire camp security, mess hall, and facilities (wooden buildings and tents). I was basically the mayor of this small city we Marines called a base camp."

Entirely ringed by triple rows of concertina barbed wire, Duong Son (2) epitomized a heavily fortified and impenetrable fortress. Out in front of the perimeter's wire were anti-personnel mines. The surrounding fields outward from the camp had been cleared for pre-registering of all types of support weaponry: artillery, 4.2 mortars, and Air Naval Gunfire Liaison Company (ANGLICO) firing. Strategically located within the camp behind the perimeter wire were two- and four-man sandbagged bunkers. Larger bunkers established the field-of-fire positions for crew-served weaponry, e.g., machine guns (.50 caliber) and anti-tank weapons (106mm Recoilless Rifles). All bunkers were manned night and day. Every Marine had a fighting hole or trench near his sleeping quarters. First Lieutenant Hand remembers it was, "in short, a ring of fire!"

Sleeping quarters were mostly large tents sandbagged around the outer walls. The mess hall could feed several hundred troops at a time. It featured a shower facility, and in the main area, buildings were constructed for a command and control center and company offices. Internal to the camp were spaces for equipment and supplies, vehicle parking, a supply warehouse, an armory, a Battalion Aid

Jesse Hand on his first tour 1965-66
~ courtesy of Sergeant John Rosenau,
Co G, 2/3

Station, the all-important Communications Center, and a helicopter landing zone with a water-purification unit close by. Large generators supplied electricity/lighting to certain areas.

A lot of 1/27's base camp defensive infrastructure had been improved prior to the Battalion's arrival by previous battalions. Sandbag bunkers were continually reinforced, and complemented with trench lines surrounding the entire perimeter, much like old-time castle moats. General Purpose (GP) tents lined up in rows, were sectioned off for the letter companies. Each Marine and Corpsman had a small open personal area with a cot for sleeping, storing his rifle, 782 web gear, a sea bag and any personal belongings. The base perimeter did require constant work in some of the weaker areas around the perimeter wire. Sandbagging was a daily routine. Tin cans and other items that made noise were hung dangling from the concertina, to alert the Marines to any movements in the wire at night. Heavy-weapon machine guns were strategically placed in interlocking fields of fire on probable avenues of approach to the CP.

After settling in as Commanding Officer of this fortress, Lieutenant Hand shuttled back and forth between the Hue City area (La Son School House, 1st Battalion field CP) and Duong Son (2) (Regimental and Battalion permanent HQ). He would become familiar with both areas in leading and administering his personnel's support in the command and control of the Battalion.

Morale at Duong Son (2) Headquarters

A night at the movies was possible in this strange and faraway land. Some nights during battalion staging in late February and early March, a current movie would be shown on a large outdoor screen. A couple of movies playing at the time were *Hang 'Em High* and *The Dirty Dozen*. Newly-popular Clint Eastwood had engaged in filming what were called "spaghetti westerns" in Italy.

1/27 Outdoor Movie Theatre
~ Courtesy of Ron Oakes, B Co, 1/27

Multi-purpose stage/screen for Movies and USO
Shows ~ Courtesy of Ron Oakes, B Co, 1/27

Hang 'Em High was about an innocent man who had survived a lynching, and returned to seek vengeance as a lawman determined to bring the vigilantes who tried to lynch him to justice. It was without a doubt one of the most popular flicks amongst the Marines of RLT-27. As the men watched, you could hear them openly cheering for Clint as he got "payback" on the bad guys.

Morale was very important for Marines. Some of the more popular venues enjoyed by Marines were the traveling entertainment groups that toured Vietnam in the 60s. Below is a group of entertainers playing for the newly arrived members of 1/27 in base camp next to the hamlet of Duong Son (2).

The USO, a privately funded organization, arranged for these tours and put on more than 5,000 shows throughout Vietnam, mostly in rear areas during the war. The best-attended were the Bob Hope shows (eight consecutive shows) in the larger rear-area base camps, e.g., Da Nang and Saigon. Most of the smaller unit areas (Regimental) would attract bands from Okinawa, Japan, or maybe the Philippines. Mini-skirts and Go-Go boots were the normal attire in most of the bands and they would all invariably play the Beatles' tune in broken English: "I wanna hole you hond!" At least that is how it sounded when they sang the tune. Most of the rear-echelon Marines in support roles attended a few of these morale builders. The average grunt in a line company might be lucky to take in one of these shows during his whole thirteen-month tour.

USO Show at Duong Son (2) ~ Courtesy of Raul E. Figueroa, H&S Co, 1/27

Helicopter Supply, Logistics, and Support

CH-46 choppers were the heavy haulers for transporting cargo point to point, landing Marines for an assault, and then resupplying them. This chopper was used for almost everything the Marines needed. Medical evacuations, resupply, and troop transport were the daily priorities. The Army had "Dustoff" units which did nothing but medical evacuations. The Marines used the "Phrog," as it was sometimes called, for many purposes, sometimes diverting the nearest "bird" into tough situations, many times under fire. These flying machines were truly the mobile workhorses of I Corps.

A CH-46 "Phrog" delivering supplies to Duong Son (2) LZ ~ Courtesy of Ron Oakes, B Co, 1/27

The Marine Corps looked upon the helicopter as sort of a landing boat (ship to shore) which would haul Marines into the combat zone in large numbers, plus resupply them and take out the wounded as they went about the harsh realities of overcoming objectives. The Army viewed their many variations of choppers as horses or as cavalry, whereby outflanking or outmaneuvering could be accomplished. In either scenario, the rotary aircraft changed the way the American military did business in this and future wars. The helicopter became an integral part of the Marine Corps in Vietnam.

While 1/27 was in-country, a debate was going on in the higher levels of the Marine air wing. Commanders had become concerned with the effectiveness of one Marine air wing in support of two Marine ground divisions. Some felt it was stretching the capability of the wing. Also in question amongst Marine air and ground officers was the control or influence the ground commander should have over helicopter operations. These issues were of ongoing discussion through the end of the war.[4]

Food Supply

Mess hall chow in Vietnam came in large cans or out of a box. Dehydrated eggs, potatoes, gravy, and milk powder mixed with water were common menu items. There was hardly any fresh food served. The only problem with this type of food was if the water had considerable amounts of chlorine; in this case, C-rations were the only reliable backup. Too much chlorine added a nasty taste to food.

Regiment & Battalion mess hall Duong Son (2)
~ Courtesy of Ron Oakes, B Co, 1/27

In the mid-1800s, Gail Borden invented canned condensed milk and thus changed how troops were fed. As an example, the daily ration of a Confederate soldier in the Civil War was a quarter pound of salt pork and a few ounces of corn meal. The corn meal was equal to about a half of a loaf of bread. That got boring after a short while. The much-improved C-ration (an individual, canned, precooked, and prepared wet ration) used in Vietnam was born out of World War II. Those first canned choices were meat and beans, meat and vegetable stew, and meat and vegetable hash. By the time Vietnam rolled around, C-rations had added more choices. Multiple canned wet rations were sometimes carried in a sock to reduce noise while on patrol.

Recalling an experience with mess halls, Eddie Ronan, Charlie Company 1/27, tells the following humorous story. Just in from the field, he made his way into the chow line at the mess hall and asked what they were serving. The word came down "shit and bubble gum." Not wanting to make trouble, he said nothing and waited, like everyone else who was extremely hungry. When he finally got to the serving line, the cook slapped a lump of mystery meat on his tray. Startled, Ronan looked at him. Before he could speak, the cook looked right back at him and blurted out, "We just ran out of bubblegum."

Sanitation and Hygiene

Almost everyone experienced a "shitter burning detail" at least once or twice during their tour. Fifty-five-gallon drums were cut in half and had handles welded onto them. These were strategically placed underneath a seating hole in a screened hooch from the backside. Some crapper hooches had two holes; some had three or maybe four, depending on the Seabees' supply of lumber at the time they were constructed. After multiple daily defecations, some unlucky Marine or Corpsman would have to drag the full half barrels out from under the hooch crapper seat, pull them a safe distance away, and fill them with diesel fuel to stir and light on fire. While burning the barrel, the Marine would place another empty barrel back under the seat hole. The stench from the black diesel smoke was an odor not to be forgotten. It stayed in your utilities (combat blouse and trousers) for days. Unforgettable is too kind of a word to describe the experience and the smell.

Bravo Company CP at Duong Son (2) –
Barrels with handles full of diesel fuel to be inserted into the seat holes through the back of the outhouse
~ Courtesy of Ron Oakes, B Co, 1/27

Toilet paper was sometimes available and other times not, therefore most enterprising Marines and Corpsmen would save the small C-ration meal TP packets for the daily ordeal of relieving and wiping themselves. TP was at a premium most of the time, and sometimes would be trading currency for a can of peaches. Canned peaches were as good as gold coins.

The daily diet of C-rations had a very high content of calories. Roughage or fiber was non-existent, so it was common to hear occasional exclamations from a Marine just off the crapper seat, "Ever thang came out alright." The most common expression all over I Corps in the lighter moments went like this: "Dude…something crawled up inside of you and died…!"

The Beer Ration Incident

Lieutenant Hand, the Company 1st Sergeant, and his Gunnery Sergeant had immediately begun supervising and maintaining the sprawling Duong Son (2) Base, which included the Regimental HQ. When Hand's 1st Battalion deployed north to the Hue City area, all rifle companies followed. One of those companies had been providing security for the Duong Son (2) complex. Security for the perimeter now had to come from another Battalion within the Regiment. First Lieutenant Hand remembered one of the side effects in maintaining constant base security. "Sometimes this caused problems for me. Why a problem? First, these companies coming out of the field had been in combat operations, patrolling, ambushes, often in direct contact with the enemy, and had suffered casualties, etc. Normally, we didn't have problems with these guys but our higher command had decreed that within the most secure areas, such as our base, that a Beer ration would be be a big morale booster. The ration was two beers per day per man. The problem with this was that every man drew his two Beers but some of the men did not drink, sooooo, they either swapped their cans of beer for something else or would give their ration to a buddy…now you had the problem of, too much to drink; that was not good!"

Working late one evening, Lieutenant Hand received a call from the Regimental Executive Officer, Lieutenant Colonel N. G. "Dusty" Rodes. The gravelly voice of Rodes shouted over the land line, "'Hand, get over to the east side of the camp, there is trouble brewing…the security company and your H&S people are pointing weapons at each other.' He ordered me to take care of it and slammed the phone down! I thought to myself, oh shit, just what I needed…"

Jesse summoned his 1st Sergeant and the two of them grabbed .45s and flashlights. Heading over to the east area he recalled, "Upon arriving at the scene we immediately determined it was worse than I had originally thought. A large group of grunts presently assigned to our security duty was standing around a fire pit with their weapons pointed at a line of my H&S guys who in turn were pointing their 16s at the grunts. Both groups were shouting insults and obscenities at each other. I knew that all it took was for one man to fire a shot and it would be a firefight, Marines against Marines."

Reverting to basic Marine Corps training, 1st Lieutenant Hand walked in between the two groups and shouted, "Knock it off!" That seemed to get everyone's attention. Hand recalled, "I then ordered 1st Sergeant to march H&S company people out of the area. The 'Top' yelled at the top of his lungs, 'H&S Company, Attention…About Face… Forward March!'"

Thankfully the H&S Company men executed the "first shirt's" command flawlessly, and moved away from the area. Lieutenant Hand then turned to the remaining grunts and asked where their Company Commander was—it turned out that he was right there with them. He walked up to Lieutenant Hand, who ordered him to get his men under control and move away from the area. Hand remembered vividly, "The Captain had obviously been drinking with his troops and told me that I could not give him that order. I identified myself as Headquarters Commandant and then told the Captain for sure that he was relieved of his command effective immediately. I then asked for the Executive Officer of the Company. It was a young Lieutenant. I told him that he was the new temporary C. O. of the company."

After all that dust settled, Lieutenant Colonel "Dusty" Rodes, the Regimental Executive Officer, strode up. He told the Captain to get his personal belongings and to come with him. Lieutenant Hand never saw this officer again during his tour.

Hand requested a meeting with Colonel Schwenk, the Regimental Commander, to discuss the event and make some recommendations. Schwenk had already considered one of them. As Hand recalled, the result of this incident brought new rules in the form of a Regimental Order. Everyone knew that these new orders would not sit well with the Battalion Commanders or the troops.

Hand recalled the resulting regulations: "While inside the base camp, there would be no loaded weapons with the exceptions of Marines on immediate security watch on the perimeter or in the event of an assault. Weapons were to be carried with bolts open and no magazines in the weapon, having ammo in a cartridge belt was permissible. No hand grenades except while on watch. Commanders at all levels were required to monitor personnel, ensuring compliance with these new rules. Beer rations would be monitored more closely and would be withdrawn if there were any incidents of drunken behavior. Officers were cautioned about their own behavior. In other words, to look at your own discipline and then to the discipline of your troops. It was the Marine Corps time-tested principle of 'lead by example.'"

Familiarization

A peaceful arrival was deceptive to the newer Marines. But William Drennan, the seasoned Delta Company Marine, knew what to do when they arrived in Vietnam, his second tour. "When we arrived at Da Nang harbor, 23 February 1968, it was the anniversary of the flag raising on Iwo Jima 1945, a battle which 1/27 had participated by storming the beaches and securing a foothold twenty-three years prior. Once on the beach, our unit was trucked to an area southwest of Da Nang [Duong Son (2)] where we began erecting more tents, putting up our cots, digging more trenching and started patrolling the area with our M14 rifles with very little ammo...but we had all the grenades we could carry. If the enemy had known our supply situation, the outcome might have been different."

Drennan tells all who listen that his biggest regret was turning in the M14 rifle for the "'Matty' Mattel M16 plastic plaything," a rifle he did not favor. Mattel, Inc., one of the top American toy manufacturers, had by the mid-1960s joined the Fortune 500 group of companies. They made toy guns for children, which were popular at the time. Once dirty with the least amount of sand, mud, or any dirt, the M16 would jam, not fire, and was not well received by the men of 1/27 who had already bonded with the M14—hence the derogatory comparison.

Liberty Road south of Da Nang on the Song Cau Do ~ Courtesy of Grady Birdsong, H&S Co, 1/27

Upon arrival, the Battalion commenced joint exercises with 2nd Battalion, 3rd Marines. Shortly after a few patrols, 1/27 took over the entire area of operation. In the first days, a considerable amount of attention focused on the northeast part of the TAOR, due to its history as an infiltration route into the city of Da Nang. The line companies were each assigned their respective areas. Combined activities were planned with the local ARVN units, and throughout March, a total of four Company-size search-and-destroy operations were conducted in conjunction with the 2nd Battalion, 51st ARVN Regiment and the 59th Regional Forces of the area.

Company C began their operations in the southern sector around the village of Nhon Tho (2) (grid coordinate BT015655), about one kilometer north and west of Highway 1 and the Tu Cau Bridge. Then-Lance Corporal Donald Moorehead of Charlie Company recalled working with an ARVN company in early March just after arriving by ship. He remembered it as if it were yesterday: "There were ARVNs camped on both sides of us where we set up our platoon patrol base [PPB]. We were south and east of the Battalion CP. On one of the first patrols we began conducting, I can remember passing through a village and all hell breaking loose. I received wounds from grenade fragments thrown by our point man. After the firefight concluded, I was carried back to our base camp next to the ARVNs and placed in a tent. That night the perimeter again was assaulted and we started being overrun by enemy combatants on one side of the perimeter. I will never forget, the unit commander burst into the tent and told me I was going to have to get outside to fight or die. I rolled off the cot, grabbed my rifle, locked and loaded, half hobbling, and barely crawled into a fighting hole. They were running everywhere and randomly exploding satchel charges. It was total mayhem. The next morning, an evacuation chopper took me to NSA in Da Nang north of our position." When Moorehead returned to the platoon, he received Corporal stripes and became a Squad Leader in Company C. He remembered, "Lieutenant Donald Gustafson, the Platoon Commander, promoted me to the position because we had lost our Squad Leader."

Then-Lieutenant Dennis Lister, Charlie Company, described his area of operation (AO). His platoon set up at the An Trach church, a short distance from the battalion CP, and began running patrols to familiarize itself with Vietnam in general. The church had been partially destroyed and was also the garrison of an ARVN Company. Lister recalled, "The ARVN Company commander held an office hour trial (non-judicial punishment) in the open churchyard while we all watched. The punishment to one of his men for whatever he had done was to place that man in a little chicken wire cage outside the inner-perimeter wire all night."

Lieutenant Lister also remembered a lighter moment when one of his Marines, "Lloyd Fernung got mad because someone stole my chicken and noodle soup. We all presumed it was one of the ARVN soldiers. Lloyd drained another can of chicken and noodle soup and pissed in it and then set it out as a trap, which was taken. We all laughed about it and speculated that some poor ARVN soldier must have said to himself, 'Man, those Americans sure like a lot of salt in their food!' "

Civil Affairs

Arriving in-country on 19 February 1968, Lieutenant Crane Davis found himself assigned to the 27th Marine Regiment, newly positioned at the Duong Son (2) hamlet, several kilometers south of the Da Nang airbase. As he traveled to his new destination, it was apparent to him and his companions that the Tet fighting of early 1968 in that area had taken a toll. He was assigned as a civil affairs officer in the regiment's S-5 section. Davis and his new assistant, Corporal Henderson, quickly set about reestablishing the liaisons between the South Vietnamese in the area and the newly arrived 27th Marines. Davis recalled, "In the period after Tet, no one was quite sure what the situation was throughout our area. Many of the friendly forces in the hamlets had withdrawn or had been overrun. It would be several months before we would understand the impact that Tet had on previous pacification efforts...Fortunately, it turned out that Da Nang was the only major city in Vietnam that was not significantly impacted by Tet. NVA forces in the Tet offensive, disorganized and late in arriving, did insignificant damage to the 27th Marines TAOR. The NVA licking their wounds withdrew into the surrounding mountains to regroup and would return later in the summer of '68." Davis would later take command of a rifle platoon and help build the infamous Fort Apache in the 27th Marines' TAOR.

In early May Lieutenant Davis found himself temporarily assigned to an Army 105 mm artillery battery located south of Go Noi Island. Operation Allen Brook had been launched. The position he first went to was located on a high ridge line overlooking the Go Noi Island delta to the north. It was known as Hill 845 (grid coordinate AT971514). He recollects, "...spending two weeks with the Army, along with my radioman, at LZ 'Hardcore,' with security provided by an Army unit, so neither of us slept a wink." Davis came down with malaria shortly after that time with the artillery unit and spent most of June in recovery in the south of Vietnam at Cam Ranh Bay.

A Marine's Tour in the Field

Marines and Corpsmen never got enough sleep in Vietnam. With unit movements, patrolling, "Rough Rider" convoys, search-and-destroy ops (later called "Clear-and-Hold Ops" under Abrams), major operations, night ambushes, listening post (LP), to unit security and night watch, sleep was extremely hard to get. This was a constant the whole time the battalion was deployed. Those that have experienced a tour with an infantry unit know of the constant fatigue and exhaustion with you always. It takes a toll on your psyche and energy, leaving you in a state of dull but constant vigilance. Adrenaline and past trauma work together to keep you awake, and then when sweet sleep comes, it is because of the trust you have in your fellow Marines and Corpsmen who will dutifully take their turn on watch. As the saying went, "I've got your 6...!" This phrase used the view of a clock, with 12 o'clock directly ahead and the 6 o'clock position behind you: your back side was the "6." You know it is covered when you are with other Marines.

"Sweet sleep after night watch" ~ Courtesy of Raul E. "Figgy" Figueroa, H&S Co, 1/27

The monsoon season in Vietnam descended upon a Marine's tour unlike anything they had ever seen in their lifetimes. Most had witnessed all the nature's seasons and what came with them; rain, snow, ice, sleet, wind, and cold, along with the heat but never anything like the rain that came down from the skies and clouds of the I Corps in the Republic of Vietnam. The rain lasted for days and nights on end. It intensified so at times visibility disappeared. The rain came down for extended periods hard enough to muffle other noises. Even though the temperatures remained warm, you still became chilled to the bone. Typhoons accompanied the monsoon season frequently, and would cause much flooding in the lowlands. Typhoons were also something most Marines had never experienced.

A tropical typhoon would last for days and shut down all activity, especially the aviation brethren, the Helicopter pilots. Nothing flew unless a dire emergency called for extraction. Vehicles could hardly move in the Vietnam mud. Red mud everywhere became part of the attire, clinging to and covering utility blouse and trousers, boots, 782 combat gear, poncho, hair, hands, plus gumming up a weapon…everywhere the Marines stepped or sat, mud was part of everything. This was the origin of the term Mud Marine. Marines learned to sleep, eat, write home, or carry on grab-ass sessions with their brother Marines in that crappy, reddish, and slimy stuff. It quickly became a normal part of daily existence.

"It rained for days…" ~ Courtesy of Hal Kennedy, H&S Co, 1/27

Regimental Landing Team-27 had made the journey to Vietnam and had "snapped in." They were now part of the III MAF, which at the beginning of 1968 had command and control of the entire I Corps area in South Vietnam. At the time, III MAF consisted of two Divisions of Marines, the 1st MarDiv and 3rd MarDiv; the 1st Marine Air Wing (MAW); Force Logistics Command (FLC); and an Army Division, which accounted for over 100,000 Marines, sailors, and soldiers. The task at hand: defend their bases and airfields; destroy Communist combat units; eliminate the in-place Communist infrastructure; and conduct Combined Action Programs (CAP) in support of the South Vietnamese government. The Marines of 1/27 had a "tough row to hoe" in the coming days, and would need every tool of the trade at their disposal.[5]

CHAPTER 4

Tools of the Trade

"If you can't carry it, eat it or shoot it, don't bring it."
~ Marine Corps saying

So, what kind of tools did the Marines use while deployed in the Republic of Vietnam? You will be introduced in this chapter to the resources, personal gear, implements and supporting weaponry that helped 1/27 throughout its journey in the fields of fire of I Corps. Many of the weapons were time tested and some were not, but the Marines grumbled a little, adjusted, and made the best of both good and bad situations with these "tools of the trade."

Transportation

M274 Mechanical Mule

The M274 Mechanical Mule was designed for carrying ammunition, cargo, weapons, chow, personnel, and sometimes mounting a 106mm recoilless rifle. The mechanical mule performed countless resupplies and was a true workhorse during 1/27's deployment. It operated in full-time four-wheel drive with a two-speed (low and high) transfer case, and had three gears forward and one in reverse.

A Mechanical Mule of Alpha Company, 1st Battalion, 27th Marines while staging at Duong Son (2) south of Da Nang 1968 ~ Courtesy of Felix Salmeron, A Co, 1/27

The Mechanical Mule was designed to operate in rugged terrain and to be helicopter or parachute dropped and driven away on any battlefield. It also had the capability to ford rivers or streams up to eighteen inches in depth. This beast of burden could carry a potential payload of up to 1,000 pounds. The steering wheel allowed adjustments for driving, walking, kneeling, and crawling. Its top speed was about 25 mph. It was truly a welcome tool during the Vietnam War.

M422 "Mighty Mite" Jeep assigned to Communications Platoon driven by Corporal Doug Setley, H&S Co, 1/27 ~ Courtesy of Hugh G. Barton, H&S Co, 1/27

M422 "Mighty Mite" Jeep

Made of aluminum, the M422 "Mighty Mite" Jeep was the lightest of small military vehicles designed with all-around independent suspension. Basically a two-seat vehicle, it could move up to six people due to fold-up seating. These little workhorses were adept for airlift, extremely rugged terrain, and the deep-water fording of rivers and streams. They were gas-powered and had a cruising range of about 240 miles. The above pictured Mighty Mite was assigned to the 1/27 Communications Platoon of H&S Company and was utilized daily by the Communications Chief and senior personnel in the Communications section.

Upon arrival in the Hue area during late March and early April 1968, 1/27 constructed their Command Post (CP) at the east edge of the La Son School building, about two kilometers directly east of the Citadel. The line companies had positioned themselves in strategic positions and began working their assigned sectors out of Platoon Patrol Bases (PPB) along Route 551 all the way to the coast, and south toward Phu Bai on National Route 1. The coastal ramp at the Tan My villages on the coast was called Col Co (Colonial Company) and had been operated by a private concern in previous years. Naval LCU vessels carried supplies and fuel from the Col Co ramp on the coast into the Naval Support Activity ramp in Hue City via the Perfume River. A pipeline had also been constructed along Route 551 from the facility to pump fuel into Hue. During one hot day in early April, the pipeline along Route 551 close to the schoolhouse burst into flames. How this happened, no one remembers. The explosion and fireball consequently injured a small girl standing close to the fuel line. Gunnery Sergeant Manuel Gomez was close to the scene and calmly commissioned Corporal Doug Setley to get the communications "Mighty Mite" Jeep while he and Corporal Grady Birdsong treated the little girl. She was suffering from second- and perhaps third-degree burns. Birdsong remembers, "When Corporal Setley and I lifted her into the back of the Mighty Mite a lot of the skin came off her arms...I had never since heard that level and intensity of screaming which emanated from that poor little child. The wailing and screaming were constant and unnerving as we raced toward the Naval Support Activity and medical facility in Phu Bai about fifteen Kilometers to the south of our CP's position." Corporal Doug Setley drove that "Mighty Mite" as fast as it would go, weaving in and out of the road traffic on Highway 1. "It was an unforgettable wild ride and I still hear that little girl screaming in my dreams at night," recalls Birdsong.

M35A2 "Six-By," aka "Deuce and a Half" Truck ~ Courtesy of "Doc" R. W. McConnell, D Co, 1/27

M35A2 "Deuce and a Half" Truck

These behemoths hauled thousands of tons of dry cargo, e.g., C-rations, ammo, water, mail, sandbags, and sometimes bulk petroleum, transporting those cargos over primitive road systems to supply points throughout the Republic of Vietnam. They also performed the gruesome task of bringing back the bodies of the dead wrapped in body bags. Of the approximately 2.5 million men that served in Vietnam, almost everyone rode in these trucks at one time or another during their tour. At least a couple of riflemen and an M60 gunner usually traveled in a convoy for security. The convoys ran through ambush-prone areas and were always subject to command-detonated mines in the roadways. Some convoys were big, up to over 100 trucks.

With a full load, the "six-by" rode okay; but on the way back, unloaded and cruising at 50 mph, you would be bouncing all over the truck bed, ricocheting off the side rails and your insides would be playing leapfrog with your tongue. When the rain came, you would be drenched and there was nothing you could do about it. It was common for a line company of grunts to be transported into an area of operation on a few of these M35A2 Deuce and a Half trucks by the "Rough Riders." This was limo service at its best for most Marines. It sure did beat "humping the bush."

An M35 "Six-By" USMC Truck damaged by a detonated mine
~ Courtesy of "Doc" David E. Bronson, D Co, 1/27

Corporal Raul Figueroa, an H&S weapon section Marine, remembers an assignment with the trucks at Liberty Bridge on the Thu Bon River south of the headquarters CP. His squad had been guarding the bridge and were ordered back to the CP. "Figgy" remembers, "Loading several fifty-five-gallon drums on the back of a 'Six-By' and the driver backed into the river until the water level started filling the barrels. The water would be used for the overhead showers at CP. Corporal Eddie Villegas, PFC Andrew Jackson, and I loaded all the drums with water, all the while the driver left the engine running. After loading the drums filled with water, Jackson sat on the rear end of the truck and lit a cigarette. Horseplay was not out of the question and the driver decided to pop the clutch on the M35 pitching Andrew backward out of the truck, asshole over elbows into the river. We laughed about that all the way back to camp."

Some of these trucks, specifically Army trucks attached to the Marines, were equipped with a truly powerful weapon system. The Quad 50 was originally designed to be an aerial defense anti-aircraft weapon. It is a gun turret with four .50-caliber machine guns and a gunner that manipulates them right in-between the barrels in an open electric-powered turret. They were first used on mobile ground mounts. Early in World War II, they were mounted on trailers and then onto half-tracks. In Vietnam, they were utilized in semi-fixed positions to protect base perimeters. Then when supply convoys became a logistical necessity, mounting the Quad 50 on trucks for convoy duty became the norm. Ambushes and roadblocks were countered with the awesome firepower of one of these beasts. The typical truck with a Quad-50 had the driver, the gunner, and some loaders. These weapons could not follow a maneuver unit, but from a road or defense position were extremely effective, especially in breaking up ambushes. The Quad-50's range and strike capability made for an ideal quick-reaction weapon against machine gun positions and small arms on heights overlooking roads. Its rate was 1,000 - 1,500 rounds per minute, with an effective range of 2,500 yards. It was truly the security of most convoys in Vietnam.

C-130 Hercules

The Lockheed C-130 Hercules, a four-engine turboprop transport aircraft, functioned in Vietnam as a troop, medevac, and cargo-transport vehicle. It entered the military in the 1950s and is still the longest-used military transport aircraft. Its design made it capable of takeoffs and landings on unprepared and short-field runways. Its superior fifteen-ton payload and an ability to offload palletized cargo put it in high demand. During the siege of Khe Sanh in 1968, the Marines surrounded by the NVA witnessed these versatile aircraft coming and going, bringing in much-needed ammo and supplies and taking the wounded out throughout the seventy-seven-day battle.

After a generation of underpowered military cargo planes, the turbine engines endowed the C-130 with plenty of power. Those turboprop power plants gave the aircraft an ability to carry more, fly faster, and land and takeoff in small, rough, backcountry airstrips.

Some of the Marine line companies of 1/27 flew to and from the Hue City area in the C-130, as described in Chapter 5.

Alpha Six (Marble Mountain) resupply by CH-46 "Sea Knight"
~ Courtesy of Raul E. Figueroa, H&S, 1/27

CH-46 Helicopters

Known as the "Phrog" by the pilots that flew them, the CH-46 (pictured above) functioned as the principal troop transport for Marines. It not only transported personnel, but also evacuated the wounded, supplied Marines with reinforcements, water, and ammunition, and also the much-needed tactical supplies. The CH-46 performed hundreds of dangerous tactical insertions and extractions of Marine reconnaissance teams.

This workhorse could carry external loads with a belly sling hook (cargo hook), which was rated at up to 10,000 pounds. The power produced by the engines limited that capability depending on altitude, air density, weights and balances already onboard, and other external variables.

This aircraft was normally manned with a crew of three (Pilot, Co-Pilot, and Crew Chief) to accomplish most missions. A pintle-mounted .50-caliber M2 machine gun was mounted on both sides of the helicopter for its defenses.

Light Weapons

7.62 Ammo, M72 LAAWs, M33s, M79 Rounds ~ Courtesy of Ronald G. Oakes, B Co, 1/27

Grenades

Grenade use (mainly M26s and M33s) was widespread amongst Marines. Grenades were usually effective in stunning, maiming, killing, or routing an NVA or VC. Every field Marine and Corpsman carried them. They were utilized in a wide variety of applications, from assaulting dug-in, well-prepared enemy positions, crew-served weapon emplacements, and bunkers, to stunning, disorienting, and capturing potential prisoners or informants.

M18 smoke grenades were instrumental in marking positions for fire effect, personnel extractions, concealment, or movement. They came in four basic colors: red, green, yellow and violet. Sometimes smoke grenades were used to help helicopters determine wind direction as well as identifying enemy/friendly positions. The smoke grenade emitted smoke for 50-90 seconds.

Tear gas (CS gas) was potent but not used to a great degree in the Vietnam War. This author has not heard of its application on 1/27 maneuvers. That is not to say there hadn't been any use of tear gas by 1/27 units or other units for that matter during the war years.

The M67 and M33 fragmentation grenade (essentially identical, except the M67 had a safety clip fitted to the safety lever), a relatively new development at the time, was spherical in shape and contained about six ounces of composition B explosive, a very potent propellant. The average Marine could throw it twenty-five to thirty-five meters, maximum. The fuse delay until detonation was four to five seconds after the spoon was released. Steel fragments from the grenade's body produced an injury radius potential of forty to forty-five feet, and a killing radius of ten to fifteen feet, depending on obstacles within the impact area. It was indeed a valuable tool.

The M26 entered service in the early 1950s and saw use in the Korean War. It resembled a lemon shape, and when detonated propelled the body's special pre-notched coiled fragments outward. It, too, used the composition B explosive. There was still a large surplus of these grenades left over from the Korean conflict to be utilized in Vietnam. In fact, it seemed to a lot of Marines and Corpsmen that most issued gear was surplus from the Korean War.

At the Alpha Six position disposing of booby trap mortar rounds using the
Raul Figueroa "Cuban" technique ~ Courtesy of Raul E. Figueroa, H&S Co, 1/27

Raul Figueroa described the "Cuban" technique he used when his squad arrived at Alpha Six close to the "Crow's Nest" around Marble Mountain. "We got to the position and on the first day swept the perimeter for mines and booby traps. We found an unexploded mortar round, lying in front of one of the old bunkers. Since we didn't have an EOD [explosive ordnance demolition] guy with us and no C4, I volunteered to blow it up…What I did was get an empty C-rations can…took out one of my grenades, pulled the pin, placed the grenade in the can, tied a string on it and got as far away as I could. I got behind the berm and pulled the string. There was a big explosion. When we checked it, there was nothing left. The mortar round was all gone."

M20 3.5-Inch Rocket Launcher (DOD Photo USMC A1866259)

M20 3.5-Inch Rocket Launcher

The M20 3.5-inch Rocket Launcher was a smooth-bore, open-tube weapon made of cast aluminum, fired by igniting a 3.5-inch rocket with an electrical current. This weapon system broke into two pieces. It was designed to fire from the shoulder, standing, sitting, kneeling, or laying down in a prone position. The ordnance used was a High Explosive Anti-Tank (HEAT) round and could penetrate the heaviest armor. It also had White Phosphorus (WP) rounds used mostly for marking positions. This launcher was used quite a lot during the Korean War.

The M20 was in most inventories of maneuver battalions in Vietnam. First Battalion had four or five of them in the inventory per the 1968 Command Chronologies. The rounds were designated as fixed ammunition. "Fixed" meant that the propellant charge was not adjustable. These weapons were known for the "back blast" created behind them. It was extremely hazardous to be behind a launcher's backside within about a forty-degree radius and anywhere up to seventy-five yards away. The rocket blast from the rear of the tube could burn for a short time after it was fired and placed all personnel, ammunition, and dry vegetation (anything flammable) behind it in danger. The M72 LAAW replaced this thirteen- to fourteen-pound "super bazooka" in the later stages of the Vietnam War.

The M20 could be fired at about 12-18 rounds per minute, maximum. Four rounds per minute was the sustained rate. Maximum range was 900 yards with a maximum effective range of 300 yards for a stationary target. Moving targets were specified at the 150 to 200-yard range. Tracy Robeson of Delta Company recalls being trained on shooting the 3.5 launcher in Hawaii in 1967. "In Hawaii, I believe a Marine by the first name of Roland and I were trained on shooting this beast, first at the firing range, and then we fired it a couple of times in Vietnam when we arrived there. I remember that the tube was light but cumbersome to carry. It stood out like a flag pole and potentially became an easy target for our M60 machine guns. I remember firing the darn thing and the sound was deafening. I also remember being taught to load the launcher with the rocket and pulling the safety pin. The back blast not only destroyed one's hearing but everything and the foliage behind it. It was actually fun to fire this darn thing!"

M72 LAAW ready for U. S. Marines to fire on NVA positions (DOD Photo USMC A192247)

The LAAW

An M72 LAAW (Light Assault Anti-Tank Weapon), usually called the LAAW, a lightweight hand-carried weapon, was soundly capable of knocking out tanks. The only problem was that there were no enemy tanks other than a sparse few toward the end of the war. Its role in Vietnam became that of a bunker-busting, building-, wall-, and machine gun-emplacement exploder. The LAAW became a very useful tool of the trade. It did have back-blast considerations, but nothing like the 106mm recoilless rifles. This compact, one-shot disposable unit was extremely portable and easy to carry. Penetration head on, through armor was approximately eleven inches; reinforced concrete, roughly thirty-six inches; and log and earth emplacement at about seventy-eight inches. It was useful to many Marines throughout their journey in the northern I CTZ.

Firing M79 into tree line where NVA are suspected to be (DOD Photo USMC A371757)

The "Blooper" M79 Grenade Launcher

This unique weapon first appeared in the early 1960s and became popular during the Vietnam War due to the simple fact that it could hurl a small explosive projectile (grenade) further than someone could throw or hand toss an M33 grenade. It was indeed more portable than a 60mm mortar and could fire a selection of 40mm rounds accurately. The choices were HE-FRAG (High Explosive-Fragmentation), anti-personnel, smoke, buckshot, flechettes, and illumination. It was affectionately referred to as the "Bloop Tube," and the "Blooper" amongst Marines and Corpsmen.

Most grunts shoulder-fired the Blooper, but it had its limitations, being a single-shot, break-action load which meant a slow rate of fire. However, it was easy to use, accurate, reliable, and lightweight, weighing in at 5.95 lbs, empty. Maximum range was around 375 meters. Its official nomenclature validated it as the *M79, 40mm Grenade Launcher* which fired a 40mm (40 mm diameter x 46 mm length) round. Most Marines loved this ugly little "dogleg" of a weapon.

Browning .50-Caliber M2 HB (Heavy Barrel) Machine Gun ~ Courtesy of Hal Kennedy, 1/27

Browning .50-Caliber M2 HB (Heavy Barrel) Machine Gun

This weapon performed throughout most of Vietnam mostly as a vehicle-mounted weapon rendering firepower for defensive positions. The M2, aka "Ma Deuce," utilized by the American military had been standardized for a long time. The M2 has varying cyclic rates of fire. The HB (Heavy Barrel) air-cooled ground gun fired at the cyclical rate of 450-575 rounds per minute (rpm). Sustained rates of fire would in most cases wear out the internal barrel bore within a few thousand rounds, which required replacement. Full automatic or single shot modes could be selected.

The maximum distance a .50-caliber projectile would travel was 7,400 feet. Maximum effective firing range was approximately 2,200 yards (6,600 feet). In a crew-served ground portable group (not fully assembled), the gun itself weighs eighty-four pounds, and with assembled M3 tripod another forty-four pounds is added. Unlike most weaponry in Vietnam, the M2 had no manual safe mode. The charging assembly (locking and loading of a live round) could be changed to either the left or right side of the gun.

Several distinct types of ammo could be fired in this weapon. It used the usual standard ball ammunition, as well as Armor-Piercing (AP), Armor-Piercing Incendiary (API), and Armor-Piercing Incendiary Tracer (APIT) rounds. All the armor-piercing ammunition was required in testing to render penetration of .875 inches of hardened steel armor plate at 100 yards and .75 inches at 547 yards.

This M2 .50-caliber gun was mostly used as a medium infantry support weapon in defensive positions, as a primary weapon on helicopters, armored fighting vehicles and on tanks and naval craft. It was rumored that the NVA thought that only tanks were more of a threat than the 50 Cal.

Small Arms

Lance Corporal Gary Jarvis, Delta Company, with an M60 during Operation Allen Brook June 1968
~ Courtesy of Gary Jarvis, D Co, 1/27

M60 Machine Gun

Gary Jarvis, later to receive his Ph.D. and author of the book, *Young Blood: A History of the 1st Battalion, 27th Marines 1968*, used an M60 machine gun in combat actions during his tour with Delta Company 1/27. From a technical perspective, the M60 is twenty-three pounds, air-cooled, and fed by a disintegrating metallic link-belt which holds standard NATO 7.62mm x 51mm full-metal-jacketed and tracer ammo. Every fifth projectile on the 100-round belts is a tracer. This magnificent weapon had a maximum effective range of 1,100 meters (approximately 1,200 yards). It was one of the most important tools in the Marine maneuver units.

The M60 was capable of firing 550 rounds per minute. A more prudent rate of sustained fire over a ten-minute period was in the range of 100 rounds per minute, after which a change of barrel was necessary. Sometimes there was not a spare barrel nearby. Often it was extremely crucial to pace bursts of fire to conserve ammunition and prevent overheating. The classic textbook scenario called for a gunner, assistant gunner, and ammo man to carry 300 rounds each. This wasn't always the case. The Marines of 1/27 made do with what they had. The 100-round bandoleers of M60 ammo weighed seven pounds each. Other Marines carried rounds also, as many as could be humanly carried.

Of all the small-arms weaponry available to an infantry company, the M60 machine gun was by far the most lethal and powerful tool utilized in the field. However, the enormous firepower yielded by the gun became a double-edged sword. The M60 machine gunner was frequently the primary enemy target, along with the radio operator and leaders.

The gun's orange tracer rounds were designed to aid in target accuracy but unfortunately, the tracer rounds could reveal a machine gun location as soon as it began firing. Jarvis recalls that while undergoing weapons training at Camp Geiger in Camp Lejeune, North Carolina they were taught that, during an intense firefight in the Vietnam War, the life expectancy of an M60 gunner was only on the average of seven to ten seconds. Jarvis confided, "This weighs heavy on an eighteen-year-old's mind."

The M60, like all machine guns, played an extremely significant role in all Marine Corps units in Vietnam and was instrumental in deterring numerically superior enemy forces. The NVA and VC would pick and choose the times in which they would attack. It was always when they felt they had the advantage.

This weapon was highly respected by both friend and foe on the battlefield. Lance Corporal Ronald Oakes, Bravo Company's chief radioman, thoughtfully remembers the M60, "We would take a radio and a machine gun, and they were the most important pieces of equipment we had to take along."

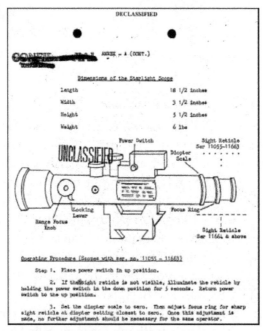

Starlight Scope – portable, battery operated, electro-optical scope for observation at night using the ambient light of the night sky for target illumination
(1st ANGLICO Command Chronologies, Aug 67-Dec 69, Annex-A, page 105)

Starlight Scope

This night vision scope used reflected light emitted from the moon and stars, thus amplifying target objects or personnel to be observed both at night and at a distance. Per the technical specifications, the ambient reflected light intensified up to about

1,000 times in the scope so that objects became more visible. It was like viewing or looking at images on a television screen that appeared mostly green. The effective range was about the same as the conventional "open sights" on an M16A1 rifle. Images would blur if the scope was moved while in use. Low levels of light, rain, fog, or smoke reduced its effectiveness. Looking directly at a visible source of light would cause it to shut down. Shooters would suffer a brief blindness from tracer fire and the flashes they produced. These scopes were known for "streaking and/or distortion" and were only reliable on a fully moonlit night and with a lot of practice.

AN/PVS-2 Night Vision Passive "Starlight" scope mounted on an M14 rifle, weighed six pounds with battery (1st Generation circa 1967-75). Effective range: same as with conventional open sights
~ Courtesy of Utah Gun Collectors Association

M14 and M16 Rifle

Most of the 1st Battalion Marines learned to shoot with an M14 rifle in boot camp and carried them through ITR up until setting foot on Vietnam soil. It did lack in the automatic firepower of being a true assault rifle, but it was a reliable, long-range, good penetration, and lethal weapon, which made it popular. Even though the M14 had seen service prior to Battalion arrival, it was considered too long in the dense vegetation and a long shooter. In heavy vegetation, contact was not further than twenty to fifty yards in a lot of cases. Most encounters in the field took place at less than 150 yards. Thus, the M16, a newly engineered rifle, quickly became its replacement. The M16 was in large part made of fiberglass, and therefore lightweight. These small rifles with a standard twenty-inch barrel (21.25 inches with flash suppressor) became the issued weapon of all Marines beginning the first part of 1968. The weight difference between the two rifles was significant. The M14 weighed approximately twelve pounds without loaded magazine compared to the M16 at 8.7 pounds. The M16 became adequate for the environment it was designed for, although it required intensive cleaning and ongoing maintenance. Comparing rifle and ammo weights, about 100 rounds accompanied the M14 versus the 250 carried with an M16.

Sarcastically called "Matty Mattels" (compared to popular Mattel children's toys), these weapons became accepted by most in a short time. There were many serious problems with the rifle during its initial introduction into the field. Several Marines lost their lives due to a jamming epidemic in mid-late 1967. A brief time after that, Congressional investigations and hearings ("Ichord Committee") on these very serious problems were held. Consequently, both the rifles and ammunition were upgraded. In layman terminology, residue from the original gunpowder used in the ammo accumulated in critical areas, causing carbon fouling of moving parts. Gunpowder in the ammunition was changed and chrome chambers implemented in all rifles, which reduced reports of malfunction considerably.[1]

Lance Corporal Bob McCulloch fires his M16 atop Alpha 6 near Marble Mountain
~ Courtesy of Raul E. "Figgy" Figueroa, H&S Co, 1/27

M40 Sniper Rifle

After looking at many different models, in 1966 the Marine Corps selected the Remington 700 bolt-action rifle as the standard-issue sniper rifle. It was designated the M40 by the Marine Corps and most of the initial seven hundred rifles ordered by the Corps were mounted with a Redfield 3-9 power variable scope. After being utilized in the field for a while it was discovered that the one-piece all-wood stocks were subject to warping. This condition ushered changes to the stock due to the humid climate encountered in the jungles of Southeast Asia.

The cartridge, a 7.62 x 51mm NATO round with a muzzle velocity of 2,550 feet per second, gave the shooter an effective firing range of 800-900 yards. This, of course, was all dependent on the sniper's experience and capability. Corporal Tommy Romo from 27th Marines Regimental S-2, was attached to 1st Battalion with his M40 Remington and actively participated in the No Name Operations, Hue area, as a scout-sniper. He and his buddy, Jim O'Connell, would form a dynamic duo scout-sniper team during April-May east of Hue.

S-2 Scout-Sniper Corporal Tommy Romo with his issued M40 Rifle
~ Courtesy of Tommy Romo, HQ Co, 27th Marine Regiment

Carlos Hathcock, the most famous Marine Corps sniper during Vietnam, used a Unertl telescopic sight (10x fixed power scope) with a mounting of his own design; at one time during a tour he converted an M2 into a long-range sniper rifle, adjusting the traverse and elevation mechanism on the tripod to get appropriate windage and elevation on a prospective target. Hathcock famously did hit targets further than 2,000 yards. During one of his tours, he set the record for the longest confirmed kill at 2,460 yards, a record held until 2002.

Lubricant, Small Arms (LSA)

When a new rifle such as the M16 appeared, it became rapidly apparent that new cleaning and lubrication methods were of the utmost importance in an infantryman's daily life. Marines had always been the habitual maintainers of the most critical of tools, their rifle. Maintaining this new weapon so that it would fire reliably when needed called for a special substance. At the infantryman level the M16 rifle, with design tolerances which produced friction contaminants, needed a lubricant which could ease the harsh conditions of steel-on-steel while also easing the burden of barrel temperatures exceeding the 2,000-degree F mark. At the other end of the gas tube, in the DI System (Direct Impingement System—internal bolt operating inside the bolt carrier, aka receiver group) the constant brief spurts of gas cycling caused the receiver group's action to reach peaks sometimes close to 1,000-degrees F. This newly minted, Eugene Stoner-designed weapon system needed an above-average lubricant.

Considering the time and material that a Marine would need to effectively clean and lubricate a sophisticated weapon

LSA – Lubricant, Small Arms

system such as the M16, LSA was developed. The resultant lubricant made its introduction into the field housed in olive-drab colored four-ounce plastic bottles. A petroleum-based substance mixed with a combination of detergent, oxidation- and corrosion-inhibitor, LSA became wildly popular amongst the riflemen of all maneuvered battalions in I CTZ. This fluid, emitting an aroma of predominantly mineral oil, part metallic with a small hint of plastic, turned out to be a truly lifesaving substance coveted by Marines and Corpsmen.

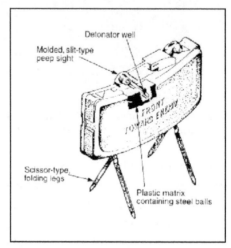

M18A1 Antipersonnel mine aka "CLAYMORE" image from ROTC training manual

M18A1 Claymore Mine

The M18A1 casing was unmistakable, with the raised wording "Front Toward Enemy" embossed on the front side of the mine. Scissor-like legs anchored it upon placing it in its lethal position. A simple open sight on the top confirmed aiming direction. The guts of the claymore contained 700 tiny steel balls ready to be propelled forward by a healthy amount of C4 plastic explosive. Its weight tipped the scales at 3.5 pounds.

Whether command or manually detonated, this deadly antipersonnel mine drove a payload forward in a shotgun-like sixty-degree arc at velocities of 3,937 feet per second. The round projectiles could reach a maximum effective range of about fifty-five yards with a 30 percent possibility of hitting a standing target at that furthest distance. It created a gigantic blast of fragments like that of an oversized shotgun. The detonating device, called the "clacker," and a 100-foot spool of M4 electrical wire, came with each bandoleer pack (called the M7).

The inventor, Norman MacLeod, named it after a historical medieval Scottish sword. The claymore could be set up to cover all approaches of a defensive perimeter and utilized to initiate ambushes or be set up as a booby trap. In a lot of cases it was all that stood between surviving an assault or being overrun.

Combat Gear/Field Equipment

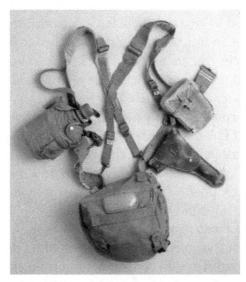

Parts of 782 Gear – Suspenders, Web Belt, Pistol and Holster, Ammo Pouch and Butt Pack utilized
by author in Vietnam 1968 and 1969 ~ Courtesy of Grady Birdsong, H&S Co 1/27

782 Gear

A web belt with suspenders allowed for essential items to be "humped" (shouldered
and carried), e.g., 1911A1 pistol and holster, ammo pouch, canteen(s), fanny pack
(aka "ass pack"), and anything else that could be attached. Per Corps history, 782
or "Deuce" gear began during WWII, and included such items as backpack, shelter
half, canteen, poncho, poncho liner, web belt, ammo pouches, and other gear when
used in maneuver; "782" refers to the official form of paperwork filled out and signed
when the equipment was issued. Officers, Radiomen, Corpsmen and M60 gunners
typically would carry the .45-caliber 1911A1 automatic pistol.

USMC 1965 Canteen ~ Courtesy of
Grady Birdsong, H&S Co, 1/27

Vietnam Era Stainless Steel Canteen Cup
~ Courtesy of David T. "Red Dog" Roberts, D Co,
1/4, 3rd Marine Division FMF

Canteen and Canteen Cup

One of the most important items for anyone engaged in a maneuver unit, the canteen system carried by Marines included a cup with some sort of handle on it which resided inside of an insulated cover that attached to a web belt by metal snap fasteners. Some Marines had canteens left over from WWII. Some were from the Korean War. Some had the latest plastic issue. Everyone had at least two canteens on their web gear. The cups were modeled on the World War I-M1910. Each man religiously carried his cup on his web gear, cradling a canteen of precious water.

Lieutenant Colonel Philip Reade's book *History of the Canteen*, compiled in 1900, points out that when a soldier is out in the field he will always learn that his best friends are his rifle or sidearm, his blanket, and his rations; this translates into the concept that food and a canteen filled with water are extremely important to him and to sustaining the military mission.[2]

Depending on the exercise or maneuver in the field, it was a given that water, ammo, and rations were the most important commodities deserving serious considerations always. Sterilized water was not always available, though water purification tablets were made available to Marines most of the time. A special compartment on the canteen cover housed those tablets.

Halazone Tabs for the canteens

Water purification tablets were carried by each individual Marine and were also available through a Corpsman. The tablets were critical. Sometimes only stream, river, or an undesirable water source was available. Then the tablets were usually added to the canteen and let set for a brief time. Halazone (p-N, N-dichlorosulfamylbenzoic acid) is a chloramine water-disinfecting agent which has a putrid and strong smell. Sometimes Kool-Aid was used to throttle the taste back to make it palatable.

L/Cpl Daniel W. Magner, M79 Grenadier, Echo 2/7, sips precious water during Operation Allen Brook
12 May 1968 ~ Courtesy of Marine Corps History Division (DOD Photo USMC A374474)

The Hand Book for U. S. Forces in Vietnam handed out to all who spent a tour in Vietnam reads, "All water in Vietnam must be assumed to be non-potable and must be boiled or disinfected with chlorine or iodine before drinking. Use water purification tablets, use one tablet per canteen if the water is clear, two if the water is cloudy. Permit the water to stand 30 minutes before drinking...Carry two canteens of water...you should drink tiny amounts of water at a time to avoid the possibility of getting stomach cramps."

Corporal Grady Birdsong remembers when his buddy, Corporal Doug Setley, wrote home and asked his parents to send Kool-Aid. "They, being the loyal and faithful parents of a good son, sent a whole case of Kool-Aid of every flavor made...I can remember becoming not so fond of Kool-Aid after that...We had Kool-Aid coming out of our asses. It seemed that from that time forward we had a never-ending supply of that stuff...and Corporal Setley in my mind became affectionately known as Corporal Kool-Aid!"

Doc William Carroll, Charlie Company, remembered drinking out of canteens and the taste of water laced with halazone. He recalled, "I hated that stuff...it tasted like crap! My parents, sisters, my girlfriends, anybody who was sending me letters, they got them to send me packets of Kool-Aid. So, my personal canteens were always full of 'Goofy Grape' or 'Crazy Cherry'...so think about that? When guys got gut-wounded, we were trained to keep the wound area moist. I would pour my canteen of Kool-Aid all over a guy's wound. I can see them nurses and doctors now back at NSA in Da Nang wondering how in the hell a Marine's wounds got to be purple or red. Only Marines and Corpsmen would get a chuckle out of this."

Poncho and Poncho Liner

Two of these unique fabric (rubber-coated) rain coats with hoods could be snapped together to make a shelter. They were olive green in color and glistened when wet from the rain. Used as shelters, ground sheets, blankets, or to carry the wounded or dead, these garments had many uses coveted by Marines and Corpsmen.

A lightweight quilted liner called a "poncho liner," made of rip-stop nylon, could be placed inside of a poncho and ended up being the standard sleeping bag arrangement of most Marine grunts.

Packs

In the 1960s there were five different packs issued for various exercises: light marching pack, marching pack, field marching pack, transport pack, field transport pack. The field transport pack was the largest and had room for a blanket roll around it. A poncho, its liner, and perhaps a shelter half would be attached as well. This arrangement conformed to field maneuver when slow-paced movement was unimportant. Every mile, every pound of equipment, the type of gear you used had a most important and serious meaning in the Vietnam War.

Author's 782 Gear consisting of Field Pack, Shelter half, Poncho and liner, Flak Jacket, Web belt, Pistol Ammo pouches, M16 Ammo Bandolier, Canteens, M17A1 Gas Mask in carrier at Col Co NSA ramp, Hue area March 1968 ~ Courtesy of Grady Birdsong, H&S Co, 1/27

M17 Gas Mask

A series of these protective masks began appearing in the 1960s. The design of the M17 mask series later allowed for drinking fluids in a chemical environment. This happened to be a good thing for someone who sweated a lot. The drinking tube addition also doubled as a resuscitation vent opening in the later M17A1 model. The negatives: the masks were burdensome and not designed to allow you to fire a weapon easily.

Referred to technically as the M17 Field Protective Mask, the gas mask was distributed to all Marines and Corpsmen who served in Vietnam, providing a degree of protection against gasses, germ warfare, and the possibility of radioactive fallout. It did not function well where oxygen was in short supply, as in or around fires, and was not sufficient protection from radiation (never considered by most Marines during this war).

The mask was mostly used when CS gas was thrown into a newly-discovered underground tunnel. A mask would be donned before entering the tunnel—with the hope that any enemy would be gone or incapacitated. This was frightening and extremely dangerous, especially wearing a device that was restrictive, susceptible to fogging up, hard to see forward in low light, and with hardly any peripheral side vision. Most Marines "chucked it" back in the rear at first chance so they would not have to carry it.

Flak Jacket – Flak Vest

Body armor worn by Marines and Corpsmen, designed to cover vital body parts, provided basic protection from shrapnel and small arms fire. The vests used by Marines and Corpsmen weighed a bit above ten pounds, and consisted of a combination of ballistic-tested nylon and fiberglass plates known as Doron. Both the M1951 and the M1952 armored vests (collarless), providing chest and abdomen protection, were standard issue for U. S. Marine Corps personnel throughout the war in Vietnam.

Korean War Issue K-Bar used by author in Vietnam ~ Courtesy of Grady Birdsong, H&S Co, 1/27

K-Bar Knife

Almost every Marine or Corpsman had a "K-Bar" knife which the Marine Corps officially designated as the *Knife, Fighting Utility*. This knife was adopted as the official USMC knife on 23 November 1942, at the outset of WWII. The K-Bar is almost always associated with the United States Marine Corps.

Originally manufactured by Union Cutlery in Olean, New York, these knives were called the Ka-Bar brand, consequently, in 1952 they renamed the company, KA-BAR Knives, Inc.

The K-Bar was used in Vietnam for many activities originally not intended for a fighting knife. It dug fighting holes, ripped the binding off C-ration boxes, stripped wire, severed time fuses and detonation cord, along with opening hundreds of C-ration cans, fashioning heat stoves from some of those cans. Many a Marine amused himself by honing his throwing skills with this knife, and the K-Bar would sometimes double as a small hammer. This sturdy instrument remained at a Marine's side, almost always.

"Bug Juice" Insect Repellent used by Marines in Vietnam ~ Courtesy of David T. "Red Dog" Roberts, D Co, 1/4, 3rd Marine Division FMF

Bug Juice

Everyone had a bottle of "Bug Juice." The small 2 oz. bottle of insect repellent *(FSN 6840-753-4963; Type II A – Int. Fed. Spec. 0-1-00503a Insect, Repellant, Clothing and Personal Application)* was carried by most Marines in the field. This "stinky" fluid worked better in removing leeches than it did for keeping mosquitoes off. It was mildly irritating to the skin, burning sometimes. Marines also used bug juice for lighting fires, as lighter fuel in cigarette lighters and cleaning weapons. Bug Juice helped maintain that small bit of sanity needed to survive in the new and strange environment of Vietnam.

Dane "Bing" Brown's Helmet ~ Courtesy of Dane Brown, H&S Co, 1/27

M1 Helmet and Cover

The M1 helmet protected the members of the United States Marine Corps from World War II until the 1980s. It is said that over one million helmets were produced during the mid-1960s. They were slightly different from the Second World War and Korean versions, featuring an improved chinstrap.

The helmet design did lead to some innovative usage: With the helmet liner out, the outer steel shell was sometimes used as an entrenching tool, a device for rudimentary hammering, a washbasin, a cooking pot, water bucket, and finally a seat.

The United States Marine Corps has consistently worn a cloth camouflage cover over the steel pot since World War II. The helmet readily identifies a Marine in each of the wars, World War II, Korea, and Vietnam. The cover featured button-hole-like openings for fastening additional camouflage materials, e.g. branches, vegetation, etc. These steel pots with covers were extremely heavy, but worth the wearing for head protection from enemy fire. Rounds would sometimes come from nowhere.

All manner of sayings and graffiti adorned the covers. By far, the most popular were peace symbols and short-timer calendars. The Marines serving in Vietnam were of the 1960s and like the college kids and demonstrators back home, they found a way to express themselves on their helmet covers.

On "Bing" Brown's helmet in the above photograph is the inscription: *"Fear not; For Not Ain't Nothing to Fear!"* and on the front, *"Crotch Sock!"* (The Marine Corps was referred to as the "Crotch" by many enlisted men.) *"SC"* toward the rear indicated Dane's home state of South Carolina. One saying stood out and would be seen occasionally in the "bush": a profound and nonetheless real but abrupt daily reality reminder inscribed on a helmet cover: *"Kill a Commie for Mommy!"*

Drawing graffiti art on helmet covers with permanent marker expressed many things: poems, slang, nicknames, art of all sorts, and anything that had personal meaning to the individual. Some would display sayings only they could understand.

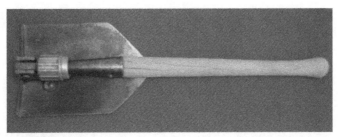

Entrenching Tool from WWII & Vietnam ~ Courtesy of Jeffery Clark, Denver, CO

E-Tool

The entrenching tool was not always carried except on extended operations, but everyone had experience with the use of an E-Tool. The E-Tool folded and the blade could be adjusted to different angles. The M1943 - M1951 E-Tool left over from WWII and the Korean War emerged throughout the Marine ranks in Vietnam. The newer version, the M1967 Tri-folding E-Tool, became prevalent throughout the Army in the later years of the war. The U. S. Army had always received the latest and the Marines always made do with older equipment.

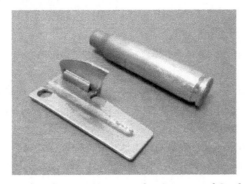

Author's P-38 can opener beside spent M16 round ~ Courtesy of Grady Birdsong, H&S Co, 1/27

P-38 Can Opener

This was a lightweight, multipurpose gadget carried by everyone. Mainly used to open C-ration cans, the P-38 would magically open a can of peaches, beans, or any of the C-ration cans in thirty-eight punctures around the circumference of the can rim. It also could double as a screwdriver or a small knife, never needing sharpening. These tools appeared with C-ration cases, a handful of new openers in each carton. All Marines and Corpsmen carried them on their person, cherishing them as a keepsake.

Zippo Lighter

During their thirteen-month tour in Vietnam, most Marines and Corpsmen carried a Zippo lighter. They were usually engraved with personal feelings and opinions about the war all the way from obscenity to the other end of the spectrum, which might include a love note for the girl waiting at home. The Zippo might have been engraved with words such as, "You Can Surf Later!" Or it may have simply stated where the

Marine had been on their tour while in the Republic of Vietnam. Unique to WWII, Korea, and the Vietnam War, the Zippo became not only a useful and dependable tool but also displayed each owner's personal artwork. Zippos were used for many tasks, from warming C-rations, illumination for reading letters, firing up a cigarette, and finally to "burning shitters."

The Zippo lighter was also a symbol of high superstition, sometimes bordering on the metaphysical. For example, lighting three cigarettes on one C-ration match was a no-no in Vietnam. Likewise, it was bad luck to light more than one cigarette without first shutting the lighter lid and then reopening it to light another's cigarette. This type of simple superstitious ritual has existed throughout most wars in one form or another, and Vietnam was no exception.

Doc David Bronson's Zippo Lighter circa 1968
~ Courtesy of HM2 David E. Bronson, D Co, 1/27

Dog Tags

An informal term assigned to identification tags worn by military personnel during the war. They were named "dog tags" due to a resemblance to animal registration tags required by municipalities throughout America. Identification of the dead or wounded clarified who was who on the battlefield. These tags had personal information pertinent to the person: name and serial number, a branch of service, blood type, gas mask size, and religion. Made of corrosion-resistant metal and issued in pairs, they were worn on the person. Marines and Corpsmen in Vietnam would typically wear one around the neck on a string or chain and the other attached to a boot shoestring.

The duplication of tags allowed identification and processing of wounded or dead bodies in chaotic situations. Accounting for Marines and Corpsmen was one of the highest priorities in each combat unit, from a squad to the line company command. It was extremely important for leaders to know their unit strength and composition always. A tag allowed rudimentary verification and processing to take place in all the triage or care units.

Almost forty years after the author served in Vietnam he received a call from a fellow Marine, Rick Johnson, in the mid-2000s. Johnson's first words on the phone were, "Hey bro, there is a woman out in California that has your dog tag, man!" Johnson had visited a website featuring recently found dog tags from the Vietnam War. Birdsong thought his buddy, Rick, aka the "Trac Rat" (he was an amphibian tractor driver in Vietnam), was funning with him.

As it turned out, this young woman had been trekking through the Da Nang area in 2000 and came across hundreds of dog tags in a small village shop south of Da Nang. Her conscience wouldn't let her go home without buying them. She bought them all (approximately 400-500) and upon returning home established a web site displaying the names on the tags, and trying to find the rightful owners, family members, or relatives.

She had Birdsong's dog tag, one of his originals. In their phone conversation, she asked Birdsong if his tag was stamped, G. T. Birdsong and the reply was a yes. As if he were still in boot camp he immediately blurted out his serial number. She verified the tag's stamped serial number and replied, "I do have your dog tag, how on earth did you lose it?" For the life of him, Birdsong could not remember losing it, when or where. He had brought the other one home and still possessed it. The area she had come across the tags was the area in which 1/27 had operated in during 1968.

Author's Dog Tag: name, serial number, blood type, service branch, gas mask size, religion
~ Courtesy of Grady T. Birdsong, H&S Co, 1/27

In their last moments on the phone, she asked one final question: "How did it get the big dent in it?" Birdsong could not recall the tag having a dent or that he had even lost it. She did send the tag to him after their phone conversation. It was indeed his original issue dog tag and is now in his possession, finding him after all those years and now carried daily on his key chain (see image above).

Fulton MX-991/U Flashlight

This flashlight, a waterproofed angle-head hand-held instrument using 2 D-cell batteries, allowed use as not only a flashlight with five different plastic lenses, but also a multi-mode Off/On switch with signaling capability. The signal switch mode allowed for signaling with Morse code. Designed for durability in the field, its tail cap contained two compartments. The first compartment contained a compressed spring and with the tail cap screwed on tight completed the direct current for two D-cell batteries in series. Underneath the spring housing a spare flashlight bulb was stored. The second portion of the tail cap is where the different colored plastic lenses were kept: two red lenses, a blue lens, one white lens and the diffuser lens. These plastic lenses were designed to enable the sending of signals using distinct colors, or diffuse and spread light in a wide glow as opposed to a narrow beam.

Fulton MX-991/U
Angle-Head Flashlight
with signaling switch

Sea Bag

One of the essential issues of gear upon completion of boot camp, when a recruit had earned the title of "Marine," was his sea bag. This singular bag brought all personal gear into one manageable container which could be carried anywhere in the world and stored in small areas. The Marine's sea bag accommodated all the necessary personal equipment to carry out daily Marine Corps life, e.g., uniform, foot gear, undergarments, socks, shaving kit, etc. It was rigorously reinforced throughout training that the bag was not a "duffel bag," but a "sea bag." The Army had "duffel" bags!

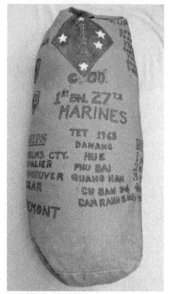

Artistically decorated Sea Bag of Richard L. Fink ~ Courtesy of Rick Fink, Charlie Co, 1/27

The seafaring bag originated in the early 1500s when a heavy type of fabric became popular in the town of Duffel, located near Antwerp, Belgium. This was a heavy textured cloth later known as canvas. This rugged and waterproof material revolutionized the essential task of repairing sails on ocean-going ships. Later these sail makers began using the leftover scraps to produce personal bags for the seagoing sailors of Spain and Portugal. Personal space was limited aboard sailing ships of the times, and sailors embraced the use of this small, sturdy, and waterproof canvas bag. Sea bags were left in rear areas and not carried in the field.

The term duffel bag came out of WWI. The duffel bag was made of canvas and was about ten inches long with a rope to cinch it shut. It was affectionately termed the "Doughboy Duffel Bag" and was like a knapsack. When fully loaded, it became difficult to carry and was therefore left in rear area trenches.

In WWII, the U.S. Army changed the pack to a longer and wider bag. It became an olive drab green bag with a strong strap, which allowed the soldier to carry a heavier load. Using metal eyelets with a grommet, a top closure could be accomplished. This allowed for a padlock to secure one's personal equipment. The bag was stenciled with the name and serial number of its owner.

Some Marines in 1/27 were adept enough to personalize their sea bag as is shown above. Richard L. Fink, a Pennsylvania Marine, artistically affirmed all pertinent information of the unit(s) he had served with, where he had been and more importantly, annotated all the WIAs in the company he so proudly served with in Vietnam, 1968. The effort in artwork by Fink on his sea bag tells an extremely powerful story of that time.

Night Illumination

Even though overhead illumination was readily available through the use of pop-up flares, it was still hard to see people in the concertina wire from a perimeter. The handheld M127A1 White Star Illumination flare (commonly referred to as a

"Pop-up" flare) gave off semi-dim light even though it burned at a 125,000 candle-power. The swinging parachute flare was shot to 400 feet above ground, and burned out in about thirty seconds, rendering partial light with a lot of shadows. Real and imagined movement in the wire was hard to decipher. It was normal to see things that weren't there with these light sources overhead.

The other handheld rocket-propelled signal flare sometimes used was the Parachute M129E1 Red Star. When this flare was deployed its signature of light would float to the ground at an approximate rate of two meters per second, giving off reddish illumination for approximately twenty-five to thirty seconds.

A Leader's Notebook

The shown Memoranda notebooks held a wide array of vital information over the course of two tours in Vietnam. Because no one can remember everything, Sal kept inventory on items such as platoon rifle numbers, pre-registered artillery overhead illumination coordinates aka "Trust Points," pre-coded grid coordinate checkpoints while on patrols called "Papa Deltas" (PD 201 = grid AT047666), items needed for resupply, and language translation, to mention just a few.

In calling for artillery illumination overhead, he would only have to call out over the radio the code name of the grid coordinate that he wanted to be lit up at night. It had all been pre-planned. Headcount along with tactical maneuvering notes were vital information that might need to be recalled at any given time.

Leader's Personal Notebook ~ courtesy of Sergeant Felix Salmeron, A Co, 1/27

Platoon data notated by Sergeant "Sal" ~ courtesy of Sergeant Felix Salmeron, A Co, 1/27

Headcount and Tactical Notes
~ courtesy of Sergeant Felix Salmeron, A Co, 1/27

Fire Support – Mortars

Lance Corporal Richard Thrush, aka "Baseplate," aside an 81mm M29 Mortar at TAOR,
Duong Son (2) South of Da Nang ~ Courtesy of Richard Thrush, H&S Co, 1/27

Mortars utilized by Marines during the Vietnam War were generally considered infantry weapons that could provide immediate fire support for company, platoon maneuver, and for pre-registering defensive positions against assault. With 60mm and 81mm mortars, Marines had to work very hard to transport and position the equipment and maintain a line of communication via radios with a Forward Observer (FO), a Company CO, and Platoon CO, who interpreted data from all inputs. These weapons generated an accurate, high-angle suppressive fire of mainly High Explosive (HE), WP, or Illumination rounds. WP mortar rounds were utilized mainly for marking target areas, HE for offensive firing, and "Illum" rounds for lighting up an area during the dark hours. The weapon was fired and its aim controlled through either fixed observation or an on-the-move controller (Company Commander, Platoon Leader, or FO), and ideally a combination of all.

James Brookhart, new to H&S 81mm Mortars in Kaneohe Bay in February 1968, found himself shipping out to Vietnam with an advance party shortly after he had checked into the Company. He had been trained on artillery fire direction control and recalls "humping" the 81mm mortar to a new position when they first got to Vietnam. "It was broken into five basic components, consisting of the tube, sight, bipod, and the outer and inner rings of the base plate. Each member of the tube crew 'humped' one of the components as well as a minimum of three, if not four rounds of High-Explosive, White Phosphorous, or Illumination. A backpack frame or ruck with lash cord was used. As the 'FNG' [F..king New Guy], I got to carry the base plate inner ring. I don't know if it was the heaviest, but it certainly was the most awkward."

When setting up a new firing position, each mortar had to be "laid in" so that all the tubes were oriented or aimed at the same azimuth (fixed point and the direction of an object). This was critical, Brookhart explained, because a crew could not see their distant target when firing. When an FO called in for a fire mission and had to adjust all available tubes to fire collectively an FFE (Fire for Effect), this ensured that they would all be aimed and firing at the same target.

Additionally, setting up likely targets (e.g., tree lines, avenues of approach) took place as soon as possible from a new location, and was termed "pre-registration." Identities were assigned by numbering each target area in the event of an assault. A commander could readily call an FFE requesting pre-assigned fire on those targets. Harassment and Interdiction (H&I), a useful tactic, would sometimes catch unsuspecting enemy combatants traveling undetected through an outlying area.

Lance Corporal James Brookhart simulating loading an HE round for firing an M29 Mortar mounted on a Baseplate ~ Courtesy of James Brookhart, H&S Co, 1/27

Lodged in Brookhart's mind to this day is the worst butt-clenching situation a mortar crewman could ever experience, aside from being under fire, and that was clearing a misfire. When a round dropped into the tube and hit the firing pin and did not fire, that round would be at the bottom of the tube with its powder charges and fuse attached. This raised every crewman's adrenaline level to a new high. The immediate procedure was to disconnect the tube from the baseplate and then one crewman would gently tilt the tube forward, careful not to let the round slide back into the tube and hit the firing pin. Another crewman would gently catch the round as the tube tilted forward, and the round could slide out. That crewman had to place his fingers and palms around the tube opening to hand-pull the "armed" round out without touching the fuse. Brookhart remembers, "We cleared several misfires in this manner without incident or accident…" Safety was getting that round neutralized as quickly as possible.

Brookhart reflects, "After a couple of month's in-country, an FO position became open. I asked what I would have to carry doing that job, and the reply was 'a map, compass, and binoculars.'" He quickly volunteered for the FO role and "…since I only weighed around 135 pounds and was humping sixty to seventy pounds as a mortar crewman, this was a job I wanted. This is when I teamed up with Bob Elliot, an RTO, and we became inseparable."

FOs and their RTO (Radio Telephone Operator) were assigned to various line companies for specific operations. Brookhart tells, "I spent a good amount of time with Bravo Company. While artillery FOs were normally officers, as were air support liaisons, 81mm FOs were enlisted men. Mortar FOs could call in 'arty' fire missions if the patrol leader trusted him and wanted artillery support. Generally, artillery FOs did not go out on small unit patrols, so on several occasions, I called in artillery fire missions. The process of calling in the fire mission and adjusting fire was the same process as for 81mm mortars."

4.2-inch M30 Mortar and baseplate ~ Courtesy of Raul E. "Figgy" Figueroa, H&S Co, 1/27

"If we encountered the enemy, I would try to physically get to whoever was leading the patrol. If the fire mission was ordered the first order of business was to identify the target and then verify on our maps our position and the target coordinates. Unfortunately, many of the maps were older, French-oriented maps and not reliable in terms of landmarks. Sometimes villages no longer existed or rivers had changed course. If we had any doubt, I would call for an illumination round (overhead). In a lot of cases the 'Illum' round went off behind or in front of us instead of near the intended target...we could then adjust the fire mission for better accuracy."

Fire Mission

The process for calling a fire mission was to radio back to where the tubes were located, announce, "fire mission," and identify yourself using your call sign. Of every fire mission request, the FO would give coordinates of the target, azimuth from him to target, and convey a "danger close" distance. This was the distance between his Marines and the intended impact area. PRC-25 radio communication was extremely critical, and clear commands were essential in relaying all the target and coordinate information. Radio traffic sometimes would become garbled due to atmospheric conditions; saying "niner" for nine, for example would most times clear the confusion. Sometimes it would require, "Say again over!"

The azimuth from the FO to a target was critical for adjusting the firing. Whoever was working the problem for the tubes had to interpret/convert and relate where the FO was in relation to the target. If the FO called in spotter rounds to begin and then had to adjust, he communicated a "right fifty" to the tube position. They adjusted fifty meters to the right based on their position and direction to the target. Once a spotter round was on target the FO would call for "fire for effect" and all available tubes would fire one or more rounds. Jim remembers, "Calling in a fire mission and adjusting spotter rounds while under fire or pinned down with the noise and confusion was a difficult process, even if everything went as planned."

80-foot Observation Tower near Tu Cau Bridge ~ Courtesy of Ronald G. Oakes, B Co, 1/27

During one part of their tour, Lance Corporal Brookhart and his H&S mortar crew teammates stood watch duty in an eighty-foot tower close to the river at the Tu Cau Bridge off Highway 1. The tower was equipped with spotter scope and radio. The duty consisted of watching for incoming mortars and rockets from a full 360-degree view. Because the tower stood well above the top of the defensive berm, the enemy used it for an aiming stake. Brookhart recalls, "Being eighty feet off the ground while enemy mortars are impacting near the tower is an experience like no other that I experienced in Vietnam!"

A Marine is Missing in Action (MIA)

Brookhart was standing watch in the eighty-foot high tower, shown above, in July of 1968. He heard shots from the bridge area below and in the distance. Checking the area with the spotter scope, he saw a Vietnamese man carrying a rifle moving rather quickly into a tree line. He looked further and observed a small group of children dragging a body across the road into the same tree line.

Brookhart recalls, "It was from this tower in late July 1968, I observed a Marine killed near the Tu Cau Bridge and his body dragged off. I reported it and the next day went with the patrol to search for the body. We never found the body." It was later learned that the Marine who was killed and never found was Lance Corporal Edward Arlo Willing; MIA 21 July 1968, later proclaimed KIA on 20 November 1978 and posthumously promoted to Gunnery Sergeant. His status in Casualty Data: "missing to died while missing." He was a member of D Battery, 2nd Battalion, 13th Marines, 1st Marine Division, a supporting Artillery unit of RLT-27.[3]

Air Support

Marine jets delivered air-to-ground ordnance and close-in support of Marines on the ground. The Air Liaison Officer assigned to advise each Battalion Commander concerned himself with the overall employment of air support, requests for support, controlling helicopter operations, and landing zones. He also was instrumental in coordinating with the Forward Air Controller (FAC) in the air and on the ground. Marine O-1s (Cessna) were used up until about 1968. Attrition was taking a toll on these aircraft, and the Cessna OV-10 was then introduced into the theater.

The big threats to the O-1 were from small arms and light machine guns. It was a slow-moving, long-endurance aircraft that could stay on station, maintaining visuals with the activity on the ground. Each aircraft had multiple radios capable of coordinating with ground forces. An FM radio was for communicating with ground troops, the UHF radio for talking with fighter aircraft, and a VHF radio for contacting the Tactical Air Control Party (TACP) to coordinate overall approvals and requests for air support.

Later, the higher speed OV-10 became the standard. It worked better against the introduction of larger-caliber weapons and man-portable surface-to-air missiles. The Marine Corps tactically employed FACs in the O-1 and OV-10 during the initial stages of the war to control all used air assets.

FACs were an air-ground team made up of ground-based or airborne personnel (above a battlefield), or a combination of the two. The jungle and heavy vegetation often required that an airborne FAC control most strikes. But there were occasions in

60mm Mortar handout to Bravo Company Marines during Hawaii Training 1967
~ Courtesy of Michael Weymouth, B Co, 1/27

Weapons cleaning detail (mortars) ~ Courtesy of III MAF Photographer (unknown) given to Raul E. "Figgy" Figueroa, H&S Co, 1/27

which ground-based FACs became very effective. During this era, the harmonization of firepower and technology pioneered new weaponry and tactics. 1/27 had an air liaison officer who had flight time as a pilot. This use of expertise from the cockpit to the ground proved to be of immense value during the battalion's tenure in Vietnam.

Corporal Laurence Ackerman recounts, "Although my training was as an RTO, I was brevetted into the position of Forward Air Controller. My understanding was that pilots were supposed to be FACs with an assigned radio operator, but unfortunately, there weren't enough of them to go around." Captain John Vogt, the battalion air liaison officer, pulled several RTOs including Ackerman together in Kaneohe Bay and held a short crash course on Air-Ground procedures. This was a worthwhile investment for what the future would bring. When Ackerman arrived in Vietnam he was assigned to Bravo Company. At first, most of the FAC activity was in extracting the wounded, which meant guiding helicopter pilots to a position using map coordinates, landmarks, and smoke grenades. Ackerman remembers when the battalion abruptly went into the Hue TAOR in March that air support activity became much more intense. "Captain Ron Allen, Bravo Company CO, needed air support on several occasions and I remember calling in fast-moving aircraft to deliver napalm and 20mm cannon fire. My favorite was napalm because it gave the longest reprieve from return fire. I did find it frustrating sometimes that the enemy would immediately return fire shortly after the aircraft had completed its pass. The overcast weather and visibility would stop us from using air support many of the times when it was needed the most."

F8 Crusader dropping its payload on Operation No Name #2, Hue Area, 13 April 1968
~ Courtesy of Corporal Dennis Fisher, 1st Marine Division Combat Photo and Correspondence Section

Support from an F4 Phantom Pilot

C. R. Cusack was an F4B pilot in 1968 based at Da Nang, RVN. Da Nang had become the busiest airport in not only Vietnam but in the entire world during the mid-1960s. By 1968, Da Nang's runways were accommodating a monthly average of over 50,000 takeoffs and landings. The units to which Cusack was assigned, Marine Fighter/Attack Squadron-542 and 122, had gained fame in the Pacific in WWII and again in Korea in 1950, and now were adding streamers to their illustrious battle flags. Ordered to Vietnam in 1966, the Tigers (VMFA-542) earned many distinctions in providing air support to ground forces in the northern I CTZ. Additionally, they flew bombing missions into both Laos and North Vietnam.

The F4 "Phantom," the main tool of VMFA-542 and 122, was an excellent bombing and strafing platform which complemented the renewed Marine Corps Air-Ground Team concept. Cusack recalls its magnificent capabilities. "You can hit targets with it and it responds quickly, when you add power, you get power. With most jets, the engines must 'spool up' before you get power…when you take power off it comes off instantaneously. It was an easy craft to fly. It had about an hour of fuel aboard, sometimes over an hour, depending on what we were doing. There were times when we had to dump fuel before we could bomb because we had to be under a certain weight in order not to overstress the aircraft."

VMFA-542 and 122 worked under the umbrella of an air control center. The center had its control tools: the "hot-pad" control (planes on the pad ready to roll and be in the air within five minutes), an "airborne hot-pad" (planes in the air ready to deploy), and "scheduled air missions." Cusack recalls, "When we were scheduled we didn't know where we were going. We would just take off and report to a particular airspace at a specific time and do what the air control center told us to do. They would then give us a Forward Air Control frequency and an approximate location. We would then hustle to that location and contact the FAC. He would then brief us and start controlling our activities. He was either on the ground, or in a Cessna L-19/O-1 [Bird Dog], or a Hughes OH-6 [Loach–Light Observation/Attack]

Captain C. R. Cusack, VMFA-122, Da Nang, RVN 1968 ~ Courtesy Major C. R. Cusack

helo or a Cessna O-2 [Skymaster]. These brave souls would then give a very brief situation report and the lay of the land. Then they would point out where the friendlies were and how he was going to identify the target they wanted us to bomb or strafe. Sometimes they would mark it and sometimes they would just describe it."

An FAC had full control of all air support activity. Before air support could be deployed, all missions had to be authorized by the controlling FAC. Every situation was different, therefore these controllers had to be aware and familiar with the kinds of ordnance the planes carried and their capabilities. For example, napalm could be dropped very close to the ground. Any type of HE ordnance had to be dropped at least 200 feet above ground level (AGL) or a pilot could blow himself right out of the air. As then-Captain Cusack recollects, "Nape, you could go right down close and put it right on the ground exactly where they wanted it. The grunts liked it…the pilots liked it…everybody liked it but the gooks…"

Briefing General Lew Walt, 1971 ~ Courtesy Major C. R. Cusack, VMFA-542

Hill 310

The majority of sorties for Cusack's unit in 1968 were close air support and direct air support. Most of these activities were scheduled. Some of them originated off what was called the "hot pad": pilots who were on call on the pad and ready to roll at a moment's notice. He remembers a not-so-fond moment on 8 August 1968. "I mostly supported grunt units in and around Da Nang. I flew support for units in those areas affectionately known as Dodge City, Arizona, and the Go Noi, also there was Charley Ridge. I flew in support of Operation Allen Brook, Mameluke Thrust, and was finally shot down around Hill 310, southwest of Da Nang, within approximately nine to ten nautical miles of the city. The NVA had been consistently setting up 122mm rocket pods and shooting them into the Da Nang airstrip from that position. The upper-level command had sent two companies of grunts out to find them and clear them out. The FAC who was on the ground with the grunts was a guy by the name of Tom Wells, TBS graduating class of 6-67."

Two companies of Marines were on the hill in a heated firefight with NVA combatants. Cusack and his flight section lead, Major Beatty, were called in to support the Marines and were controlled by Wells who was embedded with the grunts. Cusack was "Dash Two" which meant he was following his lead, Major Beatty, "Dash One" who had already made a 20mm pass. "I made one run on the hill where Captain Wells directed me to go. Then I made my second run. I made both of my runs on the hillside in an east to west direction. As I pulled up out of the second run, within a couple of seconds after I pulled up, I felt a heavy thud on the aircraft. And, eh…that is not a good sound. I am now watching my fuel gauge and I could see it wavering a bit. Then the fire warning light comes on...and then the second light comes on...so now I know I have been hit and then all four of the fire warning lights are on. By that time I am headed straight for the downtown area of Da Nang. I then thought about it for a few seconds and thought that I had better not point the nose at that area. I did not want to go free falling into a populated area...so I swung her around wide over Elephant Valley and then pointed the nose toward Da Nang Bay. With all the lights and alarms on I am still flying and most of everything is working and the engines are running and it is still airborne. I have a backseat Radar Intercept Officer with me. I radioed to my lead, Major Beatty, that we are on fire. My guy in the backseat says... 'Are we on fire?' I replied, 'Yeah, we're on fire,' and he says, 'Let's jump out!' And I ask him, 'You want to walk to Hanoi? We are still over the NVA in Elephant Valley.' And he finally tells me, 'No, let's not jump!' The engines didn't quit until we were well over the bay. THEN we jumped!"

Parachuting into Da Nang Bay

Captain Cusack managed to fly the F4 due east out over Da Nang Bay and when the engines quit he and his RIO ejected. The RIO parachuted safely into the bay waters and was picked up by an Air Force rescue chopper. Cusack, much to his surprise, was pulled out of the bay by an Air Force guy and three Marines who were out water skiing for the day.

The Stars and Stripes of Sunday, 1 September 1968 (Volume 24, No. 243) reported that *"Captain Charles R. Cusack, pilot (Ft. Collins, Colo.) and his RIO, Captain Stephen M. Creal, (Lincoln, Neb.) were rescued by the crew of a small boat in the bay of Da Nang...The Marine Fighter-Attack Squadron-122 crew was conducting air strikes on*
an enemy automatic weapons position when they were hit. A .50 caliber machine gun position, on a ridge near Happy Valley, riddled the jet as it released its load of ordnance."

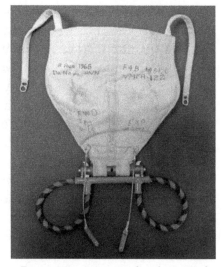

The article goes on to capture Captain Cusack's comments, *"I was pulling out of a steep bank when I felt the aircraft jolt...about five seconds later the left engine fire warning light flashed on indicating a fire in the engine compartment...my main concern at the time was to get over water where we would be free of the ground and any enemy activity."*

This face protector curtain was part of every ejection system manufactured by the Martin-Baker Aircraft Company, Ltd. It sits high on the back of the pilot's seat above his head, hand accessible. The F-4 ejection seat

Face protector curtain placed on top of
an ejection seat of F4B Phantom
~ Courtesy Major C. R. Cusack,
VMFA-542 and 122

saved quite a few lives during the Vietnam War. A Phantom parked on a runway, in theory, had the capability of catapulting a pilot or his backseat rider 300 feet in the air; then chutes would open and float them safely back to the ground. Captain Cusack managed to keep this particular face curtain as a memento of that action-filled day, 8 August 1968, when he ejected as his Phantom plunged into Da Nang Bay.

"Puff the Magic Dragon"

Almost everyone in I Corps either witnessed or had heard about "Puff the Magic Dragon," or "Spooky," as it was known. These AC-47s or DC-3s, aka "Gooney Birds," equipped with machine guns out an opening on the side, could pour out firepower at the rate of 18,000 rounds per minute. The steady stream of bullets coming from this weapon was so awesome that the enemy called them "Dragon Ships." It was often remarked that these aircraft could "rototill an entire football field" in a short minute. One of Spooky's principal missions was to provide night security around large airbases like the Da Nang airstrip. It also played a key role in performing search and rescue missions of downed pilots. Along with providing awesome firepower, Spooky dropped flares over a battlefield. Each flare provided about three minutes of light over an area. Spooky was a spectacle to the eye and ear if you were close to where it was "working out." It appeared in the night sky as a dragon-like shape, roaring and spitting fire.

One of Spooky's Calling Cards ~ Courtesy of 1st Lt. Bob Averill, H Co, 2/9 (DMZ)
and 3rd CAG, 4th Company in the Hue Area, 1968-1969

Utilizing Spooky on 2/9's perimeter at Ca Lu (Route 9 on the DMZ) in April of 1968, then-First Lieutenant Averill recounts, "We had used Spooky on the perimeter…it was so impressive watching it 'deleaf' the area and send the NVA running, leaving the usual blood trail evidence…next time in Da Nang I had to stop in their HQ to tell them thanks, that is when I got their calling card and a cup of Joe."

Sergeant Andy Boyko also remembered his introduction to Spooky. He recalled, "I can't remember the situation we were in but it occurred during Operation Allen Brook. It was at nightfall and I was in a fighting hole. I suddenly experienced what looked like a streak of steady light coming out of the pitch-black night sky. It was distinctly an intense red-colored beam going on and off…and the next thing I heard was the delayed humming sound after the light was on for a few seconds. It was not like any kind of gunfire I had ever heard but produced an on and off hmmm...holy shit, it kept doing that for the longest time. It kept illuminating the sky's ceiling with streaks of undulating light hurtling to the ground and delayed hmmmms...My mind began thinking bizarre thoughts. Perhaps, I had been in the bush too long and that I was just imagining this! In my Marine Corps brain 'housing group,' I thought Martians were really landing. I did not know we had this new weapon which had earned the nickname of 'Puff the Magic Dragon.' I had never seen this type of shooting display before. This was my first exposure witnessing these new Gatling gun cannons mounted in a slow-moving aircraft which circled overhead 'on station' controlled by ground troops."

Spooky DC-3 at Da Nang airbase 1968 ~ Courtesy of Raul E. Figueroa, H&S Co, 1/27

Ron Oakes, Bravo Company's RTO recollects, "We were on Operation Allen Brook in early summer and had set up a Company-sized hasty defense...sometime after dark. A squad leader on the north side of the perimeter called me up on the radio and requested that a platoon commander comes over to that position. I was the Company Commander's RTO at the time. I went to that position with the LT. The squad leader said there were bonfires to the north of us...so we go and look and sure enough to the north of us on the other side of the rice paddies were huge bonfires. We had been on this operation for what seemed like weeks and knew that the NVA were out there somewhere in that area. So why would they build bonfires? The thinking was that it was a distraction...they were trying to divert our attention and hit us where we least expected on our south side. A command decision was then made to reposition every other man from the north side back to the south side.

"Meanwhile, we put a call in for Puff. It took the aircraft less than an hour and it was overhead. You could hear Spooky lumbering overhead in the dark and could see the exhausts sparking out of those cylindrical engines as it started flying circles over our tactical area. It was a moonlit night and you could see its extraordinary image as it lurked above. Suddenly, the red arrows started flowing down from the sky. Spooky was shooting its mini-canons and all you could hear was a loud hummmmmmmmm… hummmmmmmmm…on and off. I think I had heard that every 5th round was a tracer round. The red arc those tracer rounds produced traveling down to the ground looked like a reddish-orange cone-shaped image that was being hand-scripted by a fiery dragon up in the sky. Whatever was within its target area on that ground didn't have a prayer…it just minced everything like it was rototilling a garden. Anyone close to those fires was mincemeat. The Marines on the northern perimeter could see what was going on and enjoyed this spectacle…This was a huge morale builder for all of us!"

Heavy Weapons Support

The Flamethrower

H&S Company retained responsibility for all supporting heavy weapons. Practice with those weapons was an ongoing training task during the time in Hawaii. The Flamethrower qualified as a useful infantry weapon for close combat situations and had been used against both fortified positions and in dug-in defenses in previous wars.

Practice with M2A1 Portable Flamethrower (Kaneohe Bay 1967)
~ Courtesy of Hugh G. Barton, H&S Co, 1/27

It weighed approximately sixty-eight to seventy-two pounds when fully filled. Additionally, it housed an ignition cylinder with five incendiary charges. Each charge when fired lasted eight to nine seconds. After all five charges ignited, the cylinder was rendered inoperable. The firing of the liquid fuel could reach a maximum range of twenty yards. Use of thickened fuel would reach forty-five yards. Needless to say, a lot of man-hours were invested in practicing with its gruesome capability.

Although used extensively in World War II, the Flamethrower did not get utilized a lot in Vietnam. As Corporal Raul Figueroa remembers its use within 1st Battalion, "We humped that heavy piece of equipment around for the whole time we were there, all seventy-three pounds of it…we carried CS [tear gas], some Napalm and most of the time regular gas in the cylinders…Raymond Coffee was the Marine that really knew them. He mixed the fuel and maintained them. He would always have them ready to go when they were called for…He was always helping everybody out and knew the ropes…He was our mentor."

It was also noted by Figueroa that, "…gas is clean when you shoot it and it spreads all over like water after it arrives at its target. Napalm stays together in a steady stream. If a person gets that stuff on them it won't come off and just clings as it will burn down to the bone."

Figueroa indicated that even though they carried the Flame Tanks on a lot of operations, they were only used twice. The first time was to burn off a cache of rice found in an NVA encampment. The second time it would not operate properly and was sent back to HQ.

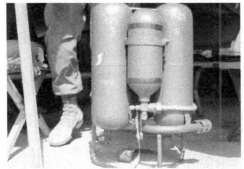

H&S Weapons M2A1 Flame Tank used in Vietnam in 1968
~ Courtesy of Raul E. "Figgy" Figueroa, H&S Co, 1/27

PFC Dane Brown remembers going on an operation when the battalion first arrived in Vietnam. Some LVTP-5 Amphibian Tractors came along in support. He recalls being called up to the front and told to flame a position. The unit had taken fire from some bunkers and spider holes. He went up and "…did the blow torch…there were a couple of fortified bunkers and a spider hole…we didn't know what all was in them. We discovered that the NVA were already dead prior to my flame assist. It was just in case so we didn't take any more fire from the NVA in them. I sure did like it when the "track-rats" told me to throw my tank up on their Amtrac. I didn't have to hump it back."

Corporal Figueroa, Flames Section, recalls being attached to the line companies and that they would "hump" the tanks on patrol waiting to be called upon. On one patrol into a village area, they spent the night by a canal. When they started to move early the next morning, Corporal Eddie Villegas was in front of "Figgy" and several rounds came cracking through the bamboo thicket they were passing through. Figueroa vividly recalls "…dropping down on one knee to get what cover I could, I noticed that Eddie in front of me with a cigarette in the mouth had lost it down the neck of his T-shirt. Eddie stood up and started beating on his flak jacket and frantically threw it off and then started beating his T-shirt to put the burning cigarette out. Although a very tense situation, when the danger passed and we started moving again, I kept laughing at him and telling him that 'Those cigarettes are going to kill you, Eddie!' "

Because of the frightening damage this device inflicted on humans, it was deemed treacherous ever since it was first used in the trench warfare of WWI. Widely used in the Pacific campaigns of WWII, it contributed to quickly and effectively taking out objectives. Flamethrowers did not receive a lot of public attention during the WWII era, but with the public distaste for Vietnam, it and Napalm came under heavy scrutiny. This weapon system was extremely dangerous and required intensive training for its effective use in the field. Mounted flamethrowers were also utilized on tanks and armored vehicles in WWII, Korea, and Vietnam. The U.S. Department of Defense terminated the use of flamethrowers voluntarily in 1978. It was, needless to say, a controversial weapon.

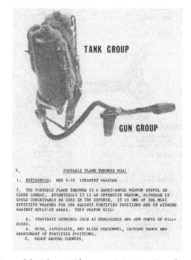

Portable Flame Thrower M2A1, Combat Handbook issued to each Marine/Corpsman, FMFPAC REPRO 1480 (1966)
~ Courtesy of Grady Birdsong, H&S Co, 1/27

67A2 Flame Tank on Operation Allen Brook 1968 ~ Courtesy of Ronald G. Oakes, B Co, 1/27

Flame Tanks damaged from mortar attack
~ Courtesy of Raul E. "Figgy" Figueroa,
H&S Co, 1/27 M40 Recoilless Rifle

106mm Recoilless Rifle arrives for Bridge Duty south of DaNang ~ Courtesy of Raul E. "Figgy" Figueroa, H&S Co, 1/27

Open breech on 106mm Recoilless Rifle ~ Courtesy of Raul E. "Figgy" Figueroa, H&S Co, 1/27

FNG ("F.....g New Guy") instruction of firing a .50-caliber spotter round atop the 106mm Recoilless Rifle at Alpha 6, August 1968 ~ Courtesy of Raul E. "Figgy" Figueroa, H&S Co, 1/27

The M40 series of recoilless rifles were extremely heavy, weighing in at 461 pounds on a tripod or mounted on mechanical mule. A typical HE round weighed thirty-seven pounds and traveled a 1,200-yard maximum effective range. These weapons generated a most deadly and massive cone-shaped back blast when fired. The blast pattern extended about seventy-five yards long and 150 yards wide behind the rifle. It was imperative that personnel not be in this danger zone during firing.

The M40 106mm recoilless rifle was an amazingly crude design. The breech block has large openings. The shell casing looks more like a cylindrical cage than a shell canister. The recoil from the propellant gasses can escape through the vents in the casing and the rear breech. This allows it to function somewhat like a rocket nozzle as the projectile with explosive is hurled toward the target.

This weapon was crew-operated and included a parallel-mounted .50-caliber spotting rifle capable of firing marking rounds that would give off puffs of smoke upon impact. That would allow for windage and elevation adjustments. The 106 was designed initially for use against tanks, and since the North Vietnamese hardly used tanks until the end of the war, the M40 found other uses. Sometimes, it was used against bunkers, though mostly as an anti-personnel weapon. The "beehive" round used functioned as a huge shotgun blast of steel dart-like flechettes fired from defensive positions.

"Figgy" Figueroa with 106mm Recoilless Rifle beehive round
~ Courtesy of Raul E. Figueroa, H&S Co, 1/27

The Ontos

The M40 recoilless rifle was also associated with the Ontos (Greek for "thing), probably the most eccentric track vehicle ever designed and used by the Marine Corps in Vietnam. This tracked, light armored, self-propelled vehicle was first developed as a tank destroyer. In Vietnam, it became more widely used for direct fire support for infantry in combat. The Ontos were used throughout I Corps, but became true Marine legend during the battle for Hue City during the Tet Offensive in 1968. The Ontos proved its worth in some of the worst urban house-to-house fighting during the battle for the Citadel in February. These "reckless rifles" were made famous by First Lieutenant Bruce "Cole" Morton's Ontos Platoon, both preceding and during the Tet Offensive, due to the mobility and awesome firepower of the six recoilless rifles mounted on the unusual weapon delivery system.

The tactic developed by his Marines in the city was to race at top speed down the narrow streets toward the intended target, slam on the brakes, pivot and aim all six rifles, firing them simultaneously, then quickly shifting into reverse and back out of the fields of fire to reload and wait for the next target. Utilized over and over by these heroes, this tactic caught the NVA rifle and machine gun emplacements totally unprepared. Accordingly, it has been said that a larger part of Fifth Marine Regiment grunts survived Hue in part because of the Ontos and the 106mm recoilless rifle crews of Morton's men. Then-Second Lieutenant Nicholas Warr, leading a platoon of 1/5

Company C Marines inside the Citadel, later wrote about Cole's Ontos support in his book, *Phase Line Green*.[4] The North Vietnamese Army and local VC units feared it.

M50A1 Ontos armored anti-tank vehicle of First Lieutenant Bruce "Cole" Morton's platoon supporting 1/27 at La Son School CP (Grid YD781269) April 1968 ~ Courtesy of Richard Thrush, H&S Co, 1/27

During Operation No Name #2, First Tank Battalion dispatched and attached three tanks and Ontos with Recoilless Rifles from Lieutenant Morton's platoon to support a search and destroy operation being conducted by 1/27 east of Hue City. The First Tank Battalion, located in Phu Bai and under the command of Task Force X-Ray, were there to assist 1/27 and the 5th Marine Regiment operating in that area during April and May.

Mid-afternoon of 12 April 1968, Alpha Company, Third Platoon Ontos set up a final block at YD818248 for the entire 1/27 sweep. Company A, Third Platoon Ontos reported firing HE rounds at many NVA fleeing the canal area. They noted many combatants falling because of their firing, but the Marine sweeping force never reached the objective to recon the area so results were not recorded. Third Platoon racked up seven NVA KIAs that were verified.

The following day, 13 April, Company B, 1/27 came in close contact with a large NVA force near YD835237 and YD831239. To their credit, Ontos Third Platoon successfully held all NVA combatants in the kill zone for later fixed-wing air and artillery strikes. The strikes repulsed the NVA and they finally moved out of the area.[5]

In the late afternoon of 17 April, the La Son Schoolhouse (1/27 CP) close by received an assault of 82mm and 60mm mortars from an unknown position. The other Third Platoon Ontos crew positioned at the schoolhouse CP sustained wounds which resulted in medical evacuation. A total of four Marines were KIA and another twenty-five

WIAs were tended to and medevac'd. A platoon of Alpha Company Marines dispatched to investigate the suspected launch sites to the southeast of the CP reported negative results.[6]

The Tanks and Ontos crews were an appreciated addition to the line companies and were welcomed with open arms. The firepower capability of these awesome behemoths and the heroes that kept them running received healthy respect from all the Marines of 1/27.

M48 Patton Tank out of service on Operation Allen Brook south of Da Nang, 1968
~ Courtesy of Hal Kennedy, H&S Co, 1/27

Tanks

The M48 Patton Tank was the mainstay tank of the Marine Corps in Vietnam. This vehicle design condensed three compartments into its interior: a driver, the gunner-loader-tank commander module, and an engine compartment. The main gun, a 90mm, had housed on it a one-million-candlepower Xenon searchlight. This searchlight generated both white light and infrared. Canister and HE were the primary ammo types. Beehive ammo, quite effective, was used but in short supply for tanks throughout the war. The M48's leading role was as infantry support, and provided extremely destructive firepower.

These behemoths offered adequate crew protection and could contend with most land mines and RPGs. However, when a breakdown occurred, repairs took lengthy periods of time and required infantry security if available. The terrain in Vietnam often stifled the full potential of the M48 tank.

Author Grady Birdsong in front of M48 Tanks at La Son Schoolhouse CP April 1968
~ Courtesy of Grady Birdsong, H&S Co, 1/27

LVTP-5 Amphibian Tractor

The Landing Vehicle, a tracked amphibian tractor, was developed in the late 1930s. During the 1940s, development rapidly increased to meet the needs of the Marines in WWII to carry both cargo and Marines across any water. Post-war modification slowed and eventually this tracked vehicle started functioning more as an armored personnel carrier on land than a landing craft. However, these LVTs were utilized in the Inchon landing in Korea (1950), and the Han River crossing to take Seoul back. The LVT (3) C was the standard tracked vehicle until 1953, when a larger and heavier improved LVTP-5 family of amphibian tractors started coming off the assembly lines. This family of amphibian tractors was widely known as "Amtracs." The largest and heaviest was used in a variety of combat roles in Southeast Asia. The most commonly seen were the LVTP-5, an armored personnel carrier capable of carrying thirty-four Marines. The other vehicle variants were for mine sweeping, command and control, and recovery. Their roles played out in rivers and coastal regions, but were also used heavily as resupply and support vehicles southwest of Da Nang, where a lot of enemy staging took place.

Dan Guenther, a Platoon Commander in 3rd Amphibian Tractor Battalion, remembers his beloved Amtracs: "The LVTP-5 amphibious tractor was a twenty-five ton, cargo-carrying tracked vehicle that was designed as a ship-to-shore unit. Upon landing in Vietnam, the Marine Corps adopted the track's mission to include transport of men and material over land. That was our mission on Hill 55, southwest of Da Nang. But it wasn't long before the grunts were using and abusing tracks for tasks outside their identified mission, exposing men to unnecessary risks, a situation that enraged my Gunnery Sergeant."

LVTP-5 Amphibian Tractor with crew ~ Courtesy of Charles F. Eckerson, H&S Co, 1/27

Tactical Maneuvers

As far back as 1944, the Marine rifle squad within the platoon came into focus and eventually evolved into a "triangular concept," which then gave its leader more control and maneuverability, considering the weapons in the Marine Corps arsenal at the time. The triangular concept positioned a squad of moving Marines in the shape of a triangle and kept the automatic weapons to the center. The position of the automatic weapons afforded better advantage in a combat engagement and the triangle formation allowed fluid flexibility for maneuver.

During Vietnam, it became doctrine that each Squad Leader had control over three "Fire Teams" with a leader and three Marines in each team. This allowed effective supervision of eleven men by the Squad Leader. Three squads made up the entire rifle platoon if it was at full strength. Usually, this was not the case in Vietnam, but nevertheless control and maneuverability with firepower in this format became a platoon or squad's strongest asset. Platoons, squads, and fire teams in 1/27 used these tactics to achieve objectives in both the Hue City TAOR and on Operation Allen Brook.

Sergeant Felix Salmeron, a 1/27 Alpha Company Platoon Sergeant, recalls his experience working with a platoon on his second tour: "I worked my people hard training them in platoon, squad, and fire team tactics. First squad's responsibility was always the nine to twelve o'clock port side [left]. The second squad took the twelve 'noon' to three o'clock starboard side [right] responsibility. The third squad provided rear security. This meant as we moved, the lead squad would always take up the nine to twelve defense. The middle squad would take the twelve to three right-side defense, and the rear squad would have responsibility for our three to nine backside defense. Command and control [leadership] always walked in the middle. As soon as we halted, everyone spread out into their designated positions on both flanks and in the rear. This way I had the guns [machine guns] behind or close to me and could maneuver them wherever they might be needed. The first time my new Lieutenant, Bill Black, saw this maneuver he was amazed. We had some shooting up forward. I immediately yelled out, 'seven defense' and the men automatically responded into their designated positions. He couldn't frigging believe it."

Often, Salmeron's Marines would employ this same concept where one squad sat up at each point of the triangle. Sergeant Salmeron would then set up his automatic weapons on each of the corners. He also taught his squad leaders to use this defensive tactic with their individual squads. These maneuver tactics served him and his Marines well; they sustained minimum casualties while performing his assigned missions.

Navy Corpsmen and Medical Support

Fleet Marine Force Corpsmen were amongst the most decorated in the United States Navy during Vietnam. There are almost 700 Corpsmen on the granite Wall in Washington, DC. A select few were assigned to Marine units both stateside and overseas. Approximately 5,000 Hospital Corpsmen served in-theater during the war. Most of those men received the Purple Heart for wounds received while serving. Their learning never stopped and they became the "go to" first medical resource in a Regiment, Battalion, Line Company, and Platoon structure, learning to live amongst Marines and earn their trust.

HM2 Danny L. Grimshaw, Corpsman, D Co, 1/27 with Unit One Bag (KIA 23 August 1968) ~ Courtesy of his brother Terry Grimshaw

Corpsmen and the Unit One Bag

The valuable tool Marine Corpsmen carried was the "Unit One," a bag with all that was needed to treat combat wounds and normal everyday maladies acquired by field Marines. These Corpsmen lived with Marines and whether they liked it or not became Marines, most of them bonding to their Marine brethren after they had been with the unit for a while.

The Hospital Corpsman's Pledge is the following:

"I solemnly pledge myself before God and these witnesses to practice faithfully all of my duties as a member of the Hospital Corps. I hold the care of the sick and injured to be a privilege and a sacred trust and will assist the Medical Officer with loyalty and honesty. I will not knowingly permit harm to come to any patient. I will not partake of nor administer any unauthorized medication. I will hold all personal matters pertaining to the private lives of patients in strict confidence. I dedicate my heart, mind, and strength to the work before me. I shall do all within my power to show in myself an example of all that is honorable and good throughout my naval career."

It was easy to know who the Corpsmen was in a unit; they carried a Unit One and usually had more canteens and an "ass pack" on their web gear than others. They went on patrols, dug fighting holes, and stood watches just as all the others did. They humped right along with the rest of the grunts and when a "Take Ten" break was called for, worked their way through the ranks of the Marines treating blisters, asking how you were doing, and checking to make sure everyone was alright.

HM3 Robert L. Taugner, B Co, 1/27 in Hue TAOR, April 1968, carrying a Unit One bag
~ Courtesy of the Cliff Broyer family photo collection

The Corpsman performed basic field medicine, from stopping the bleeding, clearing the airway, starting the breathing, and protecting the wound all the way to treating and preventing shock. He was the "Doc!" Corpsmen trained to manage multiple casualties under fire. The daily routine often included treating heat casualties to administering malaria and salt tabs. While there are many stories of Corpsmen that you won't hear, these men were held in high regard by virtually all Marines who served in Vietnam. They took the dying and wounding the hardest of all, mentally. It was their job to save lives and stabilize the wounded. They did not want to fail their fellow Marines. Of all combat Veterans, Corpsmen suffered the deep hurt and immense emotional pain of losing a Marine because they were right there and close to all the action. A cry of "Corpsman up!" meant that someone was down and needed immediate help. That cry was both dreaded but also a signal of hope that a Corpsman was on the way and would stabilize a wounded Marine.

The Medical Civic Action Programs (MEDCAPs) were another duty of both Marines and Corpsmen. Marines went along into the villages to provide security while Corpsmen held "sick bay" by setting up a temporary field clinic for all the villagers. Sick bay provided treatments for cuts, colds, inoculations, dental work, and instructions on sanitary health procedures, and so on. The primary goal was to win the "hearts and minds" of the people by providing outpatient medical care. Bill "Doc" Carroll, Charlie Company, 1/27 recalled one MEDCAP where "This little child came up to me and I noticed it was a little girl. She couldn't have been more than five years old...

and we had done something for her or one of her family members…treated her for something, maybe her mother, and she hugged me and said something in Vietnamese that I know was a 'Thank you.' Made me feel, wow, you know…that it was all worth what we had been dealing with."

Doc Carroll recollects, "Mostly us Corpsmen would do the mundane tasks, like make sure everyone took their salt tablets…the gamma globulin shots were up-to-date on everyone. I was always checking everyone's feet. That was most important. I did not think of myself any different from anyone else. My job as Corpsman was to keep my Marines healthy and humping. I remember Sergeant Larry Stone took a patrol out and I, of all people had dysentery on that day. He told me I didn't have to go, but I did. He kept telling me, that I was slowing them down…The Doc with the shits, dropping my drawers and slowing things down. We had a good laugh."

The Docs were always burning leeches off Marines after they walked through water. Doc Carroll recalls, "…that we all smoked. The interesting thing, we never quit…Somebody back in the 'World' just kept sending cigarettes and cigars in the SP packs of C-rations…We would use cigarettes to burn the leeches off or bug juice to back them off when guys got leeches, you know: just touch their tail and watch them fall off."

Naval Support Activity

Medical services provided by several different organizational elements supported the Marines. The maneuver Battalions and Regiments employed aid stations, while both the First and Third Divisions called upon a separate Medical Battalion with Hospital Companies. The Battalions and Regimental aid stations provided mainly first aid, routine sick call, and an up to seventy-two-hour holding capability.

Naval Support Activity (NSA) collection and clearing companies became established in Da Nang, Chu Lai, and Phu Bai early on and later developed into field hospitals. Later other field hospitals were established in Quang Tri and Dong Ha close to the demilitarized zone (DMZ). It is recorded that during 1968 more than 24,000 men were hospitalized in these facilities. Of all of those admitted, 43 percent were returned to active duty and the residual were transferred either to the main NSA hospital in Da Nang or to offshore medical facilities, the USS Repose or the USS Sanctuary. These offshore ships had the ability to maneuver close to battle activity and had helicopter landing capability. Mortality averaged less than one per cent in all combined facilities.[7]

Navy Chaplain Corps

Beginning 28 November 1775, when Navy Regulations were adopted, the following statement gave birth to the Chaplain Corps in the nation's new Navy. It began, "the Commanders of the ships of the thirteen United Colonies are to take care that divine services be performed twice a day on board and a sermon preached on Sundays unless bad weather or other extraordinary accidents prevent." Though Chaplains were not mentioned in the regulation, it is implicit that the intention was to place a man of faith on each ship.

In 1802, a new edition of Naval Regulations extended the duties of the chaplain. It read, "He is to read prayers at stated periods; perform all funeral ceremonies; perform the duty of schoolmaster instructing the midshipmen and volunteers in writing, arithmetic, navigation and whatever else they might need to make them proficient; and teach the other youths of the ship as the captain orders."

Due to their teaching skills, when the various "academies" in central ports were established, chaplains naturally evolved into administrators. One of those Chaplains, Reverend and Professor George Jones (Episcopal Church), began an early campaign for a central Naval Academy in 1839. His initial efforts led to the establishment of the United States Naval Academy at Annapolis in 1845, and him becoming its first Chaplain and Head of English Studies.

By the early 1900s, the Chaplain Corps of the United States Navy had established guidelines which required the commissioning of chaplains with college and seminary degrees, and who had appeared before a board to be endorsed.[8]

Chaplains with the 27th Marines

The mobilization of the 27th Marine Regiment reinforcement during the Tet Offensive of 1968 in Vietnam taxed all unit Chaplains. Regimental Chaplain, Lieutenant Merrill C. Leonard (Southern Baptist) recalled, "I had the utmost cooperation of the command in carrying out my duties." Lieutenant Marlin E. Huebschman (United Church of Christ), assigned to 2/27, received a phone call from the assistant 5th Marine Division chaplain at Camp Pendleton on the evening of 12 February 1968 and found himself in Da Nang ninety-six hours later. Lieutenant Michael P. O'Neil (Roman Catholic) assigned to 3/27, had just returned from an earlier Vietnam tour. He did not have to go back, but did. He explained, "I was here again because if I had not signed a waiver, the regiment would not have had Roman Catholic coverage, as I was the only priest in the 27th Regiment. Besides, if so many of these 27th Marines could return, so would I." Lieutenant Walter J. Brown (Episcopal) traveled with 1/27 to the Hue TAOR and then back south to serve during Operation Allen Brook before being sent home with the Regiment in September.

Regimental Chaplain O'Neil, in the History and Museum Division book by Commander Herbert L. Bergsma, *Chaplains with Marines in Vietnam 1962-1971*, commented on the number of casualties. His regiment saw some of the fiercest of the Tet Offensive fighting, suffering the heaviest of casualties while controlling the most difficult of TAORs during the early part of 1968. Bergsma's book documents how the Chaplains of the 27th cherished their contributions to the history of the regiment.[9]

Chaplain Walter J. Brown in a "playful moment" with his flock ~ Courtesy of Al "Doc" Blair, H&S Co, 1/27

Bob Taugner, a Corpsman with Bravo Company, had become close to Chaplain Brown both in Hawaii during training, and later in Vietnam when the chips were down. Doc Taugner recalls that Brown had kept him on the "straight and narrow" both before Vietnam and when they returned to Hawaii in late 1968. "We were talking about his personal life and I had found that he was originally a Corpsman prior to becoming a Chaplain. He had been in Kaneohe Bay in the early days. Another Corpsman told me that Brown worked on what we called the 'meat truck' which was a crash truck on standby in the event of a plane crash. Allegedly, prior to my arrival, Walter responded to a situation in which a pilot was trapped in a burning aircraft and he helped pull a pilot out of the fire…and received a medal for it."

Later, Corpsman Walter Brown left the service and entered theology school, met his wife, fell in love, found a life of religion, and came back into the Navy as a Chaplain to serve with Marines. Chaplain Brown was always there for all his 1/27 Marines.

Doc Taugner remembers being comforted by Chaplain Brown after the terrible ordeal of 13 April (Operation No Name #2) on the canal. Taugner had been one of the last men in Bravo Company to come out of that area on the medical evacuation. As the Corpsmen at the CP began triage on the Marines in sick bay, he recalls his thoughts, "I am sitting against the wall…and they won't let me do anything…Chaplain Brown is sitting next to me with his arm around me…he is calming me down, talking to me. I don't know where he got them but handed me a couple of beers. I was extremely tense because I have some seriously wounded people in there…my guys. I am hearing stuff on the radio [tactical net] and the overall picture is beginning to unravel. I am finding out facts…of other platoons, of Captain Allen. I hear that Doc Dodsworth is KIA and Captain Allen has lost a hand. This all is trickling into my conscience and Chaplain Brown is talking to me in a low calming voice, trying to reassure me that I had done all I could…I wanted to hear these things but I didn't want to hear them. He had a unique way, very earthy…not exactly a religious zealot. The next thing I remember, he disappeared and then the Doctor is asking me to roll up my sleeve to give me a shot. That was all I remember until the next day."

After a few days, Chaplain Brown came up to him and asked for a cigarette. Everyone smoked because various brands of cigarettes accompanied the C-ration packs and were readily available. After giving Brown a cigarette, Taugner remembers the Chaplain presenting him with a Zippo lighter. "When he handed me the lighter he kept his hand on it and told me, that since we were friends and I had gone through hell a few days ago, and that he didn't want things to get to me...he wanted me to keep this memento and that every time I got a little anxious about things to look at this and laugh. I said OK, took it and turned it over. On the lighter was an engraved picture of Snoopy on his dog house laying on the roof with his nose up in the air with a little balloon above with the saying, 'F..k It.' That was Chaplain Brown. I still miss him!"

Zippo Lighter presented to Bob "Doc" Taugner by Chaplain Walter Brown in 1968 ~ Courtesy of Bob "Doc" Taugner, B Co, 1/27

Maps and Location Tools

Topographical Maps

Considering the amount of vegetation and topographical obstacles in South Vietnam, it was deemed early on in Southeast Asia that mapping was important to American advisors. Early in the American advisory role, older French maps created during French colonial rule were the only available representations of the countryside. These maps had not been updated for some time and were not adequate for the United States military in its new advisory role.

The United States Army Map Service, later the U. S. Army Topographic Command, began mapping agreements in 1956 with the Republic of Vietnam, undertaking a joint-mapping program encompassing the entirety of South Vietnam.

Many problems arose during this period. Viet Cong insurgency hampered the mapping program. Aerial photography and positions on the land-surface-collecting operations (geodesy) were essential for geographical naming, natural and other features to be placed on the mapping. The increase of enemy operations in the south hampered the completion of this essential fieldwork and was finally curtailed in the early 1960s.

Considering the many obstacles, the Army Map Service and the United States Army, Pacific (1959-1965) were still able to produce larger scale maps, in the 1:50,000 and 1:250,000-scale resolutions, of the Republic of Vietnam. In 1965-1966 when the war intensified with American commitment on the ground, both North and South mapping topography was updated with overlays from the newly collected aerial photography taken during that time.[10]

As the use of helicopters became prevalent, altogether changing tactical operations, more detail, positioning, and identification of features had to be quickly compiled. New maps drawn at a 1:25,000 scale utilized imagery which replicated approximate color and major topographical features. These maps began showing up after 1968 and continuing into the 1970s. This new technique was made possible by aerial photography overlaid on established mapping.

Compass

The "Lensatic Compass" utilized by Platoon Leaders and Squad Leaders derived its name from the magnifying lens mounted in the eyepiece (U. S. Compass, Magnetic FSN 6605-846-7618). The compass was mainly used to navigate, maneuver, and call in artillery or mortar support.

This device's directional needle (in a waterproof case) would home on magnetic north and allow the determination of an azimuth. "*Shooting an azimuth*" orients the horizontal direction along one of the 360 degrees of the compass to a designated point, which resolves/determines position or direction for the Squad, Platoon, or Company.

Used in conjunction with topographical maps, the compass helped pinpoint positions by comparing and contrasting terrain features with contours, stream directions, shapes of hedgerows, or changes in vegetation. Dead reckoning with a compass required that starting points be accurately established. The compass accommodated all field maneuvers.

Two methods of "shooting an azimuth" were used in the field. The compass-to-cheek method entailed holding the device level, orienting it to magnetic north, and then sighting the compass while looking through the eyepiece and noting the line-of-sight degree. The second center-hold method was executed by holding the device level and to the front of the chest with both hands.

To keep from going off course when maneuvering, Marines would recheck the azimuth to the original object or point from time to time. Sometimes a quick compass back azimuth was needed to navigate or refresh dead reckoning. A back azimuth is simply the opposite direction of the original azimuth. To calculate a back azimuth, add 180 degrees if the azimuth is 180 degrees or less; subtract 180 degrees if the azimuth is 180 degrees or more.

Determining azimuth and maneuvering toward an object aids a good dead-reckoning movement. However, when the line of sight in difficult terrain becomes obscured, a back azimuth may be necessary to aid in moving toward an objective. Establishing a back azimuth along with the forward-objective azimuth before starting was always advisable in Vietnam. These sturdy and reliable navigation tools of the trade were sometimes worth their weight in gold in enemy territory.

Lensatic Compass ~ Courtesy of David T. "Red Dog" Roberts, D Co, 1/4

UTM

The grid system adopted after WWII for American military use throughout the world is called the Universal Transverse Mercator (UTM) grid. The former Defense Mapping Agency developed this special grid system for military use. UTM was used by all field units on the ground and in the air during Vietnam. This simple methodology divides the world into sixty north-south zones, each six degrees wide in longitude on the outlay. Inside these zones, a UTM grid overlay divides down into one-kilometer squares. The UTM grid has more lines than the latitude and longitude grid lines, which simplifies finding a precise position on the map. There is no need to convert kilometers to miles or feet. Measurements are simply in tenths, which allow a position on the map to be quickly identified by intersecting grid numbering and topographical features.[11]

In UTM coordinates, the "easting" numbers are always given first, and then "northing." This means reading the coordinate numbering from the west going east, then the "northing" numbers from the bottom up. The axiom, "to the right (east) and up (north)," is an effective way to quickly remember how to read and pinpoint a UTM grid location. "Read Right Up" is the simple rule taught to Marines. Six- and sometimes eight-digit numbering helped locate precise points on a map in Vietnam. In six-digit grids the first three were "easting" and the next three were "northing." The intersection of the first three with the second three pinpoints the grid position.[12]

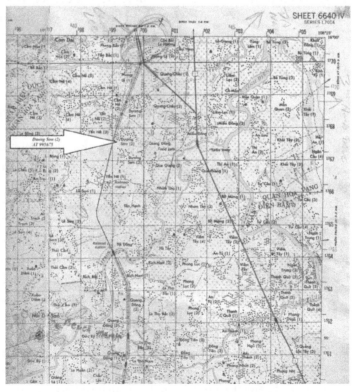

Dai Loc Map, DMA Series L-7014, a 1:50,000 Scale map with UTM grids showing 1/27 HQ CP at AT995675 ~ Courtesy of Captain Dan Guenther, 3rd Amphibian Tractor Battalion, 1st Marine Division, RVN 1968 – 1969

The two-character alpha designator characters in front of the six- or eight-digit grid numbers denoted the UTM grid zone (zones were 100 x 100 kilometers). There is a zone map for all of Vietnam, the *SVN UTM Grid Zone Overlay*. Some of the two-character designators utilized in I Corps were YD, AT, ZC, BT, AU, and YC, to name a few.

Contour intervals and their value were important and clearly marked in the map legends. The contour interval is the distance in vertical altitude between contour lines drawn on the topographic map. Most of the maps used in Vietnam were the DMA L-7014 Series, scale 1:50,000, with contour intervals of twenty meters. Those intervals were drawn as solid lines. When the slopes were gradual, supplementary contour intervals (ten meters on the L-7014 Series) were expressed by dotted lines.[13]

Tactical Communications

Radio Equipment and Operators

The AN/PRC-25 Radio (Portable Radio Communications—Model 25) was the main tactical communications radio of the Vietnam War. PRC-10s from the Korean War had been used by units earlier in Vietnam and phased out of the field. The number "25" meant it was the twenty-fifth model of field radio the military had standardized. Marines invariably called it the "Prick 25" for short. You could say that the PRC-25 was the most valuable tool of the maneuver Rifle Battalions, Line Companies, Platoons, and Squads in Vietnam. Its reliability and functionality were critical to all Marines and Corpsmen who humped the "bush."

The PRC-25 was almost the size of a case of beer and weighed twenty-five pounds with battery and accessories (antenna and handset). The radio was engineered to withstand very rugged use in a field environment. You could drop it from a helicopter at fifty feet or submerge it in water for lengthy periods of time, then pull it out and it would work. The weak part of this tactical system was the handset. It was a telephone handset, with a "push to talk" button. A hook on the backside of the handset allowed it to be hung on your 782 web gear. The handset could not get wet. Crossing streams, the handset had to be held up out of the water. Moisture was a fundamental problem and was dealt with by putting the handset in a plastic bag if one was available. Battery life was about a day when used casually, listening to normal tactical network message flow. Intense use shortened the battery life to two to three hours. Other grunts carried spare batteries for backup. The PRC-25 battery, when depleted, had to be destroyed. Inside was a series of dry cell flashlight batteries, which the enemy could and would use to ignite command-detonated bombs. RTOs were for the most part formally schooled, however, some of them learned by OJT (on the job training).

A few different antennas were used in the field. The Tape (three-feet-long) was the most popular and had an approximate range of three miles. This depended on many variables, e.g., a line of sight for the radio signal to transmit and receive messages, the strength of the battery, and weather, to name the most important. The Whip antenna (ten-feet-long) had a five-mile range of use depending on the mentioned variables. Mountainous topographies played havoc with radio signals.

An RTO with a tape or whip antenna on his radio was a high-value target and signified to enemy combatants that an officer or leader was nearby. These Marines were some of the first targets fired upon. The RTO carried and operated an important lifeline for requesting resupply of food, water, ammo, and medical evacuations, along with air and artillery strikes and reenforcement when needed. Losing a trained RTO often forced other grunts to take over; while most of them had little or no training, they usually did well in that role.

Marines in a unit looked after each other. They all shared the same lot in life and the daily hardships. As Ron Oakes, a veteran RTO from Bravo Company remembers, "New replacements aka FNGs coming into a unit had to prove themselves to the rest of the unit whether they were veteran replacements or raw recruits straight out of Infantry Training Regiment." It was extremely important that each Marine knew the basic operation of a PRC-25. Everyone's lives depended on it. The workhorse of tactical communications was without a doubt the PRC-25 backpack radio.

Cpl Joseph Roysdon on Radio watch (PRC-25 Radio) ~ Courtesy of Hugh G. Barton, H&S Co, 1/27

An actual story from the summer of 1968 had to do with communications and an RTO carrying a PRC-25 while Operation Allen Brook was in progress. An RTO was accompanying a Commanding Officer when they made contact with combatants. In the heat of this operation, the officer, trying to get another subordinate to follow his orders, became extremely frustrated. It may have been that the transmission or receive links had become garbled which caused the anger, although this scenario is pure speculation.

In a state of anger, the Commanding Officer threw the PRC-25 handset as hard as he could into the air, which severed the handset cord completely from the radio and the RTO. The RTO quickly regained his composure and began looking for another handset. Luckily there happened to be another radio with handset intact in the area, which was quickly commissioned as the only backup remaining. The conflict was indeed an issue of communication between the two men and illustrates the possibility of many variables affecting the communication links between tactical field radios. This was remembered as a tense situation indeed.

The tactical radio network of 1/27 in early 1968 used the following Call Signs, Frequencies, and Designators:

1st Battalion, 27th Marine Regiment
Tactical Network Call Signs, Frequencies & Designators

Unit	Call Sign	Frequency	Designator
1/27 Tac Net	Pickwick Paper	65.85 & 44.7	M-977
Co A	Pickwick Paper Alfa	71.65	M-1082
Co B	Pickwick Paper Bravo	75.5	M-742
Co C	Pickwick Paper Charlie	78.5	M-1119
Co D	Pickwick Paper Delta	72.0	M-509
81mm COF	Pickwick Paper Whisky	71.15	M-839
TACP	Pickwick Paper	43.40	HQ-Command
Med Evac	Vermillion Alfa	45.7	

Source: 1st Battalion, 27th Marines Command Chronologies, April 1968, Appendix D

Then-Captain Ronald Gruenberg, S-3 operations, was responsible for the creation/compiling of the Battalion Command Chronologies through 6 June, when he took command of Charlie Company. He recorded this Call Sign, Frequency, and Designator information into the reports.

PFC William Lampkin (WIA 7 June 1968) & L/Cpl Ron Oakes with PRC-25 Radios performing radio checks ~ Courtesy of Ronald G. Oakes, B Co, 1/27

Part of the job of the Radioman was to make sure that all the radios going out on patrol were working correctly and that they had at least one spare battery as shown in the photograph. The batteries were usually in a cardboard box and sealed in plastic by the manufacturer. Every radio had connections for two types of antennas. Ron Oakes explained, "We had a dipole for long distance, and then we had the short tape antennas for short line-of-sight distances. Most of the time you attached the radio's microphone to your utility blouse or onto your web gear. Whichever antenna you were using was bent forward parallel to the ground. You did not want to become that urgent target. The batteries were heavy…depending on what we were doing some others would carry extra batteries. If we were going to be out a long time it was not unusual to have a couple in my backpack. Others carried them also…We spread them out. You never went on a patrol without another spare radio and spare handsets. The handsets always seemed to be in short supply…but the batteries were the main thing! They were good for twenty-four hours. There was no recharging a battery. Once you got a weak signal, the PRC-25 went down. You really didn't have any warning, they just went. We would replace the battery with the spares we carried. It was a simple process. The depleted battery needed to be destroyed. We took an E-tool and cut them in half or sometimes in fourths. We then dug a hole and buried them because you didn't want the enemy, particularly the Viet Cong to take one of these batteries and use it to detonate an explosive 'booby trap.' It did not take much current to set off a charge rigged to an explosive device. They were strong batteries designed for the worst conditions."

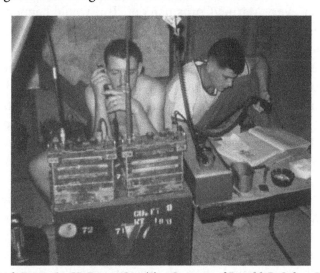

Radio Watch Bravo Co CP, Duong Son (2) ~ Courtesy of Ronald G. Oakes, B Co, 1/27

Oakes remembers, "When I first got there our call sign was 'Wedgewood Bravo 3.' The numeral three was for the Third Platoon. And likewise, you would have squad numbers. If you had a Second Squad, Third Platoon on the net they were assigned the call sign of 'Wedgewood Bravo 3 dash 2. Later our call signs changed to Pickwick Paper."

The RTO had checkpoints to call in on every monitored patrol. This protocol was strictly followed day or night. The radios were in constant use. Marines had to make sure they were working and turn in the ones that weren't for repair. "At the time the radios we used were getting a lot of use and we didn't have many…no modern technology came to us and these radios were pretty beaten up. One radio would come in with one patrol and it would go right back out with another patrol, different men…it was like a hot swap."

Oakes emphasized, "A radio and a machine gun (the M60) were your most important pieces of equipment we had to take along on a patrol. We had the primary frequency, the medical evacuation frequency, the alternate frequency, the emergency frequency, and all of those changed almost every day. When we left a base, you had to request permission to enter the tactical net. Whenever a new radio would come online you would get a radio check [test by transmitting back and forth] standard procedure before you left the wire."

At Platoon and Company level someone was on radio watch 24/7 monitoring the tactical network. Oakes reminisces, "I was somewhat lucky most of the time. I could rely on the Platoon Sergeant, Platoon Commander, and Corpsman to help with watches during the night. We would set up two-hour watches so all got at least some sleep. The radio watch from 0600 to 2200 was always the RTO. It was his job. If there was enemy action no one got any sleep. On big operations, you learned to function on two to four hours of sleep. I always would accompany the Platoon Leader around the perimeter to check every Marine/Corpsman out. This would happen in all situations whether under fire or not. I tried very hard to make sure as many Marines knew how to operate the radio in case it became necessary."

He remembered one of his first patrols in-country. There was heavy rain falling and only seven on the patrol. "We had come to a huge tree that had fallen when we started taking sniper rounds. Some of them hit the tree. While on the deck waiting for the shooting to stop, I was listening to my PRC-25 speaker and I kept hearing a 'click…click…click.' The Gooks had one of our radios and the frequency we were utilizing. They were jamming it by pressing their handsets to transmit, keying on and off continuously. I started going to the other frequencies and they were jamming them also with the 'click…click…click!' Not being able to get out on any frequency, we just lay there…they had us cold. We could not communicate and that showed me just how important these radios were to us Marines. This was one of the few times I got just a little scared! When you are with many people you feel safe. It was just seven of us at that time and with no communication, and we got just a little panicky!"

Radio Protocol and the Phonetic Alphabet

The Marine Corps relied heavily on a uniform phonetic alphabet to pass information back and forth over the tactical network. In a critical combat situation, a verbal message that is not understood can have consequences. The quality of signal and surrounding noises sometimes influenced a message transmitted over the airwaves.

The phonetic descriptors helped to simplify messages and minimized confusion. The following phonetic alphabet was used throughout Vietnam:

A – Alfa	J – Juliet	S – Sierra	1 – Wun
B – Bravo	K – Kilo	T – Tango	2 – Two
C – Charlie	L – Lima	U – Uniform	3 – Thuh-Ree
D – Delta	M – Mike	V – Victor	4 – Fo-wer
E – Echo	N – November	W – Whisky	5 – Fi-yiv
F – Foxtrot	O – Oscar	X – X-Ray	6 – Six
G – Golf	P – Papa	Y – Yankee	7 – Seven
H – Hotel	Q – Quebec	Z – Zulu	8 – Ate
I – India	R – Romeo	0 – Zero	9 – Ni-ner

Frequently used and shortened phrases would convey distinct meanings. For example, "Over," simply meant, *"This is the end of my transmission to you and a response is necessary."* "Say again" conveyed, *"Say that again, all of your last transmission."* The term "Correction," sent a simplified signal that *"An error has been made in this transmission, the correction is…"* The use of the word, "Wilco," implied, *"I have understood what you said and will comply."* The use of "Out," meant, *"This is the end of my transmission, no reply is necessary."*

Signaling Mirror

Then-Sergeant Felix Salmeron served three tours of Vietnam and functioned as not only an infantryman but also as a Reconnaissance Marine. The mirror to the right is a lightweight and essential piece of equipment he carried on his person throughout his multiple tours in Vietnam.

These signaling mirrors were a versatile piece of communication and survival equipment. Even at night and used with a flashlight, it could produce an effective signal for position identification up to an aircraft. Likewise, visible signal flashes could be created in overcast conditions by continually sweeping the horizon to maximize the chance of being located. On sunny days, a flash

Mirror, Emergency Signaling, Mark 3
~ Courtesy of Sergeant Felix Salmeron,
A Co, 1/27

could be seen up to 100 miles away. The instructions were to hold the mirror close to your eyes and look through the sighting aperture. After visualizing a target point through the light spot (center hole), you could slowly turn it so that the projecting light beam reflection moved onto the target. These mirrors were designed to be aimed with a minimum of practice and skill in a small amount of time. Instructions were printed in big letters on the back side of some of the mirrors.

The issued signaling mirrors were made of laminated glass with a retroreflective mesh aimer. The mirror has been issued to the military since 1949 and is registered with U. S. Patent 2,557,108. These mirrors came in two sizes: 2" x 3" (Type I) and 3" x 5" (Type II). They were manufactured to MilSpec standards by Revere Glass Company and Libby Owen Ford during the 1960s.

Tactical Ground Radar

Ground Radar surveillance was trialed in Vietnam and every maneuver Battalion had them in their inventory. Properly utilized and positioned, these radars afforded the capability to detect enemy movement, especially in defensive positions. This was especially useful at night.

The AN/TPS-33, AN/TPS-25, AN/TPS-21, AN/PPS-6, 5 and 4 radars were employed throughout the Vietnam War by both Marine and Army units. This equipment vectored patrols and ambush teams within the rocket belt around the Da Nang airstrip perimeter, and monitored enemy trails throughout the war. Their degree of use depended upon topographical considerations due to the line of sight trajectory required.

Student Handout for Radar Set AN/PPS-6 ~ Courtesy of Hal Kennedy, H&S Co, 1/27

The above-pictured student pamphlet of the AN/PPS-6 specifies ranges of 1,500 meters to detect moving personnel and 3,000 meters for moving vehicles. The older AN/TPS-21 units had approximate detection ranges of five kilometers (people movement) to ten kilometers (vehicles). Ideal terrain was flat, with little or no vegetation. Use of the radars required a three-man team. The rechargeable batteries kept a charge for up to about twenty hours.

Corporal Hal Kennedy standing next to a Radar Surveillance system atop Marble Mountain
~ Courtesy of Hal Kennedy, H&S Co, 1/27

The previous photo shows an older generation TPS-21. As Hal Kennedy, a radar specialist, remembers, "The TPS-21, belonging to another Battalion, shown placed on top of the 'Crow's Nest' on Marble Mountain, needed a small generator to power it electrically and was very heavy. This unit arrived by helicopter. It would have been almost impossible to carry it by hand up the side of this Marble Mountain with its 360-degree observation point. The TPS-21 was developed in the late 1950s and the PPS-6 came along ready for the field in 1967 to replace it. The PPS-6 was more portable, a fairly new development and was still evolving."

Kennedy confirms, "These radar sets produced noise in the headset that a trained operator could readily identify as a person, walking or running. You could also decide between animal and vehicle passing through the area while the radar unit was operational. They were state-of-the-art instruments at the time."

He recollects, "We were issued six of the lightweight, transistorized, battery-powered PPS-6 radar units after we had arrived in-country. The units were not taken to the Hue area with the Battalion. I estimate that it would have required at least three Marines per unit to become trained in the operation, use and care of the portable PPS-6 radar units."

Kennedy remembers deploying with the command group on one occasion into the Go Noi Island area during Operation Allen Brook to operate the portable PPS-6 unit. He remembered being told by the Battalion Commander, Lieutenant Colonel Greenwood, that there were more pressing issues at hand and it would not be necessary to use the PPS-6 he had brought along because of the additional manpower required to secure and operate it. He recalls, "Even though I was ready with a radar unit, I detected he had a serious situation at hand and didn't have the resources at the time to devote to a technology still new to all of us."

Atop the Crow's Nest in the village of Nui Kim San ~ Courtesy of Hal Kennedy, H&S Co, 1/27

Use of these devices atop the "crow's nest" on the tallest of the five Marble Mountains south of the Da Nang air base started about 1967-68. This high observation point also afforded the Marines a clear 360-degree line of sight capability. At night, Marines would determine rocket launching sites within seconds with quick azimuth sightings by providing an audible of those compass headings to an Artillery Plotting Command (called the Flash-Bang method). Many Marines from 1/27 spent watch on the Crow's Nest looking for 122mm rocket launches.

Detecting Set, Intrusion

Several types of ground sensors were developed during the Vietnam War. U. S. forces used several distinct types of sensors: seismic, acoustic, and infrared. In some cases, they were taken on recon patrols into remote areas. Documentation on these types of sensors and their use is scarce. Originally, these anti-intrusion devices were for troop movements and trucks moving along the Ho Chi Minh Trail. Later they were used as infiltration detectors around perimeters.

Detection of approaching personnel, vibrations, or footsteps without the intruder being aware of detection was done by the very reliable hard-wired Detecting Set, Intrusion, AN/PSR-1A. This detecting set was a rugged, portable, weather-proof unit designed to receive and record earth vibrations caused by surface movement. It was battery powered, and only operated for short periods before the batteries needed changing. These devices connected to seismic probes about the size of a tent peg via long strands of communications wire. With four separate wire inputs from sensors, the unit detected approaching footsteps, animal and human, and vibrations of vehicle movement. Once an operator using a headset became familiar with characteristics of incoming signals they could distinguish between the approaching footsteps of a man or woman, children playing, deer, trucks, and even tunneling. It became very easy to tell which section of sensors signaled activity.

Explosive Ordnance Demolition

Explosive Ordnance Demolition (EOD) came of age during the Vietnam War. Training for this dangerous line of duty began during WWII and expanded in scope during the Korean War. It then grew very rapidly in the mid-1960s, due to our involvement in Southeast Asia. The largest task at hand then was to make hazardous explosives harmless whenever encountered. Most munitions worked as they were intended; however, some malfunctioned, some were never used, and some of them were left in storage. All munitions, whatever their conditions, were subject to degradation, chemical reaction, and rust over time. All munitions become hazardous at some point, which creates a potential danger to both civilian and military personnel. Knowledgeable people are required to handle them, whatever their condition.

One of the main concepts in handling munitions is the fuse. Each fuse has its own explosive charge, which in turn sets off the main explosive device, be it a bomb, shell, mine, etc. Detonating the fuse explodes the main explosive munition. Some are fused for impact, or set electrically, magnetically, barometrically, or chemically for timed explosion. The ordnance dropped from aircraft was hung from the wings or loaded in a bay, and the fuse became armed after being launched by the pilot.

The overall and never-ending task was to make these munitions harmless, either by disarmament or exploding them in place. Although routine, these tasks were often extremely delicate. All explosive munitions encountered by EOD personnel were considered armed and dangerous. Training, knowledge, practice, improvisation, common sense, ability to work under stressful conditions, and the ability to think quickly were all necessary skills. Rarely were the conditions safe, due to unfamiliar foreign devices and homemade explosives in Vietnam.

In the Rifle Battalions, most of the main munitions were small arms (5.56 and 45 ACP), M72 LAAW rocket launchers, mortars (60mm and 81mm), claymores, C4, and distinct types of grenades. The Military Occupational Specialty (MOS) for dealing with munitions of this sort was the Ammunition Technician (2311) and an Explosive Ordnance Disposal Technician (2335).

Andrew Boyko had been on his first tour of Vietnam in 1965 and 1966 with ASP 1 and the 9th Marines as an ammo technician, and had returned to Camp Pendleton to join the newly formed 3/27 of the 5th Marine Division. The 3rd Battalion had a challenging time finding 0311 personnel, so it started filling its ranks with other MOS personnel. They used sundry specialties to fill those open billets. Boyko readily became a Fire Team Leader of Second Platoon of India Company, and the Ammo Tech for that Company. He remembers one of his first experiences with India Company: "When I first arrived the platoon sergeant asked if anyone had demolition experience. I replied yes, that I had blown things up on my first tour and that my primary MOS was ammunition technician. To find out what I knew, they issued me a demolition kit which contained explosive, time fuse, and blasting caps. Normally there is a crimping tool which secures the blasting cap from falling off while it's being burned. This kit did not have that tool. I asked for a crimping tool and was informed there was none available at the time. I said to myself, improvise, you're the demo man and I did, biting down on the hollow end of the blasting cap with my teeth to secure the time fuse. Later I was issued C4 which was much easier to work with. I guess I must have proved myself while there because they all started coming to me with munitions and ordnance problems after that."

Sergeant Andrew Boyko, EOD man in 1/27 ~ Courtesy of Andy Boyko, H&S Co, 1/27

Because of an overabundance of multi-MOS personnel within the 3rd Battalion shortly after arriving in Vietnam, some specialty people were siphoned off and sent to other units. Boyko was sent to 1st Battalion, 27th Marines and assigned to H&S Company, reporting to Lieutenant Thad Wiener, in charge of all Ammo supplies. The unit had just arrived in-country and was in the process of staging and readying itself for combat operations. They needed an Ammo Tech and as Boyko recalls, "…a big part of my responsibilities was to keep the Battalion resupplied with ammunition at all times, segregate it, issuing and storing all munitions, along with disposing of grade-three and captured ordnance when needed."

Marine Engineers rigging C4 to detonate unusable ammo
~ Courtesy of Gerald Risner, FLC attached to 2/5

During the months of March, April, and most of May the First Battalion operated to the east of Hue City, in the Phu Vang district and out to the Col Co JP4 fuel depot on the coast. The Battalion CP had been set up at the La Son School building, fairly close to the Perfume River and about a "klick" to the east of the Citadel. The unit began making some heavy contact with enemy combatants firmly entrenched in the area.

During this time Boyko recounts one disposal mission in which he needed to expend a cache. "I took the munitions and ordnance out on the road to the east of our position far enough out that it would not affect ongoing operations at the CP. Setting guards at both ends of the road to prevent anyone from entering the blast area, I primed the main charge with a time fuse, informing the guards to halt all people on the road. Lighting the fuse, I began to time the burn, and from nowhere an old man with his family came out of the treeline and headed straight for the main charge. Alarmed I ran toward the man and his family and motioned for them to 'di-di mau' and get back. The old man was perplexed and did not know what I was trying to say that there would be an explosion. Trying to pantomime and use words like 'Boom,' and 'Numba Ten Boom' he finally said, 'Mina?' "I confirmed saying, 'Yes, yes' and 'Get down'…After what seemed like an eternity the charge erupted with a deafening and gigantic fireball which shook us all up a little. After the sky rained debris on all of us, I stood up and signaled that he and his family could go on their way… He suddenly jumped up yelling, 'Mina, Mina, Mina!' and ran off into the tree line like a scalded cat, never to be seen again."

Disposal of ordnance by EOD ~ Courtesy of Gerald Risner, FLC attached to 2/5

In May, the Battalion returned to the Duong Son (2) TAOR south of Da Nang and began Operation Allen Brook, one of the largest operations of 1968 in I Corps (1/27's participation in Operation Allen Brook is covered in detail in Chapter 6). By that time Boyko became attached to 81mm Mortars as their demolitions man. They were operating in the Go Noi area to the east of Liberty Bridge. "The mortarmen had the rounds unpacked from the fiber containers and strapped to their 'rucks' due to anticipated combat expectations. When on the Island (actually was not an Island...just surrounded by two rivers), a sudden squall of rain fell for fifteen minutes straight and soaked us all to the bone as well as the exposed mortar rounds. We continued on and when the rain stopped I observed several Marines approaching us from the battle area of the Island. As they walked toward us they appeared to be in extreme shock. The tanks accompanying them coming out were covered with bodies of dead Marines. I spotted one of my former Fire Team members, Coporal Eggers, and asked what happened. He replied, 'The elephant grass was so thick, the gooks were everywhere and sometimes three feet away from you and you'd never know they were there.' We conversed quickly as we continued walking away from one another.

"I suddenly felt chilled and didn't know if it was from the rain or from fear. I fell in behind the tank going in toward the combat zone, trying to stay warm from the exhaust. There were craters large enough to hide this supporting tank in... The column was finally halted and I was informed there was captured ordnance up ahead that needed destroying along with our own 81mm mortar rounds that had their increments soaked from the rain... I began the fragile routine of ordnance disposal and blew it with C-4 which I had brought along."

C4, or Composition 4, as it was known, became the main explosive used during Vietnam to blow up a lot of things: bunkers, munitions, enemy ordnance, etc. Claymore mines, used extensively by the line grunts, consisted of a large amount of C4 with embedded ball bearings. C4 could be molded into any shape or form. Detonation could only be accomplished by a detonator; C4 could not be set off by jarring it or dropping it or exposing it to fire. It was an extremely stable charge. This made it somewhat safe to handle, and a small amount became extremely powerful and destructive when primed correctly. Marines used it in tiny amounts to heat C-ration cans, lighting it with their Zippo lighters. It would burn slowly at a high intensity and quickly heat up a can of C-rations or cup of coffee, a practice frowned upon by some of the officers.

Captured 122 Rockets at Bravo Company CP, Duong Son (2) ~ Courtesy of Ronald G. Oakes, B Co, 1/27

Enemy Tools of the Trade

Rockets and Tactics

The atypical, Russian-designed rockets shown above were used by both the NVA and VC. This was their artillery capability. Even though heavy when assembled, they were as transportable as the Marine 60mm mortars. They could be broken down into sections, did not require much maintenance, and could be carried through the rough terrain of Quang Nam province. This was strategic for the NVA and VC units operating in the area because because arty (artillery) pieces were cumbersome and not easily transported or camouflaged in the terrain outlying from Da Nang. Likewise, these 122 Rockets could be concealed from overhead aerial observation.

This rocket was quite effective but not highly accurate, because they were mostly launched from makeshift launch pods of crossed stakes, bamboo frames, or even dirt berms in a hurry. If the launch tubes were available, then greater accuracy could be achieved, usually not the case in I Corps during 1968. They were used to inflict whatever random death or damage that could be achieved while hopefully instilling fear amongst the survivors.

The rocket itself when assembled was just over six feet in length, weighed a bit over 100 pounds, and had fins for stabilization in flight. It had the longest range of any hand-carried weapon in the NVA or VC field arsenal. The warhead carried about fifteen pounds of explosive composition. These rockets had a range of about 12,000 meters (seven miles). Usually, multiple rockets were launched from a hasty setup launch site. The launch crew could assemble, set up, aim, and fire a group of them in thirty minutes or less. The VC rocketeers would then quickly leave the launch area. If the rocket entrails were spotted and an azimuth acquired and forwarded to an active artillery unit, U.S. forces would often counter fire and any enemy combatant in that immediate area would become subject to serious incoming.

On impact, the 122-warhead explosion was lethal within a twenty-five to thirty-foot radius. A fuse on the point of the rocket could be set for an airburst or a delay, thus the blast area would kill or maim anyone close to the impact. The thrust of the delayed-fuse explosion went forward at impact. The concussion from these deadly rockets could also cause severe injury or death. The 122s could be seen at night and would give off an orange glow as they traveled toward a target area. The sound was loud, like a freight train coming toward you if you were near its trajectory. Because they could often be heard coming from a distance, this gave some time for finding cover.

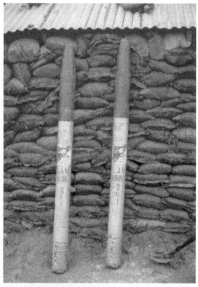

Assembled 122 Rockets at B Company CP, Duong Son (2) ~ Courtesy of Ron Oakes, B Co, 1/27

The Crow's Nest at Marble Mountain where many 1/27 Marines saw temporary duty served as the 24/7 watchtower for any of these rockets aimed at the Da Nang airbase.

Captured Viet Cong rifles and equipment ~ Courtesy of Raul E. Figueroa, H&S Co, 1/27

Enemy Small Arms

The AK-47s shown above were often referred to as the "peasant's weapon," principally because they had been Communist-supplied. A large amount of these weapons in the RVN were the offspring of the original Russian design by Mikhail Kalashnikov. The Russian rifle became officially known as *Avtomat Kalashnikova*, or Automatic Kalashnikov. Communist forces in Vietnam used a Chinese variant designated as the Type 56-1 (the 56-designation meant it was released in 1956). Most of these Chinese versions had folding bayonets underneath the muzzle and a chrome-lined barrel/receiver group. Most combatants during the latter years of the war carried the AK-47.

The SKS, a semi-automatic carbine, was also well-suited for the type of warfare carried out in Vietnam, and was used for long-range sniping, spoiling attacks, and ambushes alongside the AK-47. Both weapons used the same 7.62 X 39mm cartridge. Like the AK-47, this weapon was designed for effective distances of between 100 to 300 yards, since most firefights took place within those ranges. However, it had a slightly longer range than the AK-47 due to the length of its barrel.

Both weapons were designed with tolerances in moving parts that enabled them to fire under the most adverse of conditions. They could be immersed in the dirt, water, mud, sand, or any combinations of the elements and still be utilized. They were made to be easily cleaned, maintained, field stripped, and cleared in short amounts of time.

Captured enemy weapons display. A Russian-Soviet Mosin-Nagant M44 Carbine in the forefront
~ Courtesy of Ronald G. Oakes, B Co, 1/27

The Mosin-Nagant M44, a potent weapon which performed as a short range .30-caliber rifle (7.62 x 54mm), is shown in the forefront above. These were not the weapon primarily utilized by North Vietnamese Army units, but provided to Viet Cong main force units, and were the most commonly encountered bolt action rifle captured on the battlefield. The Chinese-made Type 53 version, and some Soviet-made rifles, were the primary weapons relegated to these Viet Cong units.

Other "Tools"

Meal Rations

The Meal, Combat, Individual (MCI) was the ration staple issued to field Marines and Corpsmen throughout the war. MCIs included not only a meal but condiments, plastic utensils, and other miscellaneous items needed in the field. They were popularly referred to as "C-rations" and came in a small box housing multiple cans. These "Tools of the Trade" were the fuels that kept the Marines and Corpsmen of 1/27 going.

The M units were meat items, the B units a bread of sorts, maybe crackers accompanied with a small flat can of spread, and the D unit was a dessert can, maybe pears or perhaps peaches. There were quite a few choices, and the Marines and Corpsmen all had their favorites. The M unit (Ham and Lima beans) was the most unpopular by far and jokingly referred to as "Ham and Mofos!"

Meal, Combat, Individual (MCI) Choices

M Units (Meat) 12 varieties in three groups:

- M-1:   Beefsteak, Chicken or Turkey, Chopped Ham & Eggs
- M-1A: Tuna Fish
- M-2:   Meat Chunks w/Beans, Ham & Lima Beans
-           Beef Slices w/Potatoes in Gravy
-           Beans w/Frankfurter Chunks in Tomato Sauce
- M-2A: Spaghetti w/Meatballs in Tomato Sauce
- M-3A: Meat Loaf

B Units (Bread) in variables of:

- B-1:   7 Crackers and 2 Chocolate chunks. Peanut Butter Spread
- B-2:   4 Biscuits and a Cookie sandwich or fudge disc
- B-3:   4 Cookies and Cocoa Powder. Jam (Apple, Grape, or Strawberry)

D Units (Dessert) offered:

- D-1:   Apricots, Peaches, Pears or Fruit Cocktail
- D-1A: Applesauce
- D-2:   Pound Cake, Fruitcake or Cinnamon Nut Roll
- D-2A: Date Pudding or Orange Nut Roll
- D-3:   White Bread

There were many recipes for field rations, but the simplest way to add zest and quickly was to sprinkle some Tabasco sauce on your Beefsteak or Tuna Fish. Mom back home was more than willing to send it in a care package and it was easily carried in your leg pockets.

The sometimes-alternative was the Chow Hall in the rear areas—still, the C-rations were a more reliable source of tasty nourishment than the mess hall. Jim Kaylor, a fellow Marine with 2nd Battalion, 26th Marines, relates some Marine Corps culinary experiences from those chow lines. "I happened to be in a chow line back in a rear area and observed an officer talking with a mess sergeant. I guess he must have been asking how the meals were going and what was being served…then I saw him take a bowl and taste some of whatever was being served. I then heard the mess sergeant ask him how it was…the officer, with a frown, looked at the cook and said, 'It's good enough for who it's for!' "

A carton of MCI, "C-rations" consisting of twelve combat meals in cardboard boxes
~ Courtesy of Tracy Robeson, D Co, 1/27

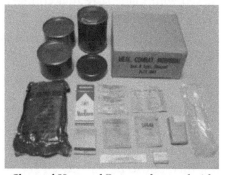

Chopped Ham and Eggs combat meal with accessories, plus cigarettes and matches

And there were the "clowns" that amplified macabre humor to its fullest. If you were in the bush with a platoon, you might hear, "Hey, look at this shit!" and shown a pack of cigarettes. On the side of the mini-pack from a C-rations box was the newly minted Surgeon General's warning, "Cigarette smoking can be hazardous to your health." "Well, no shit!" These grunts had more than likely just escaped a firefight that not one of them understood how they had survived. A bit of humor from a joker in the ranks could take the mind off serious subjects, like death and rigor mortis. It did help a difficult day in the "bush" pass more quickly.

Tracy Robeson, Delta Company, recalls his favorite meal was chopped Ham & Eggs with pound cake. "I would put jelly on the pound cake and would add peanut butter to the Ham & Eggs can and warm it with C4 explosive." When time permitted, he and squad members would dump whatever ration cans they had into a steel helmet, add some water, Tabasco hot sauce, and salt/pepper, cooking it using either the fast burning C4 or a campfire with wood when available.

Lance Corporal Ron Oakes guarding Third Platoon, Bravo Company's C-rations
at the bridge on Route 1 south of Hue ~ Courtesy of Ronald G. Oakes, B Co, 1/27

Ronald Oakes recalls, "As platoon RTO, it was my assigned duty to dish out the mail and C-rations. This tended to make me a very popular person in my immediate circle of Marines. I rarely got into a 'beef' with anyone in the platoon. They all knew who had the connection to the outside world for help if we needed it. The Marines I served with made sure that connection was well protected and I took great pains to make sure they knew that I had their backside!"

Food packages received from home were huge morale boosters. When someone received a package from home it was shared throughout the immediate squad or platoon.

Payday in the Field with Military Payment Certificates

In lieu of using U. S. dollars, the military issued MPC for the express purpose of discouraging the black markets that functioned throughout South Vietnam. This did not turn out to be an end-all solution to the problem, although it did remedy the situation somewhat. How did Marines buy necessities such as toothpaste, soap, and extra items needed for personal hygiene? Items like a small personal transistor radio, which brought morale into the ranks? Military Payment Certificates, referred to as "Monopoly Money," became the currency of all the troops stationed in the Republic of South Vietnam.

Military Payment Certificate Series 681 front & back sides.
~ Courtesy of Grady Birdsong, H&S Co, 1/27

Series 681 payment certificates were the most numerous in the late 1960s. They were in circulation from August of 1969 through October of 1970. Series 661 were in circulation from October of 1968 until August 1969. These certificates were lithographed and not printed like regular currency. There were thirteen series of these monies issued. When a series changed from one to the next, a Conversion-Day (C-Day) was announced on very short notice, intended to surprise and hopefully keep fraud or profiteering in check.

The idea behind this monetary system was to keep the U. S. dollars out of the local economies. However, many of the indigenous people in Vietnam accepted MPC in lieu of U. S. dollars and then would use this form of currency on the black market. To prevent MPC from being used as the main currency, the banknotes were frequently changed out thus imploding a black market overnight.[14]

Rest and Relaxation

A Rest and Relaxation (R&R) scheduled trip away from the war zone became one of the mental tools that kept Marines and Corpsmen sane. This was a major morale builder for most serving in Southeast Asia. Almost everyone able visited at least one of the areas designated as an official U. S. Military R&R site. You had to be in-country for thirty days to be eligible. After that you had the possibility of drawing one of the following destinations:

- Hawaii
- Sydney, Australia
- Bangkok, Thailand
- Hong Kong
- Penang, Malaysia
- Kuala Lumpur
- Manila, Philippines
- Singapore
- Taipei, Taiwan
- Tokyo, Japan
- Okinawa, Japan

These brief respites away from Vietnam required orders that came from the higher command structure. This perk could not be taken away from any service member serving in theater. Everyone was guaranteed R&R at one of the destinations. There were some mitigating circumstances that might have kept a few from participating, but for the most part everyone went on R&R if they weren't wounded or killed. You put in your choice, and would be assigned when that opening became available. Typically, when you were to go depended on how many names were on the list ahead of you. There were only so many assignments called for every week. The longest list was, without a doubt, Australia.

Marines or Corpsmen might be summoned from a combat zone on little notice to be sent back to the base area and readied to fly to Tan Son Nhut, Cam Rahn Bay, or Da Nang. From those airports, a chartered commercial airliner would whisk you to a waiting civilization. Hawaii was where most of the married men went because wives could meet them there. Bangkok and Hong Kong were where the electronic gear was for the music equipment connoisseurs. If you were into stereo equipment these were the choice destinations.

Sydney, Australia was a westernized city and quite popular amongst Marines and Corpsmen. However, it was a rather formal place. When you arrived and cleared customs you were subjected to a communal lecture on the do's and don'ts for a couple of hours. You could also exchange your money for the local currency. You were required to wear civilian clothes and required to rent a hotel room or have a place to stay before leaving the R&R center.

If some had the inclination, they could select from several volunteer citizens who lived in the Outback who would welcome military personnel to stay with them for a few days. This was usually facilitated by farmers and large landowners who wanted to meet Americans and show them around their part of the country. This gave some the chance to visit homes and join in family outings in a rural scene. The serviceman had to pay his own transportation out to these areas.

If you wanted to take in Sydney, there was King's Cross, which catered to those into the bar scene. This is where most of the R&R military personnel conglomerated. This area catered specifically to the American GIs. The hottest bar in that section of town during the mid-1960s was the famous *Whisky a Go Go*. Everyone who traveled to Australia on R&R went to the *Whisky a Go Go*.

Through luck of the draw, Charlie Company grunt Eddie Ronan finagled his R&R in August of 1968. He chose Penang, Malaysia, a little-known place north of Kuala Lumpur, and flew there on 24 August 1968. This was a day after the NVA and VC combatants in the Da Nang TAOR assaulted several fortified battalion positions throughout the area. The assault has since been coined the "Mini-Tet" of 1968 in the history books. Looking back on it, Ronan had felt guilty at the time, leaving his fellow Marines under such circumstances. Chaos and disruption reigned for the first few hours in the area around Da Nang.

THE BARBARIAN COCKTAIL BAR

PHONE 28 1887
FOR RESERVATIONS

FERDI & GEORGE
PROPRIETORS

THE BARBARIAN
FULLY LICENSED RESTAURANT

OPEN

11.30 am TO 3pm
5.30pm TO 12 pm

SUNDAY
6pm MIDNIGHT
CASUAL GEAR

The Barbarian on 300 George Street, King's Cross (postcard front & back)
~ Courtesy of Grady Birdsong, H&S Co, 1/27

Ronan recalls catching a direct flight from Da Nang airstrip to Penang the day after the NVA hit. "We flew into what was a Royal Australian Air Force base. The flight was full of Marines and Corpsmen with no Army personnel. As we disembarked in Penang, there at the bottom of the steps appeared an Australian Army Sergeant, waving at us. He had a jeep with a trailer on the back filled to the brim with ice and those large Foster's Lager cans of beer...what a sight! As we walked down the ramp and approached him, he handed each man two cans of Foster's and cheerily said, 'Welcome Mate!' "

Once the men all staged on the flight deck and were gulping down the Foster's Lager, a large bus took them to a giant movie theater on base where the local R&R officials gave them a short speech on what to do and what not to do during their stay. They were then shown pictures of the different hotels and told the cost, and then instructed to come forward to a desk and select their hotel choice. After the brief introduction and administrative session, everyone went outside to catch the bus going to their hotel.

Once at the hotel, here is how Ronan, an articulate enlisted Marine, explained his once-in-a-lifetime R&R experience: "Even before I had checked into my room, I went downstairs to the hotel lobby...It was a big-assed hotel, a very nice place, a paradise all of its own and they had tailor shops galore in the basement. It was the first thing I did. I ordered myself, you know, a couple of pairs of pants, a shirt, and everything I would need for the week there in Penang. I even ordered a handkerchief. They measured me and told me to come back in an hour or two...go up to the bar and have a few tall ones and when I came back, he would have an outfit for me to wear. It was first class, man."

Most R&R places had strict rules about not wearing the United States military uniform while on leave in that country. The same went for Penang. Once these Marines and Corpsmen got situated with hotels and clothing, they proceeded to invade the city. Ronan remembers, "I had hooked up with this Marine on the plane. I don't think he was from my unit, the 27th Marines. I believe he was with the 7th Marines. Once we got all our shit together and rallying at the hotel done, we rented some 'cycle rickshaws,' you know them 'cyclos' or 'pedicabs'...the ones that the locals had to pedal. Each of us had one to ourselves. We started having rickshaw races in front of the hotel, raising all kinds of hell going up and down the street...yelling and screaming at the top of our lungs. Then we decided to have the drivers take us to a place where we could get a cold beer, steaks, and lobster. They found an excellent place for us... in fact, I ate there every night the whole time I was there."

One of the days before returning, Ronan and his R&R buddies decided to tour the area and see the sights. Four of the Marines he was with decided to take in the temple of the Reclining Buddha (Wat Chayamangkalaram), also known as the Sleeping Buddha. The Buddha loomed large inside of an ornate building, as big as an oversized church. Eddie tells about the sightseeing venture, "This thing was a big-assed thing. I don't know if it was real gold or polished brass but it was huge, that I know. We all got our pictures taken in front of it and then with a monk blessing us at its entrance. We were on our knees and this monk is giving us a Buddhist blessing. We all thought that was really cool..." The Marines were told that this statue reputedly is the largest Buddha in the world. It was supposed to represent Buddha at death, and a symbol reflecting the peaceful moment achieved when one reaches enlightenment or Nirvana.

And of course, where could Marines meet women, the coquettish type, while visiting this fascinating city? Most of them worked out of nightclubs. One would find a covey of these girls on the dance floor dancing with each other or in a circular arrangement of chairs in the many clubs. A Marine could walk over and pick the one he liked, or a "mama-san" would bring a gigantic photo album around with pictures of all the girls that were available. A Marine could choose an arranged partnership for an hour or a day or for however long he wanted. Some Marines were known to have had their photo taken chest deep in a tub of hot bubble bath, bubbles ascending into the air, smoking a big Cuban cigar while holding up a bottle of expensive champagne with these Penang debutantes. It just might have been a Marine or Corpsman's last celebration while on earth.

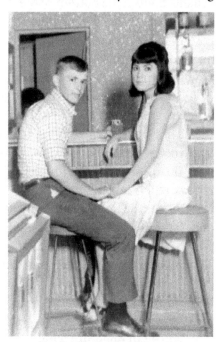

Stephen E. Austin, C Co, 1/27
(KIA 8 June 1968) relaxing on R&R
~ Courtesy of his brother Allen Austin

"Doc" William Carroll, Charlie Company, was one of the lucky ones who was assigned a billet for Australia. He recollects, "I am not sure how I got to do an R&R in Australia. I was out in the field and got a call via the LT's radio, asking if I wanted to go to Australia. It happened to be the only place I wanted to go on R&R. I yelled out, "Yeah, let me outta here...Send me to the world of round eyes. Send me to the Blonds, the Brunettes, and the Redheads. Yes, send me to those English-speaking women whom I longed for so dearly!'"

Doc Carroll spent his seven-day R&R in Sydney having the time of his life. He returned ready to join his Marines again. A fellow Corpsman, HM3 Charles R. Golling, had been sent out to replace him while he was gone. Upon return, Doc Carroll became devastated when he learned that Doc Charles Golling had been KIA on 23 August. Carroll recalls thinking, "They sent him out to replace me while I was gone on R&R and he died in place of me...I guess they mortared the area and he was hit... when I got back, it was the first thing they told me; I just wanted to vomit. I felt so bad. I felt like I had let my guys down...I felt like it wouldn't have happened had I not gone on R&R. It was 'Number Ten,' a total guilt trip for me even to this day."

Tools of the Trade Evolve

Warfare has evolved over the centuries and so have the tools of war: from the Peloponnesian War (431 - 404 BC), an all-out struggle of city-states and the use of the long spear (Doru) and short swords (Xiphos), to the present-day modern rifle in Vietnam. In 1966, a cloud of controversy surrounded the M16 rifle. The rifle was first standardized in 1967, and noticeable problems began surfacing right away in the form of a jamming epidemic in the field throughout Vietnam that year. These malfunctions began to seriously erode troop confidence in this brand-new weapon.

A Congressional inquiry into the matter began in May 1967. Although the military quickly pointed to improper cleaning and maintenance, the committee quickly determined that ammunition—specifically, gunpowder—was at the root of the problem. Back at the test ranges, receiver chambers were suspect and ultimately, it was determined that high port pressure, extreme chamber pressure, and carbon corrosion (carbon build-up) were to blame. The introduction and replacement of a modified recoil buffer, a chromed chamber, and a new ball-powder propellant reduced malfunction reports and the jamming reports began going away.

The Marine Corps is almost wholly made up of riflemen. The rifle is one of the most important tools of a Marine and the reputation of this new tool suffered during the Vietnam War. The Ichord Committee, headed by U.S. Representative Richard H. Ichord of Texas during the 90th Congress, performed the all-important task of investigating, highlighting, and helping to resolve this serious rifle-jamming problem. This modern-day evolution resulted in honing a "Tool of the Trade" that would be desperately needed in 1/27's next deployment to the Hue City area, OPCON to Task Force X-Ray.[15]

CHAPTER 5

Deployed to Task Force X-Ray, Phu Vang District

"Admiration of the Nation
We're the finest ever seen
And we glory in the title
Of United States Marines."
~ from the "Marines' Hymn"

Task Force X-Ray began expanding its operation at Phu Bai as early as mid-January 1968. Initially, Operation Checkers began planning movements of units from the south to the DMZ in late 1967. Talk was that more units from the southern areas were needed in the northern areas of I CTZ. Staff planners considered sending 1st Marine Division units and placing them under the control of 3rd Marine Division units. Major General Donn J. Robertson, 1st Marine Division Commander, recommended that his 1st Marine Division expand their influence into Thua Thien Province, which would relieve some of the pressure moving those 3rd Marine Division units already in the area further north where they were badly needed.

General Cushman concurred with Robertson and started bolstering Task Force X-Ray. General Robertson placed his assistant 1st Marine Division Commander, Brigadier General Foster C. LaHue, at the helm of the command to carry out its provisional mission.

Task Force X-Ray was to be fully responsible for all Thua Thien Province and General LaHue was to·coordinate with Brigadier General Ngo Quang Truong, Commander of the 1st ARVN Division responsible for that area.[1]

OPCON to Task Force X-Ray

On 31 March 1968, the 1/27 Battalion Command Group arrived in Phu Vang District, just north and east of the outskirts of Hue City, and established a temporary Command Post (CP) at the Phu Vang District HQ building. Lieutenant Colonel John E. Greenwood began dispatching his line companies to their respective areas of operation within the assigned Tactical Area Of Responsibility (TAOR).

On 3 April, the Battalion CP moved from the temporary Phu Vang District Headquarters (grid coordinate YD781269) and set up in the La Son School (grid coordinate YD781249) on Communal Route 552.

The City of Hue is two distinct parts. The city's interior, called the Citadel, is a miniature replica of the ancient Imperial City in Beijing, China referred to as "The Forbidden City." Built in the early 1800s, the Citadel contained many ancient and revered structures, and had served as the home of early Annamese emperors. It rests next to the banks of the Perfume River, surrounded by high surrounding walls and moats. The outer city on the southern banks of the river housed the other third of the city's residents. Militarily, Hue was important, with a railroad, nearby seaport, and the National Highway 1 passing through, allowing supplies to arrive and proceed on to the DMZ. A large population—approaching 140,000 in 1968—made it South Vietnam's third-largest city. By late January of 1968, many thousands of visitors were arriving to participate in the Lunar New Year festivities with family and friends.

Hue had reigned as the cultural, spiritual, and educational center of the country for centuries. Most of the city's local religious and intellectual leaders believed in traditional Vietnamese values and were not in sync with Ho Chi Minh's government in Hanoi, nor the U.S. backed South Vietnam government.

Task Force X-Ray (an element of the 1st MarDiv) had been given responsibility for the area between Da Nang (Hai Van Pass) to Hue City. Brigadier General Foster C. LaHue had taken command with a mission to protect that area, keep Highway 1 open and monitor the western approaches off the Ho Chi Minh Trail and its offshoots meandering through the A Shau Valley into Hue.

The senior leaders of North Vietnam viewed Hue as a weak link. General Vo Nguyen Giap (Commander of the Vietnam People's Army) directed his forces to infiltrate key areas south of the DMZ and attack during the 1968 Tet celebration. The infiltration of Hue City began in late January, and an almost-coordinated attack was launched during the early morning hours of 31 January. The NVA carried out planned executions in Hue of local and national officials, intellectuals, soldiers, and prominent families. The extent of these killings would not be learned until the battle's aftermath. The North expected that the people of South Vietnam would join in a general uprising, and the NVA, as a result. That did not happen.

Task Force X-Ray command dispatched Company A, 1st Battalion, 1st Marines (1/1), to proceed up Route 1 from the Phu Bai airport and relieve the surrounded advisers in the MACV compound on the Perfume River across from the Citadel. At the time, it was believed there were only a small contingent of NVA in the city. Upon entering the southern entrance to the city, the Marines of Lt. Col. Marcus J. Gravel's Alpha 1/1 became pinned down just shy of the adviser compound. One of Alpha's grunts, PFC William M. Purcell, remembers moving into the south end of the city. "Right in front of us was a huge, elevated causeway that went several hundred yards over rice paddies of nasty mud. On the far end of it were buildings, big structures, and we had to get to there, because the MACV compound was somewhere in there, and they were calling for help." Purcell recalls that his people had been told there was only about a company of NVA in the city and to go investigate. Unbeknownst to Purcell and the other Marines of Alpha, all hell would break loose in the following hours.

More Marines from Company G, 2/5 joined in and fought on to the MACV compound. It was later that upper-level commanders began realizing what they were up against. For the next four weeks, a force of almost 2,000 Marines (1/1 and 5th Marines) fought street-by-street, building-by-building to secure the entire city. It is estimated that close to 10,000 NVA and supporting VC soldiers had overwhelmed that area during the Tet celebrations. There was virtually no air support, and restrictions were put on larger weaponry due to Hue's political and cultural heritage, meaning they did not want structures to be destroyed. NVA firing from palace walls could only be encountered by rifle fire. The rest is history; this epic battle for Hue left the city in ruins, and most of its residences homeless. Over 5,000 civilian residents were reported killed or missing. Ultimately, the overall large-scale offensive resulted in huge losses of Communist forces throughout South Vietnam, forcing a strategic withdrawal.

Captain Tom Hoffman, U. S. Army Quartermaster Corps, had been reassigned to General Creighton Abrams's staff in the J-4 section as a petroleum supply officer at MACV Forward in Phu Bai. Staff like Hoffman had been drawn from MACV and USARV headquarters in III CTZ and began arriving at Phu Bai in early February. Hoffman recalls, "Arriving at Phu Bai during the intense fighting for the Citadel, I was hooked up with a Major. Someone high up in the MACV staff passed the word down to get someone out there and see what we had left. Our job was to go out and see what fuel supply facilities were still intact and report back...we would go out and eyeball everything we could get to."

The battle for the Hue became even more intense while Captain Hoffman acclimated. He tells of "...sitting in the old Marine Corps hooch, a jungle building whatever kind of structures they were there at Phu Bai...sitting in a folding chair at a folding table...and the entire upper-level brass would attend the morning briefings with Abrams. I never got to go to one...and the word would filter down as to what was going on. I guess Abrams at the time was really pissed off because it sounded like to me, (I can't give you an exact quote) but there was this competition going on between the Marines and the Army. The Marines wanted to retake the city and Abrams was concerned that they were taking a lot of casualties. It sounded as if Abrams was getting a lot of pressure from Westmoreland and Thieu to preserve the Citadel, a historical landmark. Abrams was extremely sensitive about the casualties and bothered by that...so he finally just...I don't know what expletive he used but it was told to me that he gave the order to take the G.. Damn city and kill the NVA. That is when they brought in more artillery, air support, and other support. Shortly after that, the Marines secured the Citadel."

Captain Hoffman also relates that toward the end of the battle for Hue in late February Westmoreland and President Thieu had told MACV headquarters and General Abrams they were going to visit the area of the battle. It filtered down through the staff appropriate quarters for a head of state and a four-star General were needed. As Hoffman explained the story, "Someone in the command structure had tracked down a couple of trailer houses in the Philippines that were in appropriate shape. So, what they were going to do was have them flown to Da Nang from the Philippines and then brought up to Phu Bai. Then someone brought up the fact that the area between Da Nang and Phu Bai on Route 1 was not secure. So, then someone comes up with a plan to Helo lift them with the Sikorsky S-64 Sky cranes from Da Nang up to the MACV compound. Someone mentioned that we did not have refueling points in-between as the Sky cranes would have to be refueled halfway...then the conversation shifted to, we would need at least a company to secure a refueling point...that was about the time I guess that General Abrams got involved and said, 'Bullshit, forget it...We are not going to do that!' General Westmoreland and President Thieu didn't come at that particular time."

Movement to the Hue Area

1/27 rifle companies traveled from the Da Nang area by truck convoy, C-130 aircraft, and seagoing vessel. Below is a Landing Ship Transport (LST) with a large part of 1st Battalion's H&S Company en route to Hue City. H&S Company Marines made a traditional beach landing, walked inland about eight kilometers to the CP area at the school, and began setting up the communications and operations center for the Battalion.

H&S Company en route on an LST to Hue City, 31 March 1968
~ Courtesy Grady Birdsong, H&S Co, 1/27

The trip from Da Nang Harbor up the coastline to the Hue area by LST was a tense and surreal experience for some of the H&S Company Marines and Corpsmen. As author Grady Birdsong, H&S Company remembers, "We were loaded into a World War II type naval vessel in Da Nang Harbor for the trip up to Hue. No one seemed to know what was going to happen. Rumors abounded like wildfire. I remember the day we boarded the LST. That day was stifling hot and would become extremely crowded onboard with all our communications gear and jeeps crammed topside. As we pulled out of the harbor and into the Gulf of Tonkin, the sea breeze became a welcome relief from the heat. There were men playing cards in small groups and some of us just stared out over the ocean, smoked and talked about our future. No one knew for sure where we were going and the discussions quickly stirred imagination which fed the rumor mill. The rumors I remember began to border on the absurd.

"At night, I remember lying on my poncho half on the steel deck topside and trying to sleep to no avail. That next morning, we all 'saddled up,' donned our issued 782 combat gear, and forming into our squad went over the side of the ship down the rope ladders into a landing craft."

The sea fog began lifting and the water was relatively calm with some chop as H&S Company disembarked. "Everyone was as nervous as a prostitute in church," Birdsong remembers. "Some Marines were jabbering away just to hear themselves talk. Some were quiet and introspective. Not knowing what to expect, I began to think the worst. What would it be like? Would we be landing under fire? Where were we going...I wondered who was in charge and how much they knew? It seemed normal that we Privates, PFCs and Lance Corporals would be the last to know what the plan would be for our movement and destination."

The company headed straight for the beach in a typical WWII beach landing. They waded ashore only to find other Marines milling around in the staging process. Birdsong remembers the LST finally pushed up on the beach as best it could, to unload the few vehicles that accompanied the Marines on the trip. "Not a thing was going on but the high humidity and heat. Once we were all on the beach we began forming into our units for the push inland. The only thing everyone seemed genuinely concerned about was how we would do under fire.

"We did not know what the enemy would do or if they would recognize the rules of war, the Geneva Convention. We had heard that they would fight to the death. The adage of 'Kill or be Killed' is not a good rule as we found out later. We found through hard lessons that we had to go on the offensive and kill the enemy, period. Later we would all learn that they were spurred on by Nationalism and 'Uncle Ho' when they did choose to fight us!"

Many of the Marines carried a lot of gear. "As we began to 'hump' inland, I can remember the sixty to seventy pounds of gear counting my own personal gear and how heavy it seemed," Birdsong recollects. "Some of the Marines were pitching stuff, comic books, 'pogey bait' [candy]… Some were loudly bitching and moaning… It was not funny at the time because the heat and humidity that day were brutal." Some Marines carried mortar baseplates, extra ammo bandoliers, rucks with mortar rounds, or extra radio batteries. No one knew how far they had to go. Birdsong's friend, Lance Corporal Richard Thrush, a mortarman, received his nickname that day. Thrush "allowed" his friend Dane Brown to carry his mortar baseplate, and became known for the rest of his life as "Baseplate."

"A lot of us were new arrivals and the first time in-country and didn't have a clue of what to expect," Birdsong recalled. "I was uncertain of my future and was scared but not to the point of panic…so we just kept on plodding westward one step after another…later we received sniper fire and took to the ground for a while until a squad deployed to hunt that sniper down."

Once H&S Company personnel arrived, they began setting up and bolstering a "hasty defense" of security around the schoolhouse and erecting the tactical communications network. Some worked on digging fighting holes on the perimeter, and some unpacked the equipment crates that had been transported by the trucks and jeeps with trailers. It would be long days and nights for all the Marines of 1/27 in days to come.

Marines in full 782 gear embarking for Hue on a C-130 ~ Courtesy of Charley F. Eckerson, H&S Co, 1/27

Some of the rifle companies found transportation by C-130 from Da Nang airstrip to Phu Bai airstrip. That was an exhilarating experience, especially for the new guys. This aircraft normally could carry about ninety passengers with full combat gear. It was uncomfortable and disorganized and usually, everyone just sat where they could and hung on for the ride. The pilots on this type of aircraft had a bad habit of making steep dives on final approach into an always too short runway, and invariably everyone and everything would get tossed around the internal cabin like dice on a crap shoot. The pilot would side-slip and try all kinds of evasive maneuvers to get anyone that might be shooting at them to miss. That would work sometimes. On the ground and toward the end of the runway it was usually a mad dash to get everyone off the aircraft as it turned around. The bird would then take off immediately in the opposite direction. If you weren't off, you were going back where you came from. This amazing aircraft was a workhorse in the Vietnam War and could move a lot of Marines.

Then-Lieutenant Roger Charles, a Platoon Commander in Alpha Company, remembered moving by C-130 from Da Nang to Phu Bai. "We were packed like sardines—no one sat, so we had over 200 Marines and Navy Corpsmen on that one flight (I recall hearing a larger number of bodies, but would not claim that was a solid number) ...I thought as we made the short trip to Phu Bai that if this bird crashed, someone would have a hell of a time justifying stuffing all these excess PAX into the aircraft!"

Segments of the other rifle companies were moved by deuce-and-a-half convoys into the Hue area. They undoubtedly traversed the infamous Hai Van pass north of Da Nang. After climbing through several hairpin curves to the top of the pass the view is about 1,600 feet above sea level. Hai Van means "Sea Clouds." When the weather is good on top there is an unobstructed view to both the north and south. The harbor of Da Nang is also visible. If the weather is inclement then there is usually fog or clouds. Coming down from the pass heading to the north, you start the descent into the Hue-Phu Bai area. This Area of Operations (AO) would be where the Battalion would begin its baptism by fire in the beginning months of 1968, the year of the Monkey.

Unloading in front of 1/27 La Son School CP ~ Courtesy of Alioth Glaettli, H&S Co, 1/27

The Mission

Commanding Brigadier General Foster C. LaHue, Task Force X-Ray, had wasted no time in assigning the Battalion its mission of providing security for the Col Co/Tam My complex, LST Ramp Operations, and the onsite Naval Support Activity (NSA) Fuel Farm. The Operation Order included Route 551 with adjacent fuel pipeline from the coast into Hue City. Additionally, the rifle companies were to ensure uninterrupted river traffic from the Col Co/Tam My complex to the Hue naval support activity ramp; provide reaction-force capability on request for the 3rd Combined Action Group, 1st ARVNs, and the District Chief. Included in the orders were bridges on National Highway 1, south and east toward Phu Bai, which the engineers were maintaining, and which needed security. This was the beginning of a series of no-name operations, No Name Numbers 1, 2, 3, 4, and 5, conducted in the newly assigned TAOR. The Battalion's secondary mission was rice denial to enemy combatants. The orders were to deploy all units of 1/27 into the adjusted TAOR east of Hue City and relieve U.S. forces already there. The security missions are identified in A through M of the Frag Order 2-68 (see following page).

Then-Major Franklin P. Eller, serving as the Battalion Executive Officer, recalled that, "The assigned tactical area of operation, east and southeast of Hue City stretching to the coast, seemed large to me...given its expanse, terrain, population in many villages, it was my opinion that a Regimental-size force would have been more appropriate... Marines don't get to choose their mission, so upon arriving we turned to and went about this very challenging task."

As he further explained, the mission was to deny free movement of the enemy within the TAOR and destroy their unit infrastructure. The line companies were assigned their own operating areas and established multiple Platoon Patrol Bases (PPB) from which they originated patrols, ambushes, and Company-sized operations. Eller further explained, "We found the enemy firmly embedded in the area and they had many supporters both willing and coerced. They could choose to fight at times and places while moving around on terrain they were familiar within this area and among populace which they had completely intimidated."

Then-Captain Ronald Gruenberg ran the S-3 Combat Operations Center (COC). He remembers the actual details of having to comply with Task Force X-Ray's order to deny the enemy freedom of movement. Their operations officer strongly insisted that every grid square (1,000 x 1,000 meters) on the map overlaying the actual TAOR be patrolled or have an ambush conducted within that square. That meant in his daily planning activity that Gruenberg had to submit patrol routes or ambush coordinates twenty-four hours in advance so they could be plotted and checked off on Task Force X-Ray's maps. He vividly recounts this daunting task: "If they observed an open grid without a 'squiggly' they would call me and insist on a patrol in that area immediately. It was extremely challenging and sometimes not doable due to our level of manpower and the large operating area we had to cover. It was an ongoing problem we had to deal with...as I learned from my earlier Midshipmen ocean-going days...Big ocean, little ship."

Telex to 1/27 Command from CG Task Force X-Ray 31 March 1968 ~ Command Chronology April 1968 (Frag Order 2-68)

2nd page of Telex to 1/27 Command from CG Task Force X-Ray 31 March 1968 ~ Command Chronology April 1968 (Frag Order 2-68)

Lieutenant Colonel John E. Greenwood, 1/27 Commanding Officer with Radiomen
~ Courtesy Sgt. Larry Broadhurst, H&S Co, 1/27

Battalion Leadership

Then-Lieutenant Colonel Greenwood, the Battalion C. O., had enlisted in the Marines at age seventeen, close to the end of WWII. Beginning his service aboard the USS Alabama (BB-60), a South Dakota Class battleship, in 1946, he received a Fleet appointment to the Naval Academy. Graduating in 1950 and accepting a commission into the Marine Corps, he then served as a junior officer with 3rd Battalion, 5th Marines during the Korean War.

Before taking command of the 1st Battalion, 27th Marines, Lieutenant Colonel Greenwood had been on the staff of both the 9th Marine Expeditionary Brigade and III MAF. During this time, he became intricately involved in the project of incorporating helicopters into amphibious doctrine and went on to become an aide-de-camp to Lieutenant General Victor H. "Brute" Krulak, who served as Commanding General, FMFPAC from 1964 to 1968.

Major Pete Eller, 1st Battalion, 27th Marines Executive Officer, 1968
~ Courtesy of Colonel Pete Eller, USMC (Ret), H&S Co, 1/27

Major Frank "Pete" Eller joined with 1st Battalion, 27th Marines at Kaneohe Bay, MCAS in November 1967 after a prior assignment as Analysis Section Head of the Navy Fleet Intelligence Center located on Ford Island, Hawaii. While there, his section of Marine Corps and Navy photo interpreters reviewed aerial photography from reconnaissance flights over North Vietnam providing real targets, and possible targets, for the Commander in Chief, Pacific Fleet, (CINCPAC) as well as current on-the-ground intelligence.

Joining the Naval Reserve at age seventeen, Eller earned an appointment to the United States Naval Academy, graduating with the class of 1955. Applying for and receiving a commission as 2nd Lieutenant in the United States Marine Corps, he later became a Platoon Commander with 9th Marines, and later a rifle Company Commander in 2nd Battalion, 6th Marines, deploying to the Caribbean during the Cuban Missile Crisis. Later assigned to 2nd Reconnaissance Battalion as a Company Commander, he moved into a senior advisor billet with 4th Battalion, Vietnamese Marine Corps as a coveted "Covan My" (American Advisor) and consequently received a Silver Star for actions on 31 December 1964 with the 4th Battalion in what was one of the major battles of the early Vietnam War.

Taking Over from Army Units in the Area

U. S. Army units had been ordered into the area by General Westmoreland beginning in mid-January through February. MACV-Forward, headquartered in Phu Bai, had seen close to 20,000 Army troops come into the I Corps area. These included the 1st Cavalry Division, some units of the 101st Airborne Division, and the 3rd Brigade of the 82nd Airborne, which had accompanied RLT-27 from the United States in February. The 82nd Airborne Brigade and 101st Airborne operated "OPCON" with 1st Marine Division Task Force X-Ray headquartered in Phu Bai. The ancient city of Hue was the largest population center in this area. First Battalion, 27th Marines would take over this area of operation from these Army units, who were then redeployed elsewhere. The transition began immediately as 1/27 arrived on the outskirts of the city in early April.

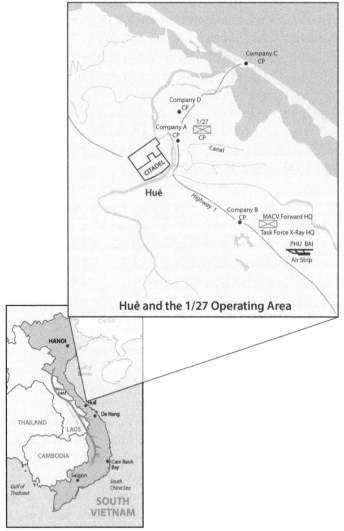

Map of Hue and 1/27's Operating Area, showing the line company CPs, MACV HQ and Task Force X-Ray HQ ~ courtesy of Nick Zelinger, NZGraphics.com

Then-Captain William Sweeney, the Battalion Intelligence Officer, remembers the move from south of Da Nang up to the Hue area. Everything went fast. All the I Corps "brass" felt a sense of urgency. The enemy had struck hard especially in Hue City and was still embedded in many pockets and needed to be routed.

Sweeney remembers the initial task of relieving the in-place Army Battalion (505th of the 82nd Airborne attached to the 101st). He recalls, "I will never forget the turnover briefing...they seemed to be undisciplined...during the briefing we were informed by the Battalion Commanding Officer that when they first took over the TAOR they had run an attack with tanks into the canal area and had been repulsed [Task Force X-Ray Intel in the Command Chronologies confirms three attempts by different units and taking moderate to heavy casualties in this specific area]. The Army Battalion C. O. warned us not to go out there or we would most definitely get into a fight.... observing facial expressions of our staff and C. O., Lieutenant Colonel John Greenwood, I detected disbelief and disgust. I knew Greenwood would not shrink from the fight."

Captain Sweeney tells that toward the end of the briefing an Army Captain informed the Marines that about 1600 every day, enemy snipers would fire on the CP area. The Army Captain added, "The best way to deal with it was to take cover, leave them alone and they would eventually leave."[2]

Captain Jim Panther, Alpha Company Commander, remembers the first day at the CP. He recalls, "When we arrived at the school house to relieve a company of the 101st Airborne, they commenced evening chow at around 1600 hours. I asked their company commander why so early and he replied that a sniper fired on them each evening from the nearby tree line. Sure enough at about 1700 hours all the Army personnel donned helmets and flak jackets and the sniper fired a few rounds. The Airborne troopers returned heavy volumes of fire into the tree line and then returned to their routine – which did not include setting up ambushes, patrols, or listening posts outside of this immediate area. Upon relieving them the next day we did commence patrolling, setting up ambushes and listening posts in the immediate area—no more evening sniper fire harassment." Night ambushes were set up and all the line companies began to take control of their respective areas.

Operations Begin

1st Battalion, 27th Marines immediately began operation in the Phu Vang District of Thua Thien-Hue Province next to the Huong Tra District.

A major element of H&S Company arrived on 3 April via LST at the Col Co/Tam My U. S. Naval Support Activity area, disembarking on landing boats and hitting the beach in typical Marine Corps amphibious landing fashion. They then swept inland on foot to the schoolhouse. Later, on 7 April, this command center would come under mortar attack from entrenched enemy forces within the area. Also on the 3rd of April the rifle companies kicked off the first significant actions on Operation No Name #1, which would last until 9 April. Several other No Name Ops would be conducted throughout April and May, with significant encounters.[3]

Huey Helicopters of the 101st Airborne picking
up elements of their troopers at La Son School
CP perimeter, April 1968

Marine H-34 Helicopter communicating
with Corporal Al Glaettli, RTO at 1/27 LZ,
east of La Son School

~ Courtesy of Alioth Glaettli, H&S Co, 1/27

Area Intelligence

Intelligence reports passed down from Division to Task Force X-Ray indicated that main force NVA and VC operated in the vicinity. It was also indicated in the reports they had mortar capability, with well-trained and hardened combatants in those units. Intel gathered and reported in April would draw attention to a larger than anticipated enemy presence for this area.

III MAF intelligence for April showed increased enemy activity, demonstrating heavy resistance, notably in the Tri-Thien/Hue Military Region. The Enemy Order of Battle in the intel reports listed the presence of the 6th NVA Regiment, the 803rd and 90th Regiments, 324B Division; the 7th and 9th Battalions, 29th Regiment, 325C NVA Division; five independent battalions and five independent companies, among them the 802nd NVA Battalion, the 804th Main Force NVA Battalion, and the 810th Local Force Battalion, aided by the C-116 VC Local Force Company, the F-116 VC Ranger Company, and elements of the C-117 Local Force Company. Some of these enemy fighters had been pushed out into the canal area during the battle for the Citadel in late February, and some of them were already there to support that effort during Tet. This enemy force concentration is what 1/27 would have to seek and destroy. The estimated enemy strength recorded in the document titled, III MAF, Enemy Order of Battle (see Command Chronology for April 68) in Thua Thien Province was 6,620.

Detaining and administering first aid for local VC suspects by Charlie Company, Col Co area
~ Courtesy of William "Doc" Carroll, C Co, 1/27

Per intelligence reports, the objective of the NVA-VC enemy combatants in this area was to maintain influence over the local indigenous population and to aggressively collect taxes during the rice harvest season. It was further learned through the intelligence network that these units had with them additional armaments; various mortars, 57mm recoilless rifles, B40 rockets, and anti-aircraft guns.

The enemy's overall tactical objective in this area was Hue. Secondarily, it was Quang Tri province. Hue was where most of the population resided. The Communists expected an uprising, and had hoped that the capture of Hue would result in South Vietnamese forces defecting. This would have left them in a strong position. The enemy did continue to challenge American and South Vietnamese troops after Tet, especially along the coastal areas, even though they had suffered enormous setbacks.

Alpha Company Executive Officer First Lieutenant John Bouldin remembered that after the Battalion arrived in the Hue area, written intelligence would come to them daily. He thought it good intel. Each report would be letter graded, A1, A2, A3 and so on. Rifle companies were to react to a report graded C3 or higher. He explained, "For example, a grade report would come in stating that a villager reported that fifteen NVA armed with such and such rifles stopped in the village at such and such a time in the night. This activity was written up by the intel people and assigned a grade before being passed down to us in the line companies."

Bouldin went on to further explain that a rifle company couldn't respond to each individual report due to manpower and area coverage. Bottom line, they mostly would look for patterns before bringing it up to the Company Commander. He also recalled, "We had pretty good general intel from Task Force X-Ray and from our line companies what was happening, but we did have an enormous area to cover which really should have been assigned to a Regiment. It was a little more than could be covered by a Battalion but we did what we were ordered to do with what we had."

Charlie Company Platoon Patrol Base (PPB) during No Name Ops in the Hue AO
~ Courtesy of William "Doc" Carroll, C Co, 1/27

An NVA stronghold

Prior to the beginning of the No Name Operations, the South Vietnamese made three attempts to enter the canal area south and east of Route 552 and the La Son Schoolhouse after the Tet offensive of February. 3rd Battalion, 3rd Regiment, 1st ARVN division made the last probe into this area and was stopped cold, sustaining heavy casualties. That move was from the south pushing northward toward Route 552. As pointed out in the Command Chronologies, guesswork, past intelligence reports, and experience showed the reasons for the heavy resistance encountered this enemy stronghold: "There were two primary considerations: 1) that the enemy is using this area inside the canal perimeter to restock his food supplies from the rice harvest and taxes from the local villagers. 2) that in consideration of the fact that this area was astride the avenue of approach that the enemy used during the Tet Offensive, he may be attempting to hold the area open to stage, assemble and resupply troops prior to a final assault on Hue for his second offensive. 3) A combination of the above.[4]

ARVN Soldier and youngster providing intelligence to Captain Jim Panther,
Alpha Company Commander ~ Courtesy of Charley F. Eckerson, A Co, 1/27

Geography and Environment of Strategic Area

Major road Routes 1, 551, 552, and the Huong River waterway (Perfume River) offered an easy approach to the Imperial City of Hue for the local population. Other approaches in the surrounding area were footpaths that were time-consuming to negotiate. The landmass to the northeast, east, and southeast of the city proper was mostly dry land, with exceptions of the canals, rivers, and streams. The average temperatures in this area ranged from 70 F to 90 F daily, producing little rain. Being close to the ocean, the area experienced high humidity levels which generally caused early morning mist and fog that affected ground visibility.

Of major importance in the coastal area to the east of Hue was the NSA complex of Tan My. It served as a control point for river and ocean traffic and consisted of a bladder fuel farm. A six-inch pipeline had been laid above ground from Tan My, aka "Col Co," toward the LCU ramp in Hue City on the Huong or Perfume River, ending at Phu Bai. This coastal complex was the ocean access for resupply to all allied troops in the area.

The Moonless Night

Upon first arriving in the Hue City area in March 1968, First Lieutenant John Bouldin, Executive Officer of Alpha Company, took a platoon of Marines on a special night mission. Strong intelligence came down to 1/27's S-2 shop that the NVA would again try to infiltrate Hue City through a specific route. Bouldin's orders were to go south of the 1/27 CP and set up an ambush on the suspected avenue of approach into the city. Bouldin recalled, "I got the word to get my men together quickly and head to a position S-3 had determined the enemy would try to pass through into Hue City. In a hurry, I stopped by S-3 for Captain Ronald Gruenberg to brief and tell me there would be no moon that night. We also pre-registered artillery and illumination grid coordinates. After squaring those details away, we proceeded to move south posthaste toward the proposed ambush site. Arriving just before dark, I found that our positions would butt up close to the city along the river. What a terrible position, I thought to myself as I got my men situated."

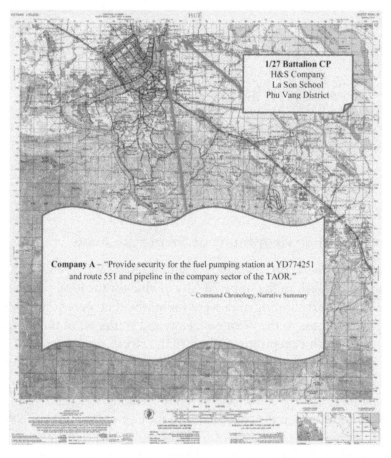

1/27 Battalion CP
H&S Company
La Son School
Phu Vang District

Company A – "Provide security for the fuel pumping station at YD774251 and route 551 and pipeline in the company sector of the TAOR."

~ Command Chronology, Narrative Summary

Vietnam – Hue City area topo map, sheet 6541 IV of HQ CP of 1st Bn, 27th Marines and Alpha Company CP, with directives compiled from 1/27 Command Chronologies beginning 1 April 1968 ~ clip art courtesy of Corporal Grady Birdsong, H&S Co, 1/27

Well into his third tour of a different kind of war, Lieutenant Bouldin placed every-one into position as best he could. Nightfall turned pitch black. Bouldin explained the unfolding detail of that night: "I had settled into some sort of a hole, all was going well when one of my new Marines came crawling up…I could hear him crawling, crawling slowly toward my position and when he found me kept saying in a muffled voice, 'Sir…Sir…Sir…there is an NVA right up against that trench line out there'…I looked and looked and then looked some more. I responded, that I would be damned if I could see an NVA out there…I kept looking and became frustrated with this new replacement. I then told him to get back to his position and to shoot the SOB… He immediately replied, 'Aye aye, Sir!' I could hear him noisily crawling back and I waited and waited… Nothing happened.

"A while later he repeated the same ordeal again. He again crawled a helluva long way to my hole to tell me that now there was no NVA out there. Almost to lose my cool, I calmly told him, 'Alright, Killer, go back to your frigging position and stay alerted!' That kid had crawled a long way both times to tell me the first time there was an NVA out there and then again to say there wasn't one out there… I have to laugh about it now…War can be hell!" To this day, John Bouldin is thankful that the ambush did not get launched that night.

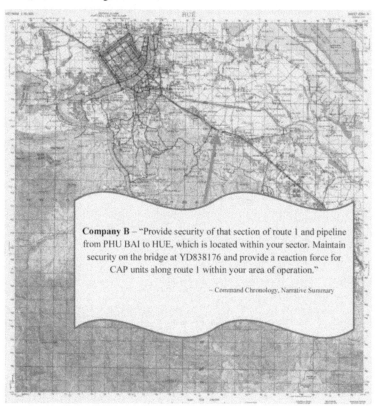

Company B – "Provide security of that section of route 1 and pipeline from PHU BAI to HUE, which is located within your sector. Maintain security on the bridge at YD838176 and provide a reaction force for CAP units along route 1 within your area of operation."

~ Command Chronology, Narrative Summary

Vietnam - Hue-Phu Bai area topo map, sheet 6541 IV of Bravo Company AO, and directives compiled from 1/27 Command Chronologies beginning 1 April 1968
~ clip art courtesy of Corporal Grady Birdsong, H&S Co, 1/27

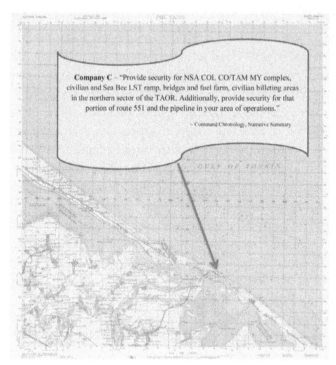

Vietnam – Hue-Col Co/Tam My area, topo map, Sheet 6542 III of Charlie Company CP,
and directives compiled from 1/27 Command Chronologies beginning 1 April 1968
~ clip art courtesy of Corporal Grady Birdsong, H&S Co, 1/27

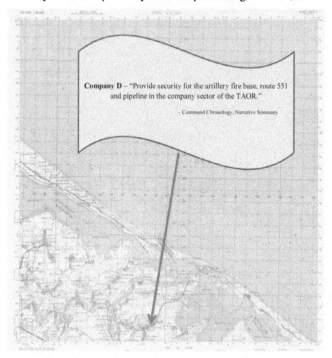

Vietnam – Hue City route 551/Pipeline area, topo map 6542 III of Delta Company CP,
and directives compiled from 1/27 Command Chronologies beginning 1 April 1968
~ clip art courtesy of Corporal Grady Birdsong, H&S Co, 1/27

Sting Ray Tactics

Upon arrival, the Battalion was introduced to a tactical concept by the Task Force X-Ray command, called "Sting Ray" teams. These Forward Observer teams, introduced earlier in the war, operated at night. Utilizing starlight scopes which increased their night visibility, 1/27 Sting Ray teams surveilled most areas in and around the canal area east of Hue city.

These teams located themselves in positions that enabled the monitoring of large open areas and watched for enemy troop movement at night. Bold enemy movements and rice gathering in this area were prevalent prior to 1/27's arrival. The Battalion Sting Ray mission was to seek, find and destroy any moving enemy with available supporting arms, mostly artillery. By combining these teams with a series of interlocking patrols and pre-planned ambushes, enemy activity was eventually curtailed. This tactic drove enemy elements further east, from the rice producing area to the more open coastal region, which tied in with Task Force X-Ray's strategy of checking off each grid (mark a "squiggly") on their overlay map.

Then-PFC Richard R. Hunt, an S-2 Battalion scout in 1/27, traveled on nightly Sting Ray forays in the Hue City TAOR. He recalls, "Our team members throughout our tour remained the same people, Sergeant Larry Broadhurst, Corporal Alexander Rios, Lance Corporal Marvin Brown, and myself. We operated pretty much where our Battalion S-2 determined the enemy was moving at night. Our mission simply put, to monitor and disrupt NVA/VC night movement on several heavily traveled routes throughout our TAOR there east of Hue City."

1/27 fielded two scout teams consisting of four men each. Each team carried two starlight scopes with mounts, a map, and a radio, with each man carrying anywhere from 300 to 500 rounds of ammo, water, and minimal first aid supplies. On any given Sting Ray patrol, the team leader reviewed all checkpoints and coordinates, and pre-registered artillery coordinates and potential escape and evasion routes prior to departure.

Hunt recollects, "Once at the site, we began our routine of setting up in our four-point box-like configuration. Close enough together where we could almost touch one another, the opposite sides, opposite corners would begin the watch. The other two would try to sleep. Every couple of hours the watch team would switch the watch to opposite corners. Each side had a starlight scope and thus had an overlapping 360-degree view. The two out-looking positions would off and on scan and sweep the area for personnel movement. One of the first things on the checklist after settling in was to sweep the area for other night sight devices. You could pick them up in a heartbeat. If you could see them that meant they could see you also…if so, time to move."

As the team monitored the area, they would occasionally power their starlight scopes off and on. As Hunt vividly remembers, "We never used our rifles…that was last resort. Our intent was to stay away from any NVA/VC troop movement but on the other hand, we would 'light them up' with on-call arty and start adjusting our fire if we caught them in our night field of vision. We operated in a 'Free-Fire Zone' in the Hue TAOR. If anyone on our team had a bad feeling about our location, we would move, no questions asked. I can remember a time when some NVA walked by us on a trail so close that I quit breathing so they would not hear me…and while concentrating on not breathing, I was afraid they would hear my heart beating."

Communications at Headquarters Command Post

The below photo shows the whole left side of the La Son School Command Post and the GP tents which housed the "Comm" equipment and personnel. The roadway in the upper right portion of the photo is Communal Route 552.

Aerial view of La Son School CP ~ Courtesy of Colonel Gene Schwartzlow (Ret), H&S Co, 1/27

Captain Ronald Allen, Bravo Company Commander, had dual responsibility for the Communications network activity of H&S Company, which he assigned in his absence to a very capable Gunnery Sergeant, Manuel J. Gomez.

In advance of the upcoming western Pacific training operation, before the Battalion was ordered to Vietnam, Captain Allen learned late February of 1968 that he had orders to meet the diverted Battalion in Da Nang. Having gone through the Communications schools in Quantico and becoming a Communications Officer after serving as an infantry officer on earlier tours, he would be taking over Battalion communications. Knowing that Allen had field command experience from previous tours, Lieutenant Colonel Greenwood asked him upon landing in Da Nang if he would volunteer to command a rifle company. Even though he did not have to, Allen wanted and took the helm of Bravo Company. When asked by Lieutenant Colonel Greenwood if Gomez could handle the communication responsibility in his absence, Captain Allen readily replied, "He, without a doubt, knows what he is doing and how to keep things up and running…!" Captain Allen had met Gomez when he arrived in Hawaii, observed his professionalism, and had assessed him as top notch.

Captain Allen with First Sgt Kendrick in 1966 while commanding Fox 2/4 under the command
of Lieutenant Colonel P. X. Kelly, 2/4 C.O. ~ Courtesy of Major Ronald Allen (Ret), B Co, 1/27

Gunnery Sergeant Manuel Gomez, Battalion Communications Chief, functioned
as a focused leader of the communication section, concerned with the setting up of all
communications equipment and orchestrating the tactical network to full functionality.
All communications personnel reported to the Gunny. His responsibility extended to
all communications links with the rear-area attachment at Regiment to the south of
Da Nang, and to Task Force X-Ray in Phu Bai.

Gunny Gomez and his people kept the Battalion tactical net up and running 24/7.
It was essential to stay linked with the Regimental Headquarters communications
network, passing critical tactical and logistical message traffic back and forth. And
the Battalion also communicated daily with the Task Force X-Ray command located
in Phu Bai a short distance to the south. First Lieutenant Gene Schwartzlow took over
Battalion communications responsibility shortly after Gunny Gomez was killed on 17
April 1968.

The high-powered radios, the AN/TRC-75 and PRC-125 mounted in the jeeps,
needed to be working and communicating with all points of designated contact. Telex
and Crypto machines needed to be in working order to pass messages on a routine
and emergency basis. Backup radios and batteries needed dry storage and checking
periodically. Ensuring the clicker-type TA-312 Telephones, placed in all the bunker
positions with wire strung throughout the entire perimeter, were fully operational,
took an inordinate amount of time. Lance Corporal Joe Roysdon, a key senior member
of Communications, remembers, "I spent a lot of time at the schoolhouse sending
'CasReps' [casualty reports] back to Regimental Headquarters south of Da Nang on my
TRC-75 mounted in my jeep. Every KIA, WIA, and MIA full names and serial numbers
went through my radio. The message center also used the TRC-75 for Teletype
transmissions."

Corporal Grady Birdsong recalls that Gunny Gomez embodied a unique leadership style. "It seemed like he worked all of the time…staying up almost all night long
making sure that everything in Communications was at its full potential. The Gunny,

a quiet but assertive man, would not put up with any 'grab ass' or joking around. He would not hesitate to get you out of your poncho in the middle of the night to check on something even if you had just come off guard duty on the perimeter. I shared a small makeshift tent-like abode with him and Staff Sergeant Raymond Johnson, so I was with and around both all day and night. We slept in our rickety makeshift tent right on the ground in our poncho liners when time allowed. In our spare time, we filled sandbags to fortify the perimeter defensive positions and everything that needed protection. Perimeter guard duty was a given at night. LP duty was also a given. The Gunny was a no-nonsense fellow and someone whom we all trusted and looked up to for leadership and consult…He had been there on a previous tour."

The move from Duong Son (2) below Da Nang to the Hue area TAOR resulted in temporary supply problems. The first weeks of April after arrival, only emergency items were addressed. The Battalion at first did not receive follow-on supplies normally shipped by Force Logistics Command from Da Nang. The breakdown was finally identified and corrected, and those critical supplies were redirected to Force Logistic Support Group "Alpha" at the Phu Bai airstrip just south of the CP. This supply group became a major supply point for not only Marine units, but also U. S. Army units operating in the area. FLSG Alpha retained support responsibility for the 1st Marine Division Task Force X-Ray elements, newly arrived in the Hue area.

CP Perimeter Defense and LPs

Once a perimeter was set up, the defense and security of that inner position was secured all hours of the day and night. The outer limits beyond the perimeter wire theoretically belonged to the enemy. The La Son School CP group sent out multiple listening posts (LPs) each evening. Usually a two-man position, LPs were set up at night outside of the perimeter away from the main body of Marines to provide an early warning against attack. Positions were set up in separate locations each night in probable avenues of approach. This activity was the least popular of all assignments for good reason; it was extremely dangerous.

On LP, Marines were expected to warn the tactical network CP radio watch in the command bunker (COC) via PRC-25 radio of any enemy activity directed toward the compound. Radio procedures indicating that the LP was set up were to key the mic twice when in position and one click every hour afterward if things were normal. If you had a serious activity, the alert was a series of repeated double clicks. LPs were not an ambush situation, but considered "doorbell" duty, and you were on your own. Passwords were given out to each LP for the possibility of coming back into the perimeter in the event of an attack.

Corporal Grady Birdsong recalls the La Son School LP experience. "As a new guy on the first one I experienced, we waited until darkness and then crept out about 300 yards to the assigned position.

"Corporal Hal Kennedy and I crawled into some tall grass which didn't feel high enough and lay down flat on our ponchos. It was such a new and naked experience laced with abject fear, that I could not sleep a wink even though I had been up for almost twenty-four hours straight. As we lay in the grass and the night got darker, things begin to happen or so we thought...We started hearing movement, and then total quiet, and then bugs droning around which put us on high alert. Cringing at every sound, I felt as if the NVA out there could hear our hearts beating...could hear my breathing... could hear my blood flowing in my veins...we knew they were out there.

"It was a terrible night, full of strange sounds, nightmarish death waiting in the shadows. But there were no NVA and when the dawn started to peek through the humidity, I started to calm down and feel like we were going to survive the terrors of the night... The images of NVA coming at us in the dark melted into the hedgerows and the increasing daylight allowed us to see more clearly...If you have ever been on LP in enemy territory the glory of a sunrise renders one of the most calming and welcoming sights you will ever know. To this day, I gain that wonderful feeling of sincere security as I witness a sunrise blossom from the first glint into full daylight."

The New Lieutenant and Lessons Learned

Mike McDade, a "salty" corporal from Pennsylvania, was on his second tour of Vietnam. PFC Dane Brown, a new guy to Vietnam, had bonded with Corporal McDade and had started sticking to him like glue because of his experience. They hit it off and became real buddies. Everyone had to spend time in the newly erected bunkers and fighting holes around the CP on security watch, which took place twenty-four hours a day. Brown recollects that he and McDade would get to serve their watch together. Their weapons Platoon Commander, Lieutenant Ralph Pineda, was good about letting Marines buddy up. Brown recalls one of the first nights that he and McDade spent on perimeter watch in the Hue area. "McDade and I set up in this recently dug fighting hole on the south side of the perimeter. McDade had served in the infantry on a previous tour and if he heard a cricket fart he would pop a hand flare or throw a grenade. He popped more flares than anyone I knew over there. He was overly jumpy and nervous as a whore in church. I always carried a grenade pouch on my right leg. I kept it filled to the brim with grenades. On every night watch if he heard something he would have me lob one out into the darkness... This was a new area and he was not going to take any chances."

As the night hours went by on this watch and the surrounding noises became seemingly amplified, Brown and McDade both heard a distant noise like someone was walking toward them. It was pitch dark and Brown recalls looking to their right and saw a small orange-like light that seemed to flicker. "I don't remember how far out it was, but the glimmering light looked to be coming closer and closer and finally we both could see a human form walking toward us...when that person got almost to our position, McDade somehow crawled out of our fighting hole, maneuvering toward that person, grabbed him by the collar around the throat, and threw him into the hole jumping on him...lo and behold it was a new lieutenant who had the perimeter watch that night and was out checking the lines, ditty-bopping around, smoking a cigar as he checked each position around the CP."

Brown recollects, "McDade told this new lieutenant in no uncertain terms that if he ever comes up on us again like that without identifying himself and a lit cigar, he would cap his ass...The cigar dropped out of his mouth...he did not say one word after receiving that lecture...he was dumbfounded. He got up, left, and went on to the next hole...I thought Mike was truly going to hurt him. I said to Mike, 'WTF, man'...Mike replied, 'I have already spent one tour in this shit hole and I am not going to let a guy like that get my ass killed...walking around with a lighted cigar in his mouth, compromising our position...' The lieutenant never spoke a word of the incident to me or McDade after that."

An Incident at the Command Post

Part of the security of the total surrounding area was the responsibility of the S-2 section, who scouted the area along with their Vietnamese associates. First Battalion, 27th Marines had three "Kit Carson" scouts, formerly members of a Viet Cong or NVA unit, on their roster. Marine units in 1966 began using former enemy soldiers as scouts, in the tradition of Kit Carson, the storied frontiersman, soldier scout, and Indian agent of the late 1800s. These "Kit Carson" scouts knew the enemy's habits and operating characteristics inside and out, and were to help evaluate and find enemy locations for the Marines.

In the early days after arriving and setting up a hasty defense CP, then-Lance Corporal Grady Birdsong and some others decided to take a chow break from the digging and sandbagging they were doing. As Birdsong remembers, "I was opening a can from my C-ration box and looked up to see our S-2 scout, the one and only, long-time Private Jim McConnell walking toward us holding up one of the Kit Carson scouts. Jim was about six feet five inches in height and towered over this little guy, the Vietnamese scout. Jim was an 'old salt,' a second-tour combat Marine with no affinity for rank. They were heading right for us as we were eating our rations.

"McConnell, obviously headed for our makeshift aid station on the east side of the La Son Schoolhouse, walked right past us. The small Vietnamese scout was stumbling and seemed to be going in and out of consciousness as 'Big Jim' held onto him as they walked. There was a Corpsman trailing them. I took a second look and was stunned. The little guy's one arm flopped around. It looked attached by only a small strand of tendon or muscle. This little man was delirious and Big Jim kept him upright as they walked right past us on toward the Aid Station. I noticed that Jim was wounded also. A couple of things struck me about this horrific scene that I had just witnessed. No one got excited or jumped up to help. All the Marines eating chow just stared in silence and kept on eating. Big Jim and the little guy just kept plodding toward the Aid Station."

Birdsong began to wonder what kind of madness this war had brought. He reflected, "Was this just a surreal event that really did not happen...I began to churn inside.

At the time, I asked myself, is this normal or is this not normal? This was the first of many more traumatic events which I would witness." As Birdsong found later, these events would become more normal. In his words, "The war would brutalize us beyond normal. I became numb like everybody else throughout my two tours."

1/27 Battalion Command Post in Hue (La Son School) with RPG hole, Grid Coordinates, YD781249 ~ Courtesy of Grady Birdsong, H&S Co, 1/27

The word was that McConnell and his Vietnamese Kit Carson Scout had been scouting the canal area to the east of the CP position and had run into an ambush. The NVA had fired a Rocket Propelled Grenade (RPG) at the Kit Carson Scout and McConnell, somehow hitting them both. Though the RPG round hadn't detonated, its trajectory had almost taken off the Vietnamese's whole arm below the shoulder. It was later reported that he was hospitalized and did lose the arm.

HM2 Bob Taugner, Company B Corpsman, also witnessed the incident. Taugner remembers, "I was sitting at the fountain right by the front gate of the CP. This Ontos comes blazing down the road and steers into the courtyard coming to a screeching halt at the fountain, hitting it. I caught a glimpse of our Vietnamese Kit Carson scout and a Marine on top of the Ontos. They were both wounded. The Marine said to me, 'Doc, just guide me, don't touch me'...the Kit Carson was going ape shit...he was screaming and running around like a chicken...I shot him with some morphine and then he calmed down. Kirkpatrick, another Corpsman, later told me that he had run into them down the road and only had one syringe of morphine so he gave it to the Marine. Neither one was bleeding bad. The trauma of the injury must have sealed their wounds. I then guided them to the Aid Station."

The "Do Not Fail" Mission

In late March or early April, Corporal Douglas Carey, Weapons Section, was summoned by his platoon commander for an unusual mission. The dilemma was that the Battalion CP had no toilets. Just arrived in the TAOR, the Marines had been using E-tools and digging their own latrines.

The Battalion Commander ordered Corporal Carey's Platoon Commander to secure an outhouse that would accommodate the Marines in the CP. He specified that he wanted a "four-hole" seating arrangement and under those seats were to be fifty-five-gallon oil drums cut in half.

These outhouses were not highly mobile and had to be transported by a heavy truck. To make matters worse, they were not readily available. After meeting the Lieutenant at his tent and receiving a "do not fail" instruction, the Lieutenant handed Carey his pistol belt and a holstered 1911A1 .45-caliber semi-automatic pistol, along with ammo, and gave him his utility cover with the officer's rank insignia on it. Carey recalls, "Off we went to find a six-by truck from motor transport. I had a few grenades, smokes, and a canteen full of Kool-Aid. We were set for this specific mission. The driver and I started driving toward the Naval Support Activity ramp in Hue City along the Perfume River which was only a couple of kilometers away.

The Seabees had a facility there and that was the best place to look for one of these 'four-hole' contraptions. Along the way, they stopped for a smoke and fired off a few rounds from their weapons just for the hell of it. As Carey recollects, "Not sure why we fired the weapons but we did. You know how young Marines are!

"We then made our way to the Seabee complex and began looking around for an outhouse. I am still surprised to this day that no one questioned our presence there. I was trying to look official and businesslike. You know, like we belonged there doing what we were doing. I was inspecting each piece of equipment like we were interested in its utility. We walked and walked, not finding a single outhouse for the longest time. We could not find even a two-hole outhouse for the life of us, and I was dreading going back empty-handed. There would be hell to pay if I failed this mission.

"Finally, after a lot of panic, we did come across an outhouse, but it was a 'six-hole' structure and could not be lifted by me, a brevetted Lieutenant, no less, and my PFC driver. It was a heavy 'mofo.' What to do? Down the road there just happened to be a Seabee working on a front-loader. I walked down to where he was working and signaled for him to stop, waving him down that I wanted to ask him a question. He shut the loader down and climbed down to talk. I told him that I had orders to pick up the 'six-hole' structure, pointing to it and told him the person we were to meet hadn't shown up, could he please help us load it onto our six-by. 'Yes, Sir,' he exclaimed, 'Right away.' He quickly loaded it on the back of the truck. I thanked him, he saluted me, I crisply returned the salute and off we went back to our CP, mission accomplished.

"That was my only experience as a United States Marine Corps officer. I immediately became wildly popular when we returned with that 'six-hole' crapper. Lieutenant-Corporal Doug Carey, imagine that! Word of deeds like this traveled rather fast. I am still amazed to this day about that phenomenon. I returned the pistol and cover to my lieutenant and he had a good hearty laugh over the whole matter. I then went back to being a more popular corporal in my platoon again. I always wondered why they called me the Wildman."

Finding a Water Supply

PFC Dane Brown, a flame-thrower Marine in H&S Company weapons section, remembers those first days after arriving at the La Son Schoolhouse. His then-platoon commander, Lieutenant Ralph Pineda, had been assigned the task of finding a water supply point where the battalion headquarters group could fill up their "water buffaloes" (a water tank on wheels pulled behind a vehicle). Brown recalls that their patrol that day included Lieutenant Pineda, their Platoon Commander, Corporal Michael McDade, Sergeant Roger Keune, a machine gunner, and himself. Brown did not remember if they knew where the water supply was located or if they were just going out to scout for a water supply point or whether they were going to escort a water buffalo filled with water back to the CP. They started walking west from the schoolhouse on Communal Road 552 toward the Perfume River, and then headed south where water canals fed to the east off the river, to the lowland areas of the coastal rice paddies.

As Brown remembers, "I wasn't carrying my flame tank that day...I had my M16 and it was hot, really hot. We walked the road beside the river for a long time, I don't recall how long. You could see Hue City on the other side. We finally came upon a village on the east side of the river that had a small canal winding eastward. The canal had large berms on both sides. We could see the entire village on the other side of the canal. Before we reached the canal, we began taking small arms fire from within the village. Moving off the roadway and onto the berm on our side of the canal, we all began returning fire into the village."

Lieutenant Pineda had a radio. A short distance away, Brown noticed him glued to the PRC-25 handset. The firefight was still going on between the Marines and enemy combatants in the village. After what seemed like a long, heated discussion the lieutenant was having on the tactical net, Brown recalled Pineda yelling at them. "He yelled out to...'Hit the deck, we have F4s coming in close.' We all heard the jets overhead. I laid on my back and looked skyward. I remember there were two of them. I don't remember if one made a 20mm cannon run first or not but I distinctly remember watching one of the Phantoms diving down toward us releasing a napalm canister... I was watching this barrel hurtling toward us, end over end, which seemed like it tumbled in slow motion. I thought for sure it was going to come right down on our position. I am saying to myself, 'Oh my God, no!' Much to my relief it sailed right over us...and impacted over in the village. Suddenly a sunny day lit up into the brightest orange and most brilliant white I have ever seen. The heat was intense, and the concussion even more horrendous, sucking the breath out of all of us."

The pilot made one napalm run. Everything in the village afterward was still burning. The Marines never crossed the canal and went into the village to assess the damage or look for KIAs. They waited against the berm for the burning to subside. Brown recalls, "No one fired at us...we stayed for what seemed like a long time. The next thing I know we got up and humped back to the schoolhouse CP...I have no idea if a water supply point was found later or not."

Operation No Name #1

Commencing the first part of April 1968, the rifle companies (in separate locations from the HQ CP) began patrol activities from their operating bases to gain familiarity with the surrounding environment; Company A (YD781249), Company B (YD808187), Company C (YD843322), and Company D (YD791271). The terrain was mostly flat with extensive rice fields—a coastal agricultural area inhabited by a few populated villages interconnected with walking paths and surrounded by thick hedgerows. This area interlinked with the main river, as well as streams and freshwater canals of two- to twelve-feet deep. Flowing water presented ongoing hazards to the patrolling Marines and Corpsmen.

The first operation of April, Operation Order 1-68 (No Name #1), ordered a search and destroy maneuver using two rifle companies and three platoons of Vietnamese Provisional Forces (VPFs): the 64th, 65th, and 118th Popular Forces (PFs). It consisted of Bravo and Charlie Companies, supported with elements from H&S Company, along with a platoon from the Anti-Tank Battalion (Ontos), elements of 1st Engineer Battalion, and the swift boats from the U. S. Navy's 12th Coastal Group Junk Fleet. External support available were two helicopter gunships and a C-47 flare ship on station, along with the local artillery battery in Phu Bai standing by on call. It was standard for an operation with only a few companies and a minimum of support involved to be recorded as a "No Name" operation in the Command Chronologies. Operations with other support elements and multiple maneuver battalions involved would usually have a meaningful name attached, i.e., Operations "Mameluke Thrust" and "Allen Brook." The area of operation: grid coordinates, YD845320 southeast along the northern coast to YD962236; then southwest to YD948217 and finally northwest along the southern coast to YD845318.[5]

Separately, Delta Company began a sweep near Thon Truyen Nam (grid YD814264) to the northeast of the Battalion CP in their own tactical area on 6 April. During this maneuver, three Marines received wounds. Corporal Pat Rider recalls approaching a tree line and taking sniper fire. "Positioned close to Sergeant Clyde Roy, I saw him take a round right through the calf of his leg. It was a clean wound. When I reached him I immediately tore his pant leg off and attempted to stop the bleeding. He bled bad all over everything, and finally I applied the right pressure which stopped the bleeding. Our Corpsman caught up to us and finished administering first aid to him."

Commencing the next day, 7 April at 0740 hours, Company B was airlifted to a blocking position at dawn. Patrol boats began to reconnoiter the southern portion of waterways and Company C, alongside the Provisional Force platoons, began to sweep to the southeast, conducting detailed search and clear activities. This was all to happen simultaneously while moving toward the blocking force. All tunnel complexes found in this area of operation were quickly destroyed. This first Operation, No Name #1, sent the first signal of intent to the dug-in combatants in this contested area. The Marines of 1/27 were ready to make contact.

Lance Corporal Donald Moorehead, Charlie Company, recalls the area his platoon was assigned. "We swept the peninsula one way and as we were coming back through the area we had walked through...and we were 'ditty-bopping' along, I became kind of worried because we were going into a tree line. The gooks would always wait until we got close in and then hit us. I remember when we finally made contact. The C. O. called for artillery and they couldn't help us for some reason. He kept calling for help and told the higher ups that we needed something...they sent tanks but it was a little late when they got there. We finally rushed the tree-line and there was not an NVA anywhere. They had left, 'di-di maued'... They had tunnels everywhere."

Doc William Carroll remembers the area on the coast. He recalled, "It was mostly a blur to me; however, I do remember a lot of concertina wire in the sand with a lot of boats coming and going. One of the first Marines I treated, Corporal Martin Garcia. We were close friends beginning in Hawaii. He had told me on the boat coming over, 'Doc, I have already been there once, follow me, do what I do and you'll be safe.' He became my first casualty in this new area we were patrolling...took a round in the thigh, a through wound. I had never taken care of anything that complicated except for bumps and scrapes. Up to that time, I had never had to worry about anyone or what I was doing. And, of course, it had to be my buddy, Martin."

Corporal Garcia was medically evacuated and did come back to the company later. Doc Carroll remembers when he did and him saying, "Doc, I have been hit; stay close to me again." Doc recollects that he gets dinged again a second time, up in the shoulder or chest area. "I remembered treating him again and saying, 'Yeah, I am supposed to stay next to you, right?' I was pretty pissed at him at the time...He is supposed to be watching over my ass and here I am patching him up again." Corporal Garcia did not return, and was a permanent medical evacuee this time.

"Snapping In"

During the intensive Battalion deployment in the Hue-Phu Bai TAOR, 3rd Platoon of Bravo Company aka, "Bravo 3," led by 2nd Lieutenant Robert J. O'Rourke, had the unique assignment of operating often independently from the rest of the unit. His platoon went on a variety of missions with their own main body of Company B, and additionally functioned as an attached platoon to Company A and D in the coming months.

Operating from Hill 78 (grid coordinate YD808187) close by National Highway 1, and from the bridge on Highway 1 (grid coordinate YD838176), his Marines and Corpsmen participated in Operation No Name #1 and #4. Most days, 3rd Platoon was running daily and nightly patrols from those Platoon Patrol Bases (PPBs). They later established and operated out of another PPB along the canal (grid coordinate YD787228) that meandered to the east of Hue city and which would become the scene of the bloody 13 April battle called Operation No Name #2.

O'Rourke recalls, "Each of the areas we operated from presented quite different tactical challenges with the platoon making contact with the enemy in each locale.

These areas were a 'baptism of fire' for my platoon, although every Squad Leader and most of the Fire Team Leaders were combat veterans from previous tours of Vietnam."

Lieutenant O'Rourke's PPBs at Hill 78 and the bridge were highly populated areas and heavily infiltrated by enemy, due to the fact both were located near the main artery of traffic going both north and south on National Highway 1. He recollects, "On Hill 78, children were frequently used as aiming stakes for mortar attacks on our positions. Nightly probes of our positions were routine. At the bridge, the village homes were within twenty meters of our defensive positions. Enemy soldiers swam within 100 meters of our position on the bridge, reconnoitering. We were lucky to obtain local intelligence from a Marine Gunnery Sergeant. He worked in the radio communications compound 200 meters from our bridge position. We were also privy to meeting with the local CAP unit and PFs supporting the locals in the area.

2nd Lieutenant Robert O'Rourke, 3rd Platoon, B Co ~ Courtesy of Ronald G. Oakes, B Co, 1/27

A Night Ambush Patrol

The Marines of 3rd Platoon carried out nightly ambush patrols from the bridge PPB. One very dark evening, a patrol set out to set up the ambush. Shortly after it had left, the remaining Marines at the PPB heard a sudden exchange of semi and automatic weapon fire which lasted thirty to forty-five seconds. The firing had come from the direction in which the ambush patrol had headed. O'Rourke describes that "After a minute of silence, the Squad Leader from the ambush patrol radioed in a soft and calm voice that they had engaged several figures moving through a path in front of them in the village."

The next day, the Marine Gunny and a PF from the radio compound came by the bridge and informed 3rd Platoon that the ambush squad had killed an enemy soldier. Lieutenant O'Rourke hastily put together a squad and had the Gunny and PF guide the squad to the location. Finding blood trails, they began following drag signs and blood and finally came upon a pagoda. Approaching it very carefully in individual rushes while mutually covering each other, they burst into a cemetery area where a small group of mourners was burying a body wrapped in fabric. Stopping and standing for a short while to show respect for the deceased and the mourners, they then headed back to the bridge with an idea of what had happened. O'Rourke recalls being briefed later that day by the Gunny's local people that "The enemy would be waiting to ambush us that night...therefore we did not send a patrol in that direction that evening or for several more nights."

7 April Attack on the CP

While early that morning, Operation No Name #1 kicked off with elements of Bravo and Charlie Company, in the early afternoon, enemy 82mm mortar rounds crashed into the Battalion CP perimeter, bringing death and destruction to the command element of 1st Battalion. This mortar barrage wore heavily on the Marines' nerves and their inability to immediately strike back. It was the first assault on the CP while 1/27 was there. The 81mm mortar section at the schoolhouse responded with Harassment and Interdiction fire (H&I) to the suspected area of origination. A search of the Thon Chiet Bi Village found no trace of the mortar team or traces of a firing area. The enemy was again elusive which frustrated the Marines, especially the second-tour Marines.

Lance Corporal Joe Roysdon remembers taking replacement radios and batteries out to the Col Co tank farm on the coast. The Col Co facility housed all the JP4 and JP5 fuel tank storage for the fuel being shipped up the coast from Da Nang. Charlie Company was providing security for that very strategic position. Roysdon tells about the return trip aboard an H-34 helicopter, "We had taken some radio equipment and batteries out to the tank farm and were returning to the CP area…we were trying to land on the east side of the schoolhouse and were waved off because they were under mortar attack…we circled for a while until we got the all-clear to land. Boy, talk about confusion when we finally landed."

The mortar barrage directed at the schoolhouse CP killed one Marine, the ever-popular Corporal Daniel Clevenger in the Communications section, and wounded eleven others. This was a heavy price to pay early in the game. The Marines were just getting acclimated to this strange new area. By the end of this ominous day, the operation in the southeastern sector of the TAOR had netted ninety-six detainees who would be intensely questioned. This was going to be a hard-fought campaign.

The Launch of Operation No Name #2

Prior to launching the second operation, a summary of the local enemy situation was made available by Task Force X-Ray command. Elements of the 804th Main Force Battalion were believed to be near Thon Zhan Hoa (grid coordinate YD787237) and two companies of local force guerrillas near Thon Cong Luong (grid coordinate YD800245).

From prior reports, the mission of these units appeared to be maintaining an influence over the local population and provide a screening force in the area. The 804th Main Force Battalion was estimated to be approximately 60 percent NVA. The overall strength was estimated at 250 to 300 personnel, maybe more. The summary report determined the Main Force Battalion was armed with 82mm mortars, 60mm mortars, 57mm recoilless rifles, B40 rockets, and anti-aircraft guns as well as ample small arms and ammunition.

This unit was purported to be very determined on the battlefield. Intel revealed that if contact was made, friendly forces could expect an unyielding fight, especially during the harvest season which fortified their food supply. The area along the canal south of Communal Road 552 was heavily entrenched with trench lines, bunkers, and fighting holes. In past ventures, attempts to cross the canals were met with heavy resistance. These combatants were known to have been reinforced by a local force north of Route 552. This was only a short distance. Three attempts by ARVN and U.S. Army units after Tet had been made and all were repulsed with moderate to heavy casualties.[6]

Operation No Name #2 was launched on 12 April. Two rifle companies began an eastward push, one on each side of the irrigation canal stretching eastward towards the ocean in the coastal rice fields of Phu Vang district. The line of departure began at YD786235. Delta Company took the north side of the canal and Alpha the south side. One platoon from Company C joined Alpha Company. The planned search-and-clear maneuver was to sweep the villages and hamlets close into the canal on both sides. Most areas away from the populated areas along the canal to the north and south were open rice fields. The original Operation Order 2-68 called for 3rd Battalion, 3rd Regiment, of the 1st ARVN Division to provide the blocking action at "Phase Line Brown" (grid coordinate YD836235). Due to unforeseen circumstances, Company B (Captain Ronald Allen, Commanding) assumed the blocking mission in the place of the ARVNs who had other operational commitments. Company B was to be the "anvil."

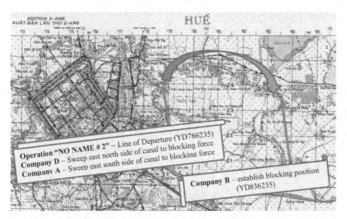

Operation No Name #2 began 12 April, Line of Departure YD786235
~ clip art courtesy of Corporal Grady Birdsong, H&S Co, 1/27

Bravo Company Encounters Heavy Resistance

As the operation proceeded, air units screened from above to deny enemy forces exiting from the sweep area, although the cloud cover that day prevented a lot of the overhead observation. At 0821 on 13 April, Bravo Company, near grid position YD833238, walked into heavy automatic, small arms, RPG, and mortar fire originating from an area northeast of their advance. As Corporal Michael Weymouth remembers, "I was Bravo Company Commander, Captain Allen's radioman. I will never forget that as we began crossing the open rice paddies heading for the village, he remarked to me, and this is a quote, 'Geez Weymouth, I am surprised we haven't been hit yet...' I responded something to the effect of what do you mean? He responded back that this was serious enemy territory we were going into, and that he was a little surprised that they had not opened fire on us. Of course, my thoughts were why we don't back up a few hundred yards and bomb the shit out of the village? The rest is history…we got all the way into the ville, found empty trenches, and that was when all hell broke loose. Dead and wounded in the open, surrounded on three sides, and we are in deep trouble. While I think Captain Allen was only thinking out loud or looking for reassurance on the decision he had already made, I still remember him asking me if I thought we should try to get out or stay and fight. I replied something like, 'We have dead out there and can't leave them.' We had no choice in the matter at this point because we were surrounded." Corporal Weymouth was seriously wounded in the volleys of fire from entrenched enemy positions, and later medically evacuated.

Dug into their trenches and bunkers, the NVA unit had been waiting for the Marines. The Marines had walked into an NVA pre-planned field of fire. Captain Allen quickly engaged the company and attempted to close with the enemy, and soon began receiving heavy volumes of fire from all directions. Marines were down everywhere. The entire Company became pinned down and unable to move.

Captain Allen began calling for "arty" support. Company A and D were monitoring the tactical net and pushed hard eastward, attempting to come to the aid of Company B. It wasn't long before Alpha point elements ran into a heavy fusillade of small arms fire themselves. Stopping briefly to call in artillery, they continued to push eastward toward Bravo's position. Company D on the north side of the canal began encountering mines and booby traps near YD820244 around 0900, which greatly slowed their movement toward the skirmish lines of Bravo Company.

All this time the KIA and WIA casualties were mounting within the rifle companies, especially in Bravo Company. Around 0950, Alpha Company started receiving excessive automatic weapon fire with small arms and rockets, resulting in a KIA and nine WIAs at YD822239. They also had become momentarily pinned and not able to continue moving toward Bravo's position. Artillery was again called in on the enemy positions. Alpha was still denied movement. At around 1130 Delta Company met up with Alpha at YD822241 where both companies were still taking heavy fire and trying to regain their original momentum. The artillery missions continued while the Marines regrouped with Bravo still surrounded.

A Change of Plan

On the 11th it was learned that the ARVN would not perform the blocking maneuver. They had a previous commitment. Captain Allen was assigned the task of sending part of his Company into the area. Per Allen, his main purpose was to maneuver his men into position and perform a blocking action for the other companies pressing toward him. Allen recalls, "Actually my main purpose in going along was that I really liked Lieutenant Alan Kettner who commanded the second platoon, and I wanted to be up there so I could see him perform more than anything else…and be a part of the command structure. That was my original intent."

The move was made early in the morning by deuce-and-a-half trucks in a non-tactical fashion. The Marines disembarked on a flat plain of rice paddies and then moved across those areas toward the canal area which had a bit of vegetation around it. Captain Allen remembers, "You drive up in a bunch of trucks and then proceed across rice paddies for several hundred yards, the entire world knows you are there…when we hit that vegetation in the village area that is when all hell broke loose. Lieutenant Kettner did a terrific job of keeping things organized and progressing. He went as far as he could which wasn't very far due to the casualties he was starting to take."

On the first day of the operation the morning began with severely overcast clouds, so almost nothing would fly. The intelligence passed to Captain Allen had indicated that there was the possibility of the enemy in this area, but nothing firm. There had been three attempts earlier in the year to enter this region, and the Army units and ARVN Battalions were repulsed with medium to extremely heavy casualties during those times. Captain Allen stated, "I knew that we could anticipate some sort of enemy force in the area. We had no idea as to the size of their force…or weaponry or what to expect. It was in no way a tactical surprise the way we approached it. We were at a disadvantage due to no air support due to the severe cloud cover. This also inhibited another important ability, that of evacuating casualties. Day one, no way any helicopters were going to fly and obviously, some of our guys would not have died had we been able to get them out of there with medical evacuation."

Ambush

To the best of his memory, Captain Allen is quite sure that he got hit by something like a rocket launcher; a direct-fire type of weapon. What hit his command group came from the enemy area right across the deepest part of the canal, which they were facing. The canal was not that deep but the banks were steep and not easy to climb. His men were not going to advance any further across those pre-determined fields of fire.

The last thing Captain Allen remembered, "I attempted to speak to Lieutenant Kettner. His platoon was off to the left of my group. This was the hardest thing for me and is stamped in my mind forever! When I called him his radio operator told me that he had been killed. I could tell his radioman was extremely upset…scared, so I began talking him through things and got him settled down…I will never forget that…and how I hated losing Kettner…it still haunts me."

Most of Kettner's platoon was surrounded and the surviving members were trying desperately to hold their positions. Ammo was in short supply and had to be consolidated and redistributed.

Captain Allen reflects, "Hindsight is always twenty-twenty and I will say that this was an ill-conceived operation given the circumstances of weather and the urgency to do this…these people were not going to run away and they had been successful before in defending this area. Had we had close air support it would have been an entirely different situation [which came later after he was wounded]. The terrain lent itself to napalm drops and strafing with 20mm. There was no doubt some heavy weaponry in that enclave and they were extremely well entrenched and waiting in ready."

Allen reminisces about being wounded, "I do not remember much after I got taken out. I did not wake up until the tracked vehicle came to our position. I had some consciousness when they were putting me aboard. I vaguely remember getting to the hospital but was out for the first couple of days after arriving." After being wounded, Captain Allen turned his command over to a trusted staff sergeant who had been in the thick of the fight and whom he considered worthy of leading his remaining Marines.

A Corpsman Remembers

One of Bravo's Corpsmen, HM2 Bob Taugner, in trace, following Captain Allen, distinctly remembered the day. He indicated that all the Marines in his platoon were on-line heading toward a village. He remembered, "...catching a glimpse out of the corner of my eye of four enemy combatants with dark uniforms and hats coming out of a building. They all came out at once, stopped and stared at us for what seemed like a long time but only milliseconds. I opened up on them. That was the start of the fight as I remember. Small arms firing broke out all over the area."

First Platoon quickly moved forward in a right-oblique maneuver. The Second Platoon did the same. The attached 60mm mortar crew and Taugner, left in-between both platoons, moved toward the canal looking right and left for a bridge. There was no bridge. Directly across the canal was an opening in the tree line. Taugner recalls, "We were all standing there talking about what was going on and out of nowhere appear four NVA walking across the opening. They were looking at us and we at them but no shots exchanged. It all happened so fast. The next thing happening were sounds in the distance, a 'bloop, bloop, bloop,' sound. I am standing there like a dumb shit. I am a new guy to Vietnam and the 60 mortar guys began hitting the deck. Before I could move, a couple of rounds hit nearby and blew me asshole over tea kettle. I thought I was OK after the attack stopped. We were laughing about it and how I hadn't moved quick enough. Later to my dismay, I found that I had taken a piece of shrapnel in my back. My pride and joy pack board given to me by an Army dude had a lot of unnecessary shit in it. It was all that unnecessary stuff, my field jacket, soft cover, poncho and socks which probably saved my life. My adrenaline was racing and I hadn't noticed until someone told me I was bleeding."

A runner from 2nd Platoon, nicknamed "Mouse," came in to where Taugner and the mortar men were. He told them that Lieutenant Kettner was dead and that the two corpsmen up front had been killed and that they needed a corpsman because there were many casualties. Taugner followed him with the mortar crew in the trace. As he remembers, "There was this one sergeant with a tube and he kept moving it...he kept peppering that village with mortar rounds...I swear they would have overrun us if it hadn't been for that Sergeant. I believe to this day that he kept the enemy down in their holes and trench lines. He was one of our unsung heroes that day. We didn't have our guns, the M60's. Lieutenant Kettner had put the two guns' side by side up front at the beginning of the maneuver...I found out later that when he was killed those machine guns were captured. The only thing we had was mortars, our M16s and one blooper [M79 Grenade Launcher]."

The Marines were not trying any offensive maneuvers and had called in Huey Gunships to make some cannon and rocket runs on the NVA in the village. Taugner remembered that didn't do any good. "The village was mostly rubble and we just kept firing whenever we had a target. A runner from another company came up to get me because I am the only Doc. Anyway, this runner's name was the 'Mouse.' I remember he was just crazy. I don't remember his name but he was of Polish descent and from Florida. He decided he wanted to find out where that .50-caliber machine gun was located. He would stand up out of the trench...stay up and look around for a while. As soon as the fifty would fire he would hit the deck on the trench floor. He would crawl down the trench line and stand up again and it would "bark" at him again. He kept doing that for a while until he found its position. He then opened up on them, the whole frigging gun crew, surprising them. I swear to God, he went toe-to-toe with them and killed them all. That gun went silent and never fired again after that. So, I don't know if the NVA gunners had any others to back them up or not. That was the end of that... The 'Mouse' was another one of our real heroes that day!"

"Mouse," HM2 Bob Taugner's buddy ~ Courtesy of Bob "Doc" Taugner, B Co, 1/27

After moving on up and coming to the trench line, Taugner and the mortar guys found some other Marines. Sergeant James May and his men were positioned along that trench. May summoned Taugner and told him there was a Marine in front of a hooch out in no man's land. He pointed out that the man was behind a mound. Next to the mound was a banana tree. Doc Taugner remembered, "May told me that guy was hit badly, to go out and take care of him while they covered me. I crawled out to him. His helmet had been knocked off him. He had been shot in the head. The poor guy was still alive. I tried to put a bandage on the wound. All I had was battle dressings and gauze. So, I put one bandage on him and it falls off. And then I put another on him and it stayed. This poor fellow was still alive and we needed to evacuate him. It was raining hard, early in the morning with heavy cloud cover. That meant no choppers and no evacuations. At about that time, I had gone from an earlier pure panic state of mind to just doing my job over the course of about an hour. I don't know how to explain it and it is not like giving up...it is not giving up. The situation we were in was inevitable and I had over that brief time just resigned myself to do my job, do what I had to do and accept what was happening. Whatever was going to be I was not going to worry about it. I just started trying to save lives...I told myself, 'Welcome to Vietnam, Doc!' "

An NVA Sniper Shoots a "Maggie's Drawers"

Everyone who has earned the title of United States Marine during the Vietnam War knows the term "Maggie's Drawers." This referred to the flag that was waved vigorously back and forth in front of the target during rifle marksmanship training at boot camp to signify a complete miss. Although the term had been used in previous wars and was a Corps-wide term for a missed shot, its origins are speculative.

Such was the circumstance when HM2 Taugner, at Sergeant James May's urging, crawled out to tend to the Marine behind the mound. Taugner still vividly recalls the way in which May was talking. "I had crawled out and gotten the Marine stabilized. May started talking to me in a muffled voice. What men do in combat conditions still baffle me. Some are loud and aggressive, and some are silent or low key. He was saying to me, calmly, almost in a whisper, 'Doc, get out of there!' He was cool and collected...and that was all he was saying. I could see him from the mound. I was puzzled, to say the least, why he was so calm? What he knew and I didn't know was there was a sniper shooting at me, the sniper who had shot the Marine I was bandaging. The sniper was in the ville on a roof which I could not see. Obviously, his aim was off because after I had dragged the wounded Marine back into the trench May later pointed out the huge banana leaf with the 'Maggie's Drawers.' That banana leaf was just inches above my head while I was out there tending to that Marine. Later walking by it I noticed that the leaf had three, maybe four bullet holes in it."

NVA Everywhere

There was a brief pause in the fighting after the initial contact. Doc Taugner and another mortar man decided to go further down the NVA-dug trench line toward where they thought Captain Allen's CP group was located. As they made their way along that narrow ditch a sniper shot at them. They had come close to a pagoda with a parapet wall. Taugner recaptured their plan to take out the sniper. "So this Marine told me, 'Doc, you go down the trench a bit and get him to shoot at you and he'll probably turn and I can see him and I can take him out.' Being a new guy, I said, 'Good plan, man.' I crouched down and started down the trench line for about twenty-five yards and started receiving rounds...so I turned and fired my M16 at the top of the wall from where the sniper was shooting from. That wall was stucco or low-grade concrete and my rounds went right through it and I saw the sniper go tumbling off that high parapet. I had not even aimed well. I was dumbfounded, so I yelled at my buddy, 'Sorry, I got him!' "

As the firefights continued sporadically, Doc Taugner continued to take care of the wounded. Regrouping, he and some others decided they needed to go out and find more downed Marines. They had tried before and had lost their "blooper" (M79) man into the canal...hit by .50-caliber fire which had spun him around and into the water. Taugner recounts that next foray. "Two Marines and I moved forward in single file. I was the last man. The NVA .50-caliber gun opened on us. The time before the big gun had fired at the last man and now again, it was zeroing in on me, the last in this group. This was one of the weirdest sensations I have ever experienced. I began spinning in a circle and my knees went numb. I was for sure that last burst of .50-caliber fire hit me. My hand started burning. I thought my hand was gone for sure. I was afraid to look. I was running as fast as I could across the opening. When I finally looked, that round had grazed the palm of my right hand and it looked like a burn mark. I still can't believe the round passing by spun me around like it did. I then found a paddy dike that protected me. I crawled over it and back to its safe side, four or five times, to look for wounded and dead Marines. I couldn't find anyone. We yelled and yelled...no one answered. Finally, we went back to the main body of Marines. I was starting to get new confidence. We had just received a bunch of the new type of grenades. The ones that looked like baseballs. I lobbed one out into the gate area in the ville. That is when we started to sense that maybe we were getting a little too far away from the main body. Talking amongst ourselves, we figured out that if we got too far out of sight we were going to get nailed. That is when we decided to go back."

As the remaining Company B Marines regrouped in their defensive positions, Doc Taugner again began the grim task of working on more wounded. One of his Marines had been shot in the face. Doc recalls the grisly situation. "He had been shot and the bullet had entered on the side of his face. It looked like the round had taken off the bottom lower jaw and half of his tongue...and most of his teeth in that area of his jaw. I was sitting there looking at his wound and thinking to myself, 'This is one they didn't teach me in Corpsmen school.' So, I did the best I could at the time. I put a medium-size battle dressing underneath his cheek and another up on top of his head. I placed it so that his mouth was just barely open and he could breathe. Then I put another where the big hole was on the side and went on around the head with it. I did the best I could with what I had. I then put him in the trench and had him sit with his back upright because he had a head wound and much of his tongue was missing. I was afraid he would swallow what he had left of his tongue. I couldn't give him any morphine. I didn't want to lose him. He was a tough one...He never grabbed me or cried out. I will never forget him."

Years later at a Battalion Reunion in Gettysburg, Pennsylvania in 2008, Sergeant Javier L. Cascos, also a Bravo Marine, told his story to Doc Taugner. Taugner asked him, "Did you ever wonder who bandaged you up that day?"

The Skies Clear

With the overhead skies clearing, a plan to evacuate the wounded began. Some of the Bravo company Marines set up a hasty defense in a dry rice paddy off the canal/village area to stage the wounded and dead and clear an LZ for the choppers. Doc Taugner remembers, "Steve Carlson, the other Corpsman with Kettner's platoon and a couple of others, had worked their way back and joined us...that is when we found out that the other Corpsman and Lieutenant Kettner were indeed dead and had been killed at the beginning of the fight. We were all talking amongst ourselves about what we were going to do if the choppers couldn't make it in to us. Anyway, from out of nowhere two F8 Crusaders come on station overhead. The one pilot, I still owe him whatever beverage he wants...We were in this circle and had given up the trench line. We were flat out in the open. We are looking up and one of them is orbiting very high. Then his partner ascends and comes in from behind us toward the village...toward the gate area where a lot of the firing was originating. I became mesmerized watching this pilot. He is coming in real slow, with his flaps down, his F8 is pouring out smoke from behind and going ever so slow...like he was going to land. Suddenly, he flips that Crusader on its side...and he is so low that we could see him waving at us...and like magic, he lights that F8 engine up and kicks in the afterburners and up he goes, straight upward into the sky. Then he goes into an inside loop maneuver and starts back down at us. As he came down toward us and almost on the deck headed for the ville, bearing in on the gook positions, he jerk/turned the plane on its side with the belly facing outward and kicked loose a canister of napalm. You could feel its concussion and heat like it was right there almost on top of our position! His wingman following behind him performed the same maneuver only exiting in the opposite direction. They then started making additional 'snake eye' bomb runs. Those F8 pilots stayed on station making more bombing runs until they had used up all their ordnance."

Alpha and Delta Companies Push Eastward

Captain Patrick Kahler, Commanding Delta Company, retraced his company's maneuvering and grim engagement on the canal. "During the day, Company D tried artillery, mortars, direct machine gun fire, LAAW fire and air support, controlled by me, on the enemy positions to the south of the canal and to our right front fewer than 200 meters. Frustrated by our lack of ability to stop the fire, Battalion sent a flame team. When we first called for mortar fire it was short and behind the Company by about 500 meters, and that irritated me. It was not the only time that the 81mm Mortar Platoon fell short. Then the flame thrower would not fire up which was probably just as well because I do not think now we could have ever gotten close enough to use it properly.

"We put a machine gun team on the top of a pagoda to put fire into the NVA trench line. That did not seem to have any effect. While all of this was going on Bravo Company was in a serious engagement to the east and had suffered many wounded, dead and missing...Captain Allen of Bravo was hit and was seriously wounded.

Lieutenant Colonel John E. Greenwood, Battalion C. O. and Captain Pat Kahler, Delta Company discuss the tactical situation ~ Courtesy of Corporal Dennis Fisher, 1st Marine Division Combat Photo and Correspondence Section

"As the day ended, the reality of not being able to prevail, having many killed, wounded, and missing Marines from the Battalion, was totally frustrating. As we went into our night defensive positions, the Provisional Reconnaissance Unit (South Vietnamese) went on a chicken hunt, which really irritated me and I threatened through an interpreter to shoot them if they did not quiet down. The night passed without incident other than a constant barrage of harassment and interdiction firing."

The area the Marines had walked into was a stronghold for the NVA and had concealed and well-fortified bunkers which could withstand direct artillery hits. Additionally, the canals off the Perfume River east of Hue adversely affected the Marines' tactical maneuvering.

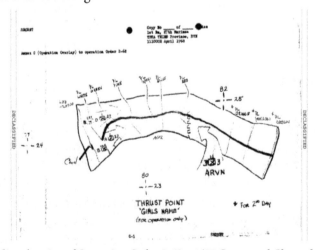

Original Battalion drawing of Operation Order 2-68 ~ 1/27 Command Chronology April 1968 (Shows original plans for ARVN unit to be the blocking force)

Then-Lieutenant Roger Charles, 3rd Platoon Commander of Alpha Company, remembers the deadly resistance that his men encountered that day. Leading the point element for Alpha Company, his Marines pushed eastward adjacent the long winding canal and were suddenly halted by intense automatic weapons and small arms firing. They had walked right into NVA pre-planned fields of fire. One of his Marines distinguished himself that 13 April. PFC Stephen J. Hinds would make the ultimate sacrifice for his fellow Marines.

Lieutenant Charles submitted an after-action report after debriefing Hind's squad mates, specifically noting Hind's bravery that day: "PFC Hinds took a position of cover and began to direct small arms fire on the enemy force which was fighting from bunkers and trench lines located across the canal from his own position. Almost immediately the leader of PFC Hinds's team was hit while attempting to gain a better position. The man was hit a second and third time...and it was apparent to PFC Hinds that emergency medical attention was required if his fellow Marine was to have any chance of survival. Without hesitation and with complete disregard for his own safety, fully recognizing the dangerousness of crossing the unsecured area to his fellow Marine, PFC Hinds ran forward reaching his fellow comrade. As he attempted to move his wounded team leader to a covered position, PFC Hinds was struck by enemy fire and killed instantly."

Lance Corporal Stephen J. Hinds was posthumously awarded the Bronze Star Medal. In part, it reads:

> *Hinds' courage, selfless concern for the welfare of his comrade and unfaltering devotion to duty were in keeping with the highest traditions of the Marine Corps and the United States Naval Service. He gallantly gave his life in the service of his country.*
> *The Combat "V" is authorized.*
> H.W. BUSE, JR.
> LIEUTENANT GENERAL USMC
> COMMANDING, FLEET MARINE FORCE, PACIFIC

By 1400 that afternoon, Bravo had lost its beloved Company Commander, Captain Ronald Allen, to severe wounds and the company had become fragmented into three positions. Two of those elements were on the south side of the canal and the other on the north near YD832239. The Battalion Commander, Lieutenant Colonel Greenwood, ordered an additional platoon from Delta Company and one from Charlie nearby to reinforce the Ontos Platoon and assist in relieving Company B. Research gathered from the Command Chronologies on 1st Tank Battalion, 3rd Platoon (Antitank) reveals that this AT Platoon quickly moved into position and began supporting the engaged Marines. They were credited with seven NVA KIAs during this engagement and in keeping the combatant NVA pinned to their positions.

Early that morning Executive Officer, First Lieutenant John Bouldin, a "Mustang officer," and First Sergeant Ronald Burtsell, following Alpha Company's Commanding

Officer, Captain James Panther, pushed eastward along the south side of the meandering canal. Approaching what appeared to be a schoolhouse around grid YD807246, Bouldin commented to Burtsell, "I don't like this one bit." On his second tour of Vietnam, he remembered that, "everything seemed deadly still. Nothing moved, no villagers, no chickens moving around…complete silence. There was something wrong here…I again spoke to 'Top' Burtsell and said, 'Let's get down and in that hole'…so we jumped into a deep depression along the path. Within seconds all hell broke loose. A hellacious firefight commenced ahead and you could hear it was close and intense.

Staff Sergeant John Bouldin on the first tour in Chu Lai, 1965
~ Courtesy of 1st Lieutenant John F. Bouldin, A Co, 1/27

"I remember jumping up and beating feet forward to join Captain Panther already inside the schoolhouse. Huddled up against the wall with his radioman he already had begun to gain control of the situation. I knew from experience that he had his hands full. This was his second tour of Vietnam and when you analyze what was happening, and the complexity of this situation we had a big tiger by the tail. One of the reports that came in immediately after things 'hit the fan' was that lead Platoon Commander Lieutenant Roger Charles had been hit and was down. That turned out not true. Roger engaged his men and was in full control."

Later as the situation intensified, Captain Panther summoned Bouldin and Burtsell to select an LZ to their rear and prepare to evacuate the wounded and dead. Lieutenant Bouldin recalls, "…Exiting the doorway, cutting left, the NVA were firing at us as we ran down the path…*zzzip*…*zzzip*…*zziip*…rounds flying overhead and missing us as we ran to a tree line. The NVA were shooting at anything that moved. These Asians were ready and waiting for us to come to them. They had pre-planned all their fields of fire in this area. I remember making my way to the next tree line and there on the other side, a square-like opening which looked like it would suffice, was our evacuation LZ. We immediately began to secure this ground to stage and accept wounded and dead Marines."

As the day progressed, "A Lance Corporal whose name I never came to know bravely stood in the middle of that landing zone controlling all helicopters coming in and out of it," Bouldin recounted. "It took a lot of skill both on his part and the pilots. That open space was tight and when they lifted off it had to be in such a manner as to fly backward instead of forward…flying forward would have put the aircraft over NVA gunners. Tedious work for my Marines but we managed to get the wounded out and to further medical care. We finally got the dead out the next day."

Bouldin knew Sergeant Fred Hayes, an S2 Scout in the reconnaissance platoon, from their Hawaii days. Hayes shuttled between Alpha and Delta Companies that morning assisting in any way he could. Hayes had earned the Chief Battalion Scout billet upon arrival in Vietnam. Lieutenant Bouldin recalled meeting Fred on the trail that morning and having a short conversation about what was going on up ahead, "He told me that he was going to move forward and join up with Delta and do what he could do in extracting some of Bravo's wounded…I briefed him with what I knew and remember telling him to keep his head down and that there was big trouble up there… He was one of those Marines you could always count on…sadly, that was the last time I saw him."

Bouldin often reminisces, "I am still amazed after all these years in observing our Company Commander, Jim Panther, on that fateful day. He quickly stabilized the company and its positions, immediately started working with the Battalion CP in obtaining air support and then coordinating what I thought to be a 'Danger Close' airstrike. Its impact close by and on target. He then arranged extraction for our wounded and dead. This man knew well what to do! I am still of the opinion that someone higher up should have recognized his leadership further exemplified by his actions under fire that day. I still believe he deserves praise above and beyond recognition for his conduct on that day!"

The PRU Incident

As the battle progressed and their eastward push continued, First Lieutenant Bouldin recollected that they were accompanied by a local Provincial Reconnaissance Unit (PRU) contingent. These local teams typically numbered fifteen to twenty men, with the purpose of eliminating the local Viet Cong and its infrastructure. Often these units were comprised of former VC (Hoi Chanh, the soldiers who rallied to the South under the Chieu Hoi amnesty program), or men looking for revenge, and were sometimes accused of atrocities. The PRU Program in South Vietnam was funded, administered, and supported by the CIA. Overall, the teams operated in forty-four provinces throughout South Vietnam and typically worked in their own local area. In most cases the local province Chief controlled their activities.

As Alpha maneuvered eastward they began taking sniper rounds. A squad of Marines, dispatched to find and silence the sniper, soon came back with the suspect. Lieutenant Bouldin recalls, "My Marines found the sniper, she was a young, attractive-looking eighteen-year-old Vietnamese brandishing a Russian SKS rifle. She kept squealing, 'Me, no VC…me, no VC.' I thought to myself, what in the hell are you doing with that Russian SKS rifle? Afterward, I turned my focus to other matters and wasn't paying too much attention while the handful of PRUs who were tagging along took her to interrogate over by the canal. When I happened to glance over their way, they had her on the slope of the canal bank. They were beating on her…with her legs spread apart, they were hitting close to her pelvic area. One of them poured water down her throat from his helmet. Another one of them little bastards had a bamboo stick pounding on her chest. I ran over there and slung the one PRU off her throwing him almost into the canal…steaming mad, I yelled at them to 'Knock it to hell off'…I then took that girl and escorted her to my Marines and had her evacuated back to our S-2 at the schoolhouse CP for our own interrogators to handle. I could not believe this happened. They were not going to hurt that girl, not on my watch, even if she was the enemy!"

Delta Company Marines L-R Bottom (kneeling): Jerolaman, Harrison; L-R Middle:
Flemming, Mahsetky, unknown, Buccola; L-R Top: Bronson, Rider, unknown, Sweet
~ Courtesy of HM2 David "Doc" Bronson, D Co, 1/27

Delta Company Engages the Enemy

HM2 David "Doc" Bronson of Delta Company, along with Chief Scout Sergeant Fred Hayes and another scout, volunteered to go forward to assist wounded Marines lying in the open. To reach the skirmish line they had to cross the canal. Sergeant David Harrison, Doc's squad leader, maneuvered his men into covering positions overlooking the canal and an open area and began laying down a base of fire as they began to move toward the wounded. Doc Bronson vividly remembers, "Staff Sergeant Hayes and the other scout had to ford the canal and then make their way forward across an unsecured area to the skirmish line. They were ahead of me and had moved much faster. As I followed them at this strangest of times I remembered that I had volunteered to do this. Additionally, remembering that I used to run well as a youngster. I had run away from my younger brother a lot when we played…I would run and would laugh my butt off because my brother could barely catch me and he was faster than I was most of the time. When you have a brother that is three inches taller, fourteen months younger and he is going to kick your Alpha Sierra Sierra…you learn how to run faster. Why then I had thought of this strikes me as strange now…

"I specifically remember that my squad mate, Patrick Rider, one of the better rifle shots in the squad, was covering my movement across the field. That thought comforted me that he was covering for us. As I began to move I could clearly hear the enemy rounds, *zip...zip...zip* flying all around me. I had kept my M16 on this op and I also had my .45 automatic service pistol. I tried to hold them in the air above my head as I waded across the canal. It was up to my waist. This was extremely difficult because I also had my B-1 bag with extra bandages along with my cigarettes which I was also frantically trying to keep dry."

Once Bronson was up to the bank and out of the canal he began to run like he had never run before. "That field had to be, oh gosh, probably two hundred yards across... I ran across it zigzagging for all I was worth. Anyway, just before I reached the wire at the far edge of the field it felt as if I had tripped over my feet. It felt as if they were trying to outrun my upper body...unbeknownst to me I had been hit by a bullet which had hit the metal cup holder and canteen on my web gear. I didn't know it at the time but that round hitting my canteen had spun me around and caused me to orbit asshole over elbows. I must have lost the canteen then. I don't remember how...reason I know is that later when I reached for it to use the water for wetting bandages...one of the wounded Marines had a lot of damage to his scalp...when I grasped for that canteen it wasn't there... and I said...ahhhhh...but luckily my other canteen had a small amount left in it...so I could pour some water over the bandage and cover the man's open wound."

Doc Bronson began treating some of the other Marines at this point. He recalls, "I think we had arrived at an old schoolhouse. We were again pinned down there for a short while. I finally went down through this hole in a wall and climbed down into a kind of yard like area...and some others were yelling, 'Get down Doc...stay down...' they kept yelling for me to hit the deck and stay put. Later, I came upon one of the Bravo Company Corpsmen. He was badly hit in the leg. He told me not to worry about him. He did have an extremely bad injury...we got him pulled out of the line of fire and bandaged. It was then I learned that Sergeant Hayes had been hit [posthumously awarded the Silver Star for his actions on this day]. He was out in the open doing my job...he was bandaging people up and was continuing to move people back out of the fields of fire and he got hit. And then I am out there and I am trying to treat the ones that I could get to...and believe me, there are a lot of them down."

Leading by Example

Sergeant Fred J. Hayes, the Chief Battalion Scout, linked up to Company D after tagging along with Alpha Company. His exemplary story of leadership and bravery can be gleaned from his Silver Star citation. On 13 April 1968, he volunteered to lead a rescue team across a fire-swept open area to retrieve wounded casualties. He received a posthumous Silver Star for his actions. The citation reads in part:

From his company's position overlooking the canal, Sergeant Hayes observed several wounded Marines lying in the open terrain and unhesitatingly volun-teered...Carefully selecting an approach route, he crossed the canal and, providing cover fire for his companions, continued to advance until he reached the wounded Marines. Repeatedly exposing himself to heavy enemy fire, Sergeant Hayes rendered first aid, directed activities of his companions and assisted in moving the casualties to covered positions. While aiding a wounded Marine, he himself was seriously wounded by enemy fire. Despite his serious injury, Sergeant Hayes continued to render medical aid until he succumbed to his wound...By his extraordinary courage, bold initiative and selfless devotion to duty, Sergeant Hayes upheld the highest traditions of the Marine Corps and of the United States Naval Service. He gallantly gave his life in the service of his country. ~ signed by Paul R. Ignatius, Secretary of the Navy

Corporal David Harrison of Delta Company tells surviving Marines now that Hayes, Bronson, and the others volunteered and did not have to go into what he called, "a definite suicide attempt to retrieve those downed Marines." He recollects that the firing was extremely heavy and precise. To this day, Harrison doesn't know how anyone made it through the horrendous ordeal in those fields of fire.

Corporal Larry Ackerman, an RTO and brevetted Forward Air Controller with Bravo Company at the time, remembered this day as his most intense day of combat. "We were engaged in an all-day struggle. A low cloud cover didn't allow us to use air support so I was not staying close to Captain Allen. We had multiple casualties and I remember attempts to retrieve wounded across the canal that were not successful. Things got so bad, Captain Allen had to call in artillery very close and he was badly injured. We thought he was dead. We soon lost effective command and became separated without any functioning officers or command NCOs.

"Eventually, I ended up with a group of injured and disorganized Marines who were out of ammo. At the time, I thought I was the only person with a working radio so I called the Battalion CO and asked for an emergency evacuation. Later I found out someone else had also called in, reenforcing our predicament. We were granted the evacuation which I directed in a minimally secure opening which we found behind the skirmish line. I remember there was one, maybe two, CH-46s that came into the LZ which I hastily selected but we had more wounded than were supposed to be evacuated and I remember thinking a few of us would be left at the LZ. The pilot decided to risk it and took us all despite the weight limitation. We were flown to the Battalion CP at the La Son School. When we landed, we got the wounded to help unload and I soon found myself being debriefed by an officer there at headquarters. I was expecting a reprimand for not following the chain of command and communications protocol but it didn't happen... much to my surprise, I later received a decoration for taking charge."

Captain Jim Panther, Alpha Company Commander, recalls that they did get an intelligence briefing but that it did not measure up to the size of the enemy and how well entrenched they were. He recollects, "They were not that far from our base... we had been sending out daily squad and platoon patrols while having almost daily contact even though it was small scale in comparison to what we encountered on 12 April.

"I do not know if we had been briefed accurately on the resistance we encountered, we would have approached the objective differently. Rather than an abreast sweep along the canal we perhaps could have leapfrogged the two lead platoons so that each could provide a base of fire in support of the other platoon…we lost communication with my one platoon and that was more than worrying!"

Laying Down Covering Fire

Corporal David Harrison, Delta Company Squad Leader, vividly remembers the day, and approaching the densely forested village when all hell broke loose. He recalled losing sight of the unit elements on his right side as his squad came upon a deep ravine (canal). "It was deep, maybe ten feet in depth. It separated my guys from them. I don't remember how far the Marines on my right were but I was intensely keeping an eye on them while they were moving forward adjacent to my squad. Those Marines on my right then came upon another canal that ran laterally right to their immediate front. The only way for them to get across it was by a small bamboo bridge. And …I didn't see it right away but then realized it was the perfect place to set up an ambush. If I had to approach it with my squad, I would have 'reconned' the area around it by fire…that meant firing into the surrounding bushes and if anyone were there they would have thought they had been seen and would have immediately fired back."

As Harrison witnessed the evolving scene, the Marines who had walked up to the bridge became targets of a pre-planned ambush. The dug-in enemy combatants began shooting Marines right and left. A lot of the Bravo Marines were caught out in the open. Harrison recounts: "This was happening to the right of us and they [the enemy] were not firing at us for whatever reason. I guess they did not want to bring us into the fray. I am just lying on the ground waiting for them to fire on us. Then, Captain Kahler tells me to move my squad up and over to the ravine that separated us from those being ambushed. So, I had to stand up and move our guys which I did sort of like sweeping-the-time-on-a clock-hand movement."

Harrison initially thought that Captain Kahler was going to send them across the ravine to kill the NVA that were killing the Marines but then made it clear that he wanted Harrison's squad to cover Sergeant Hayes, Doc Bronson, and the other volunteers going across to help the downed Bravo Company Marines.

Corporal Harrison had his squad members move quickly into position and start firing on the enemy combatants providing as much fire coverage as they could muster. He recalls, "I could see one machine gun firing…I could see the muzzle flashes coming out of the vegetation so I kept firing my M79 'blooper' into his position. I probably fired eight or ten rounds. So, I either hit him or he left. And then they all in unison quit firing."

Corporal Pat Rider recounts the events of the day as Delta Company pushed along the canal before making contact with a dug-in enemy. Rider can still recall, "After stopping, I was on the edge of that canal within hand grenade range of the NVA, throwing those new 'baseball' shaped grenades. Sergeant Arthur Smith walked around forward of our position in the open just like in a John Wayne movie…I couldn't believe him. We then began maneuvering and climbing up on some of the hut roofs looking down into NVA trench lines shooting rifle and rocket fire toward enemy machine gun emplacements. I can remember laying down covering fire for Doc Bronson and Hayes as they ran across the canal out into open ground to recover some of our wounded. Then the Phantoms and Crusaders came in close overhead. It felt as if we could touch them as they passed by…their 20mm shell casings dropping all around us like confetti. Hot and humid that day, the stench of death all around us didn't keep the mosquitoes and flies from continually stinging and biting."

Doc David Bronson reflects on the aftermath of that day's events. He remembered that nightfall was setting in and that they had a couple of Vietnamese Chieu Hois (Kit Carson Scouts) with them and "…a little fire going and were heating up some rations and we had secured our position for the night. Lieutenant O'Brien brought me aside from the Vietnamese fire and pointed out that I had two holes in my utility jacket and one hole in the canteen pouch or whatever was left of it…that is when I fully realized what we had gone through."

Then-HM3 David "Doc" Bronson with mortar round ~ Courtesy of "Doc" David E. Bronson, D Co, 1/27

Delta Company spent the night halting all movement and setting up "hasty defense" positions. The next morning Corporal Harrison's squad was ordered to move forward on the north side of the canal and recon ahead of the main body. He recalled, "It was definitely a nerve-racking situation…we moved out eastward and were to make sure there wasn't anybody to the front of us."

Gunship Fire Support Accident

After moving forward and clearing the north side of the canal, David Harrison's squad set up in a tree line waiting for further orders. Remnants of Bravo Company had again run into more gooks up ahead. Helo Gunships had been called in and were firing into the area where they had more NVA trapped.

Corporal Harrison recollects, "The gunships were flying really low, making me really nervous because they were firing rockets right over my men. I knew from my previous tour and experiences that this was not safe." He quickly got up from his position and tried to find his Platoon Commander, Lieutenant O'Brien, and his radioman to stop the rocket fire. As soon as he began moving toward O'Brien one of the gunship rockets fell short, hitting close to three of his squad members and wounding them.

Feeling guilt for not being able to stop it and becoming very angry, Harrison started motioning with his rifle barrel for the gunship to circle around and land. He remembers, "I just waved madly at them and they flew off and circled. I got so mad that I started pointing my rifle at them when they came around again. Lieutenant O'Brien yelled at me, 'Don't shoot them,'...I replied to him that I wanted them to know that I was serious and was trying to get them to back off...that my guys had been wounded." One of the helicopters finally landed so that they could medically evacuate the wounded Marines.

During the evacuation, Harrison and his Marines carried one of his wounded on a poncho to the helicopter, all the while having his finger stuck in the man's chest wound. The man had suffered a 'sucking chest' wound and was having trouble breathing. As the whoop-whoop-whoop of the chopper rotors signaled the pending liftoff, Harrison recalls frantically telling the crew chief on the chopper to put his finger in the wound so that his man could breathe.

Charlie Company Dispatched

Lance Corporal John Thompson, a grunt with Charlie Company, recalls that his platoon was ordered to provide security for the Ontos Platoon and a flame tank that had been dispatched to support the operation. "It took an entire day or a day and a half to get there, to get to them. It wasn't like we walked up there a short distance. When we got there the 'gooks' had a lot of underground things like those spider holes. We had spent the night before in one of them little schoolhouses in a ville. I think it was a school, I am not sure...I, Rick Coonfield and Chuck Self started hearing noises. We tossed a grenade in the direction of where the noises were coming from. The damn wall of that school house caved on us...I guess the concussion from the blast made it cave. Nothing happened after that. The next day we were still with the Ontos and we had a problem getting them across the canal. A small bridge was the problem. That is what was holding everything up and we had to find another route. That is what took so long to get to Bravo Company."

John tells of what he witnessed when they arrived. "We took some fire and finally got to Bravo's position and most of the dead were in really bad shape. They had walked into some bad shit. I don't know exactly what had happened but it was obvious that the enemy had some big weapons, like .50-caliber type guns and recoilless rifles. Those men had been cut to pieces. I don't think any of those Bravo Marines who survived came out of that without wounds." As they went about the grisly task of extracting the bodies, John remembers saying to one of his squad members, 'Let's take a smoke break,' …and a Marine who we thought was dead started crying. He must have been paralyzed or in shock and wasn't talking. That got to me…That stopped the smoke break and we got the corpsman to attend to him. I don't know who the Marine was… I don't even know if he made it or not…I hope he did."

Operation No Name #2 battle area ~ Courtesy of John M. Thompson, C Co, 1/27

Alpha Company Engages

Sergeant Felix Salmeron, Platoon Sergeant in Alpha Company, recaptured the action of that early morning summons. "We got word that Bravo was in a bad way and we were to move as fast as we could to reach them and help out. As we moved east, one platoon cleared the tree line and came on a tall grass area. This area was about seventy-five, maybe one hundred yards wide and a hundred yards deep. The area was all open fields with no cover. When the point of the first platoon cleared this grassy area, the enemy opened fire. They had positioned themselves directly in front and across a wide and deep canal from where we were tracking. One of the first to die was Sergeant Glennis 'Lucky' Kellams who was with the first squad of the first platoon. He was acting Platoon Sergeant. The enemy had set up a field of fire with machine gun and automatic rifle positions. Our two platoons in the lead were caught in the open. We had to hastily move back to the tree line as fast as we could…"

60mm mortar crew firing, with Lance Corporal Scott Nesbitt holding the mounting assembly
~ Courtesy of Corporal Dennis Fisher, 1st Marine Division Combat Photo, and Correspondence Section

A Changing Battlefield

Second Lieutenant Dennis Lister, the Platoon Leader of First Platoon Company C, recaptures the events of 12 and 13 April. "I had been attached to Delta and Captain Kahler on the afternoon of 11 April. Company C Headquarters and 3rd Platoon stayed on Col Co Island at the Seabee Fuel Farm/LST Ramp, which was Company Command Post. 2nd Lt. Donald Gustafson, 2nd Platoon Leader was also attached to Delta. On 12 April, Alpha and Delta Companies began moving east, pushing on the south and north side of the canal, respectively. A good bit of ground was covered on 12 April, with sporadic enemy contact. Most of the day, my 1st Platoon of Charlie, 'Charlie One,' was in company reserve. Two platoons of Delta were moving abreast through the thick villages on the north side of the canal. With no significant contact during the day that I saw, Delta set up in a company perimeter for the night in the ville adjacent to the canal. One of the platoons of Delta Company was on the canal bank and had visual contact with Alpha Company on the south bank.

"The next morning, 13 April, Captain Kahler dispatched Charlie One before first light, to the extremely large open rice-paddy area on the north flank, outside the village, the trees, and vegetation. Charlie One was to stay in visual contact with the left flank of Delta and to screen the force to the north. I discussed this for a time with Captain Kahler and headed to the north and somewhat 'ahead' of the eastward progress of Delta Company's main body. Delta was pushing and staying abreast with Alpha on the south bank, moving to squeeze the NVA forces into the 'anvil' or blocking force that Bravo was to set up that morning. Phase Line Brown was at the far eastern end of the large S-curve in the canal which was to be Bravo's blocking position [anvil] in the Op. My understanding of our mission on the flank was to ensure that the enemy had no escape into the large open rice-paddy area. I positioned the platoon over a thousand meters north and about the same distance east (or ahead of the eastward movement) of the sweeping force [hammer]."

Canal area close to Bravo Company position on Op No Name #2
~ Courtesy of Michael Weymouth, B Co, 1/27 (Photo taken in 2002)

Lieutenant Lister watched the left flank of Delta as a Marine visibly anchored the company on the edge of the thick vegetation of the north bank village. Several times during the morning, he had to contact Delta on the radio when he lost sight of the company flank. The varying width of the village caused the left flank Marine to be pulled into the village to maintain his interval and thus, be lost from Lister's view.

"The boredom of a full morning of watching the progress of Delta was broken by two incidents before noon. First, through my binoculars, I saw the movement of what had to be enemy soldiers moving toward Delta's flank. They were in front of the approaching Marines and I caught only a glimpse of maybe a dozen, brown-looking figures moving quickly and disappearing into the tree line about a hundred meters from the Delta line. It was obvious what was happening. I quickly contacted Captain Kahler on the net and advised him. He, in turn, advised his left flank platoon. As I watched that exact position where I had seen the enemy I expected firing to break out. Nothing happened. It appeared that the enemy was going underground and avoiding the confrontation.

"A second incident occurred when I observed enemy movement away from Delta to their front and to the east. After consulting Captain Kahler again, I called for artillery fire support…moving through the impact zone, Delta Company Marines found no enemy casualties. I was disappointed. It looked as though the artillery had gone off directly over their heads.

"At about noon, two things happened. First, I became aware, from the radio tactical net and from the distant noise. Delta had begun to make contact. I also was contacted by Captain Kahler that Charlie One was to be utilized to help Bravo Company evacuate some of its casualties. He advised shifting tactical frequency. I don't recall him telling me that we were to be 'OPCON' to Bravo or not? If we discussed that, I don't remember. I did not detect a sense of urgency in his request at the time.

"I did not realize at the time, but I would not regain contact with Delta command until six or seven hours later. I then called Bravo Six on the radio and discovered that I was talking to the Company Commander, Captain Ron Allen. He advised me that they had some wounded and needed Charlie One to set up an LZ and send some of my Marines to carry his casualties from just south of the canal, through the village, and to the north side of the village where we would set up that LZ. Bravo was at Phase Line Brown, but only south of the canal. In other words, they were only blocking on Alpha's side. Did I think this odd? I wondered how the north side was blocked for Delta's push. I didn't know it then but realized within the next hour that Bravo was fighting for their lives and had been for hours. In hindsight, I can dissect events and understand that 'the fog of war' was covering a lot of what was taking place and that my understanding of the full picture was deficient. I was digesting a lot of information, trying to balance competing priorities, and trying to keep my platoon intact."

Charlie One began to move toward Phase Line Brown to set up the LZ and begin the evacuation of the wounded. Lister's plan was to set up in the open rice-paddy area, using one squad as LZ security, and to send two squads toward Bravo. One of those would provide security along the 200-300 yards between the LZ and where Bravo's position was on the canal bank and Phase Line Brown. The other squad would carry the casualties to the LZ for evacuation.

"I was really beginning to get uneasy about this…there was no blocking force on the north side of the canal…my two squads were going into an unknown between the open rice paddy and the canal…a very congested bombed-out village and Delta Company was beginning to make contact and drive the combatants toward our positions."

About the time when this activity was starting to come together, a platoon of Ontos anti-tank vehicles with their 106mm recoilless rifles arrived from the west on the road running parallel to the village. The Platoon Commander of the Ontos told Lieutenant Lister that he had been sent to provide support for him and Delta Company. Lister confided in hindsight that "I didn't take any real comfort in their arrival, since his vehicles could cover only the unsecured area, but couldn't bear down on the several-hundred meters of the village that had to be traversed to get to Bravo Company.

"An ominous event took place just as my two squads were about to head toward Bravo's position. The Bravo Company Commander called me on the radio and asked me to hold up temporarily. He had a problem that he had to take care of and had to fire an artillery mission. 'Roger that.' I heard the rounds come out of the tubes several klicks away and soon heard them impact where I supposed Bravo to be on the south side of the canal. The only good thing about this development was that the impacting rounds were near Bravo—at least my guys going in for security and casualty carrying wouldn't have a problem finding them. Bravo Company was where they said they were. The fact that the CO had to shoot arty close to his position, though, told me something was wrong.

"After not hearing from the Bravo Co for twenty to thirty minutes, I called him to find out if our assistance mission could now proceed. Someone using a call sign I had not previously heard answered the radio: 'Bravo Five Assist.' This really puzzled me. I asked straight out: 'Let me speak with Bravo Six Actual—the Company Commander.' 'Sorry, he's unavailable.'"

In the ensuing minutes of radio conversation, Lieutenant Lister learned very little about the tactical situation of Bravo Six Actual. "It finally dawned on me that Captain Allen had probably become a casualty. It was understandable that the company radio operator didn't want to state that fact or even hint at it. It was then that I dispatched the squads toward Bravo's position.

"I went along and moved with my security squad. We met no resistance and found a route through the bombed-out village and thick vegetation to the canal. I then dispatched Sergeant Simon Waiau's squad to cross the canal and carry the wounded back across. His men preceded me. I was about halfway to the canal from the open rice-paddy area when I received a SitRep from Sergeant Waiau. He told me on the radio that 'They got Reid's team' and that he thought I should come to the Bravo position ASAP [PFC Donald Mansfield and William Parker were in Joe Reid's fire team]. The whole situation was deteriorating so fast I could not believe it. Making my way through a jumbled mass of broken trees and large bomb craters I finally arrived at the Bravo CP. Looking east from the CP was a concrete bridge across the canal. No one crossed it, that I saw, because of the exposure. Those who crossed the canal waded. It was waist deep at its deepest.

"Upon reaching Bravo's CP, I jumped down into a trench where the company Gunnery Sergeant was with the company radio operator. The 'Gunny' was the senior man not wounded or KIA. The two of them briefed me on the situation: one platoon, 2nd Lieutenant Kettner's platoon, had been pinned down on the edge of the rice paddy on the south side of the canal since around 0830 that morning. 2nd Lieutenant Kettner was KIA. There were heavy casualties in his platoon. Only two platoons and the company HQ were on the operation—one platoon was left behind to secure the company's base HQ south and west of the canal on National Route 1. This was the southern portion of the Battalion's TAOR. The remaining platoon and Company CP were clustered around the canal in trenches dug by the NVA. They were situated along the south bank of the canal.

"The pinned-down remnants of Kettner's platoon were southwest of the CP out about 100 yards. There were a few Marines scattered along the connecting pathway. Right in front of the trench was one of Bravo's Navy Corpsmen minus his legs. He was on a makeshift stretcher but had died sometime prior to my arrival. I looked for the CO but didn't see him. I was told that he was badly hurt when he had called the artillery right in on top of the position. Apparently, he had no choice."

Heavy Resistance

In the first minutes of Lieutenant Lister's arrival, there was no enemy activity. That would change shortly. First, the newly arrived Marines in the Bravo CP group began to take fire from the east and south, mostly. It was hard for the Marines to pinpoint the source of fire because of all the wreckage and limited fields of vision. It was after this initial assessment that Lister determined the only reasonably secure terrain was in the direction they had come from. He then called the LZ security squad to move toward him and the Bravo CP to keep a route of escape open. After becoming oriented by the Gunny and his radioman, he found Sergeant Waiau and asked him what had happened to Reid's fire team. He told Lieutenant Lister that they had crossed the canal before him to retrieve the casualties in the Kettner platoon and that all three had been KIA before he had a chance to assess the situation.

"The next three to four hours were spent by me in and around the Bravo CP. While we were attempting to evacuate all the casualties and hold on, Alpha and Delta Companies were pushing forward [eastward] toward our position on the south and north side of the canal.

"Our blocking force was in serious disarray and hanging on by fingernails. The pushing by both 'hammer' companies seemed to be successful, with close air support now being heavily utilized. For a period in the mid to late afternoon, there seemed to be a constant stream of aircraft dropping ordnance into the area. The bad guys were being pushed into us. They came in waves and gave us fits from time to time and it would quiet down for a while. I believe most of them went around our, by now, inadequate blocking position. Sergeant Junior L. Short, my platoon guide, kept things together on the north side of the canal, stretching back to the open rice-paddy area and road. He told me that they had about the same problem on the north side of the canal, keeping a route open and at times shooting it out with those enemies being driven into them.

"After consulting with the Battalion Commander, the remnants of Kettner's platoon, which we had pretty much lost direct physical contact within the Bravo CP, were lifted out by helicopters in an 'emergency extraction.' Once this was accomplished, the Bravo CP and rifle platoon followed by Charlie One pulled out along our escape route and regrouped in the north rice-paddy area before heading west to rejoin the battalion. All of the casualties in the Bravo CP area on that south side of the canal were carried out by Bravo Company and Charlie One Marines."

Lieutenant Lister surmised that what started out as an apparently simple assist to Bravo became a complex combat situation. By the time the regrouped Bravo/Charlie One element headed back to the battalion, it was almost dark. The group was assisted by the Ontos Platoon vehicles, which carried some of the casualties. The Battalion Commander, Lieutenant Colonel John E. Greenwood, had come down the road in a jeep to Phase Line Brown to ensure the orderly movement back to the Battalion CP at the La Son School. Lister further reflected upon Operation No Name #2 as "what I believe had to be the toughest fight 1/27 had been in during its deployment to Vietnam, to date."

A Hasty Rescue

Rick Fink of Charlie Company remembers No Name #2 as a dire situation. His Platoon Staff Sergeant Darrel Scott sent him, along with Lance Corporal Lloyd Fernung, Corporal Charles Weaver, and three other Marines back into the unsecured area and ambush zone where a large Marine from Bravo Company was lying.

Fernung had made three previous mad dashes into the hell zone to bring out other wounded and dead Marines. Fink remembered overhearing Staff Sergeant Scott telling Fernung that he was going to put him in for a Silver Star. This was again going to be another extremely dangerous mission just as the previous forays into the killing zone had been. As PFC Fink recalls, "We went in and found the Marine. He was a very big fella. We made it in alright with no fire in our direction. He had been hit in the face… so we turned him face down in the poncho. We then relieved him of all his ammo and everything we needed.

The gooks waited until we picked up the poncho and started back. They opened firing on all of us. They had been waiting for us to be in that situation. There was nowhere to run but back the way we came. We started to run for all we were worth. I am not sure who was leapfrogging and firing but I think it was Lloyd and Weaver.

I was tripping as I ran carrying the poncho. Lloyd finally grabbed the poncho from me and then it was Charlie and me doing the leapfrogging and covering fire. We finally made it back OK and no one was hit."

After the fighting subsided, the next day PFC Fink and another Marine were on an LP along the canal when the word came down that they were to move back into the ambush area in the hamlet and look for their own, Reid, Mansfield, and Parker. They came to some hooches and there was a cement wall about three feet in height. Fink recollects, "Everyone was pointing at it…there was something painted on it… and when we got close it read, GO HOME AMERICAN PUPPET SOLDIERS!"

Fink doesn't know which operation was worse; this one east of Hue city or Operation Allen Brook conducted later that summer. He further recounts that they had some air support late in this operation east of Hue. "I remember some of the bombs hitting so close that the shrapnel winging through the air sounded like a bear going through the woods knocking branches off trees. Some of it missed me a couple of times…one missed my arm and the reason I knew was I could feel the heat…plus the ground was steaming close to my arm."

The importance of the area became clear to him. This was a rice-rich area and a food source for the enemy combatants. Fink tells of their further excursion. "As soon as we came to the next area, we found an underground cache of rice, a lot of it. I was the chosen one to search it. I remember a piece of metal over it probably to protect it. When I crawled in, it went down and then turned to my right. I went about fifteen to twenty feet and came into a large room that was lined with bamboo…There were tons of rice bags in this underground hiding place. At the end of the room, there was another hole and that is when Staff Sergeant Scott began screaming to get out. I got out and the shit was hitting the fan…the gooks had opened up on us again."

Division Combat Photographers and Correspondents

The job of a Marine Corps photographer and correspondent was to document action and record images for Marine Corps history. These photo and correspondent Marines took the same risks and suffered the same grind as did the grunts they were photographing and writing about. They showed the Marines in battle—most of them teenagers—coping with their heavy 782 gear, weaponry and ammo, the heat and humidity, along with the rain, mud, and an elusive enemy whose booby traps and guns could have also brought a photographer or correspondent's life to an end at any moment. These Marines worked very hard to document the Vietnam battle histories covering a variety of units, situations, and unusual operations throughout I Corps. They scoured the 1st Marine Division and supporting units to record most occurrences of importance. A lot of those images, showing most aspects of the Vietnam War, are now available in the National Archives because of these dedicated men. Determined photographers and correspondents from Division Headquarters were there amongst the Marines of 1/27 on Operation No Name #2 in April of 1968 and later for Operation Allen Brook on Go Noi Island south of Da Nang.

Corporal Dennis Fisher, a two-tour photographer with 1st Marine Division's Combat Photo and Correspondents in the ISO section, tells how the photographers and correspondents received their assignments in 1968. Operating out of MACV Forward Headquarters at the Phu Bai Combat Base, Fisher recounts, "While at Phu Bai with Task Force X-Ray we operated with the Marine units in the general vicinity. Mostly the 5th Marines and later the 27th Marines. We really didn't have a dedicated photo officer at Phu Bai. Both the correspondents and photographers worked out of the same ISO office under Lieutenant Larry LePage. The brief time we spent with the 27th they were in some heavy contact, which was for me some of the heaviest combat I had been involved in other than the battle for the Citadel in downtown Hue City earlier in February."

Corporal Dennis Fisher, Combat Photographer 1st Marine Division ~ Courtesy of Corporal R. J. DelVecchio, 1st Marine Division Combat Photo and Correspondence section

Dennis came in-country December 1966, extending his first thirteen-month tour into another six months. He had already been on multiple operations and wounded by the time the Tet Offensive started 31 January 1968. Dennis remembered the scuttlebutt that had been going around amongst the correspondents and photographers at that time. "They were saying that the 27th Marines, a new unit in-country, hadn't been in the field and the comments from some photographers and correspondents were, 'Are you really sure you want to go out with them?'" As it turned out Corporal Fisher gained great admiration for 1/27 after traveling with them. He now tells many, "I had been with a lot of units to date. The thing that impressed me most was their discipline and the way they could secure an area plus take care of their wounded. They moved on despite all they encountered. They seemed to have been working together for a while and well trained. It is discouraging to see so many Marines go down..They kept going. Those poor Marines and Corpsmen of Bravo Company really got hammered! I had never been in an operation where I saw so many Marines getting killed or wounded in such a brief time."

Lieutenant Larry LePage, the officer in charge of the combat photo and correspondent section, would attend the briefings at Task Force X-Ray in Phu Bai to hear about what unit operations were coming up and what was going to happen. He would make the decisions to send photographers and correspondents based on the possibility of good stories and good-photo potentials with a unit. Fisher recalled, "He typically would tell us who he wanted us to travel with and under normal circumstances we would arrive there early before the operation started. That would enable us to introduce ourselves to the Commanders, and allow us to start meeting the Marines in the unit. We would capture names and pertinent information into our notebooks beforehand. You needed data like that to caption your photos when you came back to process the film. It was very difficult to do all of this in the confusion of a firefight."

During the Tet Offensive of 1968, the combat tempo increased dramatically and all the preplanning and preparation was put aside. Corporal Fisher remembers, "A 'No notice' assignment started becoming the norm so we kept our equipment and a few days' worth of rations in our packs ready to deploy. I was teamed with Lance Corporal Earl Gerheim at the time, a combat correspondent, and had covered many operations with him previously. Photographers and correspondents frequently traveled in pairs with the sometimes addition of a motion-picture photographer."

Coverage of 1/27's "No Name #2" operation was assigned to Fisher and Gerheim. Fisher remembers, "We were asked to head out east of Hue City to the Phu Vang District where 1/27's line companies were already in heavy contact with a large NVA force. When we arrived at 1/27's CP we were told that there weren't any choppers flying due to heavy ground fire and overcast skies. We learned there was an ammo resupply truck leaving soon and we could ride out with them."

During this time in Vietnam, it was luck of the draw to acquire any type of transportation to go anywhere. The photographers and correspondents finally made their way eastward on Communal Road 552 from 1/27's CP in a deuce-and-a-half truck loaded with ammo to find the action. Shooting became audible in the distance as the ammo truck drove eastward. Fisher remembers they reached a point on the road near some rice paddies where the truck stopped and they all got off only to be greeted with sniper fire, "The replacement Marines on this resupply run seemed to know where the companies were located, so Earl and I, not wanting to get left behind, grabbed the rope handles of the remaining cases of 60mm mortar rounds that had been tossed off the truck, headed across the paddy dikes following the others at a quick pace and headed toward a bamboo tree line about five hundred yards in the distance." The already in-progress battle was happening alongside the east-west running canal from where the ammo truck had stopped. He further recalled, "By the time we arrived at Company D's CP on the north side of the canal the shooting had temporarily died down. We checked in with Captain Pat Kahler to tell him we had been assigned to travel with his company to document their participation in the op. No sooner than we had introduced ourselves when the firefight began again. We began taking fire from the other side of the canal. It was about twenty to thirty feet wide with steep banks. The enemy and Alpha Company were engaged on the other side. I immediately started taking pictures, moving from one location to another—wherever a good photo opportunity presented itself. As a former infantryman, I also started helping lay down a base of fire with my .45-caliber grease gun. The sound it made drew some interesting looks from the Marines around me. There was a lot more incoming fire than I was normally used to and I began to worry that it might be part of a maneuver to turn our flank. When I started maneuvering with the company the first thing I saw and photographed were some Marines with Alpha Company carrying their dead back to the rear. I took the picture from across the canal with my telephoto lens. I knew then from experience that this was going to be a bad fight. Later in the day it only got worse...and the next day it seemed to continue."

"Humping" much-needed ammo to the skirmish line ~ Courtesy of Corporal Dennis Fisher, 1st Marine Division Combat Photo and Correspondence Section

The work of a photographer could be doubly hard. You were not yet an accepted member of the unit. You had to be alert to any danger and at the same time looking for candid shots with your camera. This visual media requires a good eye for composition, lighting, the angle of view, and the ability to capture the critical moment of an event. Applying these basics under combat conditions was always a challenge. Fisher recaptures his thinking back then, "Of course as a photographer you are trying your best to show the courage and skill of the Marines, capturing good shots of them in action with no hamming or posing for the camera. You need to capture the true action! Therefore, you try to be inconspicuous. I also think my picture taking was a morale booster for the grunts and it gave them some confidence that what they were doing was appreciated and was being documented for all to see. Also, you do try and make friends. The truth is that if you get wounded you want someone to come get your ass...You know, 'Maybe we should drag that photographer back in out of the firing...'"

1/27 Marines of Alpha Company carrying their dead ~ Courtesy of Corporal Dennis Fisher, 1st Marine Division Combat Photo and Correspondence Section

Delta Company's temporary CP was located on the grounds of a pagoda. Fisher seized on another subject of interest and began documenting PFC Geoffrey T Rowson, an M60 machine gunner, who had positioned himself on the roof of the pagoda to lay down a base of fire across the canal toward the enemy. Fisher recalled, "It was a very exposed position and I feared that it wouldn't be long before the NVA would zero in on him. This photograph would eventually wind up in the National Archives [DOD Photo USMC A371498]."

PFC Geoffrey T. Rowson (KIA 19 June 1968) fires an M60 from Pagoda rooftop ~ Courtesy of Corporal Dennis Fisher, 1st Marine Division Combat Photo and Correspondence Section

Next Fisher moved outside the pagoda wall to watch as a Vietnamese interpreter with Captain Kahler's command group questioned villagers. At the time, Fisher captioned the photograph as "French/Vietnamese doctor points out V.C. escape route to Captain Kahler, the CO of D Co, 1/27." As Fisher recalled, "He would only speak French even though he was fluent in Vietnamese. I don't think he wanted us to confuse him with the combatants."

Captain Pat Kahler (center), Radioman Lance Corporal Eddie Mahseet and Vietnamese interpreter conferring with villagers about NVA escape route ~ Courtesy of Corporal Dennis Fisher, 1st Marine Division Combat Photo and Correspondence Section

Once the weather improved a little later in the day the fast movers came to the aid of the Marines. Fisher remembers there were two aircraft circling, an F4 Phantom, and an F8 Crusader. He recalled, "The shot of the F4 was with a normal lens and not a telephoto lens. So, that will tell you how close the aircraft were to the ground and me...They were literally making their runs on the other side of the canal. The bombs were falling not more than a couple hundred yards away. The one plane appeared to have the 323rd insignia on its tail, the 'Death Rattlers' squadron [VMFA-323] but I couldn't be sure. That squadron was based in Da Nang. Boy, Alpha Company on the other side of the canal had a front-row seat right close to the explosions."

The equipment a photographer used then was rudimentary by today's standard. Fisher traveled with a 35mm Nikon F and three lenses—a wide angle, a normal, and a medium telephoto. Normally he shot black and white and sometimes color. The Ektachrome used for color was a transparency (slide) film and came in either twenty-four or thirty-six exposures. With one camera, Fisher had to choose whether to shoot black and white, or color. The photographers processed their own film when returning from an operation. Photo selections were made for submission to HQ Marine Corps, for hometown news releases, or in-country publications like Sea Tiger or Stars and Stripes. If something of intel value was recorded it would be enlarged and submitted for analysis.

F4 Phantom dropping "snake eye" bombs on target south side of canal
~ Courtesy of Corporal Dennis Fisher, 1st Marine Division Combat Photo and Correspondence Section

Exploding aftermath of bomb run on south side of canal in front of Alpha Company
~ Courtesy of Corporal Dennis Fisher, 1st Marine Division Combat Photo and Correspondence Section

Fisher recaptures his last day with 1/27 as the Marines were finally securing the AO. It was late in the day and Delta Company had made radio contact with a Huey Gunship passing through the airspace. He recalls, "I had heard that the chopper was returning to base and had ordnance that he wanted to expend. So, Delta put him on station and the mortar guys marked some suspect positions with smoke rounds. It was then the Huey pilot made a run firing his rockets. Some of the rockets found the target but an errant rocket fell short and into our lines. It was my recollection that the pilot saw what had happened and immediately set down and took on the casualties and transported them to NSA at Phu Bai. As a matter of fact, after I returned to base camp in Phu Bai the following day I made it a point to go over to the hospital and check on those guys. I remember when they loaded the wounded onto the chopper, one Marine had a big piece of shrapnel probably six or eight inches long, like a knife sticking right through his flak jacket and into his chest. When I got to the hospital to find out if he made it or not...amazingly, he had. I heard that another WIA did not make it and had died."

Even though photographers, both still and motion picture, had a unique mission to fulfill that required a great deal of self-motivation, professional skill, and initiative, there were no leaders in the field to direct the actions of a photographer or correspondent. It was up to the individual to accomplish the task. "Our mission was to visually document the operations with an eye for events that might: be of immediate interest for print-media stories generated by accompanying correspondents, anything discovered on an op that would be of interest to a command staff or the intel folks, and the general conduct of the operation for historical purpose. We had repeat travel orders and could pretty much go anywhere in I Corps to cover a story. While in the field, I was frequently asked, 'What are you doing out here?' or 'Is taking pictures your job?' or 'What do you do with the pictures?' My short answer was, 'It's my job.' Most of the field Marines didn't see combat photographers or correspondents at all so it was a rarity for them to have us along on an op. Photo taking was prevalent in the rear areas...It was something that I truly enjoyed doing!"

Situation Report to Regimental HQ

On 13 April, 1705 Zulu time, a Telex from First Battalion, 27th Marines CP communications center was sent to Task Force X-Ray to report on the operation. It reads, in part:[7]

> *Significant small unit contacts. By 131400H [April 13, 2:00 P.M.] Company B was without officers and fragmented into three positions, two south of and one north of the canal in vicinity YD 832239. The Battalion Commander proceeded to the scene and moved an additional platoon from Company D to reinforce the Ontos platoon and an additional platoon from company C at 131554H [April 13, 3:54 P.M]. Wounded from 3 Companies were evacuated from north of the canal. Then trying to maintain contact...At 131554H fixed wing arrived on station. Company A positioned vicinity Phase Line Orange north of canal and*

receiving heavy small arms fire...the situation remained a stalemate...

D. Nine artillery missions fired in support of units expending a total of 143 rounds of mixed types...

E. Air support provided included 3 section missions for fixed wing...UH-1E Gunships. 3 Medevac Helos which shuttled WIA's. Helo resupply (1900 lbs.) and one Helo used for air command...

F. Many of the enemy engaged so far during this operation were wearing dark green uniforms. They were well equipped. Some carried gas masks. Some wore helmets and flak jackets. They were disciplined under fire and were aggressive. No patches or other unit insignias were noticed on clothing. The enemy fought from bunkers, trenches and fighting holes positioned along both sides of the canal that run parallel to and 300 to 500 meters south of route 552. The adjacent hamlets were also well fortified. Enemy weapons included 60 and 82 mortars, rockets, B40s, 50 Cal machine guns and small arms and auto weapons...in consideration of the information and past and current intel, it is probable that judging from their determination...to keep friendly forces out of this area. They are protecting and guarding something of vital importance to them in this area such as a troop staging area, logistical staging area or some form of the base of operations area somewhere east of grids 8226. 8225. 8224. 8223.

Marine casualties in the aftermath of the battle were recorded in the Battalion Command Chronology record as twenty-six KIA and forty-six WIA while confirming sixty-two enemies KIA along with numerous captured weapons and personal equipment. It is still an unknown as to how many additional of the enemy KIAs and WIAs were dragged or carried off the battlefield. The next two days Delta and Alpha Companies continued to sweep the canal. Bravo Company underwent a "stand down" and complete reorganization.

Change of Command

On 15 April Combat Operation No Name #2 was concluded and Captain William Sweeney, then S-2, became Bravo Company Commander due to the loss of Captain Ronald Allen. Sweeney remembers making a quick visit to visit Captain Allen at the Phu Bai NSA to pay his respects. He recollects, "I had known Ron since we were basic school students together in Quantico, VA in 1961. I knew him to be a professional and an aggressive combat leader. What struck me during my visit with Ron, he was more concerned that he had to leave the company and his men than he was about his very serious wounds [losing part of an arm and hand]."

When Sweeney took command of Bravo Company, it had seen a lot of combat and had taken a lot of casualties. The new company CP position was on a hill overlooking Highway 1 south of Hue and embraced a pipeline running adjacent to the highway with a perfect 360-degree view. The hill itself, per Captain Sweeney, was steep and rounded at the top. He recollects that since the company had not been there long enough to prepare defensive positions and dig fighting holes that everyone on the hill was skylined. "My first order was to dig fighting holes around the military crest of the position... I remember feeling bad for the troops because they had lost a lot of friends and fellow Marines just two days before. The ground was hard and difficult to dig. I felt like a hard ass but it still had to be done."

The first night Bravo Marines threw quite a few hand grenades down the hill. Captain Sweeney was concerned about coming up short on grenades for future use. He recalls giving a firm order to everyone on the hill, "that if they really thought that a VC or an NVA was approaching their position to throw the grenade but then they had to crawl down and drag the body up for confirmation. This quickly put an end to gratuitous grenade throwing."[8]

Bizarre Daily Experiences

After standing down briefly, Bravo Company began running daily patrols again. The men of Bob O'Rourke's 3rd Platoon had the responsibility for bridge security and keeping National Highway 1 traffic flowing both north and south. Army supply trucks often would stop at the bridge and give his Marines some of the food they were hauling to the MACV compound in Hue City. He remembered one occasion on 16 April when, returning from a long patrol and a nasty firefight with NVA, his platoon sergeant, Staff Sergeant John Storzum, had ice cold beer and potato chips waiting for the men who had been on the patrol. The welcome beer, chips, and ice were courtesy of the Army truckers passing through on the highway. O'Rourke recaptures those poignant moments, "As we drank the beer, I engaged a local Vietnamese male in conversation. As we sat there on the steps of a home that was close to our PPB, I couldn't help but notice that he was closely observing us and our positions. He spoke excellent English and during our visit inadvertently blurted out, that we Marines had killed a lot of people. This was just after the battle of the Citadel at Hue in February. I could not shake that comment and later reflected on this encounter that he was likely a VC."

O'Rourke and his men, a few days earlier, had witnessed a firefight that local friendly forces, the ARVNs, had encountered as they looked eastward in the distance from their position on Hill 78. The ARVNs had become pinned down in an open rice-paddy area by NVA firing from a tree line.

Later, after Operation No Name #2, on 16 April, he and his men were ordered to reconnoiter that area. Before beginning the patrol, he pre-registered artillery targets where he thought the enemy would likely attack.

As he suspected, the firefight began when O'Rourke ordered his machine gunner to reconnoiter by firing at the tree line (grid coordinate YD850195) where they had witnessed the earlier skirmish involving the ARVN local forces. When the enemy returned fire, he brought in the 8-inch gun batteries from nearby Phu Bai and destroyed the tree line. As they began the assault, O'Rourke recalled, "We were ankle deep in the rice paddy where the leeches had attached themselves to our legs. There was nothing we could do about them until we finally broke contact and found dry land. Burning cigarettes worked to get them to release their hold. By that time, they had grown into small balloon-like blobs on the skin. It was an uncomfortable feeling being engaged with the NVA in a full-fledged firefight and feeling those slippery little creatures getting bigger from sucking our blood."

3rd Platoon suffered only one non-critical WIA during the fight. Lieutenant O'Rourke was thankful for Captain Ronald Allen, his Company Commander's earlier advice to reconnoiter by fire in such circumstances. O'Rourke recalls visiting him in the hospital at Phu Bai the day before this encounter where he was recovering from the 13 April battle where he had lost an arm. "That advice and action saved a lot of lives as we were able to destroy an ambush that was clearly waiting for us."

Bravo Company Reassigned

In late April, 3rd Platoon, Bravo Company established a new platoon patrol base at the confluence of two canals (Thon Dien Thai), approximately two kilometers south of the battalion CP and three kilometers east of the Hue Citadel (grid coordinate YD787228). They became attached to Alpha Company and were located south of an Alpha Company platoon patrol base lead by 2nd Lieutenant Roger Charles. Unlike their previous PPB at Hill 78 and the bridge, this area was sparsely populated with mostly uninhabited homes.

O'Rourke's platoon immediately dug in and constructed a low profile, covered fighting holes with interconnecting trenches. They pre-planned their defense by pre-registering artillery impact areas which would be crucial in an attack on their base in early May.

From this small base of operation, the platoon conducted daily patrols and began setting up nightly ambushes. Contact with the enemy during this period was very light and consisted of daily and nightly probes. O'Rourke remembers one of those evenings, "We were entertained by rocks being thrown into our positions. We returned the favor by also throwing rocks back until finally, I suggested that we end the game with a few grenades. That did end the fun, and it demonstrated good fire discipline, not revealing our locations. This would prove a valuable lesson several days later during Operation No Name #4."

17 April Attack on the CP

The NVA wreaked havoc and death upon the CP group of Marines dug in at the La San Schoolhouse. Another assault got underway late in the afternoon of 17 April. An intense wave of well-aimed mortar rounds impacted in a close grouping that was indicative of practiced marksmanship.

The confusion in the schoolyard was overwhelming. A lot of Marines were down and badly wounded. The small world of the Marines seemed to be a nightmare of violent explosions, fragments of steel whirring through the air. Everything was blurred. The assault seemed to go on for hours. In truth, it lasted only a few minutes. The Marines of H&S Company were numbed and in shock when the attack lifted. Corporal

Birdsong remembered that he ran immediately to his makeshift tent. Gunnery Sergeant Gomez had been killed instantly in the initial barrage. Staff Sergeant Raymond Johnson lay in the dirt inside their shelter, critically wounded, holding his stomach and crying out, "Birdsong, it burns…it burns so fucking bad…Oh my God it hurts…Help me…" Staff Sergeant Johnson was put on an evacuation helicopter that afternoon by Corporal Birdsong and other Marines.

The schoolhouse was adjacent to a local road heading out to the coast, with a labyrinth of canals supplying water from the Perfume River to the rice crops in this fertile area. The back side of the school harbored an elongated lily pond. There were many hedgerows in and around the hooches surrounding the schoolhouse. The circular defensive perimeter set up surrounding the schoolhouse and partially in hedgerows did not allow a 360-degree view from all sections. The Marine Corps tactical term "hasty defense" position aptly described this improvised situation.

Lance Corporal Joe Roysdon, one of the senior Radio Operators in the Communications Platoon, recaptured the beginning moments of the mortar assault on the school CP. "I had gone to the supply section on the far west side of the schoolhouse to obtain our section's C-rations. As I came out of Supply, I heard a 'ka-rump' and rocks started flying all over the place. I remember diving for cover and staying put while the mortar barrage continued. It seemed like a long time. When we finally all came out after the barrages lifted, I noted that a couple of the engineers were digging up one of the first mortar rounds that hadn't detonated." Roysdon indicated that it had landed in the front of the schoolhouse entrance by the medical and supply section of the building. Corporal Doug Setley, a Communications Platoon member walking to sick bay, immediately knew the score when it plummeted into the ground next to him.

La Son Schoolhouse, Phu Vang District, detainees, March 1968
~ Courtesy of Sergeant Larry Broadhurst, H&S Co, 1/27

Lance Corporal Roysdon describes the anguish he had to overcome when he found most of the tactical radio network had been destroyed. "The attack knocked out most of our tactical radios in the Battalion CP. Knowing that I had to get the radio net up and running probably kept me sane for that period of chaos. It was a gargantuan job…

my AN/TRC-75 Jeep radio, one of our more important pieces of radio communications equipment, was on the east end of the schoolhouse and next to the switchboard. It was badly damaged! The rudimentary telephone switchboard in the Communications tent had a radio that had taken a direct hit that killed Corporal John J. Vennard who was on radio watch. We had to get replacement radios from Supply and get them up and running again. We worked frantically to get all the radios in and antennas up and finally got back on the tactical network communicating with the line companies…I didn't think we would ever get things running."

Once the radios were up and communicating, medical evacuations were called for and arrived in relays of three extractions. The arrival of the evacuation helicopters seemed to take forever. The critical were staged for the first evacuations and the least critical along with the KIAs were on the last chopper out that evening. All the wounded were hustled aboard unceremoniously as the choppers waited to lift off. The men of H&S Company were in an almost total state of shock. The sapping, humid heat had taken a toll also. Tropical pastels of light invaded the surrounding foliage, signaling the coming of sundown and nighttime. Some turned to help with rebuilding and some withdrew into themselves. It had been the first bad taste of what was to come later.

As soon as the attack lifted and fortifying the outer perimeter began, Captain Ronald Gruenberg, an S-3 Operations Officer, and another S-3 First Lieutenant named Cox, immediately began analyzing numerous mortar impacts to determine the origin of the mortar attack. Once the direction was established, a patrol immediately searched the suspected village area for the launch site. As Gruenberg later told others, "Spotting aiming stakes in the rice paddy to the east of our position in a direct line from village to schoolhouse CP, was a clear indicator that our friendly villagers knew something."

There was debate amongst the leadership about the placement and relocation of the CP.

Gruenberg, a second-tour combat officer, contended to his superiors that the CP was a landmark and stood out like a sore thumb, thus easily targeted. Battalion Commander Greenwood insisted that it remain, and later an Engineer detachment arrived and reinforced the Combat Operation Center (COC) segment of the building with sandbags.

Gruenberg remembered, "The COC became an airtight bunker with no circulation and light discipline at night making it oven like…which made it the 'Black Hole of Calcutta.' As I recall, a week or two later, we again received another mortar attack."

A SitRep finally called into Regiment HQ south of Da Nang detailed that Battalion H&S Company had taken four USMC KIAs and twenty-five WIAs at the Hue CP. Fifteen wounded Marines were medically evacuated along with the KIAs by helicopter, and ten were non-evacuees. It had been not a good day for the Marines of H&S Company.

Dane "Bing" Brown and Doug "Wildman" Carey aboard the "Mike Boat" on Operation "No Name #3"
~ Courtesy of Doug Carey, H&S Co, 1/27

Operation No Name #3

The next operation to follow was No Name #3, commencing on 28 April. The area of focus was in the extreme northwestern sector of the Battalion TAOR, just to the north of Hue City and the Citadel about six klicks. Charlie and Delta companies were transported by LCM-8 (mechanized landing craft aka "Mike Boat") and landed at YD767307 on the Song Huong River with the mission of performing a sweep of the villages in that sector along a side waterway just off the main Song Huong. The Song Huong aka Perfume River flows from the south to the northeast. In the autumn, flowers from orchards fall into the river giving it a perfume-like aroma, hence the descriptive name.

Two Regional Force Companies from the Huong Tra District provided the blocking force at YD745300 while the National Police Force Company conducted a thorough search of the villages. Prior to and during this operation, the battalion conducted a Psychological Operation that employed a leaflet drop and an airborne public-address system announcing to the people in the area to cooperate with the Marine forces.

Several types of leaflets and Chieu Hoi chits (phamplets) were distributed to the villages along the main Route 551. Chieu Hoi meant "open arms" in Vietnamese and promised clemency and financial aid to Viet Cong, NVA soldiers, and the cadres who stopped fighting and came over to the South Vietnamese government. Some of the leaflet subject matter pointed out the danger of the fuel in the roadway pipeline along Route 551. The leaflets also addressed the importance of turning in arms caches, mine locations, and enemy positions. Additionally, the Province Chief of Thua Thien Province encouraged citizens to stay in the city limits of Hue.

Two examples of Safe-Conduct Passes ~ Courtesy of Grady Birdsong, H&S Co, 1/27

Col Co Island Security

Company C First Platoon Commander, Lieutenant Dennis Lister, described their responsibility upon arrival to this area. Task Force X-Ray assigned 1/27 a TAOR east, south, and southeast of Hue City. Lister recalled, "The Battalion split its line companies into sectors, with each rifle company patrolling its own area giving us, Charlie Company, probably, the best area. We set up on a barrier island, across a sound that was almost identical in geographical makeup to the Outer Banks of North Carolina. It stretched south for approximately twenty miles, maybe a thousand meters wide on the north and about two miles wide on the south end. On the north end stood a Seabee base, which operated a fuel farm with several large round storage tanks maybe 100,000 gallons of fuel of all types. This area retained the name Col Co, short for Colonial Company from French colonial days. The Seabees operated the 'ramp' on the mainland side of the sound, which allowed LST and LCU boat traffic to unload cargo destined for the Hue-Phu Bai area of operations. The mainland ramp connected to the barrier island by a Navy-run ferry. The Seabees had not enough manpower to man all bunkers on the perimeter of the fuel farm. So, we provided most of their security and patrolled the numerous villages and hamlets to the south, populated primarily by fishermen and an NVA/VC unit."

Officers Charlie Company; L-R: Donald Gustafson, Dennis Lister, Martin Farmer (CO), Pete Schutz (XO), Jay Kispert ~ Courtesy of Dennis Lister, C Co, 1/27

A Marine Amtrac Platoon resided at the Seabee base, but did not run foot patrols. They provided occasional transport for 1/27 and others. In early May, Charlie Company received a battalion order to move inland and participate in a multi-company No Name operation. Left behind, Lister's first Platoon continued base security for the fuel farm under the command of Executive Officer First Lieutenant Pete Schutz. Lieutenant Lister vividly remembers those days, "The second day after most of the company had been absent, late afternoon, two mortar rounds impacted, one on each side of the steel fuel tanks, perfectly 'bracketing' the tanks. The mortar rounds came from 'down island.' After that nothing further happened. Pete and I discussed possibilities. Did they have us in their sights? Would they attack that night? These were questions that couldn't be readily answered. We knew that a mortar attack was near certain—that they had the range. The only question, timing and when? With a minimum force, what were our options? I volunteered to lead a patrol at least as far as the maximum range of a Soviet 82mm mortar. That was the probable weapon they were firing."

A Soviet 82mm mortar tube fires a mortar round the maximum distance of 3,040 meters (3,320 yards). This placed the probable launch site in the large fishing village of Thon An Duong south of the base. Lister now tells, "In hindsight, I'm not sure this was a promising idea, but at the time it didn't seem like there were many options. I hastily gathered a patrol from the already few Marines that manned the perimeter. Fire support, Delta Battery, a 105mm howitzer crew close to Hue City covered our area but were not within our PRC-25 radio's range. Luckily, we had an attached 81mm mortar crew with an FO and RTO. So, we had our own fire support."

Lieutenant Lister gathered his seventeen-man patrol shortly after the mortar attack and mounted the Amtracs at dusk, heading south along the beach's edge and travelling three kilometers almost to the large fishing village. The village was "an innocent-looking fishing village but I knew we were vulnerable going by it on the beach. There was no time to be safe, seeking another approach, so we just walked by it hoping that no enemy combatants were watching. It worked. We proceeded another 1000 meters past the fishing village. Right on the open beach where the waves broke, the sand damp, hard-packed, and easy to walk on I halted the platoon to orientate and look for a safe place. A short distance from the surf we looked up at a steep embankment, which topped and leveled into pure sand dunes. The sand stretched probably 600 to 700 meters inland to the spine of the island, which was roughly 1500 meters (almost one mile) wide at this point."

Holding the patrol on the beach, Lister took a couple of his Marines up the embankment to scan the area. It was dark, but not pitch black. They sighted no movement or combatants on the first look. Lance Corporal Tyrone James scanned again with binoculars, alerting Lieutenant Lister that he could see three silhouettes seventy-five meters inland out on the sand. James handed the binoculars to Lieutenant Lister for him to confirm. Lister recalls, "There they were, and while I started thinking about the best course of action, preempting my thoughts, AK bursts began zipping over our heads. Returning fire, the silhouettes quickly disappeared. In the chaos of those moments I momentarily looked down the embankment and on the beach one of my men was flailing around. I thought, oh, no, someone got hit. It turned out my Corpsman had dropped his .45-caliber automatic service pistol in the sand and was frantically looking for it. 'Doc, forget it, we are moving out.' My Corpsman frantically replied, 'No, I can't leave my weapon.' Just as I began to move him forward he found his pistol. Quickly, I had the patrol execute a 90-degree right turn, scramble up the embankment and head inland over the sand dunes toward some pine trees in the middle of the island."

The overhead cloud cover disappeared and a full moon overhead lit everything. The Marines had successfully driven the combatants away, at least temporarily, but

Lister's men needed to find concealment immediately. He put a trusted Lance Corporal on point, giving him the azimuth he wanted the patrol to move toward. Trudging right behind him, Lister recalled the next few minutes, "We moved quickly, not at double-time, but as fast we could in loose sand. We moved about half of the way to the pine trees. Bang! My point man fired a round and hit the deck. The rest of the platoon dropped while I crab-crawled to the point man's position. 'What have you got?' I asked, out of breath. The answer, 'Accidental discharge, Sir.' With an adrenaline rush and too scared to respond in any way other than 'Keep Going,' I quickly decided this wasn't the time to scold. My point man was a good Marine, what could I say? Not an appropriate time to make a mistake and we needed to move right then. That incident did illustrate the pressure we all felt. Of the many scary times I experienced on my tour in Vietnam, that moment was one of my worst."

The patrol continued toward the pine thickets inland. Upon reaching the tree line, the patrol paused. Hidden in the pines they found a cemetery surrounded by a two-foot high concrete wall. On the high ground in the trees, with 360-degree views into the open areas, it offered the sanctuary they needed, at least for a short while. Settling and setting up a hasty defense, Lister recalled the next minutes, which seemed hours. "Several of my men spotted enemy movement but those turned out brief and sketchy in detail. The enemy was out there but not yet close. After about thirty minutes, enemy soldiers moved toward our position from the south, where we knew they were in force for sure. They did not know exactly where we were and these combatants started firing periodically into the tree line. They were doing what we Marines called 'recon by fire,' shooting into the trees and waiting for our return fire. I passed the word not to return fire. I reasoned that they would see the cemetery and come to check it out. They approached to within about thirty to forty meters and turned back south. That surprised me. I thought we would have to kill them thus giving our position away. In the back of my mind, 'How far could their main unit have been from our present position?'"

Lister changed the patrol's position several times after the first "recon by fire" incident. Several times the men saw a lot of flashing light coming from the south. It looked like a searchlight, moving at ground level. Lister recalls thinking, "Maybe it was a vehicle, but we had never seen Viet Cong or NVA this aggressive and looking for us. They appeared brazen, but it made sense. This territory belonged to them and they probably knew that we had no reinforcements."

After hours of moving the patrol to multiple positions back toward the large fishing village between them and the fuel farm, Lieutenant Lister made the decision to beeline back to basecamp. Cloud cover overhead made visibility and walking difficult. Lister explained his decision, "We just moved north straight through the village, rather than take the beach route as the enemy would expect us to do. I figured that the chances of being ambushed in the fishing ville were slim to none and the worst danger, a dog bite. We moved quickly through and headed to camp arriving early, maybe 0400. All of us, worn, barely able to put one foot in front of the other. This happens when you expend all your adrenaline. We had walked a total of probably five or six miles, not much for young men, but due to circumstance that night we were exhausted. As we approached our base establishing contact with the perimeter bunkers that we were friendlies, the 81mm Mortar Platoon RTO behind me yelled, 'Lieutenant, you almost got our asses killed!' Tired and not wanting a confrontation, I just simply said, 'Shut up, Marine, I don't want to hear about it.'"

In the remaining days, the Seabee Camp received no mortar attacks while Charlie Company had security for that area. Lister recounted meeting the RTO in the 81mm Mortar Platoon at a reunion in Tennessee in 2006. "I noticed a Marine that looked familiar but could not place him. We talked a while and he told me his name was Victor DeCurtis and that he was with the FO team in 81mm Mortars. We both got to discussing Col Co Island and he remembered the incident and what he had said to me. We both had a hearty laugh and relived the story. Later, we had great fellowship at the following reunions in Dallas and San Diego. Victor was a character, the kind of Marine you really liked. Victor passed in 2014; we miss him. God rest his soul."

The "Fun House"

During the time Charlie Company had a presence in the Col Co area, providing security for the fuel farm and the NSA facility there, Corporal Gabe Komanec remembers running nightly patrols. He recaptures one of the more memorable night patrols: "We had just left the perimeter at dusk...It was close to a village area. I remember we had traveled about 150 to 200 yards out of our wire and I sighted some Vietnamese walking single file down in the field off in the distance. I looked them over carefully and said to myself, oh shit, these dudes were up to no good...One of them kind of semi-turned around and I could see his rifle slung on his shoulder...He had an AK upside-down holding it close to his body. He was about 150-200 yards out from us. I signaled all my Marines to 'get on-line' and on my command to lay down a base of fire on them; they were NVA...We positioned ourselves into a sort of a trench-like berm and opened fire on them big time... We killed one...The rest just scattered...They didn't come back into our lines after that... I think that they were scouting our lines big time...and were about to set up an ambush."

Komanec recounts that there were so many incidents like this one when they first arrived that he sometimes didn't even report them. He indicated that a lot of the time his squad was out so far from help that they didn't fire on the enemy for fear of giving away their position, not knowing the size of the enemy unit.

On another occasion, he recollects conducting a night patrol which originated from the NSA/Seabee fuel farm. "We had to patrol the southern area away from the facility and there happened to be a 'fun house' about 300-400 yards from the main gate in the ville. I think I had twelve or thirteen Marines and as we approached the Ville, I stopped 'em and said to my guys, 'You want to get your pipes cleaned out?' The response from most of them was, 'Oh hell yeah...yes...!' A well-known place to most in the area, the women in this place received regular inspections by the Corpsmen at the NSA facility. Anyway, I positioned my guys in a 160 and took my assistant in to arrange things. Mama-san met us at the door and I could tell there was something wrong...She was whispering and there were two girls behind her..Their faces gave me the impression something was up. I told Mama-san we had beaucoup Marines and would like to have some fun tonight. She immediately started 'Oh no, no!' This alarmed me so I immediately went back out and alerted my guys I thought there may be NVA or VC already in the house. I told them that I was gonna search the house. I gave orders that if there was any firing that I was going to drop to the deck and to fire about three feet off the ground and level that hooch...I go back in and confront Mama-san telling her I thought they had VC in the hooch. I told her, 'I wanna search...We are gonna search your house!' She babbled back, 'No, no, no VC'... I said, 'Bullshit, move over there and sit down while I search your house.' I then hear a voice in the back room, 'Who the hell are ya?' I yelled back, 'We are Marines,' and the voice says, 'I have a shotgun leveled on your ass...' I replied, 'I have a squad of Marines surrounding this house and if they hear one shot they are gonna level this place with you in it!' "

It turned out that one of the Navy guys from the NSA facility had decided to spend the night and had thought Komanec and his Marines were the NVA. He had paid Mama-san for an all-night with one of her girls. Komanec recalls telling him in no uncertain terms, 'I was not going to say anything about this to his upper command and to get his ass back in the wire that he was not supposed to be out here.' I added that if we had seen him out here at night walking on the trail we would have considered him a bad guy and shot him dead. And to consider himself very lucky he is alive now!"

Operation C-Ration

The Battalion subsisted solely on C-rations while operationally controlled by Task Force X-Ray in the Hue TAOR. On 23 April, some mess equipment and cooks were brought into the La Son Command Post from battalion rear at Duong Son (2) south of Da Nang. By 25 April a rudimentary field mess was operational at the La Son School CP which served hot coffee, soup, and light menu items to CP personnel. C-Rats remained the main staple of most Marines and Corpsmen in the field on the No Name operations.

First Lieutenant John Bouldin recalled that, "Lieutenant Thad Wiener in H&S, quite the 'procurement specialist,' somehow arranged for a pallet of canned sardines to be delivered to our schoolhouse CP. Evidently, he knew a Seabee at the NSA ramp on Col Co Island who was with 1/27 on Iwo Jima in WWII and they had become fast friends. The old Seabee had a soft spot in his heart for 1/27. We ended up with sardines in mustard sauce, in tomato sauce and even in olive oil...we had sardines running out our ears! Ole Thad was quite the guy and would come up with some of the most unusual and unsuspecting items at odd times. He even procured some sunglasses that I think were made in Hong Kong for all the Marines to wear while on Operation Allen Brook."

Also because of the lack of culinary opportunities, Corporal Pat Rider and buddies sent away for the much-heralded Tabasco Sauce C-Ration Cook Book by mail order.

Due to Delta Company's bland dietary situation, an imagination and a recipe book would liven up a daily diet of C-Rats, or so they thought. Rider recollects, "After receiving the cookbook, which was really a pamphlet, we would always find that the recipes called for at least a couple of ingredients that we didn't have. Buying or bartering with the locals or the 'Cowboys' [ARVNs] we could usually come up with steamed rice, onions and once even a live chicken."

"The Tabasco C-Ration Cookbook," published by McIlhenny Company (makers of Tabasco hot sauce) provided reading humor and distinctive-tasting C-rations for the fighting man in the field. One of those recipes, Soup Du Jour, a non-favorite amongst Marines and Corpsmen, called for a can of ham and lima beans, mashed. One equal can of hot water…salt and pepper to taste…a generous dash or two or three or four of Tabasco pepper sauce, three plastic spoons of green onions, chopped and sautéed in butter or oil or fat. Add fried bread croutons (if available) or crumbled saltine crackers. The recipe went on to point out, "There is soup du jour on every menu in every American restaurant from Maine to Frisco. There is no reason why the Armed Forces should be an exception. The front-line fighting man has one advantage. He knows what goes into his soup du jour…Bon Appetite!"

Company D's "C-Rat Taste Tester," Corporal Pat Rider ~ Courtesy of Tracy Robeson, D Co, 1/27

Beginning of Operation No Name #4

BLT-127 Command Chronologies of May 1968 record two additional Battalion-level operations. Operation No Name #4 commenced 3 May and concluded on 7 May, and made contact with NVA elements still intent on remaining in the TAOR.

Operational Order 4-68 was patterned to conduct an intensive push along the canal network in the central sector of the Battalion TAOR where the concentration of NVA and VC were suspected of regrouping and staging. The secondary mission was that of rice denial to those enemy combatants. The operation was to be executed in three phases.

In Phase 1, Companies C and D were to begin sweeping westward from the far eastern side of the canal toward Company A already in blocking position, preventing enemy egress to the west. In Phase 2, Company D would thrust to the northeastern peninsula area toward the coast, searching for residual enemy elements. Company C would remain in defensive posture along the canal conducting patrol activity, west, south, and southeast from that position. After those actions, Company C and D were to conduct a search and clear operation in the villages along the canal from YD833230 to YD830218. This movement would navigate the banks of the waterway in a southerly direction into a relatively unexplored area. This was to conclude Phase 3 and the operation.

When the operation kicked off and all units were on the line of departure (Phase Line Brown), Task Force X-Ray directed 1/27 to divert and support an ARVN operation. Companies C and D with tanks attached moved to the requested block position, and held for the 39th ARVN Ranger Battalion to complete their maneuver. After being relieved of that duty Companies C and D moved into defensive positions and dug in for the night. The next day the same activity was repeated, however the block was reoriented to the southwest which produced negative results and no contact with the enemy. Phase 1 was put on hold while these blocking actions were performed.

After completing the blocking obligation, Companies C and D, with armor in tow, executed the original plan of Phase 2. Completing that activity, both Companies set into their night defensive position the night of 4 May.

Blocking Action by Bravo 3

In the early morning hours of 3 May, a squad from Alpha Company moved south to Bravo Company's 3rd Platoon PPB at Thon Dien Thai (grid coordinate YD787228) to take over that base so that they could join Charlie and Delta Companies in the ensuing operation. The squad from Alpha Company was ambushed several hundred meters out from the PPB. They suffered severe casualties. Lieutenant O'Rourke sent one of his squads with a Corpsman to aid them while he called for an emergency medevac. Once that situation was under control, 3rd Platoon became attached to Charlie and Delta Companies to start the operation.

Four of O'Rourke's platoon members remained at the PPB along with the remainder of the Alpha Company squad. The four had medical conditions that precluded them from operating in the field.

The initial action plan was to seize the village, Cho Sam, the scene of battle on 13 April (grid coordinate YD833237). A heavy artillery preparatory fire and A-4 Skyhawk bombing were called in prior to the maneuver. Lieutenant O'Rourke's Marines in the 3rd Platoon was assigned the mission of securing the village on both sides of the canal while Charlie and Delta conducted search and clear operations to the east. After securing the ville, his platoon dug in and waited. Later in the day, they began receiving automatic weapons fire from an unknown location. Fire discipline was held since they could not identify the source of the firing. The platoon was well concealed and took no casualties.

Lieutenant O'Rourke thought about the probe earlier that day and as darkness fell decided to act. "It had occurred to me that quite possibly the enemy might have concluded that the village was not occupied, since we had not disclosed our presence. Considering this, I speculated that the enemy might try to move into or through the ville."

Charlie Company had set up and occupied the south side of the canal while Bravo 3 held the north side. Delta Company dug in about 400 meters to the northeast in their nighttime perimeter. O'Rourke ordered a squad to move eastward along the canal 200 meters and set up an ambush should the enemy decide to attack from that direction. He recalled, "It was not a long wait as the Squad Leader radioed that he heard voices and movement to his front. They held their fire until the enemy was directly in their position, then executed a short, violent ambush. The squad maintained its position in case of a follow-on force, listening to the cries of the wounded enemy. It was estimated there were six NVA in the group. After a lengthy period of quiet, I ordered the squad to return and solidified our perimeter. We waited until dawn to have a look at the ambush site. No bodies were found but the blood trails were much in evidence as they had been obviously dragged from the area."

More Enemy Action

On 5 May during the pre-dawn at 0330 hours, Company D's defensive positions were assaulted from the northeast by a large force of seasoned NVA regulars. Their pre-planned mortar barrage and precise rocket-propelled grenade fire signaled the start of the attacks. The attack was well orchestrated and heavy. The initial assault was repulsed; however, a second wave of attacks shifted and came from the northwest. This second thrust penetrated Company D defensive lines.

The penetration was sealed and contained, reestablishing the defensive perimeter around 0445 hours of the early morning. Five enemy bodies, makeshift stretchers, and many blood trails leading east and northwest were discovered in the aftermath. Assault rifles, twenty-five undetonated satchel charges and miscellaneous equipment were collected and cataloged for Intel from the entire battlefield. An extensive search of the entire defensive perimeter and its outlying areas ensued after the sun rose. The enemy took heavy casualties, as evidenced by extensive drag and blood trails leading away from the perimeter.

5 May 1968, a Long Night

At dusk on the evening of 4 May, Company D set up defensive positions for the night. The "hasty defense" perimeter encompassed the north and south sides of Community Road 552 running east and west. It was near a graveyard which was to the east. The group consisted of Delta Company's 2nd Platoon, its command group, Captain Pat Kahler in command, and a two-tube section of 81mm mortars. Traveling with this element were two armored Ontos track vehicles with their six mounted 106mm recoilless rifles.

L-R: Delta Company Marines, Robert Weinberger, Gary Jarvis, Scott Nesbitt and Dennis Malvasi below
~ Courtesy Tracy Robeson, D Co, 1/27

Two M60 machine gun teams were placed on the southeast and northwest sides of the perimeter. Both pointed outwardly, providing an advantageous 270-degree field of fire. Listening posts were also dispatched a short distance from each side of the road to the north and south. Then-Lance Corporal Gary Jarvis, a Company D rifleman, reminisces, "I had only been in the country for less than a month after turning eighteen years old. I, along with PFC Gifford Davis and PFC George Carrattini, walked about 100 yards outside the perimeter and set up an LP near the graveyard, on the northeast side of our main defensive positions. We were to be the doorbell for any visitors who came to visit our main force."

As Jarvis recalls, "At around 0300 hours enemy activity began to happen. Within minutes all three of us verified that enemy combatants were passing through and using the nearby graveyard as cover. We estimated that approximately half of a reinforced company of NVA had crossed in front of our position."

Gary and his teammates began verbally yelling to the 81mm crew to "pop illumination" to expose the enemy on the north side of the perimeter. There was a problem with the mortar tubes which prevented illumination rounds from being placed overhead. Corporal Matthew Greer heard the yelling and immediately rushed out to the LP and fired an M79 grenade launcher illumination round to shed light on what was the beginning of an assault.

Jarvis describes what happened next. "After Greer lit up the sky with the illumination flare, the NVA opened up on the entire perimeter and us in the LP position with small arms, machine guns, RPGs and mortars, and began to advance toward our positions. Corporal Greer was hit immediately after he fired his M79 and died next to me. Simultaneously, both machine gun positions were hit with heavy concentrations of fire and RPGs."

In the defensive perimeter, PFC Louis Chimeri was instantly killed and the others with him were severely wounded, including PFC Charles Blythe, PFC Tyrone Douglas, and PFC Donald Ingram. Another M60 team leader, Corporal John Hayden, was also wounded during the initial assault. Jarvis surmised, "This group of enemy combatants had gathered intelligence on our gun positions prior to the attack, which was later confirmed by a notebook found on the C117 Local Main Force Company Commander who had been killed inside our platoon's defensive perimeter."

During the initial attack, Jarvis's LP team briefly returned fire, grabbed all their ammunition and sprinted back into the platoon perimeter yelling they were coming inward. Jarvis remembers, "The enemy right behind us made an on-line assault toward the northeast and east side [road] of the main defensive position. As we approached the platoon defensive wire, PFC Gifford Davis received a round to his chest. I was wounded by either a hand grenade or rocket-propelled grenade fragment which briefly knocked me down and unconscious."

Coming to and getting up, Jarvis, became aware of an extreme pain in his right hand, which was also bleeding profusely. The tip of his right thumb had been shot off or severed by shrapnel, exposing the bone. He recalls, "The three of us eventually made it back into the north side of our perimeter safely. Small bits of shrapnel had penetrated other areas of my body."

Once Lance Corporal Jarvis was inside the perimeter, crawling along the western boundary, he began looking for Gunnery Sergeant Jesse Dobson. While scrambling around he observed an RPG round impact one of the Ontos tracked vehicles attached to the platoon. This weaponry was basically a carrier of six very large shotguns with extreme knockdown power, which had been taken out of commission by the RPG explosion. He thought to himself, "Oh, hell, we could have used that Ontos for what was coming at us..."

Jarvis recaptures the tumultuous situation of that dark early morning assault: "There were many enemies near and in our perimeter. Some you could see and others not. I heard PFC Ingram yelling for help. Lieutenant John Lancaster and I attempted to make our way out to Ingram's location. Lieutenant Lancaster took an AK-47 round which had unfortunately hit his spinal cord. I don't remember who but another Marine carried him back to the command center for medical help. I kept trying to go to Ingram and was finally able to reach him and PFC Douglas's position."

The enemy continued their attack on the perimeter while Lance Corporal Jarvis dragged both Ingram and Douglas one by one to a bomb crater east of their original position. Jarvis vividly recollects that Douglas, "screamed as I drug him away from the gun emplacement. Most of both feet had been blown off. The crater was already being utilized by PFC David Roberts. I set my gun up on the western edge of the crater and hastily made two more trips back to retrieve all of the ammunition and a semi-automatic service pistol in its holster left hanging on a tree limb by PFC Ingram."

Jarvis quickly set up the M60 gun. He held his fire until he could see the enemy combatants. "I started firing only short bursts to conserve ammo and prevent over-heating of the barrel. I was very aware that the tracer rounds would attract enemy incoming fire, including B-40 rockets, satchel charges, and hand grenades."

While the battle raged, friendly artillery rounds impacted near the outer boundary of the Marines' position. The overhead artillery illumination rounds helped expose enemy movements in the rice paddy and tree line. This was helpful in exposing the attacking NVA and slowing down all incoming fire on the Marine position.

The battle went in cycles. There were moments of quiet and then activity would pick back up. About an hour into the initial assault from the northeast, the enemy launched another attack, this time advancing on the western side. Lance Corporal Jarvis remembers, "I started seeing what looked like a platoon or maybe more of NVA advancing toward my position while in the crater. From both a standing and prone position, I fired long bursts. My barrel began heating up. I noticed that their advance began to slow and then halt. Most of them were on the ground in a prone position in a dry paddy area directly in front of me. I could not tell if they were alive or dead. Waiting for my barrel to cool, I began firing my M16 rifle and the .45-caliber service pistol at those prone figures lying in the rice paddy."

After his machine gun barrel had cooled enough to use it again, Jarvis "placed a new belt in the gun and started firing at NVA advancing into the tree line to my right. Some of them made it into the tree cover. Carratinni and Roberts continued firing madly at the advancing enemy. PFC Roberts attempted to throw a hand grenade and was shot in the neck as he was throwing. He died within minutes. The NVA soldier who had shot him was also killed."

A squad dispatched from Charlie Company arrived to reinforce the beleaguered Marines, immediately moving toward the NVA already in the tree line. The Charlie Team Leader and another Marine were wounded in their advance toward the trees. They eventually secured that area and came back to the main defensive perimeter to help with the wounded.

Jarvis keenly remembers, "When the dawn came, the NVA had retreated and things were quiet again. I had fired more than a thousand rounds during that assault. There is no doubt my M60 played a significant role in repelling this numerically superior enemy force. I was medically evacuated and spent the next three weeks in the hospital before returning to Delta Company."

Lance Corporal Gary Jarvis led that night by example and answered the call of duty far above normal bravery. His courage, example, and devotion to his fellow Marines were in keeping with the exacting standards and motto of the Marine Corps, *Semper Fidelis* or "Always Faithful." Like most M60 gunners, he, an 0311 rifleman, knew that weapon inside and out and understood its awesome capabilities. Years later, Jarvis would write the first history book of 1st Battalion, 27th Marines in Vietnam, *Young Blood: A History of the 1st Battalion, 27th Marines.*

Sting Ray Patrol Activity Close to Delta Company CP

Sergeant Larry Broadhurst, now Chief Battalion Scout, remembers preparation for a Sting Ray patrol in Delta's area in early May. The day before Delta was assaulted, Sergeant Broadhurst was told by his Platoon Commander to pick a good spot for a night ambush and was taken up in a helicopter to view the area around Delta's CP. Late afternoon the next day he, Richard Hunt, Alexander Rios and another Marine rode out to Delta Company in a jeep and were dropped off for their assignment to set up a Sting-Ray-style ambush once it got dark.

Broadhurst recalls, "It was about 0300 in the morning when the attack came and we had set up about 500 yards east of Delta's position. We had plenty of ammo, a PRC-25 radio, and a starlight scope. Delta Company got hit hard and fast when the NVA assault began. We had set up our ambush in a drainage ditch about fifty yards away from a cemetery. I know Captain Kahler had to call artillery in close to his own position because the NVA had overrun certain sections of his lines. When the rounds started impacting, some of them were hitting very close to our position. We had to lay completely flat in the ditch while the artillery was coming in... It was pretty hairy for quite a while." After the attack, Sergeant Broadhurst remembers that about four or five NVA came into the cemetery area close to where they were set up. He called for illumination rounds to verify if they were friendlies or NVA. He didn't want to make any mistakes. The request for illumination took too long and the individuals were gone before they got the artillery flares overhead. He recalls thinking, "I am almost sure they were NVA. They left quickly and seemed familiar with where they were going. I am guessing they had spider traps to hide in or tunnels for a quick escape. The enemy was just really thick all over this area to the east of our Battalion schoolhouse CP."

Communal Road 552 Looking East ~ Courtesy of Larry Broadhurst, H&S Co, 1/27

The following morning when the sun rose, Broadhurst and his Sting Ray Marines got up out of their positions and hiked over to Delta Company's CP to help police the area, carry the wounded, and stage the dead. After regrouping, the four Marines in Sergeant Broadhurst's team started walking west on Communal Road 552 toward the La Son Schoolhouse CP. A tree line to the south of them caused some concern and as Broadhurst recalls, "As I suspicioned we started taking small arms fire from a wooden structure just barely visible in the trees. It was back into the trees therefore mostly hidden from our view. Supporting tanks happened to be sweeping the road for mines ahead of us… I got the tank's attention and motioned him to an advantageous position.

I picked up on the outside telephone on the tank and started directing his fire with machine gun toward the source."

Sergeant Broadhurst then ran off the road and jumped into a drainage ditch which ran parallel along the communal road to further direct his Marines. They had provided covering fire and were beginning to suppress the small arms firing on them. As Broadhurst remembers, "I hadn't paid attention to the tank and what it was doing after it had provided fire support. Once in the ditch and assessing the situation I hadn't noticed the tank had pivoted and come up directly behind me on the edge of the ditch...luckily, he stopped close to me and fired a 90mm canister round right over my head, taking the hooch out. During this maneuver and firing overhead, the concussion blew me almost out of the ditch. I lost my hearing for a long time the rest of that day. That took care of the ambush problem and we did not receive any more fire after that. We were lucky that the tanks were doing the sweep that morning."

Friendly Fire

On 5 May, Lieutenant Bob O'Rourke noted in his log that Delta Company's position was attacked from the northeast by a well-manned and armed enemy force. His own 3rd Platoon observed on the flank from about 300-400 meters south and prepared to reinforce if necessary. Bravo 3 briefly provided flanking fire in support, but were radioed by Delta Company Commander, Captain Pat Kahler, to cease fire since it was confusing his men that it might be additional enemy fire. As O'Rourke recounts, "Charlie Company sent a squad through our lines to reinforce Delta. The battle lasted until dawn and was buttressed by heavy artillery support and an orbiting 'Puff the Magic Dragon' gunship which streamed red tracers at the enemy and continually dropped illumination flares keeping the battlefield lit up continuously."

Lieutenant O'Rourke with his men, OP No Name #4 ~ Courtesy of Ronald G. Oakes, B Co, 1/27

As Delta Company evacuated its dead and wounded and policed up the battlefield, Captain Kahler, C.O. of Delta, ordered the attached Bravo 3 Platoon to sweep toward the northeast from which the attack originated. Countless blood trails and personal gear were observed along the path of the enemy retreat. 2nd Lieutenant O'Rourke remembers watching a Vietnamese Air Force AD Skyraider orbiting over a village off to the northeast during the sweep. The village of Thon Xuan O (1) (grid coordinate YD855250) was the target of the bombing. He recalls, "Villagers began streaming out of the area. We began taking light automatic weapons fire from a tree line just south of that village. We then called in 8-inch artillery on the tree line and began an on-line assault, informing Captain Kahler of our action. We reached the tree line without incident, and suddenly saw a red 2.75-inch rocket explosion launched by an airborne Forward Air Controller twenty meters out directly to our front. It was immediately obvious that the FAC was aiming at us and about to order a bomb run."

Lieutenant O'Rourke immediately radioed Captain Kahler and tried to contact the Tactical Air Control Party (TACP) network. As he was frantically trying to cancel this bombing run he saw the first of two A-4 Skyhawks rolling in on them. As O'Rourke remembers, "We popped as much yellow smoke as we could to mark our position. Each pilot is trained to put his bombs right on top of the red smoke. Fortunately, there was a berm no more than one to two feet high between our position and where the bombs impacted. That was enough to shield against concussion and flying fragments. Finally, we made radio contact with Delta Company and had the airstrike halted."

No Marines were hit. Years later at Marine Corps Air Station Iwakuni, Japan, O'Rourke would run into the 1st Battalion, 27th Marine air officer at the O-Club bar that had controlled that mission. They talked about the incident, which the officer well remembered. He related to O'Rourke that he cleared the mission for the FAC from the battalion CP after ascertaining that there were no friendlies in the area. O'Rourke afterward thought that "Somewhere along the line there was clearly a break-down in coordination since earlier the battalion Fire Support Coordination Center (FSCC) had cleared an artillery attack on the same location."

Lieutenant O'Rourke called off an assault on the village. He felt that it was likely occupied by NVA, including their dead and wounded. He confides that, "My decision was based on my concern that our position was not well known by higher-ups and that we would have a challenging time as a single platoon in enemy contact two kilo-meters away from reinforcements. To this day, I feel it was the right decision, but also believe that a company-size unit of Marines could have inflicted a decisive defeat on an enemy that was likely trying to recover and reorganize from a disastrous attack the night before. I also came away with a deeper understanding of the use and limits of airpower. The Marine A-4 pilots were precise, based on the red smoke marker, but it could have been catastrophic had the bombs been off just a little or had detonated in the air overhead."

Alpha Company Assaulted 6 May 1968

The 2nd Platoon of Company A was attacked and then overrun beginning at 0230 on 6 May. They were due west of Delta Company's 2nd Platoon, who were also assaulted at approximately the same time. An estimated company of NVA hit the Alpha perimeter first with RPGs, and then ran through it, placing satchel charges in pre-planned positions. The events of Company A's courageous actions that and the following night is best described by Sergeant Felix Salmeron, a second-tour Platoon Sergeant. "Sergeant Sal," as he was called, remembers the battle: "My 2nd Platoon was at a company designated Platoon Patrol Base [grid coordinate YD798245]. The platoon straddled the canal with a squad, a machine gun team and an attached 106 recoilless rifle team on the north side, the other two squads with machine guns and rocket teams on the south side. There was a building inside our perimeter. A deep trench line ran along the length of the canal all the way west to Hue City and the Perfume River. The trench line had [foliage] coverage and could not be seen from aerial observation. The NVA often moved through the area in this trench. Our presence put a stop to their movement. There were lots of tunnels off the trench used as living quarters and escape vents. We had not found this trench until after the April 12th encounter with the NVA. We then ran considerable squad patrols [not full strength] to the east along the canal. We had a sniper team along and they were observing movement in the tree lines to the southwest of our PPB. My first thoughts, we should never have positioned at this location the way we were set up. It was not an ideal situation."[9]

Lance Corporal Ed Singletary, Sergeant Salmeron's radioman, distinctly remembers setting up. "Our unit was split up by the canal. There was that little fifty-five-gallon drum flotation bridge that went across from one side to the other. I was close to Sergeant Sal and Lieutenant Black next to our CP hole lying on the ground. I was not down in the hole. I had fallen asleep while Lieutenant Black had gone out to check the perimeter. I was awakened by an RPG that came screaming across me and exploding in the tree line on the other side. I immediately jumped down in the hole with Sergeant Sal. We soon had illumination rounds going off overhead. After a while, I could see Lieutenant Black running back toward our CP across the bridge bent over holding his stomach. I believe someone was helping him. I knew he'd been shot. Our Corpsman, Allen Sentner, was in the hole and quickly started administering to the Lieutenant's wound. Lieutenant Black had evidently surprised the NVA on the edge of our perimeter while checking our lines after receiving the RPG. It was after that our perimeter got shot up pretty bad that night."

Sergeant Felix Salmeron recalled what happened next, after the 106mm recoilless rifle team reported that they had been fired upon by an RPG hitting their position (PFC Ricky Lee Doye of Prophetstown, Illinois manning the 106 Recoilless Rifle position was killed in that attack 05/05/1968). "Lieutenant Black immediately grabbed his M16, traversing the pontoon bridge and crossed the canal to investigate. Within fifteen to twenty minutes, considerable contact was made. Lieutenant Black was one of the first to be shot and badly wounded. He made it back across the bridge to the south side. We managed to keep him stable and started calling in arty. It seemed forever to get the artillery fire support mission established. It finally arrived and the first impacts landed to our northeast. From that point, I guided the artillery battery, moving the barrage to the south and just east of our perimeter. The action finally broke around 0330 hours."

PFC John Hill, a scout sniper from S-2 attached to Salmeron's platoon, and his spotter watched the open areas and tree lines religiously from the PPB. They spotted NVA movement going and coming all day long. Hill indicated they looked to be squad-size groups. A "mule" brought ammo out to the Marines and to retrieve the 106mm recoilless rifle, taking it back to the Battalion CP. Hill and his spotter left with that mule around 1630 going back to headquarters. Salmeron then had his men set up Claymores, pulling positions into a tighter perimeter, and awaited the expected second assault that evening.

On that second night, 6 May, the LP seventy-five meters south of the perimeter called Sergeant Sal, now acting Platoon Commander, asking if any patrols were out. They reported hearing a voice saying, "Patrol coming in." That LP withdrew to the perimeter. As Sergeant Sal walked over to talk with them, he remembered, "All hell broke loose. We received incoming automatic and small arms fire from the south and east. It lasted about an hour. I had my radioman, Ed Singletary, call in overhead illumination. Realizing that the NVA had penetrated our perimeter, I immediately called for the pre-registered arty around our own position, telling everyone to get down and stay down. It seemed an eternity before those rounds impacted. I counted six incoming rounds. Finally, about 0330 complete silence and all fighting had ceased. By 0530 we could see the results. I had a wounded Marine, Private Artous S. Woods, who needed evacuation. We began to regroup and assess. Several enemy weapons were recovered from within the perimeter. We noted the numerous trails indicated that the NVA had left dragging their dead and wounded with them. The night before I had lost our Platoon Commander, Lieutenant Black and Lance Corporal Carl Crites to critical wounds and evacuation. We were ready to get out of this position. It was not an ideal position. My CO Captain Panther told me to hang tight and he would get us out of there soon."

Sergeant Sal's radioman, Lance Corporal Ed Singletary, remembered that, "We had been at this position quite a while before being attacked. We kind of got comfortable in that position now that I look back. I think that was a problem for us...we had ARVNs close by and they would come right through our area. I remember them coming through the day before we got hit. A whole squad of them...maybe fifteen or twenty of them. In fact, I recall that the last Vietnamese soldier in line had an army rucksack on and he had a duck in it. A live duck with its head sticking out and it was squawking. We all laughed at that comical scene. Now that I think back, I think they were gathering intel, taking notes on our positions and the entire layout...that was just my assumption...I didn't trust any of 'em."

Phase 3 of Operation No Name #4

Phase 3 of the operation began 0900 on the morning of 6 May from the village that Bravo and Charlie Companies had occupied. Charlie Company took the right flank on the south side of the canal, and Bravo 3 (3rd Platoon) was on the north side with Delta Company on their outside flank. The maneuver was accompanied by an

M48 tank which tracked adjacent to Delta. The sweep moved toward a village located to the east and then turned south (grid coordinate YD823219) which was suspected to be a major enemy stronghold.

Dug into fortified positions, the enemy awaited their advance. By 1130 hours the canal itself prevented Company D's final advance. The only avenue of approach for the main body was a bridge crossing the canal. The NVA had started an intense firefight, halting the advance. Around 1600 hours the point element of the company, followed by the rest, traversed the bridge under a rolling artillery barrage and began a house-to-house sweep of the village.

As Bravo 3 moved southeast along the canal they came into a cleared rice-paddy area with a tree line about 150 meters directly to their front (grid coordinate YD833228). Bravo 3 had a fire team well in front operating as point security. As the fire team entered the tree line, they came under intense automatic weapons fire from dug-in positions. O'Rourke recaptures these moments and some macabre humor, "I ordered an immediate frontal assault on the tree line to reinforce our lead fire team. Within thirty seconds, the entire platoon was in the tree line and engaged with the enemy who was no more than ten to twenty meters to our front, well dug in and concealed. There was a small irrigation canal that separated my platoon from the combatants. The point fire team had gotten to the other side of the irrigation canal, and I realized immediately that our most pressing task was to get them back on our side and treat the wounded. We did this quickly but took a few more wounded in the process, including one of our Corpsmen. I recall during this intense battle, that the wounded Corpsman, Bennett, started joking with me that he had the 'Million Dollar' wound, a gunshot wound through the fleshy part of his arm, oblivious to what was going on all around the battlefield."

Forward Observer, Johnson and "Doc" Kirkpatrick with Bravo 3
~ Courtesy of Ronald G. Oakes, B Co, 1/27

Bravo 3 had walked into a hornet's nest of enemy activity. The fight was extremely close in and intense, the noise deafening. Grenades and rockets were used by both sides and while the local vegetation gave some concealment, it was being cut to shreds by the gunfire. Lieutenant O'Rourke recalls, "Dirt was kicking up in our faces from the enemy bullets. My Marines fought bravely and professionally. We kept moving our machine gun positions to avoid them getting pinpointed. We had come to a stalemate and were too close to the enemy to use air support or artillery, with causalities mounting on both sides. This seemed to be their normal tactics, get us in and close at hand so we could not use our air or arty resources. HM2 Michael D. 'Doc' Kirkpatrick was the only functioning Corpsman and was doing a heroic job of taking care of our wounded under the heavy fusillades of fire."

Dinged

Lieutenant Robert O'Rourke recollects an exhilarating moment when, "Sometime during the battle, I turned my head to motion a fire team forward when I felt a sharp, powerful blow to the back of my head. It literally spun me violently facedown into the dirt, and my helmet was knocked forward covering my face. After a few seconds from literally being stunned, I began feeling my head for blood. Relieved that there was no bleeding, I noticed that only the top of my head was pretty tender."

O'Rourke reminds people now of Winston Churchill's quote from the past, "There is nothing more exhilarating than to be shot at with no result." He remembers that when he lifted his head up he had immediately glanced at one of his faithful riflemen, Lance Corporal Kermit Evans, weapon in the firing position staring down at him with eyes as big as banjos. "We grinned at each other in this moment of relief and kept on fighting."

Lieutenant Bob O'Rourke firing at NVA ~ Courtesy of Ronald G. Oakes, Bravo Co, 1/27

The back of his helmet had a dent and hole and the front had a huge dent. The bullet had entered the back of the helmet and was stopped dead in the front. It tore through marker panels and other items that O'Rourke had stored in his helmet. He now reflects, "Somehow, the helmet deflected the projectile enough so that it did not penetrate my skull."

Time to "Di Di Mau"

Bravo 3 had their hands full in this tree line. Captain Kahler, the Company D Commander, called O'Rourke on the net and asked him if he would like to have tank support. He also suggested that he withdraw his platoon so that air and artillery could soften up the area in which they had made contact with a significant number of enemy combatants. Lieutenant O'Rourke recalls that he had no direct radio communication with the tank, "so we relayed instructions through Captain Kahler's radioman. The tank came right up close, positioning to my left. I requested through Kahler's radioman that the tank fire five beehive rounds [gigantic shotgun blast of thousands of flechettes] into the enemy, which they did. Those of us, who were under or next to the tank's muzzle, were very much stunned by the concussive shock wave from the outgoing blast. Lance Corporal Evans grabbed his ears and rolled around on the ground in pain from the percussion. My own ears were throbbing badly."

Under covering fire from the tank, Bravo 3 pulled out of the tree line with all their wounded. Lieutenant O'Rourke and Staff Sergeant Storzum lagged behind the men to lay down covering fire, and finally sprinted back to Delta's position where they reassembled.

Divine Intervention

Five Bravo 3 Marines and one Corpsman had been wounded in the firefight. The six required a medevac. One of the tank crewmen had been killed. Once the dead and wounded were evacuated artillery and air support was called in to pummel the area. During a lull in that action, Lieutenant O'Rourke remembers spotting movement in the enemy-held tree line. He remembers distinctly taking the target under fire, "To my great frustration, none of us could bring that moving person down. We ceased firing when the target broke out of the vegetation and moved toward us now in full view. Oh Jesus, we now realized that our moving target was a young mother who was holding her baby. One of our Vietnamese soldiers with us ran into the open rice paddy and escorted her to our lines and safety. A moment of humanity on the part of the enemy could have been a major tragedy caused by us. I still cannot understand how we could have missed her and must ascribe some divine intervention to this most fortunate outcome!"

A Second and Third Assault on the Tree Line

Again Bravo 3 was ordered into the breach. The second assault failed to reach the tree line objective because the platoon started taking heavy fire while moving across the rice paddy toward the dug-in enemy. PFC Johnnie Smith received an abdominal wound. Realizing that his platoon was in a "world of hurt," pinned down, and unable to move forward, O'Rourke sprinted to the tank to get it into the fight. As he recollects, "I became an immediate target, but by using a series of very short two second rushes, I was able to finally reach the tank. During the sprint, I could hear those familiar snaps over my head just as I hit the ground each time."

O'Rourke tried using the external phone located on the right rear of the tank. He had no success in contacting the tank commander inside at first. So, he climbed onto the turret and frantically banged on the hatch. The tank crew was buttoned up tight due to enemy fire. As O'Rourke remembers with glee, the tank commander had heard the banging and by great coincidence opened the hatch. When he did, "we recognized each other as classmates from Officers Basic School. He calmly asked me, 'O'Rourke, what the fuck are you doing here?'"

It was no time for conversation, as O'Rourke remembers, but "a humorous encounter upon reflection." The tank's subsequent main gun and heavy machine gun fire enabled O'Rourke's platoon to withdraw to cover and attempt to get PFC Johnnie Smith medevac'd, which did not happen in time. Sadly, Smith died just before the helicopter landed. O'Rourke remembers, "He had just joined our platoon and had made such a good first impression on all of us. We sincerely hated losing him! I hated this part of the war, losing such good men."

More artillery was called in firing for effect and the third assault began. Delta Company and Bravo 3 conducted a frontal on-line assault against no opposition. As Lieutenant O'Rourke describes, "I was positioned on the tank with Staff Sergeant Storzum directing the platoon. All the enemy combatants except four had been killed in the artillery barrage and previous assaults. The surviving four attempted an escape but were taken under fire from the tank, which leveled the house into which they ran."

After policing the battle area, the Marines of Delta and Bravo went back to the original starting positions for the night. The battle had lasted an entire day and had claimed the lives of two Marines and at least fifteen or twenty enemies. O'Rourke reflects, "My platoon suffered six evacuated WIA in addition to PFC Johnnie Smith KIA. Operation No Name #4 came to an end the next morning. Then we temporarily spent the night of 7 May at battalion CP schoolhouse. We then returned to our old positions [Grid Coordinate YD787228] of 3 May 1968."

Concluding the operation on 7 May, the Battalion executed what was originally planned as Phase 1 of the operation. Companies C and D pushed toward a designated blocking point manned by a platoon of Company A Marines. A methodical house-to-house search of the hamlets along the canal discovered excessive amounts of rice, the main staple of the enemy. Some villagers indicated that many combatants had left the area after the initial battles. Many weapons, mortars and mortar rounds, and RPG launchers, along with a large supply of ammunition, was confiscated, logged and then sent back to HQ Intel. A detailed sketch of the existing defensive trench system and emplacements were recorded and sent back to Battalion for analysis.[10]

Standing Down

In the time afterward, O'Rourke started noticing that he was having some blurred vision problems and was ordered by his Executive Officer, First Lieutenant Dick Wozar, to be medevac'd to Da Nang for examination. The medical analysis was that Lieutenant O'Rourke had suffered a mild concussion. Coming back from Da Nang he returned to Phu Bai via C-130 to rejoin his platoon, which was now bivouacked at the canal platoon patrol base. He fondly remembers that, "I stopped in the Phu Bai medical facility to visit some of my Marines who had been medevac'd and were still there. That was particularly emotional for me since I had had the time to think about the previous week's combat action and our losses. I could not have felt more pride in how well they had conducted themselves."

Upon returning to the platoon, O'Rourke was pleased to see how well they had operated and was briefed on past and current operations. There had been an attack on their base on the night of 5 May that was repulsed with no casualties. The pre-planned artillery mission registering had played a key role in the defense of the PPB.

An Investigation

However, not all had gone well while Lieutenant was gone. Four of his Marines informed Lieutenant O'Rourke of a tragic incident. Before and after the 5 May assault on the PPB, they told him that five Vietnamese men had been taken prisoner by members of a squad from Alpha Company. All five of the Vietnamese were murdered. As O'Rourke recollects, "I had a tough time comprehending what I was being told but became convinced when they showed me the bodies of the men in the canal and described in detail how they had been killed. My Marines stated that they had not participated in the killing, and were concerned for their own safety if they had tried to stop it."

Early the next morning, O'Rourke gathered the four Marines and walked two kilometers to the Battalion and Alpha Company Command Posts located at the schoolhouse. He reported the incident to Alpha Company XO, First Lieutenant John Bouldin, and had his Marines tell their story.

First Lieutenant Bouldin acted immediately and without hesitation. He summoned the Alpha Company Marines involved to report to the CP where they readily admitted to the murders. The response from Regimental Headquarters was also extremely quick as O'Rourke remembers, "Before my men and I left the Battalion CP for our patrol base, investigators arrived by helicopter. A military court tried and convicted the accused Marines in Da Nang at Division Headquarters. While the tragic murders were a serious blemish on the Battalion's record, I am proud that there was never a hint of cover up or hesitation in reporting it up the line. We had pretty clear rules of engagement, especially when there were unarmed civilians potentially involved."

Operation No Name #5

Operation Order 5-68, Operation No Name #5, commenced on 11 May 1968. This maneuver was to secure the outer coastal region in the northeastern sector of 1/27's TAOR. The plan had Companies A and C being helo-lifted into the hamlets of the outer banks along the coastal strand of the South China Sea. Both Companies were to push to the northwest, tracking the coast.

The Vietnamese National Police Field Force followed in trace of (behind) the assault companies and was to conduct a thorough house-to-house search in the hamlets of Thon Ke Sung, Thon Cu Lai, and Thon An Duong. The 64th and 65th Popular Force Platoons of Phu Vang District provided a blocking force at the northwestern end of the strand, accompanied by tanks and Ontos.

The South Vietnamese 12th Coastal Group Junk Fleet, along with U. S. Navy Patrol River Forces, surveilled the inland waterways along this coastal strand for enemy movement away from the operation. No significant contacts were made during this operation; however, considerable weapons and munitions collection was recorded and sent to Battalion headquarters, along with thirty-one suspicious detainees and one Viet Cong KIA.

Mike Tracy, Bravo Company on a coastal area patrol ~ Courtesy of the Cliff Broyer family

Corporal Gabe Komanec, Company C, had control of his squad on this operation. His Company had run into some resistance north of the fuel farm. Komanec recalls coming into an open rice paddy area and engaging in a firefight with the NVA and some of the locals that had been recruited by them. He remembers, "Some of them had tried to escape by wading out into the rice paddies lying under water thinking we would pass by them. We had a chopper overhead who would spot them and drop smoke grenades on their positions. My guys would go out and retrieve them so we could send them back to the rear for interrogation. One of them kept trying to escape. I had one of my Marines watching him and finally I told my guy, just let him go as we were getting some heavier fire and I needed him to engage the enemy. Sure enough, the local VC got up and ran. He did not make it very far because one of his own 'capped' him as he was running back to them."

On Patrol with a Scout-Sniper Team

The S-2 section in a maneuver Battalion is responsible for all intelligence gathering, and analyzing all available information about the enemy to determine their location and intent. Additionally, this section is tasked with providing strategic protection and security for the "mother" unit and serves as the "eyes and ears" of the Battalion. The S-2 intel people were constantly probing the area for anything they could piece together about the VC and NVA units operating in the area.

An article from Stars and Stripes (the military newspaper for the troops in Vietnam) of 23 May 1968 highlighted two Marines, one a member of 1/27 and the other attached to 1/27 from HQ Company, 27th Marine Regiment, and explained the routine of an S-2 scout-sniper team operating in the Hue-Phu Bai TAOR during Operations No Name #1-#5:

The first member, Private Jim McConnell, 23, of Sparks, NV, the 1/27 battalion scout leading the patrol, stands six-foot-five and weighs 250 pounds, with 32 months of combat experience. He was fighting in Vietnam when most of his men were in high school. The men look up to him. Since most of them are new to Vietnam, McConnell takes the lead as they move out.

Tommy Romo and Jim McConnell surveilling a target ~ Courtesy of Tommy Romo, S2, HQ Co, 27th Marine Regiment (DOD USMC Photo was given to T. Romo)

Presently assigned to the 1st Bn., 27th Marines, McConnell has 19 months' experience as a reconnaissance Marine. Deer-stalking stealth and the ability to move undetected in the enemy country are his specialties.

McConnell is always followed by Nguyen Ton...The "Hoi Chanh" (Viet Cong returned) scout has sworn to avenge the murder of his wife and seven children by North Vietnamese troops during the Tet offensive. Except for one brother, all his relatives died during earlier offensives.

The terrain the scorpion patrol moved through was mostly open...The objective was an old pagoda, and the Marines quickly fanned out around it for perimeter security. The sniper and spotter worked their way through dense brush and settled in...McConnell decided it was too quiet, so he and the other sniper team moved out. They ran across the road and disappeared...Later, 700 meters from their old position, the team stopped near three dirt mounds. Finding an NVA hat, McConnell assembled the team...The spotter and sniper settled into their surveillance routine.

A half hour later the sniper, Corporal Tommy Romo [S2, HQ Company, 27th Marine Regiment], 21, of San Antonio, Texas spotted movement... "I've spotted somebody in that hooch next to the banana tree," Romo reported. "He has a machine gun. No, wait—there are four, all with weapons!"

The range was at least 1,000 yards. Romo had once killed an NVA at 1,000 yards. He adjusted for range and windage and fired. A puff of dirt exploded a foot away from the enemy soldier, who quickly disappeared inside the hut.

McConnell radioed for a mortar fire mission. When the initial round landed, McConnell adjusted— "200 meters to the right…and fire for effect." The 81mm mortar rounds exploded in and around the hut… "Scratch four 'Charlie's,'" yelled McConnell into the radio…He then told his men that the NVA knew they were there and that they needed to "Di di mau, most ricky tick!"

The NVA waited until the Marines were in the middle of the paddy…Then an enemy mortar round landed nearby. The Marines hit the deck, but McConnell started screaming, "Move out! Move out!" Everyone followed McConnell, heading for a small bridge and gully 500 yards away.

A second mortar round landed closer. Gasping, out of breath, the Marines dove into the gully as a third shell exploded a hundred yards ahead.

McConnell checked for casualties and found one man missing. It was the last man and no one had seen him fall. McConnell ran out to the area where the mortars had first landed…as he reached the fallen Marine the man was coming around. The concussion had knocked him out, but the shrapnel had not touched him.

The two had begun to walk back when a sniper fired at them. Instantly, McConnell dropped to one knee and fired the light antitank assault weapon he had carried along…The rocket left the tube with a roar and slammed into the nearby tree line. Other Marines laid down a base of fire, under which McConnell and the other Marine reached safety.

It had been a close call on a three-hour patrol, one of many that U. S. Marines go through daily…It was getting dark as the scorpion patrol reached friendly lines. The password was exchanged and the 12 Marines passed through the wire.

Corporal Tommy Romo, Scout-Sniper with his M40 Rifle in a Vietnamese village
~ Courtesy of Corporal Tommy Romo, S-2, HQ Co, 27th Marine Regiment

The Ambush

The ambush technique was a multi-faceted concept that brought in basic tactical intelligence about the enemy and how they operated in the TAOR. A lot of times luck was with the Marines in the field as they carried out not only their daily security of covering the area but also the night ambushes that had to be set up. One such incident tells a lucky story and an enemy plan of attack that was spoiled.

Corporal Gabe Komanec of Charlie Company took out eleven Marines one night to set up an L-shaped ambush in Charlie Company's area of operation. Corporal Komanec reflects on that particular night, "We were taking turns sleeping, half on, half off...We would sleep for a couple of hours and then relieve the other guys. It was my turn to sleep and one of my Marines poked me and said there were some gooks coming into our ambush. I am up immediately and see this head coming down the path. It was dark and hard to see well. I passed the word to alert all the others sleeping and get them on-line. Well, they heard us in our haste to get up and ready. You could hear them trotting down the path, running away flopping sandals. I then ordered all the Marines to turn around and di di mau toward our Platoon Patrol Base perimeter. I had no idea how many of them there were. I lobbed three rounds of M79 into where I thought they were. You could hear them jabbering and screeching amongst themselves. I lobbed a couple more into the middle of where the voices were coming from. That got their heads down...I then turned towards base, bringing up the rear."

Back in the security of the Platoon Patrol Base perimeter with the rest of the platoon, Komanec explained what had happened. He told everyone that, "We had run into a fairly large force out there from what I could tell. We had foiled them with the element of surprise as they were about to set up for an assault on the PPB. It spoiled their plans and we beat them to the punch!"

No Rest for the Battalion

On 15 May, elements of the 2nd Brigade, 101st Airborne returned to the Hue TAOR and relieved 1st Battalion, 27th Marines of its security duty at the Naval Support Activity complex on the coast. Company C began their extraction out of the area on 14 May. Along with the Battalion Command Group minus the Battalion Commander, they helo-lifted back to the 3rd Battalion, 27th Marine CP (grid coordinates BT070656) named LZ 413, south of Da Nang.

The rest of the line companies began their exit from their respective PPBs early in the morning hours on the 15th. Company B extracted from the Phu Bai airfield south of Hue City and returned to the new TAOR to begin Operation Allen Brook. Company D and H&S Company, with most of the supplies and equipment, departed from the NSA tank farm at Tam My (Col Co) for Da Nang harbor by a Navy LST.

The Battalion began new offensive operations on 16 May, taking over the 3rd Battalion, 27th Marines' tactical area of operations south of Da Nang. Captain William Sweeney recalls the events, "As 15 May dawned we began to move out of the

Hue TAOR via helicopter to the 3rd Battalion, 27th Marines CP about ten kilometers south of Da Nang city proper. As soon as we landed, I attended a Commander and Staff meeting hosted by Headquarters 3/27. They were moving out the next morning to Go Noi Island, beginning their part in the multi-battalion Operation Allen Brook. Our mission was to take over security in an area west of Highway 1 which included the Tu Cau Bridge over the S. Vinh Dien River."[11]

Bravo Company began patrolling the new AO day and night. Firefights were few but the area was infested with booby traps. There would be no rest for anyone, especially for Bravo 3, which began patrolling the booby-trapped area. Also, the Korean Marines' CP was located just across the southern border of Bravo's TAOR, and inadvertent artillery fire into Bravo's area from the Koreans became a real threat during the first days of adjusting to the area.

The memory of the days at Hue come back to Lieutenant O'Rourke, Commander of Bravo Company's 3rd Platoon: "Morale in the platoon was high, although our numbers greatly diminished by operating in the Hue-Phu Bai area. The platoon considered itself battle-hardened and competent. I remain to this day in awe of my men and their courage, esprit, and discipline under fire. I felt lucky to be with them in battle!"

The month went fast, with periodic enemy contacts and a few skirmishes. Captain William Sweeney remembers that Lieutenant O'Rourke's 3rd Platoon was "the most engaged of Bravo Company spending a lot of its time OPCON to the other line companies."

Subversion, Terrorism, and Sabotage in the Countryside

The III MAF Command Chronologies of May 1968 note, "The VC propaganda activity doubled from the preceding month of March. Leaflets, mandatory village lectures, and several instances of loudspeaker broadcasts were reported throughout I Corps."

Viet Cong terrorism reports in I Corps rose dramatically during May. Terrorist action against village and hamlet officials and Vietnamese nationals accused of aiding ARVN and III MAF forces increased in frequency. Abductions of key individuals also increased and the desperate effort to rebuild and supply tactical units with rice and manpower expanded noticeably. The same May, Command Chronology log recorded that, "VC/NVA Forces abducted over 1,780 civilians; almost six times the number abducted during the preceding month."

Incidents of espionage, which involved low-level-agent collection of information on ARVN, U. S., and ROK Military Forces and their installations, were ongoing. Sabotage in May 1968 doubled from March.

The Marine Corps Combined Action Company in 1/27's Area of Operations

Not only were 1st Battalion, 27th Marines to provide security for the NSA complex at Tam My/Col Co, they also were to watch over the Tam My to Phu Bai pipeline, bridges along Routes 1 and 551, and additionally to provide a quick-reaction force for the CAP units in this TAOR.

The Combined Action Group was a sincere effort by the Marine Corps in Vietnam to conduct another kind of war. As was pointed out in the introduction to Lt. Colonel William R. Corson's book, *Betrayal*, by William J. Lederer, parallel to all the combat action, protecting and promoting stability would ensure a more peaceful solution. He pointed out that this program was designed to gain the confidence of the indigenous people of South Vietnam while the war was ongoing. According to Lederer, the effort by the Marines to restore stability, peace, and maintaining law and order in the villages and hamlets gave the people "a stake in the land and its political system."

Initially designed with flexibility and to help the South Vietnamese people, these units steadily earned loyalty away from the Viet Cong. Marines who served in this program were volunteers and specially culled by the Marine Corps. Unit objectives within their areas steadily destroyed the Viet Cong infrastructure, provided security for that area, organized a useful intelligence network, and promoted the civic activities of the villages and hamlets. Secondly, these units denied supplies to the enemy, mainly the access to food. The VC would extort or take rice and the Combined Action Platoon seriously deterred those activities. Another goal of the CAP was denial of recruits (young men from the villages) into the ranks of the VC.

Captain Bob Averill, a Combined Action Company Commander, remembers the aftermath of Tet and the May Offensive in the Hue area in 1968. Having spent his first six months on the DMZ with a rifle company as a Platoon Commander and then XO/Acting CO, he was offered a billet with Combined Action Program in the Hue area by his then 9th Marines Regimental Commander, Colonel Robert H. Barrow. In abbreviated time, he found himself in the middle of a newly targeted area to set up a Combined Action Company within a short distance of the La Son Schoolhouse in Phu Vang District. "My District was Huong Tra District in Thua Thien Province. My TAOR was from the north and west walls of the Citadel in Hue City to the base of the mountains leading into the A-Shau valley. When the NVA had taken Hue in February they made Thon La Chu their HQs which then became my tactical area of responsibility."

Major Nguyen van Hu De, Major Phelps, U. S. Army, MACV and First Lt. Bob Averill
~ Courtesy of Bob Averill, H Co, 2/9 & 3rd CAG

As Averill recalls in discussions with the MACV advisor who had been in the area before and during Tet, this was a rich agricultural area, prosperous and loyal to the government of Vietnam (GVN). It was a strong Catholic area. When the NVA arrived for Tet they had filtered down from the A-Shau and used every available route, mostly at night and including the sewers, to position themselves throughout the city. When Tet broke out, a clear majority of the citizenry fled to the east of National Highway 1 and some into the neighboring Phu Vang District. There they came under the protective sheath of the 81mm mortar fan provided by the District Chief, Major Nguyen De, who happened to be a Battery Commander for the Viet Minh at Dien Bien Phu in 1954. His younger brother was also there as a Viet Minh Infantry Commander and was later killed by the Communists. Major De was instrumental in gathering Catholics in that area at the time, and moving south to the Hue area to start a new life. He had worked his way up in the GVN organization and had become the Military District Chief of Huong Tra.

Each district had a civilian Chief and a military Chief. These were co-shared responsibilities in most instances, with the military Chief making the daily security and military decisions. When First Lieutenant Averill arrived at this new assignment he learned that the neighboring Phu Vang district had an extremely strong NVA and VC influence to his east. The Combined Action Company Commander, Al Hitchens, whom Averill coordinated with regularly, confided in him that half of his PF forces were VC and that the district chief was a VC. It became an ongoing problem for Hitchens in the daily security and relations with the citizens of that area.

Per First Lieutenant Averill, Major De became a legend amongst the regional forces and the people of the district during the Tet offensive. After the NVA had moved in and taken the strategic strong points he immediately maneuvered one of his regional force companies of "Rough Puffs" and performed a non-supported, non-illuminated night attack on Hill 211. Hill 211 was the ARVN 105mm artillery battery fan for the area. The NVA had overrun it during the battle for the Citadel in February and used it to support their infantry within the city limits of Hue and the surrounding area.

First Lieutenant Bob Averill's Combined Action Company in Huong Tra District
~ Courtesy of Captain Bob Averill, H Co, 2/9 & 3rd CAG

As First Lieutenant Averill recounts, "When I got there everything was pretty much cleared by Agent Orange…I mean this countryside was a mess. All the villagers were living along National Highway #1 in shacks, makeshift hooches…four posts…cardboard…tin on the roof. They were basically refugees. Major De was a very strong District Chief who really cared for his people. I learned that the Army operated throughout the area. First Cavalry…101st Airborne was in the area. As I understood from talking with others, the Marine Corps had wanted to put a Combined Action Company in this area prior to Tet but never got around to it. I was the first to come into this area. The CAP units that were in and around Hue took the brunt of the NVA attack during Tet as did many civilians. When I reported to Da Nang to start this assignment I met with Lieutenant Colonel Bill Corson. We talked about, what I thought was a long time, maybe an hour. I really didn't know any of the histories of Combined Action Groups. He surprised me by asking my thoughts. He made the comment that the CAP units in fixed positions really got hammered. My thoughts as I recall telling him…Well, yeah, any time you have fixed positions you are vulnerable. In my previous world, life was better outside the wire moving from point to point… much like a fish in the ocean."

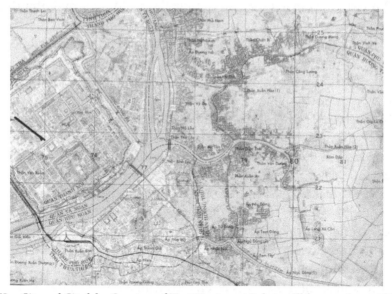

Map of Hue City and Citadel ~ Courtesy of First Lieutenant Bob Averill (personal map 1968-1969)

First Lieutenant Averill had various groups of squads and PFs throughout the District numbering about 200 people in total. The structure was a squad and a Navy Corpsman. Coupled to that squad was anywhere from sixteen to twenty-five Provisional Forces. The task was to provide security, bond with the people, and help them with their projects if possible. Captain Averill recalls there was no guidance from HQs and he could do as he pleased. The guidance came in the form of a Battalion staff meeting where all the Company Commanders would meet regularly and discuss problems, solutions, sharing ideas and different tactics. The company operated with no fixed positions except for the headquarters, which was situated on the northeastern corner of the Citadel, bordering Phu Vang District. "Major De's advice to me—be a benevolent dictator in the villages and the people will support you and your Marines. We did some things that weren't conventional. For instance, we armed every villager with a shotgun if they were older. The females were issued M1 Carbines. We created hamlet defense forces and trained them within the villages in my area. After a while, I came to realize that there was no love for the NVA! An individual could not move through these villages without being detected. These people simply wanted to live in a secure environment, raise their crops, sell their merchandise and raise their families."

"I remember one situation which got my attention early on…one of my nineteen-year-old E-5 Sergeants came to me and proclaimed that he couldn't get flak jackets for his PFs. He simply wanted to have all his Marines shed their flak vests to set an example. He made a statement to me that 'We are in this together…' I thought that was pretty square of him for thinking outside the box. So, I procured a building that wasn't used, had my Marines' flak vests hung up on bamboo poles so they wouldn't mildew. Later an inspection team complete with a General had heard about us and wanted to visit. This General had heard about the flak jacket dilemma and wanted to see for himself. I arranged for him to tour the building. I told him that my PFs don't have jackets and if we are going to work with them we need to have the same level of functioning to set a good example. That worked for him and he thought it a great idea."

"We had mostly success in our time there while De was District Chief. He was promoted to Assistant Province Chief of Quang Tri later in my tour and my new District Chief was the nephew of President Thieu, who had almost no military experience. I was warned by De before he departed that this new kid would bring trouble to the District. He was right. I spent the last two months of my tour countering moves that he instituted. The day I rotated out of Huong Tra District, my best two Vietnamese Lieutenants were killed, one on the street, the other in a church in the village."

These activities due to the CAP unit presence throughout I Corps began to show reliable results in the latter part of 1968. Consequently, the lesson was that if you gained the popular support of the peasant through well-intended civic action, security, and stability, enemy activity would decline. Sadly, although this program became successful at the grassroots level, it continued to be ignored by higher-ups and U. S. political leaders.

One of the duties assigned to 1/27 by Task Force X-Ray along with its daily activities was to prepare and be ready to provide a reaction force if required by the CAP units positioned along Route 1. 1/27 was also responsible for the defense of Hue City. Company B located at the bridge on Highway 1 (YD838176) primarily provided that ready-in-waiting support for the CAPs.

The battle for Hue City and its aftermath had been a huge setback for the enemy in this strategic area of I Corps. The sudden and quick attack by overwhelming numbers of NVA soldiers had caught both the South Vietnamese and the American commands off guard. At first the Marines sent too few troops to drive the NVA out of the city. There had been an underestimation of enemy strength and with Khe Sanh as the main distraction, the action in Hue did not get full attention at the beginning. A lot of remaining NVA not killed in the Hue City operation were forced eastward into the canal area. It was a baptism by fire for 1st Battalion, 27th Marines to go after these combatants, but the lessons learned from these battles was that the best tactic was to immediately take the offense in securing an objective. The experience of learned aggressive action would be needed for the upcoming battles looming south of Da Nang on Operation Allen Brook.

CHAPTER 6

Operation Allen Brook

"Come what come may, time and the hour runs through the roughest day."
~ *Macbeth* by William Shakespeare

After Tet, in the northern region, the 3rd Marine Division was still heavily engaged in confronting the incursions of NVA coming into South Vietnam off the Ho Chi Minh Trail corridors from Laos. While MACV had bolstered I Corps with additional troops early in 1968 and had sent the 1st Air Cavalry and the 101st Airborne Divisions north into Hue and the A Shau Valley, things were starting to heat up south and southwest of Da Nang in Quang Nam Province. Rumors circulated through upper echelon command that a second Tet offensive would launch in the spring. Preparation for that possibility began in April.

After Tet erupted in February of 1968, it became apparent to 1st Marine Division Commander Major General Robertson that the enemy had reinforced their troop strength in the Go Noi area southwest of Da Nang. "Go Noi Island," as it was called, encompassed the delta area straight west of Hoi An, the ancient village of the original Cham people nestled on the coast. Go Noi was not an island, but an area surrounded and formed by the seasonal waters of the Thu Bon, Chiem Son, and Ky Lam Rivers. The monsoon season would fill the rivers to the brim every year. Highway 1 and the national railroad dominated the eastern boundaries of this well-used NVA staging area. The activity in this area and the outlying regions compelled Robertson's staff to begin planning in earnest.

In March of 1968, General Robertson, now with additional manpower, determined it would be advantageous to take the fight directly to the NVA in this area. On 4 May, the Operation Allen Brook offensive began with the 7th Marine Regiment launching the initial attack, under the command of Colonel Reverdy M. Hall.

Some of the Marine Corp's fiercest operations in I Corps had already peaked in the earlier days of 1968 (Battle for Hue City and Khe Sanh). Two more major operations, Operation Allen Brook (officially 4 May – 24 Aug 1968) and Mameluke Thrust (officially 18 May – 23 Oct 1968), became multi-battalion exercises and among the larger operations conducted in Quang Nam Province and I Corps during 1968. Operation Allen Brook netted over 1,100 enemy KIAs (Mameluke Thrust had a kill count of almost 3,000 enemy combatants; this operation lasted for a longer time span due to the area it covered).[1]

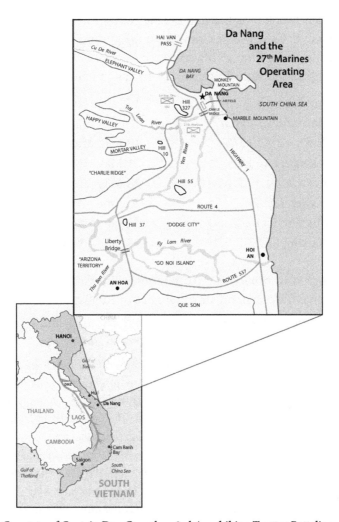

Courtesy of Captain Dan Guenther, 3rd Amphibian Tractor Battalion,
and Nick Zelinger, NZGraphics.com

7th Marines press east toward the railroad tracks, Go Noi ~ Courtesy of Ron Dorsey, Fox 2/7,
given to him by an unknown USMC photographer (DOD Photo)

Operation Allen Brook took place in Quang Nam Province, RVN, to the southwest of Da Nang. Colonel A. G. Schwenk, Commanding Officer of the 27th Marine Regiment, was senior reporting officer from 17 May through 3 August 1968. The following Battalion Commanders fielded their units in this multi-battalion operation on the dates shown:

LtCol T. J. Woodham, Jr., CO of 3/27	17 - 28 May and 16 – 31 July
LtCol R. H. Barnard, CO of 3/7	15 – 18 May
LtCol D. N. Rexroad, CO 3/5	18 – 31 May
LtCol F. J. McEwan, CO 1/26	21 May – 6 June
LtCol J. E. Greenwood, CO 1/27	28 May – 22 June
LtCol A. W. Keller, CO 2/27	23 June – 16 July
LtCol C. E. Mueller, CO 2/7	4 May – 15 May and 24 – 28 July
LtCol L. E. Watson, CO 2/7	29 July – 3 August

Colonel Schwenk summarizes the operation in his Commander's Analysis of the 27th Marine Regiment Command Chronologies of August 1968:

a. *...17 May – 6 June during which heavy contact was made with large, very well trained and well equipped NVA and Main Force VC units...*

b. *... During the period of 17 June to 3 August 1968, Allen Brook was oriented towards simultaneously accomplishing extensive land clearing/fortification reduction and conducting wide-ranging offensive operations to deny the enemy the use of Go Noi Island as a base area. The salient lesson learned was that close coordination of both tasks is essential. Since the area contiguous to Go Noi Island was not under effective allied control, the enemy had relative freedom of movement. Therefore, it was essential that offensive operations were aggressively pursued to preclude attacks by fire and harassing ground attacks... The need for constant maneuver and rapid movement to keep the enemy off balance, together with the extreme heat encountered, heavily taxed the endurance of the individual Marine. Frequent rotation of units in and out of the Allen Brook AO was accomplished in order to reduce the effects of fatigue... Flak jackets were not used and each man carried three canteens of water at all times...*

c. *The technique of using small teams consisting of snipers, artillery forward observers, and air control teams proved effective in interdicting enemy movement, particularly on the periphery of the AO...*

d. *The relative impact of the enemy's use of mines and booby traps on overall conduct of the operation increased significantly as the enemy's own movement in the area declined...Over 30% of the total casualties encountered came from mines or booby traps. The most effective counter to this threat was to deny to the enemy movement in the area. However, the strong VC ties to the civilian population in the area made complete removal of this threat impossible.*

Signed: A. G. Schwenk

Liberty Bridge and the Go Noi

Liberty Bridge spanning the Thu Bon River became the de facto field communications command post for most battalions participating in Allen Brook. It was the starting point for a lot of the operations in the region. An Hoa, a few miles south of the bridge, was at the southern edge of the 1st Marine Division's area of operations. Destruction of the bridge in May of 1968 by fire became a significant challenge in continuing logistical supply of Marines. Liberty Bridge was the major bridge connecting a supply route to the all-important An Hoa combat base. The immediate rebuilding of the bridge began by Marine combat engineers of the 1st Marine Division.

The terrain in the Go Noi area was generally flat while villages were overgrown with scrub vegetation, tree lines, and hedgerows. Dry river beds with sandy areas receded into elephant grass ranging from three to six feet in height. The elephant grass featured long slender palms of razor sharp edges which produced small cuts when pushing through the grass. It was excellent cover for enemy combatants. This grass evoked evil spirits; it was the bane of the Marine rifleman.

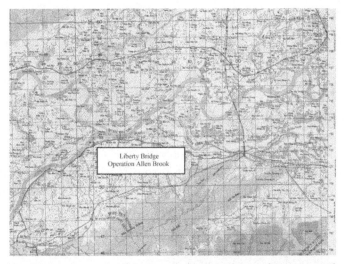

Liberty Bridge (AT925532) on west side of Go Noi, approximately 20 Kilometers southwest of Da Nang, where Operation Allen Brook originated ~ 1965 Dai Loc, Vietnam Map, Sheet 6640 IV

The maneuvering of battalions in the Go Noi Island area close to Liberty Bridge during 1968 became much like a game of chess. On 4 May 2nd Battalion, 7th Marines commanded by Lieutenant Colonel Charles E. Mueller kicked off Operation Allen Brook from the western side of the Go Noi, moving in an eastward direction. Intermittent contacts were made and on 9 May the battalion collided with a large enemy force at the railroad bridge over the Ky Lam River near the hamlet of Xuan Dai (2). This was the first of many battles during Allen Brook. This major contact resulted in close to one hundred KIAs and an unknown quantity of WIAs amongst the enemy combatants. The enemy would police up their dead and wounded and disappear, sometimes leaving distinct blood trails. The Marines regrouped after each contact, evacuated their wounded and dead, and again pushed forward in the heat and humidity. It was going to be a long campaign.[2]

Marines Ferry Supplies across river ~ Courtesy of Gerald Risner, FLC attached 2/5

A few days into the operation, 3rd Battalion of the 7th Marines took operational control from 2nd Battalion, reversing the direction of attack and pushing back due west. On 16 May Lieutenant Colonel Roger H. Barnard's 3rd Battalion surrounded remnants of the NVA regiments in that push. They had been operating freely throughout the Go Noi territory. They were dug in with excellent fields of fire and fortified positions and ready for battle as 3/7 engaged them in combat.

When that fierce battle subsided Barnard indicated they had uncovered a Regimental Headquarters and a major staging area for supplies. Years later Barnard recalled the supplies and equipment they captured was so extensive that they could not evacuate all of it to the rear for an Intelligence analysis. They set about destroying what they could not send back to the rear. He indicated it had indeed been a major staging area for the NVA. This reconfirmed the earlier Intel reports of enemy activity.

Delta Company, 1/7 advancing with prep fire crossing river 24 May 1968
~ courtesy Marine Corps History Division (DOD Photo USMC A371543)

In the very initial stages of the operation, Marines made light contact with local force and VC units. Then as the operation continued, the elusive NVA began to resist more strongly, especially when their caches and supplies were in jeopardy. This began the long-drawn-out search for an evasive enemy and their logistical infrastructure within the confines of this unique tract of land.

Late in the day on 16 May, Colonel Adolf Schwenk, 27th Marine Regimental Commander, took control of Allen Brook and the next, larger phase began in earnest. He immediately began deploying his battalions along with the attached 1st Battalion, 26th Marines (fresh from the battle of Khe Sanh) into the area.[3]

An Act of Cowardice

As the line companies of 1st Battalion, 27th Marines patrolled the rocket belt, preparation was being made for each of the battalions in the 27th Regiment to serve their time on the Operation. On the eve of 1st Battalion jumping off for its turn, Captain William Sweeney, Bravo Company recaptures what he described as, "witnessing my first and only unmitigated act of cowardice. It was not a Marine. It happened to be the Battalion Surgeon [Navy]. He was in Lieutenant Colonel Greenwood's hooch as I approached to discuss a tactical situation with Greenwood, our Battalion Commander. The surgeon was yelling and screaming that he wouldn't go with us to Go Noi Island because his education was too expensive to allow him to risk his life. What I heard and what he articulated in so many words was that his life was more valuable than any of the Marines in the unit and he wasn't going to risk his on the battlefield."

Sweeney indicated that during the exchange Greenwood was very calm and collected, telling the surgeon he was relieved of his duty and to expect a court martial and to get the hell out of his quarters. The surgeon came bolting out of the hooch, saw Sweeney and told him how unreasonable Greenwood had been. This behavior is not heard of amongst Marines. Everyone is screened and thoroughly tested before being allowed to claim the title of U. S. Marine. Sweeney recollects, "telling this man, this surgeon that he was a coward and that he should leave quickly...to get away from me!"

Another Naval Medical Doctor who proved to be both brave and competent replaced the first Battalion surgeon. The new surgeon did accompany the Battalion onto the Go Noi Island battlefields.[4]

Enemy Morale and Organization in Quang Nam Province

Enemy Units in the Go Noi

Information gathered from interrogations of captured NVA, ongoing III MAF intelligence collections, and from the 7th Marines' initial sweep of the Island provided an initial assessment of the current enemy-unit estimates. It was surmised at that time three separate NVA battalions were operating in the Go Noi. Those enemy combatants were initially identified as 2nd Battalion, 38th Regiment; 2nd Battalion, 68th Regiment;

and the 3rd Battalion, 16th Regiment. Other units would be identified and noted as the operation gained momentum.

The Communists controlled the Go Noi in the years prior to 1968, although they were periodically routed from this natural stronghold by Marines. The Communists maintained a political infrastructure throughout the region, making it a place to stage incoming units coming off the Ho Chi Minh Trail outlets from in Laos. The route off the trail coming inland was rough going but the thick jungle gave ample protection.

Until now the enemy foothold in Go Noi had been confined to guerilla tactics, but with new orders from the high command in the north, the VC and the NVA units began building for the bigger objective. That major focus emphasized the Da Nang airfield and the vast supplies of the Marines. This spring's initiative was to be a Mini-Tet Offensive, continuing the main Tet thrust that started 31 January of 1968.[5]

The local population southwest of Da Nang maintained strong loyalties to the Communists throughout the war. The continued existence of both a political and hidden military infrastructure over the years made this area a relatively safe place for enemy staging and operations. III MAF intelligence knew for sure that it was a sanctuary to three local Viet Cong units, the R-20 Battalion, V-25 Battalion, and T-3 Sapper Battalion, along with Group 44, the headquarters group commanding all VC operations in Quang Nam Province.[6]

The NVA/VC Sapper units were a type of special commando. These units were given the most difficult of missions: to penetrate a perimeter in advance of a ground attack. The Sapper would typically infiltrate and initiate battle from within the defensive base, while at the same time another ground unit would attack from the outer perimeter. This caused American units to fight on two fronts, internal and external, taking away battle focus and creating confusion. The Sapper unit personnel were trained in breaching obstacles, booby trap removal, explosives and demolitions, and in digging, tunneling, and the art of sapping. Their weapon of choice was primarily the satchel charge.

Morale in the Wider Province

Interrogation of prisoners revealed the makeup and morale of NVA units operating in the province. One such detainee from the 2nd Battalion, 38th Regiment stated, that his unit had been in South Vietnam only three to four days prior to his capture on 20 May 1968. His unit had infiltrated from the North through Laos. The trip through Laos took approximately one month. He had been in the NVA Army for only one year prior to coming south and the only training he had received were instructions on how to fire and maintain his AK-47 assault rifle. He was told that the area he was in was a training area until coming under attack by U. S. Forces. The size of his battalion on arrival in South Vietnam, he estimated at approximately 400 strong. He further indicated, "Morale in the battalion was low due to a shortage of food and medical supplies."

Battlefield detainee brought in for questioning during Operation Allen Brook
~ Courtesy of Hal Kennedy, H&S Co, 1/27

The detainee also revealed that within the unit they possessed three heavy machine guns, but had no knowledge of mortars or other weaponry. Another prisoner revealed that he belonged to the 2nd Battalion, 68th Regiment and the unit "operated with four 82mm mortars; nineteen 60mm mortars; nine heavy machine guns; fifteen to twenty light machine guns; RPGs; twenty, maybe thirty, Browning Automatic Rifles [captured]. The rest of the unit was armed with AK-47s, over half of which were newly issued. The morale in his battalion was low, due mainly to air strikes."

Extensive questioning revealed that some of these new men in the NVA battalions expressed a desire to "Chieu Hoi" (come over to the South Vietnamese side) but did not know what procedure to follow. Also, some of the NVA wanted to come over to the South but were afraid Marines would shoot them if they did. Interrogators noted that most of the equipment captured was in new condition. Their field packs were well stocked with medical supplies contrary to statements of low supplies.[7]

The Chieu Hoi campaign had produced 236 "ralliers" countrywide in May, compared to a total of 202 for the month of April. "Ralliers" were NVA or VC combatants who took advantage of the "Open Arms" program welcoming defectors to the South Vietnamese government.[8]

Lieutenant Colonel Frederick J. McEwan, CO of 1/26, had a different take on the NVA his troops fought against. He remembered, "Not many VC, they were mostly NVA and clean, had good fingernails, had tea in their canteens (indicative of good supplies). When they pulled out of a skirmish they did so in an orderly manner. They tried to extract all their dead and wounded. We pressed them hard. They had good equipment but we overpowered and overwhelmed them by our assaults. They were young, too...and they were well disciplined and good soldiers, well led! We did not take prisoners. If we took prisoners, then I would lose two Marines. They would have to take them back to the rear. But, if Regiment wanted a prisoner we would get them one."

Intel on Enemy Movements

According to the III MAF Command Chronologies, May 1968, Marine Corps counterintelligence began anticipating heightened activity in Da Nang City proper and the outlying areas. With its sea and airport access, Da Nang City promoted a natural base with ample defenses of all incoming supplies to the Marines and Army units.

Reports asserted that the local VC was instructing their agents to disguise themselves as Buddhists for participating in the demonstrations on 11 May 1968, a holiday honoring Buddha's Birthday. Other reports revealed that female agents, disguised as merchants, were infiltrating explosive devices into the city hidden in hollowed out fruits and foodstuffs.

Additionally, reports filtered in from informants throughout I CTZ that Communist insurgents perpetrated over 1,300 civilian abductions during May. A 9 May report indicated that four VC suspects were observed performing detailed reconnaissance just off the Han River in southeastern Da Nang City between Marble Mountain and the Nhye Bridge for mining and destroying it.

The May 1968 III MAF Command Chronologies also point out that an adept Communist political cadre (political commissars) was fully organized in most VC and NVA units. Their methods filtered into both strategic and tactical assignments of all units. The report asserted that this embedded political group provided a strong message of the Communist national strategy for victory in South Vietnam.

The participating political officer within a VC or NVA unit had as much or more power as did the unit field commander. The political officer's duty was to ensure that all decisions made by the field commander were politically correct and loyal to the cause. He observed all in his company, battalion, or regiment, controlling the lower political cadres within the unit. The task was to motivate, indoctrinate, and keep all cadres under scrutiny, analyzing their ideological strengths and/or weaknesses. Reeducation classes for relearning party loyalty and ideology were at the discretion of the political officer.

Espionage contributed to the Communist effort. In a May report from the 525th Military Intelligence Group (U. S. Army), the Viet Cong of the Quang Da Province Committee had established an intelligence course at Bao An Dong in the Go Noi area (grid coordinates AT985530). This location lay in the southeastern sector of the Go Noi, close to the coastal seaport of Hoi An. It further reported that approximately 350 young people (mostly teen women) were to be trained as espionage agents. After completion of the course, they would be instructed to seek employment at the various military installations in Da Nang City to gain intelligence information.

Prostitution and low-level espionage dominated many areas of I Corps. One such area in Da Nang accommodated these activities, a suburb named after the ramshackle small town of "Dogpatch" in the comic strip series *Li'l Abner* created by Al Capp. This area became the most talked about place in I Corps amongst Marines/Corpsmen and others who served in that area. Anyone who served in I Corps of the Republic of Vietnam could tell you a little or a lot about "Dogpatch!" The neighborhood captured the imagination of almost all who transited through Da Nang. There were those who participated in various exploits in "Dogpatch." And those stories were told, retold and sometimes embellished by those who had been there.

Another report from the Government of Vietnam Intelligence Service during this time revealed that the Viet Cong of Quang Da Province Committee had formulated plans to smuggle men and weapons into the cities of Hoi An and Da Nang. This called for weapons to be placed in coffins, carried in motor vehicles, and would enhance the perfect cover for VC agents masquerading as a mourning relative. The purpose: infiltration and attack of the various U. S. installations.[9]

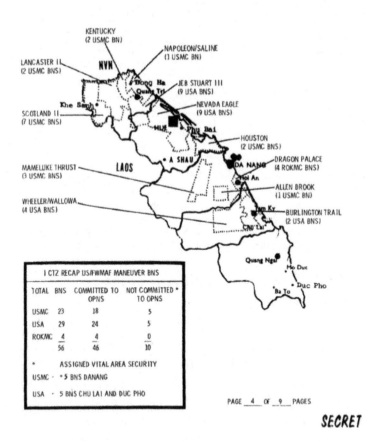

MAJOR OPERATIONS IN PROGRESS

I CTZ RECAP US/FWMAF MANEUVER BNS		
TOTAL BNS	COMMITTED TO OPNS	NOT COMMITTED * TO OPNS
USMC 23	18	5
USA 29	24	5
ROKMC 4	4	0
56	46	10

* ASSIGNED VITAL AREA SECURITY

USMC - *5 BNS DANANG

USA - 5 BNS CHU LAI AND DUC PHO

PAGE 4 OF 9 PAGES

Major Ops Summary prepared for HQ U. S. Marine Corps for period of 17 – 18 June 1968
~ Operations Files, USMC History Division - Item #120106427

SECRET
SUMMARY OF MAJOR OPERATIONS

OPERATION (DATE COMMENCED)	UNITS INVOLVED	LOCATION	CASUALTIES AS OF: 162400H JUN 68 FRIENDLY KIA	FRIENDLY WIA	ENEMY KIA
SCOTLAND II (15APR68)	1ST MAR, 1/1, 2/1, 2/3, 1/4, 3/4, 3/9, & BLT 2/4	KHE SANH AREA	* 267 25 USA	*1,317 2 MIA 359 USA	*1,598
LANCASTER II (21JAN68)	9TH MAR, 1/9 & 2/9	CAMP CARROLL, ROCKPILE & CA LU AREA	171	1,058 3 USA	493
KENTUCKY (1NOV67)	9TH MAR, 2/26 & 1/3	CON THIEN & DONG HA AREA	420	*2,181 1 MIA	2,612
NAPOLEON/SALINE (5NOV67)	3RD MAR, 3/3 & 1ST AMTRAC BN	MOUTH OF CUA VIET RIVER	339 33 USA	1,776 121 USA 1 USA MIA	3,111
JEB STUART III (17MAY68)	1ST CAV DIV (AM) WITH 9 USA BNS	QUANG TRI & THUA THIEN PROVINCES	71 USA	448 USA 2 USA MIA	*410
NEVADA EAGLE (17MAY68)	101ST ABN DIV WITH 9 USA BNS	THUA THIEN PROVINCE	73 USA	*568 USA	878
HOUSTON (26FEB68)	5TH MAR, 1/5 & 2/5	27 KM SSE OF PHU BAI	83 2 USA 2 USN	482 38 USA 7 USN	*461
MAMELUKE THRUST (18MAY68)	1ST MAR DIV, 3/5, 3/26 & 3/7	15 KM WEST OF DANANG	*92	*441	672
DRAGON PALACE (2JUN68)	20 ROKMC BDE WITH 4 ROKMC BNS	HOI AN AREA	1 20 ROKMC 1 ROKA	4 61 ROKMC 1 ROKA	65
ALLEN BROOK (4MAY68)	27TH MAR, 1/27	13 KM WSW OF HOI AN	147 2 USN	826 1 USA	748
WHEELER/WALLOWA (11NOV67)	196TH INF BDE WITH 4 USA BNS	WEST OF TAM KY	641 USA 1 USAF	2 3,265 USA	8,497
BURLINGTON TRAIL (8APR68)	198TH INF BDE WITH 2 USA BNS)	QUANG TIN PROVINCE	48 USA	411 USA	524

ALL FRIENDLY CASUALTIES ARE USMC UNLESS DESIGNATED.
* - ADJUSTED
f - FINAL CUMULATIVE CASUALTIES

PAGE 5 OF 9 PAGES

SECRET

DECLASSIFIED

Major Ops Summary prepared for HQ U. S. Marine Corps for period 16 June 1968
~ Operations Files, USMC History Division - Item #120106427

3rd Battalion, 27th Marine Regiment Joins Operation Allen Brook

On 17 May, Lieutenant Colonel Tullis J. Woodham, Jr. airlifted his 3rd Battalion, 27th Marines into the southwest side of Go Noi Island. Woodham's men ran head on into another dug-in NVA unit later identified as the 36th and 38th Regiments of the 308th NVA Division. The fighting moved northward toward the multiple hamlets of Le Bac and Cu Ban where the battle culminated in the destruction of these NVA Regiments. It was a frenzied battle to the east of the only bridge in the area. The Marines' Liberty Bridge rear CP lay approximately one kilometer to the west of this village complex. The enemy was constantly moving in and throughout the entire area, not staying in one place for long.

The temperatures soared to above 110 degrees and the heat casualties were almost as many as the battle wounded and KIAs. While the battle casualties started to mount, the Marines believed they had stalled the build up to a "Mini Tet" which was being discussed amongst the upper MACV commanders. By the middle of May, the second so-called Mini-Tet Offensive was declared curtailed by the Marine command in Quang Nam Province. A few attempts of occasional rocket, mortar, and ground assaults against major allied facilities continued in the region.

Liberty Bridge over Thu Bon River looking west from Helicopter
~ Courtesy of Gerald Risner, FLC attached to 2/5

Contact

Lieutenant Colonel Woodham's command group along with two rifle companies, Kilo and Lima, were helo-lifted into an area just south and east of Liberty Bridge close to An Tam (1) (grid coordinate AT961516). The overall concept of this maneuver was to alleviate pressure on the committed 3rd Battalion, 7th Marine Regiment to the north, engaged in heavy contact during most of 17 May. Woodham's line Company I, under the control of 3/7, had suffered some heavy casualties.

The losses would have been much more significant had it not been for Private First Class Robert C. Burke. Burke, an M60 machine gunner with 3/27, Company I, quickly reacted to the enemy's withering fire by personally assaulting enemy positions, pinning them down. His selfless act of courage allowed for his fellow Marines to fully extract the wounded. He continued his one-man assaults until he was finally killed by concentrated enemy fire. Burke was posthumously awarded the Medal of Honor.

The Search for the NVA Continues

At dawn on 19 May patrols began scouring the vacant battlefield for equipment and intelligence. Additional NVA dead were discovered with a large assortment of weaponry and equipment, along with a substantial amount of rice and corn. Another prisoner was found hiding on the battlefield who claimed to be a cook for the combatants. All the captured equipment and the prisoner were evacuated to 27th Marine Regimental Headquarters for analysis and interrogation.

Preoperational air and artillery missions were again called in on the skirmish areas. Once those strikes subsided, Company L began another search of the same area for the elusive NVA. Spotting a young Vietnamese male fleeing into tall elephant grass next to a village, the pursuing Marines came across several smoldering camp fires. It became obvious there were still significant remnants of the combatants in the area. There would be more to come.

Standard practice for NVA preparing for battle was first to move equipment and food into an area and hide it in caches. These activities would take weeks or months, and then the NVA would quickly rush fresh troops in, uncovering those supplies to focus on an objective. It became incumbent on the Marines involved in this "cat and mouse" game to comb the area not only to find the enemy but also to uncover all staging areas and cached supplies.

Company Reserves Up

Reserve Company M moved up into the now deadly firefight and started helping evacuate Kilo Company's wounded and dead. After they extracted the casualties, all companies withdrew to the north, leaving the area for supporting artillery to demolished everything above ground. Air strikes neutralized many of the enemy positions. Again, the elusive NVA had withdrawn from the battlefield policing up the scene and leaving little sign of their own losses.

On 25 May artillery, preparatory fire rained in on Le Bac (1) Village. Air missions followed. Later mid-morning more artillery impacted on the village of Le Bac (1). Afterward Company L swept forward through the lead companies. Receiving casualties, they withdrew, calling in more air support. The battalion then shifted and moved toward the Thu Bon River to set up its CP with hasty defense. A resupply conducted in the late afternoon went without problems and the air and artillery fire on the village continued into the evening hours. It was obvious they were engaged with experienced combatants.

Beginning the morning of 26 May, Companies L and M together with tanks again maneuvered toward Le Bac (1). Preparatory air and artillery fire continued to pound the enemy in the village. Moving in, the Marines found many dead NVA and twenty-two freshly dug but uncovered graves with dead NVA in them. Moving further into the village, Company L started taking mortar fire, wounding six Marines. Marine mortarmen returned the fire on suspected positions and called for more air strikes.

In the early afternoon, Mike Company made contact with an unknown size enemy force, again taking small arms and automatic weapons fire from them. The tanks along in support began taking RPG fire. Returning volleys of fire and an advance toward the embedded enemy curtailed the firefight. The NVA feared the tanks and did not want to engage them. An unexpected torrential rain stopped further skirmishing, allowing the enemy to break contact and leave the area.

By the end of that day, Marine casualties tallied fifty-six killed, many wounded, with nine missing. Enemy casualties reported at the time came to one hundred sixty-seven

NVA dead and five detainees. Night positions again were established and the battalion dug in until the next day, 27 May.[10]

3rd Battalion, 7th Marines maneuvering in Go Noi Island
~ Courtesy of Marine Corps History Division (DOD Photo USMC A371607)

1st Battalion, 27th Marines Takes Control in Operation Allen Brook

On 25 May, 1st Marine Division headquarters ordered 1st Battalion, 26th Marines commanded by Lieutenant Colonel Frederick J. McEwan, the veterans of a seventy-seven-day siege at Khe Sanh, and Lieutenant Colonel John E. Greenwood's 1st Battalion, 27th Marines, just back from the Hue City area, to completely relieve maneuver battalions 3/27 and 3/5 and continue prosecuting Operation Allen Brook. This called for further "chess board" movements throughout the difficult Go Noi Island territory.

Lieutenant Colonel McEwan and his men had been under siege at the Khe Sanh combat base in the northwest sector of I Corps surrounded by a reported 20,000-man force of NVA soldiers. McEwan remembers all so well, "We came out of Khe Sanh in April and fought around Leatherneck Square, Gio Linh, Dong Ha and Con Tien and suddenly we were ordered to get on some 'Rough Rider convoys' in May and were trucked down to 1st Marine Division in Da Nang. I put one company in the 'trenches' for security and the Sergeant Major asked me, 'What are we going to do with the rest of 'em?' I said, 'Tell 'em to be here in the morning'...and I took most of my officers to the O-Club. That next morning the troops were back and my assistant S-3, John Kaheny, had a C-Rat carton full of Purple Heart medals and we had a really quick formation and gave out I don't know how many Purple Heart Medals...and then broke it up and the next day found us almost in the mountains southwest of Da Nang in the 1st Marine Division's TAOR."

Colonel McEwan fondly remembers Colonel Reverdy M. Hall, CO of the 7th Marine Regiment. The 1/26 CP was set up close to their Regimental HQ. McEwan describes Hall's receiving of his battalion into the area, "He was terrific with us. His words to me were, 'What can we do for you, for your battalion?' We had already reported to the 27th Marines before that...Colonel Schwenk was their Commanding Officer. I remember relieving 3/5 and that was near and dear to me because I had been a Company Commander in 3/5 back in 1956. But in my mind, Colonel Hall was outstanding and stood out amongst all of the Regimental Commanders at the time."

Daily throughout the operation the Marines endured extreme temperatures, torrential rains, head-high elephant grass, as well as unfriendly locals, "beau-coup" booby-traps, and mined explosive devices. Heavy vegetation in most areas impaired movement and ground observation. The thick underbrush was prevalent in the area and excellent for concealment of booby traps and mines. The Marines were confronted with a succession of tree lines which concealed snipers and small harassing elements of the enemy. This made the operation extremely tedious and slow going. The daily expectations while sweeping the area could go from a tedious routine of searching to overwhelming fear in a heartbeat. The Marines quickly became acutely vigilant in an abbreviated time span.

To make matters worse, on 1 June, a flight of C-130 Hercules aircraft began dropping more than 30,000 gallons of fuel in fifty-five-gallon drums with igniters. The plan was to burn a substantial portion of Go Noi's foliage and resume the Operation. This undertaking failed miserably, due to heavy thunderstorm activity following the dropping of the fuel drums.

When the downpour subsided the two maneuver battalions resumed the daunting task of searching for the elusive NVA, tracking from east to west and then reversing direction. Colonel Adolph G. Schwenk, the 27th Marines commander, recalled that the NVA and local forces did not go on the offense during this operation; that they defended their caches and "fought back tenaciously" from trench lines, spider traps, and tree lines in and around the hamlets. He also added that luring the Marines into fields of fire limited the Marine commanders in the field from properly utilizing artillery and close air support. The Marines quickly learned these lessons and started using preparatory fire from naval gunships offshore, and artillery in unison with air support, before moving into an area. This became the Standard Operating Procedure during this operation whenever possible.

The Marines typically would find little sign of the enemy after these skirmishes. In most cases they had pre-planned their escape routes prior to an ambush and would drag their wounded, dead, and equipment with them in retreat, leaving little trace of a battle or signs of their losses. This was disconcerting to the Marines in the line companies.[11]

Company C, 1/27 Enters the Go Noi

Another unit exchange took place on 27 May. Charlie Company from the 1st Battalion, 27th Marines helo-lifted into the Liberty Bridge area and two companies from 3/27 were extracted on a turnaround. Companies I and L remained, continuing to sweep the village area of Le Bac (1). This movement produced the discovery of copious quantities of weapons, ammunition, 122mm rockets, and documents, together with large containers of rice and peanuts. Company C also provided a platoon to guard an H-34 helicopter, which had made a forced landing close by. Because of this event a needed resupply and the extraction of the downed chopper was initiated. As the bird was being extracted, the Marines went about distributing needed water, ammo, and supplies and settled in for the night.

Dawn on 28 May brought orders to 3/27 that the main element of 1/27 would relieve them at a rendezvous close to Liberty Bridge. Charlie Company of 1st Battalion, now back with its own battalion, turned attention toward aiding Company B, 1/26 who had tangled with a large NVA force near Liberty Bridge. Assaulting that combatant force Charlie Company dislodged the entrenched NVA with a frontal advance.[12]

Delta Company 1/27 during Operation Allen Brook crossing Thu Bon River near Liberty Bridge, PFC Daniel C. Corlew sitting ~ Courtesy of Raul Figueroa, H&S Co, 1/27

1st Battalion Headquarters group and Company B arrived at Liberty Bridge (grid coordinate AT925532) on 28 May 1968. Quickly crossing the Thu Bon River by motorized barge, they linked up with 3rd Battalion, 27th Marines and took operational control of Company C who had accompanied 3/27 to the planned changeover location. First Battalion then began their first grisly task of accounting for the eleven missing-in-action Marines from 3/27's India Company killed in the previous day's engagement.

Company C immediately began sweeping the battlefield around the village, Cu Ban (4), where the missing Marine dead were reported to have been killed. The Marines luckily found eight of the bodies, withdrawing from the battle scene at dark. The following day on 29 May, Company C resumed the search but was soon diverted to help Bravo Company 1/26.

Bravo 1/26 had engaged an entrenched NVA force nearby. Upon entering the fray, Company C assaulted the enemy positions, routing them, and discovered the remaining dead Marines. This time the NVA left various weapons and personal equipment behind in their haste. Those items were quickly gathered, logged, and dispatched to the rear for Intel analysis. This was an unusual turn of events. A small sign implying the enemy was starting to become overwhelmed and possibly in disarray.

Lieutenant Colonel Frederick McEwan, 1/26 Commanding Officer, recalls the pressure of the situation at the time: "Colonel Schwenk got my S-3 on the horn and was asking, 'What the heck are you doing...What is the holdup...Why aren't you moving?' He had all sorts of questions and we were in a very serious contact with the NVA. I didn't talk directly with him... Charles Davis, my S-3 at that time, was conversing with him. I was down with Bravo Company in the trenches. I thought it more important to be with the troops and doing what they were doing and monitoring what was going on...My job was to be with my men, encourage them and push them along...And we had many outstanding Marines in my Battalion. At that time, Jim Champion was my Company Commander, call sign 'Black Bud Bravo Six' and did an outstanding job of sorting things out and getting things under control in that particular situation."

Colonel McEwan went on to explain that the Intel was not the greatest but that it really did not matter. He recollects, "We moved so fast, we didn't have to look very far to find the NVA...They were in their spider holes and gave us plenty of intelligence because they shot at us right away. And that is when we got in there with them, routed them and ascertained the situation."

On 30 and 31 May, the two battalions now on the Island swept eastward in unison from grid line 94 all the way to 03 on the eastern edge of Go Noi. There were no significant engagements other than several sniper incidents. Once 1/27 crossed the north to south National Railroad tracks, it changed its sweep, heading from due east to a northeasterly direction. 1/26 remained on an easterly track and both battalions halted at the north-south 02 grid line approximately two kilometers beyond the railroad tracks. Battalion HQ group established a hasty defense CP near Ban Lanh (2) village (grid coordinate BT019548).

1/27 Begins the Search and Destroy Operation

Chief Battalion Scout Sergeant Larry Broadhurst remembers in early June, "We were near a large bridge [Liberty Bridge] south of Da Nang. I remember seeing a couple, maybe, three tanks idling as we passed through that area. As an S-2 Scout, I traveled with the Battalion command group. Lieutenant Colonel John Greenwood had taken over as the operation's ground commander at this stage of Allen Brook. I distinctly remember that he had his radioman call back to the tanks we had gone by at the bridge and having them come forward to support us as we began the sweep into this area...I then remember forming the assault line. It was really long as I looked to my left and right...I have no idea what happened in the other sections of that line when we all began to move forward."

During this phase of the operation, 1/27 began to sweep an open rice field east of the big bridge. The open field of rice had been harvested and was dry, making it easy to walk through. Colonel Greenwood passed the word down to his Marines to begin the maneuver. Broadhurst vividly remembers those first minutes of what later would become a deadly assault: "A Lieutenant came up to me and said, 'Sergeant, get the men up on-line, we are moving forward.' I remember the tanks started moving with us as we began executing the forward movement. Shortly after beginning, the NVA started sniping at us sporadically and then their small arms firing became more intense. One of the radio operators in front of me was hit. He took a round through the neck and went down. A Corpsman came up immediately and pulled him back off the skirmish line and started administering first aid to him. I can remember they lost him for a bit and then resuscitated him back to life...simultaneously another radioman was calling for a medevac chopper. It became evident that we were beginning to meet heavy resistance and to take casualties."

Broadhurst distinctly remembered the young Marine radioman who had been badly wounded in the neck. He had begun crying out for his mother and cursing the situation while the Corpsman frantically worked on his wound. It was to no avail. Broadhurst still vividly remembers, "I was witnessing this young man's death before his mother or father even knew...That bothered me." The young Marine died during the first minutes of the operation. As the battle intensified, more Marines were wounded and the enemy dead mounted. After the assault was over Marines started carrying the dead enemy combatants out of the tree line emplacements. Broadhurst recollects, "Some of the Marines were using bamboo poles to carry the dead NVA out of the tree line...My recollection is that we lost quite a few Marines that day, both wounded and KIA. I don't remember the exact count but twenty to twenty-five Marines sticks in my mind. I remember the dead Marines' combat equipment being put in a stack as well as some of the captured weapons which would be inventoried for Intel...A lot of things happened on that day and is still hard for me to remember."

Taking inventory after the assault ~ courtesy of Larry Broadhurst, H&S Co, 1/27

After regrouping and resupply, the search and destroy resumed. Broadhurst remembers that the command group started walking eastward and were following tank tracks. The Colonel was walking in-between the tread marks and his radio operator was on the right walking right on the actual tread's track. It was just after they started following these tread marks that Broadhurst witnessed the radioman stepping on a mine. "It broke both of his legs...he took shrapnel all over the front part of his body...His situation was serious and he had to be evacuated immediately."

Charlie and Alpha Company Make Contact

On 5 June, Captain Martin Farmer, Charlie Company CO, and his next-in-command, Lieutenant John Kispert, moved their men toward known enemy positions in the Cu Bans, an area they had swept previously in late May. Their objective, to link up with Bravo Company 1/26, now heavily engaged with the NVA. They were to relieve pressure on Company B of 1/26, thus allowing its disengagement to continue cleaning out other pockets of resistance. As Charlie Company moved south from grid position AT948553 to make that link, both leaders, Farmer and Kispert, were wounded as they made contact with an entrenched and waiting enemy force. Charlie Company became unable to maneuver or call in air or artillery support due to the proximity of the engagement, and called on nearby Alpha Company for aid, which was providing support for Engineers in the area. Along with a section of Tanks, a platoon from Alpha quickly moved toward Charlie Company's position.[13]

Sergeant Felix Salmeron, an Alpha Company Platoon Sergeant, recalled moving into the area, "We began sweeping toward Charlie Company's position. The Tanks couldn't cross the water where we crossed and had to find another crossing. When we reached Charlie's position, they were pinned down and had been trying to pull some bodies back out of an unsecured area. They had been caught out in that tall grass and a lot of their men were down. One of the first Marines I came across was Sergeant Danny Ruiz. He and his men, regrouping and assessing their losses, began briefing me on the layout, what had happened and where the enemy combatants were dug in. We then moved forward. I decided not to take the same approach Charlie Company had tried and diverted my guys to the right and executed a flank maneuver onto the battle area. We moved rapidly towards the hedgerows where the enemy was and had pinned down Charlie Company. We discovered some NVA in the trenches, but most had left. When we reached the objective and started searching, we began finding dead and wounded Marines and started pulling them back to our rear. After securing the area, the rest of Charlie Company's wounded and some of Bravo 1/26 men were evacuated. Fortunately, we had overwhelmed the remaining NVA and they di-di'd [left the area]."

What Are You Doing Here?

William "Doc" Carroll, a Corpsman with Charlie Company, had grown up in Tonawanda, New York, close to Niagara Falls. Fond memories of his childhood and high school years were the last thing on his mind as he and other Marines struggled to make it through the days and nights of June in the Go Noi area. Doc recalls, "I had written on my helmet, my hometown, Tonawanda, NY. Everyone had some sort of writing on them, their helmet or flak jacket. I was proud of where I was from. Well, some tanks came in the area to support us and I don't know who came over to me, but he told me that there was some asshole with tanks that was from that Indian town in NY, my town. So, ever curious, I went over to this tank that had 'Tonawanda, New York' painted on it and there he was, my close friend from home, Jerry Cain. He looks at me like he was seeing an apparition, and exclaims, 'What the hell are doing here?' I said something like my work is here, man! We couldn't believe it…He and I had gone to high school together and I can still see him to this day standing in front of me in homeroom. This was not supposed to happen in the Nam. Here we were getting our head and ass handed to us and here he and his guys are, towing us out." PFC Jerome F. Cain was later awarded the Silver Star on 15 June 1968 while serving with Company B, 5th Tank Battalion.

Doc Carroll's close buddy, Sergeant Simon Waiau, returned that same day to the unit after being wounded. Carroll remembered Waiau walking up to him and asking, "Who is in charge?" I looked at him and replied, "You're a Sergeant, right?" I remember saying something to the effect, "You do not want me in charge; I am a Corpsman and you are a Sergeant…I know how to patch people up. I don't know tactics." He laughed and replied something like…"Well, if it isn't you, it must be me…Oh Hell!"

That same day Charlie Company engaged in a hellacious firefight and Doc's guys, Lloyd Fernung and Rick Fink, got wounded close to a tree line in tall grass when it started. Doc remembers that "They were yelling for me, 'Corpsman up' and I knew who was yelling for me…We all had been close since Hawaii. I immediately started running across the open ground. Diving into the tall grass where I thought they were, I startled them both. Even though they were lying down, they were both locked and loaded thinking I was a gook. Later, they revealed that they almost blew my ass away. I had missed their location by about five yards, startling them. One of them yelled a lot of profanities at me, like, 'Where the fuck is you, Doc?' I finally found them in the elephant grass. So, I patched them up and started dragging Rick back across open ground. I think Lloyd was running…Lloyd could move on his own. The faster Lloyd moved, the faster I drug poor Rick. We were all hollering profanities and scared to death. That was about as close as I came to getting my ass killed. Simon Waiau, Jerry Cain, Rick and Lloyd all in the same day." Then-HM3 William E. Carroll was awarded the Bronze Star Medal with Combat V for Valor on 5 June 1968.

Bravo Company 1/27 Maneuvers onto Go Noi Island

Company B convoyed by trucks to Liberty Bridge to find that they would have to cross it on a barge. Captain William T. Sweeney recalls, "The bridge was unusable, so I experienced my only amphibious landing in combat with my whole company on a very open deck of a large flatboat ferry being winched from shore to shore. I am sure my men felt vulnerable as we crossed the river to the tunes of heavy gunfire from elements of 3/27 who were engaged and trying to break contact."

Reaching the battle area, Company B and C were on the point: Company C on the left flank on the banks of the Thu Bon River with Company B on the right flank. As they moved into the attack they began experiencing some minor engagements and booby traps. A tank company attached to 3/27 had previously laid down its track prints, and tread tracks were leading into the contested area. Captain Sweeney recalls thinking about a previous tour with the Vietnamese Rangers in 1965 where the VC had used the tread tracks to plant booby traps. "They knew most troops found the tread tracks easy to walk on. I put the word out to stay out of the tread tracks. Sure enough, a Marine ignored the order I had passed down and walking in a tread mark, set off a booby trap and had to be medevac'd."

Sweeney, an enlisted Korean War Veteran and now a "Mustang" commissioned officer, extremely confident in his Marines and their capabilities, moved his under-strength company forward. They began meeting resistance. After taking sniper fire from the tree lines and hedgerows, Sweeney noted to himself, "True to form, as soon as my Marines would begin taking fire, on their own initiative, they would charge the sniper positions. The problem with this was the NVA had set up booby traps to their approaches...After the second time this happened I ordered that no one charge these sniper positions until LAAWS and M79 rounds had been fired into the sniper emplacement exploding all possible booby traps surrounding the area. This began working and we eradicated a few snipers also in the process."[14]

As Company B progressed eastward, about a thousand meters from the national railroad bridge they encountered stiff resistance in the form of heavy machine gun and automatic weapons fire. That could only mean one thing. The NVA were in mass and had laid out pre-planned fields of fire.

Captain Sweeney vividly remembers the day, "the cracking sound of rounds flying through the air and flying dirt around me from the impacting rounds at my feet. We were quickly pinned down and halted. I could see NVA soldiers shooting at us from approximately seventy to eighty yards to my direct front. The ones I could see were under an old dead tree stump. I immediately started collecting my thoughts and fortunately overhead flew a brace of fast-movers circling and waiting for targets. My FAC, a young Lance Corporal, was at my side patiently waiting for direction."

"Because the NVA were so close, he was hesitant to call in air support and told me so. I told him I'd rather risk a few casualties from friendly ordnance than a lot from encountering the NVA. He then went to work and directed the planes to the target in front of us, the old dead tree stump. I had passed the word for every swinging dick to hug the deck because we were bringing close air support in on the target in front of us...as I watched their approach, they came in low, fast and furious and I could plainly see the face of the pilot on the first aircraft. On that first run, they released napalm. I watched as the first napalm tank hit the dead tree trunk and exploded. The heat was searing as the waves pushed out from the flames. It was a rush of extreme heat I was not expecting. On their next run, they dropped 500-pound drag bombs, again right on target. The concussions were horrific. It reminded me of an earthquake. When it was over, there was nothing left where the old tree trunk had been. Everything was barren and no one was shooting at us. From that experience, I vowed that I would use air whenever I could in lieu of artillery. I've bragged about Marine Close Air support ever since…It never failed me…and I was extremely proud of my Lance Corporal FAC that day!"

Company B kept the attack going eastward, taking a few casualties as they maneuvered. They crossed the old National Railroad track bridge, continuing until linking up with an ARVN Battalion. Sweeney recalls his thoughts at the time, "We were raunchy, and some Marines had their bare asses showing through the seat of their utilities. The ARVN, in contrast, looked very clean and well-fed. They looked like they had been doing garrison duty for too long and were rear echelon troops. They apparently were operating in a safe environment. After we conferred and confirmed the link-up with Headquarters we turned the troops around and again commenced in attack mode westward back toward Liberty Bridge."[15]

Hit in the Ass

As the elements moved westward through the villages and hedgerows, sweeping the same areas they had passed through days before, resistance mysteriously picked up again. On 4 June elements of 2nd Platoon became seriously engaged with some NVA in a tree line 100 yards to their west. Receiving a radio call from 2nd Platoon Commander Lieutenant Ralph Pineda, Captain Sweeney learned his Platoon Commander and men are pinned down and taking heavy casualties. Sweeney remembers running to his position as quickly as he could. The only way to get there was to run along top a berm as a high-profile target for the NVA. They tried but didn't wound me…I did what I had to do to get to him. As I ran down into the depression where they were, I noticed a lot of wounded. I also noticed a gulley leading north out of the depression which could be used to flank the NVA position. One of Pineda's great traits is that he really cared for his Marines. He was a popular leader…Ralph was pissed that I had exposed myself to get there."

The gulley offered concealment and would work for a flanking maneuver. Sweeney ordered Lieutenant Pineda to have his Marines lay down a base of fire forward and get some men moving up the gulley to attack the flank. As the attack began, a loud explosion curtailed all movement. An entire squad had been taken out by a booby-trapped 105 round in the gulley. Several Marines were all down, seriously wounded but no KIAs. Shortly, mortar rounds started raining down on the Marines. One standout Squad Leader, Sergeant James May from Arkansas, had been wounded in the chest and kidney and was slowly trying to move away from the impact zone crawling on all fours. Sweeney recollects thinking, "If he moves he may cause more serious internal injury and bleed to death. I yelled at him not to move. Then I made a leap for him to try and cover him. As he crawled away from me, I landed at his side with my hands on him. It was then that I felt a hot searing piece of steel hit me square in the ass. I recall saying, 'Oh shit I've been hit.' Sergeant May then asked me, 'Where are you hit, Skipper?' I replied, 'In my ass!' May started laughing out loud and yelling as loud as he could, 'The Skipper's been hit in the ass!' That must have served a good purpose in that it broke the tense moments we were having in the middle of an assault and mortar barrage. Everyone busted out laughing."

Captain William T. Sweeney - 1/27 Bravo Company CO
~ Courtesy of Colonel William T. Sweeney, USMC (Ret)

Meantime, to make matters worse, an airborne FAC rolled in and dropped some red smoke to mark the battle area for an air strike. Everyone could see that the fast movers were turning into final approach for a run on the smoke marked area. Sweeney recalls, "My fast-thinking Lance Corporal FAC called the air strike off before they could finish their run and blow us to kingdom come. By this time with rounds cracking overhead and the bleeding wounded lying all about, I ran another airstrike to my frontal area followed by an assault, driving the remaining NVA off us."

It had been a heavy engagement and Captain Sweeney immediately became more concerned with getting his wounded out than counting NVA dead. The enemy again had policed the area of bodies but plenty of blood trails told the story. As Sweeney administered getting the wounded Marines out on relays of medical-evacuation helicopters, one of Bravo's Corpsmen noticed blood on Captain Sweeney's rear end and told him to drop his utilities. Sweeney vividly remembers that his Doc had "observed that a sliver of metal had punctured an area close to my femoral artery. "My Doc indicated that I was going to be evacuated. So, I conceded...As I recall, three choppers came in one by one and got my men out as quickly as they could. I went out as the last man on the third bird. The deck was covered with heavy blood and bleeding bodies. I happened to notice one of my Marines had been hit with shrapnel from the booby trap 105 round.

His neck appeared to be almost severed. I could plainly see his trachea and could see his carotid artery pulsing. To my surprise, he made it back to Da Nang triage still struggling. As we exited the chopper I refused a stretcher and walked across the tarmac into the hospital area. I immediately went to check on my Marines. Finally, I got the good news; the Marine with the open neck wound was going to make it."

The Corpsmen, doctors, and nurses at NSA Hospital in Da Nang attended to Captain Sweeney's Marines and then looked after him. The doctor pulled a long thin sliver of steel out of his rear end and cleaned the wound. He remembers being taken to a clean bed and told to rest. He recalls them telling him he would be there for a few days so they could watch for infection. They put his clothing on a chair next to his bed and left. Captain Sweeney briskly put his utilities back on walked out of NSA and as luck would have it, hitched a truck ride south to regimental CP at Duong Son (2). The next day he caught the resupply chopper back out to his beloved Company B on Go Noi Island.[16]

Back in the Saddle

As the resupply chopper hovered over the LZ, it began taking rounds from nearby NVA positions. The helo dropped low enough for an exchange of dead bodies for ammo, supplies, and Captain Sweeney's return. Captain Ron Gruenberg had taken over for Sweeney in his absence and would leave on this same bird but under fire. Sweeney recaptures the confusion he felt after hitting the ground, "I was completely disoriented. The company had moved the day before. Rounds were cracking all around. This didn't bother me so much as the fact I couldn't find my command. Finally, I saw an antenna sticking up above a rounded grave mound. I ran towards it; the whole time being chased by enemy fire. Finally, I was in the welcome arms of my company CP. It took a couple of minutes to orient and locate my platoons. Once oriented, First and Second Platoons on the right and Third to my west, I immediately ordered a flanking move by Pineda's Second Platoon and ordered Third to lay down a base of covering fire. Ed Shore, First Platoon, called me and stated he could see people moving in the hooches to his direct front. He couldn't give me a positive ID on them to fire a LAAW. I did not want to take a chance on killing women or children, so I told him to check fire."[17]

The conditions worsened for the Battalion. The third time over the same terrain became tougher than the first pass. As the month of June wore on it became hotter and more humid. No shower for weeks. Eating cold C-rations became boring and tasteless. Sweeney remembers vividly, "I was eating ham and mofos twice a day because that is all there was left over after the C's were distributed amongst my men. Mother's cookies, coffee, and chocolate from home showing up in 'care packages' became bartering items. Small quick firefights several times a day became the norm. We began using C4 explosive in lieu of heat tabs to quickly heat our rations and not spend a lot of time eating. Our trousers in tatters were beginning to rot and fall apart. The soles of our boots were coming apart, either falling off altogether or flapping freely against the bottom of the boot. It was becoming a miserable operation for all of us."[18]

Do It Again

About 13 June, the Battalion was ordered to turn around and resume their attack eastward toward the old National Railroad bridge and clear the hamlets around it as they went through them. Approaching the area, Captain Sweeney remembers hearing an overly loud explosion to his left. One of the tanks attached to the sweep had hit an anti-tank mine. He vividly recalls the incident as if it happened in slow motion. "The road wheel from the tank's tread track had begun a slow spiral skyward directly over a shocked-looking young Marine. My company Gunny and I were observing this first-hand and I remember the dilemma coming to my mind of, should I yell at him...Time stood still as we watched the wheel's descent...As I held my breath and let fate play out, that wheel hit within feet directly in front of the Marine. I recall him making without a doubt the highest standing high jump in history. What a relief! Every one of us nearby except the young Marine laughed (with relief) that it did not hit him."

Shortly after this incident and getting the order to sweep and hold the hamlet, Bravo began taking fire. As the Marines swept through they noticed small fires and the hot food on them. The elephant grass came right up to the edge of the village. Sweeney remembers thinking, "The enemy could crawl through that grass and be on us before we could react. As hot and tired as my Marines were, I had them cut the grass back to where we could see the ground and could establish a reasonable field of fire. I remember the muttering and complaining of the Marines. It was not a popular decision at that moment but saved our ass a couple of nights later."

Regrouping, Sweeney had less than seventy Marines left in Bravo. His trusted Second Platoon Commander Pineda had been recalled back to Battalion. That left him and Lieutenant Ed Shore of First Platoon as the only officers in the field with two Staff Sergeants at platoon and company level leadership. That night they set in their defensive perimeter and Sweeney personally supervised every machine-gun placement and its field of fire. He had the platoons send out patrols and set up LPs. They received some probes from the south and the west later in the night. The next day broke hot and humid but quiet on all fronts. Sweeney recollects finding a well with water near the edge of the hamlet. He said to his acting Gunny, "Let's take a bath." They both stripped naked. As they stood next to the well, Sweeney suddenly looked off in the distance and noticed a sniper about to draw a bead on him... He vividly remembers his thinking, "Talk about a strange feeling, bare naked, no weapon and a VC holding me in his sight picture? I heard the round crack in as I hit the deck. At the same time, I hear this horrific war cry and look up and I see my Platoon Commander, Ed Shore, charging across a rice paddy with no shoes on, shirtless and waving a 1911 A1 .45-caliber service pistol in the air. I look again and the VC is running away into a tree line. When I think of it today I chuckle and am reminded of the Irish mythological warrior hero, Cu Chulainn [pronounced kooh koo-LANE] terrorizing his foes with blood-curdling war cries as he charged into battle. It was a sight to behold."

The night of 14 June, Bravo Company again prepared for the worst. At 2400 (midnight), Sweeney checked his entire perimeter. A short while later, Lieutenant

Shore reported NVA at the edge of the grass directly to his front. The night was balmy with a bright moon. Visibility was very good. Hand grenades then started coming in and the concussion from one knocked Shore and his radioman to the ground. Shore was up and engaging his platoon in no time. The NVA started the assault and came charging inward. First Platoon cut them to pieces. Captain Sweeney recalls, "I started the 60mm mortars firing and then called in arty that I had registered when we first arrived at the position. The artillery put the impacts behind the attack force so we could hold them in position and kill them."

The attacks seemed relentless. Grenades from the NVA were hitting all around. The Marines killed some of the enemies in hand-to-hand combat. The other Second and Third Platoons were not under attack. The NVA were focusing their effort on the First Platoon situated on the eastern flank facing the railroad tracks. Captain Sweeney noticed they were burning up a lot of ammo and told his Gunny to redistribute some of the ammo from the other platoons. He then called Battalion and requested a resupply. The new Battalion Executive Officer denied his request. The next thing Sweeney remembers, "My concept of time during our fight was nonexistent. After my request for ammo and it being denied, magically in the illumination of artillery flares, under heavy fire, a chopper appears over our position and kicks out beaucoup ammo boxes and three five-gallon cans of vanilla ice cream. All of it was retrieved and carried into the CP for distribution."

The fight continued at close quarters and then suddenly stopped. Everything went quiet. Hearing the assault and firefight, one of Ed Shore's squads out on a short patrol tried to come back in the wire to reinforce the company. As they were coming in they began taking fire from the NVA outside the wire. Sweeney remembers, "I ordered Ed to clear our direct front for the incoming squad to come in...Suddenly, there came a shower of green tracers going over the berm from the railroad tracks...I recall thinking, the poor little bastards don't know how to shoot at night...Before I knew it Ed had elements of the First Platoon flanking them outside the wire and were moving amongst them killing them as they walked through them...We had no sooner gotten regrouped back on our lines and we started taking more NVA fire from the northeast corner of the perimeter. I told Ed to stand by for another assault when I gave the word. I then brought in my LAAW man, Corporal Richard Lopez, and had him place a LAAW round into the source of the fire. That interrupted them immediately. The next thing I see is Lieutenant Shore again shirtless, bleeding about his back, pistol waving and leading one of his squads in an aggressive assault right amongst the enemy. The fight ended quickly and in my mind our victory that night was never in question. My Marines and Ed Shore's leadership, in particular, were magnificent!"[18]

A New Marine Endures the Probe

In this fight during the early morning hours of 15 June, PFC Tom Shabel, newly arrived a couple of weeks earlier, vividly remembers the early morning probe. "My fighting hole was about ten yards from the M60 gunner. As the probe began the machine gunner opened fire without receiving the appropriate authority from the Platoon Commander. This was a big no-no because it allowed the NVA to ascertain where the gun was—one of the objectives of their probe. After receiving an on the spot physical disciplining, the gunner and his weapon were pulled out of the hole and I swapped positions with him."

Minutes later, the assault began in force and Shabel recalled being ringed in his "new hole" with several RPG rounds, blowing him left, right, forward, and then backward. He was peppered with shrapnel from the RPG rounds in the face, neck, and chest. He describes in detail, "I knew I had been hit, but I did not have time to dwell on it as the NVA followed that with a ground assault. Our guys responded with a heavy volume of disciplined small arms fire, 60mm mortars and finally artillery which had been pre-registered. The NVA then saw the attack fruitless and broke off. We were then ordered to lock and load, get out of our fighting holes and go after them. The result, I remember, was the recovery of twenty-one NVA dead. Many of them had been drug off...Bravo Company had taken only WIAs in this attack. It was a decisive victory for us and our morale that night! I was sent to the Battalion Aid Station back in the rear, patched up, and returned to the Company."

Victory Isn't Always Glorious

The dawn came slowly as the NVA continued to engage Bravo Company with sporadic firing to retrieve their dead and wounded. Bravo miraculously had suffered only five casualties up to this point. Taking a head count, Sweeney was down to sixty-three Marines and himself as the only officer left in the field. As Sweeney recalled, three of the wounded, including Lieutenant Shore, were from NVA hand grenades. "As the sun slowly rose, I walked over my CP area and happened to glance down at the three five-gallon cans of melted vanilla ice cream with the tops ripped off. All three of them had streaks of blood on the surface where Marines, getting their ammo resupply, had reached in with bloody hands and snatched up some of the ice cream. It looked like strawberry swirl, which at the time was my favorite. I've since switched to other flavors."

The enemy dead was twenty-four enemy bodies on the ground, with one captured. The captured NVA, a Captain, through an interpreter, expressed extreme anger at his men for leaving him on the battlefield. Sweeney recounts what he assessed after the night battle, "The enemy dead had fresh haircuts, decent uniforms, and most had belts of explosives around their waists which indicated that we had been hit by a Sapper Battalion. One NVA was cut clean in two at the waist without a drop of blood showing. We couldn't find his legs. It appeared that he may have been hit dead on the explosive belt and prematurely blown in half. There were many bloody drag marks leading away to the northeast. I estimated that we killed thirty-five to fifty NVA and wounded at least that many."

PFC Tom Shabel recollects, "We pulled a night ambush after this firefight and while coming in the next morning, we accidentally tripped over the missing legs which Captain Sweeney talked about...we called it in on the radio and were told to drag what was left of that NVA back to the perimeter. One of those life experiences you do not forget."

Back at it in the early morning, the wounded were starting to be medevac'd and Bravo received some replacements. The 1/27 Battalion Commander called Sweeney on the radio and gave him the order to continue attacking east across the railroad berm. Sweeney recollects, "I had the sense that he had no concept of what we had just been through. I objected on the basis that my Marines were exhausted and needed some rest. He then granted us a three-hour period to rest before we began our attack. Just finishing the conversation with him, we started taking 81mm mortar rounds. Two of my new replacement Corpsmen were instantly killed. We then began taking small arms fire from NVA still near the berm. I looked out towards the length of the berm and saw an NVA standing skylined on the top...He looked fresh and lethal and was not with the unit that we had just fought. I called my sniper team up...Their first day of combat and enemy rounds cracking all around us...The sniper kept ducking. Finally, I yelled at him, 'Give me that damned rifle.' I had the NVA in the crosshairs of the scope and was pulling final squeeze when I was shot through the upper left arm. I felt like someone had ripped it off me and then hit it with a sledgehammer! The round had cut the artery and the ulnar nerve. Fortunately, instead of augering straight through my chest, the bullet angled down and exited through the crotch of my trousers. Sergeant Isell was there and ripped my utility pants off checking my family jewels which were untouched. I handed the sniper rifle to a big Marine next to me and ordered him to kill the NVA. I then grabbed my arm above the wound and stopped the bleeding. Then a Corpsman came over and put a tourniquet on it."

Captain Sweeney radioed the Battalion Commander and informed him that he was out of commission. Sweeney strongly advised him to send Company D forward to link up with his right front and run a two-company assault forward. He also advised him that they were still up against a sizable force based on what they had encountered and with no officers in Company B. The Battalion Commander agreed with him and immediately dispatched Company D forward. Sweeney refused to be medevac'd until Delta Company arrived at his position.

Sweeney vividly remembers while they waited for Company D's arrival they again began taking mortar rounds. "Three or four Marines grabbed me and threw me into a fighting hole and then jumped on top of me. I appreciated the gesture but they damned near smothered me to death. Company D finally arrived and Captain Pat Kahler came running over to my position and took one look at me and started laughing, 'Sweeney, I knew you were going to get it.' I don't recall my retort but it probably wasn't respectable. Shortly afterward I was medevac'd out and eventually wound up in Balboa Naval Hospital in San Diego, California with serious nerve damage in my left arm. Captain Kahler, years later, became my Executive Officer when I was Commanding Officer of the 4th Marine Regiment stateside. I hold him to this day in very high regard and consider him a good friend despite his unsympathetic remark back then. Actually, I was laughing with him."[18]

The First Battalion of the 27th Marines remained on the operation throughout most of the month until 23 June. It spent most of that time thoroughly searching and clearing villages between the north-south grid lines of 94 and 03, a total distance of about nine kilometers. After the sister unit, 1st Battalion, 26th Marines received orders for another mission and withdrew on 5 June, Operation Allen Brook became a one-battalion endeavor until 23 June.[19]

Just Another Operation

Sergeant David Harrison of Delta Company did not know the name of the operation when they embarked into the Go Noi area. He remembered the general area from his first tour in 1965. It was not important to know the details and names attached to the operation by the higher-ups, only that the enemy was out there and ready to kill Marines. Harrison knew from hard experience what tactics to use with the men under him.

Harrison remembered when he was discharged and went home that he still didn't know the operation's name because there was no one to talk with about it. No one in the unit knew what the operation was named. Most did not care and had the harsh reality of surviving on their minds. It was years later that he learned from others about Operation Allen Brook's historical significance and some of the other events that took place during the overall operation.

Harrison and his platoon landed in the Go Noi area about the middle of June 1968. As he recollects, "We got off the choppers and there was no firing. We then all got on-line and the whole battalion started a coordinated movement to the east. At times, we would get snipers, we would get down...and then we would get up and walk on. We would end up walking a long way. I knew it was going to be a long and tedious maneuver."

Sergeant Harrison remembers coming up into the first tree line and everyone was standing around. Captain Pat Kahler, the CO of Delta, was going over the maps, plotting their position and figuring out which direction to proceed when the word was passed down over the radio. Harrison recalled, "We were just sitting there and sitting there...I was acting Platoon Sergeant at the time. I had walked into the tree line to our front...I had walked into it four times checking and double checking my entire platoon. The fourth trip I was almost in the tree line and for some reason I turned around, spotting a bottle cap laying on the ground half buried. One of my men, Pete Jerolaman was reaching down to pick that bottle cap up. I immediately yelled at him... 'Don't fucking touch that Jerolaman,' he recoiled instantly and looked at me as if I had gone crazy."

Harrison knew from past experiences that it was more than likely a booby trap. Everyone froze but soon understood the seriousness. Harrison started asking if anyone had any C4 explosive. No one had any, so one of his squad leaders, Corporal Bill Drennan, volunteered to roll a hand grenade onto it and jump into a hole nearby.

Harrison remembers asking Corporal Drennan, "What if it has a 500-pound bomb attached to it?" Drennan didn't seem too concerned since the hole he would get into looked deep and secure. Harrison recalls that Corporal Drennan dropped the grenade on it and dove for the hole. "That damn thing went off and almost knocked me out! It had to have been an 81mm mortar round...it made a huge hole...I had walked over that bottle cap four times before I ever noticed it... anyway, Drennan solved our problem. Everyone was shook up over that incident and it had turned out bigger than everyone thought."

Link-Up with Bravo Company

Delta Company continued moving to the east until they reached the National Railroad tracks. The tracks were on high ground and up on a berm fifteen feet above the landscape. The whole company turned right and walked towards Bravo Company's position. Bravo had spent the previous night in a position close to the railroad berm and had been almost overrun. They had killed quite a lot of NVA and were still hauling off the bodies. Sergeant Harrison remembers the scene, "There were so many of them that it had been just like shooting fish in a barrel."

The order then came for Delta to move on beyond Bravo's position. Sergeant Harrison was doing double duty as acting Platoon Sergeant and had his normal squad. He recalls going over to a new guy, PFC Lloyd Tucker, and asking him to become a Squad Leader. Harrison remembers the conversation as "He was telling me he couldn't handle it...I was telling him I would help him...And I was standing next to him which is a no-no and I knew it. You make a bigger target. So, then we are getting ready to move and Tucker gets shot in the leg, twice. I stand up and yelled to my men, 'Cover us,' and drag him off into the bushes... I felt extremely bad because I felt it was my fault he got hit. I kept telling him he would be OK... 'Just think of the clean sheets and a nice bed tonight when you get to the hospital in the rear,' I told him. I also am thinking to myself, I would take those two rounds to be in a nice clean bed tonight."

This had always been a bad area, even on Harrison's first tour. Harrison observed that the Go Noi had been previously bombed by B-52s. Everything was torn asunder. Bomb craters were everywhere. Some were twenty and thirty feet in diameter and twelve- to fifteen-feet deep in the center.

On 19 June, Bravo X-Ray (consisting of a platoon and command group from Company B and a platoon from Company D) encountered the enemy at grid coordinates BT023550, close to the hamlet of Bac Dong Ban just south of the Ky Lam River.[20]

Harrison related that Bravo had walked into that new un-swept area, and before they knew it they became heavily engaged. They radioed back for reinforcements. Lieutenant John J. O'Brien rallied his men and immediately went toward that area. Sergeant Harrison remembers, "The Bravo Marines were pinned down. A lot of them were shot, some were dead...some just strung out between rice-paddy dikes and the tree line. We came up and got behind the rice-paddy dikes. Lieutenant O'Brien took off forward with two Marines. I thought their intentions were to go out and help the wounded. I later found out that O'Brien was going forward to find First Lieutenant Richard Wozar, the now Commanding Officer of Bravo, to assess the situation."

While running, O'Brien was shot in the ankle. Harrison watched in dismay as he did a complete flip in mid-air. The two Marines with O'Brien ran back to the paddy dike. Harrison recalls, "It was just an automatic reaction for them to seek cover. I yelled at them to go back and drag his ass back to where I was...So they ran back out and drug him over to my position behind the dike. He had been shot in the ankle again where he was wounded the month before on 9 May in the Hue area. He had taken shrapnel in the ankle then and this time it was a rifle round."

L-R: D. Harrison, H. Sweet, and J. Buccola ~ Courtesy of David Harrison, D Co, 1/27

Frontal Assault

Regrouping around O'Brien, Harrison was told to take command of the platoon and orchestrate a frontal assault into the tree line in front of them. Sergeant Harrison vividly remembers, "It is over 100 degrees Fahrenheit, I am completely out of breath and I am thinking a frontal assault, what in the fuck? So, I figure, OK...I get the platoon ready and I tell the Squad Leaders, 'We are moving forward into the tree line, and to 'Get on-line, First Squad, Second Squad and Third Squad rushes...I tell them, 'I will yell to each of you when it is your turn, the other two squads will provide supporting bases of fire.' So, I start calling em out! 'First Squad!' 'Second Squad!' And finally, the 'Third Squad.' We succeeded in moving up to about forty yards from the tree line. I kept looking for the NVA in the tree line. I could not see them anywhere. They had totally concealed themselves. And then I look over to my left flank and am noticing that Bravo Company is not advancing. So, what I thought was happening, was not happening. I am thinking that maybe Bravo did not get the word? Or maybe they are not going to do the assault? Am I now confused and worried? My thoughts are, we cannot go into that tree line by ourselves. There are not enough of us. I know everyone in my platoon is worried and looking to me for guidance. Our whole left flank is open...Do we really want to go into that area not knowing what or how many NVA are in there?"

The firing and counter-firing was continuous. A machine gun team crawled up to the paddy dike and the machine gunner was immediately killed. The assistant gunner took over the gun. It wasn't long before he was killed while trying to lay down a base of fire. Harrison observed the situation and thought, "We are just too close and they have concealed machine-gun emplacements in that tree line. To make matters worse, one of my men freaks out and starts screaming at the top of his lungs. I am thinking he has been shot...I later discern that he is in shock. He had seen two of his buddies get killed and he is unnerving the rest of the men. So, I yell at a couple of my Marines, 'Pick him up and haul his ass back to the rear.' He had everyone really shook up."

The assault had stalled. Lieutenant O'Brien's radioman, PFC Richard Pixley, moved within shouting distance of Sergeant Harrison and began yelling messages from the command group. Why hadn't they moved forward and taken the tree line? He yelled to Harrison that the order still stood. Harrison recollects, "Do they really want us to go into that tree line by ourselves, with the whole left flank open? I am thinking to myself, that is not going to happen...I am not going to get my whole platoon wiped out...So I did not answer back immediately. In a little while, the command group had gotten artillery and air support on-line and Pixley and I continue to yell back and forth... I started guiding the artillery strikes on target by yelling back the adjustments. Then we got lucky and a fast mover came in with a napalm canister. That napalm exploded so close it scared the bejesus out of me...and everyone else in the front row...and the heat from it was almost unbearable. I thought for sure we were going to have some burn casualties from that napalm strike. After that subsided, I am almost sure everyone who is in the tree line was cooked."

While the artillery strikes impacted into the tree line, Harrison encountered a Staff Sergeant who came from his backside and yelled at him, "What is going on?" Sergeant Harrison was thinking, "Who in the hell is this? What are you doing out here?" I had never seen this dude before and he is standing up the whole time while the NVA are shooting at him. Rounds are impacting all around him in the ground. I say to him, "Do you know they are shooting at you?" And he says, "Yeah, I know it!" And then Bam, the NVA shoot him right in the stomach. He doubled over and started yelling at me, "I'm hit...I am a bleeder!" Doc David Bronson is laying right next to me and says to me, "I am going to go back and help him"...and I say "No" emphatically, "You stay right where you are!" The enemy had a gun trained right on us and I am telling Doc he wouldn't make it three steps before he would be shot all to hell...Doc kept pleading with me and I said it again, "Doc, I am ordering you to stay right where you are!" That was enough to relieve him of his conscience at the time. Finally, some other Marines drug the Staff Sergeant out of the line of fire and got him evacuated.

After the fight and napalm run were over, the Marines prepared to do a damage assessment in the tree line where the enemy combatants were positioned. Harrison's Marines were ordered to move forward and sweep the area and stage all the dead NVA bodies that had not been dragged away. Harrison was ready to begin the sweep when he looked back and realized that one of his squads was missing. He thought to himself, "That is almost half my platoon...so I stalled. Then I stood up and drug our dead Marines' bodies back toward the rear. Then Alpha Company comes in from our right and sweeps the tree line back and forth from one end to the other...Luckily, they had given us word to pull back while they swept it. I didn't have a full platoon and who knows what could have happened. Later I confronted the missing Squad Leader and asked him where in the hell he was when we were ordered to sweep the tree line?"

The missing squad leader related the following to Harrison, "He told me that a chopper had landed with ammo and water and asked me if I had seen it? He told me that he took his squad there to fill their canteens. I was so angry with him and had not seen any helicopters landing during the fight. I said to him, 'Did you know two of our guys got killed and others were wounded and you were gone when we were about to do a frontal assault and you went and got water? I should have your ass court-martialed!' I was so pissed off...I could not see straight! I chewed him out because I wanted him to think about what he had done to the security of our platoon."

The next day the Marines rose with the sun and walked all day long searching for where in that area the NVA had disappeared. Harrison happened to be out of water as he had given one of his canteens to a wounded man the previous day and the other he carried was empty. Potable water was nowhere to be found. The temperature was well over the 100-degree mark. When they returned to their base camp it was dark and someone in the higher echelons of the Battalion had ordered ice cream to be flown out to the troops.

Harrison recollects that he was still covered with dried blood from carrying wounded and dead bodies and caring for the wounded. "When I feasted my eyes on that ice cream, I remember dishing it out for my guys. We didn't care if we were filthy dirty or not. We just dug into that ice cream, dirty hands and all. I am thinking to myself, this is unbelievable, we are eating ice cream out here, after all we had been through? This was unrealistic! I couldn't believe it! I don't have any idea what they were thinking and why they sent it out but it tasted good...really good and there was enough for everybody...I am thinking to myself we are in a surreal movie that won't end. Here we are eating ice cream in the middle of a battlefield...It did not make sense. I still cannot get over that."

Night Ambush Patrol at the Railroad Bridge

Sergeant Harrison remembers taking a night patrol out with about two squads of Marines during the operation. That night the destination was the railroad trestle with a covered bridge. To get there the Marines had to stay off the tracks because the NVA were active in and around the railroad. He recollects not being able to walk on the tracks, "because of the silhouette a body would have. We could not walk along the side of the berm the tracks were on because the enemy could lob grenades in on us. So, I had to plan my walk overland right to the covered bridge. We hit it just right. I put men down at the bottom and some of them up topside. I went up top and got everyone quiet and settled in for a night ambush. Soon, artillery rounds started impacting close by within about forty yards of our positions. These rounds are planned Harassment and Interdiction artillery rounds and are showering us with shrapnel. I immediately called Captain Kahler on the net. He did some checking and comes back with, 'I think you have your men at the wrong bridge, over...' I now must decide; do I want to walk my men to the proper ambush site or stay here. So, I decide to stay put. I told everyone to lay low and if the H&I started again and were close that we would move quickly. All night we lay there and received intermittent showers of shrapnel. The next morning Doc Bronson comes to me and shows me a nasty blister on his hand. He had been burned by some falling shrapnel from the H&I arty rounds."

It was later learned that during that patrol, both Delta and Bravo's night positions were dangerously close to each other. Harrison and his men had heard voices close by which they thought were the NVA. When they were fired on later from the direction the voices came from, the red tracer round gave everyone the indication that it was a spotter round from a 106mm recoilless rifle. Bravo Company had set up night positions dangerously close to Harrison's men that night. Lucky for both they didn't engage.

Bac Dong Ban Hamlet

On the sweep below the Ky Lam River, two platoons from Bravo Company came into the village area of Bac Dong Ban (grid coordinate BT023550) early in the morning of 19 June. Now under the command of the Executive Officer, 1st Lieutenant R. M. Wozar, lead elements became pinned down. Numerous artillery and air strikes were called for but failed to negate the dug-in NVA positions. The Battalion Command group located near grid AT980535 crossed the railroad, proceeding to close with Bravo X-Ray (Bravo Company Commander), committing two platoons from Delta and Alpha Companies along with one platoon from Charlie Company.

PFC Tom Shabel's squad was walking point that day and as he recalls, "I was assigned right flank security and walking about fifty yards to the right of the main element when we were suddenly hit with heavy automatic weapons fire. Six Marines in the main body were either wounded or killed and lying out in the open. Advancing forward I ran up to a paddy dike and started laying down a base of fire to cover my own advancing squad. Noticing an NVA in the village area with an RPG next to a pagoda, I unleashed three rounds into him eliminating that threat. Suddenly there were plenty of other targets popping up and we had become pinned down under sudden withering fire coming from that hamlet."

Shabel immediately started looking for targets of opportunity. He spotted an NVA moving between two bunkers and started firing at him until his rifle went empty. The NVA had escaped his firing. He slammed a new magazine into his M16, stood up and took another bead on another bunker expecting to fire semi-automatic measured fire, and only one round went off. Shabel recalls, "My rifle had double fed and I immediately hit the deck and tried to clear my rifle. It was an all too often occurrence with these new M16s we had been issued. The next thing I knew an explosion occurred near my head area. Some time later, I came to and had blood in my eyes and covering my entire face and chest. I touched my face and felt a flap of skin over my eye socket. Feeling it at the time it felt like a nickel sized puncture wound. My initial reaction was that I had been hit in the head. I knew if you get shot in the head you die. Amazingly, I felt calm. I remember looking at my watch…It was 0830 am. I now look back and believe that I was prematurely recording the time of my death."

PFC Shabel, now wounded and lying up front next to a paddy dike, was all by himself. His fellow Marines in the rice paddy field within yelling distance were in one hell of a firefight. He lay there for some time and started applying a battle dressing to stop the bleeding. He recollects, "I didn't really feel all that bad and quickly decided that I was not going to die. Once I realized I was going to live, my mood changed into anger and I thought to myself, they cannot do this to me, I am an American Marine!"

Gathering himself as best he could, Shabel grabbed his M16 rifle and took a bead on a target, squeezing the trigger, the fragmented trigger housing fell to the ground. He looked down at his rifle and there was a hole you could put a fist through in the middle of his rifle. Shabel in reflection is convinced one of the NVA had taken a shot at him while he was clearing his rifle, missing him, while hitting and exploding the receiver housing group of his rifle.

With a non-operative rifle, Shabel took inventory. He still had M16 ammo, a bayonet, six grenades and an M72 LAAW left to utilize. He remembered thinking, "This LAAW is the only weapon I have to reach out and touch someone. So, I decided to hit the bunker that had the heavy .51-caliber machine gun emplacement holding the rest of the company down."

PFC Shabel stood up, placed the front sight on the bunker, and squeezed the firing mechanism. Nothing happened. Like a robot in training, he went down again, followed rearming procedure, stood up again, drew a sight picture on the targeted bunker, squeezed the firing mechanism and still nothing. Hitting the deck, he scrutinized the weapon more closely. The firing cable was swinging in the breeze. Shabel came to the realization that the weapon had not fired and was armed and hot. He remembers thinking, "I have no control over this frigging beast. I am trying my damnedest to remember what they told me in training but this was one situation that they had not covered. However, they had trained me not to leave anything on the battlefield. I knew that I was going to have to hump all this shit and my sorry butt out of here, once I figured out how I was going to get out of this shitty place. So, I prepared for the worst. I shod my rifle with bayonet, grabbed two grenades and placed the four others within easy reach. My thought was if assaulted, I could take some of them out. Me, having all of two weeks in-country and getting real life on-the-job experience, pulled the pins on the two grenades I was holding in my left hand. I was thinking that I would be ready when the time came. Time not being recorded began to wear on and before long those grenades got heavy. I had dropped the pins in a foot of grass and there was no way I was going to find them. I had no choice but to lob the grenades over the rice paddy dike. When they went off the NVA knew I was still kicking and renewed their interest in me. A few well-placed bursts from that .51-caliber into my position gave me ample incentive to melt back into the ground."

It was apparent to PFC Shabel that the only way out of this field of fire would be solely up to him. He knew it was going to be a long fight so he started to crawl to his left where the main body of his squad had been. The rice-paddy dike gave adequate cover. Reaching a perpendicular rice-paddy dike he could see that he was getting close to the others but a tracked vehicle had come through earlier and destroyed the protective part of the dike. It was an open area of about eight or ten yards. Shabel remembers, "I made the decision to just low crawl across the open area and when I reached the cross-paddy dike, I would just roll over it. I remember thinking, Gee, they have not shot at me for a while so they probably don't know I am here...I had no more started low-crawling across that open area and the .51-caliber opened up on me again! I have no recollection of running, nor diving over the dike. I do have a strong memory of the rounds impacting in front of me and then suddenly sliding head first into a crater full of water. I remember thrashing around—pulled down by all my gear and trying to figure which way was to the surface. Grasping for air, I am thinking that I am now going to drown in Vietnam in a bomb crater. Fortune smiled on me again, the drown proofing exercises in boot camp kicked in and I remembered to look for the bubbles and follow them upward."

Having finally reached the safety of the other Bravo Marines, Shabel was grabbed by the flak jacket and pulled from the bomb crater. The Marines were still under heavy fire but PFC Shabel would acquire another functioning rifle. He recalls that later that day, "I was medically evacuated around 1630. This time I was in the hospital in Da Nang for six weeks. Our two platoons had taken six KIAs and nineteen WIAs that day and there was only one Marine in my squad who was not killed or wounded. He had been on the left flank security and somehow the NVA had missed him."

Alpha Company Does the Unimaginable

Under the leadership of Lieutenant David Boillot, Third Platoon and Lieutenant Bill Jones and Sergeant Felix Salmeron, Second Platoon, the two platoons from Alpha Company secured the objective at grid BT025547. Securing that ground around 1800 hours on 19 June they immediately pivoted to the north while Companies B and D covered their move to the next objective. The two Alpha Company platoons moved their Marines across open ground toward enemy fortifications while line companies A and D provided a covering base of fire. Salmeron recalls those moments in vivid detail. "We moved eastward toward the first objective and secured it, sitting for a while. As I looked north toward our next objective I could see it was probably 400 yards between where we were and the tree line we were ordered to take...It was open ground all the way. We could see Bravo Company's position and the only thing we could do was move across that open expanse...Bravo knew we would come across. A

Sergeant Felix Salmeron & Lieutenant Bill Jones ~ Courtesy of Felix Salmeron, A Co, 1/27

lot of people would say that is daring to do, but if taught and learned properly in the basic schools it could work. What I did was make sure every one of my men knew and understood we were going to assault across the field. I had every other man shooting as we moved so if someone ran out of ammo the other could pick up the slack. As we crossed, we stepped up the pace. Bravo and Delta, laying down fire, kept their heads down as we proceeded. We caught a lot of the enemy in their fighting holes and trenches by surprise. They didn't expect us to be that aggressive. When we got to the tree line I had the guys set up a hasty defense and there were 'crispy critters' all over the place. Air and Arty had earlier prepped the area. That must have gotten most of them because the NVA would typically drag their dead away in retreat. Once the area was secured and the remaining NVA had di-di'd, Bravo and Delta Companies stayed to search the area for weapons' caches and we went back to guarding the engineers doing their plow work."[21]

This maneuver required strong leadership and was reinforced with past experience. Salmeron's quick and decisive order to move and move quickly over dangerous and open ground was all that was needed to reach this dangerous objective. It proved successful without loss.

A Previous Wound Brings Bad Luck

During clearing of the Go Noi during Operation Allen Brook, Corporal Gabe Komanec of Charlie Company revealed to his Corpsman that he had a piece of shrapnel still lodged in his leg from his first tour in 1966 with 3rd Battalion, 7th Marines. It had begun to bother him a bit. So, the Corpsman sent Corporal Komanec to Da Nang Naval Support Activity Hospital to have it looked at. When Komanec arrived via chopper, he recalls, "The doctor looked at it and told me not to worry about it. The small piece of the muscle wasn't going to move anyplace. He then told me to get my ass back out to my people...He said they needed me! Then he asked me, 'Is there anything else bothering me physically?' So, I say, 'Well, when I am running with a full pack, my leg hyper extends.' I then said, 'Let me show you,' and stood up and extended it backward. That must have gotten his attention because he immediately took me to an X-ray table and had the techs take pictures of it from all different angles."

After examining the X-rays, the doctors came back into the room to consult with Komanec. He remembers the conversation with the doctor as follows, "How in the hell did you get here to Vietnam?" Komanec recalls he was a Lieutenant Commander in rank and replied to the doctor, "I came over with my unit and had been training with them in Hawaii and here I am." The Doctor said, "You aren't even supposed to be in the Military let alone, here in Vietnam with a leg like that…You are unfit for this kind of duty!" Komanec then replied, "The Corpsman in my unit told me when he looked at it to let someone know if it bothers me and have it checked out!" He then told the Doctor, "It hadn't really bothered me and I just thought I would mention it since you asked."

Komanec was then sent to the Philippines to Clark Air Force Base where he remained under observation for approximately twenty days. The Marine Corps decided that after two tours, Corporal Komanec would be sent to Bremerton, Washington where he would spend three months on light duty. It was then finally decided he would be sent home and placed on the temporary medical disabled list and told that if his condition improved he could be called back to active duty. By 1972 he received a final Medical Discharge from the United States Marine Corps. Komanec recollects the bad feelings he had at the time he left his men, "I went on a bad guilt trip and this became a depressing time for me because I felt like I had abandoned my guys."

A Different Kind of Mission

Early in June, 1/27 split its CP group and relocated much of the command element back to Regimental Headquarters at Duong Son (2). The rear echelon of the field command group remained at Liberty Bridge utilizing the existing CP and in-place communications network left by 27th Regiment Marines.

On 6 June elements of the 1st Engineer Battalion (per 1st Engineer Battalion June Command Chronology, "B" Company, 5th Engineer Battalion, attached to 1st Engineer Battalion) reached the north side of the Thu Bon River, traveled down Liberty Road, and ferried across the river to link up with 1/27's CP group. Their new orders were to clear the Go Noi Island operations area of all structures, underground caves, trench lines, and spider holes. It was known that NVA weapons, munitions, medical supplies, and foodstuffs would undoubtedly still be in underground caches and uncovered in the coming days. This ground had an unprecedented history of enemy activity. The 27th Marines, transitioned from a full-scale operational mode into providing security for the engineering detachment, overall coordination of the clearing effort, and control/domination of the Go Noi Island area.[22] The Engineers proceeded with the task by using Caterpillar tractors with frontal "Rome" plow attachments to demolish all the NVA efforts from the past.

The mission concept of destroying the area called for the elimination of all-natural assembly areas, concealing foliage, tree lines, bamboo groves, and hedgerows. The orders were to systematically destroy all trench lines, fighting holes, caves, bunkers, tunnel complexes, and structures either natural or man-made which provided cover for the enemy. A thorough crushing and burning of all bunker material such as concrete blocks, beams, posts, pillars, and tree trunks would deprive the enemy of future use.

First Engineer Commanders named their support of the 27th Marines and Allen Brook "Project Woodpecker." The engineers' June 1968 Command Chronology noted that 659,000 total square meters of land were cleared on Go Noi because of this project. The area cleared east of Liberty Bridge equaled about a quarter of a square mile, over 160 acres. Abundant quantities of enemy and captured U. S. ordnance were found and destroyed by the engineers. After being catalogued, the inventory included the following: 500-pound bombs, 250-pound bombs, 105mm and 155mm artillery rounds, LAAWs, M26 grenades, 82mm mortar rounds, M79 rounds, flame throwers, very large amounts of small arms munitions, and an assortment of box mines. Multinational rifles along with NVA uniforms and medical supplies were also inventoried and sent to Regiment Intel. Over 300 bunkers of distinct size and type and close to 400 spider holes were bulldozed and destroyed in the month of June. This was the beginning. Ordnance and weaponry discovered and destroyed in July was beyond alarming.[23]

Captain Ronald Gruenberg remembers taking over Charlie Company on 6 June. He had been told prior that if any of the line company commanders were out that he was next in line. He recalled that when Captain Farmer, Company C Commander, was wounded, he was simply told to immediately go out and take over. He hitched a ride down to Liberty Bridge and had to walk out alone to where the company was in the Cu Bans east of the bridge. As he remembers, "My orders were to simply replace Farmer and that was it...and then we had to immediately go and find the dead Marines that had been left on the battlefield by another line company in a recent skirmish. Then we were diverted to help 1/26. I remember as we were going in one of the companies in 1/26 was still in the attack position...'Black Bud Bravo 6' was the Commander's call sign and he put us in a 'Check Fire' situation and that caused us some concern...but then after a while we eventually assaulted and took the tree line to our front."

What stood out in Gruenberg's mind was the concept of literally flattening the whole sector of this area all the way to the railroad bridge. The landmass between two rivers was quite large. He commented, "It was something unique and I don't think it gets much attention in the annals of our history other than we Charlie Company Marines chased down some of the enemies, but the really herculean effort of those engineers doing their thing on the Dozers really struck me as extraordinary... I remember Captain Lou Rice, the guy in charge of this project and how his men worked twenty-four hours a day plowing, leveling, digging bunkers and rice caches up, plowing anything in the way, and the billowing clouds of smoke...When I first met Lou he informed me that his orders were to make this island a parking lot...That was when we began to provide security for these amazing and hardworking engineers."

The initial clearing had eradicated a lot of the well-constructed NVA fortifications. Some featured concrete. Some were hand dug, constructed with railroad ties from the nearby National Railroad, and could withstand large aerial bombs if detonated close-in. Embedded firing pits with slits at ground level for controlling a field of fire were also found. These emplacements typified many of the fighting positions. The tactical emplacements throughout the whole area embodied a well-thought-out planning process.

In a firefight, the Marines who were unlucky enough to approach these uniquely constructed emplacements found themselves totally helpless once in the NVA fields of fire. It was eerie walking through these sanctuaries. The men had begun to develop instincts and grew vigilant on every approach into these areas. Flashes of gunfire would begin zipping through the hedges. Whooshing sounds fell from the sky, followed by impacts—"ka-rump" very close to them. Shock waves flattened foliage and dirt burst into the air. The Marines would hit the deck and wrap their arms over their helmets. When the chaos subsided, the Marines were up looking for where the firing had originated. It was time to move and go on the offensive...That is what Marines do. This maneuvering against fortified bunkers and spider holes was unlike anything these Marines had encountered previously.

What the Engineers plowed up and destroyed during the two exercises named "Woodpecker I and II" defied imagination. They found enemy fortifications and zig-zagging trench lines totaling over six miles, along with numerous ammunition and ordnance caches which had to be destroyed in the process.

The 1st Engineers continued the daily land clearing in support of the entire Allen Brook Operation throughout June, July, and into August. At the end of July 1968, a second land-clearing team (Woodpecker II) was assigned to conduct the razing of suspected rocket-launching areas. Again, in this sizable area, almost a square mile had been bulldozed and more caches of enemy ordnance and munitions were still being discovered and destroyed.

The security plans for the Engineers placed two companies from the battalion near the plowing to furnish them work-area security. One company would set up close in next to the demolition work while another company reinforced the outlying security by conducting longer-range patrolling. This lessened the possibility of the project being interrupted.

The first clearing project began in the Cu Bans. These villages close to and on the east side of Liberty Bridge were where most of the initial engagements had taken place. They gained priority in Project Woodpecker. The idea was to work out from the bridge and move to where the most predominant enemy staging areas were known to be. This would secure the CP and the bridge flank, quickly allowing the engineers to progress eastward into the island proper. After that first task in the Cu Bans reached completion, the work moved further east to the villages of Cu Ban (6), Le Nam (1) and Le Nam (2). By 12 June these villages and most standing structures in the immediate surroundings had been razed.[24]

Mine clearing LVTE-1 Amtracs on Go Noi ~ Courtesy of Raul E. Figueroa, H&S Co, 1/27

Early on the morning of 13 June, the engineers and the companies began work near Le Bac (1) and (2). That same day, Company D rejoined the battalion after being on an "opcon" assignment with III MAF in the Da Nang area. Delta had been working with 1st MPs (Military Police) in Da Nang.

The next phase called for the continued demolition of the embedded NVA logistical infrastructure within the hamlets of Phu Dong (1) and (2). The plows kept up the daily vigil of moving dirt, clanking with dust billowing up into the air.

Moving East from the Bridge: The End of Allen Brook

By mid-June, all the preliminary engineering work close to Liberty Bridge was completed. The engineers and CP Group with the now two supporting companies, Company B and D, maneuvered into Phu Dong (2) and (1) to again begin the plowing.

Bravo Company, which was positioned in the outer defensive vicinity of Ky Lam Nam, encountered an early morning assault into their night perimeter. Utilizing small arms, automatic weapons, and B40 rockets, the enemy launched an all-out assault on Bravo. It began with rounds piercing the air everywhere. Rifles barked with single shots and then picked up with two- and three-round bursts. Some of the B40 rockets had impacted, wounding Company B Marines. The NVA were attempting both a frontal and flank maneuver simultaneously. Bravo Marines savagely repulsed the attack by immediately going on the offensive. Bravo riflemen moved forward with disciplined squad tactics, killing twenty-four enemy combatants.

By 19 June, operating east of the National Railroad near Bac Dong Ban (grid coordinates BT025554), elements of Company B, 1/27 suddenly encountered heavy resistance. The lead platoon became pinned down. Numerous artillery and air missions were called in but failed to soften the enemy positions. Additional platoons from Companies B and D were committed and began flanking maneuvers. Company A attacked to the east and secured the intermediate objective at BT025547. Both Companies B and D then provided a continuous and coordinated base of fire upon a dug-in enemy. Company A then assaulted the enemy emplacements, securing the contested ground.

On 21 June, the Battalion executed its final major maneuver of Operation Allen Brook. The overall maneuver would involve three Companies: B on the left, A in the middle, D on the right, with Company C and the Battalion Command Group in the trace. A series of phase lines were established; Phase Line Red, White, Blue, Green, and finally Phase Line Black by which the final search for enemy combatants would be conducted. Preparation with artillery fire and air strikes preceded the maneuver. The movement would be a wide-sweeping circular movement, north to the river's edge, then toward the east and pivoting back south, encompassing the entire eastern end of Go Noi Island. All line companies performed the task well and on 23 June the Battalion was relieved by Sister Battalion 2/27. Second Battalion assumed control in the final clearing of Go Noi with the Engineering Clearing Team. Additional fortified wooded areas not cleared by 1/27 were completely leveled during the last days of June.

1/27 resumed combined patrols with elements of the 1st Battalion and the 4th Battalion, of the 51st ARVN Regiment in the original area of operation. Their focus was to saturate the rocket and mortar belt around the Da Nang airstrip with constant patrolling.

FMF Pacific Headquarters staff recorded all enemy attacks in I CTZ in each Province from August of 1967 through July of 1968. Quang Tri, Thua Thien, and Quang Nam, the northernmost Provinces, took the brunt of most of the attacks from February through June. It was clear that most of the enemy activity in I CTZ happened in Thua Thien and Quang Nam Provinces. The multi-battalion operations of Allen Brook and the extended Mameluke Thrust in Quang Nam Province seriously eroded the enemy's ability to replace and replenish their staging areas in the An Hoa basin and the rocket and mortar belt" southwest of the Da Nang airfield. The Marines large multi-battalion effort beginning in May thwarted all planning for the area laid out by the North Vietnamese upper echelons in Hanoi (see Exhibit C, pg. 398).

DECLASSIFIED

SECRET

CG 1st MarDiv Frag Order 228-68 dtd 071440Z July 1968
(MAMELUKE THRUST and ALLEN BROOK)

1. For 27th Marines

a. Deploy ALLEN BROOK south of 53 E/W grid line prior to 090645H July 1968 until herbicide mission is completed. Confirm completion with headquarters.

b. Insure persons are instructed that herbicide is not, repeat, not harmful. Take the following action.

(1) Wash Herbicide from exposed skin.

(2) Do not eat food exposed to herbicide.

Excerpt from 2nd Battalion, 27th Marines Command Chronology of July 1968 (p 134)

As a side note, the Commanding General of 1st Marine Division issued Frag Order 228-68 on 7 July 1968 for the entire 27th Marine Regiment engaged on both Operations

Mameluke Thrust and Allen Brook. The herbicide mission referred to above in the Frag Order is now known as the chemical "Agent Orange." This was a powerful mixture of chemical defoliants that, when sprayed by aircraft, eliminated cover for NVA and Viet Cong troops and the crops used to feed them. It later was revealed to cause serious health issues among returning U. S. servicemen and their families as well as among the Vietnamese population.

Operation Woodpecker I and II Summary

From the July 1968 Fleet Marine Force Pacific Command Chronologies, the following was recorded summarizing the result of land clearing by 1st Engineers toward the end of Operation Allen Brook:

> *Project Woodpecker land clearing operations to eradicate the enemy's fortifica-tions on Go Noi Island continued into July. Thus, far during the two-month effort, potential ambush sites and concealment for defensive positions have been cleared from an area equivalent to almost one square mile; 6.7 miles of fighting trenches have been filled and 633 bunkers, 22 caves, and 705 spider holes have been destroyed. During 6 July, 303 man-hours and 738 equipment-hours were expended by Marines assigned to this project.*[25]

An Amtrac Grunt Recalls Duty on Operation Allen Brook

Sergeant John Sontag of H&S Company, 3rd Amphibian Tractor Battalion, remem-bers becoming attached to 1st Engineers during Allen Brook. He recalls an event during that operation in the Go Noi as if it were yesterday. "My Amtrac, an LVTE-1, the engineering version of the LVTP5, provided support to a small engineer group assigned to bulldoze an NVA staging area east of Liberty Bridge. We were there along with one tank and some grunts who were our security. We set up on the river one of the nights along the bank. I remembered that a Warrant Officer oversaw the engineers. Grunt patrols went out that night. As the Marines were returning from patrolling the area somehow the gooks filed in right behind them...The perimeter guards let a few of them in not detecting what was going on at first. The gooks then began overrunning our defensive positions, trying to destroy the tracked vehicles. One RPG round took out the tank fifty feet away from my Amtrac. It was a direct hit and the Marines inside did not have a chance. The round hit the turret killing them all. Another RPG round aimed at my tractor hit the starboard side above the rear sprocket. That round, creasing the outer armor, deflected into a large bucket of sprocket grease bursting it. Running for cover to my Amtrac, diving for the hatch, and about to shut the lid, I was splattered all over my upper body with globs of grease. At first, I thought for sure I had been hit and was bleeding profusely, thinking my brains had scattered all over my upper torso. But I soon realized that it was not blood and brains but sprocket grease that oozed down my face and shoulders. I really thought I had taken that hit but when I finally realized it was grease I began laughing."

During the confusion, it became apparent to all who were alive that the NVA had fully breached the perimeter. Sergeant Sontag quickly positioned himself in the Cupola of the Amtrac and began to lay down a base of fire with the air-cooled .30-caliber machine gun. After witnessing the RPG hit on the tank and the explosion in the turret he could see the NVA running throughout their area, shooting at everything and anybody, some with satchel charges. One climbed up on his track on the side ladder. As that NVA peeked over the top deck, Sontag shot at him and watched him jump back to the ground. Sontag described the next few moments of what seemed like an eternity. "I had missed him on that first shot with my 1911 A1 .45 service pistol so I jumped up looking down at him and fired three more times aiming for his chest mass. I hit him once in the thigh, once in the right chest and missed the other shot. Pop-up flares and mortar flares kept the night lit up continually so at least we could see but not well. There were a lot more of them than us. They probably could have killed us all but suddenly left the perimeter. Medical evacuation choppers never came that night and by God's grace, I am here today. Not till it was over did we realize how much damage they had done."

The Landing Vehicle, Tracked, Engineer, Mark 1 (LVTE-1), an engineering/breaching tracked vehicle which Sontag commanded while on this duty, enhanced the tedious process of finding mines and booby traps prior to bulldozing the area. The area had a history of being heavily mined. This vehicle was there for a purpose. The large front-mounted excavator blade with teeth could push through a suspected minefield and clear a path, sixteen inches deep and twelve feet wide. It carried two rocket-propelled line-charge launchers for "close-in" breaching which were mounted on each side of the cargo department. They could be elevated hydraulically and then fired to the front of the vehicle. Those rocket-propelled launchers carried the coiled line, resembling connected sausage links (fireproof nylon covering) with C4 explosives which could be detonated on the ground. When fired, the rocket would carry the exploding line forward 350 feet. The explosion cleared mines and a lane forward. These behemoths were needed in this area at the time.

Sergeant Sontag recollects, "After a rocket went as far as it could the line would stop as it reached the full length and the rocket fell to the ground. There were two buttons to be pushed to detonate the complete line with multiple charges. The first button unlocked the system and the second button pushed by the Crew Chief sent an electrical pulse exploding the line charges...sometimes to clear more brush I would elevate the launcher high and do an air burst at the top of trees to clear more jungle. Sometimes if I shot it close to the ground it would set off enemy land mines. If some of the charges did not explode, one man, usually me, would run out to the charge, usually to the third or fourth block of C4 toward the end of the line, and place a couple of blasting caps with fuse in the C4 blocks, light them and run like hell back to the tractor before it exploded."

Sontag recalls doing that exercise a few times during Operation Allen Brook. Indelible in his mind is his first experience with the buttons, the faulty line charges, and the backup process to detonate the line charge. "One of my first times I had to run out there and place the blasting caps...I remember hearing some strange buzzing sounds and splats on the banana tree next to me. The second time the splats appeared I noticed two pencil-sized holes dripping sap out of the tree trunk. I suddenly realized that I was being shot at and I think that I beat all the top track and field sprinters in America with an all-time-best dash in running those 70-100 yards back to the Amtrac."

John Sontag reflects that he was the only person in his unit that had been trained in the States on this engineer version of Amtrac and ended up doing most of the patrols out with the grunts and engineers. He recalls, "Everyone that I trained always caught on very quickly."

Fort Apache

Returning to the 27th Marines in early July, Lieutenant Crane Davis took over his TBS classmate's platoon in Company C. Second Lieutenant John Kispert, 3rd Platoon commander had been seriously wounded on Go Noi Island during Allen Brook. Captain Ronald Gruenberg placed Davis and his platoon in an area within the 1st Battalion's original TAOR, north of Go Noi Island. They were again patrolling the "rocket belt," running out the clock, waiting for final orders for when the Regiment would return Stateside.

Lieutenant Davis remembered the new and widely spread out assignment, "The three squads assumed a regular rotation. One of my squads was based at a construction site close to the Ha Dong Bridge [AT 991641], where engineers were building a dam. My second squad was several klicks to the west, in the An Trach villages' area, building a new platoon patrol base aptly named 'Fort Apache.' The third squad was based on a wooden tower located on the south side of the Cau Do River, east of the Cam Le Bridge on the south entrance to Da Nang and they patrolled from there."

By mid to end of July, Davis and his men became attached to 7th Engineer Battalion and provided security for a detachment of engineers operating in the northern sector of the Republic of Korea Marine TAOR. The engineers had been engaged in constructing a security barrier at the southern end of 27th Marine's TAOR which adjoined the ROK Marines' TAOR.

On 22 August, a squad of Marines leaving Fort Apache led by Corporal Rodney Edrozo orchestrated a night ambush close by in a graveyard near An Trach (2) (grid coordinate AT 970650). Around 2000 hours, five enemy combatants were spotted moving rather fast into the ambush zone. When the ambush subsided, two of the combatants were dead, with one Marine wounded, who was later evacuated. Along with the weaponry captured was a messenger pouch containing important documents, which were immediately sent back to the battalion intelligence section (S-2). It was later revealed that the five combatants were an advance scouting party for the main force in the trace. It was further learned that they had firm orders to assault and hold the Cam Le Bridge on the southern entrance of Da Nang City. This intercepted information fit with the intel that had been collected earlier about the enemy's overall objective, the "X2 Offensive" aka "The Third Offensive."

Lieutenant Davis recaptures further events of that night: "Corporal Edrozo's squad returned to Fort Apache, where we spent much of that evening listening to the fire-fights at two ARVN patrol bases nearby. At 0315 Hours on 23 August, three sappers hit us with what I later determined was a diversionary tactic to keep us pinned down while the main force passed on its way to the Cam Le Bridge. Two of the sappers managed to infiltrate our wire and throw grenades into the outer perimeter bunkers built into a berm. Our beloved Charles 'Doc' Golling was killed by an enemy grenade during the assault. Fourteen Marines received minor wounds in this action."

For the next few days, Marine and ARVN forces in the area south of Da Nang tracked and destroyed much of the enemy force which had tried to take the city. By 26 August, most of Lieutenant Davis's platoon had returned to headquarters and had begun to administratively process going to other units in-country and finishing their thirteen-month tours or if eligible, returning stateside with the regimental colors. Davis recaptures his last day at Fort Apache: "I was still at Fort Apache with a fire team, along with elements of another platoon from Company C, led by Staff Sergeant Darrell W. Scott. Around 1350, I heard gunfire erupting from the area where Corporal Edrozo had conducted the successful ambush nights before. A squad from Scott's platoon had run into remnants of the retreating enemy force. I immediately rounded up elements from both platoons to go and relieve them. When we arrived, we found the squad pinned in an open field by the enemy firing from a tree line fifty meters to their north. As we arrived from the south, a mortar crew was setting up northeast of us and prepar-ing to drop rounds on the squad in the open. Fortunately, we had a LAAW with us, and I could place it very close to their tube position, forcing them to withdraw. The entire force then withdrew and we entered the tree line looking for bodies. We found the bodies of Lance Corporal William J. Bilbo and PFC Gary L. Clapp who had been killed at the outset of the engagement."

Lieutenant Crane Davis was transferred to the 1st Marine Regiment which arrived late August to take over TAOR responsibility from the 27th Marines. Most of the Marines in Lieutenant Davis's platoon still had their thirteen-month obligation to fulfill and were dispersed to units needing infantrymen.

A Helicopter Pilot Remembers Allen Brook and Mameluke Thrust

Perfecting the use of the helicopters in warfare began in Vietnam. It is difficult now to imagine how the military would have fought in that country's terrain without them. Late in the 1940s, after WWII, the Marine Corps pioneered helicopter usage in Korea. Later, into the '50s and '60s the helicopter was again studied as a natural addition to an amphibious operational doctrine that involved ship-to-shore maneuvers. Thus, the helicopter was introduced into the Vietnam theater early in 1962 and continually examined. Later, two types were settled on, one for medium lift and another for heavy lift operations. Those early units were the UH-34 and CH-37. They bore a load of Marine Corps operations in 1965 and 1966. It would be a long shakedown period for the CH-46 and CH-53 throughout 1966 into 1968 when these newer models transitioned.

The transition from the earlier medium and heavy lift models to the newer aircraft, even though welcomed, presented many problems in the mid 1960s. Training pilots and the maintenance people, along with learning and developing the newer aircraft capabilities and establishing adequate parts supply lines, clearly begged immediate attention.

Then-Captain Richard Rosser began his first tour in Vietnam in August 1967. He had been trained in the CH-46 stateside, and upon arriving found, "They had brought in the new CH-46 models in 1966. They were now discovering that stress on the frames was causing aft rotor head problems which caused the rotor blades to come apart. It was ascertained that there was some basic design weakness in the aircraft with respect to transmission mounting and distribution of transmission stresses to the airframe. So, they sent all CH-46 aircraft to Okinawa for retrofit right before I arrived. Since there were no CH-46 aircraft in-country, and the retrofit would take three more months to get them back, six of us CH-46 pilots went to VMO-6 and flew Huey UH-1E gunships. We automatically became copilots. There was no training. If we could land it without crashing, we were good to go...I was flying gunships my first four months in-country."

This major retrofit of the CH-46s produced a strain in the established H-34 Squadrons. They became extremely burdened and undermanned. Around January of 1968, the retrofitted CH-46s arrived back in Phu Bai at HMM-164. Rosser was trans-ferred into the squadron to fly the CH-46A models. Over time Captain Rosser would fly all three editions, the A, D, and finally the Super D. As he pointed out, the differ-ences were not significant. The biggest issue in flying any of the models were the loads they could carry, in aviation terminology, "weights and balances." As Rosser pointed out, "Because of the hot and moist climate in Vietnam we could not carry as much as in a colder climate. The outside temperature and barometric pressure, called 'density altitude,' determined how much upward thrust your power plant would develop and would ultimately lift."

The helicopter squadrons in I Corps were controlled by the Direct Air Support Center (DASC) and "Land Shark" was their call sign during 1968. Most missions were assigned in the ready room of the squadron. Rosser tells, "You were briefed by Operations [S-3] regarding grid coordinates, call signs, and frequencies of the units on the ground." Many times, returning from a mission a pilot would receive a call from "Land Shark" (DASC) about another mission, usually an emergency medevac or emer-gency recon extract. The pilot would copy the information, relay the information to his wingman and gunship support aircraft then divert immediately to the unit in need.

Most helicopters had easily a two-hour flying time of fuel when full. If fuel was too low and a source of fuel was nearby a pilot could "hot refuel" without shutting down. This allowed for quick turnarounds to continue their support role.

Captain Rosser described in lay terms how he calculated what he could carry in his chopper. "For weight issues, we calculated each Marine at 240 pounds which included their 782-combat gear. It was just a rough estimate...you knew that you could lift ten Marines easily...Then you started working your way up with the numbers...And if you were full of gas then it became a little harder with more than ten Marines. A pilot could also choose to jettison fuel to increase lifting capability. When I had to pull Marines out of a 'hot' zone and there was more weight than the aircraft could lift, jettisoning fuel was the best option. I never left fewer Marines than could defend themselves alone in the bush. There were times when I would grit my teeth and take them all...and then jettisoned fuel to keep the helicopter in the air."

The most Rosser ever took off with was a count of twenty-six...A combination of ARVNs and some combat Marines. "I was down to 200 pounds of fuel which are about twenty minutes of flight time. We were not that far from Da Nang and I had jettisoned the bulk of my fuel before landing on a very narrow ridgeline. I could not in good conscience take ten or twelve and leave the rest...They would have gotten overran. So, I gritted my teeth and took them all. When I lifted off the ridge I knew I was going to sink (lose altitude) until I had a transitional lift and enough airspeed to maintain level flight. The helicopter started to descend with full power, but I was lucky enough to stay above the tree line down the hill following the terrain, then gained enough airspeed to finally recover. That troop lift was one of those butt clinchers you vividly remember, but combat is always high risk."

Captain Richard Rosser spent thirteen months of his tour from August 1967 through September 1968 on missions all over I Corps, including flying Studies and Observation Group missions (SOG) into Laos, and in and out of the Khe Sanh combat base during its siege. Most of his missions were troop lifts and resupply. Each resupply mission went out with ammo, water, and C-rations along with essential personnel. Every mission would require bringing back some sort of medical evacuees. Most casualties needed further medical help and there were the inevitable KIAs.

Rosser recalls supporting 1/27 in both the Hue area during the Tet Offensive as well as during Operation Allen Brook. He specifically remembers "Pickwick Paper," 1st Battalion, 27th Marines inclusive call sign. "The Arizona Territory, which was close to An Hoa, Liberty Bridge, Go Noi Island, Hill 55, Hill 65, Charlie Ridge...those areas. The last three months of my tour, I was in and out of them constantly. From the air, the areas are easier to know where you are because you can see the big picture...And I learned where all the units were operating. We didn't pay too much attention to what the operations were called because our missions each day were specific to one unit. There was a reason we went, medevac, resupply, taking troops in or out...Transporting troops was most of what we did."

May 1968: HMM-164 flew 336 sorties carrying 861 troops, lifting 53.1 tons of cargo, evacuating 139 battlefield casualties in support of Allen Brook.

June 1968: HMM-164 flew 472 sorties carrying 1294 troops, lifting 84.8 tons of cargo, evacuating 44 casualties in support of Allen Brook.

July 1968: HMM-164 flew 1272 sorties carrying 1726 troops, lifting 295.7 tons of cargo, evacuating 111 battlefield casualties in support of Allen Brook.

August 1968: HMM-164 flew 142 sorties carrying 76 troops, lifting 52.3 tons of cargo, evacuating 8 battlefield casualties in support of Allen Brook.

Sorties conducted by HMM-164 May – August 1968 [26]

Three Missing Marines

As the multi-battalion operation Allen Brook began winding down, Operation Mameluke Thrust shifted its focus further south to An Hoa in July. The 5th Marine Regiment found themselves in the middle of a major NVA staging area. It was becoming evident to the upper command that enemy preparations meant a third offensive against the Da Nang airstrip was eminent.

Captain Richard Rosser and his crew woke up on the morning of 18 July 1968 to find themselves assigned to support a quick reaction force. This concept had recently been adapted by the Marine Corps and was now being utilized on a regular basis. A reconnaissance team operating in what was called the Arizona Territory had discovered some NVA in the open and had called their coordinates into the 5th Marines Command. The NVA position was plotted and Bravo Company, 1st Battalion, 5th Marines became the assigned quick reaction force to find those NVA and eradicate them.

Captain Rosser remembers the day his flight of four CH-46s took Bravo Company Marines into the landing zone: "We had taken 105 Marines out there and it had taken several trips. I was call sign 'Press, Dash Two' behind our flight leader, Captain Jim 'Smedley' Butler, the 'Dash One' that day. It is primitive but the crew chief keeps a verbal count always telling me how many guys are either getting on or off...Then the pilots pass the count to the flight leader so he can tally the total count."

Rosser describes that it had taken quite a few trips to get them all into the rice paddy and he observed after they had lifted out of the first insert the Marines came under immediate attack. He recollects, "They were basically surrounded. I found out later that there was a Regimental Command CP out there somewhere in the area...We did observe tank tracks on the ground...So we came back with the second load and there is four of us going in...We would go in two at a time and drop them off...Jesus, it got so crowded in that rice paddy, we had a hard time putting everybody in there...Every time we went in we got shot at and what we didn't realize until later was that those Marines were probably outnumbered ten to one."

On the last turnaround at the An Hoa combat base airstrip, Captain Rosser encountered a Colonel as he was refueling who asked him to load a 106 Recoilless Rifle on its platform into Rosser's helicopter. Knowing the actual situation on the ground of this commander's men, Rosser explained to him that, "'Your guys are surrounded—are getting their asses shot off and it is getting dark and you need to consider pulling them out!' It was not what he wanted to hear from me, a Captain...I perceived he did not know what was really going on!"

Shortly after that encounter, the leader of the flight, Captain Butler, "Dash One," began the extraction of the beleaguered Marines. The flight of four helicopters began extracting the Marines and bringing them back to An Hoa combat base a short distance away. While on the airstrip Captain Rosser recalls going through the count with his crew chief and conferring with the other pilots. "After that last trip we come up three Marines short...The radio goes silent...I am waiting for a decision. I am not in charge on this flight...I normally am...still, radio silence...I am also down on fuel."

After what seemed like a long time of radio silence, Captain Rosser made the decision, "I say to my copilot, Major Wilson, who was a brand-new transition pilot, we are going back for those three Marines...We cannot wait for someone to make this decision. I can tell he is extremely stressed. I announce over the radio, 'This is Dash Two...I have two hundred pounds of fuel; we have just dropped our last load and we are going back out to look for the three missing Marines.'"

Captain Rosser, his copilot, Major D. D. Wilson, and his crew chief and gunner Corporal Black went back to look for the missing Marines. They found the area where they had extracted 1/5, call sign "Millbrook Bravo" Marines, and hovered from rice paddy to rice paddy looking for the missing men. All the while VMO-2 gunships covered them as they went from dike to dike searching, telling Rosser that the NVA

had them surrounded and were shooting at them. Rosser vividly remembers, "I couldn't find those men and 'Hostage' [call sign for the gunships of VMO-2] told me over the radio that the NVA were on top of me...That is when I took most of the hits to the fuselage and rotors. Corporal Black was wounded...We finally pulled out and made it back to An Hoa fueled and returned to our home base. When we were firmly on the ground at Marble Mountain airstrip the aircraft had taken over sixty hits. My CO was waiting for us when we landed and after debriefing took me to the O-Club for drinks. Over drinks, he told me that our Commanding General wanted to see me the next day but did not tell me why. I am thinking, 'What did I do now?' The General wanted to thank me personally for what I had done for those Marines on the ground."

Captain Richard C. Rosser Jr, HMM-164
~ Courtesy of Colonel Dick Rosser,
USMC (Ret)

Captain Richard C. Rosser, Jr is one of a very few USMC Vietnam helicopter pilots to receive two Silver Stars. Both citations were recommended for award by the infantry units he supported, 1st Battalion, 5th Marines and 1st Force Recon Battalion. In 1984, then-Lieutenant Colonel Rosser met a Colonel at Camp Pendleton, who after visiting with him determined that Rosser had indeed inserted and extracted his then-Company B, 1/5 Marines, call sign "Millbrook Bravo" on 18 July 1968. Colonel J. S. Pipkin thanked Rosser for extracting his Marines and Corpsmen that day and going back to look for the missing men. Rosser learned then that the count was off and that there had been no missing Marines.

Operation Allen Brook lasted three and one-half months, resulting in over 1,000 enemy combatants killed. Friendly losses to secure the Go Noi Island area rose close to almost 200 Marines and Sailors killed with over 1,100 wounded. Even more men were subjected to heat stroke, heat exhaustion, disease, snakebite, and accidents. Land-clearing operations in the Go Noi area by the Marines and engineers continued until the "Third Offensive" launched and halted that activity. First Marine Division terminated Allen Brook and deployed those Marines to battle enemy forces engaged in their attempt to destroy the Da Nang airstrip in the much-expected "Third Offensive." This mini-offensive was designed to influence the ongoing Paris Peace talks, but faltered and was quickly brought under control. It failed to affect the talks nor change the sound security circling the airstrip.

CHAPTER 7

A Third Offensive – Altering the Paris Peace Talks – Return of the Regimental Colors

"If you're going through hell, keep going."
~ Winston Churchill

Rumors abounded of a major Communist offensive in the summer of 1968. With the siege of Khe Sanh ending 14 April 1968 on the western region of the DMZ and events in northern parts of I CTZ stabilizing, Marine commanders observed that the Communist focus shifted to Da Nang and its strategic airstrip. The intelligence showed that in June and July enemy forces were in motion and using the approaching new moon to prepare for another attack on southern I Corps installations with the main target, the airstrip and supporting units in and around Da Nang. Ho Chi Minh mentioned this briefly in a speech to his countrymen on 20 July 1968. U. S. Intel picked up on his remarks when he virtually stated in the speech the following final words, "a final victory during the Third Offensive."[1]

Late in July, III MAF Intel personnel gathered information from captured prisoners and documents, which, coupled with reconnaissance intel, gave a glimpse of what the Communists were planning. The Vietnamese National Police in Da Nang had captured a North Vietnamese officer who revealed some detail of the impending attack, referred to by its code name "X2 Offensive." The prisoner claimed that the objective of this upcoming offensive was to create favorable political leverage for the North Vietnam Delegation engaged in the Paris Peace talks in May of 1968. The plan was for Communist forces to overtake the military base and military facilities throughout the area, assassinate key South Vietnamese officials, and coordinate with the National Liberation Front. The Communist timetable was not known.[2]

The offensive plans had all the appearances of a considerable effort. One of the ralliers questioned told of North Vietnamese tanks and aircraft being used as a last resort. Marine Recon teams and air observance reported sightings of enemy armored fighting vehicles west of An Hoa. Intel originally had the offensive pegged for the middle of July when the moon was almost dark. When that did not materialize, it was then readjusted to 22-23 August to fit the next moon phase. Later an unsuspecting prisoner told Intel officials that August would bring a decisive battle in the North's revolutionary history.[3]

The "Third Offensive" began 18 August. The main target was Da Nang. Sporadic rocket and mortar attacks against provincial and district military installations began followed by a few sapper attacks. By 22 August, ARVN units had made contact with the 38th NVA Regiment eight miles south of Da Nang. The NVA movement had been discovered by Marine units throughout the "Rocket Belt," while the local Viet Cong units had secretly infiltrated into and had taken up positions throughout the city. The August 1968 FMFPAC Command Chronologies noted, "Motivated by the high echelon appeals, and the possibility of establishing exploitable breaches in allied defense networks, eleven ground attacks, and ten attacks-by-fire were launched south of Hai Van pass from 20 to 24 August. Climaxing on the night of 22-23 August, this spasmodic effort, immediately splintered and defeated by IIIMAF and ARVN units, lacked both the staying-power of the Tet attacks and, again reflecting enemy command and control problems, full-enemy-force participation...By end-August, the enemy drive had resulted in 16 of the month's 19 ground assaults, and 21 of the month's total of 32 attacks-by-fire being launched against IIIMAF, ARVN, and GVN positions in the southern three provinces of I CTZ."[4]

Even though the NVA had been discovered by ARVN Rangers and Marines just to the south of Da Nang and delayed, the more elusive VC had slipped inside the city limits. The Cam Le Bridge was the key to the city and elements of the 1st Military Police Battalion stoically held onto that strategic piece of real estate until elements of 1/27 nearby could come to their aid and retake the bridge.

The Cam Le Bridge

The Cam Le Bridge was a major choke point on the southern boundary in and out of Da Nang. The bridge, on National Route 1, was seized in the early morning hours of 23 August. The Viet Cong had slipped north across the bridge and assaulted the Hoa Vang District Headquarters just south of the air base, while establishing a foothold on the south side of the bridge. Marine MPs from Company C, 1st Military Police Battalion, moved quickly to secure and seal the north side, stopping any enemy advancement across the bridge.

Early, around 0300 hours, two of 1/27's platoon patrol bases to the west of the bridge were simultaneously attacked by mortars, followed by ground assaults. 1/27's then-Commanding Officer, Major Kenneth Skipper, felt that these were diversionary tactics meant to draw focus away from the main objective. At 0530 hours, word was passed down from the regiment that the Cam Le Bridge had fallen into enemy hands. Major Skipper was directed to "exert maximum effort" in regaining the vital Cam Le Bridge artery. A platoon from Company A was dispatched and moved toward the bridge to determine enemy strength and positions. By 0915 hours the platoon advanced to within 150 meters of the enemy-held bunker and defensive positions before being pinned down by small arms fire and automatic weapons. Skipper's 1st Battalion, 27th Marines CP was within striking distance of the bridge, and most of Company A and D were garrisoned at 1/27 HQ CP area. Skipper wasted no time ordering both line companies to initiate a convergence of force toward the bridge. First Lieutenant Robert Baribeau, Delta's CO, left the battalion compound with three platoons to attack from west to east. Captain William O. Moore, Alpha Company, hastily left with two reinforced squads with intent to attack from south to north.[5]

Then-2nd Lieutenant Dan Guenther, newly arrived in-country, commanded a provisional rifle platoon of "Am-grunts" in H&S Company of 3rd Amphibian Tractor Battalion (Rein). The night of 22 August 1968 when the Cam Le Bridge was overrun and other surrounding unit positions assaulted, Guenther remembered, "The 5th Special Forces, Command, and Control North for MACV-SOG [Military Assistance Command, Vietnam - Studies and Observations Group], had a base close to one of the Marble Mountains called the 'Chin Strap' and had been overrun. We had security responsibility in that TAOR. The Green Berets there had a mobile strike force, where they had 'hatchet teams' made up of Nung [ethnic minority in Vietnam whose name means Natives] mercenaries, and some Bru tribesmen [ethnic minority which means "people living in the woods"]. The main force VC Sapper unit had assaulted the place. I had heard it was an inside job...They burnt up some choppers on the pads, kicked in the air conditioning roof units of the Combat Operations Center, and stuffed some satchel charges inside. They were running around the place causing all kinds of havoc so my rifle platoon and other provisional rifle platoons went down to Nui Kim Son and headed up the road to the front gate to provide them some relief. There was a Captain up in a tower with the base that we were talking to on the radios. I guess there was a VC mortar position discovered in a coastal village called Xom Son Thuy that had fired some mortars into the compound to start the attack. Their base was on high ground close to the Marble and Limestone Mountains."

View from Helicopter - Marble Mountain, "Crow's Nest" lookout on right
~ Courtesy of Gerald Risner, FLC attached to 2/5

Guenther's platoon reacted quickly, setting up a blocking force maneuver to monitor the roads and river traffic just west of the marble/karst outcroppings. He further recalled, "We were kind of strung out that night and were to prevent any infiltration from the Cam Le Bridge area, concentrating on the river and any combatants backtracking south. There was some river traffic and we had gunships overhead. Puff came on station and put out the big basketball-like flares. That is when everyone di di mau'd to take cover. We did take some small arms fire through the night but nothing significant. There was a lot of fighting going on to the North of our position."

Retaking the Cam Le Bridge

At 1230 on 23 August a platoon from Alpha Company 1/27 swept up from the south of the Cam Le Bridge (grid coordinate BT015701) and began receiving rocket and small arms fire from its southern entrance. Along with four tanks attached to Company E, that Alpha Company Platoon assaulted the enemy positions utilizing the tanks' firepower. Together they succeeded in killing twenty-two of the enemy and capturing six, regaining control of the bridge later in the day.[6]

Bob Taugner, a Corpsman who had transferred into Alpha Company from Bravo, was amongst the Marines approaching from the south with the tanks. Captain W. O. Moore, Jr., the Commanding Officer of Alpha at the time, was on the right flank and Taugner, the senior enlisted man, was on the left. Taugner still remembers that cautious sweep toward the Cam Le Bridge.

"We were not a full platoon but really two reinforced squads. We were in a kind of an echelon maneuver and had tanks on the road moving slowly northward. It was a narrow road [National Route 1]. We were coming into a village and the two point Marines on my side started taking intense small arms fire. They made their way to an overturned vehicle, one of them buses [sic] with a motorcycle-like front end that had been blown up. The typical ones you saw on the roads hauling passengers, farm animals, chickens, produce, etc. The two point Marines used it for cover. I didn't know if they were wounded or were killed. We could not see them. I found later that day they survived and were not wounded.

"Captain Moore stopped to assess the situation. While we were stopped, an RPG came winging out of the village on my side of the road and exploded right in front of the tank. I first thought it had hit the tank. The tank's turret immediately pivoted and fired. And then another RPG round goes sailing over the same tank. As a senior guy in my squad, I started positioning my guys. We were in a dried-up rice paddy and most of them had found cover against paddy dikes. We were then taking fire and a lot of it. I crawled up close to the road.

"The road was elevated about six- or seven-feet high...As I am scrambling on my hands and knees, the tank closest to me swung the turret and barrel directly over me and fired a round into the village. I didn't know he was going to do that and was just underneath the muzzle blast. I was knocked down, asshole over elbows, completely stunned, surprised, and thus was not going to be able to hear well for another three or four days. I wanted to get up on the road behind the tank and get on their intercom and direct his fire. I could see which hooch the RPGs had come from but the small arms fire was too intense so I stayed put."

HM2 Taugner was in contact with Captain Moore via radio, communicating the situation from his side of the road. After a while, the lead tanks pulled off to the side of the road and the last tank moved forward toward the village. As Taugner recalls, "This thing was moving and I noticed it had a stubby little barrel on it. Well, the next thing I know is that the ville is on fire. It was a flame tank...It lit that whole place up and the next thing that happens right before our eyes reminded me of hunting a covey of quail. The enemy was coming out of that ville like quail being jumped out of a thicket. I mean there were 'Charlie' everywhere...All heading back northward toward the bridge...And then the assault was on...The tanks started moving, we started moving on-line. That is when some reinforcements joined up from our rear...They caught up with us and we all assaulted the bridge. When the MPs left the bridge in the early hours of the morning they had left a .50-caliber gun on the bridge...We had to overcome that also...Charlie wanted that bridge bad and was shooting that bad boy at us big time."

One of the dead enemy combatants that Taugner examined while the Marines were policing up the battle area and staging the wounded was a dead woman wearing white pajamas. After searching her for documents and explosives he found six grenades strapped to her back. On another of the dead combatants, Taugner retrieved a brand new AK-47. The weapon was exceptional with an unusual wood stock: an assault rifle you wouldn't expect to see on the battlefield. He kept the rifle as a souvenir. Doc Taugner recalled his intentions for the weapon at the time and the plight of the unusual AK-47, "The stock was a reddish wood, and it wasn't one of those pieces of crap, Chinese models. This one was really a showpiece weapon. I threw it on my back and humped it back to the rear and took it back to Hawaii with me. I later took a picture of it and still have the photo. We were staging a firepower demonstration for some Senators who came to inspect us while training at K-Bay in 1969. Hey, why would a Senator go to just any Marine Corps base for a firepower demonstration like say, Camp Pendleton or Camp Lejeune when you could visit Kaneohe Bay in Hawaii? The AK eventually found its way into the Marine Corps Museum at K-Bay."

Bob "Doc" Taugner with prized AK-47 in Hawaii ~ Courtesy of Bob Taugner, B Co, 1/27

Lance Corporal Ed Singletary, a radioman from New Jersey, recaptures some of the tenser moments of the push to the Cam Le Bridge.

"We started walking alongside a straight road that went directly to the Cam Le Bridge. There were rice paddies on both sides of this oiled dirt road. I remember being on the left side and coming to a brick factory. We paused there and took cover for quite a while behind a stack of bricks. I was busy communicating with an overhead Forward Air Controller in what we called a "Birddog" aircraft. I was relaying information back and forth between him and Sergeant Sal [Felix Salmeron] our platoon Sergeant. The FAC was flying way up over and above the bridge. There was a village in front of the bridge on the south side. Then the tanks came forward on the road. We were sloshing around in the muddy rice paddy close by the road. Sal was yelling at me to make sure the tank was a 'Zippo' tank [flame tank]. When it came up it stopped about thirty feet from us. Sal went over and started directing the tank.

"When the tank fired his flame, I was not ready for the heat. I thought I had done gone to hell...It was hot. I couldn't believe the heat coming from that flame. The actual stream of jellied gasoline (a form of napalm) had a range of twenty to thirty feet. When it had fired all that it had, they retreated and another regular tank came forward. It stopped in about the same position. Sal kept yelling at me to get the tanks on the radio. I couldn't raise them on the tactical network. He wanted to direct their firing. After a while, he told me to get up to the back of the tank and talk to them through the intercom system mounted on the outside. He wanted them to put a round in the bunker aperture [a window]. Sal was yelling, 'You tell them that he has got to get that round in the aperture of that bunker.' There was an old French bunker right by the bridge. I think the first round that was fired missed. The second one went right into the bunker through the aperture. That was it, the enemy holding the bunker were killed."

After that direct hit, the tank received another RPG round from another direction. Singletary remembered that it hit the spare tread mounted on the turret. He recalls, "When it hit those treads they just went every which way...They kept them mounted on the turret probably for some sort of secondary protection. When that round exploded, I just held my breath. I said to myself, 'Oh, Lord that is it, that tank is gone'...Well, that tank turret came alive and pivoted and fired another round. Holy Shit, that was great...The tank was alive and that is when we saw the MPs coming from the north across the bridge towards us."

Delta Company Attacks from the West

Early in the morning hours Company D, under the command of 1st Lieutenant Baribeau, a "Mustang" officer known for his tactical ability, began the on-line sweep from grid coordinates BT007704 toward the bridge. About 900 meters out from the bridge, his Marines started taking small arms and automatic weapon fire from an entrenched enemy in a tree line, halting their advance. Air strikes were then called in to soften the enemy positions. In a furious exchange of weapons fire, three Company D Marines were wounded. After the fast movers made their 20mm cannon runs the enemy combatants retreated to the east. Company D aggressively following the fleeing NVA in trace and caught sporadic sniper fire to slow their advance. The left-behind sniper tactic did little to deter the Marines' advance.

It took approximately three hours to advance through five-hundred meters of enemy occupied ground. At 1215 Barribeau's Delta Company Marines were at grid coordinate BT012705. The bridge was still about 400 meters out and again small arms and automatic weapons firing had halted their advance. The enemy had held back their fire until the Marines were within about 100 meters from their concealed positions.

This time the Marines started to take heavier fire and witnessed many of their fellow Marines hit the dirt, falling to the ground wounded. As the fusillade increased, Danny "Doc" Grimshaw, a combat-weary Navy Corpsman, took cover behind a rice-paddy dike next to M60 gunner Lance Corporal John Sloatman III. As they assessed the situation together, Doc Grimshaw spotted two wounded Marines trapped in the enemy's field of fire beyond their position. Doc decided he would go to their aid. Sloatman pleaded with him to stay put. He told him, "Doc, don't go out there...Wait until the firing dies down." Grimshaw refused to wait and bounded over the rice-paddy dike toward the wounded men under a hail of small arms fire.. Unfortunately, "Doc" Grimshaw's past personal thoughts played out again in real time. He had earlier lamented, "...being able to walk down the street and not think about the next tree line...or if somebody is going to yell, 'Corpsman up' and I have to go charging up to them...some of them messed up pretty badly." Doc Grimshaw went forward like he always did. He was one you could always count on...Miraculously, he made it to the first downed man and immediately began treating him. As he was administering aid to the fallen Marine an enemy round struck him in the head and he died instantly. It was then that his platoon mates laid down a devastating base of fire and angrily assaulted the enemy positions. Overwhelmed again, the enemy fled, dragging their dead and wounded, escaping to the northeast. This time they had left three of their dead behind.

Before the day was over, all the Marine dead and wounded were carried out by hand. The beloved Danny "Doc" Grimshaw was hand-carried in a poncho by three of his close buddies, Lance Corporal Billy Frye, Lance Corporal Gary Jarvis, and PFC Donald Carrico from the battlefield all the way back to Battalion CP, approximately three kilometers. Then-Lance Corporal Gary Jarvis exclaims, "It was an extremely painful and unforgettable experience for us...And out of profound respect, Lieutenant Baribeau personally turned over Danny's body to the battalion corpsmen as we entered the Battalion compound. Danny had volunteered for this dangerous mission and had paid the supreme price. We had lost a truly good man." Senior Corpsman Danny Lee Grimshaw was posthumously awarded the Bronze Star Medal with Combat V for his more than heroic actions on 23 August 1968.[7]

First Lieutenant Robert "Bob" Baribeau, CO of Company D at the time, recalled his men's role in retaking the strategic Cam Le Bridge during the "Third Offensive" on 23 August 1968 and wrote in Author Dr. Gary Jarvis's history book, *Young Blood*:

"At approximately 0530, I was summoned into the Combat Operations Center where Major Skipper informed me that the Cam Le Bridge had been taken by NVA. I was given orders to take Delta Company and proceed as quickly as possible and attack from west to east. Alpha Company was to attack from South to North. Our mission was to retake the southern end of the bridge. I moved the company down the road from the battalion CP, as it was the most direct and fastest route. We then moved off the road and went due east toward the Bridge. We arrived at an open rice paddy. On the other side of the paddy was a small village. I sent First Platoon B Company to the right to cross the paddy and enter the tree line. I had Third Platoon cover the left flank. They also moved toward the tree line in the village. I kept Second Platoon (-) in reserve along with my command group. First Platoon received fire and became pinned down. As Third Platoon moved forward, they too received fire. Two of the Marines from Third Platoon moved by fire and maneuvered to approximately 100 yards of the tree line becoming pinned down and unable to advance.

"I received a call from Air overhead, asking if they could help. I replied in the affirmative. Ordnance [bombs] could not be used as the south end of the bridge was on the other side of the village and they feared damaging the bridge. However, they informed me they could use their guns [20mm canons]. I instructed Lieutenant Charles Collins, Company B First Platoon Commander, to have the most forward Marine place an air panel directly in front of him. I subsequently informed the pilot that he could strafe forward of the air panel. After that canon run, I then ordered the platoon to move forward approximately twenty-five to forty yards and place the air panel further to the front of their most forward Marines. I again notified the pilot that he could again strafe the most forward area in front of the air panel. I repeated the forward advance move one more time so that we could reach the tree line at the village. After First Platoon reached the tree line, First Platoon swept to the left and Third Platoon moved to the tree line. Second Platoon then followed with command group in the trace.

"Once in the village, we moved toward the bridge. We managed to evacuate our wounded at that time. As we battled forward, Delta Company flushed several NVA who ran into a pagoda. A flame tank attached to Alpha Company moved forward and torched the building with the NVA inside. Subsequently, I then received a radio call from the battalion, informing me that they were going to TOT [Time on Target by artillery] the area and that I was to evacuate my Marines immediately. I radioed back to battalion and informed them that I could not execute their order because our Corpsman, Danny Grimshaw, had been killed and his body was still lying out on the battlefield where we were to pull back from. I told them to hold, that we were not moving until I recovered my Corpsman. We were always taught and strongly believed that we always bring back our dead and our wounded. Once Danny's body had been recovered, I then informed the battalion CP that all dead and wounded were retrieved and I was moving my men from the area so that the TOT could be executed...The artillery performed their Time on Target, using the artillery battalion in its full capacity. Subsequently, we received our order to return to the battalion CP."[8]

Blocking Force Deployed

Then-Lance Corporal Richard Hunt, one of the battalion scouts, remembered being assembled into an H&S Company blocking force that was hastily sent northward from the Battalion CP toward the bridge area. He recalls, "Midday on 23 August 1968, PFC Otto Ostenfeld, another scout, and myself having returned from an earlier patrol, were summoned to join a patrol being put together of all able-bodied Marines at Battalion headquarters. An aerial spotter we knew as a 'bird dog' working overhead of the Cam Le Bridge had observed an enemy group of unknown size moving away from the bridge traveling south toward 1/27's CP." The three groups of this H&S element moved quickly northward. Passing through a tree line in the center prong of the patrol, Hunt and Ostenfeld observed enemy combatants to the left sitting in wait to ambush the left flank. Immediately engaging and killing several of them, Hunt's element found one combatant with an RPG, safety off and ready to fire at the flank patrol. He recollected, "Another Viet Cong was wounded who had shot one of our Marines in the neck and head. That enemy died in the exchange. The wounded Marine needed emergency medical attention. The medical evacuation protocol for emergencies at the time was for any close aircraft (helicopter) in the air, not already on an emergency, would assume the medical evacuation. I discovered much to my surprise the chopper coming to us carried the Commanding General of the 1st Marine Division, Major General Carl A. Youngdale [27 June – 20 Dec 1968]. Flying close by our position he had allowed his Command and Control Helicopter to be utilized for this emergency. Ready for battle when he emerged from the H-34, the General jumped off the chopper brandishing a .45-caliber Tommy gun. Obviously, he had seen some action in his younger day. I was witnessing our Commanding General willing to evacuate our wounded and combat ready, something I hadn't anticipated that day."

After evacuating their wounded, the Marines swept the nearby village for more enemy and returned to the CP. Hunt remembers, "The results of that engagement, I think were about six enemy KIAs and two wounded Marines. One of the guys noticed moist blood on my one hand and all over my rifle. The blood, still moist. After working with the wounded, blood dries and gets crusty. It was then the realization came to me that I had been wounded sometime during that firefight."[9]

Four miles directly south of the Cam Le Bridge, the 38th NVA Regiment became engaged first with the 1st Battalion, 51st ARVN Regiment and then the Marines. Company F, 2nd Battalion, 27th Marines finished off the NVA on 25 August in sharp fighting. It was reported that the NVA and local VC units lost over 1,000 dead in the Da Nang area from 22 to 31 August. Overall the "Third Offensive" had some minor effects but in the end, had faltered.[10]

Meanwhile in the United States on 28 August 1968, the Democratic National Convention held in Chicago experienced riots in the streets by almost 10,000 anti-war protesters who were confronted by police and National Guard troops. The protest was covered live on network TV. This particular event marked a peak of social unrest not seen since the American Civil War in the mid 1800s.

1/27's Final Months In-Country

Originally, RLT-27 was supposed to spend only three months in-country and then return to CONUS (Continental United States). They had been sent to Vietnam for the emergency measure when Tet of 1968 erupted. The proposed duration of their three months' stay in Vietnam was duly annotated in the Impact Assessment, *Marine Corps Southeast Asia Forces* of October 1968 sent to the Deputy Secretary of Defense generated by the Commandant of the Marine Corps. That predetermined length of stay quickly changed when it was realized that the Marine Corps needed to maintain reasonable troop levels in the I Corps area due to increased enemy activity. President Johnson and his advisors made the decision to extend their stay until mid July.

To maintain troop strength levels in that area the Defense Department designated the 1st Brigade, 5th Infantry Division (Mechanized), located at Fort Carson, Colorado, to relieve RLT-27.

This Army unit's training and orientation schedule conflicted with the new scheduled rotation in July of RLT-27 back to the States. The Mechanized "Red Devils" did not arrive in the country until 31 July 1968 which ultimately delayed the 27th Marines' return to CONUS beyond the planned timetable. It would now be mid September until Relief and Redeployment could be carried out.[11]

During this time, while continuing to operate in the southern Da Nang TAOR, the 27th Marine Regiment relinquished command and control of Operation Allen Brook on Go Noi Island. It then returned to its original TAOR and resumed saturation patrolling of the Rocket Belt. Major General Carl A. Youngdale, CG 1st Marine Division, issued Frag Order 281-68 in early August, "Directing 27th Marines to pass OPCON of BLT 1/27 and control of Op Allen Brook to 5th Marines effective 031200H [3 August at 1200 hours]."[12]

Enemy contact for the first part of August started out light and became moderate toward the last of the month. Most means of enemy warfare during this time were the employment of mines and booby traps coupled with sporadic guerrilla tactics. Again, this was a new environment for the Marines who had locked horns with the NVA in the Hue area and became used to search-and-clear tactics on Go Noi Island.

Bald Eagle Company

Alpha Company, assigned to provide security in 2/27's previous TAOR, took up positions in that operating area in August. Lieutenant John Bouldin remembers, "Basically, we stood by on a nearby LZ ready to deploy on a moment's notice if the 26th Marines would call for help. Operating in the Que Son mountains to our west, we would wait for the call to assist or reinforce. We were much like the Bald Eagle and would swoop in if called upon. I can remember not having a single map of the mountain area where they deployed. So, we sent Lieutenant Blankenship back to Division, which was not far, to fetch maps, 26th Marine unit call signs and frequencies, and any other pertinent information available. We sat there on the LZ for a long time. I finally called Battalion and asked them if they knew where Blankenship was. They did not know. My friend Captain Pat Kahler was by then in the Regimental S-3 operations shop. Beside myself, with no sign of Lieutenant Blankenship, maps, call signs or frequencies...Anxious is too tame of a word...Captain Pat Kahler told me that my company was going to be committed with or without the call signs, maps, or frequencies if the call came. I can't tell you how tight my ass was puckered that day. It crossed my mind to refuse the order, however, the call never came and luckily I did not have to make a decision."

Returning the Regimental Colors to CONUS

On 2 August 1968, Regimental Landing Team-27 including Battalion Landing Team 1/27 (all three battalions of the 27th Marine Regiment) were ordered by the Commanding General, 1st Marine Division, FMF to begin planning for redeployment to the United States and Hawaii respectively. Second and Third Battalions were home-based in Camp Pendleton, California on the mainland and First Battalion would return to its base at Kaneohe Bay, Hawaii.

As August closed, the Regimental Headquarters and 3rd Battalion became fully relieved of all tactical responsibility and started full preparation for redeployment. On 24 August, 1st Marine Division Operation Order 305-68 directed 1st Marine Regiment to transition a relief of the entire 27th Marine Regiment. Starting 28 August through 30 August, Third and Second Battalions of the 27th Marines handed responsibility of their TAOR to the maneuver battalions of 1st Marine Regiment. 3/27 was relieved by 2nd Battalion, 1st Marine Regiment (2/1) and 2/27 handed over control of their TAOR to 1st Battalion, 1st Marine Regiment (1/1). BLT 1/27 along with 2/27 remained in a reserve/on-call status to 1st Marine Regiment until departure from the RVN. On 7 September, the 1st Marine Division Commanding General issued Frag Order 353-68 (Relief and Redeployment of RLT-27) relieving the total responsibility of the 27th Marine Regiment. RLT-27 was homeward bound.[13]

Changing of the Command Color Guard August 1968 ~ Courtesy of Jesse Hand, H&S Co 1/27
(Rich Thrush, second from right)

Throughout August, RLT-27 Headquarters staff attended numerous meetings with 1st Marine Division and III MAF Headquarter staffs. They began the arduous task of sorting out logistical and manpower reassignments and publishing a logistical time schedule to include all events in the redeployment. III MAF HQ's requested both sealift and airlift to CONUS and Hawaii for personnel and equipment which would be returning. Civil Affairs Officers of the three RLT-27 units began briefing the 1st Marine Regiment's S-5 on their existing programs, problem areas, and activities, handing over acquired intelligence and files.

Beginning 28 August, all non-deployable personnel of 3rd Battalion began transferring to other 1st and 3rd Marine Division units throughout I Corps. Under "Operation Mixmaster" all Marines had to serve the full thirteen-month tour-of-duty in the Republic of Vietnam. "Public announcements by the Marine Corps made it clear that most of the Marines were staying in Vietnam and that the return of RLT-27 did not represent the beginning of a withdrawal from Vietnam."[14]

In truth, many the 27th Marines with time left to serve on their full tour transferred to other Battalions in-country. Some of the Marines and Corpsmen went to units on the DMZ. The author and other Marines were sent by truck up Route 1 to 2nd Battalion, 9th Marines in Quang Tri. Marines and Corpsmen that had a DEROS (Date Eligible for Return from Overseas) of early September were transferred into RLT-27 for the journey home. Essential leadership and short-time personnel already embedded stayed with the regiment and escorted its Colors and remaining equipment back to the Continental United States and Hawaii.

On 16 September, the last remnants of Marines and Sailors (a total of 699 men) from the 27th arrived in California, and on the 17th of September, the last group of 101 men arrived in Hawaii at 1st Battalion's home base in Kaneohe Bay. Nearly 400 Marines from other units who had finished their 13-month tour in Vietnam also returned to CONUS with RLT-27.[15]

Awards Ceremony August 1968 – L-R: 1st Sergeant Herman, 1st Lt J. Hand, CO, Major Kenneth J. Skipper, 1/27 ~ Courtesy of Jesse Hand, H&S Co 1/27

Upon returning to Camp Pendleton, California, the 27th Marine Regiment settled into the area of the base known as Camp Margarita or Area 33. Now back at home in the 5th Marine Division, the Regiment was honored with a homecoming parade in downtown San Diego a short distance south of Camp Pendleton. The purpose of the parade was to pay tribute to the lives the Regiment had lost in Vietnam in 1968. For the coming days into 1969 and before retiring the Colors, the 27th Marines became home to short-timers and Marines transitioning out of the Marine Corps.

A Southern California newspaper of September 1968 printed the following quote with parade pictures: "San Diegans turned out by the thousands to honor the first Marine Regiment (RLT-27) to return from Vietnam…On the reviewing stand were Navy Secretary Paul R. Ignatius; Commandant of the Marine Corps, General Leonard F. Chapman Jr.; MCRD Commander, Major General Lowell English; 5th Marine Division Commander, Brigadier General Leon J. Dulacki and Vietnamese Consul General, Luong Nhi Ky. They were backed by eight Marines and two Navy hospital men, all ambulatory wounded in casts, on crutches, and in wheelchairs."

In a Norwalk, Connecticut newspaper *The Norwalk Hour* of 10 September 1968, the following was printed: "In nearly seven months of combat, the 4,500-man regiment claimed over 2,000 of the enemy killed, many prisoners and captured weapons. The regiment lost 292 dead and handed out over 1,900 Purple Hearts for battlefield wounds. 'I'd say 21 months here is quite enough,' said second timer Corporal Bruce Finley, 22, of Newton, Massachusetts."

And Finally...

There was a common saying amongst the men who served and fought in the Vietnam War. It was an everyday saying; said thousands of times, passed back and forth as a matter of course. Dissected at a psychological level this saying could be looked at as a betrayal, an absence of commitment, and lack of leadership at the highest levels of our government in the prosecution of the Vietnam War. Symbolically bequeathed in each of these four simple words lay the many true sacrifices, personal commitments to each other, valor and courage carried out by these men daily. Most that served in Vietnam considered these four words to mean that we were not there to win: *"It don't mean nothing!"*

However, had these Marines and Corpsmen been asked to form up on-line and attack north toward Hanoi, almost every one of them would have volunteered. They will tell you above all else to this day that they were "Semper Fi" to the Garys, the Steves, the Larrys, the Jims, the Eds, the Ricks, the Rons, the Davids, the Docs, the Skippers, the LTs, the Gunnys, the Sergeants, the Corporals, and the Marines and Corpsmen who were in their fire teams, squads, and platoons... "To the sound of the guns!"

Personal Combat Decorations

Combat decorations for 1st Battalion, 27th Marines are listed below. Gary Jarvis, Ph.D., Company D, personally researched and compiled the following list of Marines who earned recognition for their heroic actions. All the following citations were derived from military records:

Silver Star Medals

Allen G. Arbogast, Cpl (A Co)
Stephen E. Austin, Cpl (C Co) KIA 6/8/68* pc
David A. Boillot, 2d Lt (A Co)
Ronald L. Burtsell, 1st Sgt (A Co)
Matthew E. Greer, Cpl (D Co) KIA 5/5/68*
Fred J. Hayes, Sgt (H&S Co attached to D Co) KIA 4/13/68*
Kenneth P. Hutchinson, Jr. L/Cpl (C Co) KIA 6/5/68*
Glennis R. Kellums, S/Sgt (A Co) KIA 4/13/68*
Samuel H. Lozano, Pvt (B Co)
James A. May, Sgt (B Co)
Samuel E. Shore, 2d Lt (B Co)
James R. Vojtisek, PFC (B Co)
Johnel N. White, PFC (B Co)

Bronze Star Medals with Combat "V"

Ronald L. Allen, Capt (B Co) md
Martin Farmer, Capt (C Co) pc
Patrick J. Kahler, Capt (D Co)
William T. Sweeney, Capt (D Co)
Robert A. Baribeau, 1st Lt (D Co)
Ralph A. Pineda, 1st Lt (B Co)
John A. Lancaster, 2d Lt (D Co) md
Dennis L. Lister, 2d Lt (C Co)
John J. Kispert, 2d Lt (C Co)
John J. O'Brien, 2d Lt (D Co)
Jesse A. Dobson, GySgt (D Co)
Joseph L. Storzum, S/Sgt (B Co) pc
Vincent Streeter, S/Sgt (H&S Co)
David O. Harrison, Sgt (D Co)
Paul W. B. Herring, Sgt (B Co)
Arthur W. Smith, Sgt (D Co) KIA 5/7/68*
Luther J. Thedford, Sgt (B Co) KIA 8/23/68*
Simon Waiau, Jr. Sgt (C Co)
James Buccola, Cpl (D Co)
Tyrone T. Douglas, L/Cpl (D Co) md
John E. Granville, L/Cpl (C Co) md
Stephen J. Hinds, L/Cpl (A Co) KIA 4/13/68*
Richard G. Pixley, L/Cpl (D Co) KIA 7/20/68*
Jerry A. Snipes, PFC (A Co) KIA 4/13/68* pc
Theartis Watts, Jr. PFC (A Co) KIA 8/17/68*

Navy Corpsmen:
David E. Bronson, HM3 (D Co)
Wilson E. Carroll, HN (C Co)
Charles R. Golling HM3 (C Co) KIA 8/23/68*
Danny L. Grimshaw, HM2 (D Co) KIA 8/23/68*

Navy Commendation Medals with Combat "V"
Roscoe D. Adams, Pvt (D Co) KIA 7/28/68*
Roger G. Charles, 2d Lt (A Co)
Rodney P. Edrozo, Cpl (C Co)
Manuel J. Gomez, GySgt (H&S Co) KIA 4/17/68*
Clifford A. Horton, Cpl (B Co)
Patrick M. Lorditch, PFC (D Co) KIA 8/6/68*
Cameron J. Milum, 1st Lt (B Co & H&S Co)
Robert J. O'Rourke, 2d Lt (B Co)
Felix Salmeron, S/Sgt (A Co)

Navy Corpsmen:
Danny L. Grimshaw, HM2 (D Co) KIA 8/23/68*
Michael D. Kirkpatrick, HM3 (B Co)
Robert Taugner, HM3 (B Co)

Navy Achievement Medals with Combat "V"
David E. Bronson, HM3 (D Co)
Gifford J. Davis, Jr. PFC (D Co)
Kenneth E. Davis, Cpl (C Co)
Lloyd L. Fernung, Cpl (C Co)
Billy R. Frye, L/Cpl (D Co)
James P. Mays, L/Cpl (C Co)
Donald L. Moorehead, Cpl (C Co)
Fred T. Spell, SgtMaj (H&S Co)
Harold D. Sweet, Cpl (D Co)
Edmond P. Tardy III, Cpl (C Co)
Jan L. Warren, Sgt (D Co)
    * Awarded Posthumously
    md - Medically Discharged
    pc - Pending Confirmation

Purple Hearts – **112 KIAs** with a total of **669** Purple Hearts awarded March through September 1968.

CHAPTER 8

Casualties of War

Cowards die many times before their deaths;
the valiant never taste of death but once.
~ William Shakespeare

"Good men must die, but death cannot kill their names." ~ Proverb

The Vietnam Veterans Memorial Wall quartered on the National Mall in Washington, D. C. was completed in 1982. It was born of and created by Vietnam Veterans. At first, the government had no hand in the memorial. The idea came from veterans themselves who wanted to honor the terrible price that was paid in blood by American boys. Its intent: to honor the "courage, sacrifice and devotion to duty and country" for those that served. The Vietnam Veterans Memorial is now to perpetually remain on the northwest corner of the National Mall, dignifying those who made the ultimate sacrifice in Vietnam. The Memorial has two black granite walls composed of seventy panels, on which are inscribed the names of over 58,000 men and a few women. It serves as a stark reminder of the staggering cost borne by American sons and daughters in one of the longer wars.

The war in Southeast Asia bore one of the higher death tolls of America's wars. Now that the war has passed, those who came home think of those days in northern I Corps in vignettes: some of those thoughts are mundane, some exotic; some are filled with remembered fear and some with deep remorse…

- The beautiful flowing Ao Dais dresses of young women.
- The smell of Nuc Mam.
- The heat, dust, and humidity.
- Hard stares from villagers.
- The smell of diesel fuel.
- The sudden crack of a rifle shot, a burst of automatic rifle fire.
- The boredom.
- The cacophonous confusion of a firefight.
- The wounded.
- The dead.

There is not a day that goes by that we Marines and Corpsmen don't think of some aspect of the boredom, the drudgery, and the chilling experiences of our daily existence during that war. The one thing we sincerely don't like to think about is the deaths we witnessed. Especially those that happened to comrades close to us. Fleeting thoughts such as, "What if he had lived…" intrude our daily thoughts at the most unexpected moments. "I wonder what he would be doing now were he alive." "Why did I survive?" These thoughts invade our minds often. At the time one did not have even moments to think about the dead or to even mourn for them. Sergeant Felix Salmeron, a platoon Sergeant in Alpha Company, solemnly reflects, "I didn't have time to grieve for them; I had others to think about and keep alive…I kept them moving!"

Human bonding borne of combat is part of the glue that holds a unit together. When one perishes, the survivor of that bonding process is forced to suppress bereavement and deal with the realities of the moment. Upon returning home most soldiers had no one around who had served or even understood the war. Grief sometimes erupted as rage. That silent rage was carried home with many and never discussed. In others, grief manifested as withdrawal from society. In a lot of instances, the grief and remembering came many years later. Men worked at careers for long hours to mute their war feelings. Some turned to drink or drugs to self-medicate the memories of combat. But everyone remembered…

Years later, the dead would begin to appear and linger, looming real again. Some Marines/Corpsmen literally blocked out painful experiences of loss. Those events were summarily buried and consciously denied because of the close bond. The experience of comradeship throughout our Corps is legendary amongst its participants. A loss had long-lasting effects especially if it could not be discussed within the trusted group. Some left the battlefield and found themselves back at home within hours with no one to relate to. This was utterly perplexing for most veterans. Most of the society at the time did not understand what their psyche had experienced or the grief they had within them when they hastily arrived back in "the world." The nation did not understand the war overall. Some in society rejected these honorable men when they returned home.

The First Battalion, 27th Marines sustained extremely heavy casualties during its short deployment in the Republic of Vietnam in the aftermath of Tet. The official count is 112 KIAs and close to 700 Purple Heart Medals awarded to Battalion members in the almost seven months the Battalion was deployed. The mentally wounded, only God knows. The entire Regiment was significantly understrength from the beginning. It had gone ashore in the Republic of Vietnam with the bare minimum of infantry billets and began operating as a functional unit. These next personal accounts of the families' grief and how they dealt with losing their loved ones are just a few of the thousands of stories that overwhelmed our nation during the Vietnam War. The author wishes he could tell everyone's story.

James Joseph Allen, KIA 5 June 1968

One such beloved Marine of the Battalion killed-in-action on 5 June of 1968 and forever remembered by his squad, platoon members, and family is James J. Allen of Charlie Company, aka "JJ" as he was called. JJ was liked by all. He made friends easily wherever he went and gained the respect of most in his circle of Marines. He was not clownish or a braggart.

Jimmy was the All-American kid from Philadelphia whose father had served honorably in World War II in Europe with the 1st Infantry Division, "the Big Red One" for 444 days without a break. His father had endured the invasion of North Africa and on to Sicily. He had landed on Omaha Beach on D-Day and slogged through the European countries of France, Belgium, Germany, and finally Czechoslovakia with the 32nd Field Artillery. His son, Jimmy, was a pride and joy to him and his wife. Together they had lovingly instilled the values of family, patriotism, and worshipping in church every Sunday. They were extremely proud of

James J. Allen, 13 years old
~ Courtesy of Robert Allen,
brother of James

their five children. Robert, the youngest, recollects, "We went to church every Sunday as a family and we were not allowed to skip out of going…The services back in those days were all in Latin. It was boring to us because we did not know what was being said…And of course, we would get questions, for example, 'What was the gospel? What was this? What was that?' And a lot of the time we didn't know the answer to the questions…But we went to church every Sunday, religiously!" Jimmy's younger brother admiringly tagged along everywhere and basked in his tutelage. Sometimes he was not allowed to hang around with Jimmy's older friends. "I was like a little puppy and he and his buddies sometimes did not want me in their world. So, I was told to leave. And sometimes they would hide from me, not wanting me to follow them. I suppose they thought I might tell on them. God knows what they were up to?"

Jimmy lived in a rough-and-tumble neighborhood of mostly blue-collar workers who were veterans of WWII. Robert remembers, "Everyone was very, very patriotic and I cannot think of a childhood friend whose father was not in the Second World War. Those values and patriotism were deeply instilled into all of us, my three older

Jimmy on the left side with neighbor kids, 1958
~ Courtesy of Robert Allen, brother of Jimmy

sisters included. I suspect that my father had PTSD as it is called nowadays. He seldom talked about the war. My mother told me years after he was gone that he would go into the basement anytime a plane would go overhead. She also said that he would take very long walks at night by himself. No one talked about it back in those days. As a child, you don't understand these things and now that I am older I can put it all together." The Allens had two sons and three older daughters. The daughters were all married by the time Jimmy enlisted in the Marines.

Prom Night 1966 – Jimmy on left with date and the same grown-up neighborhood kids
~ Courtesy of Robert Allen, brother of James

Jimmy started out in Catholic school and for a while did fine. However, as his younger brother points out, "These schools in the 1950s were pretty strict. The three older sisters all went to this school and Jimmy followed in their footsteps. I can remember when he was disciplined by one of the Nuns at the school. The sister had grabbed him and tried to get his attention and he pushed her back…That was the end of his parochial schooling. My mother took him out and placed him in public school. Subsequently, I followed in his footsteps. We attended Henry Armand Brown Elementary School then on to John Paul Jones Junior High and finally to Thomas Edison High School. Jimmy was very protective of me. I can remember being bullied by another kid one day on the playground. The kid that was confronting me was an older kid around Jimmy's age. He just kept messing with me and taunting me and finally Jimmy just mopped the playground up with him. It wasn't long after that, I was walking around the playground with my chest out and just daring someone else to mess with me… Nobody gave Jimmy any guff… He was not a bully and he would stand up for anyone being bullied…I remember that he was outspoken about that subject…about fairness and things like that."

Jimmy was the popular kid amongst his peers and participated in all the sports in the neighborhood. Robert remembers some of those times. "Looking back, we played pickup games which were very popular. We played on rough fields; they were not grass or dirt, they were cinder…Keep in mind this was the inner city…We didn't have any parks or open spaces that you see in the suburbs today. Jimmy was well into unorganized sports; football, basketball, baseball. We had local teams and if you wanted to call it organized we did play other neighborhoods."

Jimmy dropped out of high school the end of his junior year. His next move was to join the Marine Corps and he went to Parris Island. Jimmy talked about joining the Marine Corps with his younger brother and told him he wanted to join the Marines because he thought they were the best. A lot of the kids in the neighborhood were joining and the Allens had relatives that were already in the Corps. Jimmy's younger brother Robert recalls, "Next thing I knew he was in the Marine Corps. He did go to recruit training at Parris Island, South Carolina and graduated in June of 1967. I remember my mother; my girlfriend, at the time, who is now my wife; and myself went to visit and observe Jimmy's platoon graduation. I can remember walking around Parris Island with Jimmy while he had leave right before the platoon graduated and he would get upset if we were doing anything unmilitary-like, like hands in the pockets, chewing gum, etc. He would correct us and show us that we had to do things the Marine Corps way. And me, especially as undisciplined as I was at the time...I was thinking to myself, 'What is your problem, Jimmy?'"

FIRST RECRUIT BATTALION   PLATOON 170   M.C.R.D., PARRIS ISLAND, S.C.
SSGT. J.H. EDWARDS, Jr.   SSGT. R.J. BEATTY   SGT. W. HOHNHORST, Jr.
GRADUATED 30 - JUNE - 1967

James J. Allen on bottom row, sixth in from right ~ Courtesy of Robert Allen, brother of James

Upon graduation, James J. Allen, like any recruit, had learned the lessons of discipline and responding to commands in the long grind of becoming a Marine. It was evident he was proud of his accomplishments at earning the title of a United States Marine Corps Rifleman. He had certainly learned the fundamentals well, as evidenced by his family. After a short, blissful leave at home, Jimmy was off to Camp Lejeune, North Carolina for Infantry Training (ITR). The family received the typical letters while he was there. As Robert recalls, "Jimmy didn't elaborate much about the training regimen. There is one significant thing I recall…He always had a group of buddies and was liked by all of them and would write us about them." After completion of ITR, Jimmy joined the 1st Battalion, 27th Marine Regiment in Kaneohe, Hawaii. This was a newly-formed unit that was training Marines in the Air-Ground Team concept, preparing for duty in Vietnam. He really enjoyed his time there, writing home that the "training was rough" and that he was "learning a lot but that it was fun!"

James Allen, June 1967 USMC
~ Courtesy of Robert Allen,
brother of James

Robert remembers the day he and his father were going someplace in the family car and his father produced a letter from Jimmy. "I could see that he was visibly upset." Prior to this Jimmy had let us know that he had embarked upon a training cruise to the South Pacific somewhere to train. And we didn't think too much of that other than it was additional training. Dad then told me what he had written. He had written to us that "By the time you read this letter, I will be in Vietnam." Shortly after receiving Jimmy's letter another letter from Lieutenant Colonel Greenwood, Battalion Commander arrived at the Allen home, which explained the diversion to Vietnam. Not much detail other than they would be deployed to RVN and conducting operations there. "I remember my Dad was sitting there in the car and fumbling with the letter…It was tough for him but now I know that he had accepted it because he had been there himself. Later when my mother was told, she became really upset… My father, trying to mitigate any anxiety for my mother, tried to calm her by saying, 'Well, he is in Da Nang; it appears to be a pretty secure base from all accounts.' I know my Dad was not ignorant about combat and was trying very hard to put her at ease."

The family started to receive letters from Jimmy about the operations his unit was conducting. The letters were somewhat vague. After a short period, Robert started noticing a change in the tone of the letters. Rereading the letters recently, Robert tells, "I know looking at the timeline of the now written history what was going on…We did start noticing the change of attitude about the time Operation Allen Brook began. It was while they were in the Go Noi area. I remember things like, 'It is so hot here, I cannot believe it and our Company Commander thinks we are Superman!' I am thinking this must have been very fatiguing…The words hot and humid stick in my mind… Those words were in all his letters. I am thinking Philadelphia is hot and humid in the summer where we grew up and if he is complaining then it must really be bad there. It seemed to me that Jimmy was hard pressed mentally and physically and it was starting to weigh on him. It was at this point about four or five months into his deployment that I saw a definite change in the tone of his letters."

Wendell "Buzzy" Cooper grew up in JJ's neighborhood; they had been friends since early childhood. It happened that Buzzy was also in the Marines and in the same area of Vietnam. The two exchanged letters and somehow met each other while on Operation Allen Brook. After meeting during Allen Brook, "Buzzy sent a letter to my parents and told them that JJ was having problems with his ears. He had problems with his ears as a child. He was always having bad ear infections. I think he had narrow drainage tubes and it caused him a lot of discomforts. It was a chronic issue for him. And now he was having those same problems again while over there. He had not mentioned any of this in his letters."

JJ's death was shortly after that meeting with "Buzzy." During the Vietnam War, casualty-notification teams of at least two people were dispatched to notify the families and loved ones. On a moment's notice, these teams were activated and sent to impart the sad news. In the early days of the war, telegrams were delivered. The process was quickly refined and teams were mandated later in the War. In most cases, at least two military officials of equal or higher rank would be involved in the notification. Sometimes a Chaplain would be present, but at least two military types would deploy. The objective was to treat loved ones with compassion, dignity, and respect while helping them cope with their loss.

In the case of his brother's death, Robert recalls that fateful day when he found out Jimmy wasn't coming home alive from Vietnam. "I was in New Jersey with my girlfriend, Kathy at a popular lake where families would go to spend the day. We were enjoying the day there and my name was announced over the intercom to come to the refreshment stand. I have blocked out most all details and can only remember bits and pieces. The next thing I remember is that we are walking up my street and there were people standing all around my house. Someone came up to me and said to me, 'Your brother got killed.' I don't recall who told me…but it was like a hammer hitting me… When I finally walked into the house my father was standing there staring upward and my mother was at the top of stairs on her knees, sobbing, almost screaming. My married sisters were all there with their husbands. I was the youngest and the only one at home with my parents. It was a scene that I don't like remembering. It was so overwhelming that I have blocked most of it out. My girlfriend, Kathy, now my wife, tells me that I didn't come out of the house so she left. She remembers me at my brother's viewing before the funeral just staring at nothing and remaining silent, which was not like me."

Some of the Allens' old neighbor friends have said that Jimmy's funeral was the biggest funeral and memorial service in the history of the neighborhood. He was laid to rest at Holy Sepulcher Cemetery on Cheltenham Avenue on the outskirts of Philadelphia. There were reports of over 200 cars in the funeral procession. Jimmy was buried with full military honors, Final Honors as it is called. Final Honors expresses a burial rite to a warrior who has died in battle and served his country faithfully. It features guards, words of condolence, flag draping over the coffin, firing of volley shots as a salute, and flag folding for presentation to a patriarch or matriarch of the family. Taps are then played as the final salute to the deceased veteran. It is a ceremony in which great respect is shown to the veteran's family and loved ones.

This was the case in James J. Allen's Final Honors. As Robert remembers, "I remember the long, long drive to Holy Sepulcher Cemetery. It seemed like it took forever. I remember seeing people in dress blues walking around but I can't remember the honor guard. I was only sixteen at the time. I am sure there was an honor guard as my father was Commander of the American Legion…I remember a letter from General Cushman. I think he was the Commanding General in Vietnam at the time. We received many letters from politicians, Senators, Congressmen, etc. I believe one came from the President, LBJ. And most of all, I remember receiving hate mail. One woman wrote that Jimmy deserved what he got. Of all the letters and there were hundreds of them…There were these protest letters and I remembered this one being the most vicious! I just couldn't believe someone would do this to us."

James J. Allen Gravestone ~ Courtesy of Robert Allen, brother of James
KIA Operation Allen Brook, 5 June 1968 – Panel 60W Line 014

The Allens' lives had been shattered after they laid their son to rest. Robert recounts he was overcome with a feeling of helplessness. He became very conflicted with the loss of his beloved older brother and wanted somehow to strike out at the cause of his and his family's loss. "This hits you and spreads all over your being and leaves you cold. It doesn't hurt physically. You cannot feel it. Numbness sets in and a feeling of helplessness wells up inside. When I turned seventeen I sought permission from my parents to join the Marine Corps. They steadfastly refused to allow me to join. I now look back and can understand my parents' anguish and their refusal for allowing me to join." Later, Robert joined and served with 3rd Battalion, 14th Marines Artillery Reserves as a wireman and field radio operator in the early 1970s as the war came to an end.

Stephen Edward Austin, KIA 8 June 1968

Stephen was into sports while he was growing up, especially baseball when he was younger, and cowboys and indians. He went to the occasional Saturday afternoon matinees to watch the favorites of those times, Gene Autry, Roy Rogers, and William Boyd aka "Hopalong" Cassidy. Steve was a Boy Scout and an exceptional athlete as a young teen, excelling in all the sports.

The Austin Boys, Allen, Dean, Lassie and Stephen   Stephen on the right as a Boy Scout 1959

~ Courtesy of Allen Austin, brother of Stephen Austin

As younger brother Allen remembers, "He had trophies in baseball, basketball and in football…and excelled in football." As a running back, Steve injured his knee in his junior year of high school. "This really did discourage him and because he wasn't able to play sports he began hanging around with an older crowd. During his high school years, he acquired a couple of girlfriends and because we didn't have a lot of money he worked and saved up his money to buy a 1951 Ford with a flathead engine. I can remember hanging out with him, riding around town waiting for the Beatles' songs to play on the radio. We cherished every one of their songs that played on the radio. He dearly loved music as did I. Steve didn't finish his senior year due to the knee injury and not being able to play sports. That is when he enlisted in the Marine Corps."

His father and mother did not want him to go, but he was determined. A parent had to sign a release for a seventeen-year-old to join any of the military branches. The Vietnam War was in the early stages and no one was paying attention to it in 1964. Signing up for the "Buddy Program" with three local friends, Steve headed for Marine Corps Recruit Depot, San Diego, California. Allen recalls, "His friend Buddy Allen was one of the guys he ran around with and it was he who convinced Dad and Mom to sign for him. Later, when Stephen was killed, Buddy was also in Vietnam at the same time in another unit. After the War, I would see Buddy occasionally. Buddy felt extremely guilty for his death and personally responsible for talking my parents into signing for Steve."

Stephen E. Austin with his beloved Lassie 1960 ~ Courtesy of Allen Austin, brother of Stephen Austin

In San Diego, Stephen injured his football knee in the early stages of boot camp and was put on medical hold. They performed surgery on his knee and placed him into rehabilitation status. He could have opted out of the Marine Corps with a medical discharge but elected to recuperate and start his recruit training over again with another platoon. He finally graduated with Platoon 330 of Third Battalion on 10 August of 1965. It was a long and arduous journey for young Stephen.

After boot camp and Infantry Training Regiment, Steve was sent to the 1st Battalion, 1st Marine Regiment, 1st Marine Division, Fleet Marine Force as a replacement. The Battalion arrived in Vietnam in August of 1965 and came under the operational control of the 3rd Marine Division. The Battalion began operating in the Chu Lai TAOR. Steve was wounded by enemy mortar fire in November 1965, shortly after arriving, and was medically evacuated. Brother Allen reflects, "It took him sixteen months to fully recover. All that time he spent with a couple of units in Okinawa, Japan. Fully ready again, he was assigned to the 28th Marine Regiment in 5th Marine Division and eventually transferred to Kaneohe Bay to fill the ranks of 1st Battalion, 27th Marines, of 5th Marine Division in Hawaii."

During Steve's last leave home from Hawaii, he spent a lot of time with a new girlfriend, Jolene Cradock, a local girl, and nice young lady. He then left home for Hawaii for the last time. What he did not know was Jolene became pregnant with his child. Allen vividly remembers, "It was on Mother's Day in 1986 that my mother ran into Jolene's mother in town and she told my Mom the truth of the matter and about Steve's biological daughter, Neily. We met Neily that Christmas and to this day I am not sure that Steve ever knew he had a daughter."

Austin Family visiting Stephen during ITR in Camp Pendleton, CA
~ Courtesy of Allen Austin; L-R: Allen, Dean, Stephen, Lorene, and Albert Austin

Stephen's father had served in the Army in two wars and retired as a Master Sergeant in 1953, continuing in the California National Guard. He had gone through Europe with Alpha Company of the 56th Armored Infantry Battalion with the 12th

Armored Division, and was later with I Company, 35th Regiment of the 1st Cavalry Division in Korea. Albert Austin was wounded while battling the Germans in the European theater. He received a Bronze Star while on the battlefield in Germany. Austin later served as a Deputy Sheriff in Tulare County, California and worked for the California Youth Authority.

Stephen's youngest brother takes us back to his high school in 1968 when Allen was about to graduate; it was Friday, 7 June 1968, the last day of school. Spring was in the air and the seniors were on top of the world. They were killing time cruising around town having a few beers before their graduation ceremony. Suddenly a news flash came across the airwaves, "Robert Kennedy has been shot." From out of nowhere, the prevailing "come-what-may" attitude was crushed, and for one in that graduating class there was even worse news yet to come.

Allen Austin recaptures that painful news, "It was Monday when I heard the knock on the door, and as I opened it there stood two Marines in uniform with a message in hand. I knew immediately why they were at our door. As they began to speak, it was to me, almost like an out-of-body experience which began to envelop me. A dark and heavy shadow fell as they announced my oldest brother, Stephen, was killed in action. After the Marines left, I waited in turmoil, teetering in and out of despair, for my parents to return home. They were away on a trip at the time and finally returned two days later. Upon returning home my Mother literally collapsed on the floor and it took two weeks for her to function again. Our doctor made a house call and put her on some medications. Looking back now, I realize my father knew all along this was possible. He was a WWII and Korean War veteran. He knew firsthand the tragedy of war and now his firstborn was gone. I was unable to talk to my father openly, especially concerning Steve. Oh, what I would give now to be able to do so. The next day Steve's final letter from Vietnam arrived in the mail. It had been on his person when he was killed and it was mailed with his blood still stained on the envelope. You can imagine the impact on our family. When his belongings arrived after his death, while opening his wallet we found a ticket to an Eric Burdon and the Animals Concert in San Diego, California." The Animals were responsible for the hit songs of this era, *We Gotta Get Out of This Place, Don't Let Me Be Misunderstood, House of the Rising Sun* and more.

In a matter of a few days, Allen Austin went from the top of the world to what felt like the bottom. The news catapulted him into a non-caring attitude, which would begin to eat away at him and would take many years for him to recover from. His dear mother never recovered from losing her firstborn son. She grieved for Stephen for the rest of her life. "It's been almost twenty-five years and it still seems as though it happened yesterday," she says, "It still hurts…The last time I ever saw him he was standing alone at Travis Air Force Base, I looked back and ran back and hugged him. They brought him home in a sealed casket and I couldn't ever see him again."

A sterile Western Union Telegram explained what had happened and how his remains would arrive home ready for burial:

MR. AND MRS. ALBERT H. AUSTIN
4057 MAIN STREET
DENAIR, CALIFORNIA

I DEEPLY REGRET TO CONFIRM THAT YOUR SON CORPORAL STEPHEN E. AUSTIN, USMC, DIED ON 8 JUNE 1968 IN THE VICINITY OF QUANG NAM, REPUBLIC OF VIETNAM. HE SUSTAINED GUNSHOT WOUNDS TO THE HEAD AND BODY FROM HOSTILE RIFLE FIRE WHILE ON AN OPERATION. THE FOLLOWING INFORMATION IS PROVIDED TO ASSIST YOU IN MAKING FUNERAL ARRANGEMENTS. HIS REMAINS WILL BE PREPARED, ENCASED, AND SHIPPED AT NO EXPENSE TO YOU, ACCOMPANIED BY AN ESCORT, EITHER TO A FUNERAL HOME OR TO A NATIONAL CEMETERY SELECTED BY YOU...

The middle son, Dean, was in the Army and had received orders for Vietnam. Mrs. Austin had to seek the help of her Congressman twice to prevent him from being sent to Vietnam.

It was years before Allen could accept, through his religion, what had transpired. In his struggle to understand what had happened in his life, he began to experience the peace and true meaning of freedom through the application of his faith. "I also was released to grieve the death of my brother and over the years acquired the real truths of the Vietnam War and a balanced sense of looking at the issues that divided us. I had never fully grieved or dealt with Steve's death. I somehow could compartmentalize it. I had anger towards it and I blamed the government and society. I would blurt out angrily whenever a reference to the War or anything related came up on this very personal subject. People were taken aback with my anger. They had no idea of the hurt in my heart over my brother. As the healing gradually began to take hold I began to truly contemplate the circumstances of my brother's death. Why was he there? Where and how did he die? Who was with him when he died? I began to reach out to the Marines and Corpsmen he served with. I created a website to honor him and his fellow Marines. I began reading all his letters, something I had avoided since his death. I never fully realized the danger he was in, as I was completely naïve about this war. I had no idea he was struggling with life and death daily. I have now finally placed it in the hands of God."

Corporal Stephen E. Austin
(KIA 8 June 1968), C Co, 1/27
~ Courtesy of Allen Austin,
Stephen's brother

Last Letter Home

7 June 1968

Dear Mom and Dad

I am sorry for not writing. But I've had very little chance to even think about writing. This is my 14th or 15th day in the field. I am on an operation south of Da Nang. The name of the operation is Allen Brook. Is there anything about it on the news? It's been going on since the 12th of last month. So far, we've captured a lot of new weapons and tons of rice. June 5th things got a little rough on my company. We took 28 wounded and six dead. So, our company is hurting for some new men. On my birthday, things didn't go too good. One of my best friends who I met in Hawaii was shot twice in the stomach and he died the following afternoon. His name was Art Sinksen. I am going to write his parents a letter soon as I go to the Battalion area. I am so sick of fighting. I've seen and helped too many boys my age or younger that was wounded or dead. I thank the lord each morning I get up. Well, I should be going on R&R any time. That's about it over here. So, say hi to everyone and take care of yourselves. Bye for now.

All My Love,
Your Son Stephen
P.S. Write Soon

Stephen E. Austin Grave site ~ Courtesy of Allen Austin

Daniel J. Clevenger, KIA 7 April 1968

Daniel Clevenger, born on 7 December 1946, in Pueblo, Colorado came into the world in an area rich with western history. Historically, Pueblo reinforced the northernmost boundaries of the Spanish and, later, Mexican influences. This area continued to be a stopping-off-place for settlers and people headed into the Rocky Mountains and the southwestern United States. Kit Carson, famous frontiersman and scout, came through the area frequently.

A Start in Life

Daniel John Clevenger's father, Harley John Clevenger, came to the Pueblo area from Clay Center, Kansas. Marrying in 1937, he and his new wife, Minerva, moved to Durango, Colorado, where he would try his luck in the silver mines. Their oldest child, Donna, born in Durango in 1938, recaptures family beginnings. "When Mother graduated from high school, she worked as a telephone operator...They married in 1937 and moved to Durango, Colorado because my father felt he could strike it big in the silver mines...After they moved back to Pueblo wouldn't you know it, the silver came in..."

C. F. & I. entrance 1950s ~ Courtesy of
Donna Clevenger-Gaasch, sister of Dan Clevenger

Founded in 1938 in a small room at the YMCA in Pueblo, the C.F. & I. Credit Union evolved into a statewide/national organization over the years. By 1945, John Clevenger had worked not only at the C.F. & I. plant where he had gained employment in the power department, but also became treasurer at the C.F. & I. Credit Union and continued working both jobs until his death in 1969. In his later years, he moved into a Director's position at the credit union. John also became an officer in the Credit Union National Association (CUNA), the largest national trade association in the U. S. serving America's credit unions.

Donna recollects, "Mother and I would ride the bus, to the credit union to pick up daily deposits and take them to the bank for father. Mother did not work at the time and sometimes would help out at the motel owned by her brother when a maid didn't make it to work." Minerva Clevenger later started working at the popular Fashion Bar, a clothing retailer, in the children's department. After establishing herself, she started a local TV show which featured youngsters modeling clothing available at the store. It became a hit with local TV viewers during that time.

After a few years, Dan and Donna's mother also worked at Lady Burlington and then finally went to work at J. C. Penney's where she retired. Minerva Clevenger had her oldest daughter working with her while Donna attended high school. Donna tells about her mother's rule of work, "I had to sell a certain amount of merchandise to get off work for a Friday-night football game. So, I had a lot of incentive to work hard."

Later, Mrs. Clevenger learned to drive and bought a Plymouth Valiant. She was the sole driver in the family because her husband, John, had suffered from severe arthritis for many years. He did not drive and took the bus everywhere. He would walk to the bus stop, take a bus, and then transfer to another, walking the last mile to his job every day.

Danny's parents were active in Masonic work. As older sister, Donna, recalls, "Dad was a devout Masonic Lodge member and a Shriner. Mother was in Order of the Eastern Star participating in all their activities." These organizations, built around fellowship and service, focused most of their activities toward charity, giving, and projects that benefited mankind. This became the Clevenger family focus throughout most of their lives.

The Clevengers had many lifelong friends in these organizations and went to many of the Shriner conventions. One of the stories told included a Jewish friend of John's who wanted to become a Mason. Learning that there

The Clevenger Family: Donna, Minerva, Harley & Danny (below)~ Courtesy of Dani Sydorenko, Dan's daughter

was reluctance in the organization for him to join, John stood up for his friend and sponsored him. The man was eventually allowed to join and became a devout lifelong Mason. This Jewish man was extremely thankful and remained a close friend of the Clevengers for many years. The Clevengers also found the time to religiously attend Bethel Methodist Church in Pueblo throughout most of their lives.

A Child is Born

Dan came along in 1946 right after the family had moved to their new home on Elizabeth Street. His older sister remembered his very curly hair and thought he was just about the cutest thing she had ever seen.

In 1952 the family moved to Saratoga Road where Daniel attended Ben Franklin Elementary School and then Risley Junior High School, close to home. Danny contracted Perthes Disease in his sixth year, which meant a lack of blood flow to his hip joint. Due to this condition, the bone area affected softens, dies, and stops growing. His treatment centered on removing pressure from the joint until the disease ran its course. Young Daniel was in a body cast for almost three years and then had to rely on crutches for another year. As his sister, Donna, tells of his

Daniel John Clevenger ~ Courtesy of Dani Sydorenko, Dan's daughter

serious malady, "He never once complained...he was homeschooled during the entire time and did not miss out on his early education."

Get-well cards descended on a surprised Dan from far off Portland, Oregon. No one could figure out how the second-grade students at Duniway School in Portland had found out about Dan Clevenger and the hipbone disease he had contracted. As the Pueblo paper reported the event, "The packages were addressed to 'Master Danny

Clevenger.' Girls and boys evidently colored the cards, drew vague Easter bunnies and kites and laboriously lettered the notes like, 'Hello Danny' and 'Get Well Soon, Easter Is Coming.' A few of the cards had a nickel or dime scotch-taped inside. The cover letter simply said that the class members heard he was sick and hoped he gets better...In the meantime, a visiting teacher instructs Danny in reading and writing...He's going to write a thank-you...but the Clevengers also would like to thank the anonymous friend who suggested the get-well packet."

Young Danny as a Cub Scout, far right, and longtime boyhood companion Bob Getts, far left
~ Courtesy of neighbor Ron Getts, Pueblo, Colorado

Ron Getts, older brother of Bob Getts of Pueblo, Colorado provided the above photograph of the Cub Scout Den which both his younger brother Bob and Dan Clevenger enjoyed in their young years. Bobby happened to be three weeks younger than Dan and they had remained steadfast companions in the neighborhood while growing up. Older brother Ron remembers Dan, "When he was a little boy I always thought he was a neat, caring little child. My brother Bobby and Danny always played together. I was four years older than they and was tasked, on occasion, to keep an eye on them so they would not get into trouble. They always had a lot of fun together and were always playing 'cowboys and indians.' Bobby served in the Navy during Vietnam and passed away at the young age of forty years old. Ironically, they both are buried at the Imperial Memorial Gardens in Pueblo, Colorado."

Rock and Roll

Geri Ellis-Graves, Danny's cousin from Denver, had fond memories of young Dan while growing up in the '50s and early '60s. She recalls that "My sister, Judy, and I adored him...He was one of the kindest and most patient young men that we had ever known." She remembered that he would let them follow him everywhere when they went to visit his family in Pueblo, Colorado.

On one visit Dan showed his cousins Geri and Judy the Clevenger family crest and how their generations went back centuries. Geri recollects that Danny was extremely proud of the fact that his father had researched and put all the family genealogy together. She further tells of Dan's intellect, "He built a radio from scratch with parts he was able to identify and buy...He was such a genius!"

Geri's favorite memory of Dan went back to their teen years. "Dan had bought a new 45-rpm record player and we ended up dancing all afternoon to it right after he had bought it. The song, 'The Lion Sleeps Tonight' had just been released and we danced and danced some more to that song with youthful and carefree joyousness that only comes when you are a kid. It remains as one of my favorite songs from the memory of Danny and the times we had back then."

Cousin Geri's world shattered when one evening in April of 1968 while she was in college, her father called, voice shaking, to tell her that Danny had been killed in Vietnam. Geri remembers thinking, "That just couldn't be! He couldn't be gone! My young heart broke that night, never to completely heal."

Geri now reflects, "Every now and then, I think of him, what he would be doing now if he were still alive? What kind of grown man would he have become? Would he be happy? I still miss his quiet, patient, kind presence all through my life. My joy lies in knowing that, in not too many years, I will see him again. 'Until God calls me, Danny, I love and still miss you!'"

Dennis McKay, Danny's first cousin, remembers Dan was also into collecting 45-rpm and 33-rpm records. Dennis briefly recaptures the '60s and Danny, "I bought 'Little Darling,' originally recorded by the Diamonds, from Danny. He and I used to cruise Main and all around Pueblo in his 1965 Chevy Bel Air...I distinctly remember that Danny really loved electronics and we would go around to all of the second-hand stores looking for old electronic equipment, especially old radios."

At Pueblo's East High School, Dan tried out for football and made the team. In his very first game, Danny broke his arm, which ended his football career. Danny, extremely popular amongst his peers, made friends easily. After high school, Dan enrolled in the local Junior College, Pueblo College, and attended classes for a short time. Shortly after discovering college wasn't what he wanted to do, Danny enlisted in the United States Marine Corps, attending boot camp at Marine Corps Recruit Depot, San Diego and then continued to Camp Pendleton for ITR. After completion of ITR, Dan attended Radio Communications School located back at the Marine Corps Recruit Depot in San Diego.

Young Daniel Clevenger
~ Courtesy of Dani Sydorenko,
Dan's daughter

A Long-Distance Love Affair

Corporal Dan Clevenger wrote his father and mother from Vietnam before his death to tell them he was to be a father. In a letter now kept by his daughter, Dani, he consoles them, "Yes, I am to be a father. When I first found out, I had every intention of telling you..." He and Star, his longtime girlfriend in Hawaii, had not yet married before the Battalion deployment. He went on to tell them, "It is not the baby's fault...for being born and the baby will have a mother and father."

In another letter saved by Dani, Dan wrote to Star, "Good night, my love, sleep tight, sweet dreams, and God is with you. Tell the girls to be good and I will bring them something when I come home, with love, Dan." Star had daughters from her first marriage. In another letter to Star, Dan buoys her with, "How are you feeling, yourself? I hope you're not having any more complications. I will bet you are getting to be quite a big pear now and cute as hell. I wish you could somehow send me a picture of yourself in your present state as you may not be that way when I see you again the way things are going here. I feel prouder each day that you are pregnant and know you are getting cuter each day that way. What I would give if we could be together right now. Give the girls my love, I love you, Dan."

Another letter, Dan states, "Am pleased that you are taking all of this without regret. Myself, I am regretful for the pain you endure...It's our responsibility to see that he never suffers just because he is alive. I pray that he will be born healthy and with the minimum of discomfort to you."

In Dani's baby book, compiled by Grandmother Clevenger (Minerva) for her granddaughter, resides a passage written by Star: "Danielle was a name I gave you after your father. He liked the name Kathleen so it was given to you as your middle name. Your father was killed on April 7, 1968, in Hue, Vietnam. It was Palm Sunday of that year. When you were 10 days old we left Hawaii, and went to Colorado to be with your Grandparents."

As Dani Clevenger recalls being told by her grandmother, "They did not know my mother at the time, but my Grandfather John sent my Grandmother Minerva to Hawaii for my birth. She stayed and watched over my half-sisters and waited for me to be born. After I came into the world, my Grandfather and Grandmother had my Mom, I and my sisters moved to Pueblo, Colorado to be near them."

Donna Clevenger with young
Dan ~ Courtesy of
Donna Clevenger-Gaasch,
sister of Dan Clevenger

Premonition

Donna, Danny's sister, still retains the vivid premonition she had when Danny was eight-days old, "I remember on that day having a vision come to me while watching my mother give baby Danny a bath. As I was watching, a voice came to me and told me that Danny was going to grow up, participate in a war and would be killed." This omen evolved into a reality in 1968.

Donna recollects, "A week before he was killed, I became very edgy, depressed and upset. I prayed that he would be okay but it wasn't to be. We received notice of his death six days after he had been killed on the 7th of April, 1968." Overwhelmed with grief, the family learned shortly after notification of Dan's death that Star was pregnant with his child, Danielle. Minerva Clevenger traveled to Hawaii to be with Star for the birth of Dan's daughter. Donna remembers, "Soon after that, my Father had Star move back to Pueblo so that he could take care of them...He saw to it that they received Dan's benefits from the Marines to help with the family."

CP Attacked

Like any other day at that time of year, 7 April 1968 started out hot and humid as the sun came up. The monsoon season was just weeks away. The rutted dirt road in front of the schoolhouse would send dust toiling upward every time a "Mule" or "Mighty Mite" Jeep drove into the 1/27 Command Post. Security watch on the outer perimeter bunkers had been changed as the sun came up and those who had the last watch would be able to catch up on lost sleep.

The Marines of 1/27 had recently bivouacking in this temporary location and were preparing for the worst. Rumors abounded and an alert that North Vietnamese Migs (jet aircraft) would strike had been just passed down the chain of command to all command and control centers.

Corporal Daniel J. Clevenger
~ Courtesy of Dani Sydorenko,
Dan's daughter

At 1415 hours, the CP began receiving 82mm mortar fire. Confusion and chaos immediately reigned throughout the CP. The old hands of previous tours would reorganize the Marines into helping the wounded and strengthening the perimeter for an attack. The ground assault never came. A little later it was determined by mortar-impact analysis that the suspected enemy mortar position was near grid coordinates YD793246, a short distance to the southeast of the CP. A squad of Marines, quickly dispatched to the suspected mortar site, found no evidence of the launch site.

The devastating result of the assault yielded one Marine KIA, six WIA (medically evacuated) and five WIA (non-medically evacuated). Daniel John Clevenger was the Marine whose luck had run out that day. The Marines who knew Dan were devastated and morale in the Communications Platoon went down to its lowest ebb. Dan was the first of many 27th Marines who would lose their lives in the coming months. A leader in the communications section, Dan was loved by all and embodied the character and makeup of all volunteers throughout the Vietnam War. He was kind and looked up to by many. He loved the little children that came to the compound looking for food. He was always finding them extra C-rations cans to take home with them. He would be hard to replace both as a Marine and close friend.

Letter of Response from Harley Clevenger's initial letter to LBJ

In mourning and grief of the loss of his only son, Harley Clevenger wrote a letter to President Lyndon B. Johnson outlining the concerns he had for the war and its prosecution by the United States in Vietnam. This is the response he received from the Assistant Secretary of the Navy:

Corporal Daniel J. Clevenger, Vietnam 1968 ~ Courtesy of Hugh Barton, H&S Co, 1/27

Dear Mr. Clevenger,

President Johnson has asked that I reply to your recent letter concerning your late son, Daniel John Clevenger.

I would first like to express my deepest sympathy for the sad loss of your son while serving his country's cause. Daniel's death remains a source of deep sadness to the President and all of your son's many friends in the Marine Corps. All Americans are indebted to Daniel who suffered the supreme sacrifice while defending the cause to which this nation has been dedicated for nearly two hundred years.

I deeply regret the mixed emotions you and your wife felt upon receiving the President's letter expressing his sympathy and his personal tribute to the courage and dedication of your son. I realize that at the time you wrote to the President you were experiencing the extreme heartache attendant to anyone who has lost a loved one on the field of battle. The President realizes that words of sympathy are not sufficient to assuage this sorrow. While speaking to another bereaved family, The President summarized his own feelings when he said: "I don't believe anyone can know the depths of another's grief. I can only know the grief I would feel if my son were lost in battle."

"But I hear a measure of that sorrow. Because I am Commander-in-Chief, I have a profound responsibility for the lives of Americans in Vietnam. I have not tried to cast off that responsibility to another. I know it is mine and I do not bear it lightly—either by day or night. I could not bear it at all if I were not sure our cause is right in that bitter conflict."

Your thoughts, Mr. Clevenger, regarding Vietnam are appreciated and understandable. Day and night, the President seeks an answer, a reasonable and honorable solution to the war in Vietnam. The President has said that he welcomes every suggestion, every plan that offers any hope of reaching peace. Whether it be from a Congressman, a committee, or private individual. All are considered through long and arduous hours in the hope of finding a way to peace in the world. Recently he said:

"We work every day of every week trying to find the answer....There are good, sincere, genuine people who believe there are plans that could bring us to peace soon. Some think we ought it get it over with, with a much wider war...we have looked at those plans and looked at them carefully...we do not think it is a wise course...there is another extreme...they say they want to do less than we are doing. But we are not doing enough to win it by the way we are doing it now, and we are constantly trying to find additional things that are reasonable, prudent and safe to do."

Again, let me extend to you and the other members of your family, my deepest sympathy in your great loss. You may be assured that a grateful nation will not forget.

> *Sincerely,*
> *Charles A. Bowsher*
> *Assistant Secretary of the Navy*

Remembering a Father

Dani's mother, Star, eventually took her daughters and moved back to Hawaii to continue her life. As Dani recalls, "I became extremely close to my Grandmother Clevenger especially in high school. I also became very close to my mother who raised us girls to value God, Family, and Country, also the love of our military. I feel that I retain a very high level of those moral values due to my Mother."

Dani is quick to tell anyone that her grandmother was the most influential person in her life and Minerva made sure that Dani knew everything there was to know about her father. Dani recollects, "She called me every Father's Day, his birthday, and was there for me through almost everything. Losing her in 1997 was one of the hardest things in

John Clevenger with granddaughter Danielle Clevenger ~ Courtesy of Dani Sydorenko

my life. I think that because I did not have my father that I relied on her and she relied on me as a part of him. When I became older and started seeing young girls with their fathers at special events, it made me start to miss him more. I would give anything to have him here now and I know he would have been a good father. I treasure the love my mother had for him and his legacy. I want to continue to keep his legacy alive by getting involved with Veterans. I missed having him at my high school and college graduation, at my wedding and throughout my life. I felt his presence when I was sleeping at my Grandmother's before I went to College. I felt him standing over my bed looking at me. I told my Grandmother and I will never forget it as long as I live. I know it was him there in the room with me."

Harley John Clevenger died of a heart attack in 1969, not long after putting his only son to rest.

Daniel J. Clevenger grave site, Pueblo Colorado ~ courtesy of daughter, Dani Sydorenko

Ricky Lee Doye, KIA 5 May 1968

Wars come to an end but the memories of those who lost loved ones never end. Ricky Lee was born to his beloved mother Lois and father LaVerne on the 24th day of June in 1949. Rick was the youngest in a family of two older brothers, Arlyn and Larry. The Doye family had the great fortune of living in the prime farming country of northwestern Illinois close to the Mississippi River. This was not only a robust agricultural area but also rich in the history of an earlier age of pre-Columbian Mississippian culture, the Cahokia civilization. Later came the era of European exploration; Frenchmen Jacques Marquette and Louis Jolliet explored this area, especially the rivers of Illinois. Illinois belonged to the French until the late 1700s and was then ruled by Britain. In 1783 this vast frontier became a part of what was known as the Northwest Territory and then by 1818, Illinois became the twenty-first state of our Union.

Ricky Lee was fortunate to have been born in this rural area. There was not only a lot of work to do on the farm which was character building, but also the learning and many sports activities that awaited him in his schooling. Rick was considered one of the best all-around athletes in the history of the school. He was All-Conference in basketball and football, and above average in track, especially in the discus competition. His mentor and teacher on the faculty at Annawan (Illinois) High School, Clarence Hughes, said of him after his death, "Doye was one of the most popular students ever to graduate from the school and when he was home on leave…he visited the school and spoke to several classes…And while Doye was a senior at Annawan he had already made up his mind to join the Marine Corps when he graduated. This is all he talked about and all he wanted to do."

The basketball coach at Annawan who coached all three Doye boys still writes to Mrs. Doye. "Rick's not forgotten…Their coach thought our three boys were special and brags on each. He keeps a picture of Rick on his office file. He went from coaching to become a College Professor. His wife was our boys' English teacher."

Ricky's mother Lois reminisces to where it all started, "Our three were close. We married in 1945, had my first son, Arlyn in 1946, the second son, Larry in 1947, and Rick in 1949. I had no sisters so I grew up playing with dolls. If someone had told me one day, I would have three boys and they would all become teenagers at the same time I would have run…Turned out to be 'The best years of my life.' My husband, LaVerne, did not want me working. 'You raise them, boys,' he told me! Our boys were busy boys, sports, activities, etc…They ate like vultures…They had chores to do, especially Saturdays. We raised cattle and hogs."

Mrs. Doye laments that the loss of a son is unforgettable. She is reminded of Rick every day in some shape or form. Pictures of Rick are in every room—next to her bed, next to the phone, and throughout the house. She remembers that the coach's wife who taught English had Rick's class write about "Democracy, what it means to me." Rick's writing assignment received First Place and was published in the local newspapers in the area. The beginning and ending of Rick's senior English paper are extremely poignant:

"Would you, as an individual, die for democracy? Or would it be your choice to live without it, rather than accept the responsibilities necessary to keep it alive? What does this nine-letter word mean to you? Ask yourself these questions…

"We, the younger set, are the key to democracy. We will be the ones owning, governing, and having to live in the world that we form. So, it is up to us whether democracy goes on living or is only a thing for our children, and our children's children to have read in the history books. It is up to us today to decide what we are going to do."

Mrs. Doye was the daughter of a farmer. "I had the best parents ever. On December 7th of 1941 I was a senior in high school. Pearl Harbor changed all our lives. I graduated from high school and went to work at the Rock Island Arsenal because the men were enlisting or getting drafted for war and the women were being hired for those jobs."

The Arsenal, a government weapons and ordnance manufacturing facility, is in northwestern Illinois between the cities of Rock Island, Illinois and Davenport, Iowa. During World War II, the Arsenal focused on artillery production and recoil mechanisms for the artillery, along with machine guns and ammo belt links. Lois Doye loved her job as a clerk typist. She and a friend lived with her Aunt and Uncle in East Moline, Illinois while they worked at the Arsenal. Her hobby in the off hours became writing to Pen Pals, writing to young men in the service. She had over forty pen pals which, as she explained, "kept me out of trouble."

Ricky Lee Doye at age six months
~ Courtesy of Mrs. Lois Doye

LaVerne was older than Lois. They began their family soon after they were married. "The boys were close in ages. Rick our youngest grew up faster as he was not left out of anything going on with the other two. He kept up with them. All three were teenagers at the same time. All three were starters on the basketball teams. All of them were in all sports. They were popular. Busy boys are better boys. Rick worked weekends at the Truck Stop and was proud of the motorcycle he had bought with his spending money. He was really proud of that cycle!"

Rick at two years of age ~ Courtesy of Mrs. Lois Doye, Ricky's mother, Prophetstown, IL

Rick had enlisted in the Marines with two other classmates from Annawan. Rick made friends all the way through boot camp. He wrote home to his parents as often as he could, mentioning the names of his friends. His mother sent packages. His older brothers also went to the service; he and his older brother Arlyn joined three days apart. Arlyn, the oldest, went to the Army and spent his time in Korea in tanks. Larry wanted to join the service, went to his physical in Chicago and was rejected. Lois exclaimed, "I had ulcers on top of ulcers with two gone from our household…

Rick and his motorcycle
Courtesy of Mrs. Lois Doye

Arlyn was deployed to Korea and was on the DMZ when the Army got a notice to him about Rick's death. The Red Cross was a great help. Arlyn didn't even have time to get any of his clothing; he was on the first cargo plane in the back part of it heading for the States. Cold, but he was finally home."

After Ricky Lee Doye's Final Honors and reality had set in, Mrs. Doye wrote to Leatherneck Magazine inquiring in the letters section if anyone knew Ricky Doye with the 27th Marines. It happened that Ricky's Platoon Commander in Alpha Company, Lieutenant Bill Black, was in the States in the hospital convalescing from his wounds received that same night Ricky was KIA. He saw the request and responded to Rick's mother. Ricky's mother recollects that "He had said that he had checked in on Rick and Michael Klinski at their position that night prior to his being

Ricky Lee Doye
Boot Camp 1967
~ Courtesy of Mrs. Lois Doye

wounded and did not know that Rick had been killed in that same assault." Black himself was seriously wounded in the initial assault and had been medically evacuated. He was at a loss for words. It stunned him that Rick, one of his Marines, was KIA.

Corporal Doug Carey manned the 106 Recoilless Rifle that night in the position next to where Rick and Mike Klinski were located. Haunted by Ricky Lee's death, Carey finally found Mrs. Doye through Lieutenant Bill Black and wrote to her. Evidently, she had been told rumors by others

Mrs. Doye's parents seated, standing L-R: Rick, Arlyn, Larry, Lois and LaVerne Doye
~ Courtesy of Mrs. Lois Doye

as to how Ricky was killed that night. To dispel those rumors Doug wanted her to know what he had personally experienced that night. He wrote her and explained what he remembered. "As you know Lieutenant Black was wounded. It was unlucky for him but lucky for us as it alerted us to an imminent assault. It is my opinion that even though Lieutenant Black was wounded (very unfortunate) that it saved many lives that night... That event alerted everyone. Ricky Lee (that's what we called him) was in a fighting hole next to mine. An RPG round suddenly hit his position. It was then that I left my position to see what had happened to him after the impact. I really don't remember how much time expired. I found Ricky some distance away from his fixed position. He had crawled from the fighting hole, where they had been, toward mine, maybe twenty or thirty feet. I have no idea how he made it that far...I did what I could for him and I believe his thoughts were of you, Mrs. Doye... Moments later NVA secured the Buddist Temple to the front of us and I went to

my 106 Rifle to respond to that threat... When I returned later to Ricky Lee, he had passed away. I have thought of your son and that night all my life wishing that I could have done something more for him...Any stories that you have heard about his death are false. Your son is a true American hero and died fighting for our God and country. He was and is still a great Marine!"

Mrs. Doye responded to Doug in a letter, "I am still amazed at you guys after forty-seven years still having all your feelings of grief on your minds. Not

Ricky Lee Doye and Michael R. Klinski (KIA 17 July 1968) reading a letter from Mom and enjoying her care package on top of a trench line east of Hue City
~ Courtesy of Mrs. Lois Doye

good for ya's. I am a Mother and this is different but wants you to know it is wonderful knowing Ricky Lee's not forgotten and thank you so very much for letting me know."

Lois recalled that she had received a letter from the committee who was responsible for constructing the Wall on the Mall in Washington, D. C. The letter indicated that someone had contributed a large amount of money toward the building of the new wall in Rick's memory. "I had to write and ask who—so I could thank them…and after they responded I found that it was Lieutenant Black and his father."

Driving her parents to winter in Florida, Lois once got to stop and finally meet Bill and Nancy Black and their three young sons. It was a true pleasure for her to meet him and his family. "He had to have been such a good officer. He had written that he'd go visit the Vietnam Wall—he did tracings of Rick's name for me."

Mrs. Doye wrote to Doug Carey thanking him for letting her know about her son, Ricky Lee. "I sure could have never, never received a letter that could mean any more to me than the one from Doug Carey…I am so relieved to learn of how it really was that 2 a.m. May 5, 1968. Mother's Day was coming up. Rick had sent a note wishing me one of the best Mother's Days. Trying to tell me of the terrible predicament there… Yes, thanks again to you—a Mother wonders and cares each day. I miss Ricky Lee constantly. His pictures are in every room and get a good night kiss…Thanks for listening and oh, so grateful for your letter!"

That day in late May when the two Marines came to her house to tell her of the tragic news of her son's death was forever etched in Lois Doye's memory. "Ricky's nineteenth birthday was about to come up in June and he had asked for a movie camera so that he could take movies while there in Vietnam. I had gotten the camera and was at the kitchen table boxing it up along with some goodies for Ricky." Mrs. Doye clearly remembers thinking the two men approaching the door were feed salesmen because they were dressed in tan shirts. She soon realized they were Marines and felt the immediate dread that all mothers feel. "My husband was out plowing. He came in from the field and we tried to deal with the unbelievable news."

Memorial Service and Final Honors for Ricky Lee Doye ~ Courtesy of Mrs. Lois Doye

Mrs. Doye remembered it took two long weeks before their son's body arrived home. Flags in the area were flown at half-mast to honor PFC Ricky Lee Doye.

The local paper reported that nearly 500 persons attended the funeral services on 18 May 1968 at the Calvary EC church at Hooppole, Illinois. The Reverend Lew Mills officiated and Ricky Lee Doye was interned in Hooppole Cemetery on that Armed Forces Day with a detachment of United States Marines present from Moline, Illinois performing Final Honors. America had lost another precious son to the fighting in South Vietnam in May of 1968, one of the worst months for casualties.

Manuel J. Gomez, KIA 17 April 1968

Gunnery Sergeant Gomez was a man of few words. When he asked Marines to do something it was clear what the task was and when it needed to be completed. "Gunny" Gomez, as he was referred to throughout Communications, ensured the 1st Battalion's entire tactical network remained active. This serious task demanded a no-nonsense leader at the forefront monitoring all that was happening within the nerve center of communications. The Gunny was that dutiful person. The equipment utilized for this task ranged in size and complexity from items like the AN/GRC-19 (Jeep-mounted radio) to the company/platoon/squad PRC-25 portable field radios. All this equipment and activity required efficient repair and backup to ensure continuing links with all the units within the Battalion and Regiment's tactical network. The generation of situation reports to Regimental Headquarters using this equipment provided Command and Control with an ongoing view of past and present events.

First Enlistment in the Navy

Manuel Gomez had joined the Navy as a young man in July of 1950. He served as a Quartermaster Class Signalman aboard the USS Princeton, CVA-37 during Korea. This duty entailed transmitting, receiving and logging all messaging traffic aboard ship. Using infrared systems, the Signalman would maneuver ships in formation, transmit emergency signals, tactical signals and routine communications.

The Princeton, an Essex-class aircraft carrier built after World War II, joined the Korean War effort and Task Force 77 off the Korean peninsula to provide combat air patrols and close air support beginning in late 1950 on through 1952. Gomez received a highly-coveted letter of recognition from the Commanding Officer of the USS Princeton for his work as a Signalman during that time. Gomez's son Gary pointed out that, "His cruise book reads like the book, *Bridges at Toko-Ri* by James Michener. The pilots were doing strikes on

Manuel Gomez aboard ship with shipmate
~ Courtesy of Gary Gomez, Manuel's son

the Korean Peninsula supporting the effort to contain the North Koreans. This was extremely dangerous but was an important support given during that conflict."

Born to Jose Gomez and Carmen Charvet-Gomez, Manuel Joseph began his life in the Bay area of California. Not much is known about his family. His father Jose was a Basque, and, it was told, had to flee Spain as a young man. In the late 1800s the Philippines had been a colony of Spain and somehow Jose ended up there. Jose married Carmen Charvet, of Filipino descent, while in the Philippines. A document from the Department of Commerce, dated 1917, that certified Jose was a lifeboat man, suggests he arrived in California in the early 1900s, and it was surmised that he probably arrived via the merchant marines.

In the 1950s Manuel lived with his father and attended school. His mother and father had divorced. As Manuel's son Gary remembers, "Dad was living with Grandfather and going to school in the Vallejo area. Back then grades 7 through 10 were classified as Junior High grades. It looks as if he graduated from Franklin Junior High in 1949. Looking at a newspaper clipping with no date, apparently, around this period there was a fire at the house where Dad and Grandfather were living. Dad was awakened by the fire. There was a kerosene heater and it caught fire somehow. Dad found his father sleeping and on fire. He somehow dragged his father out of the house, going back in to extinguish the flames. The fire department was called and it turned out that his father, Jose had first-degree burns. He had to be hospitalized."

Manuel's last days in the Navy were spent on the USS Jupiter AVS-8, a supply ship. Gomez decided to execute an inter-service transfer, being discharged from the Navy on 7 September 1955 as an E-4 and then receiving a "promotion" to PFC in the United States Marine Corps on 8 September 1955. This was a gutsy move which required mandatory Marine Corps Boot Camp before anything would be guaranteed. The transfer was a unique and healthy commitment to his future. Son Gary, going over his records and certificates, recites, "He graduated at the top of his class in the Radio-Telegraph-Operator's course. He had already acquired the basics from the Navy. He quickly made rank and by 1957 found himself as an E-5 Sergeant. In the late 1950s, he could remain in the southern California area. As an instructor in both Communications School at Marine Corps Recruit Depot-San Diego and Amphibious Training Command in Coronado he learned both the basics and intricacies of communications in the Marine Corps."

It turns out that Manuel somehow attended Vallejo Junior College in the Bay area before receiving his High School Diploma in San Diego in 1967. While still in the Navy he attended night classes. He lettered in football and baseball at the Junior College. His

Manuel J. Gomez playing football
~ Courtesy Gary Gomez,
Manuel's son

school was crowned Conference Champs in 1954. He also received a certificate of athletic achievement in baseball. He was very athletic and enjoyed sports.

Manuel met his wife-to-be in school there in Vallejo. She was Norwegian with the maiden name of Larsen. Her parents did not endorse the courtship at first, but after they were married and Manuel went into the Marine Corps they ended up loving him as one of their own. Gary recalls, "It was a neat story there…My Mother passed away from cancer in 1988. It was an aggressive brain cancer…Mom didn't talk much about Dad because it pained her to lose him. Although, she did tell me stories about Dad when I asked about him."

Manuel and Catherine Gomez
~ Courtesy of Gary Gomez,
their son

Gary remembered as a boy John F. Kennedy. Gary had watched the news on their black and white television when they lived at MCRD in San Diego. Kennedy had flown into San Diego and visited Marine Corps Recruit Depot to get a haircut. There were not large crowds in those days. Manuel had heard about it and put the whole family in the car and they drove to the barber shop with hopes of seeing JFK there. Gary recalls, "We just missed him… and my father was really disappointed. So, we got back in the car and went home. I was watching the news again on our TV and it showed him departing San Diego airport. So, I ran outside and got to see the president's Air Force One taking off…"

Manuel deployed for Japan in the early 1960s where he took up Judo and became a black belt. Looking through his memorabilia, Gary notes, "There are a lot of certificates from Japanese instructors. I think it was close to Camp Fuji. This was an unaccompanied tour [no family]. That was when my sister Laura and I lived with my Mother's parents in Vallejo."

Gary recalls the night Manuel made Staff Sergeant. "He at the time was also working as a baseball umpire for Little League and working part time as a bartender in the Staff NCO Club. The night he was pinned with his Staff Sergeant Chevrons, obviously, he had been celebrating. I had developed a fever that night. It was a bad fever and my temperature was off the charts…Mom called the Club and told him she needed him to come home and help. She was almost frantic over my condition and needed him there as moral support more than anything else. Dad was in his 'Alphas' (dress uniform) as I recall when he came home…He was always even-keeled, calm and collected. He instructs my mother and helps a little but doesn't get too involved… They give me a cold bath, reduce my temperature, dry me off and out the door, he goes back to the celebration. As Mother said, 'He was very predictable and never got overly excited about most things.' "

Staff Sergeant Manuel Gomez ~ Courtesy of Gary Gomez, son of Manuel

Staff Sergeant Gomez was with 2nd Battalion, 9th Marines on his first tour of the Republic of South Vietnam. He participated in Operation Hastings and as Gary recalls took a lot of photographs. Gary reminisces that, "He was a prodigious photographer and brought home a walking stick from that tour. That tour was in 1966. He made Gunnery Sergeant in 1967."

A Second Tour

As a Gunny, Manuel went to further communications schooling in San Diego. Shortly after that, the family settled in 29 Palms. Gary recalls they lived in a trailer and that was where he discovered giant desert turtles right outside of their home. Gary remembers distinctly overhearing his Mother and Father discussing his new orders for Vietnam. "I remember hearing them talking about it…Apparently, the orders came for another Communications Staff NCO to go…I remember this vividly because Mom and Dad were doing dishes. I could hear them in the next room. Dad wasn't overly disturbed but he was like… 'I can't believe this…' Apparently, this Staff NCO complained a lot and the short of the long was somehow Dad had to go in his place.

Gary, Dad, and Laura ~ Courtesy of Gary Gomez, Manuel's son

It was not Father's turn. He had just gotten back recently from his first tour. But my father didn't complain."

The Gomez family went to live with their Grandfather Larsen in Vallejo when Manuel deployed to Hawaii to join the 1st Battalion, 27th Marines prior to their deployment to Vietnam.

Gunnery Sergeant Manuel J. Gomez, Hue, April 1968 ~ Courtesy Gary Gomez, Manuel's son

Gunny Gomez ran a "tight ship" as the Marines under him used to say to each other. Each day was a long one for all Marines under his watchful eye. There was always something to do and when a Marine had a spare moment, sandbags needed filling. Watch at night was a 'given' most of time. There were not many nights that the Marines in the Communications Platoon had to themselves. When there were spare moments there were letters to write and to reread. The H&S Company Communication Marines went right to the field and conducted themselves as a rifle company would while also fulfilling their communications functions and duties.

The late afternoon of 17 April 1968 would turn ugly. The sun was ever present and the heat and humidity had become almost too much for most as the day was winding down. Everyone was concerned with their clear and present duties and the alarming news of Bravo Company walking into the NVA enclave a couple of klicks to the east of the CP. It had been a bloodbath.

Mortar Assault on the CP

Late in the afternoon author Corporal Grady Birdsong, who lived with the Gunny and was at his side constantly, was told by him to go to the Communication center. As Birdsong recalls:

"I remember this day. We were in our small living space in a makeshift tent east of the main schoolhouse CP. Staff Sergeant Johnson was doing paperwork or writing a letter as he sat legs crossed on his poncho. We did not have cots. We just slept on the ground with the poncho laid down. We didn't have many personal belongings other than our 782 gear with rifles and ammo. The small tent was nothing more than an oversized shade to shelter you from the rain. Gunnery Sergeant Gomez was standing next to the sandbags that ringed our makeshift shelter. I believe he was reading a letter he had just received from home. We had pulled the sides of the tent up to allow the light and any sort of a breeze there might be flow through our shelter. Gunny told me to go check on or retrieve something at the 'Comm Shack.'

"I started toward the Communications Center located in the midsection of the school building about twenty yards away. Startled by a sudden 'swoosh,' a thud hit the ground right in front of me. It happened so quick that I was at first curious, but within short seconds reacting to the following incoming rounds of enemy 82mm mortars and their impacts. That round that hit in front of me was a dud round. After that round impacted, all hell had broken loose and there was nowhere to go but hit the deck immediately. As soon as I was on the ground my legs began shaking uncontrollably. It seemed like forever that my legs shook; however, now that I look back it was only for a few short seconds. When the incoming rounds ceased I immediately got up and ran to a pre-dug trench close by toward the front of the school. Then came the second barrage and the third and a fourth and more...I became really scared. It seemed like the mortars would never stop raining down on us. They were landing all throughout the CP area with deadly accuracy destroying everything and downing anyone standing. A few of the rounds hit the roof of the school house. I wondered if anyone had made it out of there alive. The thought that I would get a direct hit while in that trench fixated my mind and it seemed like forever that I retained that thought. I couldn't get that thought out of my mind. Shortly after the barrage lifted, I ran back to my area only to find Staff Sergeant Johnson badly wounded and the Gunny lifeless."

When the assault ended, everyone stayed in their positions even though there was a lot of screaming and yelling. Everyone was preparing for a human ground assault next. That did not happen. The chaos of everyone running to the wounded and the screaming was extraordinary. Bodies were lying everywhere. Some of the second-tour Corpsmen and Marines in the Battalion finally brought order to the situation and began a much-needed, orderly process to treat the most seriously wounded, and form a makeshift triage process.

The target area was the nerve center of the Battalion where most of the Communications and Headquarter Marines functioned. Amongst the dead and wounded lay the beloved Gunnery Sergeant in charge of Battalion Communications, Manuel Gomez. The Gunny had been killed by one of the first explosions impacting almost where he was standing reading a letter from home.

The Marines of 1st Battalion had lost five KIAs and twenty-four WIAs, their best men in that late afternoon mortar assault. It seemed like the end of the world for some.

The Visitors

The dreaded knock on the door by the Casualty Affairs personnel reached the Larsen household within hours of Manuel's death. His wife and children, Gary and Laura, were living with Catherine's father in Vallejo, California. Gary remembers vividly when the knock came. "I happened to have just taken a bath. I was eleven years old at the time. I knew somebody had knocked and come inside. I could hear the unfamiliar male voices. I recall it had an 'introductory tone' to it. Grandpa quickly came into the bathroom and told me, 'You need to come on out here, Son!' So, I wrapped a towel around myself and as I was walking out into the room, I remember hearing the Marine Captain exclaim, 'Oh my gosh...' A Chaplain accompanied the Captain and went right into a script. He informed us of the details, reading it from a paper he had in hand."

Catherine broke down sobbing uncontrollably. Laura started crying too as Gary recalls, "I think it was because Mom was crying...my little sister was only four years old. The Captain and Chaplain did not stay long which struck me as appropriate. I was glad because we were all consumed by the news and not fully believing this was happening."

Gunnery Sergeant Manuel Joseph Gomez was laid to final rest in Golden Gate National Cemetery, San Bruno, California. Almost all of the family came for the services. Roy Gallihugh, a decorated Marine, had married Manuel's aunt. Roy had completed two tours in Vietnam and had run into Manuel while each was there on previous tours. He also attended the funeral and Final Honors.

Laura, Catherine, and Gary Gomez receiving
Manuel's awards ~ Courtesy of Gary Gomez

Gary was surprised when his family was summoned to the Naval Base in Vallejo, California, after the burial. Manuel had received a Navy Commendation Medal with Combat V posthumously. Gary tells of that day, "There were a band and a platoon of Marines. The three of us, my mother and my sister attended. There was a Colonel and he read the citation. At the time, I did not know the order of precedence of medals. And I read the whole thing, what had happened. Lieutenant Jesse Hand, the H&S Company Commander, had sent a note of what had happened. For me, at the time it was like my father was receiving the Medal of Honor. It was an impressive ceremony, what they did for my family, considering what had happened. Everything in my mind now is that...all this process was 'properly attended to.'"

The Navy Commendation Medal Citation reads:

For meritorious service, while serving as Communications Chief of the First Battalion, Twenty-Seventh Marines, First Marine Division from 23 February to 17 April 1968. During this period, Gunnery Sergeant GOMEZ performed his duties in an exemplary and highly professional manner. Displaying exceptional initiative, he developed and administered the plan of communication support for the battalion and tirelessly trained his personnel to react in a timely and effective manner to any situation. Exhibiting sound judgment and managerial skill, he obtained optimum utilization of personnel, supplies, and equipment, contributing significantly to the efficient operation of his unit. On 17 April, Gunnery Sergeant GOMEZ was mortally wounded during an enemy mortar

attack. Due to his thorough training and foresight, his section maintained vital communications throughout the remainder of the battle. By his outstanding leadership, resourcefulness and unfaltering devotion to duty, Gunnery Sergeant GOMEZ upheld the highest traditions of the United States Naval Service.
The Combat "V" is authorized.
FOR THE SECRETARY OF THE NAVY
JOHN J. HYLAND
ADMIRAL, U. S. NAVY
COMMANDER IN CHIEF U.S. PACIFIC FLEET

Gary Gomez enlisted in the Marine Corps in 1975, serving as an enlisted mortar man and M60 machine gunner. He was commissioned a Second Lieutenant in 1980 and after a brief tour as a rifle Platoon Commander with 3/6, Gary was accepted to Naval Flight School, earning his wings and served as an F-4S Phantom pilot with Marine Fighter Attack Squadron VMFA-235, in Marine Corps Air Station Kaneohe Bay, Hawaii. Transitioning into the Navy, Gary became an F-14 Tomcat pilot with the U. S. Navy Fighter Squadron VF-84, Naval Air Station in Oceana, Virginia. Flying combat missions in Desert Storm, Gary was awarded the Strike Air Medal and Navy Commendation Medal with Combat "V." Gary proudly proclaims, "I never thought I would receive the same Medal that my father had received years earlier."

Gary did not feel at the time his father was killed that he was destined to go into the Marine Corps. In hindsight, Gary believed more than anything that he just wished for an understanding of what his father had gone through. "I was reading everything about what was going on in Vietnam…What was the environment like over there for them?…Where is this place?…What are they doing?…sort of like the chants of the students in the 1960s, 'What are we fighting for?' I was watching all of the movies, *Coming Home* with Jane Fonda, *The Boys in Company C*… The closest thing I could do as an adult was go and do the same thing… And so I enlisted."

Grady Birdsong tells his remaining Marine buddies that, "Gunny Gomez would be extremely proud of his son's accomplishments as a Marine and Naval aviator!"

Gunnery Sergeant Manuel J. Gomez grave marker ~ photo courtesy of Shawn Chiasson & Larry Panzica, friends of the author

Danny Lee Grimshaw, KIA 23 August 1968

Danny Lee Grimshaw began life close to the banks of the Columbia River in southeastern Washington. Lewis and Clark had made their epic trek through the area 144 years before in the early 1800s. Bobbi, Danny's oldest sister by five years, recalls the birth of her little brother, "My mother was lying on the couch and there was this tiny monkey-looking kid. That was Danny. That was my first impression of him. I thought that he was just about the cutest little tiny monkey kid I had ever seen…!" Both of his older sisters would continue to dote on this little guy throughout all his growing years.

Danny Lee singing with sisters ~ Courtesy of Bobbi Grimshaw-Nagel, sister of Danny

Danny had a wonderful childhood with a family that loved him immensely and grandparents that watched over him most of his young life. Danny was destined to be a loyal and loving young son of this close-knit family.

Young Danny began learning the basics of music at an early age. His older sisters both grew to become accomplished musicians. In wanting to be a part of their world of music, Danny began developing his singing ability and became by all standards a very good singer. In high school Danny joined a group called the "Mad Hatters," an award-winning vocal ensemble. His younger brother tells of his music ability, "His voice could be picked out of any group on just about any song. I believe he was known for his perfect pitch."

His mother's father, a hardworking farm laborer, always took Danny with him to the fields as a young boy. His younger brother Terry always tagged along, too. During the summer, the potato crops had to be irrigated with hand-placed siphon tubes into the rows. Danny and Terry loved going with Grandpa and helping him. His grandmother would pack a lunch for everyone, including a small thermos with watered-down coffee laced with a lot of milk for the boys.

Danny Lee Grimshaw as a child ~ Courtesy of Terry Grimshaw, younger brother of Danny

The younger Terry remembers going to the fields with them both and goofing around the truck all day long while Danny and Grandpa worked the irrigation rows. He recalls,

"There was nobody like my Grandfather. He loved us kids and we loved him and being with him. It was the highlight of our lives back then. My mother worked a lot of hours as a nurse and my father was working in Seattle. Our grandparents basically raised us during those days. My mother worked very hard most of her life. I can remember that she worked shifts so her closet, when you walked into it, would be full of white nurse uniforms. She didn't have a lot of time for herself. She always was concerned about us her whole life and making sure we got raised and had all the necessities. I can still remember when Grandpa would take us down to the drug store for a special treat. They had a little soda fountain there and he would put us up on that fountain counter. In those days, he wore PayDay coveralls and one of those small brim LBJ type hats. He never carried a wallet but always had his coin purse on him and would shuffle those coins out and buy us something special at that fountain. It was really something when he did that for us."

SCHOOL DAYS 1957-58
EASTGATE

Danny Grimshaw, Grade School years ~ Courtesy of Bobbi J. Nagel, oldest sister

Danny was lucky to be surrounded by his musically talented sisters who both played the violin. His older sister, Bobbi (married name Nagel) pursued the fiddle quite vigorously. She became a National Champion Fiddler in 2010, winning the National Old-time Fiddlers' Championship in the senior division that year at Weiser, Idaho. She tells of that experience, "I have gone there off and on over the years and most generally, I have placed in the top five fiddlers. The 2010 Championship was my swan song."

Terry and Danny were close even though they were seven years apart in age. Danny always looked after his younger brother. Terry recalls an outbuilding at their grandparent's home which they called the "Cabin," a workshop where Danny and Terry would stay quite a lot. It was an adventure for them to be away from the house and the elders. The cabin had a dirt floor and a small bedroom off to the side. Terry tells of the times that his mother would bring home used heavy-glass IV bottles from the hospital, "Danny would make worm beds with dirt, burlap sacks and used coffee grounds. He would, for the fun of it, hook up the IV bottles filled with water and adjust them to drip into the worm beds. He would raise worms to sell to

L-R: Danny, Jerry, & Bobbi with their violins ~ Courtesy of Terry Grimshaw, brother of Danny

people that would come down the road who were going fishing. I thought it was more for entertainment than anything."

Danny attended Kennewick High School and graduated in 1965. It was the same high school that his mother had graduated from in 1939. His mother's graduating class was very small as was Danny's. Danny excelled and enjoyed participating in most musical events at Kennewick High. Sister Bobbi recollects Danny's childhood, "I remember when we posed for a picture and Danny had a little fiddle. I don't remember him playing that much but he had a beautiful singing voice. Later in high school, he was close to the music teacher. The music teacher was Mr. William H. Ames. He was one of those music teachers loved by the entire community. I remember him very well because he sang at Danny's funeral."

MAD HATTER BOYS

LOCATION RECORDING SERVICE · 2201 BURBANK BLVD. · BURBANK, CALIFORNIA

The Mad Hatter Boys of Kennewick High School ~ Courtesy of Terry Grimshaw
(Danny top row, second in from right)

Bobbi, the oldest, has kept Danny's memory with her all these years. "He was like what you might call the 'golden child!' I am not saying that just because he is gone or that he was my brother…He was just a really, special little person. Everyone gravitated toward him because of his personality. He was just real family oriented…loved his family, especially very close to our mother. He was always there; he was always very giving. I don't ever remember him being mean in any way. He didn't tease others. It is really hard to put into words."

Danny received a wood-burning set for Christmas one year as a youngster. They were the popular thing to have in the 1950s. Bobbi told of the cherished little plaque that she has held dear for her all of the past years, "Danny gave me a little plaque that he had made for me with his wood-burning set. I don't know where he found that odd shaped piece of wood. It was light-colored wood and it had a notch in one corner. It must have been a left-over piece of wood? He wrote me what amounts to a letter on it. I just recently gave it to our youngest brother, Terry. I wanted him to have it for a keepsake."

His middle sister Jerry was not only close in years to Danny but close to him as most brothers and sister become as children. Jerry reminisces, "When Danny and I weren't running through the fields or fighting over who got the most batter licking the cake bowl, I was his 'little mother.' I was always teaching him something, usually what I was learning in school myself, i.e., Spanish. Every night I would read to him; his favorite (and mine to read) was *The Little Engine That Could*. Once I helped him enter a contest to name a TV cartoon character—a beaver that we named Bartholomew. He won Second Place. We thought of course, that it should have come in First…In playground skirmishes; he was called 'Dirty Shirt Dan.' I was shocked! My tender-hearted little brother, in fights? Well, boys will be boys. He was sometimes a daredevil, careening down the street on the handlebars of a friend's bicycle. Next thing you know there's a screeching trip to the ER, to stitch up his head. Prophetic, perhaps."

Jerry further recalls that when their Grandfather Carpenter died, Danny was sent home on leave. Instead of connecting with friends, she remembered that he spent his entire leave with family—her sons, reading them stories and promising camping trips when he came home again. "One Saturday he took me dancing. At the time, the bars in Washington closed at midnight. So, we piled into his car and drove to Oregon, where the bars were open until 2:00 a.m. While I danced, he sat alone out in the bar area, drinking Cokes and talking to the bartender." That was the last time Jerry was together with her brother, Danny.

Danny had enlisted in the Navy for the Nursing Program right after High School. Terry tells of Danny enlisting in the Navy, "Danny was a very good young man and wanted to go into nursing so he signed up for the Navy for their Nursing Program. I think he was inspired a lot by my mother's career in nursing. Of course, the Marine Corps gets their Corpsmen from the Navy. As far as him going into the Marines, I am not sure he would have volunteered for the Marines but was put there by fate. I am sure, had he lived, he would have been proud of his service with Marines. I sure am proud of him."

Danny had a tape recorder that he purchased while in Vietnam and sent tapes home to his family often. Through this device, he could tell the family back home what was going on, his feelings about the country and the people, and his future. Vietnam, at the time, was not a progressive country and was still basically an agricultural economy. Everything was centered on rice. In one of the tapes he explains his view of the country: "The Vietnamese have a poor economic situation over here. Everything is rice. You can walk for miles and miles and miles…and all you will see is rice. Everywhere you go there is rice. Some of the other areas there is sugar; some have coffee or rubber trees but all I have seen in my humping is rice. One rice paddy after another and the climate is such that they grow it all year long or so it seems. I never see the entire countryside stripped of growing at the same time. One of the farmers will be growing rice and another will be harvesting and another one will be planting it. They are good farmers. They work constantly. They will flood whole rice fields…"

In another segment, Danny comments on the Vietnamese women, "I don't know if I have told you in my letters or not…take the average Vietnamese woman about twenty-five years old…and this woman is liable to be walking down the street carrying something and if she feels the call of nature she will stop right there, roll up her pant leg and let it trickle down…And she chews beetle nut and her teeth are black and filthy looking, they look terrible. I am sitting here in my hooch and I can watch some farmers across the way irrigate a field. They are doing it probably like they did back in Christ's time…They are taking buckets of water and throwing the water up into the field. There are about twenty people working on it. They don't seem to want progress. I mean all of this is just my opinion."

Life in the field with a line company of Marines was Spartan, to say the least. There was not the time for anything other than to look for the enemy. And that was harrowing for the most part because the area the Marines operated in had booby traps. Marines became wary and untrusting of the Vietnamese still out in the "villes" and hamlets of the countryside. The local people walked the paths and trails day in and day out and never tripped the booby traps. They knew where they were placed. When the Marines walked through the area they tripped them and either got killed or wounded.

Danny angrily exclaims in his tape to his family, "We know these people know where the booby traps are at…We sweep through the villes and there are always children and old women. On one sweep, there were about four children and one old woman lying in one of the hooches. Before we went into that village we had called in arty on it because they were shooting at us from the damn place. When you do that, the combatants will leave. Well, this old woman and these children hadn't left. A lot of these people won't get out. It is their home place. They will take their chances and they all have bomb shelters. Every home has a hole dug down into the ground where they can go if they come under attack. When we walked into this village these children had some serious shrapnel wounds that were days old. I treated them as best I could. I am not sure what happened to them after we left."

The Vietnamese people in the area where Danny served, south of Da Nang and Go Noi, were for the most part sympathetic to the Communists and were living from hand to mouth. Little children would beg for anything: food, cigarettes, and chocolates. They would follow the Marines and shout out, "You give me chop-chop?" Or they would beg for cigarettes, "You, give me one cigarette?" The familiar question would always come from some of them, "You, souvenir me?" The Marines could always find a Ham and Beans to give them because that was the most disliked of all the C-rations. Most Marines felt sorry for the kids and gave in to their demands.

In another segment of the tapes sent home, Danny described that as a senior Corpsman he had seven other Corpsmen working under him and indicated that they did most of the field work and he was responsible for the admin work. "I do take patrols for them and I do go out and relieve them whenever possible and give them a break. They work their ass off…That is a fact! And it isn't right that I set in the rear constantly because I picked up a little rate and they are constantly on patrols. So, I do take patrols to relieve them whenever I can."

HM2 Danny L. Grimshaw, D Co, treating a child ~ Courtesy of Terry Grimshaw

Writing and receiving letters brought mixed emotions for some. Danny preferred to talk on the tape recorder and send the tapes in the mail rather than sit down and write a letter. However, he indicated in his tapes that he was very glad to get letters from loved ones. His mother had placed his APO address in the local newspaper and Danny began receiving letters from many in his hometown of Kennewick, Washington. Danny revealed his mixed feelings about receiving letters from some of those people. "I am going to start a letter to Carol; she is some sweet five foot, five inches, 175-pound girl that decided she wanted to write to me and uh, she has got a pleasant personality, simple, but pleasant, very pleasant so I write her. Somebody put my name in the newspaper and I received 'beaucoup' letters, many, many letters…some girls and about twenty or thirty of them in fact. Most of them were tiny-boppers and childish or something… and… eh… wrote with this, 'We got a poor serviceman in Vietnam' attitude and it made me sick. And I already got a bunch of sick Vietnamese kids here to take care of…And Mother, I don't want any more so don't tell the paper."

Rumors knew no boundaries for the Marines in I Corps. Most came from within the ranks. There was one rumor floating around throughout the Battalion that 1st Battalion would return to CONUS starting 15 July. Danny sets the record straight in a segment of his tape home, "There was a rumor that we would go back July 15th. Well, it is now July 27th, so the rumor wasn't a good one. I should say accurately: This lag in time comes from the fact that the Army unit that took our place arrived on time but they requested thirty days' time to get acclimated with the area before they took over our TAOR…Tactical Area of Responsibility. So they extended it up to thirty days at least so we will be here until August 15th at the very earliest. And if this Battalion goes back to Hawaii then I have good chances of going back there with them. And I will be too short or too little time for them to bring me back to Nam again if that happens."

Hope springs eternal with all combatants in any war, and the chance for a respite from the daily grind is on the minds of everyone. Danny's thoughts not only of rotating back to Hawaii but of also being sent on R&R enter into the conversation on a taping session to his folks back home, "I am not sending any money back from this paycheck. I have $300 and some odd dollars coming to this paycheck. With R&R coming up, I am going to have to have some money in my pocket. I am going to try and go to Bangkok and have myself a devil of a time. Bangkok is noted for being able to show servicemen a good time, especially on R&R. I chose it above Tokyo, Australia, or Hawaii, simply because more people ask for those places…And I stand a better chance of getting mine sooner. I am overdue in fact; most people have already had R&R so almost any day now I should be going…It is seven days of pure rest and relaxation and wasting time and money. And I will go through those $300. And I think it will be well worth it."

As with everyone the thought of rotating back to "the world," as it was referred to, entered the daily thought process. Along with dreams of going back home came the wishful thinking of safety and comfort. Danny ruminates on the tape, "I dream of being able to walk down the street with a pair of trousers that are light and comfortable with a pair of light shoes, not combat boots and have a nice shirt on…being able to walk down the street and not think the next tree line is going to have somebody in it…or walk through the park and not step on something that is going to blow up on me…or if somebody is going to yell, 'Corpsman up' and I have to go charging up to them…Some of the guys I have seen have been pretty badly messed up. It is a bit of a nightmare at times. I don't want to paint a bad picture but there have been times that I have been so scared that I could scream. Most of the time it has been spent in waiting or going to someplace…And a small percent of the time you are actually getting shot at and in contact with the enemy. Most of our time is spent in looking for an elusive enemy."

He continues on with his daydreams about what he will do when he returns home. "I daydream a lot. I dream about going home, taking a girl to a movie, taking a girl to a drive-in movie, taking a girl to dinner or to a dance or just taking her anyplace she wants to go. I daydream about buying me a camper, a pickup camper. I want one of those real bad and I probably can't afford one…I don't have a lot in the bank. I have to think of college. I think I am not going to be up for it when the time comes. I am almost afraid of college. I am not up to the study-for-the-course work. I think about the time and effort that I am going to have to put into it. I am sure that I am intelligent enough, but have I got the patience? Have I got the drive to stick with it? I will have to get a job to pay my way. I just can't go home and live with my mother now. I am a grown man…I have been lucky, I have been real lucky. Somebody upstairs is on my side…I tried very hard a few times to get into the area where things were happening, where people were getting wounded and killed and every time I transferred into that area it subsided…It was always the other Platoon Patrol Bases that were getting hit, never the one where I was at the time."

On 23 August 1968, the Marines and Corpsmen of Delta Company were ordered by 1st Battalion, 27th Marines Commanding Officer Major Kenneth Skipper to counter-attack and retake the Cam Le Bridge on Route 1 south of Da Nang. An offensive had again erupted all over the Da Nang area in the early morning hours. Nineteen units in the Da Nang area recorded hundreds of mortar and 122mm rocket rounds in and around their positions. Three company positions held by the 27th Marine Regiment, headquarters of the 11th Marines, and three Combined Action Platoons in the 7th Marines' TAOR endured probes and assaults on their positions. Sappers penetrated many perimeters and positions in the surrounding southern area close to the Marble Mountain Air Facility.[1]

This was a bad day for the Marines of Delta Company, 1/27. Their beloved senior Corpsman, Danny Lee Grimshaw, died from wounds sustained from enemy rifle fire as he moved to the front of the skirmish line to tend to one of his wounded Marines.

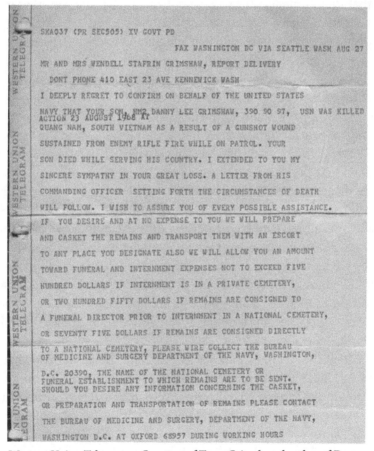

Western Union Telegram ~ Courtesy of Terry Grimshaw, brother of Danny

Danny's younger brother Terry recounts the night he learned of his older brother's death. "My parents were in Seattle at the time…I was living with Grandmother and had laid down for the night and a knock came on the door. I thought it strange and listened intently and I remember hearing my grand-mother letting out a gasp. It was a low screaming type of gasp and that startled me because I had never heard her do that before. I immediately got out of bed and went down the hallway and into the living room. My Uncle Don, my father's brother was there with another man. From their conversation, I learned right there that Danny had been killed. And you know, I knew what it meant but it just did not register."

Bobbi, the oldest sister, was married with two tiny girls living in Everett, Washington and was pregnant with her son at the time. "My mom called me…I could tell right away from her voice, she could barely talk, that something terrible had happened. She told me that the men who had come to tell them that Danny had been killed were there with her. She wanted me to talk with them…I didn't want to talk with them…"

Terry remembers that his mother aged quickly after the news of Danny's death and never was the same again. She talked about how there had been mistakes made in transporting the dead home from Vietnam and that possibly there had been a mistake made with Danny and it wasn't really him in the casket.

Bobbi recalls, "My girls and I got on a Greyhound bus and went home to be with the family…The whole family was there and was just in turmoil. I know my mom probably had a hard time feeding everybody. The military was so kind and help-ful. However, they would not let her look at Danny in the casket. She was bound and determined to see him. I remember seeing one of the telegrams and it stated 'remains not viewable.' She thought there had been a mistake. I had an aunt who was close to the family and she even asked if she could see him or see his hands and they wouldn't allow her to view him either. Bottom line, I was always grateful they didn't let her view him."

She also added that a young sailor was escorting the casket and that he did not know Danny, but that he had been with Danny's casket all the way home. Almost all of the family was at the funeral. The flag was presented to Terry, Danny's little brother. To honor her younger brother, Bobbi gave her son, born a few months later, the middle name Lee after Danny's middle name.

Sister Jerry tells, "The shock of his death had just begun to abate when two weeks later, the young sailor who had accompanied his body home came knocking on our door. We all felt sorry for this young man and the onerous duty he had been assigned. The grieving started anew…Danny's death descended a blanket of grief on an entire family, one that has never lifted—and never will."

In Memory Of
DANNY LEE GRIMSHAW

Born
February 15, 1947

Passed Away
August 23, 1968

Services At
Mueller's Chapel Of The Falls
Kennewick, Washington
Saturday, September 7, 1968, 2:00 P. M.

Bishop Louis Marsden, Officiating
Assisted By
Roy King, Norris Brown and Ken Allen

Ermenie Ditch, Organist

William Ames, Soloist

Casket Bearers
Steven Grimshaw   Dick Capistrant
Michael Blair   Roy Hutchins
Bob Kubick   Don Nagel

Color Bearers and Firing Squad
By U. S. Navy Personnel

Concluding Services
Desert Lawn Memorial Park
Kennewick, Washington

Memorial Service Program
~ Courtesy of Bobbi J. Nagel,
Danny's sister

Terry never cried about his brother's death until years later when he visited the Vietnam Veterans Memorial in Washington, D. C. "When I approached it you really couldn't see it…other than it was a large V notched out in the dirt. We had to go around the end of it to see the hundreds of names on the front side of it…And there were more men than I had ever seen before standing in front of it…some in wheelchairs, some standing, some kneeling, some crying…A lot of them had parts of uniforms and medals on them, all there at the base of that granite wall. There were grown men bawling their eyes out. It must have been hard for the men that survived and had lived through that war. It was there that I think I finally had closure on my brother's death!"

Bobbi reminisces, "My daughter visited recently and we went through Danny's things, his awards, pictures, and newspaper clippings…We organized everything in an archival arrangement. His letters home are displayed so that you can read them without touching them. There were letters that he had written to my mother and his grandmother. Danny sent tapes home. It is still very difficult for me to listen to those tapes. He was so optimistic in the tapes. He was making plans…He was only twenty-one years old."

Terry still has vivid memories of his beloved mother. She would frequently touch him on the shoulders and make him look into her eyes and exclaim, "Terry, don't ever do that to me…do not join the service…" She died at seventy-six years of age, a broken heart still grieving for her oldest son, Danny Lee.

Letter to Danny's parents from Captain M. T. Farmer ~ Courtesy of Terry Grimshaw, Danny's brother

Danny Lee Grimshaw grave site ~ Courtesy of the Grimshaw family

Letters were sent to family members detailing how their loved one died. Then-H&S Company Commander, 1st Lieutenant Jesse Hand, recalls, "The deceased Marine/Corpsman's family notified by a telegram received an immediate visit by a Marine representative, perhaps a local reserve officer or Chaplain or both, whoever was on duty in that area. A signed 'death letter' following those visits was then generated by the H&S Company Commanding Officer. Line Company Commanders in the field had other concerns and relied on the support of these H&S Commanders."

Lieutenant Hand explained that this process evolved from previous wars and that helping the family move toward "closure" was the goal. The reporting officer would have to do some homework, like finding out about the personal traits of the KIA from the men and officers that knew him, before constructing a letter. It was important that the entire chain of command become involved and the incident of death was reviewed by everyone before being sent to the family. The task was daunting, but designed to omit false reporting. The procedure eventually developed into the present Military Personnel Casualty Matters, Policies, and Procedures, DOD Instruction 1300.18.

Danny was eventually awarded the Bronze Star medal for a truly heroic action on the last day of his life:

> *Observing a companion attempting to remove the wounded man from a position dangerously exposed to the hostile fire, Petty Officer Grimshaw fearlessly rushed forward to render assistance. Realizing that the man would probably die without immediate medical attention, he disregarded the intense enemy fire impacting near him as he entered the hazardous area and began treating the casualty. Refusing to allow others to endanger themselves in further attempts to move the injured man, Petty Officer Grimshaw remained in the fire-swept area administering the life-sustaining first aid until he was mortally wounded by the hostile fire.*
>
> *The Combat "V" is authorized.*
>
> H.W. BUSE, JR.
> LIEUTENANT GENERAL, USMC
> COMMANDING, FLEET MARINE FORCE, PACIFIC

Danny was truly one of the heroes of our 27th Marines!

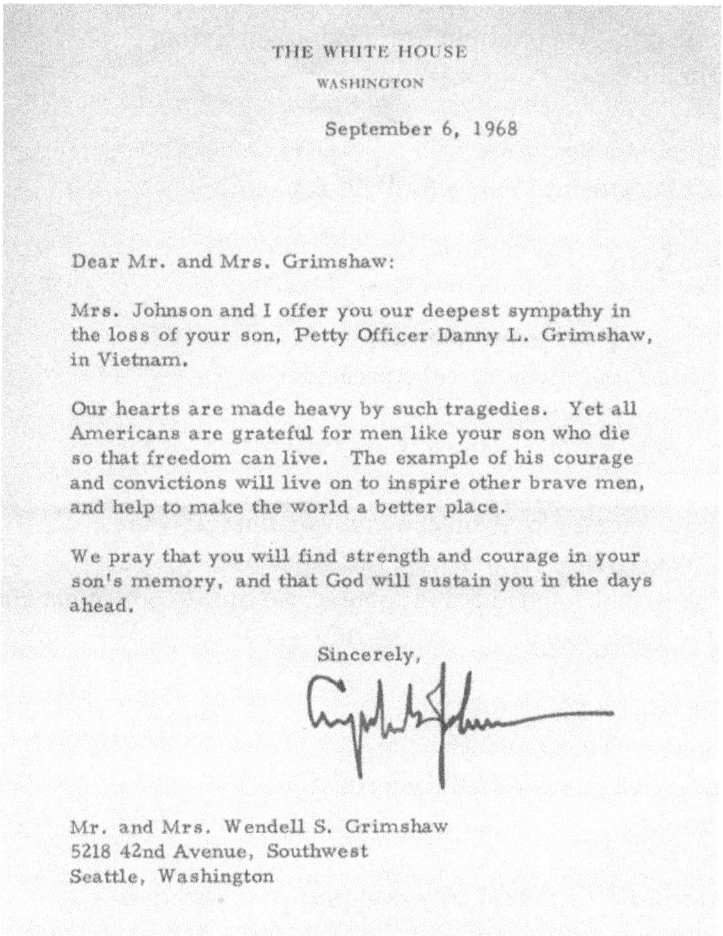

THE WHITE HOUSE
WASHINGTON

September 6, 1968

Dear Mr. and Mrs. Grimshaw:

Mrs. Johnson and I offer you our deepest sympathy in
the loss of your son, Petty Officer Danny L. Grimshaw,
in Vietnam.

Our hearts are made heavy by such tragedies. Yet all
Americans are grateful for men like your son who die
so that freedom can live. The example of his courage
and convictions will live on to inspire other brave men,
and help to make the world a better place.

We pray that you will find strength and courage in your
son's memory, and that God will sustain you in the days
ahead.

Sincerely,

Mr. and Mrs. Wendell S. Grimshaw
5218 42nd Avenue, Southwest
Seattle, Washington

Letter signed by President Lyndon B. Johnson ~ Courtesy of Terry Grimshaw

Danny's older sister and "little Mother," Jerry Grimshaw Beamer, composed the following poem for Danny many years after his death.

TEN MINUTES AGO

After all these years, I still miss you.
I wouldn't recognize you,
But see you often: in a rainstorm, a foggy winter day,
A familiar song.

I think of our footprints in the cement, hopscotch,
Post office, frozen tag. As my children played, I wondered
Did I give them what you would have yours?
Chase a butterfly.

We camped and fished and dreamed and wished. Older and wiser,
I read to you, taught you Spanish, scolded your clumsiness.
It's forgotten now—even the punishment for whispering
Together in the dark.

I can laugh now at your forgetfulness,
The hours of practicing "Yellow Bird" off key.
I hear it now,
And weep silently.

I published your poetry, my meticulous typewriter and I,
Our one gift to your memory. No one cared.
Your class reunion didn't want it—
Too much "sadness," "that senseless war."

But dammit! You *died* for them and *that* war. But they were
Too busy. Waterskiing, reminiscing, getting drunk,
Comparing wrinkles and kids and spouses. No time to remember you
Grinning from ear to ear.

I don't visit you on Memorial Day.
Others look at me curiously when I say,
"Oh, I prefer Valentine's Day, the Fourth of July,
A dozen roses."

You loved roses. Valentine's Day was almost your birthday.
On the Fourth, we made sand castles and celebrated independence.
Wasn't *that* why you died? Independence? No one understands,
So I give up, shrugging.

Driving through a stormy cloudy sunset many autumns ago, finally
I knew you were somehow content. In that moment, I buried my sorrow,
Relinquishing it to the storm, losing it in silent, lonely,
Private memories.

Your loving sister,
Jerry

Gregory Woods, KIA 23 August 1968 – A Debt Remembered

Gregory Woods was killed on 23 August of 1968 along with two other Marines on a Platoon Patrol Base close to the village of Cam Ne (4). His Bravo Company Platoon was assaulted by combined NVA/VC forces, which they successfully repulsed, although with Marine losses. Amongst the dead were PFC Ricky G. Harrison, PFC Robert J. Miller, and PFC Gregory Woods. Five other Marines were wounded in the attack.

PFC John T. Shabel, known as "Tom" to most, was very close to Gregory Woods. Tom reminisced about his buddy Greg and how they had come through the Corps together, "He was my friend and a great guy. We had gone through BITS, ITR, and Staging together and were assigned to Company B, 1/27. What made it even greater was the fact that we were in the same platoon and squad but in different Fire Teams. Our platoon had security in an area of known enemy activity that August [grid coordinate AT970697]. It was about to be the beginning of the 'Third Offensive,' unknown to us. That night my Fire Team drew ambush duty and Greg's team had perimeter watch. My team was out on the ambush when the gooks hit our patrol base perimeter. The attack began with RPGs. The Sappers were almost on top of the M60 gunner's position before he realized it was gooks. They had fired a green star cluster and he thought it was an ambush coming into the wire. The NVA Sappers made their way into the perimeter throwing a satchel charge into Woods' fighting hole, killing him and the other two Marines instantly. When I returned from ambush duty that early morning, I helped put my buddy Greg on the chopper. I was devastated!"

Greg Woods had a girlfriend back home in St. Louis, Missouri who happened to be pregnant with his child when he was killed. Tom had only heard Greg talk about his girlfriend and did not know her personally. When Greg had been killed, Tom still owed him five dollars that he had borrowed earlier in their tour together. It bothered Tom that he still owed Greg the five even though he was now dead. Five dollars was a lot of money to an enlisted Marine in 1968. When Shabel moved to St. Louis in the 1970s he decided to try and find Greg's family. Tom recalls, "I tried all the Woods in the entire metropolitan area. You have no idea how many Woods there were in St. Louis at that time. So, with no luck after a good college try, I kind of gave up. Several years ago, I saw a posting on our 27th Marine web page. There was a Marine who was looking for information on Greg Woods with the 1st Battalion, 27th Marines. He had some pictures of Woods and wanted to give them to the family. I emailed the Marine and together we began the search anew. As luck would have it, after some time in searching we found his son. The son was living in Denver. I emailed him and introduced myself and asked for his address. I told him that I had something to send him."

Tom Shabel then called his banker and asked him to run the compound interest on five dollars from 23 August 1968, to the present. The banker quickly responded and Shabel wrote a check for that amount and placed it in a letter to the son, telling him what it was all about. Shabel recalls, "The boy was flabbergasted to get the check and I received a heartfelt thank you from Greg's son. I felt very pleased and relieved that I was able to find his son, tell him about my close buddy, his father and clear my debt while remaining Semper Fi to Greg!"

Epilogue

"There are no great men.
Just great challenges which ordinary men,
Out of necessity, are forced by circumstances to meet."
~ Admiral William R. "Bull" Halsey, USN WWI & II

Out of War: A Renewal of Semper Fidelis

During its deployment in South Vietnam, the United States Marine Corps found itself involved in most major engagements and immersed in a diverse range of environments. From the first beach landings in 1965 to hellacious humps through triple-canopy jungles, rice paddies and thick hedgerows, Marines went directly to the enemy wherever they were throughout Vietnam. Though hamstrung by politics and unclear strategies for winning the war, these men performed above and beyond the call of duty.

Whatever the mission—in the case of 1/27, securing the Hue City canal area out to the coast and then deploying south of Da Nang to secure the Go Noi Island area while conducting Operation Allen Brook—these 1/27 warriors marched "To the sound of the Guns" as did earlier Marines on Iwo Jima.

Marine Corps traditions which began in the American Revolution have continued throughout all of America's wars and are "time-tested." Despite all the challenges these men faced, they consistently demonstrated the single dominant characteristic that bond Marine brethren of every generation and their traditions closely together like glue—"Semper Fidelis," Always Faithful.

Most Marine combat veterans of the Vietnam War will not talk in a lot of detail about their tour(s). Especially not with strangers or those who were not there. Even though they had to live in adverse conditions: the mud, rain or both for days on end, sometimes humping heavy loads for hours, these veterans don't share their war past, easily. Those feats are etched forever in memory, shining like badges of honor. Living like animals day in and day out, sometimes with little to eat or drink; their stories, if revealed, are usually downplayed.

If they trust you, they will tell you they were often scared and sometimes feared for their lives. They might also tell you that a tedious and boring day could sometimes unexpectedly erupt into instantaneous terror. Some will tell you that they did not expect to make it through their tour. Others would say they had hope of making it back home, to the "world." Most will tell you that after being in-country and losing close buddies, that they chose to not get close to others later in their tour. Some might give indications that they experience survivor guilt. All of them remember their dead buddies with somber reverence. Most of them will tell you that even though the living conditions bordered on the extreme, it was the best of times in their young lives, because they were amongst Marines and Corpsmen whom they trusted.

These men, mostly teenagers in the 1960s, came from all across America eager not only to prove themselves but to serve their nation. They were for the most part working-class American sons, the source of an immense national pride. Their attitudes were conducive to becoming part of what they called at the time the "Green Machine."

This rite of passage, joining the finest military organization in the world, epitomized the foundation and spirit of our great nation and its history. Most of their fathers and grandfathers had served in one branch or another. It is what able, proud, and brave men do!

In the 2000s most of the living veterans who came home from the war were in their fifties and sixties. Their families grown, their careers nearing an end, some felt a renewed urge to remember, to reconnect, to remember fallen comrades. The need to bond with the men who they had endured Vietnam with in both good and bad times came bubbling to the surface. It was from those past war experiences that friendships once again formed with this yearning to reunite. They knew each other well. That was because once upon a time long ago they had been willing to die for one another.

There have been several 1/27 reunions since the first one in 2000 which was held in Washington, D. C. William Drennan and his wife, Maria, coordinated the first reunion along with Dr. Gary Jarvis (both of Company D), with assistance from John Bouldin, CO of Alpha Company and Pat Kahler, CO of Delta Company. Since that time, thanks to those Marines, the able veterans of 1/27 reunite every two years at locations around the United States. Felix Salmeron, Alpha Company, a retired Marine First Sergeant, stepped up to lead this renewal of brotherhood forged long ago. He and select others rally the remaining veterans, family and friends, making 1/27 reunions popular events.

These living men, all answering our country's call in the 1960s, had come home to a nation which did not understand their service or sacrifice, but still these uncommon heroes dutifully took their place back in society and further released themselves to their individual destinies… They assimilated without fanfare or notice and began their next journey as citizens of our great nation.

These fine men of 1/27, both the living and the dead came from the heartland of America…

Sons, brothers, fathers, and husbands,
Called upon to serve as had their forefathers.
Unselfishly gave their all,
In obedience to duty,
As they understood it…

Gratitude Since Vietnam

I wish to recognize Dr. Gary Jarvis, a Company D 1/27 infantryman, for an unselfish quest early in his life after Vietnam in keeping the legacy and history of 1st Battalion, 27th Marines alive. He aptly wrote the first book about us combatants in *Young Blood*, a detailed and chronological history of the United States Marines who trained for and served in Vietnam during the peak and defining year of the war, 1968. Dr. Gary Jarvis documented the sacrifices of the many men who adroitly contributed, participated and suffered in the most significant and pivotal time of the Vietnam War, the Tet of 1968 and its aftermath. Dr. Jarvis led the way in telling our history and is one of my heroes. I have looked up to him as a shining example of leadership in soldiering, citizenship, a career in Medical Doctoring and finally authoring. I will always be grateful to him, his advice and his friendship.

I also want to recognize the men, friends and family members who took the time to talk with me and share their recollections about the past and our journey into the unknown. I am truly grateful for their help in compiling this history of our time on the line in Vietnam. All contributors are noted in the appendix.

Likewise, it is my hope to post remembrance of those men who were killed but also recognize those who survived and came home from their tour of Vietnam. These men will always be my heroes! It is these men who transitioned as best they could back into a society that did not understand what they had endured. It was these men who continued to contribute to America long after this divisive war ended.

I know in my heart, that the men who survived never for one moment of their lives forgot those who had sacrificed their all. We all think about them and our time in Vietnam every day of our lives. It is these men both dead and living whom I will always truly admire and respect as long as I breathe. I am truly honored and humbled to have walked amongst them.

Grady T. Birdsong

USMC Vietnam 1968 - 1969

Exhibits

Exhibit A: An Overview of the USMC Table of Organization

"Not only do Marines fight, they fight far more often and in far more places than any other branch."
~ Anonymous

"We didn't promise you a rose garden."
~ 1970s USMC Recruiting poster

United States Marine Corps Organizational History

How are Divisions, Regiments, and Battalions structured to make up the United States Marine Corps in its entirety? This segment addresses only infantry/artillery units and not air, logistical, or support elements. This information is intended to show the simplicity of Marine Corps unit structure with simple numbering. The United States Marine Corps is a department within the Department of the Navy, which is headed by the Secretary of the Navy (SECNAV). The Commandant of the Marine Corps is responsible for the entire USMC organization, recruiting, training, and equipping of all units so that it is ready for operation on a moment's notice.

The Table of Organization (T/O) of the Marine Corps lays out the organizational structure and the equipment required to function. The T/O started out as a chart-like document published by the War Department during WWII, prescribing the organic structure and equipment of units from divisional strength on down to the smallest operational entities, i.e., Platoons, Squads, and Fire Teams. Prior to 1943, organization and equipment were in Tables of Organization (T/Os) and Tables of Basic Allowances (T/BAs). Beginning in August of 1943, to ensure coordination between organization and equipment, a consolidated Table of Organization & Equipment (T/O&E) was instituted for each standard unit throughout the military.

Let us use 1/27 because it is the unit of discussion in this history. It is referred to amongst Marines as a member Battalion of the 27th Marine Regiment. The 27th Marine Infantry Regiment (commanded by a Colonel) when activated consisted of a Headquarters and Service Company and three rifle infantry battalions, the First, Second, and Third Battalions. With three Regiments in a Division, accordingly, the 26th, 27th, and 28th Marine Regiments reported operationally and administratively to the 5th Marine Division (Commanded by a Brigadier General). All Marine Regiments are structured in the same modality. To simplify the naming of all Marine Corps Regiments, they were given numerals with the addition of **Marines**: thus 1/27 aka First Battalion, 27th **Marines**, meaning the First Battalion of the 27th Marine Regiment; 2/26 for Second Battalion, 26th **Marines** or 26th Marine Regiment, and so on.

To give the reader an overview of the United States Marine Corps in its entirety and full personnel potential (Infantry & Artillery only), this following rudimentary T/O (Table of Organization) example from World War II shows Division and Regimental makeup at full capacity:

1st Division: 1st, 5th and 7th   **Marines** (infantry); 11th Marines (artillery)
2d Division: 2nd, 6th and 8th   **Marines** (infantry); 10th Marines (artillery)
3d Division: 3rd, 9th and 21st   **Marines** (infantry); 12th Marines (artillery)
4th Division: 23rd, 24th and 25th   **Marines** (infantry); 14th Marines (artillery)
5th Division: 26th, 27th and 28th   **Marines** (infantry); 13th Marines (artillery)
6th Division: 4th, 22nd, and 29th   **Marines** (infantry); 15th Marines (artillery)

Both the 5th and 6th Divisions were decommissioned after WWII and the 4th Division evolved into our Marine Corps Reserve units to this present day.

The 4th, 22nd, and 29th Marine Infantry Regiments were already combat-proven units and became subordinate units of the 6th Marine Division assembled in September 1944. The 15th Marines, artillery regiment was also activated and thus placed in the 6th Marine Division. The Sixth Marine Division never set foot in the United States—being formed in the Pacific, fought in the Pacific, and disbanded (colors retired) there.

When assembled, the Sixth Division was a grouping of already battle-hardened regiments who had been tested back to the beginning of the war in the Pacific. The 4th Marines were the Raider Battalions; 22nd Marines fought on Eniwetok; and the 29th Marines had been on Saipan. They were independent roving units in the past, now chosen for upcoming Pacific battles. Major General Lemuel C. Shepherd, Jr., whose experience went all the way back to WWI, was their leader. Along with the 5th Marine Division, they were destined for historical greatness toward the end of the war in the Pacific. The 27th Marine Regiment was formed in January of 1944 and saw first action on Iwo Jima in the Pacific as a Regiment of the 5th Marine Division. The "Easy" Company Marines of 2/28 of the 5th Division were responsible for raising the flag on Iwo Jima twice. After the war, the entire 5th Marine Division was deactivated in 1946.

The 26th, 27th, and the 28th Regiments of the 5th Division were reactivated again during the Vietnam War in 1966. The 26th Regiment, sent to Vietnam in March of 1966, played a prominent role in the northern I Corps area of the Republic of South Vietnam. It was attached to both the 1st and 3rd Marine Divisions at various times during its deployment. The 27th and 28th Regiments trained personnel as replacements for the units already in Vietnam. The 27th Marine Regiment was ordered to Vietnam in early February of 1968 by Lieutenant General Victor H. "Brute" Krulak, Commanding General, Fleet Marine Force-Pacific (FMF-PAC) when he received notification through the chain of command to send additional Marines. The 28th Marine Regiment remained in California as the Division reserve and training element.

The above listings of Divisions and their Regiments identify for the reader a mental arrangement of the basic Marine Corp's infantry and artillery structure of the Division's T/O when it was at its zenith during WWII. During Vietnam personnel strength and Regiments functioned differently. The new acronyms OPCON (Operationally Controlled) and ADCON (Administratively Controlled) came into use to maneuver the units throughout I CTZ in Vietnam. The 1st and 3rd Marine Divisions were assigned to the combat zone of the I CTZ while the 2nd Division remained on the east coast, and whose missions focused toward the Atlantic and eastward. The 4th Marine Division was the Reserves.

The USMC Table of Organization and Equipment in present day operates with only the first four Divisions. The 4th Division functions as the home of the United States Marine Corps Reserve. The 5th and 6th Divisions exist only on paper and in history with their colors in retirement at Marine Corps Headquarters.

Each Division during the Vietnam War represented a combat force on average of roughly 22,000 – 25,000 personnel, and fluctuated in troop strength monthly due to tour rotations, KIAs, and WIAs. Of course, there were support organizations such as Engineers, Logistics, Air-Ground Support, and Intel. They were and are indeed extremely important organizations linked to the success of the Marine Corps mission but are not shown in this overview.

Exhibit B: Remembering 1/27's KIAs

"If everyone does not come home, none of us can ever fully come home."
~ Anonymous

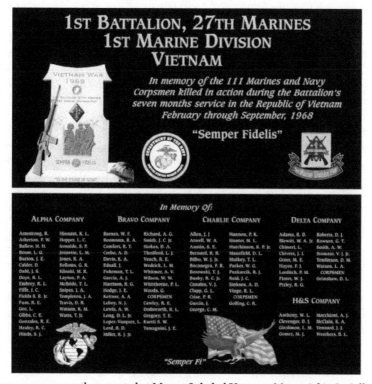

These Plaques are permanently mounted at Mount Soledad Veterans Memorial in La Jolla, California, dedicated there by the surviving members of 1st Battalion, 27th Marines in September of 2012.

This was made possible by the combined efforts of Felix Salmeron and Gary Jarvis, who collaborated in the design of the plaques, Mr. Allen Austin (brother of one of 1/27's Marines whose name appears on the plaque) who offered the use of his copyrighted emblem in the design, Colonel Pete Eller who coordinated the overall effort and by the many members of the Battalion, family members, and friends who contributed to the substantial cost of the plaques.

Gary E. Jarvis Ph.D., (Delta Company 1/27) personally researched and compiled all KIA Marines/Corpsmen of 1/27 in 1968 and recorded them in his book, *Young Blood: A History of the 1st Battalion, 27th Marines in Vietnam.* Ronald A. Skelton, Alpha Company was wounded 3 May 1968 and later died 22 July 1968; he does not appear on this memorial. He is on the Vietnam Wall and now listed on the 1/27 Honor Roll.

HONOR ROLL

Casualties in each Company of 1st Battalion, 27th Marines during 1968

The following Honor Roll was laboriously researched and compiled by Gary E. Jarvis, Ph.D. (Delta Company 1/27) for his book, *Young Blood: A History of the 1st Battalion, 27th Marines Vietnam 1968.* Gary has graciously allowed this author to display his research in this book.

ALPHA COMPANY

Name	Home Town	DOB	Rank	Died
Armstrong, Raymond	Cleveland, OH	01/14/1950	PFC	04/13/1968
Atherton, Frank	Templeton, PA	03/06/1950	PFC	04/13/1968
Ballew, Henry H.	South Roxana, IL	06/13/1950	L/CPL	08/23/1968
Bosse, Laurier G.	Providence, RI	05/18/1947	L/CPL	05/23/1968
Burton, Jack E.	Whites Creek, TN	02/16/1950	L/CPL	07/17/1968
Caulder, Durwood	Florence, SC	2/12/1950	L/CPL	07/27/1968
Dahl, James S.	Milwaukee, WI	05/22/1949	PFC	05/14/1968
Doye, Ricky Lee	Prophetstown, IL	06/24/1949	PFC	05/05/1968
Embrey, Richard L.	Warren, AZ	07/25/1946	L/CPL	04/13/1968
Fiffe, John C.	Albany, NY	02/04/1950	PFC	05/08/1968
Fields, Sherman	Dallas, NC	07/25/1947	CPL	05/17/1968
Fuss, Robert E.	Lincoln, NE	04/05/1946	CPL	04/27/1968
Gee, Leroy	East St. Louis, MO	10/09/1949	PVT	07/09/1968
Gibbs, Charles E.	Buffalo, NY	01/13/1950	PFC	05/06/1968
Gonzalez, Robert E.	Fresno, CA	07/20/1947	PFC	05/23/1968
Healey, Robert C.	Trenton, NJ	12/20/1949	PFC	04/13/1968
Hinds, Stephen J.	Osseo, MN	10/06/1946	L/CPL	04/13/1968
Hinnant, Kenneth L.	Johnson City, TN	11/24/1947	PFC	04/13/1968
Hopper, Larry C.	Ontario, CA	04/09/1948	PFC	04/13/1968
Ironside, Stephen P.	Vallejo, CA	02/24/1948	PFC	07/10/1968
Jennette, Leo Miller	Buxton, NC	06/15/1947	L/CPL	08/23/1968
Jones, Richard A.	Morenci, MI	01/19/1949	PFC	06/24/1968
Kellams, Glennis R.	New Albany, IN	05/11/1942	SGT	04/13/1968
Klinski, Michael R.	Auburn, MI	4/22/1948	PFC	07/17/1968

ALPHA COMPANY

Name	Home Town	DOB	Rank	Died
Layton, Patrick A.	Kansas City, MO	11/27/1949	PFC	05/27/1968
McBride, Thomas L.	Evansville, IN	11/12/1949	L/CPL	06/05/1968
Skelton, Ronald A.	Lowell, MA	06/22/1948	PFC	07/22/1968*
Snipes, Jerry A.	Albemarle, NC	01/18/1950	PFC	04/13/1968
Templeton, John A.	Lake Bluff, IL	01/10/1946	2dLT	07/18/1968
Travis, Dallas R.	Gary, IN	06/16/1948	PFC	07/17/1968
Watson, Kenneth M.	Toledo, OH	08/16/1945	CPL	04/13/1968
Watts, Theartis Jr	Philadelphia, PA	10/18/1949	PFC	08/17/1968

*Died 07/22/1968 from 05/03/1968 wounds

BRAVO COMPANY

Name	Home Town	DOB	Rank	Died
Barnes, Walter F.	San Bernardino, CA	10/20/1946	CPL	04/30/1968
Boomsma, Roger A.	Arcadia, CA	03/24/1949	PFC	04/13/1968
Comfort, Ray T.	Northumberland, PA	01/26/1950	PVT	04/13/1968
Corbo, Al D.	Harrah, OK	03/24/1948	L/CPL	10/13/1968*
Davis, Kinsey A.	Dover, NC	08/09/1948	PFC	08/11/1968
Edsall, James	Honesdale, PA	03/12/1949	L/CPL	07/27/1968
Fuhrman, Terry Lee	Fort Wayne, IN	11/16/1945	L/CPL	04/14/1968
Garcia, Augusto Jose	Chattanooga, TN	03/02/1942	CPL	07/17/1968
Harrison, Ricky Gene	Thomaston, GA	02/21/1950	PFC	08/23/1968
Hodge, James Edward	Macksburg, OH	01/01/1948	CPL	04/13/1968
Kettner, Alan Arthur	Springfield, MN	08/22/1943	2dLT	04/13/1968
Laboy, Neftale John	New York, NY	01/09/1950	PFC	06/19/1968
Lewis, Allen Wayne	Fremont, CA	03/08/1950	L/CPL	06/17/1968
Long, Douglas L. Jr	Savannah, GA	02/10/1950	PFC	04/13/1968
Lopez-Vazquez, Leonardo	Chicago, IL	11/06/1947	PVT	06/19/1968
Lord, Barry David	Findlay, OH	08/24/1946	PFC	04/13/1968
Miller, Robert J. Jr	Galion, OH	10/07/1949	PFC	08/23/1968
Richard, Andrew Gus	Elkhart, IL	10/11/1946	PFC	06/19/1968
Smith, Johnnie C. Jr	Columbus, OH	05/16/1948	PFC	05/06/1968
Stokes, David Alan	Council Bluffs, IA	01/23/1947	CPL	06/05/1968
Thedford, Luther J.	Cleveland, OH	05/25/1943	SGT	08/23/1968
Veach, Robert Eugene	Lebanon, IN	12/20/1949	L/CPL	06/19/1968
Wedrick, Lonnie Mark	White Salmon, WA	10/03/1947	PFC	06/04/1968
Whitmer, Alfred Van	Morenci, AZ	05/02/1947	L/CPL	04/13/1968
Wilson, William W.	St Marys, WV	02/28/1950	PFC	04/13/1968
Whitthorne, Paul L. Jr	Memphis, TN	01/04/1947	PFC	04/13/1968
Woods, Gregory	St Louis, MO	05/01/1950	PFC	08/23/1968

Corpsmen: KIA while attached to Bravo Company

Name	Home Town	DOB	Rank	Died
Cawley, Richard E.	St Joseph, MO	05/18/1947	HN	04/13/1968
Dodsworth, Robert L.	Franklin, IL	08/23/1946	HN3	04/13/1968
Gregory, Thomas E.	Endwell, NY	08/27/1947	HN	06/15/1968
Kurtti, Stephen W.	Salem, OR	06/11/1945	HM3	06/17/1968
Tamagnini, Joseph E.	Edison, NJ	07/10/1946	HM3	06/15/1968

* Died 10/13/1968 from 08/23/68 wounds

CHARLIE COMPANY

Name	Home Town	DOB	Rank	Died
Allen, James Joseph	Philadelphia, PA	11/03/1949	PFC	06/05/1968
Atwell, William A.	Oja, AZ	12/13/1948	PFC	07/27/1968
Austin, Stephen E.	Denair, CA	06/01/1947	CPL	06/08/1968
Bernard, Rodney R.	Garden City, MI	01/08/1947	L/CPL	06/05/1968
Bilbo, William J. Jr	New Brighton, PA	08/04/1948	L/CPL	08/26/1968
Bocanegra, Felix R.	Venice, CA	08/09/1949	L/CPL	06/05/1968
Borowski, Tadeusz J.	South Bend, IN	03/28/1947	CPL	06/04/1968
Busby, Richard C. Jr	Fort Worth, TX	03/15/1948	PFC	06/30/1968
Canales, Victor J.	Fennville, MO	09/07/1945	PFC	06/05/1968
Clapp, Gary Lyn	Grand Ledge, MI	04/23/1949	PFC	08/26/1968
Crise, Perry R.	Fredonia, NY	07/20/1949	PFC	07/26/1968
Garcia, Jerome	Sacramento, CA	02/24/1950	PFC	06/25/1968
George, Claude M.	Hammond, IN	04/16/1949	PFC	06/05/1968
Granville, John E.	Los Angeles, CA	01/07/1947	L/CPL	04/26/2007*
Hannon, Patrick K.	West Mifflin, PA	12/20/1949	PFC	06/16/1968
Hunter, Marvin Lynn	New York, NY	01/01/1950	L/CPL	07/17/1968
Hutchinson, Kenneth P.	Huntington, WV	12/13/1949	L/CPL	06/05/1968
Mansfield, Donald L.	Rockland, ME	07/18/1949	PFC	04/13/1968
Mulkey, Terry Lee	Smyrna, GA	02/19/1949	PFC	06/05/1968
Parker, William Gene	Detroit, MI	08/11/1949	PFC	04/13/1968
Puskarcik, Ronald J.	Campbell, OH	09/19/1949	PFC	07/18/1968
Reid, Joseph C.	Baton Rouge, LA	12/10/1948	CPL	04/13/1968
Sinksen, Arthur Dale	Rock Island, IL	02/06/1946	CPL	06/02/1968
Vinge, Richard L.	Seattle, WA	04/05/1947	PVT	06/05/1968

Corpsmen: KIA while attached to Charlie Company

Golling, Charles R.	Nevada, OH	06/17/1946	HN3	08/23/1968

*John E. Granville was WIA on 06/12/1968 and DOW (Died of Wounds) on April 26, 2007. Complications from his wounds caused him heart disease that led to his death in 2007. His name was added to the Vietnam Wall in Washington, DC as families and service members gathered there to join the Chairman, Joint Chiefs of Staff in honoring him and five others on Memorial Day observance May 31, 2010.

DELTA COMPANY

Name	Home Town	DOB	Rank	Died
Adams, Roscoe D.	Longview, TX	11/28/1949	PFC	07/28/1968
Blewitt, William A. Jr	Wayne, PA	03/04/1950	PVT	06/19/1968
Chimeri, Louis	Island Park, NY	03/29/1950	PFC	05/05/1968
Chivers, James Lee	Dayton, OH	02/04/1945	SGT	06/15/1968
Greer, Matthew E.	East Palatka, FL	09/07/1946	CPL	05/05/1968
Hayes, Fred J.	Walnut Creek, CA	09/07/1942	SGT	04/13/1968*
Lorditch, Patrick M.	Leicester, MA	10/18/1949	PFC	08/06/1968
Pinter, William J.	Bellamy, VA	11/25/1948	PFC	09/12/1968°
Pixley, Richard G.	Franklinville, NY	10/15/1949	L/CPL	07/20/1968
Roberts, David J.	Miami, FL	01/14/1950	L/CPL	05/05/1968
Rowson, Geoffrey T.	N. Grosvenor Dale, CT	10/24/1949	L/CPL	06/19/1968
Smith, Arthur W.	Liverpool, OH	07/06/1947	SGT	05/07/1968
Stamato, Vincent J. Jr	Philadelphia, PA	11/28/1949	PFC	05/17/1968

DELTA COMPANY

Name	Home Town	DOB	Rank	Died
Tomlinson, David M.	Cypress, CA	02/12/1946	PFC	04/11/1968
Watson, Lester A.	Sturgis, SD	08/22/1937	2dLT	07/20/1968

Corpsmen: KIA while attached to Charlie Company

Grimshaw, Danny L.	Seattle, WA	02/15/1947	HM2	08/23/1968♦

*Fred J. Hayes, Chief Battalion Scout, H&S Company was attached to Delta Company at the time of his death.

°William J. Pinter died 09/12/1968 from wounds received on 04/14/1968 while with Delta Company.

♦Danny Lee Grimshaw was born in Kennewick, WA and lived most of his life growing up in that area. His home of record where his parents lived at the time of death was Seattle, WA. Therefore, his hometown on the Vietnam Wall is given as Seattle, WA.

Note: Private Ronald Jay Lockhart of Louisville, KY DOB, 05/16/1950 spent a brief time with Delta Company and was transferred to Alpha Company, 1st MP Battalion, 1st FSR, FLC, III MAF. Lockhart was a casualty of drowning on 06/17/1968.

Note: PFC Dennis Lynn Cook of Yoder, IN DOB 07/02/1947 with A Company, 1st Tank Battalion, 1st MarDiv was attached to Delta Company in the Hue City area when he was killed on 05/06/1968.

H&S COMPANY

Name	Home Town	DOB	Rank	Died
Anthony, Ward L.	Canton, OH	08/21/1946	CPL0	4/17/1968
Clevenger, Daniel	Pueblo, CO	12/07/1946	CPL	04/07/1968
Girolimon, Louis M.	Peabody, MA	01/24/1949	L/CPL	06/10/1968
Gomez, Manuel J.	Vallejo, CA	03/25/1933	GYSGT	04/17/1968
Macchioni, Alphonse J.	Johnston, RI	12/09/1945	CPL	05/30/1968
McClain, Kenneth A.	Exira, IA	12/24/1945	L/CPL	04/17/1968
Vennard, John J.	Albany, NY	11/30/1933	CPL	04/17/1968
Weathers, Bobby L.	Longview, TX	02/04/1948	L/CPL	03/17/1968

CASUALTY STATISTICS
(March through September 1968)

KIA Total = 112

1st Time WIA = 497
2nd Time WIA = 59
3rd Time WIA = 2
Total = 557 WIAs

WIA = 557
KIA = 112
Total = 669 Purple Heart Awards

Exhibit C: Enemy Activity
August 1967-July 1968

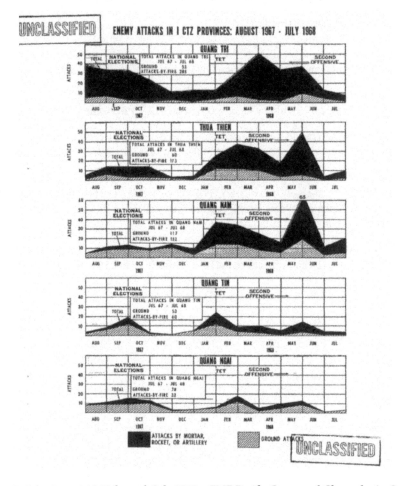

Enemy Activity August 1967 through July 1968 ~ FMF Pacific Command Chronologies July 1968

During February through July of 1968, enemy combatants increased their activities in the lowland area west, south, and southwest of Da Nang in Quang Nam Province. Operations Allen Brook and Mameluke Thrust beginning in May slowed the flow of food, munitions and troop replacements into the enemy staging and operating areas of Go Noi Island, An Hoa basin, Hill 55, Charlie Ridge, Dodge City and the Arizona combat areas of the Province. Ground Attack count on the Quang Nam graph illustrates the degree of effort needed and was thus applied by 1st Marine Division in multi-unit operations and counter guerrilla tactics.

Marine Corps Casualty Count for the Vietnam War: 13,067 KIA, 88,633 WIA

Exhibit D: Vietnam War Statistics

US Causalities (as of the late 1990s)
Hostile deaths: 47,359
Accidental deaths: 10,797

58,272: Total names on the black granite wall, latest additions on 2011 (source: The Wall-USA.com).

US Wounded
Wounded: 303,704
Severely disabled: 75,000
Totally disabled: 23,214
Single limb amputations: 5,283
Multiple limb amputations: 1,081

Draftees
25% of the total U. S. forces activated
Marine Corps draftees: 42,633

Socioeconomic Status
76% of the men sent to Vietnam were from lower-middle/working class.
75% of the men sent to Vietnam had family incomes above the poverty level.
50% of the men sent to Vietnam were from middle income backgrounds.
23% of Vietnam veterans had fathers in professional careers.
79% of Vietnam veterans had a high school education.
Deaths by region per 100,000 of population: South—31%; West—29.9%; Midwest—28.4%;
Northeast—23.5%

Honorable Service
97% of Vietnam-era Veterans were honorably discharged.
74% indicate they would serve again, even knowing the outcome.
82% of veterans who saw heavy combat strongly believe the war was lost due to lack of political will.

Race Composition
88.4% Caucasian
10.6% African-American
1% listed as others

86.3% Caucasians were of war dead.
12.5% African-Americans were of war dead.

Total US Forces 1959-1971

Year	Forces
1959	650
1960	900
1961	3,200
1962	11,300
1963	16,300
1964	23,300

1965	184,000
1966	485,300
1967	485,600
1968	536,100
1969	474,400
1970	335,800
1971	250,900

The Department of Defense Vietnam War Service Index officially provided by the War Library originally reported with errors that 2,709,918 U.S. military personnel served in-country. Corrections added 358 not originally listed. Interesting past Census statistics and claims of service in Vietnam found 9,492,958 Americans falsely claiming to have served in-country.

201 Army and 77 Marines were convicted of crimes against the Vietnamese. Isolated atrocities committed by American Soldiers produced torrents of outrage from anti-war critics and the news media while Communist atrocities were so common that they received hardly any media at all. The United States sought to minimize and prevent attacks on civilians while North Vietnam made attacks on civilians a centerpiece of its strategy. Americans who deliberately killed civilians received prison sentences while Communists who did so received commendations.

These statistics were taken from a variety of sources: The VFW Magazine, the Public Information Office, and Headquarter CP Forward Observer – 1st Recon of 12 April 1997.

Exhibit E: Timeline of Deployment, Operations and Noteworthy Events Involving 1/27

1967 – 1st Battalion, 27th Marines (Rein) stage and train at Marine Corps Air Station, Kaneohe Bay, Oahu, Hawaii; LtCol J. E. Greenwood, CO; Major Franklin P. Eller, XO.

10 February 1968 – Approximately half of the command departed Hawaii on USS Vancouver to be followed by remaining Marines on 12 February aboard USS Bexar and USS Washburn destined for training in WestPac.

13 February 1968 – 1/27 scheduled for a four-month deployment. Scheduled for training on Okinawa and on to exercises in Operation *Former Champ* with Taiwan military units and Operation *Tamaraw* with Philippine military forces. Those operations canceled and 1/27 diverted to "deadhead" to Da Nang Harbor, RVN. 2/27 and 3/27 located at Camp Pendleton, CA were ordered to deploy to RVN by air and surface and to report for Operational and Administrative (OPCON & ADCON) control by the 1st Marine Division (Rein).

23 February 1968 – First elements of 1/27 arrive Da Nang harbor: H&S Company (-), Company C and Company D on USS Vancouver.

27 February 1968 – Remaining elements of H&S Company (-), Company A, and Company B arrive on the USS Bexar.

28 February 1968 – Remaining sections of H&S Company (-) and supporting units arrive at Da Nang harbor to embark by truck to Duong Son (2) CP.

29 February 1968 – 1/27 began staging and commenced joint training operation with 2/3 and then deployed to the Hue City area. An established camp located at Duong Son (2) village was shared by 27th Marines Regimental HQ, 1/27 (the entire battalion), and a small rear echelon of 2/3 at grid coordinates AT992677.

1-5 March 1968 – Company A provided a platoon for "Rough Rider" convoy duty from Da Nang to Hue City.

9 March 1968 – Company A detached reporting to operational control of 1st Military Police Battalion in Da Nang. They remained with 1st MPs until 30 March 1968.

18 March 1968 – Med CAP conducted in Tho Trong Loung (Medical care provided for villagers).

18-19 March 1968 – Company B established blocking position at Phong Le (1). Conducted search and destroy mission in that area with 2nd Battalion, 51st ARVN Regiment.

25 March 1968 – Med CAP conducted in Thon Con Dau, Lo Giang, and Trung Luong.

March 1968 – The Battalion took an active part in staging, learning "Lessons Learned" from 2/3 and defending the southern sector of the Da Nang TAOR. A total of 505 patrols, 213 ambushes and 8 Company-size search and destroy operations were conducted as the Battalion "snapped in." The 1/27 Battalion TAOR was classified as the "Rocket and Mortar Belt."

29 March 1968 – Commanding General, 1st Marine Division at 2349Z hours directed 1/27 to report OPCON to Task Force X-Ray in Hue City area. 2/27 and 3/27 would remain in the TAOR south of Da Nang.

31 March 1968 – The Battalion Command Group and four rifle companies arrive in the Hue City area, immediately relieving elements of the 101st Airborne Division.

Commanding General, Task Force X-Ray orders 1/27 to formulate operational plan and prosecute aggressive offensive operations, extensive patrolling, and minimize fixed security installations in area east of Hue City.

Company A – to provide security for fuel pumping station at YD774251 and pipeline along Route 551.

Company B – to provide security on Route 1 between Hue City and Phu Bai. Maintain security at bridge on Route 1 grid coordinate YD838176. Additionally, provide reaction force backup for CAP units along Route 1.

Company C – provide security for NSA Col Co/Tam My complex (civilian and Seabee LST ramp), bridge, and fuel farm area in NE sector of TAOR. Also, provide security for pipeline in that area.

Company D – provide security for artillery fire base, Route 551 and pipeline in that sector.

3 April 1968 – H&S Communications section and other elements arrived by LST at Col Co/Tam My at 0900. Battalion CP relocated to La Son schoolhouse grid coordinate YD781249.

7 April 1968 – Assault (mortars) on 1/27 CP at La Son schoolhouse. Grid coordinate YD781249. USMC casualties, 1 KIA and 8 WIA.

5-30 April 1968 – Company D assigned security for Engineer road clearance detail on Route 551 from Col Co/Tam My to fuel pumping station at grid coordinate YD774251.

7-9 April 1968 – Operation Order 1-68, Operation *NO NAME #1*. Operation conducted along the NE coast employing two companies and three platoons from the Phu Vang District Popular Forces. Company B and Company C with PF forces performed a detailed search and clear employing sweep into a blocking force. Results netted enemy KIA's and assorted weapons, ordnance and rice caches with no USMC casualties. General area grid coordinate YD930250 in the village of Phuong Dien.

12-15 April 1968 – Operation Order 2-68, Operation *NO NAME #2*. This operation planned a search and clear north and south sides of a canal off the Perfume River stretching eastward toward the coast. From YD786239 east to YD836235 with Company D on north side and Company A on south side moving toward Company B setting up a blocking force at grid coordinate YD812245 and YD812247. Significant contact and heavy resistance slowed progress of Companies D and A moving eastward along the canal. Company B attempting to set up the blocking position ran into a coordinated, pre-planned NVA field of fire and becoming pinned down and unable to move, taking heavy losses.

The sky cleared and fixed wing air support arrived on station around 1630 hours. Company B taking heavy casualties returned to the Battalion CP via Route 552, arriving 2130 hours to stand down. Companies D and A consolidated their positions at YD817243 and YD818245. The following day, both swept forward to YD833240 with negative contact. The embedded enemy had vanished.

Summary: USMC casualties: 26 KIAs and 46 WIAs. 62 enemy confirmed KIAs, numerous AK and SKS weapons, crew-served weapons, personal combat gear, and rice caches were captured. Many drag marks and blood trails were reported.

17 April 1968 – Assault (mortars) on 1/27 CP at La Son School house. Grid coordinate YD781249. USMC casualties, 4 KIAs and 25 WIAs. Helo support was called for to Med Evac casualties.

18 April 1968 – Company A (-) and B (-) conducted another search and destroy along canal from YD790245 to YD798288 into one company of 39th Ranger Battalion (RVN) providing a blocking force at YD786239 to YD798248. No contact with negative results.

19-21 April 1968 – Company D OPCON to 2/5 to provide blocking force in support of Operation *Baxter Garden* at grid coordinates YD795270 and YD820268.

27 April 1968 – Company B (-) reinforced with PF Forces conducted search and clear astride Loi Hong canal from YD813202 to YD875181. Ran into snipers, mines, and booby traps.

28 April 1968 – Operation Order 3-68, Operation *NO NAME #3*. A sweep of three villages in the NW sector of TAOR conducted by Companies C and D. Landing by LCM-8 from river at YD767307 and moved through grid coordinates YD7531, YD7631, and YD7632. Two PF Companies from Huong Tri District provided blocking force at YD745300. The area showed no signs of enemy presence or prepared defenses.

28-30 April 1968 – Med CAP conducted at refugee camp grid coordinate YD833323. Treated approximately 450 Vietnamese during this period.

3-7 May 1968 – Operation Order 4-68, Operation *NO NAME #4*. The general concept for this op was to conduct offensive sweeps along the canal network in the central sector of the 1/27 TAOR. The secondary mission to invoke rice denial (destroy all rice caches found). The operation was executed in three phases:

Phase I – Companies C and D swept westward and Company A to block denying enemy egress out of the area. Both companies moved into a blocking position from YD849220 to YD867237 to support a sweep by the 39th ARVN Ranger Bn. 3 May 1715 hours, C and D were relieved of blocking mission. No contact made with enemy.

Phase II – 4 May 1968 Company D conducted offensive operation in the northeast section of the TAOR within grid lines YD8424 to YD8727. Company C to remain in defensive position astride canal at YD833238 conducting patrol activity west, south and southeast. Both companies with tank support executed Phase II plan. Company D moved to YD872265, establishing blocking position. Company C swept village of Thon Xuan O at YD855255, moving toward Company D blocking position. No contacts were made. Companies returned to PL Brown to set up night defensive positions. In the early morning hours of 5 May Company D was assaulted on their NE perimeter by a large enemy force. Using mortars, RPGs, and sappers, NVA regular troops attempted to assault through the NE perimeter. That initial attack was repulsed using supporting arms, 81mm mortars, artillery, and small arms fire. The second attack came through the NW sector of the perimeter penetrating through Company D's lines. The assault was sealed off and repulsed by hand-to-hand fighting, 81mm mortars, artillery, and small arms. Numerous weapons, 25 satchel charges (unexploded), miscellaneous personal military gear, assault rifles, and dead NVA bodies were left in the aftermath. The discovery of numerous blood trails and drag marks was also recorded.

Also on 5 May in the early morning hours Second Platoon of Company A in the blocking position was attacked and overrun. Due west of Delta Company an estimated company of NVA regulars hit their perimeter with RPGs, mortars, and satchel charges in pre-designated positions. The attack was repulsed by small arms, 106 recoilless rifle fire, claymore mines, and hand-to-hand fighting. Artillery fire support was called in at "Danger Close" distances.

The Phase II objective was postponed until 6 May to enable a thorough search of the battlefield and the reorganization of the companies.

Phase III – 6 May 1968 Companies C and D began moving again with preparatory fire delivered in support of the thrust along the canal at grids YD8323, YD8322, YD8222. Company B (-) blocked at YD814201. Initial contact with NVA was made by Company D at 0915 hours in the vicinity of YD837233. Company D resumed moving and received heavy small arms, and automatic weapons fire from YD835223. The main obstacle, another canal running north and south was too deep to wade across. The only approach was a bridge which was heavily defended. Company D crossed via the bridge under rolling artillery support and began to sweep the heavily defended village on the far side. The Company policed up the battlefield, recording numerous enemy KIAs, weaponry, assorted ammunitions, B40 rockets, mortar rounds and miscellaneous military gear. Drag marks and blood trails were numerous.

7 May 1968 Companies C and D began a search and destroy along the canal from YD833238 to YD804248. Company A placed a blocking force near YD803246 on both sides of the canal. They thoroughly searched each hamlet and excessive amounts of rice were discovered. No enemy contact made and a villager reported that the enemy had left prior to the Marines' arrival. During the sweeps, detailed sketches of the trench and defensive positions were noted.

11 May 1968 – Operation Order 5-68, Operation *NO NAME #5*, An offensive operation in the NE sector of the TAOR. Company A and C were helo-lifted to Landing Zone YD935254 to commence sweeping to the northwest. The Vietnamese National Police Field Force were landed by helo in trace of the assault companies to conduct detailed searches of the hamlets along the azimuth of advance. The 64th and 65th Popular Force of Phu Vang District provided the blocking force with support from Tanks and Ontos units at grids YD862298 and YD870305. The Vietnamese 12th Coastal Group Junk Fleet provided coastal water surveillance and the U. S. Navy Patrol River Force the inland waterway surveillance. The operation resulted with no significant contact. One VC KIA, some weaponry captured, and 31 detainees rounded up for questioning.

1-15 May 1968 – The Battalion introduced into its operational tactics forward observer teams (four-man teams) known as "Sting Rays." Three teams had the capability of on-call artillery support. The teams were dispatched during dark and established themselves in large open rice paddies to provide surveillance of likely avenues of approach into Hue City. These teams, combined with a series of planned interlocking patrols, and ambushes, curtailed the enemy's movement during the night.

15 May 1968 – Elements of the 2nd Brigade, 101st Airborne Division relieved 1/27 of the Hue TAOR with the 1st Battalion returning to the area south of Da Nang. In 45 days, the Battalion drove the enemy out of the canal area they had previously dominated and denied the, freedom of movement, pushing them even further into the extreme eastern coastal regions where there was little support.

16 May 1968 – The Battalion left the Hue City TAOR and traveled by sea, surface, and air to occupy 3/27's CP located at grid coordinate BT070656 and took responsibility of that TAOR. Three line companies began coordinating and patrolling their respective sectors. Company D began OPCON to III MAF assigned to 1st Military Police Battalion duty in Da Nang City until 31 May. The Battalion encountered a new and different environment. The confrontation with an enemy of any appreciable size became non-existent. The Marines were now confronted with the threat of booby traps and mines daily. The Da Nang TAOR, termed the "Rocket and Mortar Belt," required constant saturation patrolling. Company C participated in combined patrol activity with 3rd Battalion, 51st Regiment, ARVN in the northern sector. Elements of Company A and C provided support for an ARVN operation in the western sector. On 25 May 1/27 received orders directing it to relieve 3/27 on Operation Allen Brook in the Go Noi TAOR.

27 May 1968 – Company C dispatched to Go Noi Island area to assist 3/27 on Operation Allen Brook.

28 May 1968 – A Battalion HQ Command group and Company B arrived at Liberty Bridge grid AT925532 and crossed the Song Thu Bon to link up with and relieve 3/27. Company C rejoined 1st Battalion and were assigned the task of accounting for MIAs left on the battle field from 3/27's Company I in a prior battle.

29 May 1968 – Company C still searching for remaining MIAs in grid area AT945532 were diverted to support Company B, 1/26 also engaged in the multi-battalion Operation *Allen Brook*. Company B, 1/26 were engaged in a fire fight with an entrenched NVA force. Company C, 1/27 assaulted the dug in enemy positions, displacing them, and located the remaining MIAs from Company I, 3/27. The Battalion mission was to conduct searches of villages in the northern sector of Go Noi Island from grid line 94 to grid line 03. No contacts were encountered for the remainder of the reporting period.

1-5 June 1968 – The mission remained the same as reported in the May Command Chronology. Conducted search and clear ops from grid lines 94 to 03 with 1st Battalion, 26th Marines.

5 June 1968 – All line companies of 1/27 were ordered to engage in Operation Allen Brook. 1/27 then split its Command Group at Liberty Bridge (taking over 3/27's communication center) to establish communications between its operating area and the Regimental/Battalion CP at Duong Son (2). 1/26 had been ordered to withdraw from Allen Brook. As they moved through Cu Ban (4) grid AT9453, they encountered NVA heavy resistance. Company C, 1/27 was directed to link up with Bravo 1/26 to relieve pressure, allowing them to disengage. The Charlie Company CO and XO were wounded. The proximity of NVA positions and restricted environment prevented arty and air support. Company A was ordered into the fight with Tanks to assault the NVA and relieve Company C. Summary: Friendly USMC KIAs, 6 and WIAs, 18 with 12 heat casualties. The NVA lost 17 KIAs (found) and numerous weaponry and personal gear captured. Blood trails and drag marks were numerous.

6 June 1968 – The new mission given to 1/27 was to provide security in the Go Noi Island TAOR for the 1st Engineer Battalion. They were ordered to clear (with bulldozers and mine sweepers) the area of useful structures (bunkers), trenches, caves, and spider holes. Additionally, to uncover any arms, ordnance, and supply caches, rendering the enemy incapable of operating in the area. This was a major staging area for the Main Force NVA and supporting VC troops.

15 June 1968 – Company B received an early morning assault while in a defensive perimeter at grid AT997538. The enemy attempted to flank with small arms, automatic weapons, and B40 rockets. The assault was negated due to good defensive perimeter plans and execution. Company B took 3 WIAs and inflicted 21 NVA KIAs (found) with numerous weaponry and personal gear captured. The Company B Commander was wounded and evacuated.

19 June 1968 – Company B moved to search the area of Bac Dong An at grid BT025554. Encountering heavy resistance, the company became pinned down. Numerous arty and air strikes were called but failed to soften enemy positions throughout the day. Two platoons from Company B and two from Company D were committed and when resistance continued, a platoon from Company A and C and the Battalion Command Group engaged in the battle. Assaulting the NVA positions yielded 17 NVA KIAs (found) with numerous weaponry, personal gear and supplies found. The day's action resulted in 6 USMC KIAs, 18 WIAs and numerous heat casualties.

21 June 1968 – The Battalion executed its final major operational maneuver as part of Operation *Allen Brook*. The tactical movement involved Company A and the Battalion Command Group moving from AT978537, linking with Bravo and Alpha Companies at BT017543. With Bravo on the left and Delta on the right, Charlie and the Command Group in trace, a series of Phase Lines were established. Line of Departure (LOD) from BT011540 and BT011548 on through PL Red, White, Blue, Green, and Black eastward to Line of Attack (LOA) at grids BT050540 to BT050550. Pre-planned prep fire preceded the advance, termed "Time on Target" missions, designed to soften any enemy positions that might be encountered. No contact was made but it was noted in the reporting that fire support coordination between air, artillery, and ground forces was well orchestrated.

22 June 1968 – 1/27 commenced to be relieved by 2/27 who would continue Operation *Allen Brook*. The 1st Battalion returned to the original 27th Marines regimental TAOR assuming responsibility for their assigned sectors. Companies B, C, and D established their command headquarters at Camp Duong Son (2) and were assigned the NW sector, W sector, and E sector respectively. Company A established a CP at the former 2/27 CP, located at grid BT013630 and took southwestern sector of 2/27's Regimental TAOR. All 1/27-line companies resumed saturation patrolling of the "Rocket and Mortar Belt." Company A provided security platoons for the Ha Dong bridge at grid AT990642 and provided security for the dam construction by engineers at grid BT003654; also, security for bridges at AT999699 and AT995688 while conducting combined patrol activity with ARVN units.

23-30 June 1968 – The Battalion operated in the combined western/central original TAOR. Battalion CP located at Duong Son (2) Village.

8 July 1968 – Company A provided platoon for blocking force action for ARVN Operation at AT988623.

10-11 July 1968 – Company A provided two platoons for blocking force action for ARVN Operation at grid AT9961.

12 July 1968 – Company B conducted search and clear with ARVN forces at AT9869.

13 July 1968 – Company A provided platoon for blocking force action for 3/26 in "Dodge City" AO at grid BT0160.

14 July 1968 – Major Kenneth J. Skipper assumed command of 1/27, relieving LtCol J. E. Greenwood.

15-16 July 1968 – Battalion assumes responsibility for a new TAOR. Company A assigned the "Riviera" AO, Company B assigned "Tu Cau Bridge" AO and Company C assigned the "Desert" AO. Company D provided platoon for "Rough Rider" convoy duty and another platoon OPCON to III MAF for security at POW compound in Da Nang City. Company C provided platoon for duty with 7th Engineer Battalion on an operation with the ROK (Republic of Korea) Marines.

17 July 1968 – Company D provided platoon to relieve Company C platoon on ROK Operation.

22-24 July 1968 – Companies B and C provided one platoon each for blocking force in conjunction with ARVN Operation at BT0367.

25 July 1968 – Company C patrols find major rocket launching site at BT055711 close to the Marble Mountain complex. Battalion CP at Duong Son (2) assaulted with 81mm and 60mm mortar fire.

29 July 1968 – Company A provided one platoon for blocking force for ARVN operation at grid BT0965.

31 July 1968 – Assumed 2/27 TAOR responsibility. Company A assigned NE sector, Company B assigned NW sector, and Company C assigned southern sector. Company D continued to provide OPCON platoons to other units. Company D's remaining platoon employed on Battalion CP perimeter security for Camp Duong Son (2), grid AT992675.

2 August 1968 – Company B, squad combat patrol located AT983691 located VC in bunker. Assaulted bunker, resulting in all VC KIA.

10 August 1968 – Company B with attached 1st Engineers sweep village at AT9868. Village was heavily booby-trapped. Cleared seven "surprise firing devices" by detonating them. USMC KIA from tripped booby trap.

11-17 August 1968 – Company B OPCON to 1st Marine Regiment.

15 August 1968 – Company A platoon with RD team captured nine VC suspects including Hamlet Chief. All detainees sent to Hoi An for interrogation. Regimental/Battalion/Division meeting held with participants from all line Companies to discuss return to CONUS.

22 August 1968 – Company C squad patrol in vicinity AT965650 made contact with enemy combatants resulting in KIAs and weaponry captured.

23 August 1968 – The enemy's long awaited "Third Phase Offensive" was launched in the early morning hours. The magnitude of the offensive was not as robust as expected. It did force all tactical units in the Da Nang TAORs to focus on countering and quelling it.

At 0300 Hours, Company B, at grid AT970697 received a ground assault by satchel charges, automatic weapons, and rocket fire. The attack was repulsed.

At 0300 Hours, Company C, at grid AT973642 received mortar fire followed by ground assault. The attack was repulsed.

At 0915 Hours, Company A, located at BT018717, moved toward Cam Le bridge which had been overrun and held by enemy NVA combatants. Company A (-) assaulted the bridge complex at 1400 hours receiving heavy small arms, B40 rockets, and automatic weapon fire, finally securing the enemy-held bunkers on the southern end of the bridge.

At 0920 Hours, Company D swept eastward toward the Cam Le Bridge at vicinity of BT007704, receiving heavy small arms and automatic weapon fire from enemy entrenched in tree line. Air support called in to suppress the combatants.

At 1215 Hours, Company B platoon attached to Company D encountered heavy fire from grid BT013705. Assaulted and overcame entrenched enemy.

At 1400 Hours, Company H&S platoon (Rein), with a recon patrol vicinity of BT003668 made contact made with unknown size of entrenched NVA, engaging and overcoming them with an assault.

24-25 August 1968 – Company C, squad combat patrol made contact with large enemy force grid BT000652. First Battalion, 51st ARVN Regiment reacted to contact. Action was heavy and continued for two days. Summary report: Approximately 200 enemy KIAs.

26 August 1968 – Various elements engaged in patrolling grid AT969656, making sporadic contact with remaining NVA forces. Company D returned to "Rough Rider" convoy duty.

27-31 August 1968 – Line Companies continued routine patrolling and maintained high alert for a possible continuation of "Third Phase Offensive."

31 August 1968 – The 27th Marine Regiment was relieved from operational control (OPCON) of the Da Nang TAOR by the 1st Marine Division and assigned to 1st Marine Regiment.

1-12 September 1968 – Battalion prepared to return to CONUS. Many Marines who had another six months to serve "in-country" were transferred to other units in bad need of manpower. Essential personnel and second-tour Marines/Corpsmen took the Battalion Colors back to Hawaii.

These events and operations were reconstructed from:

Command Chronologies, 1st Battalion, 27th Marines, February – August 1968, Declassified by the USMC History Division. Available at the *US Marine Corps History Division Vietnam War Documents Collection* at The Vietnam Center and Archive, Texas Tech University.

http://www.recordsofwar.com/vietnam/usmc/USMC_Rvn.htm

Notes

Introduction

1. *The Encyclopedia Britannica: A Dictionary of Arts, Sciences and General Literature*, 9th ed., s.v. "Étienne Maurice Gérard – Count (1773-1852)," by Thomas Spencer Baynes, Volume 10, pg. 440; and Bernard Cornwell, *Waterloo: The History of Four Days, Three Armies, and Three Battles* (New York: Harper Collins Publishers, 2014), 150.

Chapter 1 – Training Begins in Hawaii

1. United States Marine Corps, *A Chronology of the United States Marine Corps 1965-1969*, PCN 19000318100, Vol IV, Historical Division HQ USMC, 1971. Historical reference pamphlet.
2. Bernard C. Nalty and Danny J. Crawford, T*he United States Marines on Iwo Jima: The Battle and the Flag Raising* (Washington DC: History and Museum Division, Headquarters US Marine Corps, 1995).
3. Andrew W. Boyko, *Parris Island Boot Camp Diary 1964*, member of Platoon 296, Company K, 2nd Recruit Training Battalion.
4. United States Marine Corps, *First Battalion, 27th Marines Command Chronologies*, February 1968, 4.
5. Ibid., 5.
6. Windward Marine, "Station, Brigade Troops Prepare for Annual FMFPac Inspection," Vol. 17(1), January 5, 1968. Provided by Taras and Dani Sydorenko.

Chapter 2 – The 1968 Tet Offensive, the Peak Year of Decisions

1. Lyndon B. Johnson, "Remarks at El Toro Marine Corps Air Station, California" (speech), from The American Presidency project, weekly compilation of presidential documents, February 17, 1968. http://www.presidency.ucsb.edu/. Accessed July 20, 2017.
2. Neil Sheenan et al., *The Pentagon Papers as published by The New York Times* (New York: Bantam Books, Inc., 1971), 607, intro ix, 652.
3. Victor H. Krulak, *First To Fight: An Inside View of the U.S. Marine Corps* (Annapolis MD: Naval Institute Press, 1984), 179.
4. Sheenan et al., *The Pentagon Papers…*, 589.
5. Ibid., 594.
6. United States Marine Corps, *FMFPAC Command Chronologies*, February 1968 (SPECAT EXCLUSIVE).
7. Jack Shulimson et al., *U.S. Marines In Vietnam: The Defining Year 1968* (Washington DC: History and Museums Division, Headquarters US Marine Corps, 1997), 4-5, 12-13.
8. Edwin H. Simmons, Brigadier General USMC, "Marine Corps Operations in Vietnam, 1968," in *The Marines In Vietnam 1954-1973: An Anthology and Annotated Bibliography*, (Washington DC: History and Museums Division, Headquarters US Marine Corps, 1985), 111.
9. Max Boot, *Invisible Armies: An Epic History of Guerrilla Warfare From Ancient Times To The Present* (Liveright Publishing Corporation, 2013), 418-421.
10. Shulimson et al., 13; Robert Coram, *Brute: The Life of Victor Krulak, U. S. Marine*, 289-290, 294.
11. William C. Westmoreland, A *Soldier Reports* (New York: Doubleday, 1976), 166.
12. Krulak, *First To Fight*, 186.
13. Ibid., 198-199.
14. Ibid., 198-200.

15. Nicholas J. Schlosser, *The Greene Papers: General Wallace M. Greene, Jr. and the Escalation of the Vietnam War, January 1964 – March 1965*, ed. History Division Marine Corps (US) (Quantico, VA: US Marine Corps, 2015), 416.
16. Bui Tin, *From Enemy to Friend: a North Vietnamese Perspective on the War* (Annapolis MD: Naval Institute Press, 2002), 74-76. Bui Tin was a combat officer, front-line journalist, confidant of NVA Generals, who fought for the North and later became a political dissident.
17. Ibid, 82.
18. Robert L. Fischer, *Guerilla Grunt: How One Enterprising Marine Helped Change the Way Marines Fight Their Wars* (Virtual Bookworm Publishing, 2013), 177.
19. Nguyen Cao Ky, *How We Lost The Vietnam War* (New York: Stein and Day/Scarborough Books Edition, 1978), 150-154.
20. William R. Corson, *The Betrayal*, (New York: Ace Books, Inc. 1968).
21. Courtesy of the VFW Magazine and Public Information Office. See Exhibit D. The statistic is: 25% (648,500 of the total forces in country) were draftees (66% of U.S. Armed Forces members were drafted in WWII).
22. Shulimson et al., *U.S. Marines In Vietnam: The Defining Year 1968*, 573.
23. Lewis Sorley, *A Better War: The Unexamined Victories and Final Tragedy of America's Last Years in Vietnam* (New York: Harcourt Brace & Company, 1999).
24. Simmons, *The Marines In Vietnam 1954-1973*, 110-111.
25. Coram, Brute, 312-315.
26. Shulimson et al., 576.

Chapter 3 – Arrival and Staging: Attached to 1st Marine Division
1. Shulimson et al., 229.
2. Ibid., 91.
3. Ibid., 251-252.
4. Ibid., 516-532.
5. Ibid., 2.

Chapter 4 – Tools of the Trade
1. From *Report of the M16 Rifle Review Panel, 1 June 1968*, Army Library Pentagon, Washington DC. Congressman Richard H. Ichord, Chairman of special subcommittee of the House Committee on Armed Services inquiry into the M16 rifle program. Colonel Crossman and Colonel Paul B. Henley field investigated. D-1 through D-98; E-1 and F-1.
2. LtCol Philip Reade, IG, USV, *History of the Military Canteen*, published by authority of The Honorable Secretary of War 1900, Printed by C. J. Burroughs, Chicago. Available online at University of California, http://www.archive.org/details/historyofmilitar00readrich. Accessed July 20, 2017.
3. Virtual Wall, www.virtualwall.org/dw/WillingEA01a.htm. Accessed July 20, 2017.
4. Nicholas Warr, *Phase Line Green; The Battle For Hue, 1968* (Annapolis, MD: Naval Institute Press, 1997), 162-165.
5. *1st Tank Battalion, FMF, Command Chronologies*, May & April 1968, 13-18 April SitRep.
6. *1st Battalion, 27th Marines, Command Chronologies*, April 1968.
7. Frank O. McClendon, Jr., Commander, "Doctors and Dentists, Nurses and Corpsmen in Vietnam," in *The Marines In Vietnam 1954-1973*, 346-355.
8. Commander Herbert L. Bergsma, *Chaplains With Marines In Vietnam 1962-1971* (History and Museums Division, Headquarters US Marine Corps, 1985), 164-166.

9. Ibid.

10. Michael P. Kelley, *Where We Were in Vietnam: A Comprehensive Guide To The Firebases, Military Installations and Naval Vessels of the Vietnam War 1945-75* (Central Point, OR: Hellgate Press, 2002), 1-1 through 1-6.

11. Jim West, *TOPO: The Stories Behind the Maps* (Lakewood, CO: Bristlecone Publishing, 2015), 79-80.

12. Kelley, *Where We Were in Vietnam*, 2-1 through 2-6.

13. Ibid.

14. Bureau of Engraving and Printing, Department of the Treasury, Historical Resource Center, available at: https://www.moneyfactory.gov/historicalresources.html. Accessed July 20, 2017.

15. From *Report of the M16 Rifle Review Panel: History of the M16 Weapon System*, D-1 through D-98; E-1 and F-1.

Chapter 5 – Deployed to Task Force X-Ray Command, Phu Vang District

1. Shulimson et al., 105-111.

2. Captain William Sweeney, "Military Experiences: A Company Commander's Perspective," in *Young Blood: A History of the 1st Battalion, 27th Marines* by Gary E. Jarvis, PhD, 245-246.

3. *27th Marine Regiment Command Chronologies*, April 1968.

4. *1st Battalion, 27th Marines Command Chronologies*, April 1968, Annex B (Intelligence) to Operation Order 3-68.

5. Ibid., Tab B Operation Order 1-68.

6. Ibid., Tab C Operation Order 2-68.

7. Ibid., 101-103.

8. Sweeney in *Young Blood*, 247.

9. Gary E. Jarvis, PhD, "Alpha Company Platoon Base Attacked," in *Young Blood*, 129-130.

10. *1st Battalion, 27th Marines Command Chronologies*, May 1968, 4-11.

11. Sweeney in *Young Blood*, 249.

Chapter 6 – Operation Allen Brook

1. Simmons, T*he Marines In Vietnam 1954-1973*, 115.

2. Shulimson et al., 328-349.

3. Ibid., 333-336.

4. Sweeney in *Young Blood*, 250.

5. *3rd Battalion, 27th Marines Command Chronologies*, May 1968, 3-4.

6. Shulimson et al., 328.

7. *3rd Battalion, 27th Marines Command Chronologies*, May 1968, 3-4.

8. Shulimson et al., 72.

9. *III MAF Command Chronologies*, May 1968, Periodic Intelligence Report #18-68 Through #22-68, USMC History Division.

10. *3rd Battalion, 27th Marines Command Chronologies*, May 1968, 3-10.

11. Shulimson et al., 334-341.

12. *1st Battalion, 27th Marines Command Chronologies*, May 1968, 5.

13. Jarvis, *Young Blood*, 177-178.

14. Sweeney, *Young Blood*, 250-251.

15. Ibid., 251-253.

16. Ibid., 253.

17. Ibid., 254.

18. Ibid., 256-261.

19.   *1st Battalion, 27th Marines Command Chronologies*, June 1968, 4-8.
20.   Shulimson et al., 339-342.
21.   *1st Battalion, 27th Marines Command Chronologies*, June 1968, 4-8; *1st Engineers Battalion Command Chronologies*, June 1968, 2-4, 7; *1st MarDiv (Rein) Command Chronologies*, June 1968, 28-36; *FMF Command Chronologies*, June 1968, 19-23.
22.   Through 25. Ibid.
26.   *HMM-164 Command Chronologies*, May 1968, 10; June 1968, 7; July 1968, 9; August 1968, 9.

Chapter 7 – A Third Offensive and Return of the Regimental Colors
1.   *FMF Pacific Command Chronologies, Operations of US Marine Forces Vietnam,* August 1968, 25.
2.   *III MAF Periodic Intelligence Reports,* August 1968, No. 32-68, No. 34-68, No. 36-68.
3.   Ibid.
4.   *FMF Pacific Command Chronologies, Operations of US Marine Forces Vietnam,* August 1968, 24-25.
5.   Jarvis, 224; Shulimson et al., 375-383.
6.   *1st Battalion, 27th Marine Command Chronologies,* August 1968, 4-5.
7.   Jarvis, 224-227.
8.   Ibid., 227-228.
9.   Ibid., 231.
10.   Simmons, 123.
11.   Shulimson et al., 578.
12.   *1st Marine Division Command Chronologies,* August 1968, 37.
13.   *1st Marine Division Command Chronologies,* September 1968, 40.
14.   Through 15. Shulimson et al., 579.

Glossary of Terms, Jargon, and Acronyms

782 Gear – 782 is the name of the form that lists all a Marine's issued personal combat gear

Actual – The term for the Commanding Officer of a unit. If a radio operator on an operation answered, "This is Alpha One," that could be anyone from that unit, First Platoon of Alpha Company. If a person answered, "This is Alpha One Actual," that meant the speaker was the actual Commander of First Platoon, Alpha Company

ADCON – Administratively Controlled

Agent Orange – A chemical with mixtures of powerful defoliants which, when sprayed by aircraft, eliminated cover for NVA and VC troops and some of the crops used as their food source

AKA – Attack Cargo Ship, re-designated Amphibious Cargo Ships (LKA) in 1969

Amtrac – LVTP-5, landing vehicle, tracked amphibian tractor to carry cargo and Marines across water

ANGLICO – Air Naval Gunfire Liaison Company, a Marine unit tasked with calling in air and arty fire support to maneuver elements of the MAGTF

AO – Area of Operation

APA – Auxiliary Personnel Attack; a naval vessel for transport of troops

ARVN – Army of the Republic of Vietnam

Arizona Territory – An area west of Thu Bon River that looked like the Arizona desert, frequented by Marines especially during Operation Mameluke Thrust

Arty – Slang for Artillery

Azimuth – A straight line from one point to another referred to as one of the 360 degrees of on a compass

Beau Coup Dinky Dau – A slang expression, mixture of French and Vietnamese used by both Vietnamese and Americans, meaning "You"

BDA – Bomb Assessment Damage

Blooper – M79 40mm Grenade Launcher

BLT – Battalion Landing Team

Bug Juice – Insect Repellant, Clothing and Personal Application

Bush – Going out into the field or going on a combat operation

C4 – Plastic explosive used for blowing things up and heating C-rats. Packaged in olive drab cellophane, the white bar explosive was about a foot long, one inch thick, and three across. Detonation was by blasting cap

CAG – Combined Action Group; in 1970, Marines had put together four CAGs. These programs were highly successful some areas in both military and civic action terms. And they were popular amongst the indigenous people

CAP – Combined Action Program; the CAP concept has roots from pacification programs in Haiti, Nicaragua, the Dominican Republic, and other places during the Banana Wars in the 19th and early 20th centuries. Despite its history and rocky start, CAP became an official, civic-action program designed to win the "hearts and minds" of the indigenous people of Vietnam and became somewhat successful in the northern I CTZ instituting the CAGs. CAP at a lower level of organizational discussion could also mean a Civil Action Platoon assigned to a village

CASREPS – Casualty Reports

CC – Command Chronology

CG – Commanding General

CH-46 – Twin rotor Helicopter, aka "Phrog," used as principle troop transport for Marines

Chieu Hoi – Meant "open arms" in Vietnamese. Chits were distributed throughout the RVN promising clemency and financial aid to VC and NVA soldiers and their cadres who stopped fighting and would come over to the South Vietnamese government; sometimes referred to as "ralliers"

CINCPAC – Commander-in-Chief Pacific

Claymore Mine – A deadly antipersonnel mine, named from the Scottish Claymore sword (M18A1)

CMC – Commandant of the Marine Corps

CO – Commanding Officer

COC – Combat Operations Center

Col Co – Abbreviation for Colonial Company; from French Colonial times

Command Chronologies – Includes records of those units that served in Vietnam with the following common sections of information: organizational data, narrative summaries of events, accomplishments and losses, sequential listings of significant events within the unit, and supporting documentation

CONUS – Continental United States

Corpsman/Corpsmen – An enlisted medical specialist of the United States Navy who also served with Marines in maneuver units; always affectionately called "Doc" by the Marine infantryman and also considered to be a full-fledged Marine

CPL – Corporal (E-4 rank)

Covan – A shortened version of the phrase "Covan My," which means "American Advisor."

CP – Command Post

C-Rat – C-rations; food packaged in a can

Crotch – A slang term Marines called the Marine Corps

CTZ – Corps Tactical Zone

Danger Close – Indicates that friendly forces are within close proximity of a firing impact area

DASC – Direct Air Support Center, is the principal aviation command and control system and air control agency responsible for the direction of air operations supporting ground forces

DEROS – Date Eligible for Return from Overseas

Di di mau – From Vietnamese meaning "Go; go quickly"; phonetically pronounced "dee-dee" and "mao"

DI – Drill Instructor

DMZ – Demilitarized Zone in Vietnam separated the north from the south. Ben Hai River ran through it

Doc – Corpsmen; All Navy Corpsmen were called "Doc" by the Marines

Dodge City – An area west of the Thu Bon River designated as such for frequent gunfights

Dog Tags – Identification tags worn by everyone for clarification of WIA and KIA; who is who on a battlefield

Dustoff – Helo units who specialized in medical evacuations

EOD – Explosive Ordnance Demolition

E-Tool – Entrenching Tool

FAC – Forward Air Controller

FFE – Fire for effect

Field Day – Scrubbing, cleaning and putting the barracks (living quarters) in proper military order.

Final Honors – Burial service for a veteran; the final goodbye

First Sergeant – E-8 rank

FLC – Force Logistics Command, supplied the field and support units with essentials

FMF – Fleet Marine Force

FMFPAC – Fleet Marine Force Pacific

FNG – F..king New Guy; slang for a new guy just arriving in-country

FO – Forward Observer

Frag Order – Fragmentary Order. This order was an addendum to a larger original order. A frag order could amend an original to extend the mission beyond the original intent

FSCC – Fire Support Coordination Center; coordination of all artillery firing exercises

GS – Grid Square; 1,000 meters x 1,000 meters used for locating specific UTM (Universal Transverse Mercator) locations on a topographical map. Pinpointing a location within a meter

Grunt – A Marine infantryman

Gunny – Gunnery Sergeant (E-7 rank)

GVN – Government of Vietnam

Ham & Mofos – Ham and Lima Beans C-rations despised by most Marines

Head – Navy and Marine Corps term for bathroom

Heat Casualty – Marines suffering from heat exhaustion or heat stroke

H&I – Harassment and Interdiction; technique of pre-assigned targets fired on at various and odd times, e.g., known enemy routes, lanes, paths, etc.

H&S Company – Headquarters and Service Company

HE – High Explosive

Heat Tabs – Came with C-rations. Blue 1,3,5-Trioxane wafers about an inch in diameter to be used in "field stoves" (C-rat cans with holes punched by a K-Bar knife). In the bush, Marines preferred using C4

Hooch – Any shelter, whether fixed or temporary. Sometimes ponchos were stretched between trees or makeshift sticks in the ground to shade or keep the rain off

HQ – Headquarters

III MAF – Third Marine Amphibious Force (in the Republic of Vietnam)

In-country – Arriving into Vietnam for a tour; residing in the country of Vietnam

ITR – Infantry Training Regiment

JCS – Joint Chiefs of Staff

K-Bar – Official Knife, Fighting Utility of the Marine Corps

K-Bay – Kaneohe Bay Hawaii

KIA – Killed in Action

Kit Carson Scout – North Vietnamese and Viet Cong soldiers who came over to the Marine units to become scouts. Often these people were not in sync with Communist ideology, or were mercenaries fighting for whoever would pay the most

Klick – Slang for kilometers; one kilometer = 1,000 meters or .6 mile

LAAW – Light Assault Anti-Tank Weapon aka "LAW" (most commonly referred to as the LAW)

LCM – Landing Craft Mechanized

L/CPL – Lance Corporal (E-3 rank)

LCVP – Landing Craft, Vehicle, Personnel Carrier

LOA – Line Of Attack

LOD – Line Of Departure

LP – Listening Post

LPD – Landing Platform Dock, a naval vessel and carrier of Marines

LSA – Lubricant, Small Arms, a combination cleaner and lubricant

LST – Landing Ship Transport

LT – Lieutenant, usually a platoon commander

LZ – Landing Zone

M2 HB – Browning .50-caliber machine gun; heavy-duty armor-piercing weapon

M14 – U. S.-made rifle of 7.62 caliber (used until 1967)

M16 – U. S.-made rifle of 5.56 caliber (introduced in 1967)

M40 – U. S.-made Remington Model 700, bolt-action 7.62 x 51mm NATO rifle used as a sniper weapon

M60 – U. S.-made machine gun of 7.62 caliber

M79 – U. S.-made grenade launcher aka "The Blooper"

MAB – Marine Amphibious Brigade

MACV – Military Assistance Command Vietnam

MAGTF – Marine Air-Ground Task Force

MARDIV – Marine Division

MAW – Marine Air Wing

MCI – Meal, Combat, Individual

MCRD – Marine Corps Recruit Depot; Two recruit training depots which train new recruits to become Marines. One at Beaufort, SC called MCRD-Parris Island and the other in San Diego, CA called MCRD-San Diego.

MEB – Marine Expeditionary Brigade

MEDCAPS – Medical Civil Action Programs

Medevac – Medical Evacuation; usually by helicopter

MEF – Marine Expeditionary Force

Mess Duty – Work duty in the dining facility excluded cooking

MIA – Missing in action

Mike-Mike – Millimeter

MoFo – Slang term of endearment amongst Marines and Corpsmen

MOS – Military Occupational Specialty

MP – Military Police

MPC – Military Payment Certificates

Mustang – Enlisted NCO who becomes an officer

NAS – Naval Air Station

Napalm – A jellied gasoline dropped from jet aircraft exploding on impact, engulfing the area in flames, sucking all the oxygen out of the air and emitting intense heat. Second use of Napalm was in flame throwers. Trying to wipe it off one's self only spreads it around

NCO – Non-Commissioned Officer; Enlisted personnel

NCOIC – Non-Commissioned Officer in charge

NSA – Naval Support Activity (usually a fuel or supply position on or close to water)

Number One – Vietnamese would use this expression to mean "good"

Number Ten – Vietnamese would use this expression to mean "bad"

NVA – North Vietnamese Army

OJT – On the Job Training

Ontos – A tracked vehicle with light armor mounted with six 106mm recoilless rifles

OPCON – Operationally Controlled

P38 – Can Opener; multipurpose used to open C-ration cans (alleged, 38 punctures to open) aka "John Wayne"

PAX – Passenger

PF – Provisional Forces; local Vietnamese militia-like forces somewhat like National Guard

PFC – Private First Class (E-2 rank)

Phase Line – aka PL, an identified line (position on a map or area) used for coordination and control of an operation

Pig – A name given to the M60 machine gun by grunts

Point – The first Marine leading a patrol. Simply the point man or the act of "walking point" and being the most vulnerable and nerve-racking job

Poncho – Rubber-coated raincoats with hood

POW – Prisoner of War

PPB – Platoon Patrol Base

Prick 25 – The PRC 25 (official nomenclature, Portable Radio Communications—Model 25)

PT – Physical Training

Puff the Magic Dragon – DC-3 WWII aircraft capable of staying overhead for long periods of time and firing 20mm canons which streamed red tracers at the enemy while continually dropping flares

PX – Post Exchange (as in military post)

Radio Alphabet Code – Alpha is "A," Bravo is "B," and on through to Zulu for "Z." The enemy was capable of listening to U. S. Military radio transmissions; therefore, this type phonetics could be used to codify messages which was difficult for most foreigners to pronounce

Rallier – An enemy defector; the term was applied to NVA or VC who turned themselves in to the Chieu Hoi aka open arms program run by the South Vietnamese Government

R&R – Rest and Relaxation; scheduled trips away from the war zone

Recon – Reconnaissance; the eyes and ears of a unit, responsible for its security by observing and reporting

Rein – Reinforced; has been augmented by additional element, i.e., an additional Tank Platoon

RIO – Radar Intercept Officer; Backseat occupant of an F4 Phantom operating the radar and communications

RLT – Regimental Landing Team

Rocket Belt – A semicircle surrounding the Da Nang airstrip and stretching out about 30-40 miles. 122 Russian-made rockets were launched toward the airfield from this area

ROE – Rules of Engagement

ROK – Republic of Korea; sent many troops to Vietnam

Rough Rider – A convoy of trucks for moving supplies and Marines

RPG – Rocket Propelled Grenade (enemy rocket launcher)

RTO – Radio Telephone Operator; they usually followed a Commander in the field providing communication to rear command and control and other maneuver units

RVN – Republic of Vietnam

S-1 – Administration Section of a Battalion

S-2 – Intelligence and Reconnaissance Section of a Battalion

S-3 – Operations Section of a Battalion

S-4 – Supply and Logistics Section of a Battalion

S-5 – Civic Affairs and Miscellaneous of a Battalion

Scuttlebutt – Gossip and rumors abounding through the unit. A scuttlebutt is a water fountain on a ship, a place where Marines and Sailors talk about what is happening

SEATO – South-East Asia Treaty Organization

SECDEF – Secretary of Defense

SECNAV – Secretary of the Navy

Semper Fi – Latin term shortened from Semper Fidelis meaning "always faithful," the Marine Corps motto; its primary meaning amongst Marines being always faithful to each other

SFD – Surprise Firing Devices aka "booby traps"

SGT – Sergeant (E-5 rank)

Short Timer – A slang expression used to denote someone would be rotating back to the "World" aka the United States soon. A person with very little time left on his tour

SITREP – Situation Reports

"SIX" – Radio code for a Commanding Officer of a unit, Company-sized and larger

Six-By – M35A2 "Deuce and a Half" Truck for hauling cargo and troops

Skipper – A term of affection and respect given by Marines and Corpsmen to the Company Commander of a maneuver battalion

Snapping In – A week during Boot Camp of robotic dry-fire (no ammo) of practice drills (finger positions, trigger squeeze, breathing and aiming techniques).

Snake eye – An unguided, low-drag, general-purpose bomb, part of the Mark 80 series used in Vietnam

SOG – Studies and Observations Group under control of MACV operating in secret. AKA "Special Operations Group" carrying out Intel gathering, Psy-Ops and Recon missions

SPECAT – Special Category Telex messages (top secret)

Spider Trap/Hole – A camouflaged hole utilized for close in fighting by the NVA/VC

S/SGT – Staff Sergeant (E-6 rank)

Starlight Scope – Night vision scope

Sting Ray Patrols – A bold concept introduced to the battlefield, becoming an influential strategy of the Vietnam War. These patrols and ambushes helped target the enemy for artillery and air strikes in a lot of instances, while sometimes capturing the enemy for much needed intelligence

Swinging Dick – A fond expression for describing Marines and Corpsmen

T/O – Table of Organization

T/O&E – Table of Organization and Equipment

TACP – Tactical Air Control Party

TAOR –Tactical Area of Responsibility

Telex – A network of switched teleprinters similar to a telephone network, for sending text-based messages. Teleprinters evolved from the telegraph systems which used Morse Code.

Tet – Vietnamese New Year is the most important celebration in Vietnamese culture. Celebrates the arrival of spring

Time-In-Grade – Restriction intended to prevent rapid promotions. A period of time at a rank coupled with competitive measures (book and test requirements).

Trace – A course or path that one follows

Tubes – A mortar round leaving the launch tube makes a distinct sound. If one hears this "tube" sound there are several seconds of time before a mortar round impacts

UA – Unauthorized Absence

UCMJ – Universal Code of Military Justice

UHF – Ultra High Frequency radio waves for air-ground control; range 300 MHz to 3 GHz

Unit One – Corpsmen's first aid kit carried on his person in the field

USMC – United States Marine Corps

USO – United Service Organization; since 1941 the USO has stood by our troops through every step of their service from deployment to rehab and reintegration. They provide help to our soldiers and their families through the support and donations from the private sector.

UTM – Universal Transverse Mercator, the military map grid-coordinate reference system

VC – Viet Cong (Cong meaning "Communist" in Vietnamese)

VHF – Very High Frequency radio waves for coordinating ground forces; range 30 MHz to 300 MHz

WESTPAC – Western Pacific

Westy – General William C. Westmoreland, USA

WIA – Wounded in Action

Wire – Usually concertina (sharp barbs) stretched around a defensive perimeter or base camp

WP – White Phosphorus aka "Willy Peter"

XO – Executive Officer of the unit; second-in-command

(-) – Symbol for understrength

Resources and Recommended Reading Publications

1st Battalion, 27th Marines Command Chronologies
2nd Battalion, 27th Marines Command Chronologies
3rd Battalion, 27th Marines Command Chronologies
1st Marine Division Command Chronologies
7th Marine Regiment/Battalion Command Chronologies
3rd Marine Regiment/Battalion Command Chronologies
5th Marine Regiment/Battalion Command Chronologies
26th Marine Regiment/Battalion Command Chronologies
27th Marine Regiment/Battalion Command Chronologies
FMFPAC Command Chronologies
Task Force X-Ray Command Chronologies
1st Engineers Command Chronologies
1st Tank Battalion Command Chronologies
1st Amtrac Battalion Command Chronologies
3rd Amtrac Battalion Command Chronologies
1st MP Battalion Command Chronologies
III MAF – Periodic Intelligence Reports
III MAF – Command Chronologies
MACV Combat Operations/After Action Reports
MAPS: http://www.recordsofwar.com/vietnam/usmc/USMC_Rvn.htm

Task Force X-Ray Command Chronologies

Combat Handbook, H&S Bn FMF Pac (FMFPAC Repro 1480 – 1966)

A Chronology of the United States Marine Corps 1965-1969 Volume IV, Marine Corps Historical Reference Pamphlet, Historical Division Headquarters, U. S. Marine Corps Washington DC, 1971

Mel Baughman, review of *Brute: The Life of Victor Krulak*, by Robert Coram, AARP the Magazine (January 21, 2011). Available at: http://www.aarp.org/entertainment/books/info-01-2011/book-review-brute.html.

http://www.ndu.edu/press/lib/images/jfq-57/berry.pdf (Understanding OPCON by Charles T. Berry, Jr.)

JP 1-02, *Department of Defense Dictionary of Military and Associated Terms* (Washington, DC: Department of Defense, April 12, 2001, as amended through October 31, 2009)

Bibliography and Recommended Reading

Cass, Bevan G., ed. *History of the Sixth Marine Division*. Nashville, TN: The Battery Press, 1987.

Coram, Robert. *Brute: The Life of Victor Krulak, U. S. Marine*. New York: Little, Brown and Company, 2010.

Corson, William R. *The Betrayal*. New York: Ace Books Inc., 1968.

DeForest, Orrin and Chanoff, David. *Slow Burn: The Rise and Bitter Fall of American Intelligence in Vietnam*. New York: Simon and Schuster, 1990.

Dictionary of United States Military Terms for Joint Usage (Washington D.C. - The Joint Staff 1950). https://www.scribd.com/document/204229894/Dictionary-of-the-United-States-Military-Terms-for-Joint-Usage.

Fall, Bernard B. *Street Without Joy: Indochina At War 1946-54*. Harrisburg PA: The Stackpole Company, 1961.

Guidebook for Marines. The Leatherneck Association, Inc., 1964 and 1965.

Hiam, C. Michael. *A Monument To Deceit: Sam Adams and the Vietnam Intelligence Wars*. ForeEdge, University Press of New England, 2014.

Jarvis, Gary E., Ph.D. Y*oung Blood: A History of the 1st Battalion 27th Marines*, Vietnam Feb – Sept, 1968. G. E. Jarvis Publishing, 2009.

Kelley, Michael P. *Where We Were in Vietnam: A Comprehensive Guide to the Firebases, Military Installations and Naval Vessels of the Vietnam War 1945-75*. Ashland, OR: Hellgate Press, 2002.

Krulak, Victor H., LtGen (Ret). *First to Fight: An Inside View of the U. S. Marine Corps*. Annapolis, MD: Naval Institute Press, 1984.

Ky, Nguyen Cao. *How We Lost The Vietnam War*, Stein and Day, NY 1976.

Lacourture, Jean. *Vietnam: Between Two Truces*, New York, NY: Random House, 1966.

McMasters, H. R. *Dereliction of Duty: Lyndon Johnson, Robert McNamara, the Joint Chief of Staff, and the Lies That Led to Vietnam*. New York: Harper Collins Publisher, 1997.

Moyar, Mark. *Triumph Forsaken: The Vietnam War, 1954-1965*. New York: Cambridge University Press, 2006.

Department of the Navy. *The Marines In Vietnam 1954-1973: An Anthology and Annotated Bibliography.* 2nd ed. Washington, DC: History and Museums Division, Headquarters, U.S. Marine Corps, 1985.

Office of the General Counsel, Department of Defense. *[Part IV. C. 6. C] Evolution of the War – U. S. Ground Strategy and Force Deployments: 1965-67, Vol III, Program 6.* National Archives Identifier: 5890507 (DJSM 259-68, Memo for the Sec of Defense). Request & Plans for Troop increases in Vietnam by Westmoreland.

Schlosser, Nicholas J. *The Greene Papers: General Wallace M. Greene Jr. and the Escalation of the Vietnam War, January 1964 – March 1965.* Quantico, VA: History Division USMC, 2015.

Simonsen, Robert A. *Every Marine: 1968 Vietnam, A Battle for Go Noi Island*, Heritage Books, Inc., 2008.

Sheehan, Neil. *The Pentagon Papers: As published by The New York Times.* New York: Bantam Books, Inc., 1971.

Shulimson, Jack, Lt. Col. Leonard A. Blasiol, Lt. Col. Charles R. Smith, and Capt. David A. Dawson. *U. S. Marines in Vietnam, 1968 The Defining Year.* Washington DC: History & Museums Division Headquarters, US Marine Corps, 1997.

Tin, Bui. *From Enemy to Friend: A North Vietnamese Perspective on the War.* Annapolis, MD: Naval Institute Press, 2002.

Warr, Nicholas. *Phase Line Green: The Battle for Hue, 1968.* Annapolis, MD: Naval Institute Press, 1997.

Woodruff, Mark W. *Unheralded Victory: The Defeat of the Viet Cong and the North Vietnamese Army 1961 – 1973.* Arlington, VA: Vandamere Press, 1999 (Presidio Press 2005).

Websites

Aircraft Losses Vietnam. http://vietnamwar-database.blogspot.com/2010/11/aircraft-losses-during-vietnam-war.html

The American Presidency Project. Established in 1999 as a collaboration of John T. Woolley and Gerhard Peters, Co-Directors of the Project, UC of Santa Barbara, Dept. of Political Science. www.presidency.ucsb.edu/.

National Archives. http://www.archives.gov/

Records of War. The primary source of these documents is the Texas Tech University's Virtual Vietnam Archive. http://www.recordsofwar.com/vietnam/usmc/USMC_Rvn.htm. All Command Chronologies of units operating in Vietnam 1965-1975 can be found here.

Texas Tech University's The Virtual Vietnam Archive is a great source of primary documents pertaining to the Vietnam War: http://www.vietnam.ttu.edu/virtualarchive/

United States Marine Corps History Division. Photos and other historical data can be resourced here. Ms. Annette D. Amerman, Branch Head, Historical Reference Branch at Marine Corps History Division. https://www.mcu.usmc.mil/historydivision/SitePages/Home.aspx.

Washington Post Archives. Accessible at: http://www.washingtonpost.com/wp-adv/archives/copyright.htm.

Contributors

Interviews and Photographs

Ackerman, Laurence – H&S Co, 1/27 Vietnam

Allen, Robert – Brother of James J. Allen, C Co, 1/27 KIA Vietnam

Allen, Ron, Major USMC (Ret) – CO of B Co, 1/27 Vietnam

Austin, Allen – Brother of Stephen E. Austin, C Co, 1/27 KIA Vietnam

Averill, Bob, 1st Lt – XO G Co, 2/9 & CO CAC, Hue Vietnam

Barton, Carol – Wife of Hugh G. Barton, H&S Co, 1/27 Vietnam

Birdsong, Grady T. – H&S Co, 1/27 Vietnam

Black, William, Lt – A Co, 1/27 Vietnam

Boyko, Andy – H&S Co, 1/27 & 3/27 Vietnam

Bouldin, John, 1st Lt – CO of A Co, 1/27 Vietnam

Broadhurst, Larry – H&S Co, 1/27 Vietnam, Chief Battalion Scout

Bronson, David E. – D Co, 1/27 Vietnam

Brookhart, James – H&S Co, 1/27 Vietnam

Brown, Dane – H&S Co, 1/27 Vietnam

Brown, Michael L. – H&S Co, 1/27 Vietnam

Broyer, Clifton L. Family – Clif was KIA 2/28/69 with C Co 1/4 Vietnam

Carey, Doug – H&S Co, 1/27 Vietnam

Carroll, William E. – C Co, 1/27 Vietnam

Charles, Roger, LtCol USMC (Ret) – A Co, 1/27 Vietnam

Clevenger-Gassch, Donna – Sister of Dan Clevenger, H&S Co, 1/27 KIA Vietnam

Cox, James J. – 1/27 Hawaii; Previous tour K Co, 3/5 Vietnam

Cusack, C. R., Major USMCR (Ret) – VMFA-122, 1st MAW Vietnam

Davis, Crane, Lt – C Co, 1/27 Vietnam

Decker, John – F Co, 2/7 Vietnam

Dorsey, Ron – F Co, 2/7 Vietnam

Doye, Lois – Mother of Ricky L. Doye, A Co, 1/27 KIA Vietnam

Drennan, Bill – D Co, 1/27 Vietnam

Eckerson, Charles F. – H&S Co, 1/27 Vietnam

Eller, Franklin P., Colonel USMC (Ret) – XO 1/27 Vietnam

Figueroa, Raul E. "Figgy" – H&S Co, 1/27 Vietnam

Fink, Rick – C Co, 1/27 Vietnam

Fischer, Robert L., Colonel USMC (Ret) – "Covan" Advisor Vietnam

Fisher, Dennis – Corporal, 1st Marine Division Photographer

Getts, Ron – Neighbor & boyhood friend of Dan Clevenger, H&S Co, 1/27 Vietnam

Gerheim, Earl – L/Cpl, 1st Marine Division Correspondent

Glaettli, Alioth – H&S Co, 1/27 Vietnam

Gomez, Gary – Son of Manuel J. Gomez, H&S Co, 1/27 KIA Vietnam

Grimshaw, Terry – Brother of Danny Grimshaw, D Co, 1/27 KIA Vietnam

Grimshaw-Nagel, Bobby and Grimshaw-Beamer, Jerry – sisters of Danny Grimshaw, D Co, 1/27

Gruenberg, Ron, LtCol USMC (Ret) – CO of C Co; S-3 H&S Co, 1/27 Vietnam

Guenther, Dan, Captain – 3rd Amphibian Tractor Battalion Vietnam

Hand, Jesse, 1st Lt – CO of H&S Co, 1/27 Vietnam

Harrison, David – D Co 1/27 Vietnam

Hoffman, Thomas, Captain – USA, MACV Vietnam

Hunt, Richard R. – H&S Co 1/27 Vietnam

Jarvis, Gary E., PhD – D Co, 1/27 Vietnam; Author, "Young Blood: History of 1/27," 1999-2009

Johnson, Rick – Alpha Co, 1st Amphibian Tractor Battalion Vietnam

Kahler, Pat, Colonel USMC (Ret) – CO of D Co, 1/27 Vietnam

Kennedy, Harold E. "Hal" – H&S Co, 1/27 Vietnam

Kirkpatrick, Michael D. – B Co, 1/27 Vietnam

Komanec, Gabe – C Co, 1/27 Vietnam

Lister, Dennis, Major USMC (Ret) – C Co, 1/27 Vietnam

Lowe, Linda – Sister of HM3 Robert L. Dodsworth, B Co, 1/27 KIA Vietnam

Mahseet, Edmond L. – D Co, 1/27 Vietnam

Matthews, Howard – A Co, 1/27 Hawaii & previous tour of Vietnam

McConnell, R. W. – D Co, 1/27 Vietnam

McEwan, Frederick J., LtCol USMC (Ret) –CO of 1/26 Vietnam

Moorehead-Sell, Donald – C Co, 1/27 Vietnam

Morton, Bruce Cole, 1st Lt – A Co, 1st Anti-Tank Bn Vietnam (supported 1/27)

O'Rourke, Bob, Lt – B Co, 1/27 Vietnam

Oakes, Ronald G. – B Co, 1/27 Vietnam

Panther, Jim, Captain – CO of A Co, 1/27 Vietnam

Peck, William – C Co, 1/27 Hawaii

Purcell, William M. – A Co, 1/1 Vietnam

Risner, Gerald – FLC attached to H&S, 2/5 Vietnam

Roberts, David T. "Red Dog" – D Co, 1/4 Vietnam

Robeson, Tracey – D Co, 1/27 Vietnam

Ronan, Ed – C Co, 1/27 Vietnam

Romo, Tommy – S-2, HQ Co, 27th Regiment (attached to 1/27) Vietnam

Rosenau, John – G Co, 2/3 Vietnam

Rosser, Richard, Colonel USMCR (Ret) – HMM-164 (supported 1/27) Vietnam

Roysdon, Joe – H&S Co, 1/27 Vietnam

Salmeron, Felix, 1st Sgt USMC (Ret) – A Co, 1/27, Vietnam

Sarlls, Tony – MACG 18, 1st MAW Vietnam (courtesy of wife, Paula)

Schaeffer, George C. Jr. – B Co, 1/27 Vietnam

Schwartzlow, Gene, Colonel USMC (Ret) – H&S Co, 1/27 & K Co, 3/27 Vietnam

Setley, Doug – H&S Co, 1/27 Vietnam

Shabel, John Thomas – B Co, 1/27 Vietnam

Singletary, Ed – A Co, 1/27 Vietnam

Sontag, John – H&S Co, 3rd Amphibian Tractor Battalion Vietnam

Sweeney, William T., Colonel USMC (Ret) – CO of B Co; S-2, 1/27 Vietnam

Sydorenko, Dani – Daughter of Dan Clevenger, H&S Co, 1/27 KIA Vietnam

Taugner, Bob – B Co, 1/27 Vietnam

Thompson, John M. – C Co, 1/27 Vietnam

Thrush, Richard – H&S Co, 1/27 Vietnam

Whaley, Raymond – Anti-Tanks attached to 1/27 Hawaii

Williams, Ronnie – Anti-Tanks attached to 1/27 Hawaii

Weinberger, Robert F. – D Co, 1/27 Vietnam

Weymouth, Michael – B Co, 1/27 Vietnam

Beta Readers and Technical Contributors

Baker, Fred G., Ph.D– Hydrologist, provided advisory/Beta reader

Blasiol, Len, Colonel USMC (Ret) – Co-Author, *US Marines in Vietnam: The Defining Year 1968*

Carter, Paul Sgt – 1st ANGLICO Vietnam, friend provided advisory/Beta reader

Chiasson, Shawn – Police Officer and close friend of author, provided photography

Clark, Jeff – Friend of author, provided E-Tool photography

Cusack, Virginia – Wife of C. R. Cusack Major USMC (Ret). Advanced Reading Copy editor

Douglass, Karen – Colorado writer, author, and teacher of creative writing

Eller, Franklin P., Colonel USMC (Ret) – XO of 1/27 and "Covan" of Vietnamese Marine Corps

Fischer, Robert L., Colonel USMC (Ret) – "Covan" Vietnamese Marine Corps, Beta reader

Hall, Tim – FLC, Vietnam 1965-66, helped with content and general edit

Hardcastle, Mark– 1982 USAFA graduate, Persian Gulf War pilot, Airline Captain, Author; Beta reader & reviewer

Jarvis, Gary E., Ph.D – D Co, 1/27, provided extensive content advisory, Beta reader

Kaylor, James – E Co, 2/26, historical advisory

Kennedy, Ian – Beta reader & son of Hal Kennedy

Love, Wesley – K Co, 3/27, historical advisory

Lynch, B. Don, Major General USMC (Ret) – Vietnam, Beta reader

McCartney, Larry – E Co, 2/26, historical advisory

Moore, Don, Lt – 7th Marines, Vietnam, Beta reader

Panzica, Larry J. – USA, 1st BDE, 5th ID (Mech), "Red Devils," friend; provided photography

Pipes, Ken, LtCol USMC (Ret) – CO of B Co, 1/26 Khe Sanh, Beta Reader & reviewer

Quinn, Larry – H&S Co, 1/ 4, Vietnam, equipment & historical advisory

Sedlack, Denny – H Co, 2/7, Vietnam, advisory on Navy Corpsmen content

Tolleson, Frederick, Colonel USMC (Ret) – CO E Co, 2/7 Vietnam, Beta reader & reviewer

Utah Gun Collectors Association

Warr, Nicholas, Lt – C Co, 1/5 Vietnam, Author "Phase Line Green," Naval Institute Press, Annapolis, MD 1997, Beta reader & reviewer

Zumwalt, James G., LtCol USMC (Ret)– CO 4th CAG Vietnam, Internationally acclaimed best-selling author, speaker and business executive on foreign policy and defense issues; Beta reader

Acknowledgments

I owe a heartfelt thank you to my wife and family who supported and encouraged me despite the time this project took away from them. I sincerely wish to express my deepest gratitude to the many Marines, Corpsmen, men, and women who have helped me with this history project; to all who provided support, talked with me about it, read the manuscript, offered comments, ideas, and those who allowed me to quote their recollections.

A special thanks to Nick Zelinger of NZGraphics who expertly designed the cover, formatted the entire book and delivered it for publication. Nick has earned an impeccable industry-wide reputation for producing award-winning covers and books.

And to my very adept editor, Alexandra O'Connell, I would like to wholeheartedly express a grateful thank you to her for outstanding advice, expertise, and guidance in bringing this manuscript to fruition. She coached, nudged, inspired, and helped me fine-tune this writing to an even higher level than I had originally anticipated. It was a pleasure to work with this fine young lady, a professional with abounding knowledge of the writing/publishing process.

Also another special thank you to Virginia Cusack, wife of Major C. R. Cusack, USMC (Ret). As an F4 Phantom pilot he supported this unit in Vietnam and is written about in this book. Still supporting her husband after all these years she diligently went through the Advanced Reading Copy editing, proofing and fine-tuning it with gusto having lived a Marine Corps life in the 1960s. My "cover" (Marine hat) is off to her for helping me and to her continued love of the English language. A sharp hand salute to her! Thank you, Virginia!

Last and not least: a sharp hand salute to the members of the Colorado Independent Publishers Association for their support, encouragement, and camaraderie while helping writers of all genres become published. And a special thanks to Dan Guenther, Captain of Marines and Author who mentored, coached and guided me into the writing process. Dan, a decorated Vietnam Veteran of two tours obtained an MFA from Coe College, Cedar Rapids, IA becoming an accomplished writer and author of seven books.

Finally, I ask forgiveness of those who have helped with this book and whose names, unintentionally, I have failed to mention.

About the Author

Grady Thane Birdsong was raised in Kansas and enlisted in the United States Marine Corps in 1966. After serving two combat tours in the Northern I Corps region of Vietnam during the Tet Offensive in 1968 and along the DMZ in 1969, he enjoyed a successful career traveling the world as an executive in engineering, marketing, and business development in the telecommunications/data, information technology, and the optical/fiber systems industries.

Grady is the author of *A Fortunate Passage: Two Families' Journey into the Heartland*, which received two EVVY awards from the Colorado Independent Publishers Association. Also, a coauthor of *The Miracle Workers of South Boulder Road: Healing the Signature Wounds of War*, won two 1st Place EVVY awards (CIPA) and was a finalist in the Best Book Awards, with Colonel Bob Fischer.

He is a veteran advocate for returning veterans of the Middle East Wars and the Rocky Mountain Hyperbaric Association for Brain Injuries, Healing Our Heroes Program, a 501c3 organization. Also, as a volunteer at the Denver Vet Center, he helped design, commission, and build a lab with a series of computer courses for veterans to learn various levels of computer basics, computer building, Windows OS, Video/Photo presentation, and Photoshop instruction. This was done with extensive help from the American Legion Department of Colorado.

Now retired, Grady lives with his wife, Pamela, in the Denver area, where he enjoys his grandchildren and spends his time writing, volunteering, and hunting big game. Grady is a graduate of Regis University in Denver, Colorado, an officer in the 1st Marine Division Association, Rocky Mountain Chapter, and Program Chair of the large Denver area monthly Marine Corps Luncheon group, "Coopers Troopers."

For more information on Grady and his books, please visit www.gradytbirdsong.com.

CPSIA information can be obtained
at www.ICGtesting.com
Printed in the USA
BVHW060737040222
627989BV00004B/41